PHARMACEUTICAL MARKETING IN INDIA

For Today and Tomorrow

25th Anniversary Edition

PHARMACEUTICAL MARKETING IN INDIA

For Today and Tomorrow

25th Anniversary Edition

Subba Rao Chaganti

PharmaMed Press
An imprint of Pharma Book Syndicate
A unit of BSP Books Pvt. Ltd.
4-4-309/316, Giriraj Lane,
Sultan Bazar, Hyderabad - 500 095.

Pharma Med
PRESS
An Imprint of
Pharma Book Syndicate

Pharmaceutical Marketing in India: For Today and Tomorrow
by *Subba Rao Chaganti*

Published by

PharmaMed Press
An imprint of Pharma Book Syndicate
A unit of BSP Books Pvt. Ltd.
4-4-309/316, Giriraj Lane, Sultan Bazar, Hyderabad - 500 095.
Phone: 040-23445600, 23445688; Fax: 91+40-23445611
E-mail: info@pharmamedpress.com
www.pharmamedpress.com/pharmamedpress.net

Cover Design
J. Siva Prasad, Hitha Design Science Pvt. Ltd.

Printed at
Aditya Offset Process (I) Pvt. Ltd.
Hyderabad.

ISBN: 978-93-88305-25-9 (Hardbound)

Dedicated

To my mother and father in their
Heavenly abode

With eternal love, deep gratitude and
appreciation

FOREWORD TO THE FIRST EDITION

1. **To the People of India:** Healthcare delivery is our common concern - we look for a healthy nation full of enthusiasm. Marketing is aspiration fulfillment. The function of marketing is to deliver an offering, which can match the aspiration. Fulfillment of one aspiration leads to the creation of another aspiration - a never ending spiraling process. Marketing becomes a dynamic concept. Delivery of healthcare becomes an engaging affair. It is in this specific context that this book should be of particular interest to an enlightened Indian.

2. **To International Publics:** India, world's largest democracy, is of interest to you in many ways. Delivery of healthcare is one major segment - conceptually speaking. If you take a look through the pages of this book, you will get the relevance.

3. **To Healthcare Industry:** Healthcare industry in India is at the crossroads - poised for growth hitherto unforeseen. Marketing assumes pivotal role in a progressively competitive, growth oriented management environment for the delivery of healthcare services. Your corporate identity in the management of healthcare services should make it imperative for you to keep this book as a compendium for ready reference.

4. **To Management Students:** Many of you are interested in a career in marketing. Healthcare industry offers good career avenue. While there are books galore on the text of marketing as a discipline, an updated book on pharmaceutical marketing, relevant in the Indian context, has since been missing. If you take even a cursory look through the book, you will be able to assess the usefulness of the book.

5. **To the Medical Profession:** You are the custodian of the health of the nation. The confident expression of your face gets the relief to the patient looking for cure. The industry delivers healthcare services through you. To serve you effectively, the industry has

got to know all that you look for, in the interest of your patient. Marketing in today's world offers the discipline of service orientation. This book should contribute towards getting the desired level of service orientation in the delivery of healthcare.

6. **To Pharma Marketing Professional:** You might take a look through the book to assess for yourself the usefulness or otherwise of the book.

7. **To others in Marketing Practice:** They talk of direct marketing - and the growing inclination toward the application of direct marketing. India has yet to make headway in this direction in consumer marketing other than in the delivery of healthcare. It is in this context, that Pharma marketing practices could be of special and specific interest to practitioners in consumer marketing, in securing guidelines for direct marketing practices.

8. **To Marketing Faculty:** Text books in marketing in the Indian context are a rare commodity. This book provides dependable treatment on Pharma marketing, and as such should furnish updated reference material with adequate case studies - particularly useful to any person teaching marketing in any management school in India.

9. **To Medical Sales Persons:** Your role is particularly important in establishing firm link between medical profession and the industry in the delivery of healthcare services. You are the moving encyclopedia of the subject. You disseminate knowledge, you create preference, you carry conviction, you generate action through scientific promotion. All this involves a deep sense of commitment to the profession. This book should get you the right insight for developing proper sense of professional commitment.

10. **To the Author:** Thank you very much indeed, Mr. Ch. S. V. R. Subba Rao, for asking me several months ago to write the foreword. As a committed student of marketing, I think you have done an excellent, pioneering job dedicated to the cause of scientific marketing in one of the major segments of the market. I am confident your work will get you tributes from all those interested in the marketing of healthcare. I am sure you will like to take some of your time to keep on updating the information base from one edition of the book to another.

Professor ChittaMitra
Calcutta, 1990

PREFACE TO THE 25TH ANNIVERSARY EDITION

It is with great humility and a deep sense of gratitude that I write this preface to this 25th anniversary edition of the book. My grateful thanks to all those marketing practitioners who have offered suggestions to update and improve the contents of this book over the years; and who have encouraged with their generous remarks stating that they found the earlier editions of the book very useful; and to those faculty members at various management institutes for using it as a study material for teaching pharmaceutical marketing in India. Thank you very much. I am indeed grateful to you all.

25 years is a long time. Twenty-five years ago, when I first wrote this book, there was a long-felt need for a text book on pharmaceutical marketing in India. A number of pharmaceutical sales and product management executives and managers wondered at that time why there was no textbook on pharmaceutical marketing in India.

Naturally, a lot of things have changed since then. The world in general and the pharmaceutical marketing world in particular have undergone a substantial change in terms of social, economic, technological social, legal and regulatory environments. Today, therefore, more than ever before there is a strong need to thoroughly update incorporating all the changes that have been taking place evolving into what we know as today's pharmaceutical marketplace or healthcare world.

In this new edition of the book, I have just attempted to do that. thoroughly update the contents. Almost re-write. To make it relevant. Up to the date. Even future-proof to some extent.Some of the new trends, which have been introduced in this book are likely to be the key elements of tomorrow's pharmaceutical marketing -mix.

The book is primarily designed for:
1. Graduate and post graduate students in pharmacy, whose background and exposure to the study of marketing is limited,

2. Those, who are actually involved in pharmaceutical marketing,
3. Anyone interested in knowing about the intricacies in marketing prescription drugs, and
4. Entrepreneurs about to enter the pharmaceutical industry.

The book clearly has an emphasis on practice. On application of proven, tested marketing concepts to real life situations. Firstly, various marketing concepts are described in the context of their applicability to marketing of pharmaceutical products. Secondly, a number of actual cases are discussed to clarify how various pharmaceutical companies have applied these marketing concepts into practices.

As regards the structure of the book, it is divided into three parts.

Part one: *The Big Picture*:   Presents the big picture of Indian pharmaceutical industry and an overview of the Indian pharmaceutical market.

Part two: T*en 'P's*: Ten 'P's revolve around the unique, multidimensional, Ten 'P' model of pharmaceutical marketing. McCarthy has suggested the classic four 'P's, namely Product, Price, Place and Promotion. Philip Kotler, the venerated marketing guru proposed a six 'P' model in his HBR article on *Mega marketing* adding two more 'P's - Power and Public Relations. Pharmaceutical marketing in India goes one step further with four more 'P's. Hence the Ten 'P' model. Is it one-upmanship? No. Certainly not. When you study the additional four 'P's of pharmaceutical marketing - Personal selling, Prescription, Policy and Patient, you will agree on their relevance. On their importance.On their indispensability.

Personal selling is a very important, in fact, crucial determinant element of the pharmaceutical marketing mix. In a me-too market place like the Indian pharmaceutical industry, the importance of personal selling becomes even more significant. It is the quality of your sales force that determines success.

For a pharmaceutical marketer, the study of the physicians' prescriptions and understanding their prescribing behavior is a must. Hence the chapter on *Prescription*. In a highly regulated and stringently controlled industry like pharmaceuticals in India, a thorough understanding of the policy is vital, whether it is to prepare a strategic plan that minimizes risks or the one that exploits opportunities. Clear understanding of the public policy in general and the drug policy in particular is essential for the pharmaceutical marketer. The chapter on *Policy* addresses this need. The role of the patients is increasing as a decision maker in today's healthcare scenario. Hence the chapter on 'Patient'.

Part Three: *Key Success Factors* deal with those few vital factors, which very often determine the success of an enterprise.

What should be new in this edition? To answer this, I had to ask myself another question. What has been changing on the pharmaceutical marketing scene for the past fifteen to twenty years? I felt it is my duty to present the changing landscape of pharmaceutical marketing in India and explore how to stay competitive in the ever changing pharmaceutical market place. I have to do this as a token of my gratitude to all those that have been using this book for over twenty-five years as an important source of information for teaching the subject and for practicing scientific Pharma marketing and also deliver a dependable tool to refer to, to the new users who are joining the world of Pharma marketing.

A lot has changed. The patent cliff, drying up of the product pipelines, generic erosion in the first world markets, rising costs and the consequent cost containment moves by virtually all governments around the world are there for everyone to see. Top it with the continuous mergers in the name of consolidation, and increasing access restrictions to physicians, which is very high in the US but it is gradually happening even in other markets around the world including India. Add to this the internet explosion and the easy access of scientific information to physicians on the go, and reducing standards of pharmaceutical selling - all these are reducing importance of personal selling function, which was considered a crucial determinant factor only a few years ago. Many physicians are of the opinion that medical representatives have very little to offer in terms of scientific information let alone a discussion.

What is more, even the Pharma reputation has been diminishing. Some of the pharmaceutical companies, who are unable to cope with the changing market needs and requirements have been resorting to a transactional model of marketing entirely based on gratification, and have been carrying on their business of marketing with not so ethical practices. Media has been bringing these to the fore. The Department of Pharmaceuticals in India is even considering actively to bring legislation to curb the increasing Pharma -physician nexus and enforce UCPMP Code, which was introduced in a voluntary mode earlier and since the industry did not pay any heed to it.

We are already in a digital era where everything is being digitized. Over half of the physicians in the country are digital natives and they are comfortable with internet and their devices to access any medical information they want. When the customers are going digital, can the industry that serves them lag behind? Obviously not. But the pharmaceutical industry around the world in general and the Indian Pharma industry in particular have been sort of laggards in adopting to the digital marketing.

A number of new marketing initiatives are already being taken to over come the challenges that the changing market place offers by pharmaceutical companies in the regulated markets and some of the Indian subsidiaries of MNC drug firms. But these are very preliminary steps.

What's new in this edition? An introduction to all aspects of changes and initiatives that are happening in the first world markets and whatever baby steps that are being taken by Indian drug majors and their MNC counterparts in India are discussed. To name a few - Changing detailing practices such as e-Detailing, iPad detailing or tablet detailing, digital marketing strategies, social media strategies for pharmaceutical industry, multichannel marketing, closed loop marketing etc.

To improve physician access, companies have been finding new ways of engaging with physicians. The new ways of engaging and building meaningful relationships with physicians effectively are Medical Sales Liaisons (MSL), key opinion leader management and key account management. All these topics have been added. The main effort is to make this edition not only relevant for today but also for tomorrow. In other words, to make it as future-proof as is possible.

Now about the style. The style of the book is simple. Direct. Jargon-free. User friendly, rather reader friendly.

The book has its limitations too. The major limitation with any book where supportive data like sales volume, growth rate, market share are presented is that it really becomes historical by the time the book reaches the reader. The interpretations, the inferences, which are valid in their own context and serve a useful purpose of providing strategic insights and the situations may have been changed. As you are reading this book, the market shares and the ranks of some of the companies discussed in the case studies may have been changed. In a dynamic marketing situation that is inevitable and it should be so. While it is possible to update these, it is not really possible to keep pace with rapidly changing market scenario.

Apart from this, responsibility for any other limitations, errors or omissions remain main alone.

A few words about *cases* discussed in this book. There are over seventy different cases presented throughout this book. The only purpose of these case studies is to provide experiential insights to the students and practitioners of pharmaceutical marketing, and not to be judgmental about their successes or failures. These cases are real and the facts have been gathered over a long period of time from various published and unpublished sources, informal discussions with the marketing personnel of different companies, doctors, dealers and academicians. It is quite possible that some marketing practitioners may disagree with he interpretations or inferences drawn depending upon their own experience and understanding. The basis for the experiential insights presented in each of these cases is the analytical framework based on the concepts discussed in the book.

I would be particularly grateful for your insights, comments and suggestions to make the future editions of this book more valuable for the pharmaceutical marketing students and practitioners alike.

One submission. I have used the male pronoun throughout this book, wherever the use of personal pronoun could not be avoided. This is only to facilitate smooth reading. This is not to be viewed as discrimination in terms of gender. In fact, there are as many bright women product managers in pharmaceutical industry as there are men.

Finally, whether one likes it or not, transactional marketing is not going to stay. What brought us here won't take it where we want to go. Into the future. The rising power of patients, and the new demands of physicians in terms of scientific interaction and value-added information that helps them treat their patients better dictate that pharmaceutical marketers rise up to the occasion. To practice science based marketing and scientific marketing. Because it is nothing new to them. They have done it the past. It is only through scientific marketing they built the huge businesses and reputation. They have to press the refresh button and go back to scientific marketing again. Every which way you look, scientific marketing is the way to go. This book shows how.

Subba Rao Chaganti
Hyderabad

ACKNOWLEDGEMENTS

A book of this magnitude can seldom be claimed as the work of one individual. A number of people have helped me in producing the very first edition of this book, more than twenty-five years ago. It is not possible to individually acknowledge all my colleagues and competitors (in the field) and teachers, who have helped me in widening my horizon and broadening my perspective of marketing in general and pharmaceutical marketing in particular.

Here are a few individuals, whose help and support have been truly significant. Without their physical, intellectual and moral support, this book still would have been in a conceptual stage. My grateful thanks to:

Late Professor ChittaMitra, academician, market researcher with a pioneering spirit for his constant criticism and for his Foreword to the first edition of this book. I am sure he is looking at this new 25th Anniversary edition from his heavenly abode with a deep sense of satisfaction that I followed his advice of updating the information in successive editions. Thank you Professor, You have been always prophetic.

Mr. J M Raju, whose irrepressible optimism has been the major source of inspiration through out the process of writing and updating this book. He and his wife Mrs. Rukmini have been responsible for bringing out this book in its printed form for the very first time twenty-five years ago. I have never known a better motivator than Mr. J M Raju, who has been constantly egging me to do more and better.

My grateful thanks are also due to Mr. Anil Shah for his faith in this project. He apart from being a publisher with vision has been virtually pushing me to bring about this edition. My sincere thanks are also due to Mr. J. Siva Prasad of Hitha Design Science, who has designed cover for this book.

I owe my grateful thanks to Mahalakshmi, my better half both literally and figuratively and my three children and their spouses (Srinivasa Phanindra, Geetha, Lavanya, Aditya, Soumya, Chaitanya) for supporting and even pushing me to bring this 25th anniversary edition. I must be grateful to my grandchildren - Aditi, Eesha and Surya who watched me with awe while I was writing this book and that inspired me a lot and gave me great joy and satisfaction.

Subba Rao Chaganti

Praise for the First Edition (1990)

" An excellent pioneering job dedicated to the cause of scientific marketing in one major segment of the market. This book provides dependable treatment of Pharma marketing and as such, should furnish updated reference material with adequate case studies."

Professor Chitta Mitra
Managing Director, C MARC (India) Pvt. Ltd. Calcutta, India

" It is an outstanding piece of work"

Professor Gerald Zaltman
The Joseph C Wilson Professor of Business Administration
Harvard University, Boston, MA, USA

"This handsomely produced and very readable book is a most useful work for practitioners and academics. It covers the pharmaceutical industry very well and it is also an introduction to marketing in general. It provides an excellent history of regulation as well as its extraordinary growth. It is a valuable addition to marketing literature in India."

Dr. Roger Bennet
Professor of Marketing, McGill University Montreal, Canada

CONTENTS

Part One: The Big Picture

A challenging environment, A brief history, The Indian systems of medicine get a shot-in-the-arm with AYUSH, Origin of Indian Pharmaceutical industry, Industry structure, The Public Sector, The Indian private Sector, The foreign sector, Manufacturing, Technology, Drug Discovery, Bundle of paradoxes, The generics policy, Wither Loan-licensing, The Policy of drug price control, Protection of IPR, The changing face of Indian pharmaceutical industry: Post-WTO, Exports, Research & Development, Positive features, Compulsory Licensing, What the big Pharma wants from India, Voluntary Licensing - An alternate strategy? IPR and its Implications for Indian Pharma, Understanding marketing environment, The economic environment, The Legal and Regulatory environment, The Social Environment, The Technological Environment, The Ecological Environment, The Ethical Environment, The Competitive Environment, Summary

Changing! Changing! Changing!, Many dimensions of the market, Three major segments, The customer and the consumer, What is your market?, Market segmentation theory, Criteria for a viable segment, Four ways of segmentation, Pharmaceutical market segmentation, Implications for the marketer, Key Questions, Market dimensions, The Served market, Market segmentation: Some more aspects, Market opportunity analysis, Elements of a market opportunity analysis, Market opportunity analysis: A step-by-step approach, Strategic Options, Concentrated marketing, Differentiated marketing, Undifferentiated marketing, Summary

Part Two: Ten 'P's

key strategic variable, Elements of promotion-mix, Push and pull strategies and prescription drugs, Promotional objectives and tasks, Principles of medical advertising, How to prepare an effective detailing story? Innovative approaches to pharmaceutical detailing, Winning with iPad detailing, Closed-loop marketing, Digital marketing, Multi-channel marketing, Omni-channel marketing, website, eMail, SMS, Search engine marketing, Online forum, Blogs, Microblogs, Social networks, Mobile, mHealth, Social media marketing, Six ways Pharma may use social media, Pharma and social media: the Indian presence, Content is king, Gamification, More apps, Summary

Crucian determinant factor, Super sales person, What do doctors expect from a medical representative? Selecting and recruiting a medical representative, Improving the effectiveness of a medical representative, Four key areas, Declining physician access, New rules of engagement, Detailing today, iPad or tablet detailing, Why iPad is Pharma's device of choice? 3 ways to get the best out of your iPad detailing, Common mistakes to avoid, Implementing iPad detailing effectively, Tablet detailing: Future outlook, Tele dealing or eDetailing, Implementing eDetailing, eDetailing strategies, eDetailing in the Indian context, Medical Sales Liaison, Tasks and responsibilities of MSLs, MSLs: The Indian context, KOL management, Identifying KOLs, Building relationships with KOLs, Effective KOL engagement, Three basic steps, Changing role of Pharma sales rep, From Obsolescence to Relevance, Summary

Symbol of power! The Prime mover! Broad spectrum of prescription, Prescribing process, Prescriber motivation; Scientific or commercial? New product adoption by physicians: A two-step approach, Communication hierarchy, Accentuate the positive, Studying prescribing behavior, Six honest serving men, Prescription research: Key questions, Ambivalent attitude, Prescription generation: Folklore and Facts, Summary

Aware! Alert! Adapt!, What is a policy?, Policy in Japanese Management, Deploying and internalizing the policy, Policy implications for the marketer, Generics-only policy: Treat the cause, not the symptom, Policy monitoring: Key Questions, Leading all the way, Summary

Image makers?, Information, Opinion, Attitudes, Pull strategy; A necessity for pharmaceutical industry, Crisis management, Publicity, What can public relations do? Reputation management, Summary

Part Three: Key Success Factors

competence, Effective segmentation, Strategy, Competitive analysis, New product development, Building a winning team, Summary

LIST OF ABBREVIATIONS

ADHD	Attention Deficit Hyperactivity Disorder
AFMSD	Armed Forces Medical Stores Depot
AIDA	Attention, Interest, Desire, Action
AIOCD	All India Organization of Chemists and Druggists
ANDA	Abbreviated New Drug Application
BCG	Boston Consulting Group
BICP	Bureau of Industrial Costs and Prices
CAGR	Compound Annual Growth Rate
CCMB	Center for Cellular and Molecular Biology
CGHS	Central Government Health Scheme
CL	Compulsory License
CLM	Closed Loop Marketing
COS	Certificate of Suitability
CRM	Customer Related Marketing
CRO	Contract Research Organization
CSIR	Council of Scientific and Industrial Research
DGS&D	Directorate General of Supplies and Disposals
DGTD	Directorate General of Technical Development
DMF	Drug Master File
DoP	Department of Pharmaceuticals
DPCO	Drug Price Control Order
EMR	Exclusive Marketing Rights
EOQ	Economic Order Quantity
EQDM	European Directorate for the Quality of Medicines and Healthcare
FDA	Federal Drug Administration
GATT	General Agreement on Tariffs and Trade
GeM	Government e- Marketplace
GMP	Good Manufacturing Practices
GoI	Government of India
GSK	GlaxoSmithKline

HCP	Healthcare Professional
IDMA	Indian Drug Manufacturers' Association
IFPMA	International Federation of Marketing Associations and Manufacturers
IP	Intellectual Property
IPA	Indian Pharmaceutical Alliance
IPR	Intellectual Property Rights
KAM	Key Account Management
KOL	Key Opinion Leader
LOC	Letter of Cooperation
MAPE	Maximum Allowable Post-manufacturing Expenses
MAT	Moving Annual Total
MCA	Medicine Control Agency
MCC	Medicines Control Council
MLC	Market Life Cycle
MNC	Multinational Corporation
MRTP	Monopolies and Restrictive Trade Practices
MRTPC	Monopolies and Restrictive Trade Practices Commission
MSD	Medical Stores Depot
MSD	Merck Sharp Dohme
NBE	New Biological Entity
NCAER	National Council of Applied Economic Research
NCE	New Chemical Entity
NCL	National Chemical Laboratory
NDDS	New Drug Delivery System
NPIL	Nicholas Piramal India Limited
NLEM	National List of Essential Medicines
NME	New Molecular Entity
NOC	No Objection Certificate
NPPA	National Pharmaceutical Pricing Authority
OPEC	Organization of Petroleum Exporting Countries
OPPI	Organization of Pharmaceutical Producers of India

OTC	Over The Counter
PLC	Product Life Cycle
R & D	Research and Development
RRL	Regional Research Laboratories
RTE	Rep-Triggered Email
SWOT	Strength, Weakness, Opportunity, Threat
TGA	Therapeutic Goods Administration
TRIPS	Trade Related Intellectual Property Rights
UCP	Unique Consumer Perception
UCPMP	Uniform Code of Pharmaceutical Marketing Practices
US FDA	United States Federal Drug Administration
USP	Unique Selling Proposition
VL	Voluntary License
WHO	World Health Organization
WTO	World Trade Organization

The Indian Pharmaceutical Industry: An Overview

A Challenging Environment

The pharmaceutical marketing environment is perhaps the most challenging one on the Industrial scene today. It is characterized by:

A. Very intense competition with over 24,000 registered pharmaceutical companies - large, big, medium and small - fighting for their own place under the sun in a rapidly growing market that is estimated to be $ 55-billion by 2020. The competition is at its fiercest point today.

B. The seemingly ever-increasing and almost never-ending governmental regulations and policy changes.

C. Stifling price controls, eroding profits and consequently a vanishing bottom line.

D. Rigorous controls on formulations and an absence of international patent protection resulting in a 'me-too' maze of products with little or no product differentiation.

In short, it is a rat race, where a 'better mouse trap' just will not do. One needs much more than that and as in any jungle-concrete or real, only the fittest survive.

A Brief History

From ancient times, two systems of medicine were vogue in India. Firstly, there was Ayurvedic medicine, which dates back to the Vedic period. Ayurvedic medicine depends largely on the combination of various herbs, minerals and metals like gold, copper etc. Secondly, there was the Arabian system of medicine. Innumerable invasions had brought the Arabian system into India. In contrast to these, two other systems of medicine, namely Allopathy and Homeopathy, were in vogue in the western part of the world.

Despite being a very advanced indigenous system of medicine, Ayurveda has not really become popular enough, probably because of a very long British rule and the consequent development of an educational system including medical education based on a typical British model. As Allopathy or modern medicine started taking roots in India, all the research and development activities the world over fueled its growth in India as well. Conversely, there was hardly any research and development activities in the area of Ayurvedic medicine. Though the government has been making some efforts to promote Ayurvedic medicine, its development seems to be a long way off. It is still popular in rural areas, mainly be because modern medicine has not reached there. In urban areas it has yet to gain importance in so far as the prescription drug market is concerned. The inclination of Allopathic doctors towards prescribing an Ayurvedic medicine is very low indeed. Of late, however, the attitude of consumers towards Ayurvedic medicines seem to be increasingly favorable. Some of the pharmaceutical companies are planning to diversify into Ayurvedic drugs mainly to improve their profitability. Ayurvedic drugs are exempted from price control.

The Indian Systems of Medicine Get A Shot-in-the-arm with AYUSH!

The Government of India has created in March 1995, a department for the Indian systems of medicine (ISM&H). This department was later re-christened as AYUSH in 2003. Ayush means Life in Sanskrit. AYUSH is an acronym that stands for Ayurveda, Yoga and Naturopathy, Unani, Siddha, and Homeopathy. AYUSH was later elevated to a ministerial level which formed, The Ministry of AYUSH on November 9, 2014. With this, the Indian systems of medicines are indeed getting the much-needed shot-in-the-arm, which is evident from the progress it has made so far. Here's a snapshot of the progress:

1. There are 627 AYUSH colleges, and four national institutes to impart education at under-graduate level and post graduate level in Ayurveda in India. The national institutes are situated at New Delhi (All India Institute of Ayurveda for Post-graduate education), Jaipur (National Institute of Ayurveda), Jamnagar (Institute of Post-graduate Training and Research), Shillong (North Eastern Institute of Ayurveda and Homeopathy for under-graduate education).

2. The government has also set up five central councils and 82 peripheral institutes or centers for undertaking research in Ayurveda, Unani, Siddha, Yoga and naturopathy, and Homeopathy. These research centers conduct research and collaborative studies in areas such as medicinal plant research (medico-ethno botanical survey, pharmacognosy, and tissue culture), drug standardization, pharmacological and clinical research.

Origin of the Indian Pharmaceutical Industry

It is not exactly known as to when the Allopathic system of medicine made its entry into the country. But it is generally believed that it happened some time during the early part of the 19th century. The medicines were imported by the British for their personal use when they came to do business. This was the beginning of the pharmaceutical industry in India. Later, when they ultimately took over the country, the imports became a regular feature. These pharmaceutical products, which were introduced in India to provide relief to the British, soon gained popularity among the people in urban areas. For the first few decades after their introduction, pharmaceutical products were being imported into the country, mostly from Germany and the United Kingdom.

Indigenous production of these medicines, however, was started in 1901 with the establishment of the Bengal Chemical and Pharmaceutical Works, due to the pioneering efforts of Acharya P.C. Ray. The world of medical treatment was witnessing some significant developments, like Louis Pasteur's discovery of pathogenic bacteria as the cause of infectious diseases, while the Indian pharmaceutical industry was in its early stage. Scientists in India undertook research in tropical diseases like malaria, typhoid and cholera. Between 1904 and 1907 four research institutes, namely The Haffkine Institute, King Institute, Central Research Institute and Pasteur Institute were established. Yet another significant development of this period was the use of chemicals for treating various diseases. Some very important drugs like aspirin and barbiturates were made available during this period. The First World War gave a real stimulus to domestic production of pharmaceuticals. There was a steep rise in demand and a drastic cut in imports. Consequently, the production of quinine salts registered a substantial increase for the first time. Production of caffeine from tea waste and manufacture of surgical dressings were also taken up during this period. However, with the resumption of imports after the war, the industry was back to square one. It received a set back, as it was unable to compete with imported products.

The Bengal Chemical and Pharmaceutical Works started production of tetanus antitoxin, a basic drug in 1930. Indigenous production till 1939 was sufficient to meet only about 13 percent of medical requirements. Thus a large part of domestic demand for drugs was still met by imports. The Second World War was another landmark in the history of Indian pharmaceutical industry. It provided a propitious atmosphere for further expansion of production.

By 1941, the industry took up the manufacture of new drugs like ido-chloro-hydroxy quinolone as well as a number of alkaloids like ephedrine and codeine. Besides, the industry made a beginning in the production of chemotherapeutic drugs like arsenicals, anti-leprotic drugs and colloidal preparations of calcium, silver, manganese and iodine. The production of glandular products like liver extracts was also undertaken. The Production of several formulations based on imported bulk drugs also showed a significant expansion during the period.

Post-war developments in the west resulted in a high degree of product obsolescence, replacing many older drugs with antibiotics and new chemotherapeutic agents. This put the fledgeling Indian pharmaceutical industry at a great disadvantage. As a result, Indian companies had to stop production of many items that were manufactured during the war years. Instead they started manufacturing formulations based on imported bulk drugs and extraction of therapeutic agents from plant sources.

Thus, at the time independence, with the small base that existed for the production of medicines, the industry could not make much headway, in the absence of consistent governmental support to a nascent industry. The estimated value of production of pharmaceuticals in 1947 was a meagre Rs. 10 Crores.

Post-Independent Era

Immediately after independence, the government addressed itself to the task of achieving a high rate of economic progress with special emphasis on speedy industrialization. When the government of independent India embarked on planned economic expansion about six decades ago, the development of the Indian pharmaceutical industry was not commensurate with the size of the country and the growing needs of its population. Since then, the progress of the pharmaceutical industry in the country has been substantial and many-sided, and can best be described as dramatic.

Dramatic Progress

From a mere US $ 31million (equivalent to Rs. 10-Crore in production value) in 1947, to a whopping US $ 29.1 billion in 2017 (estimated), pharmaceutical industry in India has come a long way. Today India manufactures over 400 bulk drugs and about 100,000 formulations. The number of pharmaceutical units too have increased from 1,752 in 1955 to about 24,000 in 2016. Furthermore, in the United Nations Industrial Development Organization (UNIDO) classification of the developing countries according to the 'state of the art' in the pharmaceutical sector India is ranked at the top.

Exports of bulk drugs and formulations too have shown a dramatic progress from a total import-dependent industry at the time of independence to a net-exporter for over eighteen years now. Pharmaceutical exports have grown from a mere US $ 24 million in 1965 to a net-exporter status in 1999-2000 with an impressive US $ 1.25 billion in 1999. Total exports of pharmaceuticals in 2016 were US $ 16.6 billion.

Industry Structure

The pharmaceutical industry is very aptly described as a 'life-line' industry. It plays a vital role in alleviating the suffering of millions of people and controlling various ailments that afflict human beings. Recognizing this, the planners of Indian economic development after independence have rightly included this industry in the core sector.

The present day Indian pharmaceutical industry has three main sectors:

1. The public sector
2. The Indian private sector
3. The foreign sector

It is estimated that there are presently 24,000 pharmaceutical units with 330 in the list of the Directorate General of Technical Development (DGTD) generally known as the organized sector.

The organized sector, which is less than two percent of the total number of manufacturing units, accounts for about 90 percent of the total value of drug production, whereas the remaining 98 percent of units account for only 10 percent of production value of drug formulations in the country. In case of bulk drugs, the contribution of the small-scale sector is even smaller.

The Public Sector

Although there are over twenty-four thousand pharmaceutical companies in India, the core of the pharmaceutical industry comprises about 250 large and medium-size pharmaceutical companies of which five are in the public sector. These Public Sector Enterprises (PSUs) are:

1. IDPL (Indian Drugs & Pharmaceuticals Limited)
2. HAL (Hindustan Antibiotics Limited)
3. RDPL (Rajasthan Drugs & Pharmaceuticals Limited)
4. KAPL (Karnataka Antibiotics & Pharmaceuticals Limited)
5. BCPL (Bengal Chemicals & Pharmaceuticals Limited)

The Public Sector Units (PSUs) in pharmaceutical industry started with the first prime minister of India, late Pandit Jawaharlal Nehru. He said: "The drug industry must be in the public sector and I think an industry of the nature of the drug industry should not be in the private sector" But over the years the pharmaceutical PSUs went through a long series of losses, became sick and their rehabilitation and revival plans never took off. Pharmaceutical PSUs have suffered because of policy apathy and it all comes down to the poor management. Jyothi Datta rightly observed in her article that - *Once crown jewels, Pharma PSUs stare into the sunset* in The Hindu Business Line January 20, 2017.

In 2016, a union cabinet meeting chaired by the prime minister Narendra Modi decided to go-head for the need-based sale of the surplus land of four pharmaceutical PSUs to settle outstanding liabilities. Once this is completed, the government would take the steps to close down IDPL, RDPL, and assess BCPL and HAL for a strategic sale.

Research Institutes in the Public Sector

Apart from PSUs, public-funded research institutes also played a pivotal role in the growth of the pharmaceutical sector. The government created a number of research institutes under the guidance of the Indian Council of Medical Research (ICMR) and the Council of Scientific and Industrial Research (CSIR). Both these research institutes played a significant role in boosting the Indian pharmaceutical sector. Here is a list of some of the more important research laboratories and institutes in the public sector;

1. CDRI (Central Drug Research Institute), Lucknow
2. Indian Institute of Chemical Technology (IICT), Hyderabad
3. National Chemical Laboratory (NCL) Pune
4. Regional Research Laboratories (RRL) Hyderabad, Jammu and Jorhat
5. Center for Cellular and Molecular Biology (CCMB) Hyderabad

In developing few innovative drugs in India, CDRI has made a significant contributions. Many of these, however could not see the light of the day due to lack of commercial orientation. CDRI, however had invented more than 100 new process technologies, which were successfully commercialized.

The significant contribution of CSIR Laboratories in fostering the technological development of the Indian pharmaceutical industry is evident from the fact that a number of Indian drug majors such as Lupin, Ranbaxy, Wockhardt, Piramal, Neuland, Sun Pharma, Orchid, SOL Pharma, J B Chemical and Aurobindo Pharma have benefited from the services of these research institutes in some way or the other.

PSUs and research institutes in the public sector have made another major contribution for the pharmaceutical industry in India, i.e., in the area of human capital. About one-third of the two hundred and odd entrepreneurs who have made the Indian pharmaceutical industry what it is today have worked in IDPL product or research and development in early part of their careers. That is where they acquired the necessary skills and knowledge that are required by the entrepreneurs of pharmaceutical industry and also through their long term association with the public sector units. They form the backbone of the modern pharmaceutical industry in India as we know today.

The Indian Private Sector

What is the major driver behind the spectacular growth of Indian pharmaceutical industry? Cost advantage, skilled manpower, increasing incidence of non-communicable diseases, increasing penetration of health insurance, large number of blockbusters going out off patent in highly regulated markets such as the US and EU (European Union) and the list can go on. But what is the single major factor that enabled

Indian Pharma reach the phenomenal heights that it has reached today? Legislation. Yes. It is the legislative changes that have paved the way for the exponential growth of pharmaceutical industry as seen today. Not convinced? Consider these facts:

A. At the time of independence, India recognized product patents. There was little or no manufacturing of pharmaceuticals immediately after independence. India was totally dependent on imports from the western world and consequently the drug prices were very high.

B. 1970. India changed its Patents Act in 1970. The Patents Act 1970 with the Patents Rules 1972, came into force on 20th April 1972 replacing the Indian Patents and Designs Act 1911. One of the major changes of the Patents Act 1970 was giving allowance only to process patents with regard to innovation relating to drugs, medicines, food and chemicals. Indian pharmaceutical entrepreneurs grabbed the opportunity, honed their reverse engineering skills and made in India a major player in the active pharmaceutical ingredients market around the globe in the following years.

C. 1994. India singed the GATT (General Agreement on Tariffs and Trade) in 1994 heralding a massive opportunity for the Indian industries in general and pharmaceutical sector in particular. Ever-increasing healthcare costs in the developed world have been literally forcing every government to contain costs. A number of blockbuster drugs with multi-billion dollar sales were going off patent throwing up a massive opportunity for generic drugs. Some of the more progressive and ambitious Indian pharmaceutical entrepreneurs have once again lapped up the opportunity and carved out a significant share of the generics market in the US and EU (European Union).

Legislative changes in India have, thus been a great enabler in creating an environment that is conducive to rapid growth. The Indian pharmaceutical sector turned the tables in the domestic market by notching up the top eight slots in the pharmaceutical league table. In the late 1960s and early 1970s there was hardly an Indian pharmaceutical company among the top ten league. In 2017, eight of the top ten pharmaceutical companies are from the Indian sector. Only two multinational companies - Abbott (Rs. 5,851-Crore) and GlaxoSmithKline (Rs-Crore 3,424) could garner a seat at the top-ten table. Top Ten Indian pharmaceutical companies are presented in Table 1.1.

Table 1.1 Top Ten Indian Pharmaceutical Companies

Company	Rs. Crore (MAT November 2017)	Market Share (%)
1. Sun Pharma (including Ranbaxy)	9,729	8.71
2. Cipla	5,069	4.54
3. Zydus Cadila	4,262	3.82
4. Mankind	3842	3.44
5. Lupin	3,793	3.40
6. Torrent (including Unichem)	3,615	3.28
7. Alkem	3414	3.06
8. Intas	3,158	2.83
9. Macleods	3,053	3.73
10. Dr. Reddy's Labs	2,500	2.24
Top Ten, Total	**42.435**	**39.05**

Source: AIOCD AWACS Pharma Trac

The Foreign Sector

The foreign sector in Indian pharmaceutical industry comprises all multinational companies operating in India. The multinational drug firms had a dominant market share at the time of independence and even till 1970s. Due to legislative and regulatory changes, they later seem to be reducing their focus on the Indian market. The Indian arms of MNC drug firms that have enjoyed premium pricing for many of their parents' innovative drugs even after losing their patent protection may have to bear the brunt of regulatory control, with price controls eating into their profits on one hand and cheaper alternate Indian generics eroding their market shares on the other hand.

The revenues and profits of multinational pharmaceutical companies have been taking a beating since 2013, post implementation of the new drug pricing policy. For instance GlaxoSmithKline Pharma's operating profit margin has dropped from 34 percent in 2010 to less than 18 percent in 2014-15, thanks to price cuts mandated by the new pricing policy. Even the other multinational pharmaceutical companies had a similar experience. The top ten MNC drug firms had a share of 17.37 percent of the Indian pharmaceutical market in 2017, which is less than half of the top ten Indian pharmaceutical companies' share of 39.05 percent (Table 1.2).

Table 1.2 Top Ten MNC Pharma Companies in India

Company	Rs. Crore (MAT November 2017)	Market Share (%)
1. Abbott (Abbott Healthcare, and Abbott)	5,851	5.24
2. Glaxo Smith Kline	3,424	3.07
3. Pfizer	2,689	2.41
4. Sanofi India	2,580	2.31
5. Novo Nordisk	1,233	1.10
6. Novartis	1,069	0.96
7. M S D	756	0.68
8. AstraZeneca	667	0.60
9. Merck	664	0.59
10. Janssen	463	0.41
Top Ten, Total	**19,396**	**17.37**

Source: AIOCD AWACS Pharma Trac

Drug Discovery

The record of Indian pharmaceutical industry in the discovery of new medicinal substances is abysmally low. The earliest drug discovered in India was urea stibamine 1922. The second drug was methaqualone, which was synthesized at the Regional Research Laboratories of Hyderabad, had the pharmacological studies conducted at Lucknow and was commercially developed in the U.K. Haymycin, an antibiotic developed by the Hindustan Antibiotics Limited, a public sector undertaking, was the third drug. The fourth drug, enfenamic acid, was synthesized at the Regional Research Laboratories, Hyderabad and was marketed by Unichem under the brand name Tromaril. Ciba-Geigy marketed the fifth drug, an anti-depressant by name Sintamil.

Compared to this, the six developed countries, namely Italy, West Germany, France, the U.K., the USA and Japan had introduced as many as 2,567 new drugs during the ten-year period between 1970-80. During the same period as many as 6,374 new compounds had undergone clinical trials.

Why is it that in seventy years the Indian pharmaceutical industry could not introduce more than a handful of new drugs?

Of course, any comparison with the developed countries is meaningless. But then, India is next only to the two super powers in terms of technically skilled manpower. The research centers are manned by some of the best scientists. What are the reasons for this dismal performance in discovering new drugs?

1. **The Cost Factor:** The prohibitively high cost of a new drug discovery is the first and foremost reason. It is estimated that a new drug discovery (from concept to commercialization) would cost on an average about US $ 1.5 billion, and has a gestation period of ten to twelve years.

2. **Low Profit Margin:** Large international pharmaceutical companies spend about 10 to 20 percent of their annual sales volume on research and development of new drugs. Most pharmaceutical companies in India would consider themselves fortunate and successful if they could make a 10 percent Net Profit Before Tax (NPBT). Research & Development expenditure in India, therefore, is around an insignificant two percent of their sales volume. However, this is changing as the Indian drug majors are able to make higher profits as they are able to get more than fifty percent of their total sales from international markets, where the price realizations are higher. Some of them are investing close to ten percent of their sales on research to stay ahead of competition.

3. **Inadequate Fiscal Incentives:** The fiscal incentives provided by the government are hardly adequate to support the high cost of research and development and the risk of uncertainty.

Rapid Strides in Research and Development (R&D)

After India became a member of WTO and product patent regime, some of the leading Indian pharmaceutical companies have stepped up their research and development effort substantially. A Pharmabiz study of 25 drug companies revealed that these companies have increased their research spend by 42 percent in the fiscal 2004 to US $ 40 million fromUS $ 27. 2 million the previous year. Companies like Ranbaxy (later acquired by Sun Pharma), Dr. Reddy's Labs, Torrent Pharmaceuticals, Sun Pharma are now spending close to ten percent of their sales on R&D. Furthermore, companies such as Lupin, Zydus Healthcare, Glenmark, Wockhardt too have invested huge amounts on R&D activity and subsequently stepped up their spend on research and development. These companies are improving their competitiveness in areas such as product development, Active Pharmaceutical Ingredients (API) synthesis, Novel Drug Delivery Systems (NDDS) and indeed even in developing new drugs.

Bundle of Paradoxes

The pharmaceutical industry in India provides a curious bundle of many paradoxes. Consider these for example:

Paradox #1: Controlled prices! Expensive drugs!

The industry has been subjected for close to five decades, to an increasingly stringent system of price controls currently covering close to eighty percent of the Indian pharmaceutical market, but the impression is still widespread that the prices of medicines are on the high side.

Paradox #2: Urban industry?

Despite the dramatic progress and the phenomenal growth over the seventy-year period, the benefits of modern medicine have not effectively reached about forty percent of the population. Even today, pharmaceutical industry in India seems to be essentially urban-oriented.

Paradox #3: Healthcare industry ailing?

Despite its apparently impressive overall growth, the industry, which produces drugs and formulations for the health of the people is not really robust, if not actually sick.

The per capita healthcare expenditure continues to be low at US $ 75 per year. Compare this with Indonesia at US $ 99 and Thailand at US $ 228. This per capita expenditure is for the total healthcare. Pharmaceuticals are only 15 - 20 percent of the total health care expenditure. If you take this into account the per capita expenditure on medicines is about US $ 11.25 - 15 only.

Paradox #4: Small scale or large scale?

Maintenance of high quality standards in the production of both bulk drugs and formula'tions is of paramount importance. Any laxity or compromise in the quality of drugs may spell the difference between life and death. It is common knowledge that many small-scale manufacturers do not possess either the requisite apparatus and equipment or the technically qualified, competent manpower necessary to ensure quality control. They are also not in a position to meet the conditions required for Good Manufacturing Practices (GMP). A number of experts in the field including Dr. B. B. Gaitonde, an eminent pharmacologist and the Regional Advisor of World Health Organization

(WHO) firmly opined that pharmaceutical production does not lend itself to small-scale operations. In spite of unequivocal opinions by experts about the inadequate and unsatisfactory quality of drugs manufactured by the small-scale sector, the units in this sector continue to increase.

Paradox #5: Proliferation of brands or manufacturing units?

It is often argued that there are too many brands, which are not necessary, and this proliferation of brands is leading to wastage of productive capacities, which could not have been used effectively for some other essential products. Secondly, the unhealthy competition between too many 'me-too' brands and the consequent increase in promotional expenditure is pushing up drug prices. Contrary to this popular belief, the proliferation is more in the number of manufacturing units in the small-scale sector that is leading to the ever increasing 'me-too' brands. In 1981, the Drug Controller of India, Dr. S. S. Ghatoskar called for a check on the proliferation of new drug units, estimated to be around 5,000 in 1981 and for a more efficient quality control programs. According to him about one-third of these units are only re-packing units. Ironically enough the number of drug units too have gone up considerably, in fact more than three times to 16,000 by 1992.

Paradox #6: Control costs on output, but not on input costs?

One of the major impediments in the progress of pharmaceutical industry in India is the Drug Price Control Order of 1969 (DPCO). This and the subsequent Drug Price Control Orders have certainly put back the Indian pharmaceutical industry by several years. What is peculiar about the pharmaceutical control is that while the prices of raw materials as well as finished products are controlled, there is absolutely no control on the input costs. The input costs seem to be ever-increasing. As a result, the mark-ups provided in the essential product categories are lower than the breakeven points. To top it all, there is even a ceiling on the profitability of the manufacturing units.

Paradox #7: Retention prices or detention prices?

Another irrational and unrealistic policy is the system of retention prices and the pooling system in case of bulk drugs. Under this system different prices for different manufacturing units are fixed for the same product based on the direct costs and actual yields of the respective companies. But a 'pooled price' is fixed for the bulk drug to be supplied in the formulations. The more efficient manufacturer who produces the drug more cost-effectively does not enjoy any extra benefit. Instead, he has to deposit the difference between the 'pooled price' and the 'lower retention price' into the Drug Price Equalization Account (DPEA) administered by the government. This amount is used to meet the claims made by the manufacturers (who could not achieve cost-effectiveness due to manufacturing inefficiency), whose retention prices are higher than the 'pooled prices'. Isn't it really a cess pool?

The Chavda Committee has strongly criticized this 'retention and pool-price system' as way of subsidizing cost-inefficient units at the cost of consumer, while penalizing the more efficient producer, who earns only a lower retention price for his efficiency on lower cost of production.

It is a disincentive for efficiency. Why should or why would any manufacturer carry out research and development for improving process efficiency and reduce production costs, when there are rewards for inefficient manufacturing and penalties for efficient manufacturing?

Paradox #8: Licensing policy or silencing policy?

What is paradoxical about the industrial licensing policy, at least in the Indian pharmaceutical industry, is that the policies designed to stimulate growth in production have actually stunted growth. A few examples amplify this:

- Reservation of some essential bulk drugs for the less efficient public sector
- Preference given to the small-scale sector, which cannot hope to achieve the economies of large-scale manufacturing
- Fragmentation of capacities for bulk drug manufacture that is inherent in the licensing policy it self. Bulk drug to formulation ratio parameters of 1:5 or 1:10 virtually force every manufacturer in the organized sector to take up bulk drug production, irrespective of efficiency of operations and consequent cost-effectiveness or ineffectiveness. The net result of all these contradictory policies has been declining profits despite increasing prices.

Paradox #9: Price control or profit control?

Large pharmaceutical companies (with a sales turnover of Rs. 6-crore or more) cannot earn profits of more than 10 percent of their sales as per the DPCO 1979. Compare this with the R&D expenditure of 10 to 20 percent of their sales turnover by pharmaceutical companies in the developed countries. At this rate can the Indian pharmaceutical industry ever become globally competitive?

The 'Generics' Policy

The government of India announced on January 17, 1981, its decision to abolish brand names for single ingredient formulations, namely Analgin, Aspirin, Chlorpromazine, Ferrous Sulphate and Piperazine and not to permit brand names for all new single-ingredient drugs. In addition, for all other branded-generic formulations, generic names should be printed on packs more conspicuously and above the brand names. The Tariff Commission as well as the Hathi Committee had examined the pros and cons of this new generic policy.

While the advocates of the generics policy felt that a major benefit of the abolition of brand names would be reduction in drug prices, the industry circles contended that in a country where the prices of 80 percent of formulations are controlled by the government the possibility of any further reduction in drug prices is unthinkable. A number of eminent doctors are against the generics-only policy for the following reasons:

- Substitution of drugs by unqualified chemists can lead to dangerous consequences.
- Brand names carry the manufacturer's assurance of quality, abolition of brand names would considerably reduce and weaken this incentive.
- Experience of similar 'generics' policies in some other countries have paved the way for sub-standard and spurious drugs.
- The abolition of brand names for new drugs will prove a strong deterrent to their introduction into the country. The generics policy is likely to benefit only the small-scale manufacturers and traders. The 'generics' experiment in 1980-81 quite clearly blocked the way the new drug introduction. In 1980-81 only 11 new drugs were introduced during the first seven-month period, as against 35 the preceding year.

Wither Loan-licensing?

The government in 1987 announced its decision to phase out and finally abolish the loan-licensing arrangements in pharmaceutical industry by 1990, which was later extended upto 1993, to ensure the adoption of Good Manufacturing Practices (GMP).

But can the government really abolish loan licensing in the pharmaceutical industry? Consider these reasons:

- Loan licensing agreements are not peculiar to India. They are present in many countries such as the US and in Europe. Loan licensing agreements in India have helped the Indian pharmaceutical industry to record very impressive growth particularly during the past four to five decades.

- Phasing out the loan licensing agreements in the pharmaceutical industry would result in closure of about 8,000 small-scale units and about three lakh people losing their jobs.

- Loan licensing system avoids under-utilization of capacities and as a result helps in checking price increases.

- Refuting the allegation that it is the loan licensing manufacturers who are mainly responsible for most of the substandard drugs produced in the country today, the small-scale manufacturers have emphatically stated that such offenses on a percentage basis are more among the medium-scale manufacturers. They had requested government to set up a committee to go into the merits and demerits of the system. A more pragmatic approach would be to enforce stricter quality control parameters and ensure their implementation.

The Policy of Drug Price Control

Price control is the most important issue that the Indian pharmaceutical industry is facing today. While the government after signing the GATT accord, liberalized policies for all other industries in the priority and non-priority areas of the economy, pharmaceuticals have been singled out to be kept under price control as well as licensing restrictions. As a result there has been a steady decline in the profitability.

Mr. T. Thomas, Chairman of Glaxo India Limited (GSK now) in his address at the company's 68th Annual General Meeting, made a thorough analysis of price control and its negative impact on the pharmaceutical industry in India. He also suggested some plausible alternatives in his speech. The highlights of his speech are given in Table 1.3.

Table 1.3 Price Control: A Policy That Fails

1. **Fallacy of controlling outputs without controlling inputs:** It is a matter of common sense that if we want to control the price of a product we should be able to control the cost of most of the inputs that go into the manufacture. In order to obtain greater rationality in price control for the items selected, it becomes necessary for government to extend its price surveillance to an increasing number of input industries and services. That is impossible even in a totalitarian state as evidenced by recently exposed economic shambles in the former Soviet Union.

2. **Inevitability of conflicts of interests and rigidity:** Price control is almost always introduced by government when there is a rise in costs and prices. The politician is more vulnerable when there is inflation, which is precisely the time when the industry will need price increases to compensate for cost escalations. The basic conflict of interest between what is rational and what is expedient, in the minds of administrators of price control and their political masters, introduces a cumulative series of distortions in pricing decisions.

3. **Quality of products deteriorate to lowest common standards:** Under price control the inevitable reaction of the manufacturers is to survive by adopting the lowest possible standards of services that they can get away with. Companies, which have high standards of quality and safety in the manufacture of drugs prefer to discontinue the manufacture of drugs, which are uneconomical rather than compromise on standards. This inevitably leads to another set of problems that arise from prolonged price controls.

4. **Shortages, black-markets, black money and spurious products:** As the rigors of price control continue, honest manufacturers will find it unviable to continue the manufacture of products. They will try to minimize their loses by reducing their production. This happened in the soap and vanaspati industries in 1974, and even the government realized the folly of price control on these items and abolished it.

Contd...

Drug companies today are heading towards the same state, that the soap and vanaspati industries were in, in the early 70's. Of late there have been many instances of drug authorities in different states busting racketeers, who were producing counterfeit and spurious medicines. Such racketeers thrive when distortions are caused in supplies due to the rigors of price control. Yet the pharmaceutical industry has been chosen to be the last remaining industry to be still convulsed under price control.

5. **Small-scale sector is kept outside price control:** The other irrational distortion in drug price control in India is that the small scale sector in the industry is kept outside price control.

In a normal economy, the small scale sector has to compete and justify its existence through lower overhead costs, better quality of service, dedicated nature of relationships etc., and not through subsidies and favorable price discrimination. Subsidization, through discriminatory pricing advantage under a price control regime is not the method to promote a healthy small-scale sector. If the logic of price discrimination in favor of the small scale sector were adopted in more industries, our country would be reverting to medieval times in terms of technology and competitiveness. In any case, how does it benefit the consumer or contain inflation, if the small-scale sector is expected to sell at higher prices while the organized sector is expected to sell at lower but unremunerative prices?

6. **Erodes resources and motivation to invest in modernization, R&D or expansion:** When an industry is kept under price control, the firms in that industry will not have the resources to invest in expansion, or in modernization and R&D. Every industry, which has been under price control for any period of time, has shown diminishing profits, increasing financial vulnerability and inability to attract fresh investment. In the last couple of years most of the essential industries have come back from the dead after price controls were lifted and are now blossoming and investing in further growth.

7. **Price control can drive an honest firm out of business:** When price control goes on for long, firms are forced into a choice between continuously compromising on quality while running into losses, or closing the business. This danger of becoming unviable has

Contd...

already been demonstrated in the case of the Indian subsidiaries of some international pharmaceutical companies. If more companies were to be forced into that situation over a period of time, it could create a shortage or monopolistic supplies by a new breed of manufacturers (as in the vanaspati industry in 1970's) who know how circumvent price control with scant regard for quality and safety standards. The Indian consumer will be the main loser in that eventuality and the very purpose of government in introducing price control would be entirely negated.

8. **Price control projects a negative among international investors:** Price control in any industrial sector in a country will act as a major negative factor in the eyes of international investors in general. The negative image caused by price control in the pharmaceutical industry is not confined to investors in that industry alone. Investors generally tend to take a negative view of a government that still maintains its belief in and commitment to the discredited system of price control. The removal of price control is a necessary part of our country's attempt to restore confidence in Indian economic policy and to attract investments from abroad.

9. **Placing government on collision course with industry:** Price control by the very nature of its administration by government machinery tends to place industry concerned on an inevitable collision course with the government. The most important lesson to be learnt by us in India from the phenomenal success of Far Eastern countries like Japan, South Korea, Taiwan, Malaysia, and Thailand is the co-operative nexus between government and industry in each of these countries. This has contributed to their high performance. Policies and practices that may create conflict between government and industry have to be eschewed if our country has to progress. Price control is one such issue and the sooner it is eliminated from our economy the better will we be placed to create such nexus and effectively compete with other market-oriented economies. When there is such a co-operative nexus between industry and government it secures the interests of consumer as well.

10. **Price control as a political liability:** When price control is first introduced to a group, it is usually on the basis of populist measures like holding the price line in the face of inflationary pressures. The

rhetoric of the politician at this stage is directed against traders and producers, who are pictured as hoarders and profiters. If by chance there are some international companies engaged in that industry they are branded as 'multinationals' (even though that epithet has lost its venom since the demise of communism in most parts of the world). The minister in-charge almost acts like the brave little Dutch boy, who put his finger in the dyke to stop the leak that could have swelled into a flood.

But as time passes by, the inevitable effects of inflation begin to create strains in the economy and all the ills of price controls begin to show up the shortage, black marketing, spurious products etc., The politician will at this stage try to play the role of King Canute. No tide can pass controllers or ministers, as the tide never respected kings. So they have to concede some price and this assumes a very high profile. Even the pricing of a humble relatively unimportant product like a washing soap was elevated in the 1970's to become a subject matter for the Central Committee of Economic Coordination of the Government of India, presided over none other than the prime minster himself. Today the pricing of multivitamin pills may hold tremors for ministers, who have to take decision. When this stage is reached, the politician begins to feel extremely nervous, like a man riding a tiger. He does not know how to get off the tiger without being eaten alive. On the other hand, he has unwittingly built up a high profile for the tiger and his ride.

But dismounting the tiger of price control requires a lot of skill and some luck. The longer a price control regime for a product continues, the more difficult it becomes to correct or dismantle it. The turmoil being faced by Mr. Yeltsin in the erstwhile Soviet Union in trying to dismantle price control is yet another strong warning against the continuance of price control in our country and calls for the dismantling of existing controls as early as possible.

Need for a Re-look

Cost of production, cost of raw materials, packaging materials, utilities, services, salaries and wages etc., continued to escalate resulting in reduced profit margins. Several leading units suffered losses or just managed to break even. Pharma sales of many companies were in the red with non-Pharma sales subsidizing the Pharma business. The unmistakable trend in profitability after the 1969 DPCO (Drug Price Control Order) can be seen in Table 1.4.

That the pharmaceutical industry is able to achieve a competitive position in spite of the stringent controls, is a positive proof of what it can achieve with the support of more pragmatic, growth-oriented policies.

NCAER's Observations

While reviewing the ailing Indian pharmaceutical industry's performance, National Council for Applied Economic Research (NCAER) very aptly made the following observations to put it back on the path to growth:

- Preference should be given, in the matter of import technology to companies with adequate research and development facilities to absorb the imported technology.
- To be effective, major part of research and development work on development of technology should be carried out in the industrial units and not in isolated government laboratories.
- To enable the industry to invest more on R&D, its profitability should be improved. Fiscal incentives are of no avail in the absence of adequate profits. Liberal bank credit should also be made available.
- The present restrictions on larger business houses should be relaxed and mergers should be encouraged in order to enable Indian companies to face international competition.
- Instead of sheltering inefficient units and obsolete technologies, vigorous competition between different sectors (public, private organized, FERA (Foreign Exchange Regulation Act), and small-scale sector should be promoted in order to improve the efficiency and bring down prices.
- A more realistic policy may be evolved to enable FERA companies to play a constructive and useful role in the achievement of national objectives.
- From a long-term point of view, a second look is needed at the patent law relating to drugs, as the radical amendments made in 1970 failed to produce any tangible results.

The details of subsequent changes in the Drug Price Control Order and its implications are discussed in detail in chapter on The Price.

Table 1.4 Profitability of Indian Pharma Industry After the 1969

Fiscal Year	Profit Before Tax (% of Sales)	Percent of Sales Sources
1969-70	15.47	Hathi Committee Report
1974-75	10.70	
1977-78	11.70	RBI Bulletins
1980-81	8.80	
1982-83	7.50	
1983-84	6.70	NACER Study
1984-85	5.80	A.F. Ferguson Study
1985-86	4.50	OPPI Estimate
1986-87	3.50	
1986-88	3.40	
1987-89	1.70	
1988-90	2.00	
1990-91	2.00	

Protection of International Patents and Intellectual Property Rights (IPR)

Intellectual Property Rights (IPR)

Intellectual property, as the name suggests, is basically a concept, an idea or thought leading to the actual invention of a product or process. Intellectual property right, therefore, is a legal protection for inventions, which are the results of the individual's ideas resulting in new products and processes. The World Intellectual Property Organization (WIPO) defines and clarifies what exactly should be the nature of 'intellectual property.' Prior to 1994, about 140 countries gave legal protection to both product patents as well as process patents as per the Paris Convention on International Patents and IPR. India along with Mexico, Brazil and China agreed to provide patent protection for products and processes, when they signed the GATT (General Agreement on Trade and Tariffs) at Morocco in 1994.

Patent

A patent is a legal protection for an invention. At the same time, not all inventions are patentable. Generally the invention must possess or meet certain criteria such as:

- It must involve some inventive step
- It must not be obvious, and
- It must be applicable industrially

Inventions can be broadly classified into two categories, namely product inventions and process inventions. The patent too, therefore, could be either a product patent or a process patent or even a combination of both. India, for example, recognizes only process patents since the amendment of the Indian Patents Act 1970.

A patent granted for an invention is an 'intellectual property,' which remains in force for a specific period of time (7 years in India and 20 years in countries, which have signed the Paris Convention of Patents and Intellectual Property Rights).

If any other person exploits the patent without prior authorization (license) of the owner of the patent, he infringes the rights and commits an illegal act. However, if the patentee does not work the patent or he does not allow others to work the same, the patent can be revoked or the patentee is forced to give a 'compulsory license,' which is an authorization to exploit the invention. The conditions of granting a compulsory license are regulated in the Act. The decision of granting a compulsory license includes fixing remuneration for the patent.

Prior to signing the GATT in 1994, India was facing the threat of trade sanctions by the U.S. for its alleged failure to adequately protect IPR. The U.S. government can identify so-called unfair trade partners under a provision named 'Super 301,' of its omnibus trade law of 1988. After naming such countries, the U.S. representative is required to negotiate with them for measures in removing market barriers to U.S. exports including those resulting from alleged theft of patented technologies. If the negotiations do not yield results to the satisfaction of of the U.S. government, it can retaliate by restricting or banning exports to the U.S. India was also listed on 'Super 301' category along with Japan, Brazil and South Korea in the early 1990s owing to the pressures exerted by IPR Alliance, U.S. Chamber of Commerce, Pharmaceutical manufacturers, Association of Motion Picture Export Association of America on the U.S. government. The U.S. government has been demanding that India should join the Paris Convention on patents as well as amend the Indian Patent Act of 1970.

Even those who support the demand that India should accede to the Paris Convention admit that it can have disastrous impact on India's booming chemical and pharmaceutical exports. India's legal luminaries are also unanimous that India should not be a party to a one-sided and discriminatory treaty, which bestows little rights on the signatory, but gives unlimited powers to patent holders.

Signing the Paris Convention on Patents would certainly give a big boost to the multinationals operating in India at the expense of Indian drug manufacturers. The prices of new drugs too, are likely to go up steeply. The domestic industry would receive a severe set back. On the positive side, the newer drugs and the latest discoveries in the field of medicine would be made available in India much sooner than now. The time lag can be minimized and India could benefit fully from the new drug discoveries in the west. More and more multinational companies may be attracted by the opportunities that India has to offer.

Experts opine that the proposed changes (as per the Dunkel Draft) in the Indian Patents Act, which seek to alter the basis of the law from process patents to product patents, would only help patent holders to monopolize commodities and foreclose research. Developing countries would be impoverished and reduced to mere markets for goods produced by developed countries.

Dunkel Draft

Arthur Dunkel, Director General of GATT, has made some compromise proposals in respect of the Uruguay Round of negotiations in the area of Trade Related Intellectual Property Rights (TRIPS). The Dunkel proposals cover a number of aspects like market access, trademarks, product and process patents, term of patent, compulsory license and transitional period.

Transitional Period

All countries save the developing countries have been given a transitional period of one-year and developing countries an additional four years. To the extent that where a developing country not extending product patent protection to the area of technology on the general date of application on the agreement, it has been provided that the developing country concerned may delay the application of the obligation in respect of patents to such areas of technology for an additional period of five years. Thus in respect of food, chemicals, pharmaceuticals, chemicals and biotechnological products, India will have the possibility of delaying the application of the obligation till 1-1-2003. However, after the date of entry into force, such countries will have to provide means by which applications for patents can be filed. These applications can be examined only when the obligations on patent protection of these products become effective. There is also a provision for exclusive marketing rights for a period of five years, after obtaining market approval for a few products.

Major Objections to Dunkel Draft

The Dunkel proposals were initially objected mainly on the grounds that:

1. Prices of affected commodities would increase substantially
2. Importation being treated as working of the patent would destroy incentives to manufacture
3. A twenty-year patent term would result in delaying introduction of new products
4. Research and development would become redundant
5. Indian exports of such products would be affected
6. Patent protection on biotechnology would have adverse consequences on preventive medicine
7. Automatic licenses of right are needed to bring about competition
8. The burden of proof in case of an infringement should not be on the defendant

Hobson's Choice

Now that almost all countries, including China have fallen in line with the international patent law, it is no longer a matter of choice whether India should be a signatory to the Paris Convention on International Patents and IPR or not. The question is, when should India sign and what changes it can possibly incorporate in the proposed Dunkel Draft? And, how much time can India get for the transition? More importantly, the Indian government should allow drug companies to make adequate profits to prepare themselves to compete internationally.

It is not possible to achieve the ambitious objectives in terms of exports that the Indian government has set for the country in the absence of an international patent protection.

The new world economic order is quite different from what it was even a few years ago. With the ever-increasing trade alliances between different countries, the unification of Germany, the disintegration of the erstwhile super power Soviet Russia, it would be impossible for any nation to function and progress in isolation. The name of the game is cooperation. Furthermore, a number of those countries, which have been important markets for Indian exports are gradually and increasingly recognizing the international patent law. In other words those markets will be closed to Indian exports sooner than later if India did not sign the GATT agreement. Really speaking, it is a Hobson's choice!

India Signs GATT Accord

India after over four years of deliberations, dilly-dallying and protracted negotiations finally signed GATT including TRIPS on 15th April, 1994. This is regarded as a turning point for Indian pharmaceutical industry.

The main impact of TRIPS on pharmaceutical patents in India are:

1. A patent term of 20 years from the date of filing
2. Recognition of product patents
3. Importation of a product to be accepted as 'working' a patent
4. Compulsory licensing to be confined to special circumstances like emergency or abuse of patent rights
5. Reversal of 'Burden of Proof' in infringement action relating to process patents (obliging the defendant to prove that the process is non-infringing)

Transitional Period

The adoption of these provisions would bring Indian patent laws close to those in the industrialized world.

However, there will be a considerable delay before the effect of fundamental changes are perceived. Like all other developing countries that have not until now (1994) recognized pharmaceutical and technology products as patentable, India too is entitled under the terms of GATT agreement to a transitional period of ten years, before having to adopt to product patents for drugs. The transitional period for India was from 1995 to 2004.

Further, there would be no product protection for pipeline drugs (drugs under development during the period under patents published elsewhere in the world).

Indian companies that currently produce drugs that would infringe a product patent, if such a patent were recognized by the government or will infringe an international product patent prior to 2005 (pipeline drugs), may continue production after 2005, provided an equitable royalty and license fee is given to the originator till the patent expires.

Exclusive Marketing Rights (EMR)

However, drugs for which patent applications are made after TRIPS came into effect will have some marketing exclusivity in India, if they are registered during the transitional period. This exclusivity will run for a maximum period of five years during the transitional period and thereafter until patent expiry.

Implications of GATT

The signing of GATT is a mere signal that heralds a major change in the business environment worldwide. The protected markets are in the process of being snapped. The markets will therefore, be fiercely competitive. Only the fittest of industries will survive.

Once the transitional clock starts ticking, things will never be the same again. Dramatic changes are ahead for the Indian pharmaceutical industry. Some of the more important changes are:

More Active Multinational Companies (MNCs)

1. End of the era of protectionism under the Indian Patents Act (1970), a key factor that helped the Indian drug companies to achieve a remarkable rate of growth and even a net-exporter status in the Pharma industry.
2. The nature and intensity of competition are likely to change significantly. Multinationals will be more active in India as they ride out the transition period before GATT comes into force.
3. There will be a total restructuring of operations to optimize product lines and to introduce newer drugs in the Indian market. Some of the multinational drug companies introduced new products,

after India signed the GATT agreement. They have been holding back these product introductions. Some of these companies are: Bayer (Adalat Oros), Hindusthan Ciba Geigy, which is Novartis now (Nitraderm Transdermal product) and Sandoz, which is Novartis now (Sandimmune Neoral).

4. Some multinationals might want to get out of manufacturing in India altogether and concentrate on marketing and licensing their products. Already some of the well known international drug majors such as Hoechst (now Sanofi Aventis), Glaxo (now GlaxoSmithKline), Hindusthan Ciba Geigy (now Novartis) have already been into third-party manufacturing for greater flexibility and profitability (lower manufacturing costs).

5. Exports of new bulk drugs will no longer be that easy. First of all, cheap manufacturing of new bulk drugs will not be possible with product patents. Secondly, many bulk drug manufacturing facilities were coming up in South East Asian region posing tough competition to Indian exporters. Tough times indeed for small and medium players and the only way out is partnering with larger Indian companies or even multinationals.

6. While the fragmentation in the domestic industry continues due to the encouragement given by the government to small-scale manufacturers, there would be some contraction as well as consolidation through takeovers by larger companies wanting to increase their capacities. Those with good manufacturing facilities and practices would become toll manufacturers for large national as well as multinational companies.

7. The passage of Indian companies from a drug 'copying' culture to a 'research-based' strategy, each with its own aspirations to eventual multinational status (e.g., Sun Pharma, Lupin, Dr. Reddy's Labs, Wockhardt, Cipla etc.).

Future Position

The bigger gain from TRIPS is qualitative in nature. The transition to a regime of product patents will result in global majors entering India in a much bigger way with R&D intensive technology. India already possesses the necessary technological infrastructure for original R&D. As Dr. Heinz Redwood, author and Pharma industry consultant from U.K. says," It is not scientific genius that is in short supply, but cash flow."

Action Agenda

Ten years may seem long so far as transition is concerned, but it is no more than the average time it takes to develop a newly patented drug to the point of market introduction. The need, therefore, is to adapt business strategy to cope with the reality of product patents. The action agenda of some of the more progressive Indian companies focuses sharply on:

A. Reaching a critical mass

B. Marketing focus

C. Upgrading technologically

D. Increasing investment levels in R & D significantly above the industry average

E. Shifting of emphasis on export thrust from bulk-drugs-mainly to move value added generic formulations and to even more value-added marketing of branded generics overseas

F. Strategically integrating backwards into key bulk drugs and intermediates to achieve control on inputs in terms of cost, availability and quality

G. Improving efficiency of operations through optimization of business process and re-engineering

The Changing Face of Indian Pharmaceutical Industry: Post - WTO Era

A number of leading Indian pharmaceutical companies have seen a wide opportunity in the Post-GATT era before it arrived. They have seen at least seven big opportunity areas that can be exploited as India integrates with the world economy by recognizing product patents. Here's the rainbow on the opportunity horizon, which these companies have envisioned:

1. Marketing of branded generics in the domestic market

2. Marketing of bulk actives and drug intermediates in the highly industrialized regulatory markets

3. Marketing of branded generics in countries with little or no IPR protection

4. Marketing of generic formulations of off-patent drugs in regulated markets with strong IPR protection

5. Opportunities for custom synthesis of newly patented molecules

6. Branded generic formulations of off-patent, yet single-source drugs that are difficult to copy

7. Contract research opportunities

Furthermore, they have even visualized that in the not-so-distant future, there would be opportunities for collaborative research including drug discovery. Their vision and dreams have become a reality thanks to their valiant efforts and some positive policy initiatives by the government of India. As a result, within a decade after joining the World Trade Organization, Indian pharmaceutical industry has achieved a dramatic progress exploiting all the opportunities that globalization has to offer and more. Table 1.5 provides a snapshot of the dramatic progress that Indian Pharma industry has achieved on several counts.

Table 1.5 Dramatic Progress of Indian Pharma Industry: A Snapshot

Area	Progress Made
1. APIs (Active Pharmaceutical Ingredients)	1. India became the third largest global API merchant market with a market share of 7.2 percent. 2. World leader in terms of Ys (Drug Master File) applications filed in the US.
2. Formulations	1. Largest exporter of generic drug formulations in the world with a 20 percent share of the export market. 2. Ranks second in terms of the number of ANDAs filed with the US FDA
3. Manufacturing	Very competent and competitive manufacturing infrastructure comprising: A. 584 manufacturing sites certified by US FDA B. 1,400 WHO GMP certified manufacturing plants C. 1,105 manufacturers with COS (Certificate of Suitability) from EQDM
4. CRAMS (Contract Research and Manufacturing Services)	1. India's share of the global CRAMS market is likely to increase to 8-9 percent by 2018 2. Indian companies operating in contract manufacturing segment are moving up the value chain and are investing in better technology and higher capacities. Global majors are likely to outsource value-added products for biotech and speciality therapy areas from Indian companies operating in CRAMS space. (Contract Research and Manufacturing Services).

Contd...

5. Bio-similars	1. The Indian Bio-similars industry has been growing at CAGR of 30 percent. There are currently 25 companies operating in this space, marketing close to 50 products. 2. The global Bio-similars market is projected to be between US $ 25 to 35 billion. 3. The early experience with developing Bio-similars is paving way to capitalize on unfolding this big global opportunity.

Source: Adapted from IBEF

Exports

Indian pharmaceutical companies have been capitalizing on export opportunities in regulated and semi-regulated markets for some time now. In 2017, India exported pharmaceutical products worth US $ 16.84 billion and this is expected to grow to US $ 20 billion by 2020. For a country that was totally import dependent at the time of independence, to US $ 16.84 billion in 2017 is a very commendable progress indeed. The progress of Indian pharmaceutical exports and the consequent reduction in imports is presented in Table 1.6.

Table 1.6 Progress of Indian Exports (US $ Billion)

Financial Year	Exports	Imports
2012	10.1	3.6
2013	12.6	4.4
2014	14.5	4.6
2015	14.9	3.7
2016	16.9	3.7
2017	16.8	NA

Source: Adapted from Pharmaceuticals, IBEF, February 2018

Indian pharmaceutical industry today has achieved the distinction of becoming the world's largest provider of generic medicines. India accounts for about a fifth of the total global exports of generic drugs in terms of volume. These achievements have earned India the sobriquet - 'the pharmacy of the world'. Indian drugs are exported to more than 200 countries in the world, with the US as the key market. Table 1.7 presents details of Indian drug exports by region.

Table 1.7 Indian Drug Exports: Key Destinations

Region	Percent of Total Indian Drug Exports
US	40.6
Europe	19.7
Africa	19.1
Asian Countries	18.8

Source: Adapted from Pharmaceuticals, IBEF, February 2018

The two major contributors for achieving this leading position in pharmaceutical exports are legislative in nature. The first one is the Indian Patents Act 1970. It has brought the process development and reverse engineering skills of the country in organic synthesis to the fore. This technological capability has propelled Indian bulk drug industry to the third largest global generic API (Active Pharmaceutical Ingredient) merchant market in 2016, with a market share of 7.2 percent and massive portfolio of over 400 bulk drugs. In addition, India today is the world's leader in terms of Drug Master File (DMF) applications with the US, the world's largest pharmaceutical market.

The second major contributor is its signing the GATT (General Agreement on Tariffs and Trade) in 1995. It has brought the superior product development and manufacturing capabilities of the Indian pharmaceutical industry to the forefront. Indian pharmaceutical industry today capitalized on the tremendous opportunities that globalization has to offer and built a huge manufacturing infrastructure of 546 US FDA approved manufacturing sites, the highest number outside the US. Interestingly Indian drug makers account for close to a third (30 percent) of all the ANDAs (Abbreviated New Drug Applications) in the US.

The spectacular growth of the Indian Pharma industry seems to have come to a grinding halt in FY 2016-17. The exports during the year were more or less static at US $ 16.84 billion. The main reasons for this no-growth situation are - price erosion and absence of blockbuster drugs for Indian Pharma players. While this is a matter of concern, it is not alarming. Indian Pharma industry is strong and capable to meet any challenges that the changing global environment may bring.

Research and Development

Historically Indian pharmaceutical companies used to spend on an average 2 percent or less of their sales on research and development. But that has been changing gradually since India joined the World

Trade Organization (WTO) in 1995. Some of the more progressive drug firms in India such as Lupin, Dr. Reddy's Labs, Sun Pharma among others have been increasing their R&D spend. The R&D spend by five top Indian pharmaceutical companies is presented in table 1.8.

Table 1.8 R&D Spend by 5 Top Indian Pharma Companies
(Rs. Crore)

Company	F Y 2010 R&D Spend	F Y 2010 R&D Spend as % of Sales	F Y 2017 R&D Spend	F Y 2017 R&D Spend as % of Sales
1. SUN Pharma	208.2	5.5	2,145.8	7.1
2. Lupin	343.8	7.2	2,310.0	13.5
3. Dr. Reddy's Labs	379.3	5.4	1,955.0	13.9
4. Cipla	228.1	4.3	1,071.0	7.5
5. Aurobindo Pharma	97.2	2.7	543.0	3.7

Source: Bloomberg

The R&D expenditure of the top five Indian drug companies has increased six-fold since F Y 2010. The R&D expenditure as can be seen from the above table constitute 9 percent of the cumulative revenues of these companies. In fact, research costs of these companies are comparable to their global peers such as Teva, Mylan and Allergan.

As a result of this increasing R&D effort, India, which has been known for the past fifteen years or so as a large exporter of APIs and generic formulations is now getting to be known for a little more than that - an emerging hub of pharmaceutical research and development.

Companies such as Dr. Reddy's Labs, Sun Pharma, Zydus Cadila, Glenmark, Lupin, Wockhardt and Cipla and a few others have been, besides building on traditional generic product pipelines, investing in research on complex generics, specialty and differentiated products. They also started investing in pre-clinical development of small molecules with novel targets and with novel mechanisms of action. Indian Pharma and Biotech companies have been able to pile of an array of more than 120 new chemical entities (NCEs) currently under various stages of pre-clinical and clinical development.

Inadequate Follow Through

As aptly observed by Dr. Makarand Jawadekar, the most monumental event in the history of pharmaceutical R&D occurred in 2005, when the country signed a new patent law as a part of joining the World Trade Organization. While this event opened the flood gates for pharmaceutical innovation in India, the follow through has not been adequate. Consider these reasons for example:

1. India continues to lack the required amount of domestic private investments as well as the academic collaborations.
2. Aggressive price controls, while improving the access to medicines, reduce the profitability and consequently their ability to invest in research and development. This stifles innovation.
3. Inadequate respect for intellectual property is slowing down the progress of India's R&D sector from making a complete transition from a generic market to a patents market.

Positive Features

While the follow through could have been better after the momentous decision of joining the WTO, the progress of pharmaceutical industry is not without positive features. Take for instance the Gross Domestic Product (GDP) of India is expected to grow by 5 percent each year for the next four decades. The economic growth coupled with its changing epidemiological profile with cardiovascular problems and other chronic diseases and availability of technically qualified and competent manpower make India a strong candidate to become an important hub for pharmaceutical R&D and manufacturing.

In addition, two governmental initiatives such as continuous improvement in healthcare infrastructure and its strong intent in making India a hub for pharmaceutical innovation at least in Southeast Asia with multi-billion dollar investment with 50 percent public spending will help Indian pharmaceutical industry in achieving strong global presence even in innovative space.

The Indian pharmaceutical industry is well positioned to surpass other BRIC (Brazil, Russia, India, and China) in the 21st century as a global hub for end-to-end drug discovery and innovation. What is needed is a well-thought out and rational policy for Intellectual Property Rights (IPR). Clarity on patent law and its enforcement are essential not only to make Indian pharmaceutical industry shine, but even for its viability.

Generics-Only Policy Revisited

Prime minister Narendra Modi said in April 2017 that the government was looking at a law that ensures doctors prescribe medicines only by their generic name to improve affordability and accessibility of medicines in a country of 1.2 billion people, where majority live on less than US $ 2 a day. Nilesh Gupta, managing director of the Indian drug major, Lupin echoed the views of the Indian pharmaceutical industry when he responded to Modi's announcement: "Generics are fine, but there has to be a proper rigorous mechanism to enforce quality, like in the US. Unless India evolves on that, it will be disastrous".

The idea of generics-only is not new. India is not prepared to implement a policy of generic prescriptions only. Consider these reasons:

1. Half the Indian pharmaceutical market is made up of combination drugs and it would be impractical to ask doctors to prescribe series of chemical names.

2. Such a 'generic prescriptions only' policy puts too much power in the hands of chemists, most of whom are not adequately qualified.

3. Chemists would dispense the drugs on which they get the highest margins. They are unlikely to pass on the discounts to patients.

Here are two blog posts (Tables 1.9 and 1.10) from buildingpharmabrands.com that explains clearly why a generic prescriptions only in India would not be appropriate.

Table 1.9 Evolution or Devolution?

Evolution or Devolution?
Medical Council of India (MCI) and the Indian government are aggressively promoting the use of generic drugs. Pharmabiz wrote in an article titled *Medical Council of India asks doctors to prescribe drugs with generic names, on* May 10, 2013. That the MCI has issued circulars to the deans of all medical colleges, directors of Post Graduate Institutes and presidents of state medical councils to give wide publicity to ensure compliance by doctors to the clause 1.5 of the Indian Medical Council (Professional Conduct, Etiquette and Ethics) Regulations, 2002.
Branded Generics to Generic-Generics?
One hears more often these days that going generics is the way to improve access to medicines. The recent wins of patent cases

Contd...

against a few of the anticancer drugs and an approval of a generic version of an MNC's anti-diabetic drug have only furthered the case for generics. Is generic prescribing a better option? Which is the logical way or a path for a branded-generics pharmaceutical industry that is poised to evolve into a research-based drug industry in future? Become a generic-generics drug industry? Would that be an evolution or devolution?

Two Assumptions

The popular themes about promotion of generic prescribing are based mainly on two assumptions:

A. It will reduce prices and improve access to medicines considerably

B. It will significantly reduce the corrupt prescribing practices

Let us examine the first assumption that generics-prescribing leads to considerable reduction in drug prices. This is more relevant to the highly regulated first-world markets such as the US, Western Europe and Japan where research-based pharmaceutical industry rules the roost. In these patent-protected markets when the patents of drugs expire, a number of generics are introduced bringing down the prices considerably depending upon the generic penetration, almost by eighty to ninety percent of the innovator-drug prices within six months of genericization.

In branded-generic markets like India, where the prices are already at 20 to 30 percent of the innovator-drug prices, a significant price reduction is unlikely to almost ninety percent of drugs as they are off-patents already. In case of new drugs the government can regulate the prices in a number of ways taking into account the socioeconomic conditions of the patient populations.

Can the generic-prescribing reduce the corrupt prescribing practices? Think for a moment what is the root cause of this problem. When you look at the hierarchy of pharmaceutical products, innovator or brand-name drugs are at the top with the maximum product differentiation, which enables them to command a price premium. Next in the pecking order are value-added generics such as drug delivery products of the same molecule with a perceptible and patentable degree of differentiation, which helps them get some price premium. Branded generics are next in the line with a lesser degree of differentiation in terms of quality perception, availability, customer service etc. Generic-

Contd...

generics are at the bottom with a commodity status with virtually no differentiation. When there is no product differentiation, gratification rules the strategic roost. That explains but doesn't justify the unabated corrupt practices by drug manufacturers in wooing the prescribers.

The prices of branded-generics and generic-generics do not vary significantly in branded generic markets such as India. The prices to retailers and hospitals may have hefty discounts, which are not passed on to patients entirely. Patients pay almost the same price while the channel members get increased margins.

Evolution or Devolution?

The modern pharmaceutical industry as we know it today has evolved over many years and contributed significantly in the discovery and development of drugs to cure many diseases that were thought untreatable. The same industry has to develop even the future cures. Therefore, it has to continuously evolve. The evolutionary path for a research-based pharmaceutical industry has been an arduous one. A firm would start off as an API manufacturer or a generic-generic manufacturer and move up the evolutionary road to become a branded-generic manufacturer to international generics manufacturer and further move up to a value-added generics to specialty Pharma and finally to a research-based pharmaceutical industry. The Pharma companies need to generate an investible surplus to move up at every stage. With each forward step during this evolutionary process, the company would be creating and increasing its ability to differentiate itself from the rest of the pack.

Going back to generic-generics is devolution or backward-evolution. De-evolution is the notion that a species can change into a more primitive form over time. In terms of modern biology, the term may be a misnomer for that concept as it presumes that there is a preferred hierarchy of structure and function, and that evolution must mean progress to more advanced organisms. However, in the context of modern pharmaceutical industry and the state and stage at which the Indian pharmaceutical industry is currently positioned going from branded generics to generic-generics instead of moving towards a research-based pharmaceutical industry is clearly devolution. It is, if not going back to primitive stage, it is likely to become primitive in future by standing still at the present stage in its present state, while the rest of the pharmaceutical world is moving forward.

Table 1.10 Are We Aligning or Are We Aping?

Are We Aligning or Aping?

The Drug Controller General of India (DCGI) has stated that manufacturing licenses will only be issued based on generic or chemical names, and not on brand names. Archana Shukla (Asst. Editor, Rural affairs and Pharmaceuticals at CNBC and TV 18 recently reported that industry is divided on whether this is fan indicator of the government's move to push generics eventually banning the brand names for drugs.

The matter seems to have been clarified with the DCGI (Drug Controller General of India) at least for the time being as stated by the Indian Pharmaceutical Alliance's secretary general, DG Shah. The main aim of this circular is to align ourselves to international standards and separate manufacturing licenses from trademarks. It is a step to deal with the similar-branding issues, as many brand names sound similar for a number of drugs which are currently in the market. It is not a step to eliminate brand names.

While this ends the ban-on-brand-names-for-drugs speculation, a number of questions and concerns remain. The government has ordered the public sector doctors to prescribe only generic names and not brands. In a country where over 90 percent of the drugs consumed are branded generics how can the move from branded generics to generic-generics is possible? Not only that, most of the country's pharmacies are staffed by unqualified personnel. How will they dispense chemical names and contend with difficulties of this change? Furthermore, more than 50 percent of the drugs currently used are combination drugs. How will the doctors prescribe a combination drug as a generic?

There is more to international standards than merely changing over to generic prescriptions. The entire eco system of the highly regulated markets is different. In the US, which is the biggest market for generics there are innovator drugs or brand-name drugs, branded-generics and generic-generics. The prices of brand-name drugs are out of price control as the drug discovery costs and risks are very high and the drug companies have to recover the investments before their

Contd...

patents expire. The first-to-file and first- to-enter the market generic drugs too have a window of 180-days of exclusivity during which period the prices are much higher than the generic- generics. The prices of generic-generics of course would be much lower.

The next question concerns the quality of the generics. There are not so many generic variations after the patent expiry. There are very stringent quality control measures to ensure that the generics are effective in treating the patients. Every generic drug should submit a bio-equivalence test comparing it with the innovator drug as they believe that therapeutic equivalence is important and chemical equivalence does not necessarily mean that it is therapeutically equivalent. Moreover, the generic applicant should conduct this test at the US FDA approved laboratory only. All this costs a lot and puts an entry barrier for fly-by-night operators.

Contrast this with the current scenario in the Indian drug regulatory environment. The technical infrastructure is not comparable and is not ready to ensure all these quality issues. Many of the reported close-to-ten-thousand drug companies do not have a manufacturing facility that conforms to and approved by WHO GMP (World Health Organization's Good Manufacturing Practices). Under the loan licensing system literally anyone with less than a million rupees can start a company marketing his own version of generics. As a result, there are companies competing at international level, national level, regional level and even local level as there are neither any barriers to their entry nor any safeguards to quality.

Yes, it is a level playing field where products with assured quality and not-so- good at quality can survive and have equal opportunities to co-exist! In such a hyper-proliferative market, without adequate infrastructure for testing and checking quality, how will the DCGI ensure that the patients get the same quality of generic-generic that is identical to that of the brand-name drug? A brand-name manufacturer has got his entire reputation at stake. A generic- generic manufacturer who is a recent entrant into the business stands to lose nothing.

All this makes one think and ask "are we aligning ourselves to international standards or simply aping them?"

Loan Licensing Revisited

The government of India took a decision to discontinue loan licensing in pharmaceutical industry in 1986 itself. Loan licensing has served a useful purpose in the past when the multinational companies wanted to get their drugs manufactured in India and market it. The Pharma MNCs utilized the indigenous manufacturing capacity. The Indian manufacturing companies too, gained experience and expertise in acquiring technology. But today, when India is almost saturated with formulation manufacturing capacities, loan licensing does not provide much benefit. Instead it raises concerns regarding quality maintenance and assurance.

The government of India, therefore, once again decided to phase out loan licensing in its 2017 draft policy pharmaceutical industry except in biopharmaceutical sector. This is because, the stage of development in biopharmaceutical sector in India is currently similar to the formulations in the 1980s.

The 2017 Pharmaceutical policy states that loan licensing will not be allowed, except in the case of biopharmaceuticals. The policy anticipates some resistance by the industry players and has a plan B, which includes:

1. Phasing out loan licensing in three years
2. Allowing loan licensing on WHO GMP-approved facilities only
3. Allowing upto 10 percent of the company's total production

Industry stakeholders however, argue that discontinuance of loan licensing makes the installed capacities of small and medium enterprises (SMEs) redundant. What is more, it is estimated that today about 40 percent of pharmaceutical production is generated through loan licensing model. If loan licensing is discontinued, the burden on local pharmaceutical companies would dramatically increase as these companies will have to invest in Capex plans. They may have to acquire these SMEs into their fold.

P2P (Product to Product) Manufacturing

There is another variant of loan licensing that is currently in practice by various pharmaceutical companies. It is P2P or product to product manufacturing. Under this scheme, one company is approved to manufacture the product for different companies, who will then market it under their respective brand names at varying prices.

This system has led to mushrooming of regional marketing companies across the country with multiple brands that add little or no value. A number of companies which have spare manufacturing capacity manufacture a number of 'me-too' products to individuals including doctors on a batch by batch basis for marketing under their own names. This so-called franchisee-system (another name for P2P) is also responsible for increasing the unethical marketing practices. Such regional marketing outfits on a franchisee system are reducing the ethical prescription drug business (prescription drugs used to be called ethical drugs in the past) to a crass commercial system that is discount and commission based between the marketers and prescribers.

The new drug policy aims to phase out the P2P practice, following the broad principle to have one manufacturer, one salt, (active pharmaceutical ingredient) one brand name and one price.

Compulsory Licensing

Compulsory license is an authorization given to a third-party by the government to make, use or sell a particular product or a particular process, which has been patented, without the need of the permission of the patent owner. Compulsory licenses, therefore work against patent holders. But then, they are given only in certain cases of national emergency and health crisis.

There are certain prerequisite conditions, which need to be fulfilled if the government wants to grant a compulsory license in favor of someone. At least three years should pass from the date of grant of patent before anyone interested to make an application to the controller for grant of compulsory license on any of the following three conditions:

A. That the reasonable requirements of the public with respect to the patented invention have not been satisfied or

B. That the patented invention is not available to the public at a reasonably affordable price or

C. That the patented invention is not worked in the territory of India.

Thus, the use of a compulsory license effectively withdraws a patent from a drug completely if it is seemed prohibitively expensive to a domestic market and a vital public health need.

The first-ever and only case of compulsory licensing case (case 1.1) in India is a landmark case. It is the case of Natco Pharma, an Indian generic drug firm and the German Pharma giant, Bayer Corporation. It explains clearly the philosophy and the rules behind that guide the compulsory licensing decision.

Case 1.1 Natco Pharma Gets the First-Ever Compulsory License for Generic Nexavar In a Landmark Decision!

Bayer, the German Pharma major invented Sorafenib (brand name: Nexavar) used in the treatment of primary kidney cancer and advanced primary liver cancer and priced it at Rs. 2.80 lakh for one-month's supply of the drug (120 tablets) in India. The price being exorbitant, the drug reached only 2 percent of the patient population.

Natco Pharma, an Indian generic company requested Bayer for voluntary license to manufacture and market the drug in India, which Bayer denied. Natco, then filed application with the Controller of Patents for grant of a compulsory license of the drug, Sorafenib. The Controller granted compulsory license to Natco to manufacture and sell a generic version of Nexavar under the following conditions.

A. Natco would pay a 6 percent royalty on the net sales every quarter to Bayer.

B. Further it could only charge Rs. 8,800 for a monthly dose of 120 tablets of the drug and

C. Donate free supplies of the drug to 600 needy patients each year.

The Controller of Patents granted compulsory license in this case as he found that all the three criteria for the grant of a compulsory license as per Indian Patents Act were satisfied.

1. Bayer supplied the drug to only 2 percent of the patient population and the reasonable requirements of the public with respect the patented drug were not met.

2. Bayer priced the drug exorbitantly high at Rs. 2.80 lakh for a month's supply of the drug. It was unreasonably high as it was many times more than the per capita income in India in 2011. The per capita income in India in 2011 was US $ 1,575 where as the cost of the drug per year was US $ 69,000. Compare this with the price of Natco's generic version of US $ 2,120.

3. Bayer did not sufficiently work the patent in India.

Later, Bayer challenged the order passed by the Intellectual Property Appellate Board (IPAB) in Bombay High Court, which upheld the IPAB Order.

Later, on April 2013, Indian Supreme Court gave a ruling that rejected a patent of another Big Pharma company, Novartis for its leukemia drug, Glivec after a six-year legal battle stating that small changes to its earlier version of the patented drug did not deserve a new patent.

Both rulings are landmark cases and have been vehemently criticized by both Big Pharma and countries, where these companies were headquartered. India, however, did not break any rules in both these cases. Its verdicts are allowed under TRIPS (Trade Related Intellectual Property Rights). It's just that no country previously dared to take such a path breaking step. What is significant now is that it is a global trend. Christian Mazzi, a partner with the New York-based international consultancy firm, Bain & Company made an interesting observation when he said:

Historically, governments have protected themselves...by preventing access to the market or by controlling price, but never by controlling patent protection. This is the next wave, if you will. And this goes to the very core of the pharmaceutical business model on their virtual monopoly created by patent protection.

But compulsory licensing has not been the only way India has adopted against Big Pharma in an attempt to control drug prices. Indian patent officials have also neutralized Intellectual property protection to some of the Big Pharma companies by not granting them patents. Table 1.11 presents a list of patents revoked by the Indian Patents Office.

Table 1.11 Big Pharma's Patents Revoked in India

Company	Patents Revoked	Reasons
1. Pfizer	Sutent (Sunitinib), a drug used in the treatment of kidney cancer was granted a patent in India in 2007. Sutent was launched in India in 2009 at a price of Rs.1.96 Lakhs for a 45-day treatment. Cipla challenged Pfizer's patent and the Indian Patent Office revoked the patent.	The reason for the revocation of the patent is that it did not have an inventive step.
2. Roche	Valcyte (Valganiciclovir) is a drug used for treating active cytomega-lovirus retinitis. The condition, if untreated, can cause blindness in patients with HIV infection. Roche was granted a patent for this in India in 2007 and launched it as at a price Rs. 1,042 per tablet. Cipla challenged the patent and offered a generic version of the drug at Rs. 245 per tablet. Indian Patent Appellate Board (IPAB) revoked the patent.	The reason for revocation is that (a) the patent application did not have an, inventive step and (b) Not patentable as increase in bio-equivalence does not necessarily mean improve-ment in efficacy
3. Merck	Dulera is a combination of three drugs - Mometasone Furoate, Formoterol and Hepta-fluro propane in an aerosol formulation for treating bronchial asthma. Its patent was revoked in 2011	The patent was revoked as there was no inventive step.
4. Bristol Myers Squibb	Baraclude (Etecavir) a leading anti-viral drug used in the treatment of Hepatitis B infection, was pre 1995-molecule for, which no patent was filed in India. Later BMS filed a patent application for its once-daily composition in 2001 and obtained patent in 2011. Natco and Glen-mark challenged the patent.	The company has entered into settle-ment with two Indian generic companies.

Tilting the Balance

Increasing drug prices and consequently the healthcare expenditure is affecting the economies of both developing and developed countries. In developing countries such as India, the issue of drug prices and affordability are even more intense. It is unlikely that the governments in developing countries will be able to resist from their own citizens and patient advocacy groups in favor of multinational drug companies.

Though the objectives of TRIPS is to benefit both the innovator and generic industries in developed and developing nations, the balance seems to be tilted towards the generic pharmaceutical industries across the world as pricing issues take priority in most of the cases.

IPR Climate and Implications for Pharma Industry

India's patent protection is weak and has adverse effects on international pharmaceutical and chemical firms. It is estimated that annual loses to the US Pharmaceutical industry are around US $ 450-million. (Table 1.12)

Indian authorities have a different perspective. They believe that western governments routinely grant patents for slightly improved versions of medicines whose patents are about to expire and help them to extend their patent lifecycles. In other words they help to evergreen the patents of these products. That enables drug makers to get many patents to upgrade their new, generally more expensive versions rather than the cheaper generic versions. This is despite the arguments of some sections of the society comprising doctors and patients that these patents of marginally improved products do not justify the costs. Some social critics called this ever greening of patents as 'therapeutic fashions'. The big Pharma too is focusing on this analogue research that is patentable and not breakthrough research as such research is becoming very expensive and even unaffordable.

Table 1.12 Major Patent Disputes Over the Past Three Years

Year	Patent Disputes
March 2012	Compulsory license for Bayer's cancer drug, Nexavar (Sorafenib) granted to Natco Pharma
June 2012	Bristol Myers Squibb's Sprycel (Dasatinib) patent infringed
September 2012	Roche's Tarceva (Erlotinib) patent infringement upheld

Contd...

Year	Patent Disputes
November 2012	Patent for Roche's Pegasys (Peg-interferon alfa 2a) is revoked
December 2012	Patent for MSD's combination aerosol dosage form (Mometasone and Formoterol) is revoked
March 2013	Patents of MSD's Januvia (Sitagliptin phosphate) and Janumet (Sitagliptin phosphate and Metformin) are infringed by Glenmark
April 2013	Supreme Court of India upholds patent denial of Novartis's Glivec (Imatinib)
June 2013	The Patent Office denies patent for Boerhinger Meinheim's Pradaxa (dabigatran etixilate)
August 2013	Patents of Allergan's Ganfort (Bimatoprost maleate and Timolol) eye drops, and Combigan (Brimonidine tartrate and timolol maleate) eye drops are revoked
June 2014	The Patent Office for the second time denies a patent to US-based Abraxis Life Sciences for their cancer drug, Abraxane (Albumin-bound Paclitaxel injectable suspension)
December 2014	The Supreme Court of India upholds the grant of Bayer's Nexavar's compulsory license
December 2014	Novartis sues Cipla for infringing patents for its respiratory drug, Ombrez (Indacaterol maleate)
January 2015	The Patent Office rejects Gilead's patent application of its Hepatitis C drug, Sovaldi (Sofosbuvir)

India, Indonesia and other developing countries, however have been bucking that trend. They have been denying patents for marginal improvements by Big Pharma companies and licensing local pharmaceutical companies to make generic versions of those drugs, which are affordable to majority of their populations. Indian patent laws are modeled or being considered by about thirty developing countries to ensure rights of their patients. It is this trend that the big Pharma is worried about. If this trend grows and spreads to other countries, the Big Pharma would find it extremely difficult to expand its markets for all the new drugs, irrespective of whether they are marginal improvements or major innovations. It is only natural that the Big Pharma would fight with all its might to prevent the countries in the emerging markets and developing world from shooting down their patents.

India's Tug-of-war with the Big Pharma

Indian Pharma's tug-of-war with the U.S. pharmaceutical companies goes back to several decades, i.e., since 1972, when India adopted the process patents regime. It allowed local drug firms to develop alternate manufacturing processes (through reverse engineering) of existing patented molecules and sell them in the domestic pharmaceutical industry as branded generic medicines. Indian Patents Act 1970 has been the genesis of India's pharmaceutical industry as we know it today. That is the reason why drug prices remain affordable to the common man in the country even today.

The flip side of this was that it encouraged the drug companies in India to continue copying patented medicines and not investing in developing new drugs. That was until India became a member of the World Trade Organization (WTO). Some of the Indian drug majors have stepped up their investment in research and development and even started their drug discovery programs ever since.

What the Big Pharma Wants from India

US-based Pharma MNCs are wary of litigation and generic companies infringing their patents.

Indian laws clearly rule out patents for:
- **A.** Molecules invented before 1995
- **B.** Incremental innovations and
- **C.** Previously known molecules

At least, 500 - 600 patents would have been denied under the section on innovation (Section 3 d) of Indian patent law. Currently, about three-fourths of the 48 patented drugs launched in India are under threat. Five patents have already been revoked and more than 11 are under challenge by way of infringement. Patents on seven more products are entangled in pending opposition proceedings. A patent on Nexavar is already on compulsory licensing.

Alliance for Fair Trade with India (AFTI) said that India did not address many critical and long standing shortcomings to its IPR policy. The big Pharma wants the following things to be changed to make the Indian pharmaceutical market a level playing field both for MNCs and domestic players:
1. Expensive and time consuming patent opposition hurdles for patent applicants.

2. Lack of an effective system for protecting data generated to obtain marketing approval for pharmaceutical, agricultural and chemical products.

3. Adequate protection for IPR holders' interests with respect to patents, copyright and trade secrets.

4. To take meaningful action to revise protectionist, forced localization policies (compulsory licenses, patent revocations etc.) that clearly aim at favoring domestic IP holders at the expense of goods, services and intellectual property from other countries.

Voluntary Licensing (VL) - An Alternate Strategy?

Voluntary licenses, as the name indicates are licenses that patent holders give at their discretion to other parties on an exclusive or non-exclusive basis, the right to manufacture, import and distribute a pharmaceutical product.

Ever since the government of India gave its first compulsory license of Bayer's Nexavar to Natco Pharma, multinational pharmaceutical companies have been rethinking about strategy to launch their new drugs in India. The strategy being voluntary licenses. The details of some of the voluntary licenses that MNC pharmaceutical companies gave to their local partners in India are as follows:

1. MSD Pharmaceuticals gave Sun Pharma an exclusive marketing license for marketing its two patented diabetes drugs - Januvia and Janumet in India.

2. Novartis, a top-ten Big Pharma company enters into a marketing tie-up with Lupin, the Indian drug major for its Onbrez inhaler.

3. Bayer plans to license most of its patented products for India to its local joint venture company, Cadila Healthcare - Bayer.

4. Gilead Life Sciences gave voluntary licenses to seven Indian generic drug manufacturers - Cadila Healthcare, Cipla, Hetero Drugs, Mylan Labs, Ranbaxy, Sequent Scientific and Strides Arcolabs for its blockbuster hepatitis-C drug Sovaldi (Sofosbuvir).

Voluntary licensing to a local partner under mutually agreed terms will not only help patent holders to expand the market but also avoid compulsory licensing action. While government intervention through a compulsory licensing will lead to a drastic reduction in price as it is typically without the consent of the patent holder, voluntary licensing may get a more remunerative price albeit much lower than its original price.

Innovative drug companies with patented drugs realize that voluntary licensing is a wiser option to avoid a likely invocation of the compulsory licensing Act. In addition, a voluntary license offers two advantages:

A. A voluntary license helps minimize loss and also ensures a better access of the patented drug to more domestic patients.

B. It helps counter one of the most common reasons for issuing a compulsory license - in adequate patient access.

IPR and Its Implications for Indian Pharma

India has achieved a dominant position as the world's leading provider of generic drugs. The country was able to attract sizable foreign direct investment (FDI) in to the pharmaceutical sector and outsourcing of research activities from the Big Pharma companies.

1. Between 2016 and 2017, investment in life sector declined by almost 59 percent from previous years.

2. The country had lost almost US $ 10-billion worth of investment by not respecting IP norms, stated Mr. Srinivas Reddy, Director, Hetero Drugs, a leading API manufacturer, who holds about 30 percent of global market for HIV drugs.

Achieving Balance

Only twelve compulsory licenses have been granted between 1995 and 2011 across the world, and most of them are for anti-retroviral drugs (ARV) used in the treatment of HIV. India has granted only one compulsory license and rejected two. India has revoked over six patents during this period. Why then this pressure on India to change its IP laws?

How achieve a balance between the two opposing interests of the patients' needs in developing countries and remunerative prices to recover the cost of the drug development in developing countries of the world?

Developing countries such as India should negotiate on pricing with multinational drug companies when it comes to life saving drugs.

The Research-based Pharmaceutical Industry (PhRMA) in the developed world should formulate some strategy for designing drug prices for the developing world so that rewards for huge investments they make on research and innovation do not get diluted.

Understanding the Marketing Environment

To size up and seize the vast opportunities that the Indian pharmaceutical market offers, a proper understanding of the marketing environment of the industry is essential. While the marketers are actively pursuing a strategy of optimizing the marketing-mix: product, price, promotion and place for specific marketing segments, one should bear in mind that many of the forces that influence marketing strategies are outside a marketer's control. These forces constitute marketing environments and exert a powerful influence over the success or failure of a marketing strategy. Marketers, therefore, should develop a clear understanding of and gain insights into these environments. These are:

1. The economic environment
2. The legal and regulatory environment
3. The social environment
4. The technological environment
5. The ecological environment
6. The competitive environment
7. The ethical environment

The Economic Environment

The national and international economic environment affects in one way or another in almost all businesses. Yet, it is the one external environment that you cannot influence. The two principal ways in which the economic environment affects your business are:

1. Its overall condition affects the growth of your markets
2. The financial conditions in the economy affect your ability to raise finances to fuel your projects and growth plans

While it is true that we cannot alter the economic environment, we can certainly make reasonable judgements about its most likely future direction and make decisions that are congenial and consistent with those assumptions.

Once these assumptions have been made explicit, you are in a position to compare them with reality as it unfolds and, when necessary, change your assumptions to match the reality. Remember that classic principle of military strategy - Forewarned is fore-armed!

Key areas to monitor

How does one monitor the economic environment?

You should monitor and keep track of all the vital areas that are likely to affect the market behavior and investment climate. A regular, systematic monitoring of these would give a proper perspective of the economic environment in which you are operating (and will be operating). The key areas to monitor are:

1. Annual growth rate of Gross National Product (GNP)
2. Annual growth in personal disposable income
3. Short-term and long-term interest rates
4. Inflation rate
5. Price / Earning ratio and the industry average
6. Average annual growth rate of the industry as a whole
7. Stock market behavior index

Projecting the Trends

Careful monitoring of these seven vital indicators for the preceding five years and projecting the trends into the next year and further period of five years would equip and enable you better to plan for the uncertain future; to plan a winning strategy and exploit the opportunities, face the threats and meet the challenges.

The Legal and Regulatory Environment

The legal and regulatory environment is another crucial aspect of a firm's environment that impinges on long-term operations and alternatives. Government regulations of business everywhere have been steadily increasing. Such regulations limit the choices that managers can make and may also affect the profitability of proposed projects.

Another area of concern in the legal and regulatory environment comprises the government's attitude toward profits, investment credits, dividends etc. The managers, who evaluate future projects must take all these aspects into account while making assumptions.

The current legal and regulatory environment of pharmaceutical industry is a result of several statues enacted over a period of more than hundred and twenty years. This statutes or enactments can broadly be categorized into two areas:

1. Those pertaining to quality control of the pharmaceutical industry in India such as quality control, safety and standards of all the drugs manufactured and marketed in the country and those imported into the country. All these are under the purview of the Union Ministry of Health (Directorate General of Health Services).
2. Those pertaining to other aspects of manufacture and marketing

of drugs such as investment, foreign collaboration, licensing of production facilities, pricing, trade marks, patents, import of capital equipment, raw materials and technology. All these aspects were under the purview of different departments like the Ministries of Petroleum, Chemicals and Fertilizers, Industry, Finance, Law, Commerce and Labor of the Central Government. Later, the government of India created a Department of Pharmaceuticals in the Ministry of Chemicals and Fertilizers on 1st July 2008, to provide greater focus for the growth of highly potential pharmaceuticals.

In addition to central laws there are controls and regulations at the state level too. State regulations of the pharmaceutical industry in India can be traced as far back as 1878, when the Opium Act was enacted. Under this Act, possession, transport, import, export and sale of opium was regulated with a view to restricting its use either as a narcotic or as a drug. Poisons Act 1919 was the next regulatory legislation, which empowered the government to regulate the possession and sale of any specified poison and the prohibition of import of any poison except under a license. The Dangerous Drugs Act 1930, the next enactment, vested in the government control over operations relating to all dangerous drugs, including opium.

Some of the more important legislations are listed in Table 1.13.

Table 1.13 The Regulatory Environment of the Pharmaceutical Industry in India

The Regulatory Environment of the Pharmaceutical Industry in India	
1.	Opium Act 1878
2.	Poisons Act 1919
3.	The Dangerous Drugs Act, 1930
4.	The Drugs and Cosmetics Act 1940
5.	The Pharmacy Act, 1948
6.	The Industrial Development & Regulation (IDRA) ACT, 1951
7.	The Drugs and Magic Remedies (Objectionable Advertisements) Act, 1954
8.	The Trade and Merchandise Marks Act, 1958
9.	The MRTP (Monopoly and Restrictive Trade Practices Act, 1969
10.	The Drug Price Control Order, 1969
11.	The Patents Act, 1970
12.	The Foreign Exchange and Regulation Act, 1973

Consumer Movement

Another important area of the regulatory environment is the consumer movement. Consumer movement is certainly intensifying. Drug Action Committee, Drug Action Forum - while these and other consumer groups, strictly speaking, do not regulate your business directly, they do generate government activity in the affairs of business. Their influence cannot be undermined, nor their importance ignored.

Monitoring the Regulatory Environment

It is obvious that you cannot predict the legal and regulatory environment of your business or for that matter any business. But you can certainly try to make some explicit assumptions about it based on careful observation and monitoring. This can influence positively the strategic plans of your business. Consider these examples:

- The government currently is trying to abolish the loan licensing system in the pharmaceutical industry. The pressure from industry circles has given the loan licensing system a new lease of life for four more years. The reason for the government's decision is to ensure that all manufacturing units implement the GMP (Good Manufacturing Practices). If you are a manufacturer, who is currently manufacturing for a number of other companies on loan license, what are the implications of such a move by the government? A number of alternatives might influence your strategic planning. The appropriate contingency plans are likely to forearm you. In any case, you are likely to be better equipped to meet the challenges.

- According to the Drug Policy 1987, the Drug Controller of India can and most certainly will insist henceforth the clinical research data of every new formulation by every company even if that formulation happens to be a 'me-too' product and an existing one. This is to check the ever-increasing brand proliferation. Till now the companies introducing new formulations of drugs already cleared by the DCI needed only to submit only the laboratory data pertaining to quality control, stability records and the like. The new Drug Policy is going to change all that. A pharmaceutical manufacturer who is alert to changing regulations like these would be better prepared to meet the task of new product introduction.

Key Questions

Correct and appropriate solutions for many a problem depend on the kind of questions you ask. Here is a list of questions, a sort of checklist, for monitoring and appraising the regulatory environment.

1. Will there be more regulation or liberalization in government policy relating to licensing, investment and foreign collaboration of your industry in the next five years?

2. Will there be more or less tax concessions? Duty drawbacks? How will they affect your profitability in the next five years?

3. What are the priorities of the next five-year plan?

4. Will there be more or less government regulations of your production processes in the next five years? What will be its impact on your costs and your competition?

5. Will there be more or less regulation in the next five years of your marketing practices like advertising and sales promotion expenditure, traveling expenditure etc.? How will you respond if there is more government regulation? How will it affect your competitors?

6. How vulnerable are you in facing the attacks by consumer groups regarding your products, their packaging, pricing, distribution, advertising etc.? What steps can you take in preventing any problems? How efficient is your corporate radar in alerting you?

7. What will be your distributors' expectations in terms of trade margins and quality of service? How well are you prepared to meet them?

8. What will be your needs in the area of public relations in the next five years? Have you a systematic plan of action such as goal-setting and measuring your public relations effort?

The Social Environment

Probably, the most significant and difficult to detect changes that will occur in the environment will be social changes. These changes may pose tremendous opportunities for new products and services to the alert, observant, responsive and responsible marketer. Equally, they may produce exceptionally difficult problems to cope with for two major areas, which a changing social environment can affect your business.

The first is the changing composition, attitudes and lifestyles of population. Even if you are an original equipment manufacturer and manufacture for the industry, you cannot ignore the fact that the ultimate market for all goods and services is the consumer. You can certainly be affected through changes in the demand for various consumer products (and services). Consider for a moment the fact that children below 14 years account for about 40 percent of the population today. Does it not suggest a large pediatric market? It is a small wonder that demand for pediatric products has been increasing during the recent past. The demand for baby care products, toys, books, baby foods, schools, teachers, primary immunization, pediatsric dosage forms of pharmaceuticals and indeed even for pediatricians has been on the increase for the past few years. Consider the ripple effect of the increasing literacy levels and the awareness of family planning at least among the urban population. The changing scenario is not difficult to visualize. Smaller-urban families, working couples open new markets like children's day-care centers, and expand the demand for many up-market products, like convenience foods, labor saving appliances etc.

In a few years, the present pediatric market will be changing to the 'youth market'. Consequently, there will be a shift in demand to sports goods, fashion clothes, colleges, personal computers, laptops, smart phones, hi-fi equipment, fitness centers etc.

Also, consider the increasing segment of senior citizens in the country. In the U.S. for example senior citizens account for the largest chunk of the disposable income. That is why many marketers have been specifically targeting their products toward this hither-to neglected segment. While graying Indians are not currently as fortunate as their U.S. counterparts, at least in urban India new opportunities like health insurance schemes, concessional train travel, holiday plans at luxury as well as budget hotels are gradually increasing. But the demand for 'geriatric products' in so far as pharmaceutical industry is concerned is growing rapidly.

Another way in which changing trends in social environment will affect business lies in the attitudes and expectations of your employees. It has become increasingly difficult to find goal congruence between the employees and the firm. The ever-increasing legislations and increased demands for workers put limitations on the strategic choices open to firms.

Here is a checklist to serve as a starting point to increase your awareness of how social changes in your firm's environment may affect its operations and options.

1. What changes in the composition of by age are likely to take place in the next five years? How are they likely to alter the demand for your products and services? What is the basis for your assumptions?

2. What changes do you envisage in the life styles and attitudes of your customers in the next five years? How are they likely to alter the demand for your products and services? What is the basis for your assumptions?

3. What changes do you foresee in age, life-styles, attitudes and expectations that are likely to affect the availability and quality of of your work force, whether they are production workers or office workers? And the supervisors and middle level managers? What is the basis for your assumptions?

Technological Environment

Technology is the most talked about subject today, from drawing rooms to the most powerful boardrooms. A major technological change is currently sweeping the world.

There are two major aspects of the technological environment that are of great concern to you. The ability of firms in your industry to innovate and find new methods of production that can substantially alter their costs and there by achieve the cost leadership.

This gives the innovative firm a definite competitive edge to nudge other firms out of the race. In the late 1990's, Cheminor drugs, a young bulk drug-manufacturing unit on a fast track offers a classic example of how technological superiority can achieve cost leadership.

Cheminor Drugs, a member of Dr. Reddy's Labs group has achieved phenomenal success with the production of ibuprofen by a different route and is mainly responsible for bringing down the price of ibuprofen below the international price level. They have repeated their success story a few years later with another drug, norfloxacin.

The second area of technological concern is the likely impact a new technology may have on your markets, products and services. For example, recent anti-ulcer agents such as cimetidine, ranitidine and famotidine have carved out a sizable market for themselves in the in 1990's. This is evident from the fact that the top two prescription drugs in the world pharmaceutical market at that time were Zantac (ranitidine of Glaxo, now Glaxo SmithKline) and Tagamet (cimetidine of SmithKline Beecham, now GlaxoSmithKline). What is the impact of these anti-ulcer drugs on the antacid market? Has the market expanded? Have these new drugs taken a major share of the antacid market? Or have they taken a share of the gastro-intestinal surgery?

In India, the introduction of new broad-spectrum antibiotics has resulted in a shrinking market for narrow-spectrum injectable antibiotics and oral penicillin. The rate of product obsolescence is very high in pharmaceutical industry since it is technology-driven. Technological advancement is not restricted to new drug discovery alone. It can be a process improvement resulting in higher yield and lower costs, or the way in which the drugs are stored and delivered, or new production methods of delivering the drug at the site of action (New Drug Delivery Systems or NDDS) and making it more acceptable, patient-friendly as it improves patient adherence.

Close Watch

You have to be very alert and keep a close watch on the technological developments that are taking place in your industry, and how they are likely to affect your products and services. The key questions to be asked and answered are:

1. What are the major therapeutic groups where the maximum number of technological achievements occurred during the past five years? How did they affect your products and services?

2. Which companies had the maximum share of these technological achievements in the past five years? What was their R&D expenditure during this period? What have been their strengths and their vulnerable points?

3. What has been your development effort in new products area? What was the record of your innovation in the past five years? How many innovations were made? How many of them were successful?

4. Based on the above information, can you project what would be the likely developmental efforts of your firm and your major competitors within the next five years in the area of technological improvement, be it in the production area, packaging area,

distribution, storage, new drug delivery systems or new product introduction? How will they affect your products and services in terms of demand levels, market share and profitability?

5. What are your developmental plans and objectives for the next five years? What might be your competitors' plans?

The Ecological Environment

Ecology is perhaps the most rapidly changing aspect that affects the business environment. The increasing concern for maintaining the ecological balance is there for everyone to see. Not very long ago farmers could use any pesticide they chose, industrial wastes could be dumped or buried anywhere, pollution and its control was discussed rarely except as a matter of academic interest.

But not any longer! Pesticides and chemicals require extensive testing. Organic is the new mantra! Licenses for chemicals and pesticides are given only in locations that are specially earmarked outside the cities and towns. Industrial wastes require effluent treatment. One sees increasing protests and demonstrations against nuclear power plants. The ecological environment continues to change and the concern to maintain an ecological balance continues to grow.

The changing ecological environment can affect your business directly. The following key questions will expand your horizon about the many ways in which the changing ecological environment can create opportunities or pose threats to your business:

1. What processes and procedures in your manufacturing could be criticized as harmful to the environment?

2. If you were forced to change such procedures what would you do?

3. What about your suppliers? Do they use any processes and procedures that might be criticized as harmful to environment?

4. If your suppliers are forced to change such practices how would they affect the prices and availability of your raw materials and packaging materials?

5. Does your packaging create any environmental problem after the consumer uses it?

6. Are there any health hazards that might occur to you production

workers at the time of manufacture? How safe are your safety standards? Can you improve them?

7. Can you anticipate any other threats to your operation from the ecological environment? What are they? What can you do about them?

The Competitive Environment

Of all the external environments, in which the firm operates, it is the competitive environment that has the most immediate impact and is the easiest to understand. Apart from customers, your competitors are the most important determinants of your market share. Yet few companies try to analyze in-depth their competitors and understand them.

It is important that you prepare as complete a profile as possible of each of your major competitors. The important questions to ask are:

1. Company history of three major competitors for each of your major products.

2. Plant location.

3. Investment history of the last five years, plant expansion, new licensed capacities, public issues etc.

4. Financial history of the last five years like net sales, cost of sales, inventory, net income, total assets, operating expenses, gross margin, net margin, inventory turnover, profitability return on investment (ROI) etc.

5. Major products of competitors accounting for about 80 percent of their sales and their growth rate in the last five years.

6. Product quality of the competitors; what is the emphasis given by your competitors for product quality? How do they compare with your product quality standards on a ten-point scale?

When you are trying to appraise and analyze the external environment of your business, you should try to project the trends rather than predict the future. No one can predict the future accurately. History has demonstrated that amply. Therefore, do not be trapped in the number game. While it is important to be as accurate as possible regarding the historical data, any attempt at precision about the future is likely to mislead you. What should concern you are general trends that you can make explicit in your planning. Your plans will be based on assumptions about the meaning of these trends. What is crucial about the whole business of projecting the needs is that you should be able to test the validity of these assumptions as the future comes to be the present.

The Ethical Environment

Pharmaceutical industry has discovered many drugs and therapies that have saved, prolonged, and improved countless lives of people over the years. However, the business exists to be profitable for itself and its shareholders in addition to existing over time. The pharmaceutical industry must constantly work to find a right balance of profitability without losing sight of its mission to discover new medicines to alleviate pain and disease of patients and to improve their health and quality of life.

Obviously, there is more to pharmaceutical marketing than marketing pharmaceuticals. Pharmaceutical marketing is significantly broader than marketing of pharmaceuticals because the justification or the reason for the existence of pharmaceutical marketing is the patient. That is why pharmaceutical marketing emphasizes that any article, service or idea needed to anticipate and remove gaps in patients' care to be included in the discussion of pharmaceutical marketing. This places a greater responsibility on pharmaceutical marketing.

From a marketing perspective, therefore, the ethical issues and influencers within the industry center on the various marketing communications by manufacturers of pharmaceuticals. Here are the ethical issues (Table 1.14).

Table 1.14 Key Ethical Issues in Pharmaceutical Industry

Area	Ethical Issues
A. Interactions with Health care professionals (HCPs)	Many healthcare professionals and their organizations have guidelines on how to interact with the pharmaceutical industry. The guidelines cover a number of areas such as: dealing with speakers, Support of CMEs, prohibition against entertainment and recreation.

Contd...

Area	Ethical Issues
B. Off-label Promotion	In all their communications with HCPs, pharmaceutical companies can only discuss approved indications. And yet, between January 2001 and 2009, pharmaceutical manufacturers in the US paid close to $ 3-billion to settle suits involved in off-label promotion and marketing of certain medicines.
C. Publication Practices	A. While the industry states that it conducts all its clinical trials in an ethical and rigorous manner, some research suggests that there is bias in industry sponsored studies that favors the companies sponsoring research. B. Research also suggests that there is not enough data transparency. And that industry publishes only clinical trials that are favorable to its product studied and hides the data that is not favorable to it. C. The ghost writing aspect of the publication practices is being scrutinized.

The pharmaceutical industry must thus walk a fine line in promoting its products, and yet still being able to promote its products to provide the best of solutions for improving the health of patients. Companies that follow the industry and guidelines and market their products and services conforming to the best ethical standards are bound to do well in the market place. Media reports in recent times have brought to the fore the nexus between HCPs and pharmaceutical companies and a host of unethical practices. They have also tarnished the reputation of pharmaceutical industry that was earlier held in high esteem. The only route to restore the lost reputation of pharmaceutical industry is to walk the ethical path.

The pharmaceutical marketers should therefore monitor the ethical environment from outside and inside out continuously and constantly and make the necessary course correction. What is needed is an uncompromising attitude. The key questions to ask before taking any marketing decision are:

A. Is this action of mine patient-centric?

B. Will this action of mine lead to an improvement in patients' condition in any manner? Be it in terms of the cure, alleviation of suffering or quality of life.

Summary

The pharmaceutical industry in India has come of age from a mere US $ 31 million in 1947 to a whopping US $ 29.1 billion in 2017. This impressive growth is not without paradoxes. It was subjected to a stringent system of price controls on the finished products while the input costs were not controlled. This resulted in erosion of profits and profitability.

It is really commendable that the Indian pharmaceutical industry despite stringent price controls and a diminishing bottom line has achieved the coveted leadership in the international generics market. It is exporting bulk drugs and formulations even to the developed countries.

This big opportunity poses challenges as well as threats to the marketer who has to operate in the fiercely competitive Indian pharmaceutical market. He has to develop a thorough understanding and sensitivity to the rapidly changing environment. The marketing environment comprises:

1. The economic environment
2. The legal and regulatory environment
3. The social environment
4. The technological environment
5. The ecological environment
6. The competitive environment
7. The ethical environment

While no one can obviously predict the future, analyzing and appraising the environments that affect the business will equip and prepare the marketer to capitalize on the opportunities, meet the challenges and face the threats. One thing is for sure. Egalitarian or not, the market place is still very much a jungle where only the fittest survive.

The Pharmaceutical Market

Changing! Changing! Changing!

That's how one would describe the Indian pharmaceutical market.

How else could one possibly describe the emergence of new markets for new products and services, and the disappearance of some of the markets that once dominated the scene? Or the once-upon-a-time leaders that have grudgingly surrendered their positions to the once fledgling-but-now mightier-than-thou companies?

Among the top twenty-five companies which accounted for about 70 percentof the total pharmaceutical sales in 2017, as many as four Indian drug firms moved up at a frenetic pace to the top five in the industry from down-under thirties in 1976 (Table 2.1). What is even more noteworthy is that Mankind Pharma, which was founded only in 1995, shot its way into the top ten at a break-neck speed.

Around the same time, more than seven companies had left their prestigious positions among the top twenty in 1976, and lost their rank and share in the market place.

There are many lessons to be learnt from the success stories of the winning companies as well as from the declining companies. One of the most obvious lessons is that the market place is unforgiving in nature and certainly not known for its tolerance. Only the vigilant and the alert companies that are quick on the draw will emerge victorious in the market.

Table 2.1 Top Ten Pharmaceutical Companies in India
(MAT, May 21, 2018)

Company	Rs. Crore	Market Share (%)
1. Sun Pharma	9,726	5.58
2. Abbott	7,015	5.24
3. Cipla	5,308	4.54
4. Zydus	4,977	3.52
5. Mankind	4,180	3.44
6. Alkem	3,924	3.06
7. Glaxo SmithKline	3,415	3.07
8. Pfizer	2,846	2.41
9. Sanofi	2,534	2.31
10. Novartis	1,075	0.96

Source: AIOCD AWACS PharmaTrac

Many Dimensions of the Market

Market like many other words in the English language, has several meanings and thus may mean many things to many people.

The key word in all these meanings and definitions of the market is 'opportunity.' Market can be defined as individuals and organizations with purchasing power, desire and authority to buy the products. The marketing practitioner would be better off with a clear understanding of the many dimensions of the market.

Where does one start? Like everything else in marketing, 'it depends.' It depends on what products or services you have to offer and to whom you want them to offer. In other words, you have to start from the very beginning i.e., from Market Opportunity Analysis (MOA). A clear, precise definition of 'market' is essential for a proper, meaningful MOA. Looking at the 'market' from different angles would certainly give you a better idea as regards its breadth, width and depth so that you can plan a more comprehensive, meaningful, and innovative strategies to defend and increase the shares of your prospective markets. The various dimensions of the pharmaceutical market are:

1. **The demographic dimension:** This comprises geographical proximity of customers and some shared socioeconomic traits such as age, income, sex, educational level and family size etc.

2. **The generic dimension:** This comprises the generic equivalents present in a number of formulations. One example is that all formulations containing 'rifampicin' will add up to the total 'rifampicin' market and not necessarily to the 'anti T B market.'

3. **The therapeutic group dimension:** This comprises all products aimed at relieving, treating and curing the same symptoms or diseases. For example, all products aimed at relieving, treating and curing 'asthma' come under one 'anti-asthmatic' therapeutic group.

4. **The competitive dimension:** Apart from the size of the market, the extent of competition, i.e. the number of competitors, their share of the market and their growth rate, are important in determining the attractiveness or unattractiveness of the market. For example, introducing yet another 'cotrimoxazole' preparation may not be an attractive proposition, though the market is large enough at Rs. 96-crore and is growing rapidly enough (end 1992). This is because over a hundred and more 'cotrimoxazole' brands, are competing with each other. Of course, it is certainly worthwhile to enter this market if you have a distinctly superior dosage form with greater safety margin etc. Furthermore, continuous monitoring of competitors' activities is crucial for success in the market place.

5. **The fifth dimension:** Timing is the fifth dimension. All those lucky winners in various therapeutic categories are those products that have been introduced at the 'right time.' It is not enough if you have a good product. You have got to be there in the market place first with your best product (with the best benefit package). You have got to be the 'firstest with the mostest!' Here is a case in point:

Case 2.1 Torrential Torrent!

Torrent Pharma provides a classic example in the Indian pharmaceutical industry of timing strategy. The phenomenal growth of 182 percent on an average during the first five years (1983-88) can be described by only one word: Torrential! Torrent truly lived up to its name. Despite the fact that it is not the original inventor or representing any original inventor in India, Torrent has many firsts to its credit. Torrent was the first company to launch many new drugs like - Diclofenac Sodium, Ketoconazole, Nifedipine, Lorazepam, Diltiazem, Ranitidine and Famotidine in India. Being the *firstest with mostest* certainly paid rich dividends to Torrent. In a short span of five years Torrent moved from the eighty-first rung to the thirty-sixth rung of the Indian pharmaceutical ladder. In the five years that followed, Torrent further accelerated its pace and galloped to the 13th position (Sales Rs. Crore 65.6 in 1992) in the Indian pharmaceutical industry.

What's even more impressive and important is Torrent's ability to pick winning products. All the segments that Torrent chose to enter since 1983 were the fastest growing segments such as cardio-vascular, antiulcerants and psychotropic drugs. As John Young, CEO of Hewlett-Packard, a leading apostle of speed and the most admired company in the information technology industry, said, "Doing it fast forces you to do it right the first time."

Timing is also very important for planning product deletion and harvesting strategies. One should also be aware of the stage and rate of product obsolescence in the market place. Research indicates that the probability of success is greater if you are one of the first three to enter the market in any therapeutic category. The early bird really catches the worm. A clear understanding and appreciation of these dimensions of the pharmaceutical market is necessary for segmenting and proper targeting of the market.

Three Major Segments

There seems to be three major segments in the pharmaceutical market.

1. One is the 'consumer market' or the 'prescription market,' which consists of individual households that go to a practicing doctor for the treatment of their ailments.

2. The other is the 'institutional market' that is made up of the hospitals in the public and private sectors that buy the product for dispensing to their patients and the government hospitals including medical college hospitals that provide free treatment to the poor.

3. The third one is 'the industrial market,' which comprises the bulk drugs that are used in formulations.

The Customer and the Consumer

There is more than mere semantics to this discussion on the customer and the consumer. The term 'consumer' is interpreted by many as the final consumer or end-user, who is not necessarily the 'customer.' Let us take the example of a housewife, who is buying breakfast cereals. The chances are that she is an 'intermediate customer' acting as an agent on behalf of the eventual consumers (her family), and in order to market the cereals effectively, it is very important to understand the wants and needs of the end-consumer as well as what the housewife wants and needs. Likewise, in pharmaceutical marketing it is the 'doctor' who acts as the agent or 'intermediate customer or Influencer' on behalf of the eventual consumer or the end-user, ie., the patient suffering from a particular ailment. The marketer, therefore, should clearly understand the needs of the patient (end-consumer) and the wants of the doctor (the intermediate customer), in order to market his products and services effectively in the pharmaceutical market.

What is Your Market?

'Elementary, my dear Watson'! do you say? Well, defining a market is neither simple nor elementary. The problem in defining a market is that most data is available as units bought, units used, prescriptions written (in the case of the pharmaceutical market), or values. As a result, market definitions are being confined to the same basis. When you consider that marketing is the process of satisfying the market needs through your products at profit, the big picture of a market emerges. The perspective broadens.

'Actual' Rather Than 'Potential'

While it is important to be aware of the 'big picture,' one should draw a subtle distinction between the 'actual' and the 'potential' market. When you are estimating the market for your product you should be concerned firstly with the volume and value of the 'actual market' rather than the 'potential market.' You should, of course, ensure that you are measuring the right things when you are measuring an 'actual market.' An example would amplify this. A company manufacturing nylon carpets for offices wants to estimate the market size for its carpets. What should the company consider as its market? Should it include 'concrete,' since concrete is in the floor covering business? Nothing could be more irrational, for concrete, although a floor covering does not satisfy the needs consumers have for warmth and color. Therefore, this (potential) is not part of its market. It should also not include woolen carpets used in the bed rooms. The appropriate market probably is an aggregate of all fiber type carpets sold to institutional outlets (actual market). To reach the potential market effectively the company may have to introduce different products and follow a product diversification strategy to meet or satisfy the needs of the consumers.

Market Identification

You cannot take the entire population as a 'potential market,' no matter what your product offering is. It is unreasonable because of the inherent differences existing among the consumers. You have to segment your markets - split your markets into smaller, more homogeneous groups and aim your production and promotional strategies at these markets.

Market Segmentation Theory

Markets usually fall into natural segments, which contain customers (and consumers), who exhibit the same broad characteristics. These segments form 'separate markets' and can often be of considerable size. The discerning marketer is conscious of this fact and fine-tunes his product offering specifically to reach these segments effectively. Market segmentation, therefore, is the means by which a company seeks to gain a differential advantage over its competitors. We have come a long way since the days of Henry Ford, the genius who gave the world its first assembly line and who said that his *customers can have a car with a color of their choice as long as it was black*. Much water has flown since then, and today, unless you are a customer-driven and marketing-oriented company, chances are that you will join Dinosaur Inc. Being customer-driven and marketing-oriented means that you have to pay attention to what your customers want and not to what you can make. You have to practice differentiated marketing. You have to segment your markets and effectively reach them with all your might. Market segmentation is crucial. It holds the key to success!

Criteria for a Viable Segment

That a segment comprises a group of consumers with similar needs and buying satisfactions is at best a basic definition and not a very practical one. One must make a clear distinction between the data that is available from all possible sources to prospective segments and the data that is needed for formulating a strategy to reach the segment cost-effectively. This is a constant task of defining and redefining your market and involves continuous research. The essential criteria for effective segmentation are:

1. **Measurability:** The segment must be measurable or definable in some specific way. You have to be able to count the members of the segment in some way to be able to know whether it is growing or declining. One can thus be certain of the potential and measure the results.

2. **Accessibility:** The segment must be reachable with your communication package in a cost-effective manner.

3. **Desirability:** The segment must be large enough to service profitably. The total consumption of the segment must be sufficient to cover the costs and to return an adequate profit to you.

4. **Homogeneity:** There should be a proper match or 'fit' between the 'need' profile of the members of the segment and the 'satisfaction' qualities or attributes of your product.

5. **Vulnerability:** The market must not be excessively vulnerable to competition.

Four Ways of Segmentation

There are four primary ways a marketer can segment a market:

1. By demographic factors
2. By usage rate
3. By perceived product benefits and
4. By lifestyle characteristics or psychographics

These four ways are commonly used for segmenting a market. They are used often in combinations since no one basis is best for all situations. These four bases for segmentation are important because, you as a marketer, must find some way of describing the customer groups in order to communicate with them effectively.

Demographic descriptors like age, sex, education, stage in family cycle and socio-economic backgrounds have been found to be most useful methods for consumer markets.

There is a very useful correlation between readership and television viewing patterns and these socio-economic groups. An understanding of this can be very helpful in communicating with the 'target market' cost-effectively through advertising.

It is obvious that we have different needs at different stages in the 'family cycle.' Banks and insurance companies use this information effectively to develop specific service packages targeted for different groups. In the pharmaceutical market, the 'needs-differentiation' at different stages in the family cycle is even more obvious. You have, for example, an 'infant market,' a 'pediatric market,' and a 'geriatric market.'

Usage-rate segmentation enables us design specific communication packages aimed at 'heavy users,' medium users,' 'light users,' and 'non-users.' This is essential because there cannot be single communication strategy that would appeal to these different consumer segments. They all have different needs.

Benefit segmentation is vital because the benefits people seek in a product are not always apparent, and may give stress on only one or two major benefits they perceive as most important. Market research, therefore, must dig deep to unearth the not-so-apparent and hidden benefits. Even from the marketing communication point of view, benefit segmentation is important. The most revered and venerated marketing guru, Theodore Levitt said, '*what the customer is looking for is not a product but the bundle of benefits that it offers.*' It is worth remembering that what the consumer is really buying is 3.24 inch hole, when he in fact (or in effect?) is buying a 3.25 inch drilling machine.

Psychographic segmentation is also becoming increasingly important because it seems to hold the key for the 'motive behind the purchase' and may have the right answer to the key question that the marketer faces - *why do people buy what they buy?*

When you understand the 'lifestyle,' the pattern of living in the world through the customers' habits, activities, interests and opinions, you have a reasonable chance of reaching them cost-effectively through your advertising communication.

Limitations

Segmenting the market is not a panacea for all marketing ills. It is a powerful tool alright but, not a cure-all. Like any powerful tool the results depend on how well it is used. One has to be careful in gathering, analyzing, interpreting the data and processing it into meaningful information for formulating a target-specific marketing strategy. Otherwise, it would be another example in favor of the classic '*Gi-Go*' (garbage-in, garbage-out) principle! An awareness and understanding of the limitations of market segmentation would therefore, be useful. The limitations are:

1. Usage-rate segmentation does not explain why the consumers fall into one category rather than another. The labels like 'heavy', 'medium', 'light' or 'low' may sometimes hide key information.

2. Psychographic segmentation is still in its early stages in our country. More people talk about it but do not actually use it. Hence the possibility of misinterpreting the results is greater and could cost the company dearly.

Pharmaceutical Market Segmentation

In order to segment a pharmaceutical market effectively, one should clearly understand the process of transactions and the inter-relationships of the marketing channel. Figure 2.1 shows this.

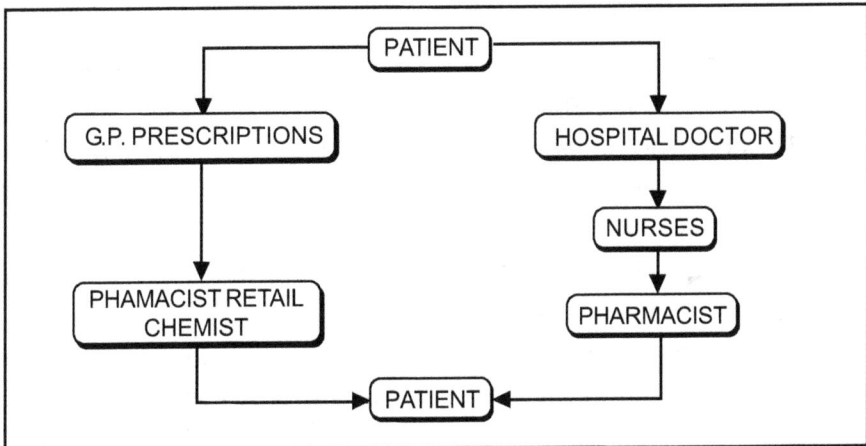

Figure 2.1 Pharmaceutical Marketing Transactions

The characteristic feature of pharmaceutical marketing is that you reach end-consumer (patient) through an intermediate customer (the physician, who advises the end-consumer through a prescription).

We can see in Figure 2.1, the two major potential target groups - patients (consumers) and doctors (customers). They have different needs. Segmentation is at the consumer (patient) level. The second logical step of segmentation is at the customer (doctor) level, whether he is a general practitioner, or a specialist or a hospital doctor, because he is the influencer. Let us look at these groups in greater detail:

A. Patients (Consumers or End-users)

1. Patients with similar illness fall under the same therapeutic group. E.g. diabetic patients, asthmatic patients, tuberculous patients etc,.

2. Patients can be classified depending on the stage at which the illness or disease has been progressing. e.g. Patients with acute or chronic bronchial asthma. Patients with mild, moderate or severe hypertension.

3. Patients according to their age group. e.g. Pediatric patients, geriatric patients etc.

4. Patients can be segmented according to sex. e.g. Male and female patients

B. Doctors (Intermediate customers, who are Influencers)

1. Doctors according to their age group

2. Doctors according to their specialty. e.g. Surgeons, Gynecologists, Cardiologists etc.

3. General practitioners, who treat mostly patients with a particular illness, common diseases, minor ailments etc.

4. Doctors according to the place where they practice. e.g. Urban, Rural, Government Hospitals, Primary Health Centers, Private Nursing Homes, Corporate Hospitals

5. Doctors according to the type of practice. e.g. Prescribing doctors, dispensing doctors etc.

6. Doctors according to the usage or prescribing rate. e.g. Heavy-users, light users, non-users, past-users

The scope for segmentation becomes clearer and broader from these examples. However, one should bear in mind that the size of the segment should be large enough to be attractive. You should never in your enthusiasm to fine-segment the market, break down the market to the ultimate degree but segment it just enough to uncover the opportunities. A segment should be viable. That is the cardinal principle.

Implications for the Marketer

The needs of a physician, who is a user and another doctor, who is a non-user are obviously different. The physician, who is a user (whether prescriber or dispensing) is currently satisfied with your products and its benefits. You don't have to sell the benefits and advantages of your products to him. What he requires from you is a continuous reassurance that choosing your product over others has been a right decision. It is worth continuing. In other words, your communication objective is to ensure continuous usage through positive reinforcement. Whereas a physician, who is a non-user, is yet to be convinced regarding the benefits your products offer to his patients. He does not believe that your product can provide the satisfaction he is seeking for his patients. He needs more information with substantial evidence. He needs positive proof, positive outcomes of the various clinical trials conducted by eminent physicians in different hospitals of repute.

Let us now take the case of a 'past user' of your product. Your product had measured up to his expectations in the past, but currently he is not using your product. What he needs is not just information and evidence of your product's superiority over the competing ones. You should investigate into all the possible reasons as to why he had stopped using your product. Is it because of competitive pressure? Or did he have any negative experience or not-so-positive experience with the product in the recent past? Is it because of non-availability of the product? Research in India shows that non-availability of the products is one of the major reasons why doctors give up prescribing products easily.

You can formulate your communication strategy to the 'past user' after ascertaining the exact reasons why he stopped using your product in the first place.

Thus, we can see that it is virtually impossible to create a single promotional communication that will satisfy the diverse needs of these three types of customers.

Similarly, you can formulate your communication strategies to patients, who have been suffering from different stages of similar illness, acute, chronic, mild or severe disease based on their needs.

The pharmaceutical marketer by using segmentation strategy creatively can:

1. Clearly identify the target group
2. Focus the promotional effort to maximize gains cost-effectively
3. Create a strong, positive product image to offset competition

Avoiding Pitfalls

While segmenting, if you maintain the essential criterion for effective segmentation, your are not likely to commit the mistakes that others have. Remember the following pitfalls of segmentation and always avoid them:

1. Choosing the wrong segment, which is not viable, too small, less attractive and declining.
2. Choosing a segment that is too small and over-crowded with competition. Such a market is fragmented rather than segmented.
3. Positioning your product as a last resort, an alternative when the leading brands fail or as a second line of treatment. That would be limiting its usage rate. You can position your brand as an essential replacement to the brand leader but not as an alternative. It is not worth playing the second fiddle.
4. Entering over-crowed segment when you cannot clearly, unambiguously and perceptibly differentiate your product.

Key Questions

Here are a few key questions to be answered while you are segmenting your market. They will help you sharpen the focus.

1. What has been the basis for segmentation?
   (a) Demographic?
   (b) Geographical?
   (c) Age group?
   (d) Sex?
   (e) Income levels?
   (f) Therapeutic group? By nature of disease?

(g) The severity of disease? Acute, chronic, recurrent, recalcitrant?

(h) The therapeutic benefits your products offer distinctly?

(I) Usage rate?

(j) The place of treatment? Home (G.P.), Nursing home, Government Hospital, or Primary Health Centre? Private Hospital? Corporate Hospital?

(k) The specialty of the doctor? Gynecologist, dermatologist, cardiologist etc.?

2. What are the needs of consumers (patients)?

3. What are the needs of intermediate customers (doctors, who are influencers)?

4. Are there any natural relationships between the consumers and the customers in the segment?

(a) Do old patients consult old doctors?

(b) Do women patients go to lady doctors?

(c) Do the highly educated, upper-income group of patients go to specialists and super specialists?

5. Are the segments attractive enough?

(a) Do they have adequate sales potential?

(b) Are they growing rapidly enough?

(c) Are they crowded with competition?

(d) Can they support your promotional costs and earn you adequate returns or profits?

6. What are the trends like? Are they static or changing?

Place of treatment: Is there any change taking place? For example, today more number of childbirths are taking place in nursing homes, rather than at homes even in rural India. This may be due to increased awareness, which is a natural consequence of increasing literacy levels. Another example is primary immunization against diseases like diphtheria, tetanus and pertussis, rubella, mumps etc, that has dramatically increased at government and private hospitals in urban areas and primary health centers in rural areas. The vaccines are distributed free of cost by the government and a massive multimedia educational campaign by health authorities is being undertaken with a missionary zeal to eradicate these diseases. What are the resultant implications for vaccine manufacturers and marketers?

7. Are there any unsatisfied needs currently in the segments, which your product can satisfy? What are they? This can certainly give you the *Unique Selling Proposition or USP* as it is popularly known and very strongly advocated by the great marketing and advertising genius, Rosser Reeves. Now, in the1990's you probably should look for *Unique Customer Perception (UCP)*. If you can un earth just one UCP, you are in business.

8. Above all, have you ranked the segments in order of importance? Have you identified priority segments?

Market Dimensions

For visualizing or sketching out a profile of your markets, you have got to view the market from all possible dimensions. Here is a checklist of the information you need to profile your markets:

1. The size of the geographical market
   (a) State-wise or district-wise if possible
   (b) How much is each state contributing to the All-India market?
   (c) What is the rate of change?
   This information is needed both in terms of volume, value and the number of prescriptions generated.

2. The size of the market by *therapeutic group*

3. The size of the market by demographics of both - the consumers, that is the number of patients treated with demographic details like age group, sex, location of treatment, income, and eduction levels etc. and the customers, i.e., by age group, sex, location, type of practice, specialty etc.

4. The size of the prescription market - the number of prescriptions written in each sub-therapeutic group of the major therapeutic category.

5. The size of the competition
   The number of competitors operating in each segment, region

with their respective shares of the total market, resources, strengths and weaknesses. The benefit packages offered by major competitors.

6. The size of the market by volume

   The dealer network, i.e., distributors, stockists, and retail chemists according to the volume of their purchases like heavy, medium, low and by location.

7. The size of the institutional market

   (a) The institutional market by nature, frequency, volume, and type of purchase, and by location

   (b) Do they call for annual tenders, periodical rate contracts?

   (c) Who are the key people involved in the buying decisions?

   (d) What are the criteria for selection?

Bird's Eye-view and the Worm's Eye-view

Now that we have got all the information we need, where and how should we begin? The best place to start in the pharmaceutical market is to segment it by the therapeutic group. By using the PharmaTrac (AIOCD AWACS) sales data or IMS Health sales data and their prescription audit or CMARC's CPR prescription data, we can ascertain and explore the marketing opportunities that are existing and dormant in various therapeutic groups. However, before working with the *nuts and bolts* in the process of pharmaceutical marketing segmentation, we should remember and understand two important concepts, namely the *bird's eye view* and the *worm's eye view*. These two concepts would enable us to develop much clearer perception regarding the market and broaden our perspective. A bird's eye view, simply stated, is the macro-view of the *market* or the big picture. When you get the big picture of the market as a whole, you would naturally develop a greater degree of sensitivity and understanding regarding the opportunities that exist, that may be dormant and how one could possibly tap and exploit them. It is like getting an aerial view of the market place. The big, large and obvious opportunities may look like tall sky-scrappers, and the seemingly small opportunities that may be lying dormant may look like patchwork on the landscape. Hence the name bird's eye view. The worm's eye view is concerned with all the minute details because the worm's view is the closest to the ground, always looking for opportunities and threats in the environment. A marketer needs to have both the bird's eye view and the worm's eye view because both the perspectives are important for him to size up and seize the opportunities in the market place.

Pareto's Law

The famous 80-20 rule, set out long ago by the famous Italian economist Vilfredo Pareto, can be seen at work even in the Indian pharmaceutical industry. Time and again, in every industry and in market after market, Pareto's law seems to be revalidated. As can be seen in the Indian pharmaceutical market, towns with a population of 50,000 and above accounted for only 18.7 of the total population of the country. But it was this significant few (towns) that accounted for a major chunk of 83.5 percent of the total pharmaceutical market in 1988. A detailed study and analysis of these town classes and their respective shares of the market in terms of both sales volume and prescriptions would be indispensable in marketing planning in terms of coverage and penetration strategies.

A Word of Caution

The usefulness of Pareto's law does not stop with this example. Its scope is much broader indeed. However, a word of caution here about Pareto's law is not out of place. Firstly, the 80-20 rule is not a golden mean - the proportion will vary while the principles won't. Secondly you can't go chopping or eliminating the insignificant many or the trivial majority; otherwise, sooner or later there won't be anything much left at all. Pareto's law is basic to better management. Even in the best-managed companies, with perfectly balanced product portfolios and the best customer profiles, Pareto's law will still apply. The dynamic nature of the market dictates that the best can never be achieved, as there will always be scope for improvement even if you think your company is the *best run* company in your industry.

A further segmentation of the major customers can be done in terms of volumes of expected business by usage (low, medium, heavy or none) and by frequency (occasional, frequent or very frequent). In the case of doctors, the volume and usage frequency would mean either purchases made or number of prescriptions written.

Segmenting by Therapeutic Group

The most important way of segmenting the pharmaceutical market is by the various therapeutic groups. The major therapeutic groups in the Indian pharmaceutical industry in 2017 are given in Table 2.2

Table 2.2 Major Therapeutic Groups in 2017 (MAT June 2017)

Therapeutic Group	Sales (Rs. Crore)	Market Share (%)
1. Anti-infectives	16,217	14.26
2. Cardiac	14,025	12.33
3. Gastro-intestinal	13,918	11.60
4. Antidiabetics	10,148	8.92
5. Vitamins/Minerals/Nutrients	9,951	8.75
6. Respiratory	8,478	7.45
7. Pain/Analgesics	7,832	6.89
8. Dermatologicals	6,859	6.03
9. Neuro/CNS	6,847	6.02
10. Gynecologicals	5,926	5.21
Total	**100,201**	**87.46**

Source: AIOCD AWACS PharmaTrac

These ten major therapeutic groups, which accounted for over 87 percentof the total pharmaceutical market, can be further segmented into over 60 sub-therapeutic groups.

Shift From Infectious Diseases to NCDs

It is an interesting and challenging time for Pharmaceutical sector since it is dynamic by nature. A gradual shift from infectious diseases to Non-Communicable Diseases (NCDs) is observable from the market data over the years. This is because populations are aging and life styles and habits are changing. Companies, therefore, need to align their product portfolios in the direction of the market.

Another way of looking at your market is to redefine and refine it. This is called *the Served Market concept*. It is a very important one, since it widens the horizon and broadens the understanding of what your market really is.

The Served Market

It is Bruce Henderson, Chairman of the famous BCG (the Boston Consulting Group), who originated the *Served Market* concept. So far all the definitions of the market have been rather implicit and included elements like your customers, products or services and your competitors' products or services. Since all customers, their needs and requirements (physical, physiological or psychological) are not alike, it is useful to think of them in terms of segments of the total market. They can be grouped in terms of homogeneity, or commonality of their needs. Such a grouping helps to sharpen your focus on customer needs of different customer groups even more effectively. This explains why so many creative and innovative marketers the world over are looking for *niches* and turning the science of segmentation into a fine art.

The served market concept is the ultimate step and the state of the art way of defining market segments and understanding market structures. This involves examination of your market segments from a competitor's point of view. In any given market there are different segments of market, comprising groups of customers with varying needs. These customer groups select the competitive offerings that best suit their needs. This process creates market segments. Each competitor, thus, has some group of customers where he holds an absolute advantage over all other competitors. This is his forte because he offers a *benefit package* of products and services that is best suited for his specific target customers. That is his *served market*. Figure 2.2 gives a graphic presentation of the served market.

What is more important to note in the served market concept is that each competitor has his own boundary lines. And by definition those areas offer zero-competitive advantages. At those boundaries, neither you nor your competitor has an advantage to offer to those particular customers. What are the implications of this to the marketer?

Firstly, all competition in a market must take place along the boundary lines of the served markets. This is because all differentiation, competitive advantages that are stronger at the core, become increasingly thinner and as you move to the periphery and they become totally imperceptible and indistinguishable at the boundaries or borders.

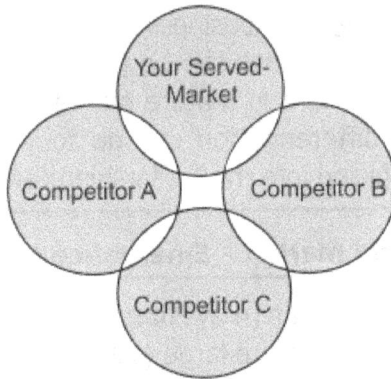

Figure 2.2 The Served Market Concept

To expand your market and increase your market share you will have to create a perceptible competitive advantage and communicate it with all your might to your customers and prospective customers around the zero-advantage boundary line and, indeed to those in your competitor's served market. That is not only necessary for growth but also essential even for survival.

Always, remember that the boundary lines of the served markets of yourself as well as your competitors' change over time since the marketing environment is such a dynamic one where change is the only constant factor. This change occurs as one competitor acquires a competitive advantage over another and occupies part of his territory. So an appropriate definition of your served market is that particular one in which, you have a combination of customers and products and services, where you have an absolute advantage over all other competitors in your market (the total market).

In order expand your served market, you have to:

A. Develop a clear understanding of your and your competitors served market.

B. Defend your served markets by communicating persuasively the advantages of your products and services to your existing customers as a positive reinforcement.

C. Create perceptible competitive advantage and clearly communicate them to persuade the customers of your competitors (and those around the zero-advantage zone).

The name of the game of business growth and market expansion, therefore, is *differentiation* that can be perceived by the customers. This is even more important in mature markets. Here is an example (case 2.2) of what differentiation can do to your product. It can catapult an obscure brand into the leadership position.

Case 2.2 Antacid market - Emergence of a new leader!

Gelusil of Warner Hindustan (now Pfizer) had been enjoying brand leadership in the Rs. 78-crore large (1992) antacid, antiflatulent market. It was a brand leader since its launch in 1973.

Its served market had been considerably large with other prominent brands like Aludrox, Divol and Digene etc. Although introduced in 1968, it was only during the 1970s that Digene created a perceptible product differentiation by adding an *antiflatulent* (Methylpolysiloxane) and pushed the product aggressively into the competitors' territory. Its volume had grown, market share had moved up significantly making Digene, the undisputed brand leader in 1992 with a 20 percent share of the antacid -antiflatulent market.

Difficult Task

Developing a clear, thorough understanding of your market is a very difficult task. You may find this a demanding or perhaps even an impossible exercise.

What you should really do is define exactly how much you understand about your business and by extension, what new information you have to acquire to develop intelligent, meaningful, appropriate competitive marketing strategies. To help you get started on this task, here is a checklist:

Defining your Served Market: A Checklist

1. Define the total market by size (volume and value), growth rate, customer-types and competitors.
2. Define your *served market* in terms of your customers' needs and how your product attributes satisfy those needs. Mention the specific competitive advantage of your product.

3. Define your competitors' served markets in terms of their respective customer needs and the competitive advantages their products offer in satisfying those needs.

4. Identify the areas of zero-competitive advantage.

5. Find out ways of creating a perceptible differentiation and turning it into a distinct competitive advantage.

6. Prepare a persuasive communication strategy to drive home the distinct competitive advantage you have created.

7. Invade with all your might into the competitors' territory.

Market segmentation : Some more aspects

While market segmentation is essential for success by creating a niche for a product, one should not splinter the market and lose sight of the opportunities that may have been lying dormant at his doorstep. This sort of tunnel vision has cost many companies very dearly. Business history, the world over is resplendent with the success stories of companies, which have been alert to spot the opportunities in time that others could not, and at the same time innumerable are the failures of those companies, who could not recognize the opportunities waiting to be tapped in front of them. Theodore Levitt, the well known Professor Emeritus of Marketing at Harvard Business School in his classic and landmark article, *The Marketing Myopia* published in 1960 has most vividly described this. It is relevant even today.

The points, therefore, you have to remember while segmenting the market are:

1. Define your *served market* and *potential market* as clearly as possible. Definition of your *potential market* includes and involves a thorough understanding of your competitors' served markets.

2. List the important characteristics and attributes that are unique to your products. Also list the important characteristics and unique attributes of your competitors' products.

3. Find out whether there are any unmet, unsatisfied needs in your competitors' served markets.

4. Monitor the changing needs and be alert to notice, recognize, and record any developments taking place in the total market. Unless you are the first to observe and recognize the changing

trends and developments, you cannot be the first to meet the changing needs of your customers (yours as well as your competitors) with an appropriate and satisfying mix of product offering. Remember the cardinal principle of marketing - *you have got to be the firstest with the mostest* if you want to reap a rich harvest in the market.

Market Opportunity Analysis

Inherent in the law of marketing success is the consistent need for Market Opportunity Analysis (MOA). Unless you constantly practice a systematic opportunity analysis and keep your antennae high and ears close to the ground, you can neither unearth the dormant opportunities nor discover those that are looming large over the hemisphere of your potential market. Here are seven cases emphasizing and amplifying the need and importance of market opportunity analysis and how crucial it is for business success in the Indian pharmaceutical industry.

Case 2.3 Anti-tubercular market: A tale of two companies!

The anti-tubercular market was Rs. 104-crore large and growing at an annual rate of 28 percent in 1972. Tuberculosis was affecting approximately 14 million people at that time. The main line of treatment in the 1970's included drugs like PAS, Isoniazid, Thiacetazone - alone or in combination of two or more drugs.

Two companies, Pfizer, a multinational on a fast track (ranked 8th with a sales volume of Rs. 89-crore in 1992) and Biological E. Limited, a medium sized Indian company with an impressive track record (ranked 44th with a sales volume of Rs. 29-crore in 1992) were acknowledged leaders in the anti-tubercular market in the seventies with their respective brands of PAS, Isoniazid, Thiacetazone and their combinations.

But the eighties had seen the emergence of new and more potent drugs such as Ethambutol (introduced in 1978 and gained significant market share in the 1980s), Pyrazinamide and Rifampicin. The earlier anti-tubercular drugs like PAS, INH, and Thiacetazone accounted for a mere 3.5 percent of the total anti-tubercular market (INH in combination with Rifampicin, however, accounted for 48 percentof the total anti T.B. market) in 1992.

But Pfizer and Biological E. Limited, the two leaders in the anti-tubercular market of the 1970s did not visualize the changes in the market and the shifts in the line treatment, in their very own served markets.

The Result: From a leadership position in the 1970's, the two companies virtually became non-entities within a few years in the anti-tubercular markets. While Pfizer in 1992 had a meager 1.4 percent share of the total anti-tubercular market as a leader in a vanishing sub-segment of anti-tubercular market, Biological E. Limited had driven itself out of the market.

Lost opportunities? Marketing Myopia? Are there any lessons to be learnt from this? You decide.

Case 2.4 Anti-tubercular market: Exploiting the opportunities - The Secret of Lupin's Success!

While the two leaders, Pfizer and Biological E. Limited, of the anti-tubercular market in the 1970's were resting on their laurels, Lupin, a fledgling company began flexing its muscles in the late seventies and was actively looking for opportunities to satiate its ravenous appetite for rapid growth. Lupin, ranked 62 with a sales volume of a mere Rs. 3-crore in 1981, took the anti-tubercular market by storm with its introduction of Rifampicin. It had introduced all other modern potent anti-tuberculous drugs like Ethambutol, Pyrazinamide and a formulation of Rifampicin and INH in quick succession. In seven years, Lupin had become an undisputed leader in the anti-tubercular market with a formidable 29.7 percent share in 1988. Lupin during this period, had also moved up to the 12th rank in the Indian pharmaceutical industry with Rs. 33.3-crore. Lupin, further went on to consolidate its already stronghold in the anti-tubercular market to a dominant position. By 1992, Lupin had achieved an invincible 50 percent share of the total anti-tubercular market in India.

Lupin's range of anti-tubercular drugs introduced since 1981 alone had accounted for over 61 percentof the increase in sales volume in these eleven years. That is what identifying, uncovering and exploiting an opportunity can do for a company!

Case 2.5 Once a leader, not always a leader! The Year: 1976.

The segment: the largest and the fastest growing segment of the lot. The Rs. 395-crore large antibacterial market. This large market had been a testing ground in the Indian pharmaceutical industry for the fluctuating fortunes of many a company.

Sarabhai Chemicals, the No. 1 pharmaceutical company in 1976, was also the leader in the antibacterial market with as many as eight of its eleven brands occupying pride of place among industry's top 120 brands. Narrow-Spectrum antibiotics and oral penicillins accounted for over forty percentof the total antibiotic sales of the company in 1976, whereas these sub-groups formed about twenty-eight percentof the systemic antibacterial group. The antibacterial market had been undergoing rapid changes since then. More potent, broad-spectrum, semi-synthetic antibiotics had been gaining prominence. Products like Ampicillin, Amoxycillin, Cephalosporins, Doxycycline, Cloxacillin combinations, Trimethoprim with Sulphamethoxazole combinations had been registering unprecedented growth rates. These newer antibiotics had grown at an average annual growth rate of over 80 percent since 1976, thus improving their share of the antibacterial market to a staggering 44 percentin 1988 from 21 percent in 1976.

About the same time, the narrow-spectrum antibiotics and the oral penicillins were losing their share of the market. The industry leader, Sarabhai Chemicals obviously did not notice the significant fall of 14 percentin the market share points. Even if it was noticed, the responses and reactions were too slow. The loss of the market share of narrow-spectrum antibiotics and oral penicillins from 28 percentin 1976 to a mere I percentin 1988 might have been a case of missing the wood for the trees, since these segments (narrow-spectrum antibiotics and oral penicillins) too had grown at a respectable pace of 20 percent per annum on an average. That may have lulled the leader into complacency in retrospect. What had led to the shrinking of the market share of the narrow-spectrum antibiotics and the oral penicillins during the period of 1976 and 1988? Well, elementary as it may seem, it is the fact that the total antibacterial market during the same period had registered an average annual growth rate of over 40 per cent, i.e., twice as fast as the narrow-spectrum antibiotics and the oral penicillins. To top it all, the newer antibiotics had grown even faster than the market! At eighty percent growth rate that is twice as fast as that of the antibacterial market. Here's a snapshot of the growth rates of the three sub-segments of the antibacterial market between 1976 and 1988:

A. Narrow-spectrum antibiotics and Oral Penicillins at **20** per cent

B. Anti-bacterial market as a whole grew at **40** per cent

C. Newer antibiotics grew at a rate of **80** per cent

The Net Result? The company that once was a leader and a sort of emperor in the antibacterial market had to contend to remain a king, who had surrendered all new markets to a one-time upstart-turned-emperor! Complacency? Lack of alertness? Whatever may be the reason, one should remember that in the market place, it is axiomatic that once a leader is not always a leader or at least, not necessarily!

Case 2.6 One company's complacency, another company's vision!

In the same anti-bacterial market around the same time (1976-88), another company, relatively small in size (rank 30, sales volume Rs 5-crore in 1976), but big in dreams, was working hard to realize them ever since. Ranbaxy laboratories (now a part of Sun Pharma) literally ran to the top of the league in Indian pharmaceutical industry in just about twelve years (rank 4, sales volume Rs. 58.6-crore in 1988). What is the secret of its success? It had unearthed, uncovered and exploited the opportunities in the rapidly changing anti-bacterial market, which was the largest and fastest growing segment of the total market. What the industry leader, Sarabhai Chemicals failed to visualize and capitalize, Ranbaxy had grabbed hard and held on to firmly. Ranbaxy in these twelve years had entered every sub-segment of the newer, potent, broad-spectrum antibiotics market and literally drove itself to success. In 1988, it had achieved the leadership position with a 10.8 percent share in the largest segment of the Indian pharmaceutical industry, which is anti-bacterials by nudging the leader Sarabhai Chemicals (market share 10.4 per cent) to second position.

Ranbaxy, obviously was not content with its achievement. Its objective was to achieve a dominant leadership position in the antibacterial segment that was large and rapidly growing. The company had chosen the fastest growing subsegment (Quinolones) of the antibacterials and pursued a very aggressive strategy with the introduction Cifran (Ciprofloxacin) in 1989. In less than four years, Cifran, had become the single most important brand for Ranbaxy accounting for about one-fourth of its domestic formulations sales. Cifran had given it the much needed competitive edge. Ranbaxy had become the unquestioned leader with a 12.7 percent share of the total anti-bacterial therapeutic group by 1992. Ranbaxy was way ahead of competition in its chosen segment with the nearest competitors - Cipla (6.9 percent and the once-upon-a-time leader Sarabhai Chemicals (Market share 6.7 per cent) trailing far behind.

The formula for success is not difficult to understand because there is no such formula. What is crucial to the whole business of winning at the market place is the ability to uncover the opportunities and the energy to exploit them!

Case 2.7 You cannot be immune to change, even if you are a leader in immunologicals!

The market for immunologicals is yet another example of a leader in the 1970s being pushed second position. The immunological market in 1976 comprised Sera and Vaccines (Anti-

Tetanus serum, Tetanus Toxoid, and DPT vaccines mainly) and Gamma Globulins. The market had grown from Rs. 1-crore in 1976 to Rs. 9-crore in 1988. In addition to this the government of India had embarked on a massive nation-wide primary immunization program against diphtheria, pertussis, tetanus and polio and measles. This would mean an addition of Rs. 5-crore to the Sera and Vaccines market making it a sizable Rs. 14-crore market. Increasing literacy levels and growing urbanization were also expanding the immunological market. The demand for other vaccines like measles vaccines, anti-rabies vaccine, oral polio drops was constantly increasing.

But, Biological E. Limited, the market leader in Immunological market in the 1970s, remained oblivious to these changes and developments. It had not introduced any new product in this category despite the numerous new product opportunities that had come its way. The company seemed to have taken its leadership position for granted and felt immune to the changes and developments. And the inevitable happened. The company was pushed to third position in 1988 with a market share of only 15.2 per cent.

The company did not see the writing on the wall, which was large and clear enough. Consequently, its share of the immunological market had further eroded to a mere 6 percent by 1992 pushing the company to fourth place.

The market place has got its own laws. First and foremost among them is that the consequence of complacency is the loss of leadership, however firmly entrenched the leader might have been once upon a time!

Case 2.8 Booster doses are essential to boost sales and market share!

As in immunology, booster doses seem to be essential in the immunological market. Because that was what Serum Institute, a young, little-known company in the early 1970s had done to climb the coveted leadership position in the immunological market in India. The company was quick on the draw and capitalized every single opportunity that had come its way. It was the first company to introduce new vaccines in all emerging categories and positioned itself strongly as the Immunologicals company. The name *Serum Institute of India* reinforced this image. The outcome? The company emerged as a leader in the immunological market in India, with no challenger in sight (market share 40.2 percentin 1988).

Perhaps this had lulled the company into complacency. It had taken its leadership position for granted and did not take cognizance of emerging competition. Hoechst (Sanofi now) and Alidac (a division of Zydus Cadila) had been obviously watching the immunological market with considerable interest.

Hoechst had entered the market with its brand of anti-rabies vaccine, Rabipur in 1986 and within a short span of six years achieved a dominant leadership position by introducing new products and by promoting its sera and vaccine range aggressively.

The market share of Serum Institute had shrunk to 16 percent by 1992 and the company had to be content with a distant No.2 position.

Another important law of the market place is that there is no time for respite. You cannot take anything for granted in marketing. Not even your leadership position however formidable it may seem to be!

Case 2.9 One is enough!

Hoechst India is another company, which conforms to the maxim of the market place, that if you uncover just one right opportunity and back it up with all your might, you are sure to be a winner.

Hoechst, though a very late entrant to the immunological market in India (December 1986), uncovered a major opportunity in the anti-rabies vaccine area and exploited it with the introduction of a truly superior product, Rabipur anti-rabies vaccine. The company had vigorously promoted the product and within a short span of two years achieved the No.2 positioning the immunological market (market share 28 percentin 1998). Surely one is enough if it is the right one!

The dramatic success of Rabipur vaccine only whetted the appetite of Hoechst for further increase in market share. The company expanded its winning range of products in the sera and vaccines market with new products like anti-RHO-D, Beriglobin, Human Albumin, and Berirab. Within six years, Hoechst had achieved the leadership position in the immunologicals market with a formidable 58 percent share of the market (1992).

Elements of Market Opportunity Analysis

The common thread that runs through these cases is that constant analysis of market opportunities is imperative to the success of any company. Market opportunity analysis includes:

A. Strengths of your product attributes (unique customer perceptions) in your served market as well as in your competitors' served markets (as opposed to their product offerings).

B. Analysis of any possible gaps between customer needs and your (as well as your competitors') product offerings. The *gap* is the opportunity area.

C. A detailed analysis of whether the identified *gaps* or *opportunities* (currently unmet needs of customers) can be exploited profitably. In other words, is the new segment viable?

D. Look for any possible weaknesses existing in your product offerings as compared to changing customer needs and the ways in which your competitors have been responding. This is necessary to prevent the invasion of your competitors into your served markets and to reinforce your product strengths by appropriate product development strategy.

E. Whether exploiting the emerging new segments or markets involves directly or indirectly any inherent threats, environmental, social, competitive or otherwise.

F. Quantitative analysis of the segment and your new product in terms of:

    (a) The demand analysis

(b) The profitability

(c) The competitive edge that it would give the company's current product-mix

(d) The likely impact it may have on your existing products - e.g., whether it would lead to cannibalization of the existing products and if so, what is the net impact on the bottomline of the company?

G. A detailed analysis of competitors and their likely responses to this new segment - like what would be the response time involved? How soon can the competition enter? What plans do you have to counter any possible attack by competitors?

H. What is your feedback system? How effective is it? What improvements are needed to improve its promptness and speed?

Once you are equipped with all this information and a determination to succeed and are quick enough on the draw, you are sure to win in the market place. This is what all successful companies have done and achieved uncommon success. Sounds simple? Well, it takes a lot of hard work!

Before deciding on any line-extension strategy, a further analysis of the available data is a must. If your brand does not enjoy a considerable strength in the market, using the same brand name for all possible line extensions with a hope of building a successful or winning flagship brand will end up only as fond hope! Like athletes need strong legs and good co-ordination to compete in a race, brands too need a strong foothold to be successful in the market place that is merciless.

While all this may sound elementary, look how many companies have ignored such opportunities even in the antacid, anti-flatulent market. Here is a case in point:

Case 2.10   Opportunity overlooked?

The industry leader Glaxo (GlaxoSmithKline now) introduced in 1977 Almacarb tablets in the antacid, anti-flatulent market, and positioned it cleverly and clearly. This earned the company a respectable share of the (over two per cent) market within a short time. Later the company had started promoting this product through its second division Allenburys, which is considerably smaller than the Glaxo Pharma division both in sales and coverage. Glaxo, which is known for its innovative marketing strategies, somehow decided to ignore the relatively larger and more prosperous segment of antacid suspension. The antacid suspension market accounted at the time for about two-thirds of the total antacid market with tablets contributing for the rest of the one-third of the market. Entering the suspension market would have been a logical decision, even an elementary one for Glaxo, particularly in the light of Almacarb's initial success and the company's marketing muscle because, the company had got an enviable combination of brain brawn! The company had been extremely successful even with 'me-too' re-launches like Piriton Expectorant in over-crowded cough and cold preparations market a few years ago!

But somehow, the company chose to ignore the larger sub-segment of antacid, anti-flatulent suspension. Opportunity overlooked?

Market Opportunity Analysis: A Step-by-Step Approach

Step One: Analyze your existing markets. What is your directly competing market?

List out all the existing markets in which you are competing in terms of market size (in units and value), growth rate, number of competitors, the top three competitors in each market, their sales in units and value, market share, the rate at which they are growing, your sales in units and value, growth rate in each market. This will give you the size of your directly competing market.

Step Two: Build on your strengths.

Have you realized, capitalized and exploited all the possible opportunities in your existing markets? Do a SWOT (Strength, Weakness, Opportunity, Threat) analysis of your products in all your existing markets. The key questions to ask are:

1. Are there any unmet needs in your existing markets, not fulfilled by you as well as your competitors?

2. Are there any major sub-segments where you do not have any product? What about your competitors? How are they faring in the sub-segments? What is the contribution of their products in these sub-segments to their total sales in the market?

3. What are the strengths and weaknesses of your products as compared with your competitors? Is there any need for product development, to create a perceptible differentiation?

4. What are the opportunities that the current markets offer? Can you plot the trends and spot any emergence of new markets early enough as Lupin did in the anti-tubercular market and Serum Institute of India in the case of the immunological market?

5. Are there any shadows or threats lurking in your markets? Do you have any early warning system so that you can pull out of the market with little or no damage? Like Schering A.G., Nicholas Piramal, and Allenburys division of Glaxo pulled out of the high dose estrogen-progesterone market, which vanished due to a government ban? These threats could be from the changing opinions of customers, shifts in the treatment pattern, or line of therapy or governmental policies. You should develop a feedback system to monitor the changing trends and the likely shifts. Developing an early warning system is as important as a stitch in time.

6. Building on strengths is crucial for success. You should reinforce your already strong position in your existing markets with new products, expand and extend your served markets. Because, if you don't, your competitors will!

Step Three: Explore new market opportunities.

Always be on the lookout for new market opportunities. Find out the fast growing markets, large markets, and the ones which are less entrenched. List out the new markets in terms of their size, growth, competitive intensity and vulnerability. Prioritize them in the order of their importance or appeal to you.

One should also analyze how the markets identified or short-listed will match with the resources of your firm. What is the level of congruence? And how will these new markets affect your existing ones? Will there be any cannibalization of the products? How many new markets can you enter?

Step Four: Evaluate new opportunities in new segments.

The main points to consider, when you are evaluating new market opportunities in new segments are:

1. Find out whether the market is large enough and is growing rapidly enough.
2. Whether the segment is over-crowded and the intensity of competition.
3. Who are the major competitors? What are their strengths? What about their coverage? How does your firm compete with them in terms of resources?
4. What about the attributes of your product (to be introduced) vis-a-vis the competitors? Have you created a differentiation that can be perceived by your prospective customers?

The answers to these questions will be helpful in giving a direction to your marketing strategy.

Market Opportunity Analysis: An Example

Assume that you want to introduce a non-steroidal anti-inflammatory drug. What should you consider as your market? Your *actual market* (directly competing market) would mean an aggregate of the sales volume of all non-steroidal anti-inflammatory drugs in the market. It adds upto limiting the market and restricting the opportunities.

Looking at the *potential* market would mean widening the horizon of opportunities. The potential market in this case would be the *anti-arthritic market* as a whole, since Non-Steroidal Anti-Inflammatory Drugs (NSAIDS) are widely used in the treatment of arthritis by virtue of their safety and efficacy. When you analyze the prescriptions of doctors, you will observe that the anti-arthritic market includes in addition to NSAIDS, muscle relaxants, steroids, topical rubifacients, anti-gout preparations and analgesics etc. With the help of prescription audit report figures, it is possible to quantify the size of each segment. You can find out exactly how many prescriptions are written for each competing product in each segment.

Consider for example the gout segment of the anti-arthritic market. The prescriptions written for gout include apart from the anti-gout preparations like Zyloric (Burroughs Wellcome then and GSK now) and Benemid (Merind then and MSD now), NSAIDs (Nonsteriodal Anti-Inflammatory Drugs) and analgesics.By referring to prescription audit you can find out the exact number of:

Prescriptions written for NSAIDs in gout;

- Prescriptions written for analgesics in gout
- In addition, to the total number of prescriptions written for the more specific anti-gout preparations

Armed with this ammunition of information, you can now aim to be going great guns with your new NSAID against a bigger anti-arthritic market (potential market) rather than confirming yourself to a smaller NSAID market (actual market).

Similarly, when you analyze each of the major segments like pain, lumbago, sciatica, bursitis, synovitis, spondylitis, sprains, osteoarthritis, rheumatic arthritis, etc, (based on diagnostic profile), you would observe that the *actual market* of NSAIDS allows itself to expand into a much larger *potential (anti-arthritic) market!*

You can do a similar analysis taking into account all the aspects of exploring and evaluating new opportunities in all the markets you want to enter.

Strategic Options

Now that you have defined, redefined and refined your market definitions and analyzed it, how should you go about deciding on your market finally? What are the strategic options?

A. **Concentrated Marketing:** Should you segment the market by the customer specialty, i.e., pediatric market, orthopedic market, psychotropic market, the gynecology market, the dermatological market etc.?

The implications of such segmentation would mean practicing the strategy of concentrated marketing. In other words you have to design a marketing-mix targeted specifically at the chosen segment and go the whole hog. The obvious advantages of concentrated marketing are:

1. You can carve out a niche for your company and its products.

2. A concentrated approach will give you a distinct and definite competitive advantage over your competitors as you will be in a better position to monitor and predict the trends and the likely shifts in the line of treatment and customer needs in the market. This is truly invaluable.

3. Consequently, your customer service will be better than your competitors' because of the specialized knowledge of your sales force, your product management and product development teams.

Of course, concentrated marketing is not without its disadvantages, the major advantage being that a failure could be devastating. It could cost the company very dearly since you are putting all your eggs in one basket. You have got to be thorough in your analysis and should have products, which are perceptibly different and distinct from the existing products. Equipped with this, when you go all out in promoting your product with an appropriate promotional mix, you are bound to succeed. But you must do a lot of homework, monitor your tactics, strategy and competitors' responses closely. As a Jewish proverb says, 'there is nothing wrong in keeping all your eggs in one basket, so long as you watch the basket closely.'

The other disadvantage with concentrated marketing is that the segment may not be viable and the company, in its enthusiasm to create a target-specific marketing-mix may be losing sight of some of the opportunities. After all even the insignificant many may also count in the long run. However, in the final analysis, concentrated marketing wins hands down when the segmentation criteria is right.

Case 2.11   Pulsar's Meteoric Rise!

Pulsar division of Glaxo (GSK now) is an example of successful concentrated marketing. Pulsar division was started in 1986 by Glaxo, the multi-division pharmaceutical giant in India, with a virtually unchallenged leadership position in the pharmaceutical industry (Sales over Rs 230-crore in 1988). The new division was started essentially to launch their celebrated anti-ulcer drug Ranitidine (original research product of Glaxo U.K. and the world's largest selling prescription drug brand Zantac with sales of over US $ 1.7 billion in 1988) in India, under the brand name *Zinetec*. Pulsar division's marketing-mix was conceived and designed in a manner befitting the winner the Zantac (the international brand name) really had been. The target audience identified consisted essentially of trendsetters and opinion makers. Top gastroenterologists from U.K. conducted seminars and audiovisual presentations to the leading gastroenterologists, physicians and surgeons in India. These specialists were received with the traditional Glaxo hospitality that was matchless in India. Zinetec was launched with great pomp and show in early 1986. The specially trained field force of Pulsar division made regular follow-up visits to all the leading specialists in the field only to promote Zinetec with heavy promotional support. After a little over one year of this concentrated marketing, Zinetec's promotion was also handed over to Glaxo Pharma division (the largest division of the company) to achieve a wider coverage simultaneously.

The result: In little over two years, Zinetec reached the top of the heap in the fast growing Rs. 31 crore large anti-ulcer market with formidable market share of 22 per cent.

In 1987, Pulsar launched another research product of Glaxo U.K., an alpha-beta blocker labetalol under the brand name Normadate. In less than two years, as a result of the massive promotional effort, Normadate had carved out for itself a respectable 10.4 percentof the market.

The rapid rise of Pulsar can only be described as meteoric!

In 1992, Glaxo, as a part of the restructuring of its marketing operations has merged two of its relatively smaller divisions (Allenburys and Pulsar) as Glaxo-Allenburys to achieve sustainable competitive advantage. The basic purpose of this merger is to achieve a greater market penetration more cost effectively (by combining the muscle of Allenburys and Pulsar) and sharper marketing focus and orientation.

Later, as a result of acquisitions and mergers with two large multinationals Burroughs Wellcome and SmithKline Beecham, Glaxo is now known as GlaxoSmithKline and has been restructured again with multiple divisions.

Case 2.12   Schering A.G. Concentrates on Gynaec Market and Beats the Retreat in Time!

Schering A.G. was concentrating only on the gynaecology market in India in the late 1960s. The company was specializing in the female sex hormones and had a number of winning brands like Primolut N, Duogynon and a wide range of oral contraceptives under the brand names - Gynovlar, Primovlar, Anovlar etc. The company's image in the gynecology segment was arguably the best in the industry. Subsequently the company had totally become a part of German Remedies and started practicing differentiated marketing, promoting even German Remedies' products. The company today does not have the special image of the company in the Gynaec market any longer.

Schering A.G.'s retreat was just in time and appropriate. The gynaec market had been undergoing a substantial change with some of the earlier hormones like progesterone and estrogen (certain esters of these hormones) coming under attack due to side effects, including the fear of breast cancer. The oral contraceptive market had not been growing fast enough. The company, was therefore, left with two options:

A. Either introduce newer and safer hormones, or

B. Pull out of the market

While the company had not withdrawn itself from the gynaec market, it pulled out of the controversial segment of high-dose combinations of estrogen and progesterone supposed to be used mainly for pregnancy diagnosis (but misused for termination of pregnancy much more often than not, much before the medical termination of pregnancy was acceptable socially and legally). The company (German Remedies), which has acquired Schering A.G. had been practicing differentiated marketing by product-market diversification (promoting other products of German Remedies) thus freeing itself from the threat of vulnerability.

Later, German Schering as the company was known later started promoting only the hormonal and other original products and not the other range of German Remedies for reasons best known to them.

In 2011, Bayer formed a 50:50 Joint ventine with Zydus cadila to market it product in India.

Today, German Schering is part of the Zydus Bayer joint venture as German Schering was acquired by Bayer.

The case of German Schering brings home one major disadvantage of practicing concentrated marketing. When you are concentrating only on one segment of the market, you may become vulnerable, if market conditions change and you do not have anything to fall back upon. What has been a major strength once, i.e., excessive specialization, may turn out to be a weakness when the market conditions change and when you are less flexible (due to excessive specialization).

B. Differentiated Marketing

The second strategic option is *Differentiated Marketing.*

When an organization markets to many segments, each with a differentiated marketing-mix, it is practicing differentiated marketing.

One major advantage of practicing differentiated marketing is that it minimizes or eliminates the vulnerability factor. It allows a firm to be more flexible. The second advantage of practicing differentiated marketing is that your major marketing costs, like selling and distribution, are spread over a number of products. This enables you to compete in relatively smaller-yet-profitable segments, more effectively.

There seems to be an increasing trend among a number of companies to practice concentrated marketing strategies mainly targeted at the institutional market in the pharmaceutical industry. A number of companies in the late 1980s and 1990s created an institutional sales division or a hospital products division. This has later evolved into a process called Key Account Management (KAM), which is a more integrated and scientific approach to focus on the institutional market that comprises large accounts, which are key to sales success.

Before deciding on any strategy or a combination of these strategies you should address the following questions:

1. What are the resources of your company? (financial, technological, manufacturing and marketing)
2. What is the competition doing?
3. Is the market new to the company?

C. Undifferentiated Marketing

Undifferentiated marketing, as the name suggests, is exactly the opposite of differentiated marketing or segmented approach to marketing. There are a few products in the consumer market and several more in the industrial market that are sold to the great mass of buyers and not to any particular sub-group. In so far as the pharmaceutical industry is concerned only the institutional market can be viewed as a mass market. While some marketers feel that in the emerging generic market too can be considered for the purpose of undifferentiated marketing, without some degree of differentiation in terms of quality or better value for money, it is not possible to market even the generics successfully. That is why the corporate-branded generics are making their presence felt, albeit at a slower pace in the so-called undifferentiated market. It is the company name and the corporate image that gives the brand status to the generic product. Undifferentiated marketing seems to be more of a myth than reality in the present day world, where branding even commodities is becoming a necessity to market them successfully.

Summary

When you define *market* as individuals and organizations with purchasing power, desire and authority to buy products and services, the focus is clearly on the opportunity. *Market* almost becomes a synonym for *opportunity*.

A constant and systematic market opportunity analysis, therefore, holds the key to success in the market place.

Understanding the many dimensions of the market, appreciating and improving the sensitivity towards the changing needs and wants of customers and consumers are more crucial today than ever before for winning at the market place that is merciless and unforgiving.

Niche marketing has become a necessity rather than a fad to succeed in the *market* that is becoming tougher by the day. Ever increasing competition, omnipresent government controls, growing consumerism place a premium on innovation and on improved efficiency and effectiveness of operations. Since it is virtually impossible to be everywhere in all the diverse markets, and to be all things to all people, market segmentation has emerged as the ideal prescription to optimize the marketing effort of the firm. It has reached the proportion of a panacea for all marketing ills.

Pharmaceutical marketing segmentation is a two-step process. One is at the level of the customer (the doctor, whether a prescriber or dispenser, he is the influencer) and at the second level or base of segmentation being the consumer (the patient, who is the end user). The pharmaceutical market can be segmented in a number of ways such as - by therapeutic category, by the severity of disease, by place of treatment, by type of practice etc. A holistic view of the segmentation process would enable the pharmaceutical marketer to develop the much-needed insight and perspective that are essential for formulating a winning strategy.

The Product

Me too! No. It is me-me-too!

How else can you describe the pharmaceutical industry in India, which is currently congested and clogged with over 100,000 products vying with each other for a share of the US $ 26.9 billion market?

Only 300 products out of this maze of 100,000 products account for about one-half of the total sales volume in Indian pharmaceutical market. How have they become the winners that they are today? What are the lessons to be learnt?

Year after year, in every therapeutic category the top five brands virtually account for well over fifty percent of the total sales volume. What is the secret of their success? How have they come to lead the rest of the pack in the first place and how are they able to maintain and sustain their lead?

A study of these factors would certainly provide useful insight for students of pharmaceutical marketing in India. In such a highly competitive situation, where one has to run as fast as he can, only to stay where he is and has been, like in the Indian pharmaceutical industry, planning and managing the *Products* become all the more crucial for organizational success.

Product and Market

Product or *Market*, which comes first, might be a classic debating issue for marketing men the world over, but in the final analysis, it is as endless and as pointless a question as an egg or hen, which comes first?

While customer-orientation is the core of the marketing concept, marketers need not be passive and silent spectators. They are players and professional players at that. Creative marketers can create the need for products. If there is a good product that is worth its while, then that is a good enough place to start from. A market can be created for such a product.

This is not to support Emerson and what he said and certainly not to say that the *world would beat path to your door, if you can make a better mousetrap*. A good product, however good that may be, does not and cannot automatically create a market for itself. First of all, a need for that product or its goodness should be felt and created. Secondly, a good product does not really become *good* until it is perceived as such by the consumers. Like *beauty, it (the goodness) lies in the beholder's eye*.

The Product Concept

What is the product may sound like a superfluous question. But, then there is more to a product than meets the eye. A product is not what it is, but what it does to the consumer. People do not buy products. They buy the benefits that the product offers. A person does not buy a TV because it is a TV. He buys it because it fulfills his need for entertainment. The needs could be real, felt or imaginary. Charles Revlon, the entrepreneurial genius behind the Revlon company said it beautifully: *in the factories we make cosmetics. In the market place we sell hope*. The hope of romance. Thus, a woman who dabs on some *Intimate* or a man who sprays some *musk* onto himself are fulfilling probably the perceived need. A person who buys some *Aspirin*, is not buying Aspirin as such, but he is buying *relief* from headache (a benefit). Similarly, when a doctor prescribes a different antibiotic like Ciprofloxacin, he is not prescribing because it is the latest antibiotic. He is prescribing it because of its superior antibacterial power and its ability to control the infection better and faster. He too is buying the benefits it offers. Thus a product can be said to be a bundle of benefits and a need-satisfying entity.

What is a Brand?

What constitutes a brand? While a generic product is an un-differentiated product, a brand is the differentiated product. For example Ranitidine, the anti-ulcer drug is a generic product, but when you call it *Zantac*, a totally different image is conjured up before us. It is the image of the world's largest selling prescription drug. A very effective anti-ulcer drug. Zantac is the brand. The next question is, what is the difference? The difference between the brand and the product - is it only in the name? No, there is more. Much more.

The brand name gives a distinct identity to the product. But this mere christening of the product does not give or create the brand image. Creating and building up a brand image is a more complex and painstaking process. This is known as branding a product. And like Rome, brands too are not built in a day!

It is the communication that makes the brand and gives it the distinct personality. Communication here includes all the internal elements of the marketing-mix, popularly known as the Four Ps - Product, Price, Promotion and Place (distribution). Each of these 4 Ps communicates and in the process creates a personality for the brand.

And until the communication about a product is transmitted and received, accepted and found rewarding, it will not become a brand. No, not for long. A product, therefore, must provide specific benefits (leading to rewarding experiences) to a large enough number of users. Only then can it become a brand.

A branded product, therefore, has the extra plus - the promise of customer satisfaction and customer satisfying benefits. A *Brand* is not a mere name that you give a generic product and put on the label for the purpose of differentiating it physically from other similar products, though the American Marketing Association has defined a brand as *a name, symbol or design or a combination of them, which is intended to identify the goods and services of one seller or groups of sellers and differentiate them from those of competitors*. But, there is certainly more to a brand than this differentiation by name. Sidney J Levy and Burleigh B Gardner emphasize this in their article on product and the brand when they say:

A brand name is more than the label employed to differentiate among the manufacturers of a product. It is a complex symbol that represents varieties of ideas and attributes. It tells the consumers many things, not only the way it sounds (and its literal meaning if it has one) but, more important, via the body of associations it has built up and acquired as a public object over a period of time.

A brand name will convey meaning, which is advertising, merchandising, promotion, publicity and even sheer length of its existence.

The net result is a public image, a character or personality that may be more important for the overall status (and sales) of the brand than many technical facts about the product.

This is an echo of what Professor Levitt of Harvard Business School has been saying for a long time that *a branded product is not what the engineers say, but also what is implied by its design; its packaging; its channels of distribution; its price and quality and activities of salesmen. It is a transaction between the seller and the buyer; a synthesis of what the seller intends and buyer perceives.*

The Augmented Product Concept

What we are discussing here about the *brand* and *branding* is similar to what Professor Levitt calls the augmented product concept. Without indulging in the game of semantics, let us decide and agree that a brand is and should be an augmented product, which is the result of voluntary improvements brought about in the product by the manufacturers. These improvements are neither suggested by the customers nor even expected by them. The marketer, on his own, augments by adding an extra facility or an extra feature to his products. This is essentially to create a significant, meaningful and perceivable differentiation in the product.

Augmentation of the product is very essential in branding, particularly in the pharmaceutical industry in India. The severe competition demands and dictates augmentation. This augmentation can be created in the basic product itself, or in the packaging, communication, and additional services or in a combination of these areas.

Product Augmentation in the Indian Pharmaceutical Industry

In the Indian pharmaceutical industry, product augmentation is a must for the survival and growth of brands. This is not because of the very high levels of research and development activity and therefore, a number of newer and newer drugs being developed making the existing products obsolete at a faster rate. The main reason is the licensing policy of the government, which encourages the small-scale sector even in sophisticated, high technology industry like pharmaceuticals. The result is the mushrooming of pharmaceutical companies churning out innumerable brands (brands here are only namesakes reduced to mere identification marks of generics; otherwise there are virtually no product differentiations). Companies, which consider that branding means augmenting the product by creating and communicating that extra plus effectively are bound to succeed. In fact, only such companies succeed.

For example, there are umpteen number of brands of Paracetamol in India (products with different names only and not brands in the real sense) but only Crocin, Calpol and Metacin are very successful in India.

Let us take different brands of B-complex in the country. They are Innumerable. But the successful brands are only a handful such as Becosules, Cobadex, and Becozyme. The situation is the same for any product group in the country.

Branding by product augmentation, in the pharmaceutical industry, is achieved by creating differentiation in the manufacturing process, changes in the formulation, packaging, communication, and by giving an appropriate, suggestive, memorable brand name. Consider these Cases:

Case 3.1 The Silent Salesman Adds Value!

An example of product augmentation by packaging is Lederle's (Pfizer now) Prenatal capsules. Prenatal capsules are hematinic capsules specially meant for pregnant women as the name

---

suggests. In fact, the name tells it all. They have brought about an innovative and voluntary improvement in the packaging. They introduced a very attractive and innovative pack of 120 capsules for their Prenatal in the shape of a feeding bottle, which is reusable. It would also ensure that the consumer buys at a time 120 capsules. The product was doing very well even before this packaging innovation. This would have probably taken the brand further up even to a brand leader position. But, the company took the pressure off this product and as a result the brand slipped from its rank and market share. Prenatal was a brand to reckon with in its heydays. The silent salesman did add value!

Case 3.2 Innovation Makes All the Difference!

Another example of product augmentation is Fefol, the pregnancy hematinic from SmithKline French known as Eskay Labs in India (Glaxo Smith Kline now). Fefol was no more than a hematinic formulation containing of 150mg of ferrous sulphate and 0.5mg of folic acid. There was nothing exciting about the formulation. There were many hematinic formulations containing these two ingredients in even higher quantities. But the product augmentation was achieved in Fefol by its superior formulation, which can be said to be the forerunner of new drug delivery systems, which are sweeping the pharmaceutical market today. Even the presentation of the product is distinctly different. It was a different kind of a capsule called *Spansule*, which contains the active ingredients in the form of tiny pellets - hundreds of them inside each transparent capsule. These pellets are coated specially to ensure timed-disintegration. Apart from the technical benefits it offers, the product too is a beautiful see-through capsule with hundreds of multi-colored time-release pellets. The benefit: freedom from side effects associated with oral iron therapy. They have very dramatically, effectively and persuasively communicated this benefit package to doctors in the country. They introduced a new brand, Fesovit (iron with multivitamins) in the same *spansule* form of capsules. They have promoted these brands vigorously and achieved a leadership position with a market share (combined for both Fefol and Fesovit) of 15 percentin 1999.

Product Vs. Brand

Branding strategy is very important because it is through a clear branding strategy alone, that a marketer can communicate the *extra plus* of his products. Thus branding is mainly a means of product identification, helping the consumer to know the differentiated, augmented product from a 'me-too' maze of innumerable products. The advantages of the brand over the product are many, particularly in the pharmaceutical industry. The case of the Indian pharmaceutical industry versus the Government of India clearly illustrates these benefits in Table 3.1.

Table 3.1 Product Vs. Brand

The Pharmaceutical Industry Wins the First Round

The Government of India took a decision to abolish the brand names for all new single ingredient drugs in 1980. All new single ingredient drugs that were to be introduced from 1980 had to be marketed under their generic names. Cimetidine, Metoprolol, Terbutaline, Ketoprofen, Nifedipine were some of the important drugs that were affected as a result of this. These drugs were the products of research by different multinational companies. Though some of the companies introduced these drugs under their generic names, the prices did not come down as the government expected.

Some of the large pharmaceutical companies (multinationals mainly) have filed a petition in the Delhi High Court against the ban on brand names.

The following excerpts from the pharmaceutical industry's advertising campaigns, the judgement of the Delhi High Court and the speech delivered by Mr. S. V. Pillai, managing director of Pfizer at the Annual General Meeting of Pfizer Limited in 1981 on the brand names issue, give useful insights, a clear picture, and make a strong case for brand names in pharmaceutical industry.

1. **The use of brand names is simpler:** *Di-hydro-ergatamine methane sulphonate* is the generic name of the drug marketed under the brand name Dyhdergot. Another jaw breaking, tongue-twisting generic name is *xylometazine hydrochloride* available under the brand name Otrivin. Brand names usually have no similarity in spelling or pronunciation.
2. **Confusion exists between generic names:** *Quinidine sulphate* is the generic name of a cardiac drug. It can easily be confused with the anti-malarial drug, *quinine sulphate.*

Contd...

3. **Efficiency:** Generic equivalence is not the same as the therapeutic equivalence. Pillai, managing director of Pfizer at that time said: *'Although such a product (generic equivalent) may contain the basic chemicals needed to fight your illness, evidence shows that often there is a real question about the potency of the ingredient, the way it has been combined with other substances, whether it dissolves satisfactorily and whether it is stable etc.'*

   Its uses will determine how much of the drug is absorbed and how rapidly it is assimilated. Other important considerations are the side effects of the drug and tolerance by patients.

4. **Reputation of the company: Quality Assurance:** When a company sells a product under a brand name, it is staking its reputation on the brand. This is a less expensive way of ensuring quality than administrative controls, according to a communist sociologist from Poland. Before a brand is cleared for marketing there are extensive clinical trials undertaken by the company concerned. The better companies maintain a 'post-launch' reporting system, a panel of doctors keeps them informed about the brand's performance when it is administered to patients. Any possible adverse effects can be detected in this manner. In a generic system this safeguard is not available.

5. **Margins rather than quality:** The doctor prescribes the drug by generic name and the patient takes it to the drug store. The dealer is likely to sell him the product from which he earns the highest trade discount. The doctor's prescription freedom and the right (to prescribe) are taken away. The dealer pays a far more important role in the sense that it is he who 'chooses' finally (some may say the doctor can insist on the company when he prescribes). The competition will no longer be on the basis of therapeutic efficiency but on the basis of the margins one can provide to the middleman. Quality is bound to suffer and the loss will be the consumers'.

   At the same time the consumer is not going to enjoy the price benefit either. In India, the price controls apply not only to branded drugs but also to generics. And the cost of promotion will not be reduced. Only the emphasis is shifted to the middleman from the doctor. So any assumptions that the abolition of brand names will bring gown the prices is unfounded.

6. **Disincentive to R & D:** The denial of the trademark protection to a drug will destroy the incentive for drug houses to develop new medicines. The cost of developing a new drug is very high and runs into millions of rupees. The discovery of an active ingredient

is not enough. This will have to be followed up by toxicity studies, experiments on animals are followed by expensive and time-consuming clinical trials.

What is that the company is left with, at the end of all this effort and expense, if it cannot have the brand system to protect its interests? Very few new drugs have been developed in India. The introduction to India of the new drugs discovered abroad has slowed down after the government adopted a policy of disincentives.

7. **Trader benefits:** Whom does the abolition of brand names benefit? Not the doctor. Since generic equivalence is not the same as therapeutic equivalence, it prevents him from giving his patients the best professional advice he can. It is also inconvenient.

   The Sainsbury Committee in the U K had proposed a ban on brand names for new drugs, but the then Labor Government rejected the proposal.

   Soviet Russia, which in the beginning used only generic names for drugs, has since the mid-1960s encouraged pharmaceutical houses to identify their products. In export markets Soviet Russia is offering products under brand names and it buys drugs from other countries including India by brand name.

   In other countries like Bulgaria, Poland, Hungary and Yugoslavia, where the pharmaceutical industry has developed fast, brand names are extensively used for drugs.

   The only country, which made a bold experiment in abolishing brand names for drugs is Pakistan. The generic scheme introduced in 1972 was a disastrous failure. It encouraged mushroom growth of drug units and the market was flooded with substandard, spurious medicines, which were not cheaper than branded drugs. The scheme was therefore scrapped under the 1976 Drugs Act.

   Unconstitutional: the Delhi High Court Judgment on this Issue

1. The banning of issue of the trade name besides being violative of provisions of Trade Marks Act, as noticed by us earlier is also violative of provisions of Article 19 (1) (g) of the constitution. This provision guarantees to every citizen the right to practice any profession or to carry on any occupation, trade of business…

2. Not allowing the brand names usage interferes with the right to carry on trade or business…

(Source: The Economic Times)

Language of Branding

A **Brand,** the American Marketing Association has defined as a *name, term symbol, design, or a combination of them which is intended to identify the goods and services of one or groups of sellers and to differentiate them from those of competitors.* Becosules, Cobadex and Basiton Forte are some of the leading brands of the therapeutic group called B-Complex Oral Solids, in India.

A **Trademark** is a brand that has been given legal protection, thus ensuring its use exclusively by one seller. A brand has to be registered with the Registrar of Trademarks to get the legal protection, i.e., the trademark. Now a days, it takes anywhere between 2 to 3 years to get a trademark registered in the pharmaceutical industry in India.

Individual Brand Strategy as the name indicates, is having a separate brand name for each product. The company can search a winning name for each of its products and can introduce a variety of brands in a single product class. If a single brand fails or proves to be inferior, the other brands of the company are not affected and victimized by the name. For instance, in the multivitamins and minerals group, Lederle in India has a number of brands like Prenatal, Vi-magna, Gevral, Folviron, Stress Caps, Autrin and Incremin.

Family Brand Strategy as the name suggests is having common brand name (family) for all related products. The main advantage here is that the company can cash in or capitalize on the image of a highly successful brand name. In the pharmaceutical industry, family brands are quite common because a number of drugs have to be used in different dosage forms for different indications and for different age groups, like in the case of pediatrics and geriatrics. Some of the highly successful family brands are - Terramycin of Pfizer, which tends to extend its image to the other products marketed in the same product class by the company. Glaxo in India has a very good image with consumers in India and the company was a household name as they manufactured baby foods, protein food supplements etc., By virtue of the heavy direct advertising, it was the best known among the pharmaceutical companies in India at the time. The company's packaging cashes in on this by displaying Glaxo in big bold letters and very prominently. Glaxo's company brands like Complex B-Glaxo, Ostocalcium-B12 Glaxo were big sellers in India.

While a corporate or company brand strategy attempts to cash in on the favorable image of the company, a brand that is extremely successful, reinforces the already well-established and favorable image of the company itself. Thus the company image and the brand image can be mutually reinforcing. Here is case in point.

Case 3.3   The Brand that Catapulted a Company into the Top Position!

Septran, an anti-bacterial drug, which is a combination of sulphamethoxazole and trimethoprim, commonly known as cotrimoxazole (generic name), was introduced in India in 1974 by Burroughs Wellcome. Cotrimoxazole was the product of a joint research program of two well-known multinational pharmaceutical companies - Burroughs Wellcome (GSK now) and Hoffman La Roche. The drug, as usual was introduced in the U.K. and some other European countries first and following its successful launch, it was introduced in India a few years later. While the drug was reasonably successful in other countries where it was introduced, in India, it was an unprecedented and spectacular success. Septran had made history. Septran remained the largest selling prescription drug in India even after fifteen years of its introduction in India. Nowhere in the world has Cotrimoxazole made to the top.

Consequently, Septran catapulted Boroughs Wellcome into the top six companies in the Indian pharmaceutical industry from a below-twenty position. Septran accounted for about 55 percent of the company's sales volume in 1988.

Boroughs Wellcome in India had pursued a very aggressive marketing strategy for Septran right from the word Go! This was rather uncharacteristic of the company, which was very conservative in the past. The image of the company in India was always very good and the company was considered to be reliable and dependable with a high quality research profile, having little or no profit orientation, as it was a subsidiary of Wellcome

Foundation, which was considered to be a nonprofit organization. Their sales force in India were also communicating the same message to the doctors in the late 1960s and even in the early 1970s.

Septran changed all this in a very big way. There was excitement. Septran promotion was backed up with specially designed visiting cards to the medical representatives, special visual-aids, booklets and product literature giving detailed prescribing information of the product, persuasive detailing by its field force, documentation of clinical trials conducted, special Septran allowances and incentives to motivate the field force to call on as many doctors and chemists as possible within the shortest time and incentive on Septran sales. The company had achieved the highest call average of customers during the Septran launch. The special visiting cards differentiated the representatives' *Septran interviews* from the regular, routine doctors' calls.

The rest was history. Although Roche, the original research partner of cotrimoxazole too had introduced their brand - Bactrim around the same time, it did not make it as big. The launch of Bactrim too was a success in India, but it had to contend with a distant second position with a sales volume that was less than half of Septran's. The success of Septran was immediately followed by a number of cotrimoxazole introductions under various brand names. There were more than two hundred cotrimoxazole brands, which were struggling to carve a place for themselves in the 1990s.

Septran has achieved about one-third of the cotrimoxazole market in India and was growing strong even after fifteen years after its introduction in India. In the process, it has made cotrimoxazole one of the biggest subgroups in the Indian pharmaceutical market. To further consolidate its position, the company has introduced a double-strength formulation of cotrimoxazole under a different brand name - *Sepmax*. This move has reinforced its already strong position in the cotrimoxazole market with a formidable and unprecedented market share of over 46 per cent.

Multiple Brand Strategy is marketing virtually the same product with two or more different brand names. The idea here is to get a bigger share of the market. This is a difficult strategy in the sense, if not planned and communicated very carefully it could lead to cannibalization of brands. Cannibalization of brands means that one brand losing prescriptions, sales and market share as a result of a new introduction by the same producer or manufacturer. In other words, one brand eating into the share of the other brand of the same company rather than taking the share of the competing brands. Multiple brand strategy as opposed to cannibalization is to ensure that both brands gain a significant share of the market and in achieve a formidable position in the market.

Glaxo had used the multiple brand strategy very successfully. It, of course, had promoted these brands through its different marketing teams (Glaxo and Allenburys divisions). Both Becadexamin (Glaxo) and Multivite FM (Allenburys) are the multivitamin and mineral capsules formulations having identical formulations. Only the brand names were different. Both the brands were late entrants to the market. Both at one time, had achieved a combined market share of 45 percent in the multivitamin minerals market (1988).

Private Brand or a middleman's brand strategy implies that the owner of the brand does not manufacture the product. The middleman or the distributor of marketer owns it. The equivalent of this private brand strategy is rapidly growing in the Indian pharmaceutical market. You see an ever-increasing number labels on cartons of new products, which read - *manufactured by so and so and marketed by so and so*. The main reason for such a proliferation of trading activity of new brands is the government's licensing policy. A small-scale manufacturer need not go through the rigmarole of registering his product with the Director General of Trade and Development (DGTD) nor is it controlled by the Drug Price Control Order (DPCO). All he needs is a drug license. To save valuable time and to avoid the fear of rejection of the license for the proposed new product, even the leading pharmaceutical companies resort to this back door method of getting the drug manufactured by a small scale manufacturer but market it themselves.

Product Item is a distinct unit within a product line that is distinguished by size, dosage form, price, appearance or some other attributes.

Product Line describes a group of related products with similar function. The depth of a product line is measured by the assortment of sizes, dosage forms, strengths, concentration of active ingredients, flavors, price range offered within each product line.

Product-Mix is a complete list of all the products offered by a company for sale. The number of product lines it offers measures the breadth of the product mix.

A Rose by Any Other Name!

What's there in a name? May be Shakespeare had his own reasons to say that there is nothing more to a name. But in marketing, that too in a the age of brands, a rose by any other name is not a rose and it does not smell as sweet! Not only do we see what we want to see, we also smell what we want to smell.

In today's 'me-too' world, a name is a very important tool that can cut through the chaos and confusion in the market place, where the number of brands multiplying can only be compared to that of rabbits.

A name is the hook that hangs the brand on the product ladder in the prospect's mind. A name should tell the prospect, what the product is and what its major benefit is.

Let us look at what Al Ries and Jack Trout, the strong advocates of the positioning strategy and in fact, who introduced the concept of positioning into the marketing lexicon. Here's what they said in their landmark article, *The Positioning Era Cometh in the Advertising Age* more than forty-five years ago:

Choosing a name is like driving a racing car. To win you have got to take chances. You have to select names that are almost, but not quite generic...A strong, generic like, descriptive name will block your me-too competitors from muscling their way into your territory. A good name is the best insurance for long term success.

What one should look for in a name is not the *goodness* but appropriateness. Would Septran by any other name, have been successful?

Would Becosules, ABDEC, Fefol have been successful? Of Course, it is difficult to say in retrospect, but the chances are that they may not have been as successful.

It is not enough if the name is short, rhyming and descriptive as illustrated below in the case of the impossible name.

Case 3.4 The Impossible Name!

Tips & Toes, understandably is a very good name for nail polish. The brand, backed by very good promotion has become a big success. Inspired by this, another company wanted to introduce a lipstick. The company was planning to launch simultaneously some cosmetics. The company wanted to have a catchy, memorable brand name for their lipstick. It should be suggestive, short and sweet. They came up with the name - *Kiss & Tell*. Suggestive, crisp, and rhyming. They promoted it vigorously. The brand was a miserable failure. Not because, the name was bad. The brand name had all the characteristics of an ideal brand name. But it was simply an impossible name. Impossible because it prevented customers from asking for the product. Can any woman walk into a store and ask for *Kiss and Tell*?

Realizing the importance of the name in branding a product, the US Department of Commerce listed out a number of characteristics of a good name, in a guide issued to developing and selling new products. An ideal brand name should meet the following criteria:

- Short
- Simple
- Easy to spell
- Easy to pronounce
- Easy to read
- Easy to recognize
- Easy to remember
- Pleasing when read
- No disagreeable sound
- Cannot be pronounced in several ways
- Does not go out of date
- Adaptable to package or label
- Can be easily connected with the trademark
- Not offensive, obscene or negative
- Descriptive, or suggestive of product and use
- Connoting a good image of the product and the company

Product Life Cycle

Products are like people. They gestate, take birth, grow, mature, become old and ultimately die. The product life cycle concept describes the product's life history starting from its birth to old age or death. In fact, it is not a cycle, but a *span*. The span popularly called *life cycle* can be divided into four phases for better understanding and study. These phases as shown in Figure 3.1 are:

1. Introductory phase
2. Growth phase
3. Maturity phase
4. Decline phase

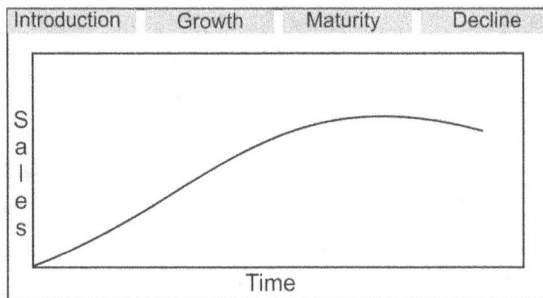

Figure 3.1 Product Life Cycle

It is said that every product has a unique life cycle very much like a human being. Just as it is difficult to predict the future of a human being, it is very difficult to predict the future life cycle of a product.

The value of the division of the Product Life Cycle (PLC) into the four phases mentioned above lies in determining the marketing inputs that are required at various stages. It is just like the human organism where the requirement of calories, proteins, carbohydrates, vitamins and minerals, and fiber are different at different stages of human life in order to maintain optimum growth. Likewise marketing inputs also vary at different stages of product life cycle.

The *introductory phase* is also the phase of market development because neither the demand for the product nor the capabilities of the product to fulfill the customers' needs are proved yet. The marketing effort here is directed towards getting the customers to try the product.

Indeed a great deal of marketing effort is needed at this stage. The sales are usually low and creep along slowly. The duration of the introductory stage depends on the complexity of the product, degree of novelty and its ability to fit into customer needs.

The *growth phase* of the new product is also allowing the growth phase of the market. The demand for the product accelerates. The *market* too expands, as potential competitors, who have been waiting and watching till now, jump into the fray. This calls for a different marketing strategy and tactics on the part of the originator. The originator is forced to change his focus from seeking ways to get the customers to *try* the product, to getting them to *prefer* his brand.

The *maturity phase* is indicative of market saturation in the sense that all the potential customers have taken to the product, except those who have decided not to adopt it. Sales growth will be on par with the population growth. The maturity phase is characterized by leveling-off the demand and intense competition. Competitors at this stage try for finer product differentiations, and resort to price wars etc. Competitive strategies include product augmentation efforts in packaging and advertising communication.

The *decline phase* is the terminal point of the product life cycle. Whether the product life cycle is to be extended by injecting new blood, thus prolonging the maturity phase and avoiding the decline phase or whether the dying the product is to be left to its fate depends on the marketers and the insight and foresight that have gone into product planning.

The key questions which a marketer should address himself are:

Key Questions

1. To what extent can the shape (or the curve) and duration of each stage be predicted?
2. How can one determine at what stage an existing product is?
3. How can this knowledge be used?

Usefulness of Product Life Cycle

The product life cycle is a theory and it seems unlikely that it can ever be proven experimentally. But this does not diminish its usefulness or importance. As the famous economist Kenneth Boulding once observed, " *there is nothing quite so useful as a theory that works."*

The product life cycle concept is useful because it helps you to anticipate future events and prepare the best response to coming changes.

The life cycle concept is of immense value for managers who are about to launch a new product. No doubt, it is very difficult to foresee or predict the slope (or the curve) and duration of each phase of the PLC very accurately. But this does not mean that one cannot make useful efforts to foresee and visualize the scope and duration of a new product's life.

Product planning can become more rational with an understanding and appreciation of the PLC concept. It helps to create the valuable lead-time for important strategic and tactical moves after the product is introduced. It can be of great help in developing a series of orderly competitive moves - be it stretching or extending the life of a product or accelerating an introductory phase, or phasing out and deleting an old product.

Market Life Cycle

So far our discussion on product life cycle has revolved around the theory rather than a brand of a particular company and its strategic implications and the likely impact on that particular company. But, when you consider a product in generic terms, you have to think in terms of a product class or therapeutic category, or indeed even as a market (segment). This is because, when a market is, say, nearing maturity it does not necessarily mean that all the companies competing in that market will have the same sales history curves. Consequently, the strategic options available to each of the competing companies are not the same. Their responses too will be predictably different.

It is reasonable to expect that in any maturing market, for that matter even in a growing or declining market, there will be major, medium and small-stake players. It is quite obvious that there will be differences in their margins, economies of scale and break-even levels.

The Market Life Cycle (MLC) concept which, simply stated, is the aggregate life cycle consisting of several competing brands and companies in a given market, therapeutic category or product class. The micro level characteristics or reality described as *higher investment needed, little or no profits, rapid growth*, *peak profit levels* refer to a product or, more specific to a brand of a particular brand of a particular company and not the market as a whole. This is schematically shown in Figure 3.2.

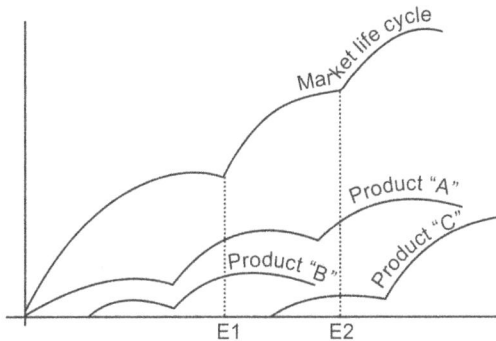

Figure 3.2 Market Life Cycle

As can be seen from Figure 3.2 the *market life cycle* has been extended twice (E1 and E2). Product 'A', which was introduced around the same time as the market was emerging had also extended its life cycle once, running almost parallel to the market life cycle, but unable to exploit the opportunities when the market started its second extension with a dramatic growth phase (E2). That was the time when product 'C' entered the growth phase, and even reinforced the growth phase of the market life cycle itself. Product 'B' never really took off in the real sense of the word, plateaued very early, and declined rather prematurely even while the *market* had been in its growth phase.

In the pharmaceutical industry, a market life cycle curve may consist of various brands and even different molecules, product classes or sub-segments in a particular therapeutic category.

Consider the case of the anti-tubercular market in India, which offers a close parallel to the schematic sequence of the market life cycle as shown in Figure 3.2.

Case 3.5 Anti-tubercular Market Extends Market Life Cycle, While Eradicating Tuberculosis!

The anti-tubercular market in India was Rs. 341-crore (1988) with an annual growth rate of 0.5 per cent. The main line of treatment consisted of drugs like streptomycin, INH, PAS and thiacetazone till the late 1970s. Subsequently, in the 1980s, newer drugs like ethambutol, pyrazinamide, and rifampicin were introduced. Since these newer drugs were more potent, the medical profession accepted them readily. These new drugs had even made it possible to treat tuberculosis at home instead of a sanatorium. Tuberculosis, which was once labeled as killer disease is not dreaded as before thanks to these newer drugs. It is curable.

Each of these newer drugs had extended the anti-tubercular market life cycle on their introduction. The conventional drugs like thiacetazone and PAS had reached their maturity phase and even started declining. Whereas INH had extended its life cycle (as a sub-segment and not as a brand) when the combination of INH with rifampicin had gained acceptance and even preference to single ingredient formulations of the newer, more potent anti-tubercular drugs. The newer anti-tubercular drugs accounted for over 90 percentof the anti-tubercular market in 1988, whereas the conventional anti-tubercular drugs accounted for a meager share of less than 10 percent as they were declining.

One can see that while the anti-tubercular *market's life cycle* was in its *mature* phase (1988), some of the products such as thiacetazone and PAS (sub-segments as these are molecules comprising a handful of brands) are in the *decline* phase. At the same time newer anti-tubercular drugs like ethambutol, rifampicin, pyrazinamide are in the growth phase of their life cycles (as these molecules are subsegments each containing a number of branded generic formulations). INH by virtue of the increasing demand of its combination with rifampicin and other newer drugs was also enjoying the extended maturity phase.

The advantages and strategic implications of the juxtaposition of the product life cycle curve and the market life cycle must now become obvious the discerning marketer. The MLC and PLC of a brand for any particular company may be close or far apart for a number of reasons. The marketing actions dictated by this juxtaposition may also correspondingly vary. The marketing actions, which would best exploit that product life cycle, are not dependent on the market alone but on the phase the individual brand is in.

The original producer or the innovator bears most of the costs and risks of the product and market development. Competitors are only waiting on the sidelines watching the product and how it is likely to behave in the market place at this stage. Therefore, the introductory stages of the product and market life cycle are virtually the same.

Once the product is accepted, others join the fray. The competition intensifies. It is at this point that the difference between curves and life cycles of the market and the product begins, with a number of competitors trying to create product differentiation, to capture as big a slice of the market as possible. The competitive pressure on the originator increases. If the originator has plotted the PLC for his new product even before its introduction, anticipating the possible entry of competition and their likely moves, he will be better off in countering the competition. This can be done by critically examining the vulnerability of the product before introduction and by planning the product development and diversification strategies accordingly. If the originator is not forearmed or well-equipped, his unit sales and contribution will be adversely affected. Consequently, there will be a premature decline for the originator's product while the market may well be on its growth or maturity phase.

A hypothetical market life cycle is graphically presented in figure 3.3. You can observe from that, while the market life cycle phase like introduction, growth, maturity and decline unquestionably depend on the aggregate of various products, these phases may differ significantly for a number of individual brands. This is because the resources, competencies, and strategies for the various brands competing in the same market differ.

The life cycle for a given market or therapeutic group may be extended when some of the competing producers innovate, extend their product usage and modify their existing products. The sum total of this expansion of the served markets of individual products results in the extension of the market life cycle. At the same time, products that are less competitive and unable to exploit the opportunities due to a slow or sluggish response may bite the dust even when the market life cycle is in its growth phase. Consider the following case (3.6) for example.

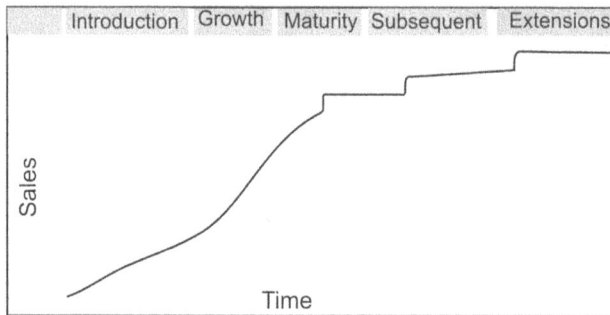

Figure 3.3 Hypothetical Market Life Cycle

Case 3.6 The Centurion Gets Younger and Stronger by the Year!

The aspirin market indicates that the market life cycle can be extended indefinitely, even to eternity. The aspirin market is over one-hundred-and-twenty-five years old (should we say young!) and is still going strong. Of course, it was not without fluctuations. It did have its share of ups and downs. But, it has withstood them all. Due to certain side effects and a creative re-positioning by Tylenol (paracetamol brand of Johnson & Johnson), it lost some of its market share to paracetamol in so far as the antipyretic and analgesic markets were concerned. But the therapeutic efficacy of aspirin was too well known to the medical and scientific profession to be ignored. Some innovative marketers introduced safer dosage forms of aspirin such as enteric-coated, buffered tablets and dispersible tablets. These brands like Dispirin (Reckitt Coleman), Microfined Aspirin (Nicholas) in India and Bufferin (in the US) made it good, while the numerous lesser known brands vanished from the market. But the market life cycle and the PLCs of successful brands had been given a new lease of life.

Research findings in the mid 1980s have given a further boost to the centurion. It is believed and proven that regular intake of aspirin will minimize and even prevent *heart attacks* in high risk patients. The aspirin market was on a growth phase once again. New bulk drug manufacturers have entered the market while the existing ones were busy expanding their capacities!

Extending the Product Life Cycle

Likewise, the life cycle of a product can be extended and decline can be averted. What one needs is a broader perspective and holistic thinking. You should think in terms of your product or products in the context of the relevant therapeutic category or product class. You should also think in terms of expanding your served markets. You should not lose sight of these and think about your products in isolation. That would only limit and restrict even the existing opportunities. Here are a few ideas as a starter to extend your product life cycle in the pharmaceutical market.

- Find out new usages for your products. What are the new indications in which you can promote your product?
- Enter new markets by covering new geographical markets or expand the existing market coverage. Expand your served markets.
- Modify existing products. Introduce different pack sizes. Introducing larger pack sizes of tonics and enzyme preparations has improved the product sales considerably and extended the growth phases of many a product.
- Introduce new flavors. New dosage forms. Introduce flanker products.
- Keep track of competition and develop your products constantly. Be alert to spot new opportunities and introduce new products early enough in your existing markets (therapeutic categories). *Update,* and *keep abreast* are the two most important watch words.

The pharmaceutical industry has countless examples of products well past their life and which in theory should be either in maturity or decline stage, but are still selling in high volume and producing acceptable profits.

You should use the PLC concept as a framework for thinking through and develop winning marketing strategies based on the phase of the product in its life cycle and for that, planning activity must take place now to preempt decline in future years, In fact, that should be the sole purpose of planning. Remember what Peter Drucker, the great management thinker said about planning? *It is the futurity of the present decisions.*

Today in the pharmaceutical industry, more than ever before, successful maintenance of mature products becomes an increasingly vital part of product planning and management. This is because the rate of new, absolutely new drug (new to the world) launches is declining.

A very important point to remember regarding the concept and application PLC in pharmaceutical product planning is that as a product is being used in different market segments, the same product is at different stage or phase in each segment. Product management decisions should be based on this.

Here are a few cases of companies that have extended the PLCs of their brands by extending their usage (promoting in new indications) successfully.

Case 3.7 Anti-allergic Stimulates Appetite for Growth!

Periactin (cyproheptadine hydrochloride) of Merck Sharp and Dhome (later Practin of Merind) was being promoted initially as an antiallergic and antipruritic. In the late 1960s, the company produced new evidence that Periactin stimulated appetite. They have gone all out in promoting Periactin as an appetite stimulant ever since. Many new brands entered this new segment. The product sales grew faster because, not only did the doctors who were using it as antiallergic and antipruritic continued to use it, but even a number of new doctors (new to the product) started prescribing it in the new-found indication of stimulating appetite.

Case 3.8 New Indication Widens Growth Spectrum!

Flagyl (metronidazole) of May & Baker (later Rhone Poulenc and now Sanofi) was being used mainly to treat *giardiasis*. The company had found out in the 1960s that their product was very effective in treating *amoebiasis*, which was very prevalent in India. The company launched an aggressive promotion of Flagyl in the treatment of amoebiasis and replaced the conventional treatment of amoebiasis with emetine hydrochloride injections. Many other brands of metronidazole joined the bandwagon. Flagyl even today remains one of the popular prescription drug brands in the treatment of amoebiasis.

Case 3.9 New Indication Attacks Competing Brands while Preventing Heart Attacks!

Betnesol (betamethasone) injections had always been one of the most important brands of Glaxo (GlaxoSmithKline now), the industry leader in the mid-1970s. Betnesol injections were lagging behind Decadron injections (dexamethasone) of MSD in the late 1960s. Glaxo, by promoting in one new indication, i.e. a ten-ampoule course in myocardial infarction, changed their position dramatically. The product image as a life saving drug got a big boost indeed and the product became a brand leader and more importantly remained a brand leader for many years!

Determining the Phase of Your Brand in PLC

Understanding the characteristics of the different phases in the life cycle concept will help the discerning marketer to determine the stage of the life cycle for his existing products. This coupled with an understanding of market life cycle will enable you to plan, preempt and execute winning strategies. Consider this case:

Case 3.10 The Antacid that Neutralized Even the Competition!

A medium-sized, rapidly growing pharmaceutical company had introduced an antacid brand 'x' in the Rs. 44-crore large antacid, anti-flatulent (actual) market. When you add the anti-peptic-ulcerants to this the (potential) market becomes larger by another Rs.31-crore (1988).

The company was well aware that the potential market (antacids, antiflatulent including anti-peptic ulcerates) was in its growth phase and there were literally more than one hundred and one brands already fighting for their survival and growth. Introducing yet another antacid at this stage was no easy task. But the company was determined to enter this large market as part of its product diversification strategy and to make the most of it.

The company had meticulously planned a new product with a perceptible differentiation - a new ingredient, new flavor, new additional benefits and a very persuasive communication package coupled with attractive sampling to induce trial, special training to the field force - in short the whole works.

In addition, the company's marketing team had stormy brainstorming session to plot the PLC for their product and to pre-empt the likely moves of competitors (top five competitors accounted for over 90 percentof the actual market) and new entrants. The launch had been a success by all standards. In less than one year the product picked up a 2.4 percent market share, which no other antacid introduced during the preceding five years had achieved. But, the product had not made any dent in the top five brands. Being alert, ever-vigilant competitors, they had responded quickly and stepped up their promotional inputs and mounted an offensive on this fledgling brand.

Since the company had pre-empted and anticipated the major moves of competitors it was not caught off-guard. The company was well prepared to meet the competitive challenge. The company had plotted the PLC and the strategic action for their brand 'x'. The company's analysis was somewhat like the one presented in Table 3.2.

While these may sound or look like over-simplified statements that is what exactly happened. The competitors' responses were indeed predictable in retrospect, for they had acted exactly as anticipated by the company even before the introduction of its brand 'x'.

Though brand 'x' was yet to achieve the pre-eminent position that it has set out to (the brand as well as the market were still in growth phase in the early 1990s). In the final analysis, brand 'x' seemed to be successful not only in neutralizing the acid, but even the competitors' offensive!

Table 3.2 PLC and Planning for a New Antacid Brand

1. **Introduction:** Brand 'x' should be different from all other antacids available in the market and should be perceived as such by our prospective customers. The differentiation should be created in:
   (a) Composition

Contd...

(b) Shape

(c) Color

(d) Flavor

(e) Pack

(f) Promotion at doctor level as well as at chemist level

(g) Price - skimming strategy. Since the active ingredient in brand 'x' was not listed at the time in any controlled categories, the company was able to fix its price.

(h) Launch itself

2. **Likely Responses of Competition:** The pharmaceutical market in India is virtually a 'me-too' market. The possibility of new competitors joining the fray once the product is accepted is certain. The major competitors , who are currently taking their respective shares of the market for granted but for a few skirmishes around the borders of their served markets, face no threats. The shares of the market leaders were more less frozen. The success of brand 'x' might shake them out of their complacency. That would mean waking up the sleeping giants. With their resources they can launch a major offensive. Brand 'x' therefore, must initiate product development and product diversification strategies before the introduction so that it need not be caught napping during the crucial growth phase.

3. **Product Development:** The company and the brand 'x' better be right the first time. Since the company is fighting the international giants in the market and the target customers are knowledgeable and enlightened, qualitative differentiation (in addition to aesthetics) is of course a must. Not only that, to counter the competitors' moves effectively during the growth phase, but also product development effort should be concentrated in major areas such as:

(a) Acid neutralizing capacity

(b) Taste. Since antacids are to be chewed, taste becomes a very important factor.

(c) The improvement and the necessary changes are to be initiated before introduction.

4. **Product Diversification:**

(a) New flavors are to be developed since the competitors might

Contd...

> try to introduce different flavors. The company should be prepared to introduce more flavors of brand 'x' during the maturity phase (essential to maintain novelty and sustain the interest of the early majority), or earlier if the competitors' moves warrant it.
>
> (b) To look for new segments and enter with necessary product modifications (like combination of local anesthetic, the small but attractive segment) to prolong, extend and indeed avert the decline phase.

New Product Adoption Process

New Product adoption process takes time and effort to fructify. Regardless of the intrinsic value of product, many potential customers will have a tendency to resist change. Some may accept change but most do not.

For many products the process of adoption follows a rather uniform pattern, from the time the new product is developed until it is widely accepted by the ultimate consumer. In the case of pharmaceutical products it is the intermediate customer, the doctor, who decides whether to accept or decline a product.

Researchers have charted a course of the new product by determining when people adopt it. Graphically presented, the adoption process looks like a simple probability curve, in cumulative as shown in Table 3.3.

Table 3.3 New Product Adoption Process

Innovators (2.5%)	Early Adopters (13.5%)	Early Majority (34%)	Late Majority (34%)	Laggards (16%)
Willing to accept risks	Regarded as role models by many others in the society	Willing to consider	Skeptics; Need enormous pressure from peer group before adopting	Thoroughly oriented to the old; diehards; may never adopt the new

A few people adopt a product first, then a few more, followed by a rather sharp increase and finally leveling off, when most of the potential consumers have adopted the product.

The adoption of a new product can be viewed as a special kind of attitude change. Almost by definition such a change encounters resistance. The product or idea usually alters or replaces something, which is already a part of the individual's pattern of thought. If the change under consideration is a major one, it is quite likely that it will encounter great resistance and consequently will take longer to adopt. The customer may even reject the idea of the product of change. On the other hand, if the change is trivial, the resistance may not be much and may take less time to adopt.

Three Major Propositions

A. The greater the complexity of change, the more resistance is aroused and the longer the period that is required for adoption.

B. The more expensive the item, the longer it takes before it is widely adopted.

C. A change, which has more rapid and obvious results, is adopted more quickly than a change with slower and less visible results.

The Individual Adoption Process

To adopt or not to adopt is not a simple question with a simple *yes* or *no* answer. It is not a simple *go* or *no go* decision either. It does not happen at once. When an individual is confronted with the possibility of a change, he goes through several mental stages before he makes up his mind to adopt or not to adopt. They are:

1. **Unawareness:** At this point the customer has no idea about the product.

2. **Awareness:** At this point the customer has a general idea about the product.

3. **Interest or Information Stage:** At this stage, he collects more information about the product. If his interest continues to grow he wants to know what the product can really do for him.

4. **Evaluation Stage:** *Would I be better off with this product? Would I be worse off without it?* The customer evaluates.

5. **Trial Stage:** This is the final stage before adoption. The trial stage appears to play a crucial role in the decision process because

a customer, who is satisfied with the trial is very likely to take up the product whole heartedly. Marketing people in general and pharmaceutical marketers in particular have been aware of the value of free trials for many years. This explains why a significant part of the promotional expenditure is spent on *Physicians'* samples.

6. **The Adoption Stage:** The customer adopts the product after a successful and satisfactory trial, at least until some other product comes along to replace it. Then the adoption process starts all over again.

Adopter Categories

Some people adopt very quickly. Others wait a long time before they take up the new product and there are some others, who never adopt. Depending upon how quickly or how slowly the new product adoption takes place, customers are categorized as:

A. Innovators
B. Early Adopters
C. Early majority
D. Late majority and
E. Laggards

Innovators are defined as the first 2.5 percent to adopt the new product. They are well educated with established practice, successful and venturesome. They are respected but not held in a very high degree of esteem, watched but not followed readily by neighbors.

Early adopters are defined as the next 13.5 percent of the people, who adopt the new product. They are relatively young, but not younger than innovators, well educated and socially active. They are the sources of information to the community.

Early majority comprises the next 34 percent of the people who adopt the new product taking the total adoption to 50 percent. The number of adoptions increase rapidly after this group begins to adopt. They are slightly above average in age, education, less active in formal activities than innovators and early adopters as leaders, but active members of their organizations. They must be sure that the new product or idea will work before they take it.

Late majority is the fourth category, which comprises the next 34 percent of the consumers, who take to new product after the early majority have adopted.

Laggards are the final 16 percent of the customers, who adopt a new product (or idea). They may even include non-adopters, if everyone does not use the product. They do not participate in community activities and are usually suspicious of sales persons.

Product Life Cycle and Adoption Process

Product life cycle and the adoption process are rather intimately linked. Product life cycle describes the rate of acceptance or rejection of a product. The adoption process explains about the individuals who adopt a product, the pace of adoption and categorizes individual adopters accordingly.

A fit of these customer categories based on the adoption process and the four phases of the product life cycle reveals these. This is shown in Table 3.4.

A. The introductory phase reflects product acceptance by the innovators.

B. In the growth phase the sales are due to the early adopters and the early majority.

C. In the maturity phase the late majority would have jumped in.

D. The laggards who almost never come in probably hasten the decline phase and those few, even if they join, are too insignificant to avert the decline.

Recognition of the fact that the phases of the life cycle of a product are closely related to its adoption process can be of great strategic importance. It enables the marketers to arrive at meaningful, responsive strategies required at different stages.

Table 3.4 Product Life Cycle and Adoption Process

Introduction	Growth	Maturity		Decline
New product adoption process & Adopter categories				
Innovators	Early adopters	Early majorities	Later majority	Laggards
2.5%	13.5%	34%	34%	16%

For instance, the identification of prospective innovators is crucial for a new product launch. The introductory phase or the market development phase can be accelerated by a proper, accurate identification of the innovators and by convincing them. The relationship of product life cycle and adoption process can be seen in Table 3.5.

Table 3.5 Product Life Cycle and New Product Adoption

Phase of Product Life Cycle	Adopter Category (%)	Cumulative Total Adopting (%)
Introduction/ Market Development	Innovators (2.5)	2.50
Growth	Early Adopters (13.5)	16.00
	Early Majority (34)	50.00
Maturity	Late Majority (34)	84.00
	Laggards (16)	
Decline	Last 16%, may or may not adopt	100.00

Implications for the Marketer

The implications for the new product planner become clearer when you understand the product life cycle concept and the new product adoption process. A few of the more important implications are:

1. When you are introducing a new product, you have to identify the innovator and the early adopters carefully and target your communication and promotional inputs specifically oriented towards them. In the pharmaceutical market how does one identify the innovators and early adopters? Apart from the psychographics profile like their educational qualifications, life styles, social affiliations, media habits, a more reliable way is to observe their prescription habits. Since the innovators and the early adopters take to new products quickly (almost instantaneously), they are also likely to give up these products quickly. Remember that these are the trendsetters and take to anything new immediately. Change, constant change in their prescribing behavior is there for the discerning observer to see. Their brand loyalty by definition is less. This is not to say that they stop prescribing your product once the *newness* is gone. The regularity and intensity of prescriptions are bound to decline unless your positive reinforcement is strong enough.

2. Therefore, you will have to identify these *trendsetters* by monitoring their prescription habits from the retail chemists. You will observe that it is this small group of doctors who have started the prescriptions of virtually every new product that has entered the market. It is therefore, imperative that your identification of these doctors is accurate and your promotional package *target specific* for your new product success in the introductory stage.

3. The next logical sequence is to increase your prescriber-base and penetrate the market. You have to persevere with your early and late majority categories of prescribers. This is because, your rate of growth is determined by these prescribers, who are clearly the majority. Another important advantage with these prescribers is, while they may take a relatively longer time to take up your product, they are equally conservative in dropping off your brand from their prescriptions. Their brand loyalty is certainly better and it is very important and essential during the growth and maturity phases of your brands' product life cycle. Like everything else, even in marketing perseverance certainly pays!

Product Portfolio Analysis

It is rather obvious that a review of a company's different products at any point would reveal different stages of growth, maturity and decline. The objective of any company is not to just make a fast buck, but also to achieve consistent growth in profitability. A regular review and analysis of the company's products and markets is essential to pursue an active and aggressive policy towards planning effective strategies for products in the growth and mature phases and an innovative new product development strategy to ensure tomorrow's profitability and to plan for divestment or harvesting of declining products in shrinking markets.

Thanks to the pioneering work done by the Boston Consulting Group (BCG), you now have a systematic procedure for classifying every product your company makes, in terms of its present position and in terms of future profit earning potential. This is known as *product portfolio analysis* and it provides a basis for allocating today's resources to optimize returns by exploiting tomorrow's business potential. The idea of a portfolio analysis for a company is to meet its objectives by balancing sales growth, cash flow and risk. There are two essential aspects to the conceptual framework of the portfolio analysis. One is the market share, relative market share to be specific, and the other is market growth.

Managing your product portfolio is very much akin to management of a portfolio of stocks. Some should be held for current dividends, some should be actively acquired for growth and some should be divested to free capital for a more profitable investment.

It is useful and simple to visualize all this on a grid with one dimension representing the relative market share and the other representing the market growth rate. That market share is a crucial element in strategic planning is universally accepted. Consider the case of Cheminor Drugs, the young Turk of the bulk drug market in India.

Case 3.11   Dr. Reddy's Laboratories and the Cost Leadership!

Cheminor Drugs and Dr. Reddy's Laboratories, the bulk drug units belonging to Dr. Reddy's Laboratories group of companies, had done remarkably well in the manufacture and marketing of bulk drugs. Within four years, the company had achieved cost leadership in manufacturing at least three bulk drugs, namely ibuprofen, methyldopa, and norfloxacin. How did the company achieve all this in such a short time? There are two reasons. Firstly, the economies of scale. The company is the third largest producer of ibuprofen and methyldopa in the world. The huge volumes had given the company the cost leadership. The second reason is that the company had also achieved technological superiority.

The case of Dr. Reddy's Laboratories clearly indicates that market share is closely related to profitability. This is because, higher market share means higher sales volume. It is a well-known fact that we become better at doing things the more we do them. This phenomenon is known as the experience or learning curve. This manifests itself with items such as labor efficiency, work specialization and methods improvement thus resulting in improved productivity and increased profitability. There is an overwhelming body of evidence supporting this experience effect.

Simply stated, this means that the greater your volume the lower your unit cost should be. In other words, if you have the largest market share (hence bigger volume), your profitability should be relatively higher. That is how and why Dr. Reddy's Laboratories were able to bring down the price of a recent antibacterial drug, norfloxacin, whereas their competitors could not. Cost leadership is crucial to competitive advantage. No, cost leadership is the competitive advantage!

The relative market share is an important dimension in portfolio analysis since it gives you an idea about the degree of competitive advantage or disadvantage that your product (or company) has in a given market. Relative market share also indicates the product's ability to generate cash as compared to the competitor's product. The relative market share is expressed as a ratio and can be arrived at by dividing your market share with the market share of your largest competitors.

Rate of market growth is the other important determinant since it indicates the direction in which the market is moving and its potential.

Boston Matrix

The Boston grid or matrix combines these concepts in a simple manner, which has profound implications for the company. It is worth noting that profit or profitability is not considered as a determinant in this matrix. This is because profits are not always an appropriate indicator of portfolio analysis and performance. Market share is chosen instead as a determinant because market share indicates that the greater your volume, the lower your unit cost should be. In other words, if you have the largest market share (hence the biggest volume) your profitability should be relatively higher than all your competitors. Profits do not always indicate the scope of future development as they often reflect changes in the liquid assets of the company as inventories, capital equipment, receivables etc. Cash flow has been taken as a key determinant factor since it reflects the cash generating ability of the company, which is essential to develop its product portfolio.

The basis of classifying your products on the Boston matrix is according to their cash generating ability and cash utilization for promotion etc. A model of the Boston matrix for your own portfolio analysis is shown in Figure 3.4.

		Star					Question Mark		
	Cash flow	+	+	+ +		Cash Flow	+	+	+ +
	Cash usage	–	–	– –		Cash Usage	– –	–	– –
	Balance		0			Balance		0	

		Cash Cow					Dog		
	Cash flow	+	+	+ +		Cash Flow	+	+	+ +
	Cash usage	–	–	– –		Cash Usage	–	–	– –
	Balance		0			Balance		0	

Market Growth — High / Low — 10%

Relative market: 4.0 2.0 1.0 0.5 0.25 — High ... Low

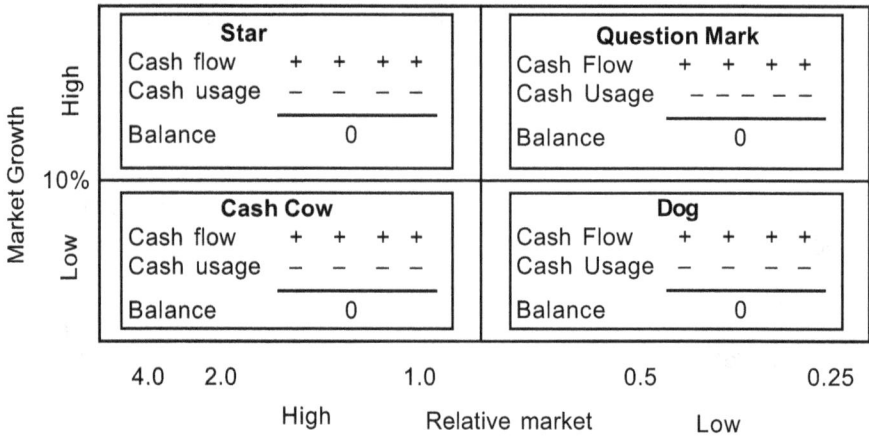

Figure 3.4 Boston Matrix and Portfolio Analysis

Though the axes on this grid are labeled arbitrarily, they are widely usable. Market growth is classified as low when it is less than ten percent and high when it is more than twenty per cent.

Relative market share is shown as a ratio. For example, if your market share is twenty percent and your major competitor's share is also twenty per cent, then the ratio is 1:1 and if your competitor's market share is only ten percent as against your twenty percent then the ratio is a more favorable (to your company) 2:1. This ratio is in fact the measure of market dominance.

The picturesque labels attached to each of the four categories of products give some indication of the prospects of the products in each quadrant. Each quadrant of the grid shown in Figure 3.4 has different strategic implications.

Quadrant - I

Products in this quadrant are appropriately named as *Stars*, as they are products with a high market share in high growth markets. They represent the basis of tomorrow's business. They may or may not generate sufficient cashflow today to finance their rapid growth. A careful analysis is needed regarding their present position, future prospects and potential. They should be carefully nurtured. They should not be starved of funds that need to fuel their growth even if their cashflow today is not so positive. That would only result in preventing them from becoming major sources of cashflow in future.

Quadrant - II

Products in this quadrant are the most difficult to deal with and often lead to the classic question that Shakespeare's Hamlet had faced - To be (promoted vigorously) or Not to be (promoted because of the low market share).

That is why they are called *Question Marks*. These products often lead to a marketing man's dilemma because their cashflows are usually not adequate to fuel their own growth. They require large transfusions of cash to build market share and increase volume, so that they may someday become major cash generators. While the market growth rate is very attractive, the investment is very large. Hence the *Question mark*.

Quadrant - III

Products in this quadrant are good sources of cash. While their market share is high, they are in slow growth markets. So building up further market share is too expensive, even prohibitive. Therefore, the cash generated by these products should be invested preferably in *Stars* (high growth products and future prospects), or even in *Question marks* after careful analysis. Since these products generate adequate cash to finance the future profit earners of the company, they are known as *Cash Cows*. There is one caution however. You should never milk these cash cows to death because there may be many productive and profitable years ahead of them. These can be exploited by the discerning marketer through creative extensions of the life cycle of these products.

Quadrant - IV

The products in this quadrant are low share products in slow or no growth markets. These products may not be earning an acceptable return on investment (ROI). They require a disproportionate amount of marketing effort. Their prospects too are very bleak. They are often a cash drain on a company. The name given to these products is *Dogs*. They are underdogs at that. While it is human nature to support the underdog, in marketing one should avoid any emotional attachment to these products (Peter Drucker very aptly called these products as *investments in managerial ego*) and dispassionately adopt a strategy of either harvesting or divesting so that funds can be freed for investing in the top dog products i.e., Stars.

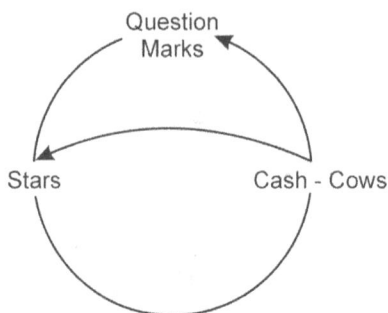

Figure 3.5 Perpetual Product Development Cycle

The art and science of product portfolio management becomes a lot clearer now than ever before. The ideal product development sequence involves developing Question marks into Stars and Stars into Cash cows. Inherent in this ideal product development sequence is the judicious usage of the surplus cash generated by the cash cows in stars, which in turn will be tomorrow's major profit earners (cash cows) and in some selected question marks, which are likely to become tomorrow's stars and perhaps, day-after-tomorrow's cash cows. This is more or less a cyclical process and the marketer should be alert while playing at this wheel of fortune. One thing about this cyclical process is that the movement is anti-clockwise, as can be seen in Figure 3.5.

The cyclical movement shown in Figure 3.5 is no doubt hypothetical. But it is useful in the sense that it indicates the likely direction and the ideal sequence in which a company's products should be developed. As physicists are obsessed with the idea of perpetual motion so are marketers with the idea of the perpetual product development cycle.

Portfolio Analysis in Pharmaceutical Marketing

It is useful to do the product portfolio analysis in pharmaceutical marketing at two levels. Firstly, at the level of the individual product or brand for each of your major brands. Secondly, for each of the therapeutic categories in which you are competing. This would help in identifying and formulating effective strategies to exploit even the relatively-small-but-could-be huge opportunities of tomorrow, that is, the star opportunities in each therapeutic category that may not be as obvious today. You have to be alert and look for the emerging sub-segments.

The concepts of PLC and product portfolio analysis are rather closely related. Product review must therefore, include both PLC and portfolio analysis. Here are some important reasons:

A. The basic premise of PLC is that it is a very useful planning tool and provides important strategic directions during the different phases of both product and market life cycles.

B. Secondly, PLC analysis also suggests the levels of promotional efforts required during the different phases of the life cycle of product and its market.

C. Thirdly, a careful study of PLC will enable a marketer to exploit the hidden or dormant opportunities by extending the life cycle of a product and indeed even of the market. PLC is thus futuristic.

D. Product portfolio analysis takes the cash generating ability of a product and cash usage into cognizance for classification of products into today's profit earners and tomorrow's potential profit earners. Thus, the product portfolio analysis essentially provides the strategic directions to the company. The basic purpose of portfolio analysis is to optimize the process of resource allocation.

The reason why the relative market share and the rate of market growth are chosen as key determinants is to identify the present position of the company's products and to decide on the desirable course of action for the future of the company's products.

Thus, on closer examination, you will observe that the major purpose of portfolio analysis is to optimize the resource allocation for the company's products based on their current position and desired future direction and determine the promotional effort needed. The basis for analysis of PLC and product portfolio and key determinant factors may be different but the purpose remains the same.

Product review and analysis from different angles, dimensions and directions would give a better idea, improved insight and a broader perspective of key strategic actions, which need to be taken at different phases of product and market life cycles. Such an analysis would enable you to bring stability to the company through present profit earners and ensure future growth opportunities by nurturing and developing the stars and by extending the product life cycle through innovative marketing strategies.

Product Positioning

Product positioning is a concept borrowed from military strategy. The earliest known writings about positioning in military strategy can be found in the writings of a Chinese general Sun Tzu, who was a contemporary of Confucius, the famous Chinese philosopher. In his classic work, *The art of War*, Sun Tzu, being the master strategist that he really was, discussed the importance of positioning in the military strategy context - *troop disposition, ground, terrain, relative strength of opposing forces and the mental attitudes of the opposition. His primary target was the mind of the opposing commander.* These concepts are very much relevant in the present-day marketing context.

Jack Trout, a strong advocate of positioning, wrote in a 1969 article entitled - *Positioning is the game people play in today's me-too market place.* What can be more 'me-too' than the pharmaceutical market in India, choking with over 100,000 products?

David Ogilvy in 1971, pointed out that *the result of our campaigns depend less on how we write our advertising than on how a product is positioned.* The 1970s have clearly ushered in a new era in marketing - the era of Positioning. Accurate positioning has become the most important step in effective marketing.

Why is Positioning a Must?

It is the information explosion that has led to this realization. It is the ever-increasing noise level in the market place, with the number of brands multiplying like rabbits that has made positioning a must for survival and growth. Let us consider the pharmaceutical industry in India. There are over 10,000 companies churning out over 100,000 products. An urban doctor on a typical working day meets about 20 to 25 medical representatives who in turn detail about 5 to 8 products. That means an exposure of anything between 100 to 200 products. Add to this the information through newspapers, magazines, professional journals, radio and television messages etc. The total number of messages that he is exposed to is truly mind-blogging. A marketer must virtually fight for the attention of the doctor for his product. While the human mind has a remarkable ability to cope with such an information overload, the ways in which it deals and processes this excessive volume of information are certainly not helpful to the marketer. One is screening and selective process of perception. The other is that the human mind rejects any information that is not related to its prior knowledge. The human mind has no room for something that is totally new, unless it is in some way related to or matches with prior information and knowledge. The simplest example is that learning alphabets of any language is essential for learning words in that language. Without the prior knowledge of alphabets new words sound like gibberish.

Furthermore, it is said that people rank objects, events and even other people in their minds. This is necessary to organize the ever-increasing information in order to cope with it. Similarly consumers rank products in their minds. If the product is distinctly different in that product category and if it fits with similar, equivalent perception of the consumer, then, only then the product is likely to be ranked higher in the consumer's mind. The closer and the more perfect the unique product-attribute and the consumer perception-fit, the higher the ranking of that product. It is here that the positioning of product is going to play a vital, crucial role. Much depends on how the product is positioned.

Positioning Prescription Drugs

Today, in the Indian pharmaceutical industry where the rate of brand proliferation is behind only that of rabbits, success of new or even modified versions of existing products depends more on proper positioning. Failure to recognize or understand positioning can lead to major marketing mistakes frequently associated with major changes in the product line:

(a) The introduction of a new or modified product fails to generate adequate sales and profits or

(b) The new product launches succeed, but at the expense of other products (illusion of success)

If undetected, this could result in misdirected marketing efforts by the company. On the other hand an appreciation and understanding of positioning can produce increased profits through marketing innovations. The importance and crucial nature of positioning is very aptly summed up by David Aaker, in the brand growth management : *Product positioning is so central and critical that it should be considered at the level of a mission statement...It comes to represent the essence of a business.*

Positioning : A Definition

Webster's dictionary describes positioning as:

(a) A relative place, situation or standing
(b) Perceived images consumers have of one product in relation to their needs
(c) Perceived images of similar products marketed by competing companies

Positioning is the process of establishing a product, person, company or even an object in the minds of the members of a target-market in such a way that it is perceived to answer the needs of that market. Positioning thus, refers to identification and communication of a differential advantage.

Profitable positioning is a strategy for creating unique product image, which increases total profits. Firms that are planning modifications of existing products or introduction of new products will naturally, in keeping with their marketing objectives strive to position their products' entry so that it will produce maximum sales and profits.

The three primary tasks of product-positioning in the drug industry are:

1. The type of conditions for which the product will be prescribed
2. The type of patient for whom the product will be considered suitable
3. The products with which the product will compete closely

Positioning and Target Market Selection

It is very important to emphasize the interaction of positioning and selection of the target market. Target market and positioning strategies are like two sides of the same coin. They are inseparable.

A brand must be positioned to appeal to a target customer segment (target market) and likewise, a consumer segment too will respond to a brand that occupies the position preferred by it.

Sustainable Differential Advantage

Uniqueness or rather perceived uniqueness is a product's only protection against commodity status. The primary task of marketers, therefore, is to create a perceivable uniqueness i.e., differential advantage. A differential advantage should satisfy three fundamental criteria.

A. It should differentiate the product from all others in the product class creating a perception of uniqueness.

B. It is important or can be made to seem important to the target audience.

C. It should be sustainable over time against competition. The primary task of marketers is to create a differential advantage. The secondary task is to defend it with all their might. There are two basic approaches to achieve this. One is to increase the importance of the product features or attributes and their benefits, which are perceived as unique. Alternatively, one can reduce the importance of the product features or attributes and the benefits of competitors' products, which are perceived as unique. Here are two cases highlighting these two approaches.

Case 3.12   The Fabulous Success Story of American Remedies in the Systemic Anti-Fungal Market!

American Remedies, one of the fastest growing companies in the Indian pharmaceutical industry had spotted an opportunity in the early 1990s (the company was later acquired by Dr. Reddy's Laboratories) in the systemic anti-fungal market. Griseofulvin was the most widely prescribed anti-fungal for systemic use (77 percentof the market in 1992). Only two companies - IDPL and Glaxo with its two brands (Grisovin FP and Dermonorm) - had accounted for over two-thirds of the total anti-fungal market. American Remedies, being a small company could not have thought of succeeding with another brand of griseofulvin in the systemic anti-fungal market. It had to do something totally different - a perceivable differential advantage not only over the other brands of griseofulvin but also over other brands of emerging new anti fungal molecules like ketoconazole etc.

After a thorough enquiry into the perceptions and the needs of the target consumers and users, the company identified a vacant, unoccupied slot in the perceptual space of the target consumers - the convenience of dosage. The recommended dosage for all griseofulvin brands was one tablet four times a day. When you consider the low levels of gastric tolerance associated with griseofulvin, suddenly a certain vacant slot becomes obvious. What other companies were oblivious to, became obvious to American Remedies. The company found out that it is possible to offer a once-a-day griseofulvin brand by reducing the particle size further, down to about 400 microns. The company introduced Gris OD (griseofulvin once-daily) and communicated this differential advantage very forcefully and persuasively. The convenient dosage regime became far more important to the prescribing physicians. This differential advantage of once-a-day brand of the well established griseofulvin molecule paved the way for the dramatic success of Gris OD. The brand was on its way to achieve the leadership position in the systemic anti-fungal market.

A seemingly simple, even obvious positioning slot, when exploited well can result in fabulous success!

Case 3.13   Undermining Others' Differential Advantage?

Zantac's pre-emptive strike against Losec (now Prilosec) offers an excellent example of undermining the differential advantage created by potential competitors. Zantac (ranitidine) of Glaxo (GSK now) had achieved the distinction of being the world's largest prescription drug brand (sales US $ 2.7 billion in 1991-92). Losec (omeprazole), an original research product of Astra, belongs to a different class of drugs (proton pump inhibitor) even though it is in the same therapeutic category of anti-ulcerants. Losec offers a distinct advantage in terms of faster ulcer healing and very low (if not totally absent) relapse rates. Glaxo sensing this, decided to undermine the differential advantage, and launched a pre-emptive strike against Losec, internationally creating a dissonance among the prescribers. It succeeded in making Losec a reserve drug to be used as a second line treatment for some time. Meanwhile, Glaxo had pursued a market development strategy by expanding the usage of Zantac in non-ulcer dyspepsia, gastritis etc. Glaxo could do this primarily from its preeminent position. It had built up a lot of credibility. Astra (AstraZeneca now) had also built up a substantial clinical evidence and got its Prilosec cleared as a first line drug in gastric ulcers.

Glaxo surely had bought time by undermining the differential advantage created by Astra and defended its leadership position for Zantac in the anti-ulcer wars!

Positioning is perception. Positioning is deciding on what your product is going to do and for whom. Having decided on this, the next step is how to make the customer perceive *it* the way you want him to. The key questions that one should ask and answer before positioning a product are:

(a) What position do we already own in the prospect's mind? for existing products)

(b) What position do we want to own?

(c) What is the *Gap* like?

(d) What companies must be out-gunned, if we are to establish that position?

(e) Do we have enough marketing resources, both in terms of money and creative talent to occupy the position we want to?

(f) Do we have the conviction and guts to stick to the one consistent position?

(g) Does our creative approach match our positioning strategy?

Ground Rules for Positioning

Let us now look at some of the ground rules for positioning a product. These are not rigid rules, but are some of the basic principles that are derived and formulated from a detailed and exhaustive study of a number of product successes and failures. Some of the important ground rules are:

1. **You cannot appeal to everyone:** There is no room for *panaceas* in the market place. A product that tries to appeal to everyone winds up appealing to no one. This attempt to appeal to everyone is in fact, the antithesis of positioning. If anyone claims that his product has lot to offer from *pediatrics to geriatrics,* in a number of conditions, a sort of *cure-all,* who is going to believe it? The credibility will be near zero if not a real zero. A number of pharmaceutical brands in India have achieved uncommon success through precise, non-ambiguous, no-nonsense positioning. Here are two cases in point:

Case 3.14   Precise Positioning Improves the Blood Picture of Two Brands in the Hematinic Market!

Let us take the multi-hematinic market in India. It is a highly fragmented market with over a hundred brands. The market size in value was around Rs. 20-crore with an annual growth rate of 1.2 percentin 1992. Majority of these brands do not have a clearly defined positioning strategy. A typical list of indications for a *no-position* hematinic looks like this:

In anaemias due to diverse causes such as increased requirements of hematinic during pregnancy, lactation, convalescence, due to malnutrition, due to restricted diet, in obesity, chronic infectious diseases, tuberculosis, anorexia nervosa, chronic diarrhea, achlorhydria, post-gastrostomy, or gastro-jejunostomy, chronic hemorrhoids, hookworm infestations etc.

Only two brands, Fefol of Eskaylabs (GSK now) and Livogen Capsules of Allenburys (GSK now), had a clear positioning strategy. Both were positioned as *pregnancy haematinics*. Since research indicated that pregnancy accounts for about 70 percentof the hematinic usage. Fefol stayed with the theme *part of the routine of pregnancy and lactation* consistently.

They had put their might behind this position (*the mother and baby contest* was one unique promotional strategy they had adopted to reinforce their positioning strategy) and reaped a rich harvest of prescriptions.

Close on their heels was Livogen Capsules, which stayed on with its very strong, persuasive and distinct theme, 11 (*blood-building factors*) *for the mother and 5* (*mg of folic acid*) *for the fetus*. This is not to say that the other hematinics were not promoted in pregnancy. Pregnancy was one of the several indications in which other hematinic brands were promoted, whereas both Fefol and Livogen Capsules were positioned only in pregnancy and stayed on with that position unwaveringly. Unflinchingly!

It has always been a neck-to-neck race for Fefol and Livogen Capsules with a negligible difference of less than one percent in terms of market share points, Fefol having a market share of 11.6 percent and Livogen Capsules having 10.9 percentin 1992.

Case 3.15   Clear Positioning Steers Glaxo Clear in Anti-Asthmatic Market!

Another case in point is Betnelan tablets of Glaxo (GSK now). Each tablet of Betnelan contains 0.5 mg of betamethasone valerate, a potent corticosteroid, which can be used in a number of conditions like: asthma, severe allergic disturbances, leukemia, rheumatoid arthritis, collagen diseases, various inflammatory skin diseases, nephrotic syndrome, ulcerative colitis, pemphigus, sarcoidses (especially with hyper calcaemia), rheumatic endocarditis, ankylosing spondylitis, blood dyscrasias, agranulocytosis and thromobo-cytopenic purpura etc.

Betnelan, introduced sometime in the 1950s was being promoted in all these conditions till 1973. The company had a relook at its marketing strategies in 1973 and positioned Betnelan in bronchial asthma and promoted it vigorously. Betnelan, not only achieved the leadership position but also remained a strong leader even after fifteen years after this clear, decisive positioning in bronchial asthma. That is what a clear, precise positioning can do to a brand.

The reason for this specific positioning and its success with a such a versatile drug like betamethasone valerate was that Glaxo at the time was also marketing it in the same strength of 0.5 mg of the drug per tablet in a soluble tablet form under a different brand name, Betnesol effervescent tablets. Betnesol tablets were positioned differently.

Glaxo, by virtue of its clear positioning strategy and the conviction with which it stayed on, achieved a formidable position in the systemic corticosteroid market, with a market share of 48 per cent. Its positioning strategy paid off handsomely in marketing the twin brands of betamethasone. Both Betnelan and Betnesol continued to grow from strength to strength. There was no cannibalization of brands either. Clear positioning had ensured harmony and growth instead.

2. You Cannot Beat Them - The Brand Leaders head On!

There are some positions, which cannot and should not be contested. You cannot make a direct, frontal attack on the brand leader who is firmly entrenched. Over 2,400 years ago Sun Tzu recognized the folly of attacking a superior and firmly entrenched competitor head-on. He said:

There are some roads not to be followed, some armies not to be attacked, some cities not to be seized, some positions not to be contested.

If you want to introduce an antacid brand now, you cannot afford to attack either Gelusil or Digene. That would be setting you on a collision course. You can take a different position, but you should create the necessary differentiation and make your brand stand out distinctly. You should of course, relate your product to competition, but only to say that it is different and better than others. The differentiation must be perceived.

Unless your communication is based on a unique idea and position, the message is often put into the mental slot reserved for the leader in that product category. That is why with every addition of a new product that is not really differentiated is a particular product group, you find that the brand leader is gaining share constantly further strengthening its position. Consider the case of a new antacid that had made the waves in the antacid, anti-flatulent market.

Case 3.16   The New Antacid's Guerrilla Warfare!

Biological E. Limited, in 1987 introduced a new antacid that jostled for space among a crowd of 151 antacid brands in a Rs. 45-crore large antacid, anti-flatulent market. The company knew beforehand that it could not fight the brand leaders Digene of Boots (market share 19.9%) and Gelusil of Warner Hindusthan (market share 13.1%) head on. Therefore, the company chose to create a perceptible product differentiation. It formulated the product differently, and promoted it as a sodium-free antacid. This caused enough dissonance since it has been common knowledge that sodium intake is restricted in hypertensive patients. Furthermore, it is highly likely that middle-aged patients who are susceptible to hypertension are also likely patients of hyperacidity. The company chose a totally different name for its brand that is suggestive and powerful enough to cut through the clutter. p*H4* is a highly suggestive name since that is the normal gastric pH level. The product became synonymous with the normal gastric pH. The company reinforced its product differentiation in a number of ways and communicated persuasively its differentiation. The net result is that the product found a *niche* for itself and gained foothold in the minds of physicians, which no other antacid introduced during the previous six years was able to. While the new brand - pH4 did not take any share from the brand leaders, it certainly awakened the sleeping giants, who stepped up their promotional efforts to defend their market share.

(*Boots later became a part of Abbott Healthcare and Warner Hindustan later became a part of Pfizer due to a series of acquisitions.*)

3. **You Can Re-position Your Brand:** Even if you do not find any gaps in the market as it is currently defined and perceived, it may be possible to alter the market map and thus create new opportunities. This may be done by introducing a new attribute and making it salient for the target market.

   This is repositioning by changing the frames of reference. You can reposition your brand against the competitor. Repositioning is undercutting an existing concept or a product. One should not be afraid of conflict or controversy while repositioning a product. Consider these cases.

Case 3.17   *Alert* makes it Good!

There are over a hundred brands of antihistamines in the anti-allergic market in India. Although, many of them contain different ingredients, customers (doctors) continued to perceive these various brands as antihistamines with little or no difference. A few differences like *price,* which is of concern to the dispensing or purchasing doctors and hospitals, and of *action of duration*, of course, existed in the served markets of different competitors. There were no major perceptible differences existed among the brands in the total market as such. The brand leaders - Avil (Hoechst, which is Sanofi now) and Foristal (Ciba Geigy, which is Novartis now) had been guarding their respective served markets zealously. All other brands had insignificant shares of the total market with very little served markets.

Enter Incidal of Bayer. Incidal contained a different ingredient. Furthermore, with a clear product differentiation and a clever repositioning strategy, Bayer literally invaded the served markets of of various competitors and grabbed the business (prescriptions) right from under their noses. They promoted Incidal as an *Alert and Daytime Histamine* vigorously. This created a strong product differentiation in the minds of customers as all other antihistamines cause drowsiness or sedation and cannot therefore, be prescribed to patients while driving vehicles and who are busy at work places during the day. With its clear and clever repositioning as a Daytime antihistamine, Incidal overcame the current limitations of all antihistamines in one stroke and stormed the antihistamine market and achieved a the second position in the marketing in a short span of few years.

Case 3.18   Repositioning Strategy Replaces an Entrenched Brand!

Here is an example of how Tylenol (brand of paracetamol) in the US was repositioned against the mighty aspirin and won the battle. The Tylenol ads said:

for millions who cannot take aspirin...if your stomach is easily upset or you have an ulcer... or you suffer from asthma, allergies, iron deficiency anemia, it would make a good sense to check with your doctor before you take aspirin,,,Aspirin can irritate stomach lining, can cause hidden gastro-intestinal bleeding... Fortunately there is Tylenol...

Tylenol is a leading brand of analgesic antipyretic in the U S and in many other countries. The repositioning strategy paid rich dividends indeed!

A few years later, an over-the-counter (OTC) brand of ibuprofen was trying to invade the served market of the mighty Tylenol brand with its own repositioning strategy.

Positioning or repositioning strategies discussed here may look obvious and over simplistic. The simplicity is deceptive. One can apply the principles of positioning strategy after thoroughly analyzing the various aspects like the current position of his brand, the desired position and the existing gap between the two. One should not mimic or imitate another product's theme just because it happens to be a similar product or falls into the same product category. Such practice of imitative strategy could be disastrous. Consider this case.

Case 3.19   'Me-too' Strategy Meets with a Disaster!

Imitation may be the best form of flattery. But, it could falter when overdone or without proper analysis in marketing.

Inspired by the success of Tylenol's classic repositioning strategy, Burroughs Wellcome (GSK now) in India marketed their brand of acetaminophen, Ridake (manufactured by Litaka Laboratories). The company had chosen the OTC route. Large ads of Ridake appeared in leading newspapers. The copy was almost similar to the copy of the Tylenol ads, when it was introduced in the U.S. many years ago. There was strong objection to these ads as they were hypercritical about the popular aspirin. Comparative (or combative) advertisements were almost non-existent at that time in India. The resistance to their advertising strategy was so high that the company had to withdraw these ads. The company finally got rid of the product that was supposed to rid the pain (hence the name Ridake)!

Case 3.20   Synergistic Power of a Successful Repositioning Strategy!

Septran, the anti-bacterial that catapulted the company, Burroughs Wellcome (GSK now) into the limelight (from a mere Rs. 4-crore company in 1973 to a Rs. 75-Crore giant in 1992) was repositioned against the mighty tetracyclines in 1973.

Septran was the Indian pharmaceutical industry's leading brand (sales Rs. 31.3-crore, growth 3.1% in 1992). Septran, a combination of sulphamethoxazole and trimethoprim positioned itself as an ideal alternative to the widely prescribed tetracyclines (rather indiscriminately used) that were reigning supreme up to the late 1970s. What is particularly noteworthy is that the synergistic power of Septran backed by unprecedented promotional effort of the company pushed the brand to the dizzy heights of the industry's *number one* position even when other sulfa drugs were on the decline.

4. **There is Not Much Room Over There!:** The human mind can no doubt store and process an incredible lot of information (about 12 billion bits of information is the estimated capacity of the human brain, but scientists say that hardly 10 percentof it is used by an average individual. The brightest seem to be using about 15 per cent). According to the Harvard psychologist, Dr. George A Miller, the average human mind cannot deal with more than seven items at a time in its working memory. Ask anyone to name all the brands he can remember in a given product category. For a high interest category, chances are that they will hardly get past seven, usually it is much less.

Your product has got to occupy one of the seven positions, to be remembered, recalled and to be successful. If your product fails to occupy one of the seven *rungs* on the product ladder in the prospect's mind, it has no chance of survival. In any product category the few top brands (usually 5 to 7) account for about 90 percentof the market. The Indian pharmaceutical industry is no exception to this.

Moving up the ladder is very difficult, particularly when the above brands are firmly entrenched and the gap is wider. A detailed analysis of the competing brands and their positions is a must before one plans to climb up the ladder.

If you have a truly new product, it is often better to tell the prospect what the product is not, rather than what it is. That is because the mind has no room for what is new and different unless it is related to the old and matches with prior knowledge.

The classic example of this is that the first-ever automobile was positioned as a *horse-less carriage*. Among cough syrups for children in India a *non-narcotic* brand was the leader in the 1990s. Patients certainly prefer (and therefore, doctors too) a *pain-free* injection. In the anti-inflammatory market a *non-steroidal* drugs are preferred. *Non-staining* ointments are highly acceptable among topical preparations as they have a cosmetic appeal. *Sodium-free* and *Sugar-free* preparations are sought after by many a health conscious person.

5. **Credibility is the Foundation for Success!:** The foundation of a successful positioning strategy is its credibility. Whether it is

possible to tell the truth, the whole truth and nothing but the truth is besides the point. Unless the consuming public believes the message conveyed by the product promotion, the positioning game is lost.

In a highly competitive, over-crowded market like the Indian pharmaceutical market, in a *me-too,* rather 'me-me-too' market there are many who claim that they are different. But merely claiming that one is different is not going to create a unique, distinct position. At best it will change the *me-too* market into a *me-different* or *me-me-different* market.

Only when the consumers perceive the *difference,* will the product be successful. The *desired position* for the product in the minds of consumers can be created only when the product differentiation is genuine, in both words and deeds.

Finally, what is axiomatic about the whole business of positioning is this: the best policy for an effective, successful positioning strategy is honesty itself.

Product Policy and Strategy

Product policy and strategy is the keystone of a marketing-mix, since a product is the most tangible and often the most important expression of any business endeavor. Customers satisfy their needs only through the use of products. Customers' image of a product and decisions to buy your products or not in future is influenced only by their experiences with your product. The satisfied customers with rewarding experiences of your products are likely to indulge in repeat purchases. Others with not-so-positive experiences may switchover to competitors' products. Decisions relating to products, therefore, are crucial to marketing strategy.

There are two main reasons why a company adds a product or two to its existing product-mix. Firstly, when it realizes that its existing products do not have the potential to attain the growth and profit objectives the company has set itself.

The second reason is that the company spots new product opportunities that can be exploited since they are matching its resources or that the company is confident of mobilizing.

It is vital that a company's product-mix must represent a dynamic equilibriums between current profitability and future growth and stability in the ever-changing market place. An adoption of the product portfolio analysis suggested by BCG is very useful for this purpose. You classify the products on the basis of their current market share, market or sales growth and profitability. When you look at products this way you will observe that:

(a) Products with high market share and low growth are today's profit earners (cash cows)

(b) Products with high market share and high growth represent tomorrow's (potential) big profit earners (stars)

(c) Products with low market share but high growth are high risk investment (question marks)

A company should have a properly balanced mix of products that includes today's as well as tomorrow's profit earners.

Governing Factors

Product strategy, therefore, is concerned with decisions on the range of products a company must offer to achieve its objective of profit, growth and market share. The policies will specify the action plans and programs that will be implemented to achieve the strategy objectives. The factors governing the product policy and strategy decisions are:

1. **Resource Utilization:** Optimum use of resources holds the key to improved profitability. Productivity must be improved. Will the product policy and strategy decisions lead to better utilization of resources in all areas such as raw materials, installed capacities, market position, corporate image, reputation and quality? Will the product decisions lead to better utilization of the existing resources?

2. **Stability:** Stability in sales, profit, return on investment, earnings per share are essential for continued success. A company, which is robust (financially speaking) and can venture to expand further must avoid excessive fluctuations and should not stretch beyond limits. Temptation to buy market share at any (promotional or otherwise) cost must be restrained. Aggression tempered with prudence pays dividends in the long run.

3. **Flexibility:** A company's product policy and strategy should be feasible enough to adapt to ever-changing customer needs and marketing environment and exploit them.

4. **Profit:** Profits are the lifeblood of a company. A company must constantly strive to improve profitability by improving performance in all areas and activities of the company. It is the profits that fuel the growth opportunities and maintain the existing business.

Product planning, therefore, is crucial for attaining marketing objectives. The key result areas are:

- A regular review of product range and product-mix becomes mandatory to ensure optimization of sales and profits of all items in each product line.

- A constant improvement in marketing and manufacturing efficiencies to improve product image, promotional effort and ensure better capacity utilization.

- To maintain a balance between price and value based on customer expectations and perceptions. Maintaining expected quality is important. Excessive quality (beyond the acceptable limits and levels) may be very costly and need not necessarily reap any additional benefits either to the customer or to the company.

- Anticipating competitors' moves, reactions and responses to your product strategies is absolutely necessary to stay ahead and defend your products' market share.

The decision regarding the product policy and strategy, therefore, affect a company's future significantly. The choice of products of a firm influences all the other elements in its marketing program and may have significant implications for such functional areas as finance, production and personnel. That is why product policy and strategy have been called the micro marketing functions that center on a firm's marketing programs, and its organizations and management of marketing. The basic interacting triad suggested by David J Luck that forms the foundation of the entire product program is:

(a) **Objectives:** Provide the ends towards which the management must steer.

(b) **Policies:** Provide the guidelines along which and the channel within which the firm should proceed towards meeting its objectives.

(c) **Strategies:** Conceptualize and direct the means whereby the firm moves towards its objectives.

Stated simply, product policy and strategy decisions center around what goods and services a firm should offer for sale and what characteristics and attributes they should have. These decisions involve matching company's resources and needs with market opportunities.

Formulation of product policy therefore, requires careful analysis of existing and potential (new) products relative to the characteristics of both the market and the firm. A checklist of all essential properties and other aspects that need to be included in reviewing a pharmaceutical product is presented in Table 3.6.

Table 3.6 Pharmaceutical Product Review - A Checklist

---

1. Physical Properties of a Product

(a) Dosage form - Capsule

What should be the color, shape, size and texture (hard gelatin or soft gelatin) of the capsule?

What are the ingredients and their strengths?

Should the brand name be printed on the capsule? Linear printing or circular printing? Are the colors selected for printing approved?

(b) Dosage form - Tablets

What should be the color, shape (round, oblong, flat, square etc.) and size of the tablets?

Should the tablets be sugar coated, film coated, enteric coated or uncoated? Should they be scored?

Should the brand name be embossed on the tablet?

What are the ingredients and their strengths?

Should they be chewable or swallow tablets? If chewable, what should be the taste and flavor?

(c) Packing for Oral Solids

Should the capsules or tablets be packed in glassine poly or aluminum foil, blister or alu alu or in blister packing? In glass bottles or plastic containers?

(d) Dosage form - Oral Liquids

Should the product be in suspension or syrup form?

Contd...

Should it be free from sugar?

What should be its color, smell, taste and flavor?

Should it be packed in glass bottles or PET containers?

Should there be a measure cup or a dropper (in case of pediatric syrups)

What is the composition?

(e) Dosage form - Parenteral

Should it be in ampoules or vials?

What is the composition? What kind of preservatives should be used?

Should it be packed in disposable syringes?

What are the storage conditions? Should it be transported through a cold chain like some vaccines?

(f) Dosage form - Topical Ointments

What should be the smell and color of the ointment?

What are the ingredients?

What should be the base? Cream or oily?

Should there be an applicator (as In the case of hemorrhoidal ointments)?

(g) Dosage form - Topical Solution

What are the ingredients?

What should be the color, smell of the topical solution?

Should it be in a glass bottle or a roll-on bottle?

(h) Dosage form - Topical Powder

What are the ingredients?

What should be the texture of the powder?

Should it be packed in glass vials, plastic containers or tins?

What should be the pack size?

2. Medical Rationale

Medical rationale for each product and for each dosage form

Details regarding why and how the product works

What is the recommended dosage?

3. Indications and Claims

What are the indications?

What are the product claims? How can they be substantiated?

What are the side effects and contradictions?

Contd...

4. Trade Mark Position

Is the trademark registered? It is always necessary to apply for trademark registration for proposed new products, at least three years in advance in India.

5. Patent Position (Basic drugs)

This is necessary if you are exporting to those countries, which are signatories to GATT on intellectual property rights.

6. Registration and Licensing Status

Have you obtained the Director General of Technical Development (DGTD) registration?

Have you received the drug license for manufacturing?

7. Pricing

What category does the proposed product fall into as per the Drug Price Control Order (DPCO)?

Have you got a price approval from the National Pharmaceutical Pricing Authority (NPPA)?

If the product does not come under the purview of price control, what pricing strategy should you adopt? Skimming the cream or penetration strategy?

8. Sizing up the Competition

What is the intensity of competition?

How many competitors are there? Their market shares?

What is the combined market share of the top three competitors?

What are their product attributes and benefits? How do they compare with yours?

What are their resources? Their promotional effort? Their distribution? Their sales force and their competence? How do they compare with yours?

How do they compare with you in terms of all resources?

9. Sales Potential

What are your sales forecasts? What is the projected profitability in the next five years?

10. Launch Plans

Detailed launch plans

New Products

Speaking of new products, Professor Stanton in his book, *Fundamentals of Marketing* states that:

It is not important to seek a very limited definition of a new product. Instead we may recognize several possible categories of new products.

The three recognizable products categories are:

A. **Innovative:** These are products, which are really innovative and truly unique like *hair-restorer*, or *cancer cure*. For these products there is real need and there are no existing satisfactory substitutes. Products, which are quite different replacements for existing goods serving existing markets, can also be included in this category. H2 Antagonists like cimetidine, ranitidine, famotidine among anti-ulcerants, anti-hypertensives such as atenolol, nifedipine, captopril and the quinolone derivatives like ciprofloxacin, norfloxacin, ofloxacin among antibacterial drugs are some notable examples of the truly innovative products in pharmaceutical industry.

B. **Replacements:** Products, which are essentially of the same type, but with a significant differentiation from the existing product, can be classified under this category. Ibuprofen sustained release capsules - Fenbid, Fenlong, Ibubid TR, and ferrous sulphate and folic acid spansules (Fefol) are some examples in this category. The basic idea here is to create a product differentiation even if the drug is the same, by combining it with another drug (to achieve synergy) or using a drug delivery system (to achieve a higher degree of safety and minimize the dose) and to achieve a bigger share of the market.

C. **Imitative:** Products in this category are new to the company but not to the market. The purpose of introducing products in this category is that a company merely wants to capture part of an existing market with yet another brand of an existing type of product. The pharmaceutical industry in India is virtually flooded with imitative products and it is this category of products that have made the pharmaceutical market in India the fiercely competitive market that it is today.

Product-Mix Decisions

Product-mix decision is an important and indeed a crucial product policy decision for a company, since it tends to reflect not only the nature of the market and the resources of the firm but also the underlying philosophy of the company's management.

There are a number of options available for a firm in this area. One firm may pursue a policy of diversification. Some other firm may prefer to concentrate and specialize in a specific area and offer a narrow product-mix. For example, Serum Institute of India specializes only in the area of immunologicals. It is important to note that market opportunities for the firm's product-mix serve to determine the upper limits of potential corporate profitability while the quality of the marketing program tends to determine the extent to which this potential is achieved.

Optimal Product-Mix

As Philip Kotler, the marketing guru says, *it is extremely difficult to define an ideal or optimal product-mix. One can say that the current product-mix is optimal, if no adjustment will enhance the company's chances of achieving its objectives and improving its performance.*

Diagnosis of a sub-optimal product-mix, therefore, is very important. Unless you regularly conduct a SWOT (Strengths, Weaknesses, Opportunities, Threats) analysis of each product in your product-mix, you would not be able to diagnose whether your product-mix is sub-optimal.

The usual symptoms are:

A. Chronic or seasonally recurring excess capacity in a firm's production and inventories of finished products. This is often due to a tapering or sluggish demand.

B. A very high proportion of profits coming from a small percentage of products.

C. Inefficient use of sales force skills.

D. Steady decline of profits and sales.

E. Steady increase in complaints from dealers about slow or non-movement of products from their shelves.

F. Steady increase in claims for refund on date-expired products

This situation, if not corrected immediately will only lead to disaster. The strategic options available to a firm for correcting this situation are:

A. **Deletion:** Deletion strategy involves decisions regarding product discontinuance or abandonment of individual items or even of an entire product line.

B. **Product Modification:** Product modification can be achieved by changing either tangible or intangible product attributes. Reformulation, redesigning, changing the pack size or shape, changing the taste or flavor and removing certain features are some of the methods commonly adopted in product modification strategies. By successfully planning and implementing product modification strategies, a number of companies have extended the life cycles of their products, resulting in a longer, healthier, more profitable lease of life for both products and the company.

C. **Introduction of New Products:** Since the introduction of new products is crucial for survival and growth of any business endeavor, we shall discuss this in a separate chapter on managing new products.

Here is a case that illustrates the importance of diagnosing the sub-optimal product-mix in time to avoid any catastrophe.

Case 3.21   Poor Diagnosis Proves Dearer!

Unichem (now acquired by Torrent Pharma) is a large pharmaceutical company in the Indian sector with a considerable reputation. The company manufactures bulk drugs and a number of formulations (about 75 stock keeping units in 1988).

Two products - Uni-enzyme tablets and E.P. Forte (high dose combination of estrogen and progesterone) accounted at one time for over one-third of the company's total sales volume. Though the company was among the first to get license to manufacture newer anti-tubercular drugs like ethambutol and rifampicin, the company had not persevered with ethambutol and had marketed rifampicin and INH combination under Anticox. Consequently, despite a head start the company had only a token share of 2.5 percentof the anti-tubercular market.

Coming back to the company's stronghold - Uni-enzyme tablets, a brand leader in the digestive preparation category for years and E.P. forte, also a brand leader in the high-dose estrogen, progesterone combinations- the company seemed to have taken its position for granted and not monitored and reviewed the changing trends or even the opportunities waiting to be tapped.

Take for example the market for digestive preparations. It was as large as Rs. 34.7-crore with an annual growth rate of 8 percentin 1988. This market comprised oral solids and liquids, with oral solids accounting for about 33 percent and the liquids for the balance 67 per cent. Uni-enzyme tablets had been enjoying the brand leadership for a number of years. The company seemed to have ignored the large oral liquids market for it did not introduce digestive enzyme syrup all these years. A line extension of Uni-enzyme brand as syrup or tonic, backed by massive promotional effort would have made the brand far more formidable. But by 1988, a number of companies entered the market with their brands of digestive enzyme syrups and took a major share of the digestive preparations oral liquids market. Aristozyme of Aristo and Bestozyme of Biological E. Limited had taken a sizable share from the veteran brands like Vitazyme of East India Pharmaceutical Works and Digeplex of TCF.

As a result, Unichem from its formidable position of brand leadership has gone to a rather vulnerable position, where even the brand leadership position was at stake in the total digestive preparations market. Had the company been alert and instituted a diagnostic screen of detecting the symptoms of the sub-optimal product mix early enough, Unichem would have reinforced its already formidable position in the digestive enzyme market as being invincible rather than turning vulnerable.

Consider now the market for a high-dose combination of estrogen and progesterone. The combination had been enjoying brand leadership for years with EP Forte. But then, the Government of India banned the formulations containing high doses of estrogen and progesterone around 1986. While other companies such as German Remedies, Nicholas and Allenburys had withdrawn their products in time and planned for some new products in other therapeutic categories, Unichem did not. Sudden withdrawal of E P Forte left a void in its product-mix. The company was unprepared to meet this sudden loss of sales.

Other companies, while their stakes in the high-dose estrogen progesterone market were not as high as they were for Unichem, their brands Duogynon Forte, Orasecron Forte, Disecron Forte, and Secrodyl contributed significantly enough to their total sales respectively. But those companies noticed the storm signals early enough and sustained their growth by concentrating on other products and by introducing new products in different product categories. But, Unichem seemed to have been caught napping without a proper diagnostic screen. It failed to detect the symptoms or perhaps was too complacent to act quickly.

The net result was that this lack of systematic review of product mixes registered a decline of about ten percent per annum for the next two years and the company's rank fell from 16th in 1986 to 22 in 1988 and slid down further to 30th position in 1992.

The importance of regular and systematic evaluation of a Company's product-mix and development of diagnostic screen to detect or spot the symptoms of a sub-optimal product-mix can never be over-emphasized. Companies that take cognizance of the early storm signals and act fast are bound to succeed. Companies that take their position for granted and close their eyes and ears to the early warning signals are sure to join the dinosaurs club.

Product Strategy

How do you go about formulating the product strategy? From the very beginning one should have a clear, precise, statement of objectives for each product, because, any decision on strategy depends upon your objective (where you want to go). Once you decide on a strategy, the means (tactics) by which you want to achieve your objective become much clearer. A detailed understanding of objective, strategy and tactics will be of help.

Objective

An objective is like your destination. A meaningful objective should be clear, precise, non-ambiguous, quantifiable, measurable, realistic and achievable. At the same time, it should not be too easy to accomplish with little or no effort.

The *stretch factor* should be built into it to make it challenging. There are three levels at which objectives are set. They are:
- (a) Corporate objectives
- (b) Marketing objectives
- (c) Product objects

Strategy

A strategy is like a route or road you want to take to reach your objective (destination). A decision on strategy, therefore, involves all aspects like your target audience, your product's key attributes, allocation of your resource-mix and the segments you will attack.

Tactics

Tactics are the means or vehicle that will take you all the way (strategy) to the destination (objectives). Tactics are the specific action plans. Deciding on tactics would mean deciding on your entire promotional mix.

Market Penetration and Market Development Strategies

Market penetration and development suggests that you increase the market share and profits of your existing products in your existing markets. Five main ways in which you can achieve this are:
1. Widen the customer base. Increase the coverage of doctors like promoting to different groups of specialists, who are not presently covered by your sales force.
2. Increase the call frequency of your sales force to top prescribing doctors.
3. Find new usage for your products. Find out new indications in which your products can be promoted. Like May & Baker did with their Flagyl when they had started promoting it in the treatment

of amoebiasis in addition to the earlier indication of giardiasis. Another example is when Merind (Merck now) started promoting their Practin (Periactin earlier), originally an anti-allergic and anti-pruritic as an appetite stimulant and anti-inflammatory drug aspirin, which is now being promoted to reduce incidence of heart attacks in high risk patients.

4. Add flanking products or line extensions in the same therapeutic category either under the same brand name (it would mutually reinforce the brand image if it is already well established) and facilitate the entry of the new product. This could also mean introducing it in another dosage form or combining it with another drug if synergy can be achieved.

5. More aggressive promotion than ever before is another way of increasing sales, profits and market share. For products with OTC profile (over-the-counter products where prescription is not needed) attractive dealer incentives will help boost the sales.

Product Development

Product development strategy should be a constant exercise. Product development aims to improve the quality and efficacy of the product or to minimize the undesirable attributes. Inherent in the product development strategy are:

A. Constant monitoring and analysis of competitors products. This is the equivalent of reverse engineering of the Japanese electronic industry, which is one of the major secrets of their success. This will enhance and sharpen your competitive edge.

B. Offering better value for money by modifying pack-sizes. Family packs for protein-food supplements, tonics and multivitamins for consumers and dispensing packs for doctors are some examples of product development.

Diversification

Diversification is both expensive and risky. Related diversification is what is recommended. A pharmaceutical company diversifying into OTC healthcare products, hospital products and animal healthcare products are a few examples of related diversification. The more unrelated the diversification to the existing business of the company, the more costly and risky it is. Here is a case in point.

Case 3.22   Unrelated Diversification Eludes Success for an Otherwise Highly Successful Company!

Cadila Laboratories is probably one of the most successful companies in Indian pharmaceutical industry. From a position of 37th in 1976 the company moved to the prestigious second position in the Indian pharmaceutical industry by 1988. The company successfully planned and implemented market penetration, market development and product development strategies in copybook style. The company also pursued an aggressive and imaginative new product planning and development strategy during these twelve years and reaped rich dividends.

Inspired by this success, the company went into a diversification program totally unrelated to its existing business. It began manufacturing color televisions and mopeds. It could not make any mark in these two unrelated areas, whereas everything the company had touched in the areas related to its core business of pharmaceuticals turned into gold. The *Midas touch* was not to be seen in the unrelated diversification and success eluded the otherwise highly successful company.

Product Management

The concept of product management or brand management originated in 1927 by Proctor & Gamble, has undergone several refinements over the years. Today, product management has carved out a niche for itself in the organizational structure of many a forward looking, dynamic and fast growing companies the world over.

Camay soap was the first-ever product in the marketing history of the world to have been assigned exclusively to a product manager in 1927. Since then, neither Camay soap nor the product management system have looked back.

Today, an ever-increasing number of consumer, pharmaceutical and industrial products are being assigned to product managers specifically with a hope to develop and nurture these products into winning brands.

What actually is product management. Is it a panacea, a sort of cure-all for all kinds of ills and problems that marketers face? No, certainly not.

Product management is a system of decentralized business management. Product management is an application of perhaps the most important marketing principle. The principle of concentration.

A product manager, when assigned with a specific responsibility for product or product line, can do some real solid, concentrated thinking on problems and opportunities that exist for his product. This concentrated thinking, in turn, is bound to result in more appropriate and better strategies for his product.

The product management system creates a focal point of planning and responsibility for individual products, says Philip Kotler. The product manager's role is to create product strategies, plans, see that they are implemented, monitor the results and take corrective action.

David Luck termed product managers as *the vital organizational loci for the focus of marketing interfaces.* The important interfaces with which product managers interact frequently are:
- The buying public
- Distributors
- Sales force
- Advertising agencies
- R & D
- Production
- Suppliers
- Finance
- Governmental agencies

The tasks of a product manager are:
1. Developing a long range and competitive strategy for the product.
2. Preparing an annual marketing plan and forecasting sales.
3. Working with advertising and merchandising agencies to develop copy, programs and campaigns
4. Stimulating interest in, and support of the product among the sales force and distributors.

5. Gathering continuous intelligence on product performance, customer and dealer attitudes, on competitors' moves, new problems and opportunities.

6. Initiating product improvements to meet changing needs.

Advantages

The product management system offers many advantages. Here are some of the important ones:

A. A product manager, because of the concentrated approach to the system facilitates, can balance and harmonize the various functional marketing inputs needed by a product.

B. A product manager is in a position to react quickly to problems in the market place without involving in several different people and lengthy meetings.

C. A product manager can also be alert to spot, identify and capitalize on the opportunities that exist for his product.

D. Smaller brands, which are otherwise neglected in a functional marketing organization, find a *champion* in a product manager who will pursue their cause.

E. Product management is an excellent training ground because it involves the manager in virtually every area of company operations. The product manager is literally the hub of the entire marketing activity.

Management by Persuasion

Product management is basically is management by persuasion. If a product manager needs special output from the sales force and the plant to gear up for a big advertising campaign, he has to sell the idea to people, who report, not to him, but to managers in charge of sales and manufacturing. If his data and instinct tell him that his product needs different packaging, a more focused commercial or a reformulation of ingredients, he must impress upon the appropriate support groups with the importance of paying particular attention to his brand. If a product manager is worried that swings in one of his basic ingredient costs will erode into his profit margin, he might go to the purchase department.

A product manager is responsible for his product's sales and profits. At the same time, he has very little authority and virtually no margin for financial risk. Still product mangers feel just about as entrepreneurial as a young executive could in an established hierarchical organization.

Competitive Edge

The product management system is necessary when:

- A company's product lines need specialized marketing programs, or
- A company markets a number of products, heterogenous in nature, which are thus beyond the capacity of a functional marketing organization. Product management does not replace the functional organization, but servers as another layer of management. Product management provides the much-needed cutting edge in the ever-increasing competition that exists in today's business world.

Product Manager as a Gardener?

A product manager is like a gardener. He owns his garden (is possessive about the garden) and at the same time he does not own it (the garden does not really belong to him and he has no right to the produce). But he sows and plants the seeds (product ideas), cares and nurtures and nourishes them (prepares plans, gets the support of other departments and campaigns for his products) and ensures their proper growth. He is happy when the plants bloom (products become winning brands). He guards them zealously from intruders and trespassers (competitors trying to take a share of his products), takes out the weeds (deletes the products that are on the road to decline and obsolescence) and ensures that his plants are healthy (profitable, that is in sound financial health).

Some Problem Areas

Product management has come to stay, because the advantages and the competitive edge the system offers are many. But product management has its own share of problems. The problems in a product management system are not insurmountable. There are some *areas of conflicts.* These are:

1. **Responsibility for Profits:** The product manager is accountable for profits. Professor George S. Dominvez in his book on *Product*

Management, calls a product manager a *profit manager*. One of the most important functions of the product manager is to ensure an increasing profit volume. The two problems that a product manager faces are:

(a) Reduced gross profit volume because of rising ex-factory costs

(b) Increasing media and promotion costs

The product manager has no control over both these costs and yet he is held responsible for the profits of the products he manages! He, therefore, has to arrive at a balance between the promotion budget he can spend and the sales he can achieve with that input.

2. **Conflicts of Costs:** As far as media and promotion costs are concerned, the product manager has to accept these and find ways of spending the promotion budget most effectively. However, when there are rising ex-factory costs, there is a conflict between product management and production/purchase management, who should be able to control costs by rationalizing production and purchasing at the most economical price.

3. **Implementation of Promotional Plans Through Field Force:** A good promotional plan can become ineffective if the implementation is improper. The product manager is responsible for the plan but, he has to get it implemented through the field force, which is not directly under his control. He, therefore, has to sell the plan to the field force and motivate and persuade them to implement the plan correctly and effectively.

4. **Conflicts with Distribution:** This conflict arises when distribution is centralized in a company handling different product lines like cosmetics and pharmaceuticals. In this case, the cosmetic range would require a wider distribution than pharmaceuticals. if, for some reason the field force does not get along with the product manager, all his promotional plans tend to be ignored. Thus the desired results are not achieved.

Let us take a specific example. A product manager planned to launch a new anti-acne cream in the top 30 towns in the first year and worked out promotional plans and sales estimates accordingly. If the field force in their anxiety to achieve the sales targets, stock up markets outside the 30 specified towns, there would be problems of shortages initially and later on complaints that stocks have not moved from dealers' shelves in those markets where promotion was not planned.

Product management may have an objective of increasing new outlets. It may so happen that distribution, in order to save costs, may set a high minimum order value. This could lead to conflicting objectives. Problems arise where the distribution function is not under the control of the marketing or product management department. Conflict arises because the product management team is anxious to sell, whereas distribution is concerned with having the lowest inventory carrying costs and waiting for the most economical transport, not realizing that the market will take stocks at time when, where and on what terms it wants.

5. **Conflict Between Product Managers:** Product managers have to compete with one another for financial and staff support for their products, even for shelf space at a dealer level. Therefore, in a product management system there could be conflicts. For example, there could be a clash of promotional plan between a product manager handling throat lozenges and another looking after a pain-relieving balm. Both would like to promote their products actively during the winter. There would be a problem of which product would receive more emphasis and which should be promoted first. This is the area where the head of marketing division or the group product manger will have to handle the situation without affecting the effectiveness of either of the product managers.

Yes, conflicts exist in product management. We, therefore, could say that a product manger is not merely a manager of products but a manager of problems and conflicts too. Perhaps, that is why product management is more challenging than most marketing tasks.

Product Management in Indian Pharmaceutical Industry

We have discussed the product management system and its growing importance. We have also discussed briefly the role, tasks and responsibilities of a product manager.

Now let us take a look at the product management system with specific reference to the Indian pharmaceutical industry; how the product management system is practiced in pharmaceutical companies in India and how product managers function, their attitudes towards their job and their aspirations etc.

There seems to be wide gap between the product management system practiced in the western world and in India, particularly in the pharmaceutical industry. Product managers in companies engaged in marketing consumer products and industrial products in India seem to be better off in terms of responsibility and support from the top management.

A study conducted among 50 product managers and product executives in the pharmaceutical industry in India (there is virtually no difference between product managers and product executives and these designations are given differently in different companies) makes the following observations:

- The product management system in the FMCG (fast moving consumer goods) companies was significantly different as they have been practicing product management as it was intended to. The same was not true in case of pharmaceutical companies in India till 1990s.

- Some large pharmaceutical companies in India used to home-grow their own brand of product mangers in the 1970s. They used to select the product managers from area sales managers and give a two or three-day orientation program internally. Some companies also followed the policy of job rotation between product managers and area sales manages every two or three years. But of late, the trend in pharmaceutical companies, particularly the young ones, is to recruit graduates or post graduates in pharmacy with diploma in business management with one or two years experience. This practice of recruiting qualified pharmacists or biochemistry postgraduates with management diplomas is increasing as more and more complex products requiring thorough scientific knowledge are being introduced. The changing complexity of product mix is making this change in recruitment practice a necessity.

- In many pharmaceutical companies, product managers are not given the specific responsibility for their products' sales and profits.

Many companies were not used to sharing the cost data even with their product managers as it is considered sensitive. This practice is however gradually changing.

- Product managers did not have much say in the annual marketing plans for their products in the real sense. Their participation in this area was moderate and restricted to do the basic tasks such as working out the preliminary details.

- There was no systematic appraisal or evaluation of product managers in many companies in India.

- A number of product managers due to lack of exposure to cost data did not seem to have the big picture of profitability. The following case gives a broad picture of how product management was being practiced in the late 1980s.

Case 3.23   The Plight of a Profit Manager!

Some time ago in 1988, a special training program on product management in pharmaceutical product management was conducted in the prestigious Administrative Staff College of India (ASCI) at Hyderabad. Some of the giants of the Indian pharmaceutical industry had sponsored their product mangers for the program. When it came to discussing the product policy and strategy alternatives, there was a sudden silence. Fictitious cost-data (for doing simulation exercises) was provided to the participants for analysis and presentation during a case study. Many a product manger drew a blank. It was for the first time that they were exposed to any cost data, fictitious or otherwise. This explains the plight of the profit managers in Indian pharmaceutical industry!

The study also points out to what product managers in the Indian pharmaceutical industry were doing mostly. Here are some of the more important tasks that pharmaceutical product managers mostly do:

1. Preparing *detailing stories* (communication) creating the product visual aids for their products

2. Preparing sampling strategy - broad guidelines to field force on what products to be sampled and in what quantities and to which doctors

3. Field work with representatives and independently to find out the movement of their products as well as competitors' products in the market place and to monitor the levels of implementation of their strategies and their impact

4. Analyzing the ORG (Operations Research Group) retail store audit (PharmaTrac AWACS or IMS data now) and prescription data from CMARC or IMS for their products and competitors' products and presenting to the management and field force every month

5. Analyzing the internal sales of the company, product-wise, region-wise and presenting it to the head of the marketing department and to respective sales managers

6. Briefing the sales force on promotional strategies at briefing sessions or cycle meetings

7. Follow-up with suppliers of gifts and other sales promotional materials

This trend however, seems to be changing with increasing competitive intensity and the role of pharmaceutical product management expanding gradually. Product managers are also involved in designing stalls or booths and in-stall activities at medical conferences and CME (Continuing Medical Education Programs). They are also involved in preparing speaker notes for key opinion leaders (KOLs) who conduct product symposia on behalf of the company at the programs sponsored by the company.

Making Product Management More Effective

Effective product management is crucial for a company's success in the market place. How to make the product mangers more effective? by giving them the responsibility, building accountability in to their jobs and by giving it due importance both in words and deeds. These approaches may seem to be simple, but the implementation often is not.

Often there is a conflict between the line and staff functions. Which is more important? It is as mindless a question as which vital organ of the body is more vital? The heart? The brain? The kidneys?

When you build a well-knit team of sales mangers and product managers who understand and appreciate their mutually supportive and reinforcing roles, you are in fact, and in effect building up a winning team that is formidable. You are enhancing the distinctive competence of your company. Here is a case of one company that found a rather unique way of nurturing and building an effective product management team.

Case 3.24   Unique Brand of Brand Managers!

A medium sized pharmaceutical company a few years ago was faced with a conflicting situation wherein divisional sales managers and product managers were up-in arms against each other. While apparently the relationships with each other were smooth, they were limited to civic courtesies. The divisional managers felt that the product managers were having a jolly good time, without any responsibility (for sales) while they (the divisional managers) were sweating out on the field.

The product managers on the other hand felt that they had been brought from the field to head office (they were field managers, that is front-line managers earlier, before they were promoted as product managers) and were given a raw deal. They were not clear about their position in the organizational hierarchy and had not advanced or progressed in their careers as they had envisaged. There was growing dissatisfaction, since they were also suspicious that the divisional managers were getting a better remuneration package and incentives on achieving sales targets. No divisional or field manager was willing to join the product management team.

The company realizing this, albeit belatedly, reacted positively. The company had clarified that the divisional managers and product mangers were and would continue to be at the same level on the organization ladder, though their functional responsibilities were different. It had also standardized their remuneration and clearly defined the job descriptions. The attributes or qualities that the company had been looking for in product managers ever since were:

A. Technical knowledge

B. Communication skills - written as well as verbal

C. Creativity

D. Inter-personal communication skills

E. Perseverance

F. Enthusiasm

G. Analytical ability

The company launched an ambitious program of building up a top team of product managers that would be a model to and envy of the industry. To communicate that the divisional managers and product managers are at the same level and are equally important, the company introduced a job rotation program between product managers and divisional managers. Such a job rotation program would lead to personal as well as organizational development. It would also develop a core team of product managers and divisional managers. They would have a better understanding, a better insight and a broader perspective of formulating and implementing marketing strategies. The quality of strategy formulation and implementation would greatly improve.

The result would be an elite regiment of *esprit de corps*, which is built on the bedrock of mutual respect based on each others' competence. This had been the logic on which the structural changes were based. The company, while sticking to its promotion from *with-in* policy in all functional areas, had recruited a few product mangers, who were technically qualified with excellent scholastic records to strengthen and fill the void of training its field force in product knowledge and also to remain ahead of competition in strategy formulation. The company was planning to enter into new therapeutic categories and wanted to improve its knowledge base.

Superior technical knowledge and information were essential in these new segments.

Furthermore, the company had given field sales assignments to its newly recruited product managers to gain perspective and insight into the dynamics of pharmaceutical selling and to get the much-needed 'hands-on' experience. The company had thus planned meticulously a blend of product managers with selling skills (promoted from within) and product managers with superior technical knowledge (recruited from the universities).

In addition, the company had planned out to the minutest detail - a one-year curriculum, which included reading assignments, marketing research assignments, field work assignments, weekly class room discussions and case study presentations. After successful completion of one year's learning while earning (on the job) the product managers would be presented a *Post Graduate Diploma in Pharmaceutical Product Management* ceremoniously. While this is not a university or any institute-recognized certificate or degree, the perceived value of this diploma would certainly not be inferior to those in any manner. The company had really planned an effective way of developing its own successful brand of brand managers and above all to retain them, which is even more difficult!

The Package

The package is perhaps the most important component of communication about your product. That is why package or pack is called *the silent salesman* of a product. A pack can make or break a producer in the self-service market. Packaging is very important, in fact, crucial for products , which are brought mainly an impulse. Like in cosmetics, well-designed successful pack has got the power of grabbing the consumer at the store. Research clearly indicates that on a number of occasions people prefer one brand over another on package alone. What constitutes a successful package? The one that appeals to both the conscious mind and the sub-conscious (or even unconscious) mind of the consumer. The package that appeals to the consumer's mind at these two levels, communicates to the consumer that this the product you have been looking for. It almost whispers to him, '*Come, I am here, buy me.*' This is because, while the conscious mind recognizes the product, the unconscious mind is motivated by the package.

This may be applicable only to consumer products but is it applicable to pharmaceutical products and more specifically the prescription drugs?

The *grabbing power* of successful package may not be as relevant to prescription drugs as it is to consumer products and products in high impulse buying. Nevertheless, the psychological cues that can reinforce the product's image (in case of existing products) or their ability to create a positive image (for new products) cannot be undermined. Research tells us even the products which require personal selling must be packaged in way to reinforce the sales representatives' claims and to induce trial (by customers and facilitate re-purchase or repeat prescriptions) once they are satisfied with the product.

The package should be capable of communicating quality, economy, prestige, relief etc. Of course, the product must live up to its expectations and deliver what the package promises.

These are all the information cues, which the consumer is looking for in a product. More often than not, the tendency of the consumer is to equate these information cues such as the package with the product itself; we all know that beauty is skin deep but we still prefer beautiful people. The liking or preference will be further reinforced if this physical attribute or characteristic is matched with an equally agile mind and an empathic heart. Likewise if an effective product is packaged in an imaginative manner, that makes it a winning combination for sure.

Major Components

Color, design, shape, size, brand name, materials, labels and typography are the components of the packaging communication process. Each of these components must interact harmoniously and synchronize to evoke the desired responses in the consumer. It is important to note that people react to the whole and not to the individual components. Proper synchronization of all the components in the packaging communication process transfers the meaning intended by the marketer subliminally.

Color communicates very strongly. The symbolic meanings of color and the effects and associations of color on moods and personalities of people are well known to psychologists and advertisers alike. Advertisers utilize these learned responses to colors, to communicate meanings to buyers. Factors that influence color are:

- **Education and Income:** There seems to be a strong correlation between higher education and income levels and preference towards delicate colors. No wonder the famous designer Shyam Ahuja's most expensive furnishings are always in delicate colors and pastel shades. They are advertised in the specialty magazines targeted at the elite of the society. Conversely, the illiterate, less educated and the impoverished seem to prefer brilliant colors.

- **Color:** Race seems to affect color preference. Black, red and golden colors are very popular in the Orient. It is generally believed that warm colors like red, brown, and yellow are very popular where there is abundant sunlight and cooler, softer colors like blue and green are preferred where there is less sunlight.
- **Age:** The color preference seems to change with age too. Babies for example prefer bright colors like red and yellow. Older children prefer red or blue and as they mature their color preference seem to change to softer tones of greens and blues.
- **Personality:** Color choice is affected by the personality of the individual. It appears that athletic people prefer red, intellectuals blue. Extroverts seem to prefer red and brown and the introvert's choice is towards blue.

Color: Ten Commandments for Its Utilization

The use of color in appealing to different emotions and evoking desirable moods is too large a field of study to discuss here. However, here are the ten commandments of effective utilization of color:

1. Use a color scheme that will attract attention. Your product should stand out in a crowd of 'me-too' products.
2. Communicate forcefully the special features of your product through effective use of color.
3. Keep the indications, dosage and instructions for usage of the product in a color that contrasts with other colors in the package.
4. Use as little copy as possible on the pack. In the pharmaceutical industry the copy is usually long and it is mandatory to give all the details (even the type-size is specified in the drug laws). You can however, keep the font and back panels free from clutter to maximize the visual impact.
5. Mention the price and batch number, date of manufacture and date of expiry clearly.
6. Use warm, bright colors on pediatric products.
7. Use pictures appropriately.
8. Build your pack around the *house colors* of your company for

immediate identification of the family brand of related products (in the same therapeutic category).

9. Use a distinct and striking color for the brand name.

10. Pretest your package.

Design

Designing is another important component of your packaging. A good design should permit a good eye-flow and movement to facilitate a point of focus. It should guide the consumer along the pre-determined path, which highlights the salient features of the product.

The length, thickness and the slope of lines on a pack evoke different reactions and responses. For example, horizontal lines suggest restfulness and evoke feelings of tranquility. This is because people move their eyes horizontally with effortless ease and the vertical movement of the eyes is less natural and produce greater strain in the eye muscles. The vertical lines, therefore, evoke feelings of strength and confidence. The slanted lines suggest upward movements to most people. Glaxo, the leader of the Indian pharmaceutical industry had changed its logo to slanted, thick lines in the late 1970s. Is it a mere coincidence that the company started its rapid and steep climb to the top position in the industry ever since? Or did it communicate its determination towards upward movement and its ravenous appetite for growth, when it changed its logo to slanted thick lines? This association of the upward movement with slanted lines is based on the fact that people in the western world read left to right and thus view the line as ascending rather than descending.

Brand name perhaps is the single most important component of a product pack. It must be treated as such. The design, the color, the visual, the typeface and size must be related to the theme of the brand name and create synergy. Even though the generic name should be set in type size that is twice as large as that of the brand name in the case of pharmaceutical products in India containing a single ingredient, creative use of color and the choice of a typeface can enhance the emphasis on the brand name.

Materials used for packaging are very important as they determine the cost of packaging, which is part of the total cost of the product. The increase in cost of packaging may be offset by a substantial increase in sales due to the attention grabbing power of a successful package in the case of products purchased on high impulse. But in case of pharmaceutical products the use of package is limited only to the mere functional aspects of packaging. The functional aspects of a package essentially are:

(a) To protect the product and its contents

(b) To provide information about the product, its composition, indications, contra-indications, dosage, storage conditions, manufacturer's name and address, drug license number, dates of manufacture and expiry etc.

(c) To provide the product a distinct identity by prominently displaying the brand name

There are two reasons why superior and better quality or premium packaging materials are not used in pharmaceutical packaging in India. They are:

(a) The pharmaceutical industry is a highly regulated industry where the government not only fixes the prices for products falling under controlled categories but also fixes the conversion norms for manufacturing and packaging. There is a limit fixed on your input costs and you cannot afford to exceed them. The paradox is that while packaging and conversion norms are fixed for pharmaceutical products, there is no control on the prices of packaging materials and other items, which are constantly increasing.

(b) The consumer (the patient) does not buy the prescription drug brands on impulse. He buys what his doctor prescribes. Packaging, therefore, has a limited role that is purely functional.

That said, it does not mean that pharmaceutical products can be packed in any manner. The importance of the quality connotation cannot be overlooked in one's anxiety to cut costs. A quality packaging reinforces strongly the efforts of the sales force of a company.

Most pharmaceutical companies discontinued the outer cartons for their bottle packs, when their profits began to erode after the 1969 Drug Price Control Order (DPCO). Removal of package inserts was the next step these companies undertook. The first cost-saving step was taken in the area of packaging when the axe of price control fell on the pharmaceutical industry. The other important steps like rationalization of product-mix, improving the efficiency of operations were quickly adopted by some of the more agile companies whose survival instincts were high.

All these point to one thing. What is crucial in packaging pharmaceutical products is imagination, creativity and utility in the total design rather than using expensive or fancy packaging material. Cost-effective packaging is vital.

Packaging Pharmaceutical Products

There are some important points to be considered while packaging pharmaceutical products. Since pharmaceutical products are concerned with the health of people, safety is the first and foremost factor to be considered. Stability of the the product is another. For example, the colors used for oral solid dosage forms like tablets and capsules and the colors for printing the brand name and the company logo should be from the colors approved by the Food And Drug Administration (FDA). The choice of packing materials like glass bottles, plastic and metal containers also depends on the stability and compatibility of the product with the packaging material. There should not be any interaction of the drug with the packing material resulting in any chemical degradation or deterioration. A check list of all important aspects to be considered while designing pharmaceutical packages is given in Table 3.7.

Table 3.7 Packaging a Pharmaceutical Product

A Checklist
1. Whether the brand name is registered?
2. Whether FDA and DCI have approved the materials chosen?
3. Whether it is mandatory to mention any warning on the pack?
4. Whether your label claim can be substantiated?
5. Whether your label claims comply with the Drugs and Cosmetics Act., and Magic Remedies and Objectionable Advertisements Act?
6. Whether you have set the generic name in a type-size that is twice as large as your brand name (in case of single ingredient formulations) and positioned it exactly above the brand name on the pack?
7. Have you included all the important details on the pack like: • Composition   • Drug license   • Manufacturing license   • Schedule according to drug laws   • Dates of manufacture and expiry   • Manufacturer's address   • Indications

- Dosage
- Batch number
- Price
- Storage conditions
- Instructions for usage
8. Whether the color coding is according to the specifications i.e., different colors for drugs under different schedules?
9. In case of physicians' samples it is necessary you mention clearly that it is 'physicians' sample - not to be smold'

The list can go on endlessly. It is important to remember that safety is of utmost importance and that safety comes first, above everything else, in the manufacturing and marketing of pharmaceutical products.

It is true that the consumers do not buy pharmaceutical products on impulse. The doctors (customers), who are the influencers, recommend and prescribe the products to their patients. The packaging norms for a number of products are fixed by the government (DPCO 1987). You have no flexibility there, since extra cost in packaging those products would erode into your margins. Even for the so-called de-controlled products, you cannot fix any price you want, as the highly competitive market place determines the price. You cannot, therefore, have an expensive, glorified packs for your products. Does that mean designing an attractive pack that stands out on the shelf need not be very expensive? What is needed is creative and imaginative designing that reinforces the efforts of product differentiation and the persuasive efforts of your sales force.

An effective, successful packaging that communicates quality and reinforces the superior product image need not necessarily be very expensive. What you should aim at is synergy and synchrony of the basic product idea and the promotional theme. While there should not be any difference in the basic pack of your product, a special gift pack of physician's sample that reinforces your product's promotional themes is bound to enhance the memorability and recall value of your brand by the people who matter in choosing your brand.

Another important aspect of successful packaging is that you should not view packaging as a cost saving means. You should not compromise on the specifications of the paper or labels, the gum for labeling, the paper board to be used for cartons, shippers, the gum tape and the strapping material etc. Fundamental as it may seem, there have been many manufacturers who have aimed at a meager cost savings in these areas and have paid dearly as the incidence of breakages in case of bottle packs, increases considerably. There is an even greater damage, which is the most expensive of all. The perceived quality of the faulty or sub-optimal packaging has been extended even to the product quality. Such a shortsighted approach can cause irreparable damage if unchecked. Even the confidence of the sales force can get adversely affected. In the final analysis, you will observe that successful, quality packaging need not be an expensive proposition. In fact, quality is free!

Safety First

Pharmaceutical products being what they are - dealing with the health and healing of people, are subjected to rigid controls and stringent regulations. Safety is of paramount importance. A product even if it is a major earner for a company or a product group that is growing rapidly, if considered unsafe may have to be withdrawn. If the government decides that the product or category itself is not safe enough, or is irrational, it may ban the use of the product or product category as the case may be.

Pharmaceutical marketers therefore, should monitor closely the changing trends of products and the lines of therapy not merely in domestic market, but on a global level. The pharmaceutical companies in developed countries closely monitor their products in terms of safety and efficacy.

This is known as the post marketing surveillance. It is important to monitor global trends because they have profound influence on the Indian pharmaceutical market. Consider the following examples.

- The Government of India banned the high-dose estrogen progesterone combinations, as they are considered unsafe and irrational.

- Combinations of analgesics and anti-inflammatory drugs with tranquilizers like diazepam are banned.

- The use of oxyphenbutazone and phenylbutazone preparations is restricted to severe inflammatory and arthritic conditions as a result of some severe side effects reported in a few European studies.

- Hindusthan Ciba Geigy withdrew its Mexaform tablets, an anti-diarrheal with sizable market share since its parent company, the Swiss giant (Ciba withdrew its diidohydroxyquinoline, which is the active ingredient in Mexaform) withdrew its products from all other countries.

- The use of Aspirin containing products is banned for pediatric usage since it is reported to cause Reye syndrome in a few cases according to some international studies.

Summary

While a Product is the most visible and tangible expression of any business endeavor, there are many intangible aspects to a branded product, which are equally important. Professor Theodore Levitt best states the intangible aspects of a branded product when he said, " *a branded product is a transaction between the seller and buyer.*" Customer perception is more important. In fact that is at the core of the branding strategy.

Decisions relating to a product policy and strategy are indeed very crucial for the success of any firm. This becomes even more important in a highly competitive market place like the Indian pharmaceutical industry with over 100,000 brands and about 10,000 companies engaged in a race to gain market share, and accelerate their growth.

In such a 'me-too' market place, the rules of the game are changed and the name of the game to be precise is product differentiation. How does one achieve that? The creation of differentiation should run through all the elements of the marketing mix like the product itself, price, promotion, place and personal selling. It is important to achieve the much-needed *synergy* and *stand out* distinctly on the chemists' shelves and in the minds of the prescribing doctors.

Clear product positioning helps you to achieve this. By studying the strategies behind some highly successful brands and by understanding the reasons why so many brands literally died a premature death on the retailers' shelves, one can formulate some ground rules for effective product positioning.

A number of analytical and planning tools like product and market life cycle concepts, product portfolio analysis etc. would be helpful to the marketer in drawing up successful strategies for developing winning brands. The insights that these concepts give are truly invaluable.

Product management seems to have come of age in India since Proctor & Gamble in the USA introduced this concept for the first time nearly ninety-years ago.

Effective product management can be of immense help in managing existing brands, nurturing new products and developing them into successful brands.

Whatever product policy and strategy decisions you may take, irrespective of the structure of your organization the maxim for success is that you manage your existing products (today's profit earners) effectively. This is not only necessary for growth but also vital even for survival.

The Price

Controls! More Controls!! Still More Controls!!!

That seems to be the only way to describe the *pricing scenario* of the Indian pharmaceutical industry.

Price is no longer a significant decision variable for the pharmaceutical marketer. There is very little choice or elbowroom for him to maneuver and formulate a meaningful pricing strategy, because, prices of all essential and important bulk drugs and formulations are fixed by the government. At the same time, neither the manufacturer nor the government seems to have any control over the input costs. They continue to skyrocket. To make matters worse, there is a ceiling on the profits. That is the price one has to pay for achieving efficiency of operations. Stifling controls on prices on the one hand, spiraling increase of input costs, almost never-ending and ever-increasing demands of trade regarding their margins on the other hand continue to tighten the noose around the neck of the industry. The result is predictable of course and that is constant erosion of profitability.

Price, simply stated, is the exchange value of a product or service. Price setting is very difficult for any product or service. It involves both objective and subjective components. Objective factors include demand, supply, costs, competition, governmental regulations etc., subjective factors involve the evaluation of the likely impact of other elements of the marketing mix and their possible responses to various pricing strategies. What makes price setting a particularly difficult task is the fact that it attempts to set monetary value upon the consumers' perceptions and the *bundle of benefits* that the product offers.

The pharmaceutical industry is highly regulated. The government controls the prices of a number of bulk drugs and formulations. There is very little for the pharmaceutical marketer in India to decide in so far as pricing is concerned. It is no exaggeration that pricing is longer an important element, strategically speaking of the marketing mix in the pharmaceutical industry. This is because, there is a ceiling price fixed for as many as 162 bulk drugs and 585 formulations. The only choice available for a pharmaceutical marketer is whether he can manufacture and market profitably within those prices fixed by the government or not. Even the conversion norms and packaging norms are fixed for the formulations.

The pricing of remaining formulations, which are treated as non-essential (and therefore as decontrolled category) is naturally governed by competitive pressures. It is a typical *between-the-devil-and-the-sea choice* that exists in the most crucial element of the marketing mix, namely the price.

History of Price Control

Since government regulation largely influences *pricing*, a historical overview of the Drug Price Control Order (DPCO) will provide the necessary insights into the extent of controls and the degree of freedom or maneuverability that is available for the pharmaceutical marketer in getting the price for his product. This understanding is essential before we discuss pricing objectives and strategies in detail.

The history of drug price controls can be traced back to fifty-five years. Here is a brief overview of drug price control, from its origin to the present and its impact on the industry.

1962

The year of the Chinese aggression and the consequent declaration of emergency was also the year of the first ever regulatory and control measures taken by the government on drug prices. The Drugs (Display of Prices) order was promulgated in 1962, under the Defense of India Act. This first-ever order regarding drug prices required the industry to publish prices of drugs and the trade to display them.

1963

Subsequently, in 1963, the Drugs (Control of Prices) Order was also promulgated under the Defense of India Act. This second order on drug prices froze prices at the levels prevailing on 1st April 1963.

The 1963 Drug Price Control Order had an understandable but undesirable result: the disappearance of voluntary price reduction. Voluntary price reductions were a regular practice before the price control order. This can be observed from the following facts:

- Between 1956 and 1963, the prices of antibiotics were reduced by 50 per cent.
- During the same period the prices of anti tubercular drugs had fallen by 67 per cent.
- A price reduction of similar magnitude was also recorded in other therapeutic categories such as antihistamines, vitamins and anti-diabetic drugs.

Sounds unbelievable? Well, that was the practice of voluntary price reduction before drug prices were frozen on 1st April 1963. This kind of reduction was possible due to increased production, economies of scale and competitive pressures.

1966

What emerged as an emergency measure continued even after the emergency and was perpetuated in 1966 as a permanent feature under the Essential Commodities Act. After the Drug Prices (Display and Control) order was promulgated in 1966. It became obligatory for manufacturers to obtain prior government approval for increasing the prices of all formulations in their product range as of 30th June 1966. Items with pharmacopeial name and new drugs, which had been developed as a result of original research, were later exempted from price approval by an amendment. But the government could revise the prices at any time. Thus the exemption of these two categories were related only to the approval of prices and not to the controls.

The machinery set up to control drug prices under the 1966 order was hardly adequate to implement the revision of prices for existing products and the approval of new product prices. As a result there was an enormous delay of anywhere between 12 and 18 months in obtaining price approvals. Another lacuna in the Drug Price Control Order was that there was no control on the input prices while the prices of finished drugs were controlled. The government, in 1966, following the industry's representation asked the Tariff Commission to study the cost structure of 18 essential bulk drugs and their formulations and recommend reasonable, realistic and fair prices accordingly.

Meanwhile, the Development Council for Drugs and Pharmaceuticals evolved some guidelines to be followed in scrutinizing and fixing drug prices. The Council recommended a mark up price of 150 to 200 percent over the ex-factory cost. This was necessary to speed up the process of scrutinizing the ever-increasing piles of applications for price revision. The government, however, continued to operate at the lower figure of 150 percent and to limit the increase in prices to unavoidable increases like in the costs of raw materials and packing materials. The other increases in costs had to be absorbed by the industry. This resulted in constant and almost never-ending erosion into the profitability of many a company.

1968

In August 1968, the Commission submitted its report to the government. The study covered 453 units manufacturing one or more of the 18 specified bulk drugs and their formulations. In the final analysis only 34 units were selected for detailed costing.

The Tariff Commission made as many as 43 recommendations and conclusions including suggestions regarding fair selling prices for 18 specified bulk drugs and their formulations. Significant among these were two broad conclusions:

- The prices of selected bulk drugs were generally much lower in most cases in other countries

- The prices of formulations in the Indian market compared favorably with prevailing prices of similar formulations in other countries.

The major factors responsible for the high prices of bulk drugs in India as compared to developed countries according to the Tariff Commission were:
1. The high cost of equipment, intermediaries and raw materials, a major part of which was imported.
2. The small size of capacities or fragmentation of capacities.

1970

The Tariff Commission's report, together with the government's decisions thereon, was placed in Parliament on 30th April 1970. The Drugs (Price Control) Order 1970 was promulgated on 16th May 1970. The objectives of the order as described by the government were:

- To bring down the prices of drugs
- To place a ceiling on the profits of manufacturers
- To fix the prices of drugs on the basis of a rational formula that can be applied uniformly to all formulations and products, and
- To provide adequate incentives to the industry to continue the growth from the basic stage, develop R&D facilities and provide more employment

The formula suggested for pricing formulations based on the 18 selected bulk drugs (identified for the purpose of a detailed study by the Tariff Commission) as well as all other formulations, is given in Table 4.1.

Furthermore, the government was specific regarding the mark-ups that were permissible. The details are given in table 4.2.

Alternatively, the companies could price their formulations independently in such a way that the total return before tax does not exceed 15 percent of the sales turnover. It is however, mandatory that the companies seek prior approval for their proposed enhanced prices from the government.

In case the return on sales exceeds 15 per cent, the excess cannot be distributed as dividends. This can be utilized with prior approval of the government for purposes of Research & development.

Table 4.1 Formula for Pricing as Per DPCO 1970

RP = (MC + CC) = PC) x (1 + MU /100), where

RP = Suggested retail price

MC = The cost of materials, including basic drugs and pharmaceuticals

CC = The cost of conversion or the cost of formulation

PC = The packing charges, includes the cost of packing materials and packing expenses

MU = The 'mark-up is meant to cover the cost of packing materials and packaging expenses, promotional expenses, after sales services if any, and trade commissions if any

Table 4.2 Mark-ups Permissible Under DPCO 1970

Type of Products	Per cent
1. Ongoing and old products	75
2. New products, but not original (not developed through extensive R & D work)	100 (for the first 3 to 5 years)
3. New products, original (developed through extensive R & D work)	150

The DPCO 1970 also specified the commissions payable to retailers. A provision was made in the 1970 Order to the effect that, in case of ethical (prescription) drugs, the retailers should be entitled to commission at the minimum rate of 12 percent and in case of non-ethical drugs, at the minimum of 10 percent.

To protect the weaker sections of the industry the 1970 Order made some provisions. Under these, manufacturing units with an annual sales turnover of Rs 5-lakh were exempted from price controls. This limit was later raised to Rs. 50-lakh.

DPCO 1970 and Industry's Reaction

The industry's growth rate, which had been 15 percent per annum hitherto, was expected to continue as per the Planning Commission's estimates. OPPI (Organization of Pharmaceutical Producers of India) commented on DPCO 1970 that, the 15 percent profit on turnover would hardly permit a growth rate of 15 per cent. Even the pre-tax profit was an illusory figure in the context of mark-ups allowed on essential drugs.

Furthermore, OPPI was apprehensive that the Order of 1970 would very likely cause a further setback in the growth and development of this industry and this would in turn have an adverse affect on the creation of job opportunities.

The pharmaceutical industry had no option but to reconcile itself to the new position and think in terms of lower margins on a higher turnover, rather than in terms of higher margins on a low turnover.

The *Economic and Political Weekly* commented aptly on the 1970 Order as *Partial solutions*:

The undesirable but understandable consequence of the 1970 Order will be the change in the industry's product pattern as producers moved to drugs with higher mark-ups and higher profit opportunities. This may mean a move away from essential to non-essential drugs...something, which had been happening anyway.

The 1970 Order allowed manufacturers to recalculate the prices of all formulations and to submit the revised prices of all formulations to the government for approval within the time limit prescribed. The government had to accord approval with or without modifications, within the prescribed time limit. If the government approvals were not given within the prescribed time limit, the prices as calculated by the manufacturers stood automatically approved. All that the manufacturers were required to do was simply to issue the approved price list in the prescribed form showing the prices to the consumers. This, understandably enough, resulted in price increases, as the government machinery was inadequate to process the numerous applications for price revision from various manufacturers. The government therefore, acting on second thoughts amended the Act and froze all prices at the levels prevailing on 16th May 1970, thus invalidating all subsequent price increases pending scrutiny and approval. The government, however, laid down a time limit for scrutiny - 31 December 1970.

In addition, the Ministry of Petroleum and Chemicals set up Drug Prices Review Cell to examine quickly the cost structure of 11,372 packs submitted by manufacturers. As a result of this exercise, prices of about 45 percent of the formulations were reduced, 36 percent were kept at the earlier level and increases were granted only in respect of 11.5 percent of finished formulations. According to the estimates of the Ministry, this exercise benefited the patient community to the extent of Rs. 20-crore by way of price reduction in a total turnover of about Rs. 200-crore in 1970.

Furthermore, the Ministry of Petroleum and Chemicals constituted a working group, headed by the Chairman of the Bureau of Industrial Costs and Prices (BICP) to examine the cost structure of 24 bulk drugs (other than the 18 bulk drugs studied by the Tariff Commission) and their formulations. The group also developed norms for their conversion, packing charges and different packs of these formulations.

1971

While the 1970 Order allowed the manufacturers to revise the prices if they did not receive the approval from the government within the stipulated period, the amendment Order of 1971 made it mandatory for the manufacturers to obtain prior approval for price increases. The 1971 amendment Order also stipulated that prior approval of government should be obtained for the selling prices of all new formulations and new packs of existing formulations. The amendment also vested in the government the power to revise the price of any formulation.

Industry's Response to the DPCO

While the industry was not happy about the DPCO 1970, its response nevertheless was positive to the 1971 amendment. Some of the innovative and aggressive companies made the necessary changes in their structure and operations to blunt or to minimize the onslaught of the DPCO. In 1972, an interesting study was conducted by Rajeswara Rao and Sushila Rao (Faculty members in Marketing Area) of the Administrative Staff College of India (ASCI), Hyderabad at the suggestion of Hyderabad Marketing Association, on the impact of the 1970 DPCO on the industry and the likely response of the industry towards these controls. The study was based on responses to a structured questionnaire from all the affected parties namely, executives, sales force, wholesalers and retailers. The study also made a predictive analysis regarding the likely courses of action that the industry might adopt and the structural adjustments that might be followed.

Their observations and predictions can broadly be classified into four areas:

A. **Cost-effectiveness:** Emphasis clearly would be on improving the cost-effectiveness, particularly in areas like packaging, product literature and personal selling efforts. Cartons and package inserts would be deleted wherever possible. Product literature would be restricted to new introductions and relatively inexpensive *leave-behind literature* would be used for existing products and in the area of personal selling more economic routing and transportation for curtailing traveling expenditure etc. would be more rigorously pursued.

B. **Rationalization:** The product-mix decisions would be rationalized rather ruthlessly. Profitable product-mix would be the operative phrase. The rationalization process would be extended even to the sales territory decisions. Which markets are to be covered and which to be deleted? What should be the minimum return from each market, for each working day and for each customer call?

C. **Optimization:** Optimizing the effectiveness in all areas of operation would be pursued with new vigor. That would be the deciding factor for survival and growth. The optimizing measures would include:
  - Attempt to improve the yield
  - Improving the economies of scale
  - Better inventory control of raw materials, packaging
  - Effective management of receivables
  - Concentrating on important customers (major prescribers) by increasing the call frequency

D. **Diversification:**The drug companies would be pursuing two main areas of diversification:
  - Introducing new products with modification or differentiation
  - Diversifying into related areas like OTC (over-the counter) formulations and Animal Health Products etc.

The consultants very rightly (in retrospect) predicted that the overall efficiency and effectiveness of the industry would be improved as a result of the DPCO. Those companies, which make the necessary structural adjustments would be the ones to succeed.

1973

During the latter part of 1973, the prices of petrochemical based materials increased considerably consequent to the oil price hike by OPEC (Organization of Petroleum Exporting Countries). Since these formed a significant proportion of pharmaceutical raw materials, this resulted in a further escalation of manufacturing cost. There was a general decline in the ratio of profitability on sales from about 15.5 percent in 1969-70 (pre-DPCO year) to about 8.4 percent in 1972-73. These findings were based on a study of profitability ratios conducted by NCAER (National Council for Applied Economic Research) on sales pertaining to 58 firms. Following representation by the industry, the government advised the BICP (Bureau of Industrial Costs and Prices) to develop a set of interim guidelines for price revision in consultation with the associations of the industry. A more detailed investigation into the pricing, the cost structure and the profitability ratio were to follow.

1974

The Hathi committee was constituted in 1974 to study the problems of pricing in detail. Prominent among the findings and recommendations of the Hathi Committee were:

- There was a decline in the profitability ratios of many companies after the 1970 DPCO.
- Non-pharmaceutical activity accounted for a significant part of the total turnover in the case of many larger companies in the years preceding the DPCO year of 1970. In fact, non-pharmaceutical products accounted for as much as 25 percent of the total sales of 25 companies, which in turn accounted for about 45 percent of the industry's total sales.
- While the operation of price control contained the profitability of companies, it did not seem to have contributed towards achieving social needs or national objectives as envisaged.
- It was desirable to exempt from price control items in which there were no imported elements and where the total sale of the bulk drug did not exceed Rs. 25-lakh.
- Fair prices should be determined for important formulations on the basis of an investigation into the costs of production of two or three leading manufacturers accounting for 60 percent or more of the total sales of the particular product. There would be no mark-up on the costs of these manufacturers. Instead, all costs including selling expenses, trade commission and freight would be taken into account. In addition, a return on sales ranging from 8 percent to 13 percent (depending on the size of the units and whether they are engaged in basic manufacture and R&D) would be allowed in arriving at a fair selling price. This system evolved as a leader price, later in the 1979 DPCO.
- The committee also observed that the average investment per year had taken a nose-dive in the decade of price controls, from Rs. 19.1-crore in 1963 to Rs. 0.87-crore in 1973.

1978

The Hathi Committee submitted its report to the government in 1978. The pricing policy statement of the 29th March 1978 took into account the government's decisions based on the Hathi Committee's findings and recommendations.

1979

Hathi Committee's recommendations resulted in DPCO 1979. It became operative from 4th April 1979 and replaced the earlier DPCO 1970. Here are the salient features of the 1979 DPCO.

- Grouping of bulk drugs coming under the purview of price controls into three categories. The return to be allowed was fixed at 14 percent post-tax on net worth for bulk drugs used in the production of category I and Category II formulations and 12 percent on net worth on other bulk drugs.

- The new bulk drugs, which have been developed through original R&D in India not to be in the purview of price control of five years.

- The provision to fix a retention price for individual manufacturers and a common sale price based on the weighted average of the retention price of bulk drugs allowed for individual manufacturers. In other words, different prices (retention prices) are allowed to different manufacturers, based on their cost structures and efficiency of operations, for the same bulk drug.

- Creation of the Drug Price Equalization Account, which will be maintained by the government. Under this provision, a manufacturer who can produce a bulk drug more efficiently and cost effectively is required to credit the difference in amount (difference between the pooled price or the common sale price and his retention price) to the Drug Price Equalization Account (DPEA). This amount would be utilized to pay the manufacturer or the importer towards the shortfall of the pooled price or the common sale price and his retention price, and to cover the expenses of the government incurred in discharging this function.

- Introduction of leader prices. The 1979 DPCO empowers the government to fix the *leader prices* for formulations in Categories I,II and III. These leader prices would be based on the costs of an efficient manufacturer. All those manufacturers, whose prices are above the leader prices are required to bring them down to that level.

The government may notify leader prices at any time it chooses to, for all single ingredient and standard formulations, according to the 1979 DPCO.

Like DPCO 1970, DPCO 1979 too had laid down a formula for calculating retail price of a formulation. The formula had two components I.e., (a) ex-factory cost and (b) mark-up. Ex-factory cost includes the cost of raw materials, packing materials and conversion charges. Certain norms were defined for the purpose of calculating conversion cost and packaging charges.

Mark-up, the second component of the retail price, is calculated as a percent of ex-factory cost and intended to meet the sales promotion expenses, distribution costs, outward freight and trade margins. The balance left after meeting the above expenses is the margin of the manufacturers. The prescribed mark-ups as per the 1979 DPCO were:

(a) 40 percent in case of Category-I formulations

(b) 55 percent in case of Category-II formulations

(c) Up to 100 percent in case of Category-III formulations

(d) All other formulations were outside the purview of price control (Category-IV)

Ceiling on Profitability

The DPCO 1979 prescribed an overall ceiling of pre-tax return on sales turnover of formulations. The rates of return applicable to different categories of manufacturers are given in Table 4.3.

Table 4.3 DPCO 1979: Profitability Ceiling

Other important aspects of DPCO 1979 were:

Criteria for Ceiling	Profitability (Per cent)
Large Units (sales turnover exceeding Rs. 6-crore per annum)	
Having no basic drug manufacturing activity and no R&D activity	8
Having basic drug activity at 5 per cent or more of turnover and no R&D activity	9
Having basic drug manufacturing activity at 5 per cent or more of turnover and engaged in approved R&D	10
Medium Size Units (Sales turnover ranging from Rs. 1 to 6-crore per annum)	
Having no basic drug manufacturing and no R&D activity	9
Having basic drug manufacturing activity at 5 per cent or more and no R&D activity	11
Having basic drug manufacturing activity at 5 per cent or more and engaged in approved R&D activity	13
Small Units (Sales turnover less than Rs.1-crore per annum)	
Having only formulations activity	12
Having basic drug manufacturing activity at 5 per cent or more of turnover	13

- Formulations not included under Categories I, II, III were to be exempted from price control.
- As regards the trade margin, the DPCO 1979 prescribed the margins for wholesalers and retailers at 2 percent and 12 percent for ethical drugs and 2 percent and 10 percent respectively for non-ethical drugs.

The Industry's Stand

The industry strongly felt that the DPCO would act as a deterrent and may slow the rate of progress. The principle stand taken by the industry against DPCO 1979 may be summed up as:

- The prices of only very essential and most commonly used formulations numbering about 117 identified by Hathi Committee should have been regulated and not 85 percent of the total formulations manufactured in the country. The DPCO 1979 brought all these formulations under price control by placing them into categories I, II, and III
- The categorization was not scientific, nor was any rational basis adopted
- The creation of Drug Price Equalization Account and the related provisions would penalize efficiency rather than place a premium on efficiency
- The mark-ups for Category I formulations were less than even the break-even mark-ups in most cases
- The ex-factory cost plus mark-up formula for pricing was misleading to the consumer, who believes that the total mark-up is the manufacturer's profit.
- This formula, therefore, should be replaced by a total cost plus return formula for pricing these formulations.
- Provision should be made for automatic revision of selling prices (both upward and downward) based on the increases or decreases of the input costs. Guidelines should be laid down for this purpose so that price changes may be announced promptly.
- The mark-ups provided for formulations in Categories I and II were considerably less than even the break-even points. A uniform mark-up of 75 percent for formulations in Categories I and II and a mark-up of 125 percent for formulations in Category III should be allowed.
- A uniform post-tax return of 14 percent on net worth should be

constantly prescribed for all bulk drugs to ensure their maximum production.

The government, however did not pay any attention to the industry's pleas and proceeded to implement the provisions of DPCO 1979. The process of fixing bulk drug prices continues even now. The prices of about 11 bulk drugs were announced in 1980. The prices of around 170 bulk drugs cost studied by BICP were being announced in installments.

Impact on Profitability

An in-depth study conducted by NCAER on profitability trends consequent to the DPCO 1979 revealed the following:

- Profitability declined by about 4.55 percent between 1978 and 1980 as a result of the increase in ex-factory cost of formulations and expenses met out of mark-ups. The increases in costs were more than the increases in sales value.
- The break-even mark-up for a number of units was around 63 percent. The mark-ups allowed by DPCO 1979 on Categories I and II were lower than the breakeven levels. Thus the mark-up allowed for units manufacturing these formulations were not sufficient even to cover the expenses.
- To minimize the loses, these units seem to have curtailed the production of formulations belonging to these categories. This resulted in shortage of certain essential drugs.

Even in the subsequent years, the profitability of many a company declined due to escalating input costs over which there was no control. The industry had been making demands persistently to review the DPCO 1979, revise and amend certain provisions. Some of the important demands of the industry were:

- Price control to be limited to the most essential formulations number ing about 135. A minimum mark-up of 95 percent to be allowed on these.
- On all other formulations there should be a self-regulatory scheme, which allows a 10 to 13 percent return on sales turnover depending upon the bulk drug manufacturing activity and R&D effort.
- A post-tax return of 16 percent on net worth should be allowed in case of bulk drugs.

- Conversion norms should be revised since these were based on the input costs of 1976-77 and there had been a sharp increase in costs since.
- Trade margins should be suitably revised and specifically fixed for all formulations. Any increase in the existing trade margins should be added to the overall mark-up.

The long awaited revisions came along with the new drug policy of 1987.

1987

DPCO 1987 replaced the earlier DPCO 1979. The government took a more pragmatic view of the price control situation and decided that the industry should maintain sound health and only then can it deliver a better quality of service. The salient features of DPCO 1987 were:

- The number of categories and the number of formulations are reduced and contain only the very essential and most commonly used ones. The basis of the categorization too has been made more scientific. For example, all drugs used for the treatment of certain diseases like tuberculosis, leprosy, trachoma, malaria, filaria, oral rehydration therapy, which are the priority areas under National Health Program, are grouped in Category I.
- Mark-up of DPCO makes way for MAPE of DPCO 1987. MAPE means Maximum Allowable Post-Manufacturing Expenses including trade margins. MAPE should not exceed:
  (a) 75 percent in the case of formulations belonging to Category I
  (b) 100 percent in the case of formulations belonging to Category II

Categorization of formulations as per DPCO 1987 was based on bulk drugs. Only bulk drugs are classified into Categories I and II. For the purpose of categorization of a formulation it shall be deemed as:

  (a) Category I formulation, if it contains any bulk drug either individually or in combination specified for Category I formulations
  (b) Category II formulation, if it contains any bulk drug either individually or in combination, specified for Category II formulations

(c) In case the formulation contains bulk drugs specified in Categories I and II, it shall be deemed as a Category I formulation

As regards, the trade margins, DPCO 1987 prescribed a margin of 16 percent to retailers and 3 percent to wholesalers for all ethical drugs.

The industry's overall reaction to DPCO 1987 has been positive. Some of the industry's recommendations have been considered in the new drug policy. Conversion norms have been revised. The DPCO 1987 and the new drug policy indicate that the government has adopted a rational and growth-oriented approach towards the pharmaceutical industry.

1995

The next drug policy came five years after the government decided to review the drug policy of 1987, a record in official dithering, DPCO 1995, replacing the drug price control order of 1987 was announced in January 1995. The response of the industry to the 1995 drug policy was rather mixed. While it is an improvement on the earlier policy, it could have been far more liberal opined the industry leaders.

The government on the other hand strongly felt that since the drug industry covers everyones' lives, the policy should balance the interests of the industry as well as the consumers' interests. There were many positive features in the 1995 drug policy.

1. Abolishes licensing requirements with a couple of exceptions like genetically engineered drugs. In addition, there is a greater flexibility for manufacturers. Since licenses are also linked to production locations, manufacturers will be free to to start producing where they wish, shift production to another plant or increase production at a plant.

2. Raises the equity ceilings for foreign companies to 51 per cent. Investments above 51 percent will be allowed on a case by case basis. Government approval for foreign technological collaborations will also be automatically cleared.

3. Introduces three criteria - turnover, monopoly and competition - for assigning whether drugs should fall in the price control basket.

   (a) The government will continue to fix prices of drugs whose annual turnover exceeds Rs. 4-crore (previous cut-off point: Rs. 5-crore). The assumption here is that these are widely used drugs.

(b) A drug is said to enjoy a monopoly when its retail sales fall in the Rs. 4-crore bracket and a single manufacturer has a market share of 90 percent or more. The main purpose of laying down these criteria is to make decisions on price control transparent.

4. Replaces the current two lists of 142 price-controlled essential drugs by a single list of 73 drugs. Consequently, the price control will cover about 50 percent of the retail pharmaceutical market as compared to the present 70 per cent.

5. Allows manufacturers a maximum mark-up of 100 percent on price-controlled drugs against current mark-up of 75 per cent. Mark-ups are not to be confused with profits, as they are meant to cover all post-manufacturing expenses such as freight, marketing, distribution, administration overheads etc.

6. Provides for fixing of ceiling prices for commonly used packs of formulations based on price-controlled drugs. These prices would be applicable to all manufacturers and also to the single ingredient formulations sold under generic name. The ceiling prices are applicable even to small-scale sector.

7. Exempts new bulk drugs that are developed indigenously from price control. In addition, the current five-year exemption from price controls is extended to ten years for new drugs produced by Indigenous R&D.

8. Proposes to set up a National Pharmaceutical Pricing Authority (NPPA) to facilitate:

(a) Faster fixation and revision of drug prices

(b) Include and exclude drugs from price control and

(c) Monitor the prices of the drugs outside the price control

The NPPA has set deadlines to clear price revision applications - two months for deciding on applications for price revision of formulations and four months for price fixation and revision of applications for bulk drugs.

9. Stipulates that the government is to notify on an annual basis the norms relating to conversion costs, packaging material costs and packaging charges.

10. Promises to set up a National Drug Authority (NDA) on the lines of the US Federal Drug Administration to look into the quality aspects of drugs. The NDA is to be funded by a cess of 1 percent of the value drugs produced on the industry, which is expected to raise about Rs. 70-crore a year. However, essential drugs and drugs produced by small-sector may escape the cess.

11. Trims the list of 15 drugs reserved for the public sector to five.

12. Proposes to set up an inter-ministerial group to decide on the introduction of tax and other incentives like excise exemption for new indigenously produced drugs, soft loans for setting up and running R&D facilities etc.

Industry's View

The industry leaders opined that the new drug policy falls short of the expectations. Some of their major apprehensions were:

(a) The Rs. 4-crore criteria for bringing a product into the price control category is not pragmatic. What incentive is there to launch new products if they are eventually brought under price control based on this turnover criteria? This will lead to uncertainty. Manufacturers will not be able to plan growth.

(b) As regards the government's estimates that the drugs covered by the price control account for only 50 percent of the retail pharmaceutical market, the industry clearly states that the data used for determining was   rather obsolete as this was based on ORG Retail Store Audit of March 1990. Since then many of the brands have improved their respective market shares considerably.

(c) The 100 percent mark-up to cover all the post manufacturing expenses is not adequate when you take into account the industry's need to invest in R&D and up-gradation of technology. The present rate of investment in R&D by Indian pharmaceutical industry is a meager 1.4 percent as compared to 12 to 18 percent of the International pharmaceutical industry.

(d) The industry is skeptical regarding the good intentions of the new policy. The question is: how far these will be implemented?

The NPPA, for example was mooted several years ago. The NDA (National Drug Authority) was first suggested in 1973, but was never set up. Several policy decisions in the past have stated that there would be drug price monitoring system, but it was still is not in place.

The new drug policy could have been more liberal in order to provide the much needed support to Indian drug industry in its effort to become a world class industry. In the post-GATT era, it is essential to achieve a world class standard even for survival.

Genesis of NPPA

National Pharmaceutical Pricing Authority (NPPA) was conceived in 1994 as part of liberalization process that started in the Drug Policy 1986. It states: *In the light of the apprehensions expressed in the parliament on the likely spurt in the prices of medicines, it has been felt that it would not be desirable to allow price revisions automatically in the pricing mechanism. The government would set up an independent body of experts to be called the National Pharmaceutical Pricing Authority (NPPA) to do the work of price fixation. This expert body would also be entrusted with the task of updating the list of drugs under price control each year on the basis of established guidelines and criteria. This body would also monitor the prices of decontrolled drugs and formulations and oversee the implementation of the provisions of DPCO.*

NPPA came into effect and became fully functional from 29th August, 1997.

Mandate and Functions of NPPA

1. Fixation and revision of scheduled bulk drugs and formulations.
2. Updating the list of drugs under price control.
3. Monitoring the prices of decontrolled drugs and formulations.
4. Monitoring the availability of drugs.
5. Collection and maintenance of data on production, exports and imports etc.
6. Implementation and enforcement of the provisions of the DPCO.
7. Getting studies on pricing of drugs and pharmaceuticals controlled.
8. Rendering advice to the central government on drug pricing policy.
9. To deal with legal matters arising out of decisions of the NPPA.

2001

India along with other member countries of WTO (World Trade

Organization) signed the Doha Declaration on public health at a ministerial conference at Doha. The declaration clarifies that the TRIPS agreement would not prevent WTO members from taking measures to protect public health and provides them the right to determine what constitutes a national emergency or circumstances of extreme urgency. The WTO members would be allowed to determine the grounds on which compulsory licenses are granted and grant them.

2002

The pharmaceutical policy of 2002 was announced in February 2002 reducing the number of drugs under price control from 74 under the earlier DPCO. With this, price coverage of the industry would have been reduced significantly. The policy, however, could not be implemented as it was under litigation.

2003

The Patents Controller granted the Exclusive Marketing Right (EMR) to Novartis India for Glivec (imatinib mesylate), Nadoxin (Nadifloxacin), and to Eli Lilly for Cialis (tadalafil).

Change in Excise Duty

In addition to the price regulations, government of India had issued a notification on the changes in excise duty. As against the earlier practice of levying excise duty (prevailing rate being 16%) on ex-factory price, the government has introduced the provision to levy excise duty on pharmaceutical products on the maximum retail price less 35% abatement (in other words, excise duty is charged at 65% of MRP). This resulted in a significant increase in the excise duty payable.

Schedule M and Schedule Y

The Drugs and Cosmetics Act 1940 and Drugs and Cosmetic Rules 1945 regulate the import, manufacture, distribution and sale of drugs in India. Schedule M of this Act, which pertains to manufacturing practices and quality norms (known as Good Manufacturing Practices or GMP) was amended and provided for up-gradation of manufacturing facilities by June 2005. Schedule Y of this Act governs the conduct of clinical trials in India. Revisions in clinical trial norms have also been introduced under Schedule Y.

DPCO2013

In the beginning, manufacturers were fixing drug prices based on their manufacturing costs. After the implementation of DPCO 1995, the government started fixing the drug prices. DPCO 2013 under NPPA brought a number of drugs under NLEM (National List of Essential Medicines) and started fixing the drug prices by their simple average prices of all marketed products of a drug, which have a market share of more than one per cent. The final MRP (Maximum Retail Price) of a drug at the retailer is increased by a factor of 16 per cent. DPCO 2013 also specified ceiling and non-ceiling prices of drugs. The patient groups, however argued that the previous cost-based pricing mechanism of 1995 was more significant than the present (2013) market-based pricing. Table 4.4 presents the main differences between 1995 and 2013 Drug Price Control Orders.

Table 4.4 Main Differences Between DPCO 1995 and 2013

DPCO 1995	DPCO 2013
Governed by Essential Commodities Act 1995	Governed by National Pharmaceutical Pricing Authority based on National List of Essential Medicines
Prices of 74 drugs were regulated by this Act	Prices of 652 drugs are regulated by this Act
Once prices are fixed, they cannot be changed as per the Act	Based on simple average price (SAP) the highest prices can be lowered depending upon the margins.
Ceiling and non-ceiling prices of drugs are not specified	Ceiling and non-ceiling prices are specified

Incentives for Domestic R & D

DPCO 2013 strives to support national research and development by giving a five-year exemption from price controls on all new innovations that are patented in India from the time they start the commercial production. The eligibility criteria for this exemption are:

    A. The drug is developed through indigenous R & D

B. The manufacturers producing new drugs patented under Indian Patents Act 1970

C. New drug products manufactured by new development process

D. New drugs involving NDDS (Novel Drug Delivery Systems)

Pros and Cons of DPCO 2013

The pros and cons of DPCO 2013 are presented in Table 4.5.

DPCO 2017

DPCO 2017 fixes ceiling prices of 851 formulations (including two coronary stents) under revised Schedule-1 based on NLEM (National List of Essential Medicines) 2015, till December 2017. It is estimated that capping of prices of medicines and medical devices including coronary stents and knee implants has helped patients save a total of Rs. 11,365.61-crore till December 2017.

Table 4.5 DPCO 2013: Pros. and Cons.

Pros.	Cons.
1. The weighted average price of brands having greater than 1 per cent market share formula will result in over 40 to 70 per cent of price reduction in 60 per cent of drugs on National List of Essential Medicines.	1. The Organization of Pharmaceutical Producers of India (OPPI) and the Indian Pharmaceutical Alliance (IPA) opined that the new Drug Policy would adversely impact the profitability of Indian Pharma companies and their competitiveness globally.
2. The Weighted Average Price (WAP) mechanism of the price of essential medicines will achieve the twin objectives of public health and industrial growth. have to reduce	2. When the policy is implemented, Indian drug makers will have to reduce their prices by 20 to 25 percent across portfolios. MNCs will their prices between 30 to 50 per cent.
3. 348 essential medicines, including cancer and HIV medicines will come under the purview of the pricing policy.	3. The big foreign Pharma companies may lose interest from investing in or expanding production capacity in India.

Is Price an Element of Pharmaceutical Marketing-Mix in India?

In a highly regulated industry like pharmaceuticals in India, can price be considered an element of marketing mix? When the prices, conversion norms, packaging norms are fixed for all essential drugs and formulations, does the pharmaceutical marketer have any option? Is there a choice, really speaking?

Of course, there is a choice, however restricted it may be. Price may not be the the most important variable in the marketing-mix of the pharmaceutical industry in India. But it is important enough. One has to make the most of all the options available. One has to exploit the residual degrees of freedom to the optimum. A brief discussion on pricing concepts, objectives and strategy would be helpful in this regard.

Pricing is a strategic decision. A number of factors influence the decision regarding what pricing strategy to use and when to use it. Some of these are:

1. Price sensitivity of different market segments.
2. Market position of product and the firm (image, market share etc.)
3. Stage of the life cycle the product is in
4. Economies of scale in production
5. Channels of distribution
6. Pricing moves by competition
7. Composition of the product-line and product-mix of the firm (number of product packs in controlled Categories I and II and in the decontrolled category, expected sales and profit volumes category-wise etc.)

Understanding these factors that influence pricing decisions is important for the pharmaceutical marketer, for it would enable him to formulate realistic and profitable pricing strategies for his products.

Pricing Objectives

You must have clearly defined objectives for price setting. The top management normally sets pricing objectives. Pricing objectives usually revolve around and are related to market share, return on investment, profit, price stability etc. Since prices of pharmaceuticals are largely regulated and controlled, the scope of pricing objectives is somewhat restricted. Improving the efficiency of operations both in manufacturing and marketing, therefore, assumes greater importance than ever before. Adequate return is what everyone talks about while on the subject of pricing. What is adequate return? How much is enough? That's difficult to say. It depends on a number of factors, like economies of scale, cost leadership, etc. Profit is what is left over after meeting all the costs and expenditure. That is why it is called the bottom line. All pricing objectives have one thing in common, a sound and healthy bottom line. Some of the important objectives of pricing are:

1. Maximization of profit. Specific objectives for short term and long term. Short-term objectives should not be short sighted I.e., they should not jeopardize the long-term objectives.
2. Growth. Sustained growth over a long period.
3. Should obtain a predetermined rate of return over a long period.
4. Achieving market leadership.
5. Should allow the firm to be ahead of competition in terms of innovation.
6. To increase market share.
7. Meeting competitive price levels.
8. To achieve a greater degree of market penetration.
9. To recover the investment faster.
10. Minimizing risks.

Pricing Decisions

Usually, there are two situations around which, almost all pricing decisions revolve. They are:

A. Setting the price for the first time, as when you launch a new product, new pack, or new dosage form. In case the new product falls into the controlled Categories of I and II, the choice of pricing is restricted to the extent of specified MAPE, i.e., to pricing it at the uppermost limit of MAPE or below. In case a leader or ceiling price exists for that particular product, the choice is once again limited to whether to price it at par with the leader or ceiling price or below that, to be more competitive. If the proposed new product belongs to the decontrolled category, the choice of pricing is relatively broader. The government, however, can bring any product into the controlled categories any time it chooses to.

B. The second situation for price setting involves the existing products. Changing circumstances necessitate a price change for some of the existing products. For example, the products hitherto failing in the decontrolled category could be brought into a controlled category. Another example is that you are likely to be forced to bring down your prices when your major competitors lower their prices considerably.

Bases for Pricing

There are four commonly used bases for approaches towards pricing a product. They are:

1. Cost based pricing
2. Demand based pricing
3. Competition based pricing
4. Market based pricing

Cost-based Pricing

Cost based pricing is an accountant's approach. As the name implies, it is based on total cost of the product, plus an allocation for overheads plus a predetermined percentage to provide for an adequate return (profit margin). The total of all these gives you the selling price. This is very much like the pricing formula suggested in DPCO. DPCO, in addition, fixed the cost norms (conversion and packaging norms) and MAPE (maximum allowable post-manufacturing expenditure) for all formulations and bulk drugs belonging to Categories I and II.

The major advantage of cost based pricing is that it can help to indicate the minimum price levels. The disadvantages of cost based pricing are that it:

A. Does not take into account the fluctuations in input costs as it is based on predetermined level of demand and production. This has been the major disadvantage with the DPCO, which does not take into account the escalation of input costs.

B. Ignores the market factors like demand and competitors' actions. This explains the reason why the pharmaceutical manufacturers stopped voluntary price reductions after DPCO 1969. The formula for pricing suggested as per DPCO 1969 was a cost based approach with an added restriction of predetermined conversion and packaging norms.

C. May lead to wrong pricing decision as overhead cost allocation based pricing can be misleading.

Demand-based Pricing

This is an economist's approach towards pricing. The economist's theory of pricing and elasticity of demand states that:

- Demand will fall as price increases
- Demand will rise as price decreases

This approach to pricing, therefore, takes into account the likely effect that different prices may have on the demand for a product. Under this method you are required to calculate the break-even points at different selling prices and different volume forecasts. After evaluating the impact of price on volume, you try to arrive at the most profitable price volume ratio. To arrive at this you must be able to forecast with a reasonable degree of accuracy the number of units of a given product you could sell at different price levels.

One major advantage with market demand-based pricing is that it takes the market realities into account while pricing product. This method is therefore, useful in pricing products profitably in a market that is price sensitive and demand elastic.

Since pharmaceuticals in general and ethical drugs in particular are not price sensitive, this may not be a very appropriate approach for the pharmaceutical marketer.

Competition-based Pricing

In so far as the pharmaceutical industry is concerned, competition-based pricing is perhaps the most commonly used method. The options that are available to the marketer are:

- Prices can be set above competitors'
- Prices can be set at par with competitors'
- Prices can be set below competitors'

It is important to estimate your competitors' costs when considering their prices for formulating your own pricing strategy. Estimating the costs of competitors is relatively easy in the Indian pharmaceutical industry since the norms for conversion and packaging are fixed. They are the upper limits and it is possible that some of your competitors may have achieved greater efficiency levels, incurring less cost than the prescribed norms. It is therefore, more important to know the real costs of the competitors and whether they have achieved cost leadership. For example, if a manufacturer of a formulation happens to be one of the largest manufacturers of the bulk drug used in that formulation this an obvious advantage. Here is a case in point.

Case 4.1 Dr. Reddy's Laboratories Create Entry Barrier with Their Cost Leadership!

Norfloxacin, a broad-spectrum antibiotic that is highly effective in urinary tract infections, was introduced in the Indian market in 1988. The market size for urological was around Rs. 16-crore in 1988 with an annual growth rate of 105 per cent. The introduction of Norfloxacin accelerated the growth rate of the category itself to a frenetic pace. A number of brands were introduced in quick succession. But Cipla's Norflox was a brand leader right from the beginning., with a formidable share of 19.3 per cent. As regards the price, almost all the brands were selling at around Rs. 8 per capsule of 400 mg strength and around Rs. 18 per capsule of 800 mg strength.

Enter Norilet brand of Norflaoxacin from Stangen, a group company of Dr. Reddy's Laboratories, a leading manufacturer of bulk drugs at Hyderabad. Dr. Reddy's Laboratories started manufacturing the bulk drug Norfloxacin and very quickly achieved cost leadership. The cost effectiveness of their Norfloxacin manufacturing was so high that they were able to market their Norfloxacin brand, Norilet, at less than half the prevailing market price. Norilet 400 mg was priced at around Rs. 4 per capsule and Norilet 800 mg at around Rs. 8 per capsule. Norilet was rapidly making inroads into competition. Not only that, it even created an entry barrier. No brand of Norfloaxacin was introduced ever since! Subsequently they became the largest manufacturers of Norfloxacin bulk drug in the world!

Price Comparison

In the Pharmaceutical industry, price comparison could be on unit basis, daily cost of therapy or the total cost of the treatment. The prices of competitors can be obtained from published sources like the Indian Pharmaceutical Guide, price lists of respective companies, MIMS, ORG Retail Store Audit etc., Prices should be analyzed at all the four levels, namely, consumer (maximum retail price), retailer (price to the retailer), wholesaler and the special hospital price, so that you can have a clear idea regarding trade margins, discounts etc. given by various competitors.

Market-based Pricing

Market-based pricing deals with the judgmental or subjective elements or pricing. The judgments, of course, will have to be based on analysis of certain facts. This basis of pricing is judgmental in the sense that it deals with the perceptions of customers in terms of the value satisfactions, or the bundle of benefits that the product might offer. They key word is perception and the important factor is the perceived value. This perceived value could be a result of:

- Performance of the product as experienced by customers and consumers
- Reputation and image of the firm
- Quality of service delivered

An accurate assessment of a market's perception of your product is crucial for success in market-based pricing. Market research is an important and invaluable tool in assessing the perceived value of your product by the market. It also helps you avoid the pitfalls of over pricing and under pricing.

Over pricing may be due to the fact that you have taken for granted your perception of according a high value (to your own product), instead of the market's perception. Perceived value by definition is a qualitative judgment made by the consumer regarding your product vis-a-vis competition, based on his experiences.

Under pricing is the result of underestimating the real value of your product of charging less than you could.

Pricing Strategies

What is the right pricing strategy for a product? Admittedly, there is no formula for arriving at a single pricing strategy that suits all products and all markets. The choice of a right or ideal pricing strategy depends on a number of factors like the objectives, the type of product and its value perceptions, the market segment it belongs to and the extent of competition etc. The three commonly used pricing strategies are:

1. **Skim the Cream Strategy:** Skim-the-cream strategy aims at the top end of the demand curve. It sets the price at the top of the acceptable price range. The skimming strategy is often used:

   - On a new product during the introductory and early part of the product life cycle in order to recover the high R&D costs faster

   - Since it is easier to reduce prices if need arises, than to increase prices, the skimming strategy is used. You are erring on the right side and playing safe when you use a skimming strategy.

   The disadvantages of the skimming strategy are that:

   - Increases vulnerability since it attracts competition

   - The higher price may result in low unit sales, which may not suit the plant output and may result in underutilization of capacities

2. **Penetration Strategy:** As the name suggests, penetration pricing strategy aims at greater and deeper market penetration by pricing at the lower end of the spectrum. Thus penetration pricing strategy takes a diametrically opposite approach to the skimming strategy. This strategy can be profitable only when the sales volumes are large. Penetration strategy is helpful in the growth and maturity phases of the product life cycle.

   Furthermore, this is a highly competitive strategy as it preempts competition. This can also be used as an entry barrier. Since the customer base is widened due to lower prices, penetration strategy can help build the sales of a product even in the long-term.

   Penetration strategy is not without disadvantages. The first and foremost disadvantage is that the payback period is longer for a new product. This is due to low profit margin. Secondly, if the product has a very short life cycle, this pricing strategy could be disastrous. Thirdly, it is often very difficult to increase prices substantially, if the initial price set is very low. The consequent psychological disadvantages of such revision can be very difficult to overcome.

3. **Marginal Cost Pricing Strategy:** Simply stated, marginal cost is *the cost of producing one more unit.* The cost of producing one more unit implies that the cost of producing the extra unit consists only of the variable costs since fixed costs are already being covered with the existing sales volumes. It should be adequate even if you make a small profit on the additional sales because this small profit would not have been there had you not obtained the extra business. By obtaining an additional order at a small profit, you are improving your capacity utilization, which would have been otherwise idle. That is why many companies use the marginal costing approach towards pricing, particularly for highly competitive business situations like large institutional tenders etc. where lower price is always an advantage. The major use of marginal cost based pricing, therefore, is not as a pricing tool but to answer the question - *should you accept this order?*

This type of pricing strategy is also used often where production capacities are high and high volumes of sales are essential to keep the fixed costs low and where the demand is price elastic.

Pricing Management

Pricing management in the pharmaceutical industry involves decisions related to setting prices for new products, implementing price changes according to the changes in governmental policies (DPCO amendments etc.) monitoring the costs of company's own products as well as those of major competitors, analyzing prices of competitors, quantity discounts, free goods and bonus offers etc.

Bonus offers or free goods on selected products, particularly seasonal products like cough and cold preparations, antidiarrhoeals etc., are a common practice in the Indian pharmaceutical market. Introductory bonus offers on new products too is common in order to achieve adequate stocking at the retail level before promotion to doctors is commenced.

Bonus offers are also given by various companies where inventories are built up and sudden increase in sales volumes is required to reduce the inventories and to liquidate them. Bonus offers are frequently used as sales promotional tools by pharmaceutical marketers to boost their sales of OTC (over the counter) drug brands, since a retail chemist can help push the sales of non-prescription drugs.

What should be the bonus offer? How many free issues to be given on the purchase of how many units of a given product? It has been the practice in the pharmaceutical industry to give *free units* of a product under a bonus offer, rather than a percentage discount. The reasons are obvious and even elementary. One is that it costs less for the manufacture to give free units, whereas the monetary value for the retailer is retained and not reduced. Secondly, the manufacturer would be reducing his inventories at a faster rate. Thirdly, the firm is able to exert a greater stock pressure at the retail level.

The number of free issues to be given for a product on bonus offer depends on factors like:

- The image and reputation of your product and the firm
- The extent of competition and their likely moves
- The price of your product
- The marketing objectives of your product
- The nature of the market in which your product is competing, for example whether its demand is price elastic?

Customers' Reactions to Price Changes

It is very important to understand the likely reactions of your customers towards price changes. Some of the important reactions of customers towards the price changes in general are:

- When the price is reduced they may think that you are downgrading the product or even deleting it subsequently, if the product is currently perceived as a premium product
- Conversely, if the price is increased, they may think that you are improving the product. This probably explains the reason why there seem to be a never-ending claims such as New Improved Formula, Improved Flavor and Taste etc. The discerning observer will notice an inevitable price increase every time such a label claim is made. This is not to say that these claims are not justified or untrue, the main purpose of these claims is to desensitize customers towards price increases.

- In case of price increase, a retailer may reduce his stock holding, delay his payments, or may substitute other brands in case of OTC products. More often than not, he may stock up more before the price increase is implemented.

- An understanding of the psychological aspects of pricing will be helpful for the marketer in planning and managing pricing strategies effectively.

Price Communicates

Price can be used as a very effective marketing communication tool. In its simplest form, price communicates the exchange value of a particular product. Price can be, however, used to communicate status, quality, low purchase risk and other ideas. Research indicates that consumers are inclined to use price as a cue to quality in evaluating brands. This tendency to equate price with quality is particularly high, where a perceptible difference in quality between brands exists. As for ethical drugs, consumers believe that the higher price reflects *hidden qualities* in the brand.

In the case of new products that are less familiar to consumers, price becomes a powerful cue in evaluating the quality of a brand. In other words, the consumer is left with little or not choice in terms of attributes to evaluate an unknown or unfamiliar brand. There are no established brands or even the companies in given product category. How does he go about evaluating a brand before making a decision to purchase or not? Price here becomes a powerful cue to quality.

In case of new products, absolutely new products, marketers can use price as a communications cue for their products since these new products have no traditional price and therefore are likely to be assessed by the consumers largely on the basis of their initial prices.

Marketers quite often use a *skimming* strategy to price their new products. We have already discussed that skimming refers to both strategy of setting high price to catch the upper portion of the demand curve, and its disadvantages. By reinforcing the price as a communications cue of the product's quality, by a careful and creative use of the elements of its marketing mix like the pack, the product itself and its promotion etc., the firm can further strengthen the consumer's beliefs about its quality. Here is a case where a large multinational pharmaceutical company has used price and reinforced it as a strong communications cue, both in international and Indian markets, to emerge victorious in the global anti-ulcer market.

Case 4.2 How Glaxo Won the Anti-Ulcer Market!

Glaxo (GSK now), the British pharmaceutical giant, had developed ranitidine and launched it under the brand name Zantac in a number of countries. SKF's (GSK now) Tagamet was reigning supreme in the anti-ulcer market with an annual sales of over US $ 950-million and was aiming to become the first-ever prescription drug to cross the US$ 1-billion. But Zantac of Glaxo shattered all those dreams for it was Zantac, which became the first-ever prescription drug to cross the US$ 1-billion mark.

How did Glaxo win with Zantac? Glaxo obtained a higher price for Zantac compared with Tagamet of SKF, which was the first of H2 antagonists and the market leader (skimming strategy to recover the high R&D investment faster). To reinforce the communications cue of quality and superiority that the relatively high price of Zantac offered, Glaxo launched a prestige campaign and differentiated their anti-ulcer drug Zantac and positioned it as superior product - in fact a *Super Tagamet* in the doctors' minds.

In India too, Glaxo followed the skimming strategy for their Zinetec brand of ranitidine, when they launched it in 1986. The company priced it very high, almost one hundred percent above the prices of many a competitor.

The company very aggressively pursued a promotional strategy aimed at desensitizing the customers to the high price and reinforcing the quality cues that the high price offered. These included seminars, lecture sessions for doctors in class I towns and metro-cities, by eminent gastroenterologists from from all over the world, persuasion by a team of highly proficient and well trained medical representatives, samples, gifts, an attractive premium looking pack and a differentiated product in the form of a specially coated tablet (all other formulations were plain tablets). Consequently Glaxo achieved brand leadership for Zinetec in the very first year of its introduction.

The company had to drastically reduce the price of Zinetec consequent to the DPCO 1987, to almost half of its introductory price. The company followed a penetration strategy (it had virtually no choice) and made the most of it, by making customers perceive it as enhanced value for their money.

The reduction in price, however, did not affect the quality image of the product since the doctors and dealers are aware that the price reduction was not voluntary but a result of a government order (DPCO 1987).

Glaxo, by following a skimming strategy for their Zinetec in India, not only recovered the development costs faster but could also afford the heavy promotional expenditure in establishing it as a market leader. When the company was forced to reduce the price of Zinetec, Glaxo valiantly pursued an aggressive market growth strategy, thereby increasing its sales volume considerably. The result was a formidable leadership position in the Indian anti-ulcer market with over 20 percent market share, growing at an impressive 18 percent (1988).

Psychological Effects of Pricing

The effects of price on demand are not restricted to price-demand relationships, or price-quality connotations. There are a number of observable yet unsatisfactorily explained, if not explicable phenomenon of price on demand. In fact, some of them are diametrically opposite to the traditional explanations or views of the economists. They are:

1. **Quantum Effect in Pricing:** It is an observable fact that increases in prices up to some point do not result in a loss of sales volume but increases beyond that point produce a sharp decline in sales. This particular point at which the rapid drop in sales occur is called the *quantum point*. Consumers do not show any resistance or sensitivity to prices up to the quantum point but appear to be hypersensitive to even moderate increases in prices beyond the quantum point. Bata, the leading shoemaker in India, is vey good example for this quantum effect in pricing. The almost proverbial Bata prices are typically at the right side of the quantum point.

   For example, you can price a new antibiotic capsule (assuming that it is in the decontrolled category) at Rs. 4.65, 4.75, 4.80 and in fact, up to Rs. 4.95 without any drop in sales. But a price

Rs. 5.05 could lead to a sharp decline in sales volume. In this case Rs. 5 is the quantum point.

2. **Price Perception in Reverse Direction:** As the name implies, consumer perceptions regarding the price work here in a reverse direction. In other words, as consumers perceive lower prices higher than higher pricers. For instance consumers may perceive a price of Rs. 4.95 as lower than a price of Rs. 4.45 for a 10-gram jar of pain-relieving ointment. How does this happen? This phenomenon can be explained in terms of reference points. Round figures serve as reference points and tell the consumer that the price of Rs. 4.95 is 5 paisa less than Rs. 5 and the price of Rs. 4.45 is 45 paisa more than Rs. 4. Thus the higher price may appear lower and lower price higher because of their relationship to their reference points.

3. **Just Price Standard**: Another observable phenomenon, which cannot be explained satisfactorily is the *just price standard*. Consumers seem to develop a just price in their minds, which serves as a *just price standard* for evaluating brands. Prices falling within this *just price standard* are acceptable to consumers. Prices above this fair price standard result in low sales. Prices below this standard are likely to reflect poor quality.

4. **Cost Price Standard:** Knowledgeable consumers often think that they can judge manufacturer's cost of a product and develop a fair price estimate based on their judgment of the manufacturer's cost plus a *reasonable profit*. This is more common in case of industrial buyers.

   Understanding the psychological effects of pricing will help the marketer in gaining insight into all aspects of pricing. This in turn will enable him to formulate strategies to desensitize the consumer to price and to find ways to overcome the price barrier.

Desensitizing the Consumer to Price

Overcoming the price barrier or desensitizing the consumer to price requires some basic understanding of consumer behavior and also of the underlying factors that are responsible for increasing this sensitivity to price. It is possible to identify the desensitizing factors once you understand the character of this sensitivity to price changes.

Sensitivity to price changes is greater where:

- There is no variance in point of sale effectiveness
- Service after sale is not important
- Personal selling is not involved
- There is little or no product differentiation
- Unit price is high

In the pharmaceutical industry sensitivity to price changes is relatively low because the products are clearly differentiated. Furthermore, personal selling is crucial differential and a medical representative, who is a more effective persuader, can often overcome the difference in price successfully by convincing the doctor about the value for money that his product offers as compared to others.

The image of the company is another differential, though it is not as important a differential as personal selling is, in the pharmaceutical industry. Multinationals seem to have a better image as producers of better quality products compared to their Indian counterparts. This may be a result of the 'halo-effect' of the significant R&D effort of multinationals on their Indian subsidiaries. The Indian sector, too, has been asserting its strong presence in this area during recent years. This is evident from the spectacular progress made by some Indian companies like Sun Pharma, Cadila, Ranbaxy (Sun Pharma now), Cipla, Torrent etc.

The major action implications for the pharmaceutical marketer in understanding the sensitivity of customers and consumers to price changes are:

1. To communicate the quality image of the company both in words and deeds.
2. To strengthen the personal selling effort by giving better training inputs and developing the sales force to become more effective and more persuasive.
3. To create a perceptible product differentiation, not merely by adopting a cosmetic change, but by instituting a systematic product development process.

Marketing history, too, has its own share of folklore. Consider this for example:

Folklore and Facts

Price is the single most motivating factor for a purchase. Consumers always prefer a lower-priced product.

Fact

The consumer simply see the price in terms of what is the cheapest. In fact, what he is really looking for is value (bundle of benefits) for his money. If this sounds like a theoretical statement, consider the following facts for evidence.

1. Take for example, any therapeutic category and check the prices of brand leaders in that category. You will find that in most cases, brand leaders are more expensive than all other brands.
2. On closer examination, you will find that even a number of hospitals in both public and private sector do not purchase products on the basis of price alone. You will find that they stock even the major brands that are more expensive than others.
3. Take the case of the dispensing doctors. You will observe that even dispensing doctors who should strictly be buying on the price, stock up some of the expensive brands along with the lower price brands.

'Me-too' Pricing Strategy for 'Me-too' Products

In the Indian pharmaceutical industry, the general practice has been to set the prices on the basis of competitive parity. There are however, a few exceptions to this. In the absence of any perceptible product differentiation, one probably feels safer for pricing his product on the basis of competitive parity.

Periodical Review

A periodical review of prices and costs is important for it will help identify the improvement areas. Comparison of your actual manufacturing costs with the conversion and packaging norms fixed by government will also throw open the gates of opportunity. How can you optimize your manufacturing costs? How can you increase your productivity? The answers to these questions will enable you to strive and achieve cost leadership, which is crucial for winning at the market place. Your focus should be on cost effectiveness rather than on cost control. A periodical review will help you in preparing an action plan to achieve this.

Summary

Pricing, one of the very important elements of the marketing-mix, is subjected to ever-increasing governmental controls. The controls are even more stringent in the case of the Indian pharmaceutical industry.

The pharmaceutical industry, for nearly five decades has been going through the thick and thin of price controls. It had been a case of more *thick* than *thin*. Until 1987, the government did not consider escalation of input costs, while arriving at drug prices. Prices of finished formulations were fixed and controlled, whereas increases in the input costs continue to rise unabated.

Consequently, the obvious and Inevitable happened. Growth rate of industry slowed down. A number of companies ended up in the red. The bottom line of many a company became thinner increasingly to a vanishing point. Pharmaceutical marketers had to be content with the residual degrees of freedom available to them. Only the decontrolled category gave them any opportunity to set prices. Even this is a misnomer because competitive forces restrict them in pricing even products belonging to the decontrolled category. Furthermore, the government can reduce the prices of these products any time it chooses to. This explains the reason why a number of companies do not enjoy higher margins even on products falling in decontrolled category as compared to the controlled categories. The difference existed only on paper and provisions, but not in practice. DPCO 1987 and the new drug policy, however, seemed to have taken a more pragmatic approach. Implemented both in letter and spirit, the new drug policy and DPCO 1987 had all the ingredients to fuel the growth of the Indian pharmaceutical industry.

Later the Government of India had set up an independent expert body, National Pharmaceutical Pricing Authority (NPPA) to fix and regulate the drug prices. The NPPA came into effect and became fully functional from August 29, 1997.

National List of Essential Medicines (NLEM), a World Health Organization resource, is one of the key instruments in balanced healthcare delivery system of a country, which among other things includes accessible, affordable quality medicines at all the primary, secondary and tertiary levels of healthcare. Realizing this, Government of India and Ministry of Health and Family Welfare (MOHFW) decided to have its own essential medicines list and prepared its first NLEM in 1996 and subsequently revised it in 2003. The revisions later became regular feature resulting in almost annual revisions.

That necessity is the mother of invention is proven one more time in the case of the Indian pharmaceutical industry. It tapped all the possible ways of improving the efficiency of operations and continues to do so. That is how and why it has survived the arduous and never-ending price controls all these years.

Does all this mean that the pharmaceutical marketer should resign himself and adopt a fatalistic attitude towards pricing? Of course not! Pricing whether highly restricted and controlled or not, will always remain an important strategic decision. If at all, restrictions and controls will make it more challenging.

A clear understanding of pricing objectives and the bases or approaches towards pricing is essential to formulate any profitable pricing strategy. The four widely used pricing approaches are:

1. Cost-based pricing
2. Demand-based pricing
3. Competition-based pricing
4. Market-based pricing

Having understood the pricing approaches the next question that a marketer should answer is whether to follow a skimming strategy or a penetration strategy in pricing his product.

While economic theories like price and demand elasticity and their inverse relationships are important and enduring, a discerning marketer should not lose sight of the psychological effects of pricing and other non-economic factors that affect pricing decisions.

Price can be used as an effective marketing communications tool. Understanding the psychological effects on pricing and the communication cues that the price of your product is signaling to consumers will help in developing strategies to reinforce those cues and desensitize consumers to the price.

What is the right price may be a difficult question, as it only leads to an endless debate. A thorough understanding of the pricing scenario of your industry, the enduring economic theories, pricing objectives, approaches and strategies, psychological effects on pricing and other non-economic factors of pricing will definitely help a marketer in setting up or arriving at the most *acceptable price.* For the key to any marketing success lies in not formulating a strategy but in making the consumers accept it. Just as the proof of the pudding is in the eating, the acceptance of the consumer of your (products') price is the only proof that the *bundle of benefits* or value satisfactions of your products are accepted in the market place.

5

The Place

Changing Complexion! Changing Dimensions!!

During the past decade, the dimensions of the marketing channels have been changing. The complexion of the trade channels too has undergone a significant change, thus adding to the complexities of the distribution of pharmaceuticals in India making it more challenging than ever before. Consider these facts:

- India is a vast country that measures over 3000 kilometers from Kashmir to Kanyakumari, with different climatic conditions and terrain, transportation and storage of certain essential drugs is indeed a challenging task, particularly during summer, when it becomes very hot. In fact as hot as 43 to even 50 degrees celsius.

- Even today close to two-thirds of the population live in rural areas. Almost half of these are villages with a population of less than one thousand. Modern medicine has not been able to reach them.

- The severe power shortages in a number of states make it difficult for retail chemists even in urban areas, to store certain essential drugs under prescribed temperature conditions. Consequently, the refrigerator (meant for cold storage of medicines) in retail pharmacies has become merely ornamental particularly during the summer months, when temperature control is most needed.

- The ever-increasing costs of distribution in the absence of appropriate price increases have been constantly eroding into the profitability of manufacturers.

- The growing power of trade associations and their not so gentle demands for increased margins makes the pharmaceutical marketer's task even more formidable.

The Pharmaceutical Market Place

Distribution activity is concerned with placing goods and services when they are needed and where they are wanted. That is why distribution traditionally has been referred to as one of the four Ps, the Vital P that is *Place*. Place or distribution is a crucial element for achieving success at the market place. However unique and beneficial your product may be, if it is not available when it is needed and where it is needed, you cannot even hope to succeed. Proper distribution is an essential prerequisite for success.

Marketing Channels

Marketing or distribution channels are the paths that products (or services) follow on their way from manufacturers to the consumer or the industrial user. In the past, services were not considered in the study of marketing channels, because the exchange of intangibles was always thought to be direct. But, today services are no longer excluded from the study of channels. Marketing scholars today strongly feel that, tangible or not, when two parties are involved in any transaction or exchange, there exists a channel. A marketing channel, therefore, requires at a minimum a seller and a buyer. The buyer may be a consumer or an industrial user. A typical marketing channel includes, besides buyers and sellers, various middlemen. There are two types of middlemen - retailers and wholesalers.

Pharmaceutical Marketing Channels

While a marketing channel requires at a minimum, two parties, in so far as the manufacturer of prescription drugs is concerned, the law requires that at least one intermediary stands between the manufacturer and the consumer - i.e., the doctor since it is illegal for the manufacturer to sell prescription drugs directly to the patient. Usually the physician is not considered to be a member of the distribution channel. Instead, he is considered as an influencer or intermediary customer and therefore is not drawn into such diagrams. He is considered only as the decision maker. Dispensing doctors, however, are members of the distribution channel. One cannot overlook the role of pharmacists and the need of their services in the process of drug distribution. The distribution channel, when you consider the role of the pharmacists looks as in Figure 5.1.

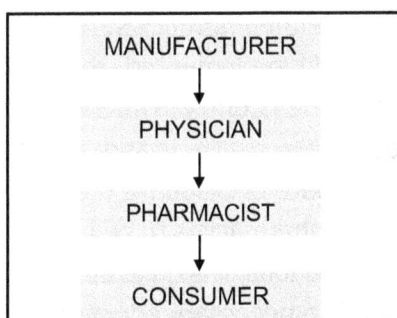

```
┌─────────────────────────────┐
│      MANUFACTURER           │
│           ↓                 │
│       PHYSICIAN             │
│           ↓                 │
│      PHARMACIST             │
│           ↓                 │
│       CONSUMER              │
└─────────────────────────────┘
```

Figure 5.1 Pharmaceutical Distribution Channels

The *pharmacist* in the distribution channel could either be a retail pharmacist, who is commonly known as a retail chemist or a hospital pharmacist.The five basic members of the distribution channel are:

1. The manufacturer
2. The physician
3. The wholesaler
4. The retailer
5. The consumer (patient)

Another characteristic feature of pharmaceutical distribution in India is that only licensed persons can manufacture and sell allopathic drugs. Law requires this. Every other systems of medicines like Ayurveda and Unani require a separate license for manufacturing. Homeopathic and Unani drugs, however are made an exception to the requirement of the Drug Technical Advisory Board and Drug Consultative Committee as per the Drugs and Cosmetics Act of 1945. It is therefore, imperative that a retail chemist or druggist should also be qualified and licensed to sell pharmaceutical preparations. The minimum qualification for a registered pharmacist, who can dispense medicines on the prescription of a medical practitioner, is a Diploma in Pharmacy (D.Pharm) in India.

Since pharmaceutical products are concerned with the health of the people, it is essential that the persons, who dispense the drugs on the prescriptions of doctors possess adequate technical knowledge.

Only then, can they interact and communicate with consumers regarding matters related to the dosage, side effects, drug interactions etc.

Currently, there are a number of unqualified but experienced persons working in various retail pharmacies. If the 1979 amendment of the Pharmacy Act is strictly implemented, there would be a severe shortage of pharmacists in the country. The 1979 amendment of the Pharmacy Act states that only qualified and registered pharmacists shall be allowed to mix, prepare or dispense medicines. Even if all the experienced but unqualified pharmacists to be trained and educated to acquire the necessary qualifications, it is quite an uphill, if not impossible task to provide them with the necessary education and training.

There are over 1,500 institutions in India offering various training programs in pharmacy education with an annual enrollment of about 100,000 students per year. While the number of pharmacy colleges and pharmacy students have increased, many of them are not choosing pharmaceutical retailing as their career. The role of a pharmacist is not perceived as an important one in the delivery of healthcare unlike their counterparts in the highly regulated markets like the US, UK and Europe. That is one of the major reasons for the shortage of qualified retail pharmacists in India.

Pharmaceutical Manufacturing

Manufacturers, as defined by the United States Census, are those engaged in the mechanical or chemical transformation of inorganic or organic substances into new products. Pharmaceutical manufacturing can be sub-divided into three classes, namely:

1. The biological products industry, which includes the production of bacterial and viral vaccines, toxoids and analogous products (such as allergy extracts) sera, plasma and other blood derivatives for human and veterinary use.

2. The medicinal and botanical industry, which includes the manufacturing of bulk medicinal organic chemicals and their derivatives and in processing (grading, grinding and milling) bulk botanical drugs and herbs. In India the botanical and herbal drugs are classified as Ayurvedic Drugs.

3. The pharmaceutical preparations industry, which includes the manufacturing or processing of drugs into pharmaceutical preparations for human or veterinary use.

The pharmaceutical preparations industry accounts for over 90 percent of the total medicines consumed in India. Ayurvedic or herbal medicine though are becoming increasingly popular, currently account for less than ten percent of the total consumption of medicines.

The Manufacturer

The characteristics of the manufacturer are important determinants in the channels of pharmaceutical distribution. These include:

A. Financial Capacity: Obviously enough, financial capacity is an important determinant of channels of distribution. The cost of selling direct or reaching the consumer or even retailer direct is prohibitive and virtually impossible today. A small-scale manufacturer cannot even think of that. That is why some large pharmaceutical companies like Glaxo, Alembic, East India Pharmaceutical Works etc., who were practicing multiple retailing in the late sixties, switched over to a more-or-less standardized distribution channel of the Indian pharmaceutical industry, i.e., manufacturer-wholesaler-retailer-consumer.

B. Reputation: Reputation is a vital characteristic, which is hard earned. It gives the manufacturer the much-needed entry into an effective distribution channel. Reputation can be built only on the bedrock of integrity, quality and fair dealing.

C. Manufacturers' Policies: Manufacturers' policies regarding all aspects of the business have a mutually reinforcing relationship in an effective distribution channel, when they are clear-cut and pragmatic.

The Physician

The physician plays a pivotal role in pharmaceutical marketing channels and indeed in pharmaceutical marketing activity as a whole. Without the prescription of a physician, no ethical drug can be dispensed by the retailer to the consumer. The physician is the decision maker and his role in the distribution channel is largely indirect in the sense that he does not buy and resell the pharmaceutical products to the patients (consumers). The dispensing doctors are an exception to this. Their involvement in the distribution channel is direct, since they purchase the pharmaceutical preparations from the manufacturers and dispense to the consumers (sell to the patients).

The Wholesaler

A wholesaler is one who purchases goods from manufacturers on his own account and resells them to other outlets like other wholesalers, and retailers , dispensing doctors, nursing homes and hospitals etc.

The wholesalers operating in the Indian pharmaceutical industry can broadly be classified into:
1. Super distributors or super stockists or distributors
2. Stockists or Accredited Wholesale Dealers
3. Wholesale Dealers or Sub-stockists
4. Clearing and Forwarding (C&F) agents

Pharmaceutical companies appoint super distributors or super stockist under an agreement. The difference, if at all, between the different terms - super distributors, super stockist and distributors - exists only in terminology or nomenclature used by different companies and not in the functions they perform. Usually, super distributors are appointed by manufacturers to look after the entire function of distribution of their products in relatively larger geographical territories like a complete state or a part of the state, depending upon certain factors like the volume of business, the product-mix, the size of the state, the degree of market penetration needed by the company etc.

A super distributor sells the products of the company or companies he is dealing with to stockists or Accredited Wholesale Dealers (AWD) appointed by the respective companies under mutually acceptable terms. He may also in addition sell the products directly to hospitals, nursing homes and dispensing doctors.

Functions of a Super Distributor

The super distributor is a very important member of the pharmaceutical distribution channel in India. Broadly speaking, the functions of super distributors are:
1. To maintain adequate stocks of the entire range of products marketed by the company.

2. To store the goods purchased from the company in an appropriate manner and at the specified temperatures required for various products.

3. To redistribute these products properly by re-selling to all the authorized stockists of the company attached to them.

4. To provide details regarding the sales (unit-wise, product-wise, and value-wise) data for each of the sales territories covered by him on a regular basis (usually every month) along with the details of stocks held by him (product-wise, pack-wise) to the company. The closing stock details help them to maintain adequate stocks and avoid possible stock-outs.

5. To provide details of stockist-wise outstandings and area-wise analysis of receivables every month. Though collection of payments from the stockist is the responsibility of the super distributor, the marketing and sales managers of the company require this information. They can probe into the reasons behind outstanding dues (if they are high and getting accumulated) and evaluate the performance of the concerned sales personnel and take corrective action.

6. To collet returned goods from the market and arrange for replacement or credit as per the policies of the company.

7. To provide feedback to the company regarding the customers' reactions towards the company's products, reactions of trade towards the company's policies, competitors' strategies and policies etc.

Thus one can observe that a super distributor functions more or less like distribution office or a depot of the company (or companies) he represents. Functionally speaking, a super distributor can be likened to a Clearing and Forwarding (C&F) agent. There is, however, one major difference. In the case of a super distributor, he purchases goods from the company and resells them to stockist appointed by the company. Therefore, the ownership of or the title to the goods change from the company to the super distributor. In the case of a C&F agent, he virtually operates like a company's distribution office or depot. He does not purchase the goods from the company. He provides the warehousing facilities, redistributes the goods to the stockists appointed by the company, and collects payments from the stockists. In other words, he manages the distribution function for the company in a given territory. The title or ownership of goods does not change in the case of a C&F agent. He is a custodian of the company's goods. He manages all the distribution functions of the company for a commission, unlike the employees of a company who draw a salary. Another difference between a C&F agent and distribution manager or a depot manager of a company is that a C&F agent of the company can also be a C&F agent for several other companies, whereas a depot manager of a company cannot have any other business interest, either directly or indirectly.

Stockist

Stockists or accredited wholesalers perform a very important function. In fact, it is the stockists, who determine the penetrative power of a company in the market place. The function of stockists, broadly speaking, include:

1. Maintenance of adequate stocks of the company's products at all times to prevent stock outs.
2. To provide proper storage facilities in terms of maintaining the specific temperature that some pharmaceutical products may require.
3. To resell the company's products among retailers, dispensing doctors, nursing homes and hospitals
4. To provide details regarding the sales (product-wise, pack-wise and value-wise) and stock held by them at the end of every month.
5. To collect the returned goods, if any from retailers and other parties as the case may be and arrange for replacement or credit as per the company's policy through the distributor or C&F Agent.
6. To provide prompt feedback to the company and its field force regarding the consumers' reactions to their products and any information on competitors' activities.

One may ask, what is the difference between a super distributor and a stockist, when both of them are essentially resellers of a company's products? The difference between super distributors and a stockist is summarized below.

A super distributor buys the goods directly from the company and caters to a larger sales territory. The order size, therefore would be considerably larger. He mainly supplies to stockists appointed and attached to him by the company, whereas a stockist under this system purchases the company's products from a super distributor and not directly from the company. He caters to a smaller sales territory. He is appointed or authorized by the company mainly to supply to retailers, dispensing doctors and nursing homes etc. He usually does not supply to wholesalers. Some stockists, however supply goods to some wholesalers who function as sub-stockists.

C&F Agent

We have already seen that a C&F agent functions more or less like a super distributor but the ownership of the goods does not change in the case of the C&F agent. Therefore, a C&F agent operates virtually like a company's own depot or distribution office. The company appoints a C&F agent under a mutually acceptable agreement. The commission payable to the C&F agent varies from company to company and usually depends upon the sales turnover of the company. The commission can be fixed as a percentage of sales turnover or as a fixed amount every month irrespective of the sales volume. Even this fixed amount is usually based on the volume of present as well as projected sales. The functions of a C&F agent are:

1. To store the company's goods safely as specified as in the various schedules of the Drugs & Cosmetics Act.
2. To execute orders promptly
3. To follow-up on accounts receivables regularly and collect payments due.
4. To follow-up the documentation procedure as per the company's instructions.
5. To provide all details pertaining to the company's sales statistics (territory-wise, product-wise, and value wise) and details of the accounts receivables analysis (party-wise and age-wise).
6. To dispatch the company's promotional material, like physicians samples and gifts, to the company's field force.
7. To submit sales tax and other returns to the respective authorities before the due date.
8. To provide feedback regarding all matters concerning the business.

These are the functions of a C&F agent in general. Since a C&F agent does not own the goods, he should display a sign board prominently, which reads: T*he goods stored in the godown are the* *property of M/s. So & So company - free of any lien and charges.* It must be noted that a C&F agent prepares an invoice on behalf of the company for the same reason. The company will take appropriate insurance cover in respect of its stocks held by a C&F agent and for goods in transit, against risk of fire, riot, strike, malicious damage, flood, explosion, earthquake, burglary etc.

The company will dispatch the goods on door delivery basis to the C&F agent. Usually it is the C&F agent who bears the transportation charges for redistribution of the goods. If the company and the C&F agent decide that the commission should not include outward-freight charges, then the freight charges will be reimbursed on actual basis. It is the practice in the Indian pharmaceutical industry to take a security deposit equivalent to one month's sale. This security could also be in the form of a bank guarantee or cash and the companies usually pay an annual interest at the prevailing bank rates. The agreement between the company and the C&F agent is usually made for a minimum three years, and is renewable.

While the commission is payable to the C&F agent varies from company to company, the industry practice is that it ranges between 1.5 percent 3 percent , including outward freight charges. This commission covers all the cost components, that the C&F agent incurred for the purpose of distributing the company's goods, for an acceptable return or compensation for services rendered. The major cost components of a C&F agent include:

- Rent for godown and office
- Cost of labor for packing (packing material is provided by the company)
- Freight cost
- Administrative costs or staff costs (stationery is provided by the company)

The Retailer

Retailers can be defined as all establishments primarily engaged in selling goods for personal and household consumption, i.e., to the ultimate consumer. Thus a retailer by definition does not sell goods or services to another business. A retail chemist or druggist, therefore, is an outlet providing drugs or health care services to the patient.

Chemists & Druggists

Retailers in the Indian pharmaceutical industry too, like elsewhere in the world, are commonly known as chemists and druggists. Even the national body of retail pharmacists in India is known as the All India Organization of Chemists and Druggists (AIOCD). Is there a difference between chemists and druggists? K. Subramanian explained the distinction between chemists and druggists in his column *Know Your English,* in *The HIndu of January 30, 1990*:

In Britain there existed a group of people subservient to physicians and they were called apothecaries. This group of people later became independent and was involved in the sale of drugs. At that time, even grocers used to sell drugs. So apothecaries obtained a charter by which grocers were prohibited from selling drugs. Apothecaries trespassed into medical practice, which led to an ACT in 1511 by which only physicians were allowed to practice medicine; but later in 1542, another Act was passed by which, anyone was allowed to practice medicine. Because of this apothecaries gave free medical advice and sold drugs. So physicians started a dispensary next to their place of work and sold medicines at much cheaper rate than apothecaries. The dispensary assistants trained by physicians were called chemists, who had wider knowledge of chemical substances involved in preparing medicines. Later chemists and druggists joined together and formed a union and from then on the two words have always been used together.

The word chemist is the short form of dispensing chemist. A chemist means one who makes powders, emulsions, mixtures etc. as per the prescription of a medical practitioner. Only a qualified pharmacist is entitled to dispense. This category is fast disappearing. Druggist means one who merely sells drugs.

While all the members of a pharmaceutical distribution channel are equally important, a retailer chemist or druggist is even more important. The reasons are:

1. It is a chemist and druggist, who dispenses the prescription of a medical practitioner and sells medicines to a patient. The availability of your product at the retail chemist level is most crucial. If a prescription is returned or dishonored for want of stocks, the doctor usually changes that prescription and suggests an alternative. Sometimes a retailer is so influential (with his consumers) that he himself may dispense an alternative brand. To make a doctor re-prescribe a brand (which he has stopped due to non-availability of the drug) is twice as difficult as getting his prescription in the first place.

2. Secondly, retailer is a very important source of information regarding the prescribing behavior of the doctors around him and the movement of products of various competitors. Successful medical representatives realize the importance of the retailers and spend an adequate amount of time with them to gather valuable information on prescribing behavior of physicians to whose prescriptions the retailers cater to. There is a wealth of information available with the retailer for the discerning observer to see, note and act. The important information cues are the shelf stocks of various products, the prescriptions brought in by the patients and the bill books (copies of the bills made while selling the drugs to consumers).

3. The retailer can help you increase the sale of OTC formulations and also prescription drugs with OTC profile, once he is convinced about your company and your products.

Services Rendered by the Retailers

A retailer renders important services to the community. Some of the important services rendered by retail chemist or druggist are:

1. Holds ready stock of various important and essential medicines needed to cater to the prescriptions of doctors.

2. Provides supplementary information required by patients regarding the dosage, side effects, etc.

Are Wholesale and Retail Middlemen Useful?

Every time the prices of essential commodities go up, a public cry goes up almost simultaneously to *eliminate the middlemen*. Every time a product passes through a distribution channel its cost goes up. The longer the channel the higher the cost. Wholesalers and retailers add to the cost of medicines about 24 to 30 percent without taking local taxes into account. While the cost of wholesaling and retailing is considerable, can anyone do away with these middlemen? The answer is an emphatic *No*. You cannot consider these costs in isolation. You must weigh them against the services rendered by these middlemen to manufacturers and consumers. Consider these reasons:

- They ensure rapid distribution and wide dispersion of new products
- Relieve manufacturers of the detail of performing non-detailing tasks.
- Ensure immediate availability of all important medicines when they are needed and where they are wanted.

It is possible for these middlemen to handle even small orders economically, because they deal in a wide assortment of products not just of one company but of various companies. In the case of retailers, they stock the products of almost all the companies whose products are prescribed by doctors in their locality.

The wholesalers' sales forces augment the selling effort of the company's sale force, particularly in case of OTC formulations and non-prescription drugs.

Wholesalers can manage the retail credit better than the manufacturer because of proximity. For any manufacturer it becomes virtually impossible to collect receivables from retailers on a national level. That is why the multiple retailing system was discontinued by a number of companies.

The distribution channel system of wholesalers and retailers help manufacturers achieve a more efficient utilization of resources and better return on investment. The manufacturers' funds are not tied up in avoidable (due to the presence of middlemen) investments such as warehouse space, higher finished inventories, account receivables etc.

Vital Function

That distribution of goods and services is absolutely essential is certainly not a debatable issue. When you want to make your products and services available at the right time, at the right place, it naturally involves expenditure i.e., costs such as packing costs, transportation costs, inventory carrying costs, warehousing costs and administrative costs. The key question to ask, therefore, is which system of distribution, direct or through middlemen is more cost-effective? Obviously the system of wholesalers and retailers is the most cost-effective.

This is possible because they can achieve the optimum utilization of time, place and space. Channels of distribution help movement of goods from one place to another i.e., from manufacturer to wholesaler and from wholesaler to retailer, thus creating place utility. The retailer, who is a member of this channel, makes it possible for the consumer (the patient) to get the product immediately as per the prescription of the doctor, thus creating time utility. The manufacturer can operate with a smaller inventory and consequently a relatively less storage space (since the goods are continuously moving in the distribution channel) and still make his products available, thus achieving space utility.

Furthermore, the total cost of making the goods available at the right time, at the right place would be higher, if there were no channels of distribution. It is also not possible for the manufacturers to provide customer service at the required level. Consider for a moment the fact even with over 850,000 retail pharmacies and 30,000 wholesalers the drug distribution channels are unable to deliver the required levels of customer service in the rural areas, where about two-thirds of the the population lives. Commenting on the inadequate service of distribution particularly in rural areas, the Hathi Committee in fact, came up with the recommendation that essential drugs may be distributed through post offices, petrol stations, kerosene depots and co-operative stores in rural areas. The Hathi Committee felt that was essential to carry the benefits of modern medicine to the rural hinterland. These recommendations, however, were never considered for implementation.

Mutual Expectations

What do members of the channels of distribution expect from each other? The manufacturers' expectations from the trade channels are:
1. To help establish new products quickly by making them available and to provide the necessary information to the consumer regarding these products.
2. To maintain adequate stocks at all times and avoid stock outs.
3. To practice fair trade.
4. To retire the documents promptly and send the payments on time.
5. To display the products prominently.

6. To provide information on consumer reactions to their products and feedback on market conditions and competitors' activities.

7. To provide service to the consumers and customers promptly.

The dealers' (wholesalers and retailers) expectations from the manufacturers are:

1. A fair return on their investment, i.e., adequate margins on the products they stock and sell.

2. Quality products from manufacturers.

3. Fair trade practices.

4. Adequate promotional support to accelerate the demand for the products they stock.

5. Prompt service regarding the dispatch of goods by the manufacturers and prompt settlement of claims etc.

Pharmaceutical Distribution Channels: Key Aspects

Selecting an Appropriate Channel

What is an ideal channel is a difficult question to answer because there is no such thing as an ideal channel. Channel selection depends upon the size of the company, the type of product-mix, the degree of market penetration required etc.

Any company competing in the Indian pharmaceutical market has a relatively simple choice in so far as distribution channels are concerned. It has become almost mandatory for every manufacturer to distribute their products through a stockist or wholesaler, who in turn re-sells them to retailers and the retailer finally sells to the consumer (patient). That is the minimum length of a distribution channel you can think of in the Indian pharmaceutical market. This is because no manufacturer can ever hope to reach even the retailers directly on a national level, let alone the consumers. The size of the market and its diverse conditions dictate that. Furthermore, the number of transactions involved in reaching the retailers direct is truly mind-blogging. That is why stockists (wholesalers) and retailers have become such vital, indispensable links in the pharmaceutical distribution channels.

The options, therefore, available to a manufacturer are whether to add one more link to the channel i.e., whether to sell to stockist through a super distributor or sell directly to the stockist. Large companies with adequate infrastructure of depots in all strategic locations and adequate financial resources preferred selling directly to the stockists in the past as an additional link in the channel would increase the cost of distribution. Not any more. Those companies who had their own depots have closed their depots and switched over to C&F agency system. Companies, which have entered the market recently, or have expanded recently and do not have their own depots, prefer to sell their products through a super distributor - wholesaler - retailer - consumer channel. Companies that do not have adequate financial resources and are short on working capital, naturally, prefer distributing the goods through super distributors because *trade deposits* from super distributors ease working capital requirements, at least temporarily.

Furthermore, receivables management can also be better with super distributors. There are only a few accounts to be managed. The inherent disadvantage is that the *accounts* though few in number are likely to be substantial in volume, thus increasing the degree of vulnerability and risk in case of default. It is also important to note that the *receivables* can only be prompt when the basic demand (prescriptions) for a company's products are high.

Super-distributor or C&F Agent?

The next option available to a manufacturer is whether to appoint a super distributor or a C&F Agent? There is an increasing trend nowadays to appoint C&F Agents rather than super-distributors. The reasons are:

- Appointing a C&F Agency is almost similar to having company's own depot. The C&F Agent manages the distribution function. The goods belong to the company. The invoicing too is done on behalf of the company. The goods are transferred from the company's warehouse to the C&F Agent. There is no sale involved. The company, therefore, does not have to pay the four percent CST (Central Sales Tax) even in the case of interstate transfers. The company's goods cost less by 4 percent to the consumer. (Now with the GST in place, CST is abolished and merged with CGST).

- Having a C&F Agent in areas where the company does not have a depot ensures a uniform distribution system throughout the country. The company will be selling to stockists directly through a C&F Agent. The company will have better control on its goods, sales and receivables and in fact, all its distribution activities.

- Another advantage of having a C&F Agent is that in certain parts of the country, trade associations are contesting that a distributor is also a wholesaler and performs more or less the same functions. Therefore, all wholesalers (whether they are called stockist, super stockist, authorized wholesale dealers, distributors, or super distributors) should be given the same margins as the super distributors. This would naturally increase the cost of distribution, which manufacturers can ill-afford.

- In addition, trade associations all over the country are pressing for the same wholesale margins of 8 percent on controlled category and 10 percent on decontrolled category products, as per the industry and trade agreement, to all wholesalers whether they are stockists appointed by a super distributor. Appointing a C&F Agent would mean reaching the stockist directly.

C&F Agent or Own Depot?

When a manufacturer decides to reach the stockist directly, whether to reach them by opening the company's own depot in a given territory or through a C&F Agent is yet another option available to him. One can observe a growing trend of appointing C&F Agents in preference to starting the company's own depots. The changing economics of distribution seem to be influencing this decision more than anything else. Consider these reasons:

- Overheads for a C&F Agent are usually less than manufacturers' because wages are usually much less for the employees of a C&F Agent.

- If a manufacturer wants to lease or buy godown space for his depot today, the prices are high particularly in business localities in all cities. Many C&F Agents already own or possess a leased godown space and therefore, warehousing costs are comparatively less for them.

- Moreover, a C&F Agent usually represents more than one company and therefore costs can be spread over the services that are shared. For the same reason, a C&F Agent can achieve a greater utility in terms of the the essential elements of distribution, namely place, time and space.

- A C&F Agent specializes in distribution and therefore, he can provide a far better service to all the channel members than a manufacturer.
- A C&F Agency system helps the company implement a uniform policy of reaching the stockist directly throughout the country, without having to start its own depots.

These are some advantages the C&F Agency system offers. A number of pharmaceutical companies have been realizing the advantages that a C&F agency system offers, and switching over to the C&F agency system. If the sales volume is very high, it would of course be profitable for the company to start its own depot or distribution office. Considering the steep increase in real estate prices (and consequently in rental charges) increasing overheads and other costs, one has to do a cost benefit analysis and above all, plan sufficiently in advance to start a depot or distribution office.

Criteria for Selection

What should be the criteria for selecting a distributor or stockist? While there are no rigid rules regarding the selection of a stockist, the following questions serve as a useful checklist:

1. Is he financially sound? Can he invest the required amount? Financial capability of the stockist is an important factor to be considered.
2. What are his marketing capabilities? How many salesmen does he have? How prompt is his customer service in terms of dispatching goods, attending to complaints of customers? What is the coverage of his markets like? How frequently does he cover all the customers? A feedback from the market and from the field force of companies (with whom he is currently dealing) is an important source for getting this information.
3. How many companies does he currently handle?

This information has two important implications. Firstly, this indicates the likely level of service you can get from him. If he is currently dealing with a number of companies, you are unlikely to get a distinct service from him. At the same time, you cannot have a stockist exclusively for your company. And the second implication is that if he is also a stockist or distributor for your major competitors, there is likely to be a conflict of interests. For example, if you are enjoying a leadership position in sera and vaccines range of products and if he is also the distributor for your major competitor, then there is bound to be a conflict of interests. This kind of conflict is likely to occur in the case of your major products and their major competing brands. It is also possible in case of competing OTC formulations and ethical brands with OTC profile.

Reaching the Institutional Market

The institutional market in India is considerably large and growing rapidly. The institutional market includes purchases made by:

- Director General of Supplies and Disposals (DGS&D)
- Medical Stores Depot (MSD)
- Railway Hospitals
- Employees State Insurance Corporation (ESIC)
- Armed Forces Medical Stores Depots (AFMSD)
- Central Government Health Scheme (CGHS)
- Hospitals in the Public Sector Undertakings like BHEL, BHPV, HAL etc.
- Hospitals Attached to Medical Colleges
- Government Hospitals
- Primary Health Centers
- Private Nursing Homes and Hospitals
- Corporate Hospitals

Medical Stores Depots, apart from their contractual purchases based on annual tenders, are authorized to purchase certain medicines locally within certain limits. These limits vary depending upon the size of the hospitals in terms of services and facilities available, and the number of beds available etc.

DGS&D calls for specific rate contracts for various categories of products to be supplied to various government hospitals, Medical Stores Depots, Army establishments and Directorates of Medical and Health Services. The options available to reach this vast institutional market are similar to those existing in the trade channels. The only difference is that an institutional wholesaler, instead of supplying to a retailer supplies to a hospital, which in turn dispenses the drug to the patient as per the prescription of the doctor. The manufacturer has two choices regarding the distribution channels of the institutional market. One is that he can sell his products directly to institutions. Alternatively, he can sell his products through a middleman (a hospital distributor to sell their products to institutions). The main reason for this seems to be the enormous delay in receiving payments from institutions in general. A few exceptions to this delay in receipt of payments are DGS &D, a few hospitals in the public sector and private hospitals. DGS&D releases 95 percent of the payment immediately on receipt of goods. That is why some companies prefer to supply the DGS&D rate contract orders directly and have separate distributors for institutional sales. Another reason for supplying the DGS&D orders directly is that the additional four percent central tax is not applicable to supplies made by the company. If goods are supplied through a distributor four percent CST had to paid. By supplying goods directly, the company can to that extent, be more competitive in its price.

Even among the hospital distributors there are two categories. Distributors, who purchase products from manufacturers and resell to hospitals belong to the first category. The second category of distributors is not distributors or wholesalers in the real sense of the word, since they neither purchase the companies' products nor sell them to hospitals. They act as liaison agents and procure business from various hospitals and also ensure that payments are remitted by the hospitals to the manufacturers within the stipulated period of time. The compensation or the discount to the first category of distributors is between 10 and 12 percent . And, for the second category of hospital distributors or liaison agents it is between 2 and 4 percent depending upon the size of the company and expected volume of business.

GeM Replaces DGS&D

In July 2017, The Ministry of Industries and Commerce of Government of India had asked industrialists, IT companies, manufacturers and vendors in all states to register on Government e-Marketing Portal (GeM), which is going to replace DGS&D, the procurement arm of GoI (Government of India) by October 31, 2017.

GeM Portal has been developed as the national procurement portal replacing DGS&D, to ensure transparency and accountability in procurement of goods and services by central and state government departments. The GeM Portal presently (July 2017) has 40,000 registered users, 33,000 products and 17 services. It is observed that the prices of goods on the Portal are lower by 15 - 20 percent on an average, compared to the corresponding rate of DGS&D contracts or even the most recent tenders floated by various government departments.

The key reason for competitive prices is easy registration of vendors and payments to be made within 10 days of successful receipt or acceptance of goods and services.

Trade Margins

In the past trade margins particularly, wholesalers' margins were only a matter of understanding between the wholesalers and respective companies they were dealing with. There was a lot of variance between the margins given by various companies. Some companies were giving a discount on a minimum order value fixed by the company. Later some companies started appointing authorized wholesale dealers with a specific agreement renewable every one or two years. The wholesalers were supposed to purchase a minimum value of goods every quarter, which was determined by the company. Only on achieving the predetermined level of purchases, would they qualify for the total discount. This was later objected by trade associations, who finally succeeded in getting this conditional discount structure changed to a straight discount on the invoice, irrespective of the value of purchases.

The trade was consistently making demands for increased margins. The industry was expressing helplessness and was representing to the government that it could not possibly absorb any additional trade margins unless the government allowed it to increase its prices proportionately. Finally, in the DPCO 1979, government specified the retail margins of 12 percent to retailers and 2 percent to the wholesalers. The industry was already paying higher margins to the wholesalers than those specified by government. No doubt, the margins specified to wholesalers by government were too low, probably the lowest in the world pharmaceutical trade.

Again, in DPCO 1987, government revised the retail margins to 16 percent and the wholesale margins to 3 percent . The industry and trade, however entered into an agreement regarding trade margins and other issues. Presently, trade margins as per the revised agreement are:

- 16 percent to retailers on products in controlled categories I & II
- 20 percent to retailers on products outside controlled categories
- 8 percent to wholesalers on products in controlled categories I & II
- 10 percent to wholesalers on products outside controlled categories

These are the margins agreed upon by the industry and the trade, whereas DPCO 1987 specified a minimum margin of 16 percent to retailers and 3 percent to wholesalers on all products whether controlled or decontrolled.

Trade United!

For years many pharmaceutical manufacturers, like the general public, have taken retail chemists for granted. For a long time some of the less powerful retailers were at the mercy of manufacturers regarding settlement of their claims. The changing scenario in the pharmaceutical industry with its ever-increasing controls, numerous new entrants and the consequent proliferation of brands many of which never took-off and ended dead as a dodo on many a chemist's shelf - all these have also taken a toll of the retail trade. Retailers gradually started to get themselves organized to protect their interests.

AIOCD

The All India Federation of Chemists and Druggists started in 1943, was not truly an all India body as it was representing chemists and druggists mainly from the four metros - Bombay, Calcutta, Madras and Delhi. Later, in 1960, with the emphasis on retail trade, an All India Retail Chemists Association (AIRCA) was formed. Both these organizations did not enjoy the enthusiastic support of their respective members. A need for organizing an all India body was felt by the key members of these two organizations and a new all India body, under the name Indian Organization of Chemists and Druggists was formed in October 1972 at Bangalore at an All India convention of chemists and druggists. And finally in December 1972, when the two organizations of chemists and druggists I.e., All India Federation of Chemists and Druggists and All India Organization of Chemists and Druggists decided that was time to patch-up their differences and to start one organization, which truly represents the interests of chemists and druggists of India. This finally resulted in the formation of the All India Organization of Chemists and Druggists (AIOCD) in 1975.

A Growing Power

A retailer is undoubtedly one of the most important links in the pharmaceutical marketing channel. While it is true that a retail pharmacist's endorsement alone cannot help a brand succeed, particularly in the ethical drug business, stubborn non-cooperation from the trade can certainly have an adverse affect on the manufacturers. The retailers were the first to realize among the trade channels that they could guide the fate of brands. With this realization they started flexing their muscles and took up the cudgels with the industry. Consider these cases:

Case 5.1 Margins Hold the Key to Success!

Johnson & Johnson, the transnational giant in the OTC healthcare business, introduced a new sanitary napkin, 'Modest' in the early 1970s to take on the pioneer Comfit of Christine Hoyden. Johnson & Johnson took their image for granted, and marketed the product. The product never really took off and was finally withdrawn. What could be the reason for the failure of a market-driven and professionally managed company like Johnson & Johnson? Surprising as it might seem, the reason was that the low retail margins the company offered!

Case 5.2 The Pharmaceutical Giant Faces the First-ever Trade Boycott!

In the 1970s, it was Sarabhai Chemicals (Squibb in those days), which faced the first-ever trade boycott. The reasons for this boycott was the company's policy regarding damaged goods. The company was apprehensive that a liberal policy for replacing damaged goods could lead to abuse and corruption and therefore was very rigid in replacing the damaged goods. Claims were getting accumulated as a result. The company did not budge and refused to give-in to the pressure from the trade. The trade used their final weapon i.e., boycott of the company's products. The entire pharmaceutical industry was waiting, watching, hoping and praying for the company's success.

The prayers went unheeded and unanswered for the trade continued the boycott. The company, which was already under considerable pressure from its sagging sales of consumer products, could not afford a further loss of sales from its bread-winning pharmaceutical division. The pressure was too much to bear and the company finally gave in.

Case 5.3 The Power of Margins in Tilting the Market Share Balance is More than Marginal!

It was the turn of Glaxo's family products division in the late 1970s to face a trade boycott. Glaxo did not increase the trade margins on their leading brand of Farex (infant food with milk and cereal) as demanded by the trade. Consequently, Farex disappeared from the shelves of retailers due to a trade boycott. Nestle's Cerelac, which was a distinct number two brand, experienced a sudden spurt in sales. It was almost a windfall for Celrelac. Glaxo subsequently conceded a revision in the trade margin. By then, it had already paid the price. A number of Farex users were already converted to Cerelac. Glaxo had been trying to regain its lost market share for Farex ever since! (Later, Wockhardt acquired the Farex brand from Glaxo)

Case 5.4 Trade Boycott Costs Rs. 7-crore to the Industry Leader!

Even after the MRTP (Monopoly and Restrictive Trade Practices) Commission hauled up the AIOCD for obstructing the free flow of medicines into the market, around October 1986, the Bengal Chemists and Druggists Association (BCDA) affiliated to AIOCD organized a trade boycott against the industry leader, Glindia's (GSK now) products for over five months during 1988 demanding higher trade margins for their betamethasone range of formulations.

Since no solution was forthcoming from government or industry associations, the company on its own held discussions with the trade associations and finally agreed to pay an additional one percent on their betamethasone range of products and settled the issue amicably. The trade boycott that lasted for about five months had cost the company around Rs. 7-crore in sales.

What are the lessons from these cases? There are at least two lessons for manufacturers and marketers in these.

- Retailers could tilt the balance in favor of any brand they choose to in case of products, which are necessities and even OTC formulations.
- Once the consumer of a brand is converted to another brand, he cannot easily be converted back.

And the important message is that you should never take the trade for granted. Be sensitive to their demands and problems. In case the demands are genuine, accept them without delay. And in case of problems settle them promptly.

The trade has realized their strength and today the relationship between the industry and the trade can best be described as one of armed truce. Both the industry and the trade have entered into an agreement covering all possible areas of conflict.

NOC and LOC

Having tasted success with earlier boycotts and after making the industry concede to virtually all its demands, the trade was not really satisfied. There was more to do. It was its new found power that probably prompted the trade to ride roughshod over manufacturers. The AIOCD insisted that manufacturers should get a *No Objection Certificate (NOC)* from the AIOCD (or its state or district committee as the case may be) every time a manufacturer introduces a new product or decides to appoint a new stockist or terminate an agreement with an existing stockist, after paying a prescribed fee. If not, their new products would not be stocked and their products would be boycotted in those areas. Subsequently, when this NOC had attracted the provisions of the MRTP Act (Monopolies and Restrictive Trade Practices), the name of the *No Objection Certificate* was changed euphemistically to *Letter of Cooperation (LOC)*. It was rather a forced cooperation!

The Indian Express reported on October 31, 1986 regarding the MRTPC's observation on the NOC or LOC of AIOCD:

The Monopolies and Restrictive Trade Practices Commission (MRTPC) has hauled up the All India Organization of Chemists and Druggists for obstructing the free flow of medicines into the market.

The AIOCD, an apex body of chemists and druggists in the country has 19 State associations and other affiliated units in different parts of the country. Whenever a drug manufacturer introduces a new product or decides to terminate or appoint a new stockist, he has to get a certificate of no objection or letter of cooperation compulsorily from the AIOCD, after paying prescribed fee.

Similar certificates have also got to be obtained from state and district associations for marketing a new product in these areas. Besides, the manufacturers often have to pay huge amounts as *donations* to these associations. Manufacturers, who refuse to comply with these *rules* find their products being totally boycotted by all members of the association. Granting an ex-party interim injunction restraining AIOCD and its associates from forcing manufacturers to take such certificates from them, MRTPC bench consisting of Justice G.R. Luthra, Chairman and Mr. S.D. Manchanda, member, observed that the r*espondents cannot be allowed to* run a parallel government, to carry on a system which affects the flow of medicines to the market.

Terminating the practice as a blatant interference with the product and the flow of trade in the manufacture and marketing of pharmaceutical products, the MRTPC said *it also* leads to distortion of competition.

Tacit Understanding

What has been the effect of the MRTPC's directive to AIOCD, an apex body of pharmaceutical trade in India? The nomenclature changed from NOC to LOC. The prescribed fee is converted to advertising tariff for publishing the new product information in the trade journal. The trade associations are more careful in drafting their letters to manufacturers on these matters. Otherwise the boycotts or threats of boycott continue. Despite an interim injunction by MRTPC to a state committee of AIOCD, the boycott of a leading pharmaceutical company continued. How did it happen? It is all because there is always a tacit understanding among the members of the trade.

Managing Trade Channels Effectively

There is no magic formula for managing trade channels effectively and getting the most out of them. Consider this back to basics approach:

- A stockist or distributor is a member of your marketing team. You should build up a profitable and lasting relationship with your stockists and distributors.

- A stockist would like to rotate his capital as fast and as many times as he can. You can help him achieve a faster rotation of his capital by increasing the demand for your products and by bringing more orders from retailers, dispensing doctors and nursing homes. Increased prescription generation, is the only way to achieve this.

- If you appoint more stockists than needed, only to achieve a short term objective of temporarily increasing ex-factory sales, that is a sure way of slowing down the rotation of the stockist's capital. Stockist appointment must be based on the market demand and the degree of market penetration required by your company. A stockist is mainly interested in an adequate return on his investment. If the sales volume is not high or at a respectable level (these depend upon your stockist's ability and the demand for your products), the stockist may lose interest in your company's business. You have to therefore, maintain and sustain the stockist's interest level in your company. This can be achieved only by increased prescription generation for your products.

- Ensure that you pay prompt attention to the complaints and problems of your stockists. You can demonstrate your interest in your stockists only by solving their problems. That can be achieved only by increased prescription generation for your products.

It is possible to manage stockists and distributors only if you see them as members of your company's marketing team, helping you in the task of distribution and not as mere middlemen, on whom you can dump some stocks and achieve your sales targets.

Physical Distribution

The tremendous physical effort needed for making the products available where and when they are needed was almost being taken granted by marketers for quite some time. The study of distribution for a long time had been centered around the channels of distribution. But not any longer. Distribution is too important an activity to be left to the distribution department of a company. Increasingly, companies are realizing the importance of physical distribution and restructuring their organograms accordingly. Physical distribution is a marketing activity that concerns the handling and movement of goods. It includes all those activities required to move finished goods effectively from the producer to the consumer.

The total cost of distribution has been going up steadily over the years. When you take trade margins into account, the total cost of distribution would be equal to your materials costs if not more. The impact of distribution on the bottom line is therefore, substantial. That is how and why the concept of total physical distribution has evolved. Under this concept, all management functions related to moving products to buyers are fully integrated. Responsibility for the various activities of distribution, which were hitherto scattered, is now centered in the physical distribution department. The company can achieve greater cost effectiveness since it is possible to take a holistic view of distribution.

Three Major Areas

Distribution, under the total physical distribution concept, is a department equal to production, and materials. The three major areas of physical distribution are:

1. Warehousing

2. Inventory control

3. Transportation

Location of the depots is a very important factor to be considered. Should they be ex-factory positioned or market-positioned? Other important aspects to consider while locating a depot are: warehousing, inventory control and management of receivables.

Warehousing

In order to achieve cost-effectiveness through warehousing, managers must take decisions as to which location is most appropriate, whether the facility is to be rented or owned and how many warehouses or depots are needed.

It has now become common practice in the Indian pharmaceutical industry to have C&F Agencies to optimize distribution costs. Earlier, till the 1990s some larger pharmaceutical companies had a combination of company-owned depots and C&F Agencies.

Another important point to remember regarding the storage of pharmaceutical products is that one should follow the Good Distribution Practice (GDP) prescribed by WHO (World Health Organization) for proper distribution of medicinal products for human use. Since pharmaceutical products are concerned with health and well being of human beings, it is important that all the standards related to the cleanliness, temperatures at which the various products are required to be stored are strictly adhered to. Some of the factors to be considered while locating the depot are:

- Availability of transport
- Quantity and quality of labor
- Cost of land
- Taxes applicable
- Services provided by the local government

Inventory Control

It is estimated that about one-third of pharmaceutical production is tied up in inventory. The figure includes materials stored for manufacture like raw materials, packing materials, work in progress and finished goods. To manage such a large share of resources effectively, distribution managers must first decide on the stock levels to be maintained. The two most important goals of inventory management are:

A. To provide an adequate level of customer service avoiding out of stock situations, and

B. To minimize the company's investment in inventory

Avoiding Stock-outs

Going out of stock of finished goods can cost a good deal to a company. Customers in most stock-out situations become disenchanted and turn to competitors. Particularly in pharmaceutical marketing, it is very difficult to persuade doctors to take up a product once they change to a competitor due to non-availability.

On the other hand, maintaining a large enough inventory to avoid any possible out-of-stock situations can be a very expensive, if not prohibitive affair. Even if you achieve a marginal increase in orders to be catered to from the existing stocks, you may have to double the inventory levels of finished products. What is needed is to achieve a balance in the flow of orders and stocks.

There is no hard and fast rule to achieve this balance. Pareto's principle can be applied even to inventory management. Usually about 20 percent of the products a company carries account for majority (80 Percent) of its sales. Products with the largest sales should always be made available so that all orders can be dispatched from stock. Lower levels of stock may be maintained for less important products.

A B C Analysis

ABC analysis is a popular and widely used technique, which identifies and classifies items in order of importance according to their sales volume. Those items that account for the largest percentage of sales are classified as 'A' products, that must be stocked at all times. Likewise, other items accounting for relatively lesser percentage of sales in the descending order are classified as 'B' and 'C' products. Understandably, relatively lower levels of stock can be maintained for 'B' and 'C' products.

Two costs should be of primary concern in effective management of inventory. They are:

A. *Acquisition costs* are expenses incurred in buying the product. In other words, these are costs for setting up for production in case of a manufacturer and the expenses of record keeping, handling the paper work for orders (invoicing, negotiating the documents etc.) in case of a distributor or stockist.

B. *Carrying costs* are the expenses involved in a maintaining the stocks over a period of time. The carrying costs include interest, storage, insurance, taxes etc. The interest charges are those that the manufacturer or the middleman pays on the investment made to acquire the stocks.

Balancing Act

As the costs of acquiring and carrying the inventory is rising, it becomes increasingly difficult to avoid stock-outs and achieve a desired or desirable level of customer service. Avoiding stock-outs on the one hand and cutting down inventory costs on the other is, indeed a delicate balancing act that requires some trade-offs.

To determine the right inventory size, the assumptions regarding the demand must be correct. Sales forecasts should be reasonably accurate. The more accurate a company's sales projections are, the less money it has to tie up in excess inventories. That is the delicate act and art balancing. Only a proper orchestration and co-ordination between sales, production, finance, materials and distribution will ensure the success of the total physical distribution from concept to implementation.

Management of Receivables

Receivables management is the responsibility of the sales force. The distribution department provides the necessary follow-up. Effective receivables management is crucial for the maintenance of the required stock centers. If the outstandings are locked up within the trade channels the company cannot afford the luxury of maintaining adequate stock levels. For any company the resources are finite. No company can afford to tie its money in excess stocks and also in receivables at the same time. Therefore, prompt collection of receivables would enable a company to maintain adequate stocks.

Keeping Track

Keeping track of inventory is essential. Knowing how stock is moving and what products are moving is important in determining how much inventory to keep on hand. Records of the amount of stock on hand and its rate of depletion are necessary to plan for their replacement. The two most commonly used record keeping methods are:

(a) **Physical count:** As the name suggests physical count involves physically taking stock of all items in the product line and comparing it with the stocks issued as per the orders received. Most companies usually carry out this exercise once a month to check if there is any discrepancy when compared with the perpetual inventory.

(b) **Perpetual inventory:** The physical count tells us about the flow of goods day-in and day-out of. A firm should keep a record of perpetual inventory, a list of all goods in stock, which is updated constantly i.e., every time stocks of particular items are issued against an order.

Economic Order Quantity (EOQ)

Using the sales forecasts, distribution managers determine the inventory that they need to order to replenish the stock. The quantity or amount to be reordered is called Economic Order Quantity (EOQ). EOQ can be defined as the amount of stock that costs the least to keep on hand in order to meet the average level of demand. EOQ thus provides the answer for maintaining the right stock levels by taking into account the ordering costs and inventory carrying costs and arriving at the lowest overall figures.

Safety Stock

The economic order quantity specifies only the stock to meet the average demand. If the sales forecast is not correct and if there is a sudden spurt in demand, a stock-out may result. This in turn may lead to losing customers. Companies therefore, maintain a safety stock above the basic stock level to prevent any likely stock-out and to meet any sudden increase in demand. That is why safety stock is also known as buffer stock. The safety stock may be needed either because the supplies don't turn up or the demand for the item involved is higher than expected.

Transportation

Transportation is often the single most difficult task that a distribution manager has to perform. It accounts for a major portion of the distribution expenditure. The total transportation charges on an average amount to anywhere between 3 to 4 percent of the sales volume in the case of pharmaceutical companies in India. It, of course, depends upon the product-mix of a company. In case of companies marketing liquid orals and protein food supplements, the transportation costs would be higher than those marketing injectables and tablets etc. Furthermore, complex logistics, different terrain, varying temperature conditions make transportation tasks difficult. While there are five modes of transportation like rail, road, water, air and pipelines to move their products to consumers, the most widely used transport is road transport in case of pharmaceutical products in India. Air freight is used only in case of certain light items like injections and certain life saving drugs where temperature control is a must.

Water transportation is used only in the case of exports of pharmaceutical products, since it provides the cheapest way of carrying bulk drugs over a long distance. Many of the companies enter into renewable annual contracts with large transport companies to achieve economy and reliability in terms of safe and speedy delivery.

Implementing the Distribution Concept

Implementing the total physical distribution concept involves a proper balancing of two objectives. One is minimizing costs to the company as a whole. The other is providing a satisfactory level of customer service.

Maintaining costs is a very difficult task for two reasons. firstly, all costs are not so obvious. There are visible costs and hidden costs. Visible costs are those expenses which can be seen on a profit and loss statement. These include direct expenses like the ones incurred for running warehouses, depots and transportation charges and also the indirect costs of insuring goods, paying property taxes, interest charges etc. Hidden costs, as the name implies are those that accounts cannot record. These include costs due to cancellation of orders or failure to supply for want of stocks. It is difficult to pinpoint which costs are minimized and if so at what cost, if only costs are specified.

Secondly, it is difficult to minimize the total cost. Doing things in the cheapest possible manner is the only way to keep the total costs down. But then, it may affect the efficiency of operations. It may result in a lower level of customer service than is acceptable. One should not think only in terms of cost reduction. The approach should be one of finding ways to improve cost effectiveness. It sometimes pays to allow costs to increase in one area to bring down costs in others. This is what is known as cost trade-off. Consider this for example:

Some pharmaceutical companies, whose main product lines are liquid orals, are having their products manufactured at a number of locations, where the demand is high (locating the plant nearer to the market) with a view to peg the ever-increasing transportation costs down. The cost trade-off here is between the increase in manufacturing costs (due to lowered economy of scale, that is smaller batches of production) and the decreased inventory level and reduced transportation costs.

Setting Standards

In today's highly competitive situation, customer satisfaction holds the key to success of any enterprise. Customer service therefore, is of paramount importance. Any cost reduction exercise to improve the financial performance in the short run should not be undertaken if it is going to result in a lowered level of customer service. One can and should set high but practical performance standards. Here is an example of performance standards for pharmaceutical distribution (Table 5.1).

Table 5.1 Performance Standards for Physical Distribution Activities

Criteria	Performance Standard
A. Inventory of finished goods	95 per cent of orders for all 'A' items should be filled from available stock
B. Accuracy in inventory	99 per cent accuracy in invoicing of the orders placed
C. Delivery of goods	A. All local orders to be delivered within 24 hours B. All outstation orders to be dispatched within 2 working days.
D. Discrepancy	To achieve a zero discrepancy level between the physical count and the perpetual inventory every week.
E. Complaint resolution	Credit notes or replacements for any damaged goods to be issued within 15 days of the receipt of the compliant.

Distribution and the Legal Environment

Over the years, a number of laws affecting the business have become operational. Understanding of this regulatory environment is essential for the marketer. The laws mainly affecting the distribution activity of a firm are given in Table 5.2.

Table 5.2 Distribution and the Regulatory Environment Act Scope

Act	Scope
1. Indian Contracts Act 1972	All decisions pertaining to the formation and execution of a contract. Covers rights and duties of a principal and an agent.
2. Indian Sale of Goods 1930	Governs the transactions of sale and purchase. Lays down the rules regarding the transfer of property in goods and the duties of the buyer, and seller, rules regarding the delivery of goods and the rights of the unpaid seller.
3. The Monopolies and Restrictive Trade Practices Act 1969 (MRTP)	Prevents concentration of economic power to the common detriment and controls monopolies, restrictive, unfair, trade practices.
4. Standards of Weights & Measures Act 1976	Specified the quantifies in which certain products can be packed. While the act does not include pharmaceutical products which cannot be linked to consumer product, prescription drugs are not excluded either.

The Changing Landscape of Pharma Retail Market

What's Up with the Indian Pharmaceutical Place? What's happening in the Indian pharmaceutical place lately? Here's a snapshot (2017) of the recent and ongoing development in the pharmaceutical retail market space. Two main factors, affordability and Acceptability are further driving the growth.

The rapidly growing Indian pharmaceutical market is likely to grow even faster. A number of factors indicate this. According to an estimate by one of the world's leading consultancy firms, McKinsey, the Indian pharmaceutical market is likely to grow to US $ 55 billion in size by 2020. Here are some of the key drivers of this significant growth:

A. Substantial increase in the patient pool due to a steady rise of the disease prevalence and a high population growth rate of about 1.3 percent per annum

B. The Government sponsored healthcare programs such as Rashtriya Swasthiya Bima Yojana (RSBY) focusing on 'Below Poverty Line' (BPL) segment are expected to provide coverage to about 380 million people

C. The planned growth in medical infrastructure and increase in government spending on healthcare to about 1.5 percent of GDP by 2020

D. Aggressive market creation by the key players, an increase in acceptance of biologicals, preventive medicine are likely to increase acceptability of modern medicine and newer therapies. What's more, the increased awareness and knowledge of life style diseases and preventive healthcare will increase propensity to self-medicate. This in turn leads to a significant increase in the consumption of over-the-counter (OTC) medicines

Retail segment accounts currently for as much as 75 to 80 percent of the total pharmaceutical market in India. Even by 2020, the retail segment is likely to remain the mainstay. The hospital segment, however, is likely to rise to a significant 25 to 30 percent of the total market in a few years.

Pharma Retail Market: Current Structure

The pharmaceutical retail market in India is highly fragmented, unorganized and dominated by small chemists. Although the margins are high, increased proliferation and fragmentation has resulted in low turnover per store. The unorganized sector accounts for over 90 to 95 percent of the total market with about 850,000 retailers. Probably, it is the fragmented state of the industry that has resulted in protectionist attitude of unorganized players, which is using the strength of its numbers towards creating entry barriers for large and efficient players.

The Pharma retail market is likely to register a double-digit growth in the coming years. Healthcare spending by the average Indian is expected to reach 13 percent in the next eight to ten years from the 9 Percent in 2015. People seem to be willing to spend on preventive healthcare, product quality and value-added services. Spending on healthcare is bound to increase as the disease burden in India is shifting from communicable to non-communicable diseases (NCD). This is due to a focus on achieving competitiveness in a fast globalizing economy. The incidence of life style diseases has been increasing with the changes in life style due to rapid urbanization and a fiercely competitive environment. India is already home to the largest number of diabetic patients in the world. Stress both at work and at home are likely to increase the number of people suffering from hypertension. This will entail medication on an ongoing basis, which in turn make continuous consumption of prescription drugs mandatory and expensive.

The Organized Sector

The organized sector, however, which has started about fifteen years ago is making a slow but steady progress. The organized Pharma retail chains operate in three models.

1. Fully owned stores (eg., Apollo Pharmacy)
2. Franchisee Model (eg., Medicine Shoppe)
3. Combination of owned and Franchisee Stores (eg., Guardian Life Pharmacy)

It is worth noting that the Franchisee model has enabled loss making stand-alone stores to be absorbed by organized retailers. This is likely to trigger consolidation. And then, there is a fourth model - Retail outlets of players like Himalaya, who sell only their products.

Players in the organized sector have started to make a difference in the market place with a number of initiatives such as loyalty schemes in the form of reward points, gifts, free health insurance and discounts, value-added services (diagnostic and pathology tests, health-related consultancy and medical insurance advisory, prescription reminder service, and free home delivery) to attract and retain customers. Table 5.3 lists the major players in the organized Pharma Retail Market.

The total number of retail outlets in the organized retail pharmacy market would be a little less than 10,000, which is a very small fraction of total number of retail pharmacies. The organized sector, however, is growing at a faster rate and should be able to improve its share of the total retail market in the next four to five years. Many of the players who are active in the Pharma retail sector are planning aggressively to increase the number of outlets and improve their geographic coverage. Some are planning to reach that magic number, the number that is considered as the critical mass, which is 5000 plus retail outlets to have a significant impact in the market place in terms of revenues, profitability, market share, number of patients and consumers served. MedPlus has even announced their dream of reaching 10,000 stores in the next 4 to 5 years!

Table 5.3 Major Players in the Organized Pharma Retail
Market in 2015

Pharmacy Retail Chain	Promoter	Total Number of Outlets
1. Apollo Pharmacy	Apollo Hospitals Enterprise Ltd.	2,220
2. MedPlus	Optival Health solutions	1,350
3. Guardian Life Care	Guardian Life Care	310
4. Fortis Health World	Fortis Healthcare	112
5. Emami Frank Ross	Emami	151
6. Trust Chemist	Trust Chemists & Druggists Ltd.	105
7. 98.4 Degrees	Global Healthline	30

Major players in the organized Pharma retail sector are making a number of strategic moves such as tie-ups with major national retailers and partnerships for rural expansion to strengthen their presence. Here are some of their winning moves:

- Apollo Pharmacy plans to tie-up with the Indian Oil Corporation to set up stores across its retail gas stations in India
- Apollo Pharmacy is also planning a partnership with Godrej Aadhar to establish pharmacies at Aadhar outlets in rural areas under the brand *Apollo Aadhar Pharmacy*. The company is also planning to partner with ITC E-Choupals (Choupal Sagar) to distribute medicines in rural areas
- Guardian Life Pharmacy plans to tie-up with Kendriya Bhandar to set up Pharma stores at its retail outlets across Delhi and NCR

region to provide medicines and health foods at discounted rates

- Guardian Life Pharmacy is planning to join hands with DCM Shriram to set up its 'Aushadhi' chains of rural Pharma outlets within the Haryali KIsan Bazaars, the rural initiative of DCM Shriram.
- Trust Chemists & Druggists have tied-up with Aditya Birla Group, who run More Supermarkets to set up pharmacies in their supermarkets in Tamilnadu.

Private Labels

In addition, some Pharma retail chains are now getting generic drugs such as paracetamol contract manufactured by licensed third-parties and then marketing under their own brand names. Private labels provide low cost alternative medicines. MedPlus Health Services plans to sell 28 drugs under its own brand name at its outlets. These drugs will be available at a 15 percent discount to comparable drugs.

Apollo Pharmacy currently has over 200 private label drugs in its portfolio and is planning to add more products to the list. The company plans to achieve 10 percent of its total pharmacy sales through private label drugs in a couple of years.

Six Major Growth Drivers

The Pharma retail market is poised for a rapid growth of 14 percent per annum. There are six major factors that will drive this growth on the two key dimensions of growth namely, affordability and accessibility.

1. Government's Foray into Pharma Retail Sector
2. Insurance Coverage Extended to below-the-poverty-line (BPL) Population
3. Growth in Private Health Insurance
4. Entry of Major Retailers into Pharma Retailing
5. Rapid Growth of OTC (Over-the-Counter) Market for Medicines
6. Online Pharmacies

Government's Foray into Pharma Retail Sector

The Government of India has started distributing essential medicines through government retail outlets, now rebranded as *Pradhan Mantri's*

Jan Aushadhi stores. These outlets sell at affordable prices unbranded versions of generic drugs including popular antibiotics, pain killers, cough and cold medications etc. The Government is planning to launch 3,000 Jan Aushadhi Stores by 2020 to improve accessibility of affordable medicines.

Insurance Coverage Extended to BPL Population

The Central Government-sponsored health insurance programs such as Rashtriya Swasthiya Bima Yojana (RSBY, Aam Admi Bima Yojana (AABY), Janashree Bima Yojana (JBY), Universal Health Insurance Scheme (UHIS) and the Insurance programs such as Aarogyasree (launched by the Government of Andhra Pradesh and is effective in Andhra Pradesh and Telangana) and the Chief Minister's Comprehensive Health Insurance Scheme launched by the Tamil Nadu Government are largely focused on 'Below-the-Poverty Line' (BPL) segment of the population. These schemes are expected to increase the coverage of health insurance to nearly 380 million people below-the-poverty line by 2020.

Growth in Private Health Insurance

The affordability of drugs will rise due to sustained growth in incomes and increased insurance coverage in the private sector. Rising income levels will drive a number of households, approximately 73 million by 2020 according to a McKinsey estimate in the middle and upper income segments. Along with income growth, increase in health insurance coverage will augment affordability.

Entry of Major Retailers into Pharma Retailing

The rapidly growing pharmaceutical market and its attractive distribution margins seem to be attracting many of the leading players in the retail industry. The margins in pharmacy retailing are attractive despite price controls (Table 5.4).

Table 5.4 Attractive Margins (per cent)

Level	Scheduled Drugs	Non-Scheduled Drugs
Wholesale (Stockist or Distributor)	8	10
Retailer	16	20

The following big retail chains are making a foray into pharmaceutical retailing.

- Reliance Retail Limited has entered pharmacy retailing through its Reliance Wellness Stores.
- 'More' Supermarkets by Aditya Birla Retail is planning to house a pharmacy
- Pantaloons' is planning pharmacy retailing in the Medicine Bazaar through Tulsi pharmacy stores

Rapid Growth of OTC Market for Medicines

The market for Over-The-Counter drugs (OTC) is poised for a rapid growth. Indian consumers have increased consumption of OTC products like analgesics, cough, cold and allergy medicines, digestive remedies, antacids, and medicated skincare products. Changing consumer attitudes towards self medication in treating a number of common ailments such as cold, fever, pain, sprains, heartburn, diarrhea and indigestion etc. are the main reasons for prescription-to-OTC - switch. From a US $ 1.9 billion in 2009, the OTC market for pharmaceuticals in India is expected to grow to US$ 11 billion by 2020 according to a PWC (Price Waterhouse Coopers) estimate.

The OTC market is expected to grow rapidly as more companies are expected to enter the market with a wide range of OTC products. Increasing income levels of the middle class, rapid growth in health and fitness awareness are likely to bring a paradigm shift to the Pharma retailing business. Tomorrow's pharmacy would be more like a *Wellness Store* with a consumer preference to high quality medicines due to behavioral changes. Recent consumer survey indicates that for minor ailments only about 24 percent of consumers visit a doctor and about 45 percent visit a Pharmacist. More than half-of-the consumers resort to self-medication for minor ailments. These changing consumer attitudes towards treating minor ailments will accelerate the growth of OTC drugs.

Another reason for the rapid growth of OTC market is wider distribution channel. Companies can sell their products outside pharmacies too. Furthermore, companies can advertise their OTC products directly to consumer using a more persuasive pitch. Magic Remedies and Objectionable Advertisements Act , however prescribes a list of diseases for which medications cannot be advertised. A more important reason perhaps is the fact that most of the active ingredients used in OTC products except drugs like acetylsalicylic acid, ephedrine hydrochloride etc, do not come under the Drug Price Control Order, making them more profitable.

Sun Pharma, Abbott Laboratories, Cipla, Zydus Cadila, Mankind Pharma, Johnson & Johnson, Novartis, Piramal Enterprises, Pfizer, Dabur, Himalaya are some of the leading companies that already have a strong presence in the OTC segment of Indian pharmaceutical market.

In the short run, the pharmacy retail market presents a compelling opportunity with increased government spending on healthcare sector along with initiatives to increase healthcare awareness and improve access to cost-effective generics to the needy patients in urban and rural India and access to healthcare to people below the poverty line. In the long run, however it is the OTC market that would drive the rapid growth as affordability and access improve significantly.

e-Pharmacy, The Next Big Opportunity

The growth of internet has given rise to various technology models to access and serve consumers in the most efficient way. Telemedicine is one such model that has enabled accessibility to the finest doctors at the click of a button. e-Pharmacy also known as Internet Pharmacy or online Pharmacy is another attractive model of innovation in the healthcare space. e-Pharmacy is a technological advancement that meets three of the most important needs of the patients, namely accessibility, affordability and convenience for getting the prescription drugs and other healthcare products at their doorstep with a single click of a button on their computers, tablets and mobile phones. Can purchasing medicines and other healthcare products be any easier than this? This confirms the deliverability of the two promises of e-Pharmacy: easy access and convenience of buying from home. In terms of affordability the cost of medicines is at least 15 to 20 percent less than the prices charged by the brick-and-mortar pharmacies.

In addition, e-Pharmacy models are well aligned to address a number of key issues in Pharmaceutical retailing. Some of these important issues are:

1. Tracking authenticity of drugs dispensed
2. Traceability of medicines procured and sold

3. Abuse prevention

4. Consumption of drugs without prescription

5. Tax loss

6. Value-added services (Disease, diagnostic and healthcare awareness, prescription reminders etc.) that empower the consumers

Global e-Pharmacy Market

The global e-Pharmacy market, led by North America and Europe was approximately US $ 29.3 billion in 2014 and has been estimated to grow at a CAGR of 17.7 percent to reach a size of US$ 128 billion by 2023. In other words, the e-Pharmacy market in North America and Europe which currently accounts for 6 percent of total Pharma market would grow rapidly to reach about 18 percent of the total Pharma market in those regions.

The e-Pharmacy market in China was around US $ 1.1 billion in 2014 and accounted for 3 percent of the total pharmaceutical market. The online pharmacy market is growing at a much faster rate than the overall pharmaceutical market and therefore is bound to garner a much higher share of the total Pharma market in the coming years.

Currently, the e-Pharmacy is at a nascent stage in India, but experts opine that it has the potential to grow and account for about 5 to 15 percent of the rapidly growing Indian pharmaceutical market (from US $ 30 billion in 2015 to US $55 billion by 2020) in the next few years.

Factors Driving Demand for e-Pharmacy

There are a number of factors that are driving demand for e-Pharmacy in India and elsewhere in the world. Consider the following for example that are specific to India:

1. Increasing internet penetration and rising number of people with unmet needs along with the growing population

2. Rapidly changing consumer behavior in terms of increasing propensity towards online shopping that is convenient, accessible and affordable

How Does An e-Pharmacy Function?

An e-Pharmacy requires two operating components for dispensing prescription medicines. One is Technology and the other is a Pharmacy Stores. Table 5.5 details the tasks of these two components.

Table 5.5 Two Components of e-Pharmacy

Technology	Pharmacy Stores
A. Web-based and mobile-based application for consumers to upload the scanned copy of their prescriptions and for placing an order for their medicines. Every order that is received has to be verified and checked by a team of registered pharmacists	A. The licensed Pharmacists of the pharmacy stores check for the validity of prescriptions and only then dispense them from a licensed premises in sealed, tamperproof pack to the patient or the patients' relatives
B. After checking, the registered pharmacists forward the validated prescriptions to the pharmacy stores, which dispenses the medicines	B. The pharmacy stores should prepare a proper invoice with batch number of the medicines dispensed, expiry date, name and address of the pharmacy with the signature of the registered pharmacist
C. The web or mobile platform has to follow and comply with all the provisions of the IT Act 2000 and only act as a platform to facilitate connection between consumer and pharmacy stores	C. The pharmacy stores should follow and comply with all the provisions of the Drugs & Cosmetics Act as it does for its normal brick & mortar stores

An e-Pharmacy model would help with better purchasing margins, better inventory management, increased reach, reduced prices and greater provision of value-added services to consumers.

Barriers to e-Pharmacy Growth

Are there any barriers to the entry and growth of e-Pharmacies in India? AIOCD (All India Organization of Chemists and Druggists), India's foremost chemists association has been trying very hard to erect barriers to the entry of e-Pharmacies since their inception a few years ago. AIOCD has even organized a nationwide strike of chemists on

April 23, 2016 to protest the entry of online drug retailing. In fact, IIPA (Indian Internet Pharmacy Association) alleged that they had to endure regulatory harassment triggered by complaints from AIOCD members. These complaints led to police investigations, regulatory raid, and the cancellation of licenses of chemist shops supplying to internet pharmacies. IIPA too, in its bid to retaliate filed about 500 complaints with Maharastra Food & Drug Administration against chemist shops that were dispensing drugs without a prescription.

Why Are Chemists So Apprehensive of e-Pharmacies?

Why the AIOCD, which is the apex body of almost 850,000 retail chemists in India is so apprehensive that it had to call for a strike, lodge numerous complaints against the burgeoning e-Pharmacy industry? Gauri Kamath in her widely popular blog 'Apothecurry' lists four probable reasons in her insightful blog post - *Why do chemists hate e-pharmacies so much?* Consider these reasons for example:

1. e-Pharmacies, if successful will consolidate and channel it with those partners, who give more favorable terms (to e-Pharmacies) and throw the smaller retailers out of business.

2. e-Pharmacies, which are basically web platforms once scaled up will squeeze partners (retail chemists) for ever greater discounts or other favorable terms. Currently, retail chemists get to keep retailer margins on drugs to themselves and dole out discounts to patients at their discretion.

3. e-Pharmacies will keep raising the bar for everyone. They are strongly advocating the transparency and traceability of the model for all its worth. They claim that their systems are robust enough to spot unethical consumer, partner behavior (buying and selling without prescription) and can help trace drugs all the way to the end-user in case of a recall.

4. e-Pharmacies, if allowed to succeed will turn standard setters both from a regulatory and customer service point of view.

5. e-Pharmacies, if allowed to grow as an organized industry may draw undue attention to those chemists and wholesalers in the supply chain who are running online pharmacies themselves - but without bending backwards to be compliant and put their way of doing business under threat. Could they be fomenting protest by fanning the insecurities of their fraternity?

All this is possible, but it is far out into the horizon. Online pharmacies still account for a minuscule share of the market. But, as

Gauri Kamath says, the AIOCD's point of view seems to be *why wait for the acorn to turn into an oak?*

Putting these reasons aside, the chemists present a cogent argument against the entry of online pharmacies. Their objections are that online pharmacies:

1. Will lead to addiction of scheduled drugs and resistance of antibiotics due to refilling of prescriptions
2. Promote sale of substandard drugs
3. Poor maintenance of records
4. May lead to medication errors that could be fatal to patients
5. Make the recall of substandard drugs impossible
6. Lead to transportation errors
7. May not maintain cold chain leading to loss of efficacy of drugs during transportation
8. Lead to unemployment of pharmacists and chemists
9. May violate the rules of sale under the Drugs Laws

All the above problems have been happening even before the advent of online pharmacies. Studies over the decades have concluded that India has an unacceptably high rate of self-medication by patients. The main reason is that seeking professional healthcare can be expensive and time consuming. Fueling this trend is the fact that chemist shops are operating in a lax regulatory environment. An analysis conducted few years ago by the Global Antibiotic Resistance Partnership and Public Health Foundation of India found that *in Delhi no prescription was presented for one-fifth of antibiotics purchased recently* (around the time of the survey). The irrational consumption of antibiotics is one of the major reasons for the increasing microbial resistance to them.

Online drug retailing in the absence of a proper, well-defined regulatory environment can be problematic. What is needed is a clear policy and detailed guidelines for registering, running and monitoring online pharmacies by the government.

Indian Internet Pharmacy Association (IIPA)

Eleven progressive minded e-Pharmacies have formed the Indian Internet Pharmacy Association with the mission to promote and protect public health by ensuring that its members operate in accordance with the existing rules of Drugs & Cosmetics Act and of the Information

Technology Act 2008 and Pharmacy Practice Regulations 2015.

IIPA will cater to public's demand for safe and easily accessible medicines at affordable prices. IIPA released its code of conduct under the ambit of FICCI (Federation of Indian Chambers of Commerce and Industry) on November 21, 2016:

We need to embrace technology, in both offline and online models. There is a great opportunity to take this eco system ahead by leveraging the India stack using existing infrastructure of Aadhaar and Digi-locker to maintain the repository of prescriptions, health records and monitor the dispensing of sensitive medicines. All pharmacies, offline or online should check prescriptions in this locker.

The eleven founder members of e-Pharmacy are the industry's top players with credible experience, who are committed to working with regulators to ensure that India has a e-Pharmacy model worth emulating. These members are:

1. Bookmeds
2. mChemist
3. Medidart
4. Medlife
5. Medstar
6. Netmeds
7. Pharmeasy
8. zigy.com (PM & Health Life Care)
9. Save-on-Medicals
10. Save My Meds
11. 1mg.com

IIPA Suggests Solutions

The members of IIPA have come forward with a number of solutions to address all these concerns and are asking the Central Drug Controller to spell out and publish norms for e-Pharmacies. They are suggesting that their online platforms may be given a separate license that can be displayed on their home page. They understand that asking for more regulations is the best way to raise their credibility and barriers to entry in one stroke - a time tested strategy used effectively by the global drug industry. It is probably this strategic intent of raising the bar for everyone by e-pharmacies that worry the off-line chemists. Table 5.6 presents the solutions suggested by IIPA Members.

Table 5.6 ePharmacies: Concerns and Solutions

Concerns	Solutions
1. Fake and illegal sites	Create a registry of e-Pharmacies with a log, which needs to be displayed by authorized players.Consumers can verify from the regulator's website about the authenticity of the players.
2. Drug Abuse	All the medicines with potential for abuse like Schedule X and other habit-forming drugs could be prohibited.All prescription medicines should only be processed against an electronic copy of valid prescription.Entire audit trail, including the name and address of the patient, should be digitally stored and tracked
3. Medication Errors	Registered pharmacist of the licensed pharmacy should be the final decision maker for dispensing a drug.The e-Pharmacy should have a team of pharmacists for validation of a prescription and handling any drug related queries from patients.Address, phone number and other contact information of pharmacists should always be disclosed for any drug related query from customers.
4. Counterfeit Drugs	All medicine purchases should be tracked effectively and subject to audits.Digital translation trails, which ensure a record of full transaction payment, valid bill and batch number of medicines should be available.
5. Substitution. What if the pres- cribed brand is not there?	e-Pharmacy should fulfill orders as per prescription of a registered medical practitioner like off-line pharmacies. As per current law, substitution is not allowed unless specifically allowed by the prescribing physician on the prescription.
6. Pharmacovigilance How can drugs be dispensed?	Maintain a record of every transaction details of patient's name, address, telephone number and email. e-Pharmacies to record batch number and expiry date for all its transactions. Drugs to be dispensed with invoice by a licensed pharmacy, thus enabling recalls

Advantages of e-Pharmacy

e-Pharmacy offers a number of benefits. Benefits to consumers or patients, regulators and off-line pharmacists. Table 5.7 presents the advantages that e-Pharmacies offer to consumers, regulators and pharmacists:

Table 5.7 Advantages of e-Pharmacy

To Patients	To Regulators	To Offline Pharmacists
Increased Convenience	Tracking the data for minimizing and even preventing drug abuse and self-medication	e-Pharmacy technology platform model enables pharmacies to serve a broader customer base hither to unserved and thus provides additional business opportunity
Improved Accessibility	Analysis of large amounts of data stored by e-Pharmacies across the nation will help the Government in planning public health policies	Inventory consolidation resulting in reduced working capital requirement, and removal of wastage from the system helps increase the overall profitability
Cost Advantage	Technology enabled tracking systems of the e-Pharmacy model assists in back-tracking the channel, manufacturer, supplier of counterfeit medicines thereby making the market a lot more transparent and authentic	Helps upgrade retail pharmacies to leverage technology to stream line processes and improve operations
Improves Compliance and Education of Patients	100 per cent of orders documented with prescription.	Enables offline pharmacies to provide improved and value-added customer service through improved knowledge of patients' diagnoses, list of drugs the patient is already taking, and established drug monitoring procedures

Contd...

To Patients	To Regulators	To Offline Pharmacists
Authenticity	Stringent documentation process ensures 100percent tax collection by the Government	

In addition, the e-Pharmacy model could be aligned to the Government's CSCs (Common Service Centers) and *Jan Aushadhi Program* across the country to improve delivery of essential health services in rural India by improving access, ensuring efficacy, transparency and reliability of services at an affordable cost.

An Allay, not An Adversary!

Currently there is a lot of misconception about e-Pharmacies impacting the traditional brick and mortar pharmacies. In reality, e-Pharmacy model enables the existing traditional pharmacies to cater to a broader set of customers who are hither to unserved thus expanding the business opportunities. Furthermore, the technology platform of e-Pharmacy also ensures that the inventory is consolidated, which reduces the requirement of working capital, and helps remove wastage from the system and helps increase overall profitability. When you think of it, e-Pharmacy is an ally and not an adversary

Consumer Perceptions of e-Pharmacy

All this is fine, but are the consumers willing to adopt the e-Pharmacy model? It is important to know the willingness of target consumers to understand its potential as it is one of the the growth drivers in addition to internet penetration, computer literacy, health awareness and purchasing power.

Bureau of Research on Industry and Economic Fundamentals (BRIEF) in India has conducted recently a primary survey titled, *e-Pharmacy - Perception of Customers* to understand consumers' perspectives towards novel concept of online pharmacy and their readiness towards adopting this technology-fueled medicine buying online. Here are some key points that the respondents of the survey mentioned:

- 20 percent of the people order their medicines over the telephone
- 50 percent of the people get medicines without any prescription

- 90 percent of the people surveyed showed inclination to purchase medicines online
- 90 percent of the physicians surveyed too perceive it as an acceptable means of sale and purchase of pharmaceutical products

A significant portion of the population seem to be willing to try purchasing medicines and related products over the internet considering the advantages it has and the additional value it creates compared to the existing retail outlets. Survey reveals that lower prices, discounts, convenience in ordering and home delivery with preferred time and address are some of the advantages that will prompt consumers to shift towards e-Pharmacy.

A Major Problem

Prima facie, consumers should love e-Pharmacies and they seem to love it as the survey indicates. But there is that bit about having a valid prescription. Some e-Pharmacies want it scanned, others come home to pick it up. But you can't buy medicines without prescription - at least not from a legit source whom you can hold accountable.

On the other hand, you can buy medicines without prescription, re-using old prescriptions from the neighborhood chemist shop getting both convenience and accountability. The question is whether the long term saving on medicine is worth spending time and energy to visit the doctor more often for prescriptions?

e-Pharmacy: The Way Ahead

Online drug retail in the absence of a proper, well-defined regulatory environment can be problematic. if unchecked, it could compound legacy problems such as self-medication and drug resistance. It could also lead to the proliferation of counterfeit and spurious drugs.

Online drug platforms can only be as good as their partners. Indian pharmacies have long been known to sell drugs without prescriptions. The only way out is a comprehensive drug regulation mechanism that governs both - offline and online pharmacies. India has a well defined drug regulatory mechanism in place in the form of Drugs & Cosmetics Act, whose implementation and enforcement need to be improved. The Government should release guidelines specifically designed for online sale of medicines. Regulators too stand to gain by implementation of these guidelines because traceability will allow a faster recall of spurious drugs and a tighter leash on the black sheep of the sector.

What is the best model of e-Pharmacy? The implementation of a fool-proof e-Pharmacy model needs to be based on four guiding principles:

1. Orderly growth of e-Commerce in India
2. Patient Safety
3. Proper Access to Medicine
4. Authenticity

FICCI (Federation of Indian Chambers of Commerce and Industry) and Frost & Sullivan, one of the internationally reputed management consulting firms in their first-ever knowledge paper prepared on e-Pharmacy conclude:

An e-Pharmacy aligns very well with the national development objectives, and clear tangible benefits to the consumers as well as the industry. Meanwhile, it has also been observed that growth of e-Commerce and retail are complimentary and reinforce each other. By leveraging technology in a smart way and under stringent control, the e-Pharmacy has a scope of adding immense value to the existing retail industry in India.

Summary

The *place* has always been an important element of the marketing mix. Making your products and services available when and where they are wanted most, is crucial for the success of any marketing operation. Increasing complexities and intensifying competitive pressures are placing a premium on the *shelf-space* of retailers.

Managing the distribution function, too is constantly changing. It has become multi-dimensional. Distribution and its effective management provide the firm the much-needed competitive edge in the market place.

The physician, whether drawn in the pharmaceutical marketing channel diagram or not, is an important member of the pharmaceutical marketing channels, in so far is prescription drugs are concerned. The typical pharmaceutical distribution channel in India includes; manufacturer - distributor - stockist - retailer (pharmacist) - consumer. The distributor could be the company's own depot, a C&F Agency or a super stockist. While there is no ideal channel, reaching the stockist directly either through the company's depot, or a C&F Agent is advisable for a number of reasons. Many companies seem to be following this.

When you consider the increasing costs of distribution, the need for a total physical distribution concept becomes obvious. The total cost of distribution probably is next only to the materials cost and in some cases may even be almost equal. That is why effective management of distribution has a positive impact on a company's bottom line. The total physical distribution management includes all important activities like inventory control, warehousing, transportation and customer service.

The growing power of trade associations is another important factor that is making the task of placing the products and services when and where they are wanted more difficult and multi-dimensional.

The demand for increased margins and the threats of trade boycotts, the almost unilateral agreements with the companies, their indifferent attitudes towards the legal machinery, the letters of cooperation in stockist management and new product introductions are certainly making distribution more than a sub-function of marketing, and marketing more than a functional discipline in the art and science of management.

The rapidly growing Indian pharmaceutical market is likely to grow even faster to a US $ 55-billion behemoth according to a McKinsey estimate. The current Pharma retail market in India is highly fragmented, unorganized and dominated by small chemists. The organized sector accounts for over 90 percent of the total retail Pharma market in India. The organized retail sector, which was started fifteen years ago, however, is making a slow but steady progress. The organized Pharma retail chains operate in three models - fully-owned stores, franchisee model, and in combination of owned and franchised stores.

Players in the organized sector have started making a small difference in the market place with a number of initiatives such as loyalty schemes in the form of reward points, free health insurance and discounts, and value based services (diagnostic and pathology tests, health-related consultancy and medical insurance advisory, prescription reminder services, free home delivery) to attract and retain customers.

The government of India has started essential medicines through government retail outlets, now branded as *Pradhan Mantri's Jan Aushadhi Stores*. These outlets sell unbranded versions of National List of Essential Medicines (NLEM), and generic drugs such as popular antibiotics, pain killers, cough and cold medicines at affordable prices. The government plans to launch over 3,000 Jan Aushadhi Stores by 2020 to improve accessibility of affordable medicines.

The market for OTC (over-the-counter) drugs too is poised for rapid growth from US $ 1.9-billion in 2009 to US $ 11-billion in 2020 according to a PWC (Price Waterhouse Coopers) estimate.

The exponential growth of internet has given rise to various technology models including on line retailing of prescription drugs called e-Pharmacy. An e-Pharmacy requires two operating components for dispensing prescription medicines online. One is technology and the other is a pharmacy stores. An e-Pharmacy model would help with better purchasing margins, better inventory management, increased reach, reduced prices and a greater provision of value-added services to consumers.

AIOCD (All India Organization of Chemists and Druggists) has been trying very hard to erect barriers to the entry of e-Pharmacies. However, a significant percent of the population seem to be wiling to try purchasing medicines online. These are exciting and challenging times for pharmaceutical distribution at the same time.

What makes pharmaceutical distribution really effective may be obvious but not apparent. The prescription and indeed even the cure for many ills that may afflict the distribution function, like mounting inventories of finished goods, and accumulating receivables, is the ability of a company to generate adequate prescriptions. Prescription generation is therefore, very crucial. It is axiomatic in pharmaceutical marketing that lack of or inadequate prescription generation can bring even a giant-wheeled juggernaut to a grinding halt.

The Promotion

Changing! Challenging!!

Yes, the role of promotion in the marketing-mix of a firm is rapidly changing. The pace of change, the increasing and intensifying competition seem to be making it more challenging.

Changing Role

Firstly, let us talk about the changing role of promotion. In the past, promotion, an important element of marketing-mix, was viewed as a form of vital communication link between the firm and its prospective buyers. Today the role of promotion must be viewed as only part of the firm's overall communications effort with consumers. It is becoming increasingly clear that the roles of product, pack, price, and place are also changing rapidly as important communication variables of a firm. We have seen that all these elements of the marketing-mix are capable of sending important communication cues or signals to the consumer and thus play an important role in his decision making process as regards the eternal dilemma he faces, that is, whether to buy a firms product or not.

A marketer, therefore, should take a holistic view of promotion as the marketing communications process and not merely think of it as advertising communications and sales promotion strategies. The role and scope of transformation become much broader when you view it as the total communications process of the entire firm. It is important that we understand this changing role of promotion to make effective use of our marketing communication process. All activities of the firm should, ideally be synchronized to formulate the marketing communications package for maximizing effectiveness. Since the broad objective of any firm is to move forward, promotion should be viewed in its broadest sense, and include all the elements of the marketing-mix and indeed all activities of the firm.

Challenging Task!

It is this changing role that makes the promotion of a firm more challenging than ever before. Add to this the omnipresent and ever intensifying competition and you get an even more formidable task of promotion. The current scenario of pharmaceutical marketing in India presents a rather undifferentiated, difficult to recognize picture. It is not only that many companies are turning out a number of 'me-too' products but also that they are formulating and implementing a 'me-too' promotional strategies. Consequently the decibel level in the market place is at its highest today. If you want your product to stand out in the market place, you must first ensure that it is heard above the current noise level. That is quite a task. It is a promotional challenge. You have to be truly imaginative and innovative in formulating your promotional strategies and have the energy to implement them. That is what gives you the much-needed synergy and the competitive edge to cut through the clutter and chaos in the market place.

Promotion means *to move forward* in its broadest sense. It is derived from the Latin word *Promovere,* 'pro' meaning *forward* and 'movere' meaning *to move.* Promotion, therefore can be defined as *marketing communication that attempts to inform and remind individuals and persuade them to accept, recommend, re-sell or use a product, service or an idea.*

Acceptance of an idea, product or service by prospective consumers is essential for moving an organization forward. Since promotion is a form of communication used by both business and non-business organizations, it is often assumed that promotion is the same as advertising. While advertising is one of the most important and visible elements of a promotional strategy, it is hardly the same.

There are two major elements in the promotional mix of any organization. They are:

(a) Personal communication, which includes personal selling. In pharmaceutical marketing, *personal selling* is perhaps the most important element of the promotional mix.

(b) Non-personal communication, which includes advertising, sales promotion, publicity and public relations.

Before, we go into the details of advertising and sales promotion, a brief discussion on the basic principles of communication will be useful. Since promotion is essentially a form of communication, understanding the process of marketing communication will give us the necessary perspective.

Marketing Communication

What is marketing communication? A marketing communication is a more specific form of communication, wherein a seller seeks to transmit information to buyer. That does not necessarily mean that communication has taken place. Communication essentially is a two way process. You can say that communication has taken place only if the receiver (in this case the potential buyer) understands, accepts and acts upon what the sender (for our purpose, the seller) is intending to say. That may not be a particularly dramatic revelation.

But when you consider the innumerable breakdowns that take place every day, you will agree that there is a definite need to understand the communication process and its barriers and gateways. A proper understanding and appreciation of these will enable us to formulate effective communication strategies. Communication is also defined as transfer of *meaning*. An oversimplified definition? Transfer of meaning is not as simple as it may seem. For a communication to be effective, it must:

1. Gain the *attention* of the receiver
2. Be understood by both the receiver and the sender in the same manner to maintain *interest*
3. Stimulate the needs (*desire*) of the receiver, and
4. Suggest an appropriate method (*action*) of satisfying those needs

This is the classic AIDA principle of communication, AIDA being the acronym for *Attention, Interest, Desire and Action.*

How Communication Works

Promotional communication is a structured and systematized form of communication. Many theorists have compared the transmission of a promotional communication process to a telephone circuit because of its orderly way of transmitting a message.

A simplified model of how communication occurs is shown in Figure 6.1.

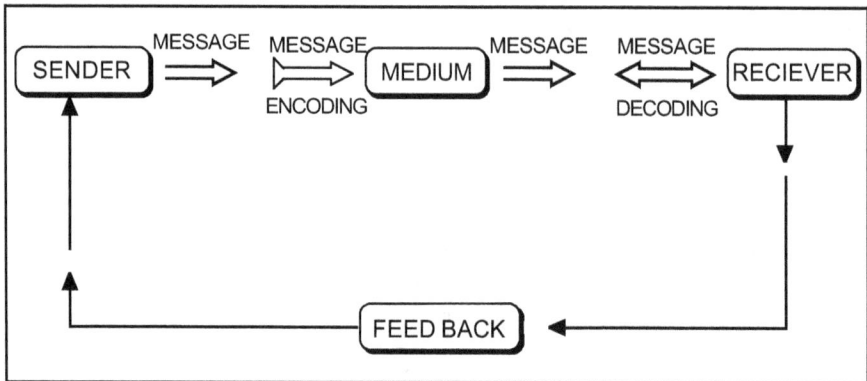

Figure 6.1 Model of Marketing Communication Process

The basic elements of this communications circuit are:

  (a) Sender: the originator or the source of the message
  (b) Message: the message itself
  (c) Medium: the means or the the vehicle by which the message is transmitted
  (d) Receiver: the ultimate destination of the message
  (e) Feedback: the signal of understanding of the message by the receiver

In a promotional communication, the *sender* encodes a message (translates the message into understandable form by the receiver) and the *receiver* in turn decodes the message (re-translates the message into his terms of understanding) and signals his understanding of the message back to the source or the sender by a *feedback.*

Sounds simple? Well, in practice there some complications. Like the message may not be understood at all or it may be understood in a way quite different from that intended. Recall the *communication game* you played in any of the communication workshops you have attended in which a group of people sits in a circle. The first person whispers a message (cigarette smoking is injurious to health: the Surgeon General's warning) to a person sitting next to him. He in turn whispers the message to the person sitting next to him. The game continues until the last receiver announces the message heard (the Inspector General warned that if you do not smoke you will have heart attacks). You may not believe that such a distortion of a message can take place, if you have not played the game earlier. In that case all you have to do is to play this game next time when you are in a group. You can try it with any message. You will not have dissimilar experience. The garbled message usually bears little resemblance to the original. There can be many barriers to the communication process.

Barriers to Communication

Here are some commonly observed barriers to effective communication:

1. **Multiple Transmitters:** There is more to a message than meets the eye. Many mistake the words of a message whether spoken or written, for the whole message. Most messages involve multiple transmitters. Take the case of medical representatives. They are very much aware of their body language. Posture, facial expression and tone of voice communicate more than spoken words. Non-verbal communication accounts for over two-thirds of our total interpersonal communication. Multiple transmission of a message is not restricted to an oral or verbal presentation. Even in print communications, secondary transmissions exist. Take for example the layout of an advertisement. It often conveys as much as the words. Try to set the same copy in classified column and a full page color advertisement. They communicate two entirely different things.

2. **Selective Perception**: Selective perception and interpretation act as barriers to effective communication. They are responsible for a number of decoding errors. People only see or hear what they want to. They simply tune out and screen out the rest of the message.

3. **Noise**: *Noise* is another barrier to effective communication. Noise can be defined as interference that is accidentally or deliberately introduced and blocks or distorts transmission of your message. Noise can be of three types.

(a) Internal noise is the kind of interference that is inherent in the message itself. If your message is transmitted in a language that is unknown to the receiver, then it is internal noise.

(b) External noise, as the name suggests, is introduced accidentally from outside the communication process.

(c) Competitive noise is deliberately introduced by another source (your competition) to gain a competitive advantage. Competition is constantly trying to distort and block your message from reaching the destination, which is common to you as well as your competition. The receiver is the prospective customer for both.

4. **Inadequate Feedback:** Inadequate feedback does not block or distort your message directly but it can stand in the way of your future communications. Without sufficient feedback, a sender (source) is totally in the dark. John Wanamaker, a famous department store founder once lamented: *I know that half of my advertising dollars are wasted. Just don't know which half!*

Gateways to Communication

Overcoming these and other barriers is essential to communicate effectively. At the same time, understanding the essential elements and crucial stages of the communication process will open the gateways to effective communication. These essential elements are:

1. Source
2. Message
3. Destination or Receiver
4. Feedback

Source

Source is a very important element of communication and can have a tremendous influence over receivers. It is common knowledge and experience that some communicators can exert a more persuasive influence over their audience than others. Even in the same product category with virtually identical products, we find that some companies are more successful because they can persuade better. What is that makes some communicators more persuasive than others? Source is one of the important factors that determine the success or failure of a communication even if it happens to be the same message. Some of the source factors that affect the process of influencing (persuading) receivers are:

Source Credibility

Credibility, perceived credibility of a source, is an important factor in influencing the receiver. The key word is perceived. If the audience perceive a source as more credible than others they are more likely to accept his message. Conversely, if the audience perceive the source as low in credibility they are likely to reject his message. It is important to remember that *source credibility* is a multifaceted concept and depends on a set of perceptions like the source's *prestige, expertise, power, trustworthiness, age* and other factors.

If an audience perceive the source as honest, then they are more likely to believe him and accept his statement. The only way to enhance your (source's) trustworthiness with your audience and to make them perceive you as honest is by *being* honest.

Source credibility is the most important attribute, which a marketer should consider because it is likely to produce the most enduring change in the receiver's opinions. When the audience perceive the source as credible, they in effect perceive him as a friend, who does not have any manipulative intent. That is why friends and particularly opinion leaders are more influential than any other source. For the same reason, the effectiveness of mass advertising is low. Partly this is due to the consumers' awareness of source's intention to manipulate. Advertisers of course, counterbalance this by trying to enhance the credibility of their communication by employing well-known personalities and celebrities as *sources* of their communication and for endorsing their brands. All this goes to prove just one thing and that is, source credibility is essential, vital and crucial. To put it more simply, *source credibility is it!*

Expertise

Expertise is a result of education, knowledge and accomplishment in any chosen area. A source that an audience perceives as an expert on a given subject is certainly more persuasive in influencing the audience's opinions pertaining to his area of expertise. Specialized sources of information are also perceived as expert sources. Specialized media like medical journals can be highly influential on an audience's opinions. Prestigious medical journals like the British Medical Journal (BMJ), Lancet, and the Journal of American Medical Association (JAMA) can have a great influence on practicing doctors' opinions. Similarly, specialized business journals like Harvard Business Review (HBR), very aptly described as the magazine for decision makers and Sloan Management Review, Fortune, Business Week etc, can greatly influence the thinking of a number of practicing managers the world over. Consider this research finding:

James Coleman, Elihu Katz and Herbert Menzel observed in their study, 'Doctors and New drugs' that physicians were more influenced by medical journals on a specific topic than by journals, which aimed at the entire profession. This is because selective audiences normally attend to a specialized source.

Likeability

Likeability is another factor that enhances source credibility. When a receiver likes a source, for whatever reason, the source will be more persuasive. The receiver's attitude to the message will become more favorable when he likes the source. This explains why pharmaceutical companies always consider a pleasing personality and good manners as essential prerequisites while selecting medical representatives.

Sources of Marketing Communications

What we have discussed so far is the importance of source credibility and its influencing power in persuading a receiver. In marketing, consumers may view the various components of the marketing system of the same company as different sources of information. This is what makes marketing communications more complex. A typical *source-mix* of a pharmaceutical company's marketing communication includes:

(a) Company
(b) Medical representative
(c) Media
(d) Trade channels

The relative importance of these components of the source-mix to a company depends upon the products it offers and the situations in which they are to be used. Very often, these sources can have a combined effect upon the response of consumers towards the company's products and services. Used creatively and judiciously, these different components of a company's source-mix, can have a mutually reinforcing effect, and give its marketing communications the much-needed synergistic power in the highly competitive market place.

Consumers usually view the *company* as a single entity having a distinct personality. This is despite the fact that a company is a collection of people and various other resources and not a single entity. People can and often do describe a company's image as honest, progressive, reliable, innovative etc. The specific image of a company depends on its advertising and public relations campaigns, its actions over a period of time like the quality of products and services it has been delivering to the public, and above all the quality and attitudes of its employees. A company that is perceived as reputable, credible, and reliable has a very valuable asset, which is reflected even on its balance sheet as good will. This good will and positive image give an edge, an advantage, in gaining entry for its new product introductions. Research indicates clearly that a company's positive image influences to a considerable extent in gaining early adoptions of its new products and brands.

In so far as the pharmaceutical industry is concerned, personal selling is a very important, in fact, vital element of a company's promotional mix. This puts a premium on medical representatives as a source of a company's marketing communications.

Theodore Levitt observed that there is an interaction effect between companies and their sales force. His conclusions based on an experiment conducted concerning the source effects in industrial selling can be summarized as:

Consumers are more likely to favor the products of the less competent sales representatives from a well-known company than those of the highly competent sales representatives from an unknown company.

This effect gives the well-known company's sales representatives an advantage at least in the short run. This effect is noticed even in the Indian pharmaceutical market. When some highly competent and successful medical representatives left the services of their earlier well-known companies and started either on their own or in senior positions with new, virtually unknown companies, they found to their dismay, that it was doubly difficult to get prescription support even from the prescribing doctors known closely to them while they were working with their earlier reputed companies. The company image certainly reinforces the credibility of the sales force. A competent sales force too, in turn reinforces the company's image.

Consumers as compared to general interest publications perceive specialized media as an expert source of information. Consequently the persuasive power of specialized media is greater.

Trade channels too can augment the image of a company. Wholesalers and retailers, who are known for their promptness in service can reinforce the positive image of a company.

Implications for the Marketer

The source credibility is a very vital component in marketing communications is an irrefutable fact. However, one should not view source in isolation. Source component interacts with many other components such as the message, the medium, and the receiver. The marketer should take this into cognizance while formulating a communication strategy for maximizing the impact. Here are a few guidelines to be considered for enhancing the source credibility:

1. Consistency must be maintained in the messages communicated through the different components of the source-mix like medical representatives, media, company advertisements etc. Since the various components of the source-mix can have a mutually reinforcing effect, a holistic approach towards communication strategy optimizes its persuasive power.

2. A positive attitude of a communicator to himself, his company's products and his audience will increase his credibility as a source of communication. Therefore, you must ensure that your medical representatives develop a positive attitude about themselves, their messages and their audience, whether they prescribing doctors, or retailers or wholesalers. Such a synchrony gives your persuasive communication the power of synergy.

3. Designing specific communication strategies to convince opinion leaders will spell sure success because opinion leaders are very influential with people. People do not perceive them as having any manipulative intent and therefore, their credibility is very high. That is why one can observe that some doctors take up some products of certain companies once they notice prescriptions of these products by their professors in medical colleges, even before the representatives of those companies introduce these products to them. Proper identification of opinion leaders and persuading them to take up your products is crucial for success in the pharmaceutical industry.

Message

While a source credibility is an essential first step to get a foot in the customer's door, the *message* component of marketing communications is no less important. When you consider the fact that each one of us is bombarded with thousands of messages every day and our ability to selectively screen out which we do not like, the *message* becomes even more important.

Before you can persuade your prospective audience to accept your point of view, you must first gain and retain their attention. Understanding how the attention process works, therefore becomes mandatory for the marketing communicator. You must also be aware of factors, which inhibit attention so that you can overcome barriers to audience attention.

Gaining and Retaining Attention

Merely seeing and hearing is not focusing your attention. That is merely a physical reception of the message. As you are going through these lines at this moment, you are probably not fully conscious of the nosies around you although you can hear them. Your attention is focused on this page. Also consider this not-so-unfamiliar situation, where a medical representative is detailing his products to a busy practitioner. The doctor is no doubt looking at the visual-aid and nodding his head to what the representative has been saying for the past five minutes. The doctor is also simultaneously writing a prescription to a patient whom he examined just a few minutes earlier. Can you say that the doctor is paying attention to the medical representative? The detailing by the representative in this case has become just a part of the background nosies. The doctor was seeing through the presentation, but was not really with him (the medical representative) and what he was saying.

Attention, therefore, can be defined as the mental process of consciously focusing on a given stimulus. Ask any doctor and he is sure to say, 'go on! I am listening'. Most of us are likely to accept this as we, though wrongly, believe that a person can focus on two different messages at the same time. After all, the human brain is more powerful than the most powerful computer known to mankind, isn't it? Contrary to this popular belief, a person cannot attend to two things at the same moment in time.

People can fluctuate rapidly between two stimuli and thus it may seem to us that it is possible at times to focus on two messages. But in reality, it is the ability of a person to change his attention rapidly from one stimulus to another, in fact so rapidly that it takes only one-fifth of a second for this shifting of attention.

Types of Attention

Attention can be classified into three types. One is *involuntary attention,* which as the name implies does not require any effort on the part of the receiver. Whether you like it or not, a stimulus intrudes into your consciousness and draws your attention by its sheer intensity.

The second type of attention is *non-voluntary attention* or spontaneous attention. This occurs when a person is attracted to a stimulus. The stimulus can sustain the attention, if it is relevant to a person's needs and interests or if it can offer some benefits to him. As a marketer, you are primarily concerned with this non-voluntary attention since consumers generally do not go about searching for advertising message. At least, not in general categories of products. They may look for information when they decide to buy high priced consumer durable or automobiles. This is called voluntary attention since the consumer is looking out for information and willfully notices a stimulus.

Attention and Competition

As you are planning and executing communication strategies to gain the attention of your prospective consumers, your competitors too are doing the same thing; trying to gain the attention of prospective consumers for their products. This naturally increases the noise level further. The bombardment of conflicting and confusing messages increases almost endlessly. As a result, the person (the prospective consumer) either:

A. Willfully selects a competing stimulus (after all, the stimuli are competing with each other) or

B. Is distracted by an intruding stimulus of greater strength

This is called *non-attention.* Your message, therefore, has to fulfill the tasks of creating non-attention towards competing stimuli by distracting him from those and compelling him to select your message. Wilbur Schramm an authority on Mass communication suggests that a potential receiver (your prospective consumer) is more likely to pay attention to your message, when the receiver perceives a high net-benefit in relation to the perceived expenditure of effort required in attending to the message. The message, therefore, should be as simple and as understandable as possible (requiring minimum expenditure of effort).

This probably explains why some of the print advertisements in magazines have very little copy and striking visuals. A long copy means a high expenditure of effort on the part of the receiver. however, in some cases, where the reader's interest level is high, he is willing to read vast amounts of copy because he perceives a high level of reward (voluntary attention).

Selective Attention

All this discussion about the attention process points out to one thing. Human beings are capable of choosing from among the several stimuli they are exposed to. This process of choosing or selecting messages is called *selective attention.* There are two factors, which influence the choice of message by a person. They are:

(a) Message or stimulus factors, and

(b) Individual factors

(a) **Message Factors**: There are a number of factors to be considered while preparing a message, which play a very important role in attracting the attention of a prospective customer. These factors often interact simultaneously to gain the attention of the receiver.

Here are some factors, which are likely to help you gain attention of your prospective customers:

Size: larger objects seem to have greater attention value. They stand out physically in a crowd and thus compel the receiver to notice them. Speaking on the attention getting power of larger size advertisements, H. J. Rudolph, the renowned advertising researcher observed a phenomenon called a *square root law*. The square root law says that the attention value of an advertisement increases as the square root of the advertisement increases. To double the attention, you must increase the size of an advertisement four times! In the Indian pharmaceutical industry, almost all companies use visual aids which are at least twice as large as the product literature they used earlier.

Color: Color tends to receive greater attention than black and white.

Contrast: Contrast is another attention-getting stimuli. Some pharmaceutical companies have gained greater attention for their products when they placed a black and white page in an otherwise multi-colored visual-aid.

Shape: Different shapes gain different amounts of attention. Tall advertisements receive greater attention than wide advertisement in print media. This can be explained by the fact that people read across a page and are more likely to notice the vertical advertisement than a horizontal one of the same size. Glaxo gained a great amount of attention when they used an orange-shaped visual-aid for their *Haliborange* (an-orange flavored multivitamin syrup) launch. Biological E. Limited drew attention of pediatricians to their pediatric range of products with their elephant-shaped visual-aid. Unichem made a mark with chest physicians for their anti-tubercular range of products with their attention-grabbing visual-aid made of some sheets of X-ray film.

Isolation: An object placed in isolation draws attention. Some companies by placing their attractive packs in the center of a page surrounded by white space have used this refreshingly fresh technique.

Multiple Sensory Messages: Messages, which affect more than one sense mode, are more effective in gaining and retaining attention than those which affect only one sense mode. This explains the greater effectiveness and overpowering influence of television advertising over radio advertising. Television affects both the visual and auditory senses whereas radio affects only the auditory senses. Today, many pharmaceutical companies are vying with each other in gaining and retaining attention of doctors with their multi-colored visual-aids and the detailing of their sales force. They are trying to appeal to both the visual and auditory senses of their potential (intermediary) customers. Some are even using scratch-and-sniff printing inks to print their visual-aids where fragrance is relevant to appeal even to olfactory sense in addition!

Position: Different Positions gain different amounts of attention. Generally speaking, in print advertisement, the upper-half page and left-hand side page get more attention than lower-half page and right-hand side page respectively. That is why the special positions have different rate structure. The importance certain positions and their greater attention-getting ability is not restricted to print advertising. Certain positions on retailers' shelves too enjoy a premium. Consumer product marketers are well aware of this. Products placed at eye-level in a retail counter or a departmental store or a supermarket, for example attract the greatest attention.

(b) Individual Factors: There are a number of individual factors, which can affect the attention. These individual factors are either inherent or learned and stored in their perceptual fields. Perception is one of the most important aspects to be considered by marketing communicators. People respond to their perceptions of the world and not to the real world itself. That is why perception is even more important than reality. This is not to say that perception can be manipulated. What it really means is that even if your product is really superior it does not become superior to your customer until you persuade him to perceive your product as superior. If you find this verbose consider this: Perception is the real thing! Since individual factors influence a person's perception, understanding these is essential. As a marketing communicator you must develop awareness of these individual factors. These are:

Personal Interests: When a person perceives an object, product or idea to be important to him, he will be more attentive to the message of that product. His attention towards the message is directly proportionate to his interest level.

Attitudes and Opinions: People are likely to pay greater attention to messages, which are supportive of their existing attitudes and opinions. Conversely, they tend to filter out messages that are opposed to their attitudes. Attitudes and opinions affect a person's selection or filtering of information both at the conscious and non-conscious level. The implications of this are quite clear for the marketer. Consider this for example - if a doctor does not believe in parenteral therapy of neuro-vitamins like B1, B6, and B12, it would be an uphill task to get a prescription from him for your brand of Vitamin B1, B6, B12 injections.

Span of Attention: The increasing digitalized life style is further lowering our attention span, which is already low to a few seconds. Couple this with our capacity for processing information. The number of objects an average human can hold in working memory is about 7 give or take two, says George A Miller, a well known Harvard psychologist. You need to grab your customer's attention faster and sustain it as long as you can. Therefore, the layout of your advertisement should be simple and uncluttered for high impact. Too much of copy and highlighting too many points reflects only your anxiety to communicate and is unlikely to get hold of the required attention.

Concentration: Research tells us that the human mind can concentrate on any object only for a very short period of time. A person tends to shift his attention at least once every four seconds. This explains the reason why there are two persons presenting the news bulletin on television, alternating the events between them. This allows the viewer to do what is natural to him - shift his attention. Many advertisers too, use two or more speakers in their commercials to gain and retain attention. Some major pharmaceutical companies train their medical representatives extensively in using their multi-colored, attractive visual-aids effectively while detailing their products, since they can not use two speakers to facilitate and capitalize on the shifting nature of their audience. therefore, they use pointing the visuals and text on the visual-aid in a logical sequence. The pointer in the dextrous hands of a persuasive representative, can track the attention (thus facilitating the shifting nature) of the viewer along a predetermined path.

Needs: People's needs affect their attention to messages. A person who is in need of a product or service is, in fact, looking for information. Even a weak stimulus like a signboard or small advertisement in the classified column of a newspaper will gain his attention.

Implications for the Marketer

1. Different stimuli have varying degrees of influence in gaining and sustaining the attention of the audience. The pharmaceutical marketer should consider these factors and their relative attention getting capabilities in formulating his communication strategy. Decisions regarding the size, shape, color, position of your advertisements, therefore, will have to depend upon the intensity of stimulus required. This naturally depends upon the kind of attention you want to get for your product. For example, if your product is in a highly competitive market, naturally you need all the attention you can get to make it stand out in a crowd.

2. Since messages that can appeal to multiple senses have a greater attention gaining and sustaining power, using multiple sensory messages will give your marketing communications a winning edge. You can probably appeal, in addition, to auditory and visual senses, to the third sensory element, namely smell. For example, in the pharmaceutical industry, when you are introducing a new product with a new, different flavor and fragrance you can use the **scratch and sniff** technique to create the same fragrance for your prospective prescribers in their own chambers when you are detailing the product. Modern, micro-encapsulation technique makes it possible to overlay numerous microscopic capsules on the printed page in your visual-aid and by scratching that picture a person can actually smell the product's fragrance and feel its flavor!

3. Knowing the personal interests of your prospective customers will help your sales force to formulate specific action plans for getting their attention.

4. Since the needs and immediate concerns of a person affect his attention, the timing and beaming of your message and establishing the need are important. Visiting doctors before they start their practice will, therefore, be more beneficial in the sense

that it will increase the attention-getting and sustaining ability of company's selling effort. A medical representative who visits a doctor before he starts his practice will have a better chance of appealing to his needs and immediate concerns. The doctor too, will have time to act upon the information immediately by sending prescriptions. For example, if a doctor is concerned with treating a patient with a chronic condition like recalcitrant ringworm that is very annoying, a representative who details a new brand of systemic anti-fungal like ketoconazole or new topical anti fungal is much more likely to get the doctor's attention than anyone else. If the representative meets the doctor before he starts his practice or immediately after he starts seeing the patients (as it is not possible to call on all doctors simultaneously before they start their practice) the doctor will have sufficient time to act on the information provided by the representative. While this may seem an unlikely coincidence, it is not too infrequent. Furthermore, the doctor will have time to act immediately on the information provided by the representative if he is met before he starts his practice and not after he retires for the day.

Destination or Receiver

The destination or receiver of your communication program is not just an important element. It is the goal of your communication. Successful marketing communicators recognize the importance of developing an understanding of the receiver and prepare communication messages and programs accordingly.

Know Thy Audience

You, as a marketing communicator, must start your communication program with an analysis of your audience. It is your audience who determine what the message should be, when and to whom it should be sent and how best it is delivered. Such a *know-thy-audience* approach will make your communication messages target-specific and more effective. Fundamental as it may seem, this basic aspect of marketing communication is very often ignored by marketers. A number of companies have paid dearly for ignoring this basic principle. Consider these cases:

Case 6.1 Inadequate Analysis of the *Destination* Costs a Company Dearly!

A medium-sized pharmaceutical company with a reasonably good track record decided to get on to the fast track. Diversification into related areas seemed a logical course and the company therefore, redefined its business as general healthcare. The company very rightly realized that speed of action was a very important element for success. It did a quick market analysis and concluded that there was an increasing trend in consumer preference towards natural products in general and herbal medicines in particular. The marketing people made a very powerful and emotionally charged presentation that the company should get into Ayurvedic formulations.

They gave details of how well Dabur and Himalaya Drug Company were doing with their herbal medicines. The top management agreed to this since Ayurvedic formulations fall into the decontrolled (out of price control) category and therefore, could be very profitable. The company quickly recruited an Ayurvedic doctor for developing the formulations and launched about five new products in quick succession. To their utter dismay and disappointment, the company found that all their new Ayurvedic formulations bombed in the market place.

How did this happen? The company had a well-trained sales force and very good image. The company did apply adequate promotional pressure. What could be the reasons for the failure? A detailed analysis by the company revealed that:

A. The company was known for its pharmaceutical preparations and had a considerable reputation in its existing marketing channels such as doctors, chemists, hospitals etc. The company was not really well-known to the general public as such, except those satisfied consumers (patients) who had been prescribed or used its products at one time or another.

B. The attitude of the company's well-trained sales force to its new Ayurvedic products was not very positive, as they were not convinced about the efficacy of the products themselves. The company did not give adequate attention to this important aspect and took the enthusiasm of their sales force for granted.

C. The company rushed into the launch of these products without adequate clinical data supporting their claims. While *speed* is a very important factor, one should not *rush* into new product launches. No, not without adequate preparation.

D. Last but not least, the company had ignored the most important element, namely, the destination or receiver. The company virtually had on its visiting list of customers all allopathic doctors. Those few Ayurvedic doctors who were on the company's visiting list had considerable allopathic practice. They were prescribing more of allopathic preparations than herbal or Ayurvedic medicines.

The general attitudes and belief systems of allopathic doctors towards Ayurvedic medicines could be at best termed as skeptical. Without adequate data and hard facts based on clinical trials conducted in reputed hospitals and institutions, these doctors would not prescribe any herbal or Ayurvedic products to their patients. The patients too, expect their allopathic doctors to prescribe a modern medicine rather than a herbal medicine.

The marketing team of the company, while considering the success story of the Himalaya Drug Company overlooked the factors that made it successful. Himalaya Drug Company's success with its herbal medicines was based on massive clinical research efforts spanning a number of years. Himalaya Drug Company has been conducting numerous clinical trials by eminent physicians in a number of reputed hospitals and institutions across the country. The Himalaya Drug Company has been improving credibility for its products by building up and communicating effectively with voluminous clinical data that convinced the medical profession in the country.

The company's failure with the new Ayurvedic formulations therefore can be attributed to one major factor: ignoring or taking for granted the important element - the destination, receiver or audience. Consequently, it could not design and implement a target specific communication program. Neither could the company select, for the same reason, the appropriate marketing channels. Companies like Dabur, Baidyanath, which were successful in marketing herbal medicines had chosen the OTC route and gained consumer acceptance.

The company for want of a clear and thorough understanding of its target audience, ignored this factor too and selected the ethical route. The failure of these new products affected the company adversely in more ways than one. Firstly, the company had lost all the developmental and marketing expenditure on all these new products. Secondly, the resultant lack of attention to its existing products due to its rushing of new product launches had affected the performance of its existing products as well.

Case 6.2 You Cannot Rub It (a new concept) in Without Proper Understanding of the *Destination*. No. Not Even If It is Hygirub!

Sarabhai Chemicals, the second largest pharmaceutical company in India had introduced in the early 1980s a new product, a new me-too product to be more specific, of course with a perceptible product differentiation that was truly innovative. The product was a rubificient ointment, a balm. The company packed their balm or ointment in strips, something like the blister packs used today for tablets and capsules. The concept was totally new at that time. The differentiation was perceptible. The advantages were obvious. For the first time, an ointment was made available in single-dose packs. The application was never more hygienic.

The packaging and the concept were innovative and rational. The brand name Hygirub too was powerful enough to cut through the clutter. The company launched it with a lusty campaign aimed at prescribing doctors and stocked the product adequately with the trade. But the product failed to take off in the marketplace, contrary to the company's expectations. The product was gathering dust on retailers' shelves for a considerable amount of time. The company, finally was forced to withdraw the product.

Hygirub was not successful despite the fact that it was an innovative concept. May be the idea itself was ahead of its time.

Being one of the largest at the time in the pharmaceutical industry, the company could afford the luxury of such an experiment. Why is that despite a new innovative product concept and with the marketing muscle of a company like Sarabhai Chemicals, Hygirub failed to takeoff? The reasons may not be very difficult to seek when you analyze thoroughly and probe deeply. The possible reasons could be:

A. Prescriptions for balms and rubificient ointments were far less as compared to their sales. A major portion of their sales was due to over-the-counter purchases by consumers. Furthermore, all major brands like Vicks, Amrutanjan, Iodex, and Zandu balm were heavily advertised and promoted as OTC brands. Sarabhai Chemicals, however, chose to promote Hygirub ethically.

B. Chemists accounted for a little over fifty percent of the total sales of these rubificient ointment and balms. General stores, grocers, departmental stores and supermarkets accounted for the rest. The company could not penetrate a major segment of the market, as almost one-half of the distribution channels could not be utilized adequately. This is perhaps due to a lack of a proper, systematic analysis of the *receiver* or *destination* factors.

Of course, it is easier to comment or lament in retrospect. It is almost like playing cricket from the commentators' box. You can very well face the fiercest fast bowler on a wintry morning or the deadliest spinner on a turning wicket from a commentators' box. Facing them on the pitch is quite a different matter altogether. Whether it is easier to comment in retrospect or not, one thing is certain. You cannot take the destination or your prospective audience for granted. A systematic analysis regarding their attitudes and perceptions to your products is crucial for the success of your products.

A marketing communicator should understand the defense mechanism of his audience. Only then can he attempt to penetrate them. The defense mechanism of your audience is not only complex but also powerful. It is equipped to resist and reject a number of unwanted messages, with a number of psychological barriers like selective attention, perception and retention. These are not mutually exclusive, for many of the same factors affect the selective process. You must be able to slip past these barriers in order to successfully persuade your prospective customers.

Attention and Perception

Attention and perception are often confused and therefore used loosely. There is a relationship between them and there is a sequence of events that are mutually reinforcing. But they are not the same. However, the same factors affect them though. Attention occurs when a person notices a stimulus; when the incoming stimuli start reacting with the accumulated experiences of one's thought process, the perception process starts, thus developing a total *image* or impression. Perception, therefore, is the total *picture* or *image* a person receives from a stimulus.

Floyd L. Ruch Professor of psychology in his book *psychology and life* describes perception as a process, which involves *a synthesis of physical stimulations, which the brain receives plus the mental activity a person engages in, to complete a thought.* Perception thus uses both sensory data from present stimulation and the learning gained from past experience.

Implications for the Marketer

Understanding the factors that are likely to cause or enhance resistance is essential for the marketing communicator. Unless you understand the defense systems of your consumers you cannot avoid attacking the defense barriers head-on. Nothing could be more disastrous than attacking a person's closely held belief systems head-on. Instead, you should recognize the psychological resistance of your consumers as an opportunity by presenting messages, which are consistent with their belief structure. You should find out ways and means of communicating your product ideas to your consumers by showing them how they can maintain, reinforce or enhance their closely held beliefs or enhance their position or status in a group.

Understanding your audience involves and implies that you listen carefully to what they are saying, what they are not saying and what they do not want to say. You have to be very alert in identifying and anticipating their needs.

Receiver and Response Process

What happens to a receiver when a message is beamed to him? He responds one way or other. Isn't it obvious? Well it is not as simple as that. Of course, he does respond to a message either positively or negatively. May be even indifferently. For all practical purposes even indifference of a receiver to a message is a negative response. But it does not seem to happen in such a straight jacket fashion. The receiver goes through a process, which is commonly known as the *buying process.* The buying process involves several stages. Many researchers have suggested various models involving a different number of stages. however, a common thread runs through all the models in so far as the basic principles are concerned. In pharmaceutical marketing the predominant receiver is the doctor. This is not to say that retailers, pharmacists and stockists are not potential receivers of the messages beamed by pharmaceutical marketers. But they mainly depend upon and cater to the prescriptions given by doctors. Therefore, doctors are to be persuaded first and foremost to prescribe your products. The typical buying process (or response process) that a physician undergoes in selecting from the innumerable messages beamed at him by various pharmaceutical companies is depicted in figure 6.2.

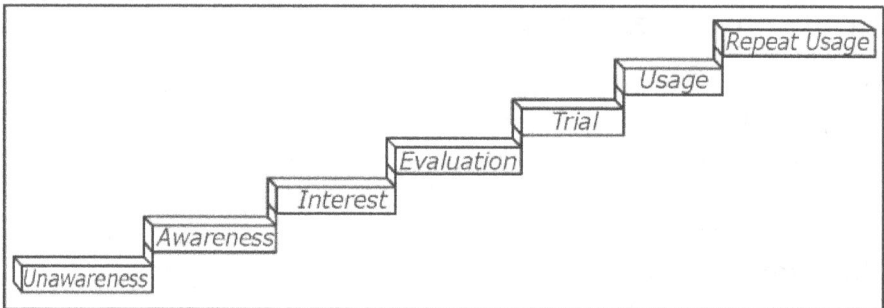

Figure 6.2 Buying Process in Pharmaceutical Marketing

Stage one: *Unawareness to Awareness*

During the first stage, that is *unawareness to awareness,* the doctor's attitude to your product is passive. He is not even aware of your product. Therefore, the doctor's major need is to be informed. Your major task at this stage is to tell the doctor and make him aware that your product exists and create an automatic association of your product with the relevant therapeutic category. Associating your brand with certain specific indications will help the doctor to recall your brand, when he thinks of prescribing a product for that particular indication.

Stage two: *Awareness to Interest*

The doctor is not passive at this stage of *awareness to interest.* He is aware of the existence of your product. But then, he is not active at the same time. You have got his attention alright by the newness of your product concept or its appearance. You need to sustain that interest by retaining his attention. You have to present your important product features succinctly, convincingly and persuasively.

Stage three: *Interest to Evaluation*

Now you are getting down to brass tacks at this stage of *interest to evaluation.* You have retained his attention. Now he is actively considering your product. The doctor will evaluate your product in terms of information provided by you vis-a-vis the competition. He will look for the distinct advantages and unique attributes of your product at this stage. Depending upon his needs he will look for safety, enhanced efficacy, economy, reliability and convenience. At this stage, you have to identify his needs and requirements, increase his confidence by substantiating your product's uniqueness and the ways in which it would fulfill his needs. You have to make an irresistible presentation of your product benefits and reassure him.

Stage four: *Evaluation to Trial*

This is a very important stage, where a doctor will be moving from a mental state of *evaluation* to a positive physical state of trial. A successful evaluation will induce the *trial.* You will have to positively reinforce the association between your product's unique attributes, the doctor's specific needs and usage opportunities like the indications in which your product is most effective.

Stage five: *Trial to Usage*

After a successful *trial* the doctor will start *using* your product. He will start prescribing your product. To ensure his continuous prescription support, you will have to provide frequent reminders of your product's positive features and benefits, which have brought it to this stage. Your brand name should be highlighted along with the specific indications and its distinct advantages. In other words, your major promotional task is to positively reinforce your product and its success factors. You will have to constantly reassure the doctor regarding the usage of your product and the resultant satisfaction.

Stage six: *Usage to Repeat Usage*

Usage to Repeat usage is the final objective of marketing. How to get a continuous prescription support from a doctor is an eternal question. To paraphrase Emerson, any marketer who finds a right answer to this, can name his price and companies will certainly make a beeline to his door. It is very difficult to get continuous prescription of your product eternally. This has been eluding pharmaceutical marketers just like perpetual motion has been eluding physicists.

You can, however, get a share of the prescriptions if you maintain the climate that has led to satisfaction. You can continue to get prescription support if you continue to maintain and improve the qualitative aspects of your product and its image.

Implications for the Marketer

At any given point of time, your prospective (intermediary) customers, that is, doctors are likely to be at different stages of buying process. Some may be in the usage stage, while some others are evaluating your product. Some of them are yet to evince interest in your product. This is because of the fact that the human adoption process towards a new product or idea is a multistage process. Based on individual characteristics some persons adopt a new product sooner while some others take a long time. Still others may never adopt. Therefore, it is only natural that you find innovators in the usage stage, early adopters in the trail stage, early majority in the evaluation stage and the late majority in the interest stage. The marketing implications of this are:

1. You should focus your research effort in deciding and determining where your target audience is in buying process.
2. Your promotional thrust and message should be different in the early stages and in the later stages as the needs of your target audiences vary.

3. To improve the effectiveness of your promotional effort, you should concentrate on those stages where the majority of your customers are present and design a target-specific communication.

Feedback

The responses of an audience to your message can be both overt (observable) and covert (unobservable and mental). You must have feedback from your doctors to know how accurately they have received your message. The feedback loop in the communication model discussed (Figure 6.1) suggests a shift in the initial sender-receiver relationship. Feedback reverses the roles of the sender and receiver. In pharmaceutical marketing, the major source of communication is personal selling, which is face-to-face communication. Therefore, the feedback, the 2overt or observable feedback is rather instantaneous. Medical representatives, who are alert can say something about their products and observe the expression on the doctor's face. A doctor, for example may smile, frown, or look puzzled or annoyed at what your representatives are saying. But this is not complete feedback, because an expression on the doctor's face does not guarantee you the most important objective of your message, namely the prescription. There may be an error in decoding the receiver's expression (non-verbal message) by the sender during the feedback. Feedback in a face-to-face- selling situation is still very important and useful, because it helps you to alter the message or channel promptly, whereas feedback of an advertising campaign might be time consuming. Consequently, any corrective decisions in terms of message or channel may be delayed.

Feedback is a very important decision tool for a marketing communicator because it tells him how well he did (or doing) in sharing a thought and transferring a meaning.

In pharmaceutical marketing the most important feedback is the prescribing behavior of the doctor. If a doctor has prescribed your product, then you have transferred the meaning of your message successfully. Otherwise, you have not communicated properly. There is some distortion somewhere in the channel, frequency, or even in the message itself. May be the noise level is very high. Feedback tells you that something is to be improved. Without prompt feedback it is not possible to transmit your message successfully. Neither would you be able to know whether your messages have reached their destination as intended. Like the proof of the pudding is in the eating, the successful transmission of your message in pharmaceutical marketing is in the prescribing behavior of the doctor. In this case the *prescription is the feedback.*

Promotion is a Key Strategic Variable

Promotion is a key consideration in strategic planning and it should be viewed as such, to capitalize and cash-in on marketing opportunities. To a large extent the use of promotion element is structured by environment, especially the nature of buyer demand. Every marketer agrees that demand is one of the most uncontrollable forces to deal with. That is why promotion is used to shift the demand and expedite the buyer's decision process. Promotion has a catalytic function. Opportunities for developing an effective promotional plan therefore, start with an analysis of markets and an understanding of underlying forces and the firm's goals.

Promotional decisions must be based on organizational goals and marketing objectives. The logical sequence of promotional decisions from a strategic perspective is:

1. Identifying target markets and audiences
2. Determining objectives and tasks
3. Preparing a promotion budget
4. Selecting the promotional mix
5. Evaluating and implementing the promotional strategy
6. Feedback

Organizational Goals and Marketing Objectives

Top management decides on the organizational goals and marketing objectives naturally depend on these. The key questions to answer at this stage are:

What is our present position? (in terms of sales and profit volumes, market share, growth, competitive advantage etc.)

Where do we want to go? (what should the company be aiming for, in terms of sales and profit objectives, market share, growth etc, in the next year? In the next three years?)

How do we get there? (this involves an analysis of strengths and weaknesses, identification of opportunities, anticipating the likely threats in the environment; preparation of an appropriate strategy and detailed tactical plan)

Understanding Promotional Decisions

Promotional decisions play a major part in the strategic and tactical plans towards reaching marketing objectives. They are the *means* to an end. Even when you keep other variables of the marketing mix (like the product, price and place) constant, promotion can direct the marketing strategy to the target market and audience. Understanding *promotion* is essential to plan and implement a winning strategy. Identification of target markets and audience is crucial for the success of any promotional strategy. If your identification of target markets and audiences is not proper, even the most creative campaign cannot get results. We have seen how two companies had paid dearly for want of a proper identification of their target markets and audiences. Promotional strategy decisions should, therefore, start with the identification and precise definition of your target markets and audiences.

Four Important Questions

Other important promotional decisions like determining promotional objectives and tasks, promotional budget, selecting the promotional mix etc. usually revolve around the following four deceptively simple questions. They are:

1. What do we want to achieve?
2. What promotional elements can we use?
3. How much can each element do?
4. What is the optimum mix?

The purpose of promotion is to generate and increase profitable sales. Every promotional activity should be related to this. Every element of the promotional mix should be justified in terms of its cost effectiveness. If it cannot be justified, it should not be done.

Elements of Promotional Mix

The promotional mix in pharmaceutical marketing includes personal selling, advertising, sales promotion and publicity. These can be further segmented for the purpose of clarity and better understanding into:

1. **Personal selling:** Medical representatives detailing the company's products to doctors, with the help of visual-aids, leave-behind-literatures, product monographs, samples, gifts etc. We shall discuss personal selling in greater detail in the next chapter, as it is the most important element of pharmaceutical promotion.

2. **Advertising:** Preparation of visual-aids, leave-behind-literature, product monographs to assist medical representatives in their detailing effort. Advertising in specialized media like medical journals and souvenirs, preparing advertising material for seminars and medical symposia; preparing mailers for doctors and dealers, preparing advertising material for print media and commercials for radio and television in case OTC formulations.

3. **Sales Promotion:** Deciding on special bonus offers, free goods and gifts to trade. Deciding on physicians' samples and gifts etc.

4. **Publicity:** Organizing medical symposia and seminars, conducting clinical trials, conducting exhibitions, designing and executing product publicity campaigns for truly innovative products. We shall discuss publicity and its role in pharmaceutical promotion separately in a chapter on Public Relations.

Evaluating the Effectiveness of Promotional Elements

Evaluating the effectiveness of various promotional elements is necessary to decide on an optimal promotional mix. In order to evaluate the promotional elements objectively, we have to understand the objectives of promotion clearly. The objectives of promotion, irrespective of the mix of elements used are to create or increase:

(a) Awareness
(b) Interest
(c) Evaluation
(d) Trial
(e) Usage
(f) Repeat usage

Let us examine the relative degrees of effectiveness of each of the promotional elements.

Advertising

When you consider the definition of advertising by the American Marketing Association as *any paid form of non-personal presentation* and promotion of ideas, goods or services by an identified sponsor, the focus is on mass media. Note the key words - *non-personal* and *paid by an identified sponsor.* This clearly rules out any face-to-face communication with customers. Advertising, therefore, can inform people, make them aware of your product, create interest and take them to the stage of evaluation. In consumer marketing, it can even stimulate the desire to buy, if a positive need exists. But in pharmaceutical marketing, the effect of advertising stops at the point where the target audience is receptive. It requires the persuasive pressure of personal selling to induce a trial. An advertising campaign can create a better climate, a favorable disposition for the sales force to move in and clinch the sale. But advertising cannot create or increase the sale directly. It can, however, reassure a convinced user and maintain usage. Advertising can be a very useful support, when used creatively and effectively.

Publicity

Publicity can be create and increase awareness and interest. It can also create a favorable disposition by improving the credibility of the company's communications. It can probably facilitate repeat usage by satisfied customers. But it can neither induce trial nor increase usage.

Sales Promotion

The most popular methods of sales promotion used in pharmaceutical marketing are:

(a) Quantity discounts or trade offers, and

(b) Gifts to retail chemists on the purchase of a pre-determined quantity of a product on value or value of an assortment of products

Sales promotion cannot increase awareness, interest, evaluation, trial or usage in general. What it can do is increase dramatically the repeat usage by dispensing doctors if the same offers are given to them. Usually, the trade offers are also extended to dispensing doctors and nursing homes. Sales promotion cannot increase the sale of a product at the retail level unless it is supported by an increase in prescriptions from doctors for those products on offer. Sales promotion, however is useful in achieving certain short-term sales objectives like reducing inventories of products and increasing the stocking with the trade. Unless adequate advertising and personal selling effort of a company to generate more prescriptions for the products on offer to backup sales promotion, it will not be able to increase even the stock levels with retailers and wholesalers. On the contrary, it may boomerang, if there are not enough prescriptions. Even in case of OTC formulations, sales promotion should be backed by adequate advertising pressure.

Personal Selling

Personal selling is the most important and effective of all the elements in a promotional mix in pharmaceutical marketing. It can increase awareness, create interest, lead the doctors to evaluate, induce them to try the product and after successful trial persuade them to use and reassure them to use repeatedly. Personal selling, to be effective, should have the support of advertising, sales promotion and publicity. These other elements of promotional mix create a favorable disposition and get the medical representative of a company the much-needed foot in the door.

The relative effectiveness of various promotional elements in pharmaceutical marketing is shown in Table 6.1.

Table 6.1 Pharmaceutical Promotional Elements and Their Attractiveness

Promotional Element	Awareness	Interest	Evaluation	Trial	Usage	Repeat Usage
Advertising	✓	✓	✓	••	••	✓
Medical Journals	✓	✓	✓	••	••	✓
Mailings	✓	✓	✓	••	••	✓
Publicity	✓	✓	✓	••	••	✓
Clinical Research	✓	✓	✓	✓	••	✓
Medical Symposia	✓	✓	✓	••	••	✓
Sales Promotion						
Samples	✓	✓	••	✓	✓	✓
Gifts	••	✓	••	••	••	✓
Personal Selling						
Individual						
Doctor Calls	✓	✓	✓	✓	✓	✓
Doctor Meetings	✓	✓	✓	✓	✓	✓

Deciding on Your Target Markets and Audiences

Deciding on your target markets is the vital first step in formulating a winning promotional strategy. After the target markets are identified, selecting the appropriate target audiences becomes the logical second step. To be effective, your promotional messages should be target-specific. This is why identification and selection of target markets and audiences precede every other strategic decision regarding the promotion. For example, if you are marketing a generic product for dispensing doctors your promotional strategy will be different from the one you would plan for a new cardiovascular drug. Your primary target audience for the new cardiovascular drug would be cardiologists and physicians. If you are introducing a specialty product for hospitals, your strategy will again be different. If you are introducing an OTC formulation, you will obviously choose a different route of promotion. Your target markets and audience determine your promotional messages and strategies. The key questions that a marketer should ask are:

1. What is the role of personal selling vs. mass advertising?
2. What type of promotional campaign will be most effective?
3. How to reach the target audiences most effectively?

Only a clear, precise, non-ambiguous definition of your target markets and audiences will help you answer these questions and sharpen your focus on formulating effective promotional strategies.

Push or Pull?

Whether to pull the product through the marketing channel by concentrating on consumers, who are the final purchasers, or whether to push it through the distribution channel by gaining the cooperation of stockists and distributors is a fundamental, strategic decision. Some marketers use a combination of these two basic strategies. In prescription drug marketing, however pull is the only way to go. Push has very little effect in the sense that it helps to stock your products with the retailers adequately when you introduce new products or run special campaigns for your products.

The Push Strategy

The push strategy got its name because it involves pushing, or urging members of marketing channel to sell a product by recommending it to consumers or by giving it an adequate display. Each channel member to promote the product to the channel below uses personal selling and trade promotion. Manufacturers, for example promote to wholesalers, wholesalers to retailers, and retailers to consumers. Manufacturers may provide special offers, discounts or gifts to dealers to gain their support.

The Pull Strategy

The pull strategy, as the name suggests, aims at pulling the customers towards the product. It attempts to create demand for a product within a channel of distribution by appealing directly to the consumer. Advertising rather than personal selling, is the primary promotional tool used for this strategy.

The Combination Strategy

Usually most consumer goods companies use a combination of push and pull strategies to achieve their goals.

Push and Pull Strategies and Prescription Drugs

While these strategies are used with great success by a number of consumer goods companies, they are not out of place in marketing prescription drugs. Every pharmaceutical marketer attempts to create a demand for his products, that is, generate prescriptions form his intermediary customers (doctors) by persuading them directly. Creating demand or generating prescriptions is in other words a pull strategy.

The pull strategy should properly be balanced with an appropriate push strategy at their dealer level. You should ensure that your products are adequately stocked with all the retailers before you implement a pull strategy to generate substantial prescriptions for your products. Every pharmaceutical marketer knows the price he has to pay for a dishonored prescription at the retail counter for want of stocks. Regenerating prescriptions for a product is twice as difficult as generating them in the first place.

That is why a combination of the push and pull strategies is the best prescription for achieving the marketing objectives of prescription drugs. A number of pharmaceutical companies formulate special campaigns, which combine push and pull strategies, mainly for some products where there is some degree of seasonality like cough and cold preparations, antidiarrhoeals etc. Furthermore, such combinations strategies are planned when the company would like to achieve a sudden increase in sales volumes or when high inventories are to be reduced to an acceptable level. It is important to remember that in the case of prescription drugs a combination strategy is useful. Unless the push strategy is supported by increased prescription generation by an effective pull strategy, the gains are merely transient. It is like transferring your stocks from your warehouse to the retailer.

That is not all. The receivables would get adversely effected. The product might get stuck with a slow-moving or non-moving image that could be dangerous. A judicious combination of push and pull strategies is essential for achieving success at the market place. Figure 6.3 indicates the push and pull strategies.

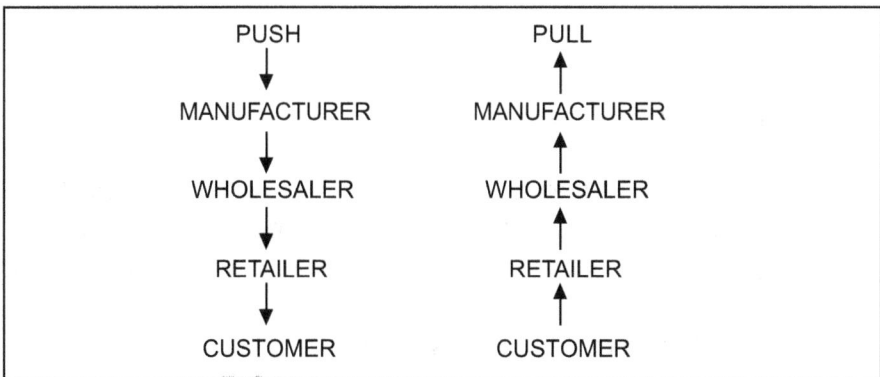

```
        PUSH                  PULL
          ↓                     ↑
    MANUFACTURER          MANUFACTURER
          ↓                     ↑
     WHOLESALER            WHOLESALER
          ↓                     ↑
      RETAILER              RETAILER
          ↓                     ↑
      CUSTOMER              CUSTOMER
```

Figure 6.3 Push and Pull Strategies

Promotional Objectives and Tasks

After deciding on the target markets and audiences, the marketer should define and determine promotional objectives and tasks.

The promotional objectives define the role of marketing communication and determine the goals in supporting the overall marketing objectives.

The promotional tasks should translate the objectives into action plans. Though promotion is marketing communication, which is largely informative and persuasive in nature, to be effective the objectives and tasks of each advertising campaign need to be clearly spelt out in measurable terms. All promotional objectives should be quantified. Not only that, all objectives and tasks should be quantified for each element of promotion. They should be based on a thorough analysis of the strengths and weaknesses, opportunities and threats (SWOT). Promotional objectives, therefore, will have to:

- Increase your strengths
- Correct your weakness
- Concentrate on opportunities
- Offset threats

Deciding on Promotional Budget

How much should a company spend on promotion? Economists say that a company should spend only up to the point of diminishing returns. Unfortunately managers find it difficult to determine this point of diminishing returns or the point at which the money spent is beginning to become counterproductive.

It is obvious that the budget should be adequate to achieve the promotional objectives and tasks. Yet a number of companies seem to be using arbitrary budgeting methods, without measuring promotional effectiveness. A lot of subjectivity prevails regarding promotional budgeting decisions. However, one can use a few thumb rules. These are:

- The level of incremental sales
- The minimum level of promotion required, taking into account the intensity of competition of promotional activities with all other elements of marketing to maximize the impact and performance.

Some of the methods commonly used in deciding on the promotional budget are:

1. Percent of sales method
2. Fixed-sum per unit method
3. Affordable funds method
4. Competitive parity method
5. Objective and task method

What is even more important than choosing any particular method is that you should constantly and consistently monitor your promotional functions. This is essential to establish more reliable parameters of cost-benefit relationships. A comparative analysis of the relative tradeoffs of these methods will help you select, modify or even evolve a promotional budgeting method that will best suit your company.

1. **The *percent of sales* Method:** Under this method, the amount to be spent on promotion is specified as a fixed percentage of historical (previous year) or forecasted year (next year) sales. This method is widely used probably because of its simplicity. The percent of sales method, however, has a number of inherent weaknesses. Some of them are:

   (a) Advertising is made dependent on sales

   (b) The company is committed to the expenditure of a certain percentage of its revenue for advertising without taking market conditions into cognizance. For example, if marketing conditions require more or less to be spent, the company may find it difficult to increase or reduce advertising expenditure. Furthermore, the percent of sales method implies little or no changes in its assumptions regarding the market conditions, which are ever changing.

   (c) The selection of percentage cannot be justified in any scientific manner.

2. **The *fixed-sum-per-unit* Method:** Some companies, which manufacture a wide variety of products with different promotional requirements, may set aside a specified amount for each of product produced. If the producer knows the promotional cost per unit in advance, the pricing is very much simplified. That is the only major advantage. But the method is highly illogical, as the past is used as an inflexible guide to future promotional expenditures.

3. **The *affordable funds* Method:** Some companies may continue to think that promotional expenditures are those business costs, which are desirable or avoidable as per the subjective judgment of the top management. Consequently, funds for promotional activities are appropriated entirely depending upon the discretion of the top management.

4. **The *competitive parity* Method:** This is a typical 'keeping-up-with-the joneses' approach towards preparing a promotional budget. This method is slightly more market-oriented than others, in the sense that it takes into account what competitors are likely to spend on promotion. This is essentially a defensive strategy.

But then, the same market conditions and challenges may not exist for all competitors.

5. **The *objective and task* Method:** This may not be as simple as the other methods but the objective and task method is certainly the most logical one. According to this approach, promotion leads and directs sales, and is tied to future objectives rather than past sales. As per this method, you have to set the objectives first and then identify the tasks necessary to achieve the objectives. Finally, you estimate the costs associated with accomplishment of each task and add other costs like research to arrive at the total promotional budget. While this is certainly the most logical of all approaches, even this is not a perfect method as objectives, tasks, strategies and estimates are subjectively derived.

The *Ideal* Method

There is no ideal method that is best suited for all companies and all industries. However, in practice, it is observed that a number of companies have been using a combination of more than one method. Quite a few companies these days are giving greater importance to the objectives and tasks method in setting their promotional budget, since it is the most logical one.

Deciding on the Promotional Mix

The most important factors to be considered while deciding on the promotional mix, include the product class, target market and competitors' strategies. Product class has a direct implication on promotional strategy. For example, ethical drugs are perfectly suited for a personal selling strategy combined with advertising in specialty media like medical journals. In case of OTC formulations, advertising in mass media coupled with push strategy through the marketing channels may be the right one.

The size, dispersion and knowledge of the target market is an important factor to be considered while formulating an effective promotional strategy to create the desired impact. The decisions regarding the weightage of the various promotional elements and the appropriate content of the promotional message depend largely on the characteristics of the target audiences. The marketing communication may have to be varied for different target audiences even in the case of the same product or product class. Consider this situation:

- Assume that you are about to launch a new NSAID (Non-Steroidal Anti-Inflammatory Drug). Orthopedics, general practitioners, physicians and surgeons can prescribe NSAIDs. Though the product features and attributes essentially remain the same, the needs of the different target audiences vary, albeit marginally. The advertising communications and the detailing messages to these different specialist doctors have to be presented in a different manner, highlighting or emphasizing the respective *benefit packages*. Only then can you achieve the upward movement for your product on the product ladder in the prescribing doctor's mind. This can aid top-of-the-mind recall, which is essential for getting his prescriptions.

- For that matter, take any product in any other therapeutic category like multi-hematinic, antibiotics and anti-hypertensives. You will observe that the information needs vary among the different (target audiences) specialists depending upon their degrees of specialization, expertise, experience and the type of practice. Therefore, a common message aimed at all the different specialist groups is not likely to elicit the same kind of response or create the same degree of impact, as a target-specific communication package would.

Principles of Medical Advertising

Medical advertising - is it in any way different from advertising in general? The Principles of communication and advertising are applicable even to medical advertising. At the same time, there are certain differences. For example, the target audience of pharmaceutical or medical advertising is not the ultimate beneficiaries (patients) of the products that are advertised. The target audience is the physicians or the intermediary customers who advise and recommend the use of the products through their prescriptions. The role of pharmaceutical advertising, therefore, is to convince the physicians that the product will help them help their patients. The same product should be perceived as benefiting both the patient and the physician. The true beneficiary, the patient, may never see the advertisement in the case of prescription drugs, since pharmaceutical advertising is primarily aimed at the physician, who will not even be purchasing the drug, but recommends it to his patients (a few dispensing doctors are the exception). Top-of-the-mind-recall becomes even more crucial in the case of ethical drug advertising. Advertising should implant a trigger mechanism in the physician's mind. When it comes to prescribing a medication, the trigger should go off. The physician should associate the patient's medical condition and symptoms with the advertised product, write out a prescription and hand it over to the patient. That is what prescription drug advertising should achieve. The medical profession combines the best of both worlds in the sense that it is altruistic in serving the needs of patients and at the same time represents a personal quest in accomplishing professional excellence. Fortunately for pharmaceutical advertisers, these two are inextricably linked. By helping his patients the physician achieves a sense of fulfillment and professional accomplishment.

Pharmaceutical advertisers, therefore, should make the doctors feel through their advertising communication that their efforts and services are directed towards enhancing the diagnostic and therapeutic skills of the physicians. This is important because physicians have a very clear and well-defined self-concept about themselves. It is, therefore, vital to appeal to this rational image of the physicians, and at the same time make a deeper appeal to their emotional factors, which really lead to action.

Physicians, as we already discussed, are rational in choosing a particular drug therapy for a specific ailment. If you are among the first to introduce it you may have to make a strong pitch with a powerful logical, *reason-why* story as a first step, followed by a subtle emotional appeal towards preferring and prescribing your brand as a second, *emotional* step.

If you are not among the first to introduce a new molecule or new drug, your approach, naturally has to be different. The doctor is not new to the drug. He is aware of it. His conviction level, however, would depend on the communication efforts of those early introducers i.e., on how strongly, powerfully and persuasively they had promoted it. If the conviction level of the physician is high, then you have to present yourself in a different light that is perceptible. You have to create a distinct differentiation in the mind of the physician.

If the physician's conviction in the drug is not strong enough, you should develop a strategy towards gaining and reinforcing confidence in the drug in the first place and then gain his preference and persuade him to prescribe your brand.

Physicians look at advertisements of pharmaceuticals critically. They identify themselves very closely with the advertisements. They accept only those advertisements, which reinforce their *self-image* that are *for me* and reject those advertisements, which they feel are appealing for the laymen and not to physicians. This probably explains why doctors are averse to prescribing OTC formulations and less interested in prescribing ethical drugs with strong OTC profile. The implication here for marketers of ethical drugs with strong OTC profile is that they should very strongly reinforce their brand image that it is a prescription drug, in the minds of prescribing physicians.

Doctors, apart from evaluating the advertisements of ethical drugs, seem to place companies also on a sliding scale. Since a number of companies manufacture and market a number similar formulations, physicians tend to evaluate the companies.

The personality of the company too, exerts considerable influence in the selection of a brand for prescription. This partly explains the reason why certain companies have an edge over others in making the doctors accept their new products faster. Some of the important pharmaceutical advertising appeals, both rational and non-rational are presented in table 6.2.

Table 6.2 A Typology of Pharmaceutical Advertising Appeals

Rational Appeals	Non-Rational Appeals
Product Related	Emotional Appeals
Economy	Empathy
Innovation	Humour
Differentiation	Curiosity
Mode of Action	Unusual Illustration (Non-clinical)
Usage	Ego-gratifying
Physician Related	
Therapeutic Aid to Physician	
Clinical Use Related	
Dependability	
Safety	
Clinical Illustration	
Patient Response	

Medical Advertising Media

Medical advertising media in India includes visual-aids for detail talks on products by medical representatives, advertising in medical journals, product literature, monographs and direct mailers. But, visual-aid for detail talk is the most important and most widely used medium in India, although the doctors interest in the visual-aid is waning. Journal advertising and direct mailers are of secondary importance. Medical representatives can use the visual aids creatively to reinforce their detail talks, by a slight variation in visuals and copy built around the same theme and the same core concept. Here are few points to ponder for improving the persuasive power of your detailing stories.

How to Prepare an Effective Detailing Story

1. Any good communication should be idea-centered and not word-centered. Do not look for play with words or puns. Instead, build your detailing story around one good, solid concept. Around the single most powerful concept that covers it all.

2. Every one of us is really obsessed with the *what-is-there-in-it-for-me* syndrome, when we are confronted with a decision making situation. Build your detailing story around the benefits that your product can provide to the doctor and his patients. Communicate your product benefits creatively, Interestingly and differently.

3. Use a strong reason - the why approach, if your product represents a really new concept in therapy. Remember, you should gain the conviction of the doctor regarding the new concept.

4. Gaining the attention of the physician in an overcrowded market is the first and most vital step. Half the battle is won, when you gain the attention of the physician. Curiosity may have killed the rat, but you have to raise the interest level, and work up to a climax to gain and sustain the doctor's attention. In the opening page, therefore, let there be no indication of what is coming in the pages which are to follow. Let him keep guessing. This will not only help to gain the doctor's attention but will help in sustaining it too! Remember, *what holds attention determines action*. Even when you have to prepare a one-page detailing story as a reminder, it is better to sell an idea and a concept rather than merely requesting the doctor to prescribe your products.

5. Your detailing story should be memorable. It should be clearly a cut above the rest. It should spontaneously and almost involuntarily be able to associate your product benefits with the medical condition or the symptoms of his patient. How to achieve this? By understanding the learning process. By applying the *principle of association* and the *principle of reinforcement* to your detailing story.

6. Once you have unearthed a really good *concept* around which you can build your product communication, stay with it unwaveringly and unflinchingly. Have the conviction. A really good concept is worth repeating. Repeat it with slight variations while retaining the central theme. That makes your message more memorable.

7. When you start your story with an interest-arousing concept, the closing of your story should be equally interesting. You should close your detailing story with a memorable *pay-off-line!* A pay-off line is a summation of your detailing story. It should be short, sweet and memorable. And yet it should convey the entire concept. A good, effective *pay-off line* enhances memorability and facilitates top-of-the-mind recall.

8. A good detailing story must first of all be heard above the competing noise level to make any impact. The various approaches to achieve this distinctive differentiation are innovative approaches, right mix of rational and emotional advertising appeals, increasing the involvement of the physician in a detailing situation, to name a few.

9. A good, creative, interesting, detailing story can only be as good and as interesting as the persuasive and enthusiastic manner in which it is detailed. It is detailing that puts life into the story. It is the quality of detailing that determines the effectiveness of your product communication. When you raise the standard of detailing, you are, in fact and in effect, maximizing the impact of your communication. Good, effective detailing can generate increased prescription support even with mediocre, 'me-too' detailing stories. But even the most innovative and creative communication strategies can virtually be killed with inept, lack-luster detailing.

Here are a few cases showing how some companies applied these communication principles effectively and created memorable campaigns for the products.

Case 6.3 Principle of Association Helps Two Brands Cruise to Top Position!

Bayer India had successfully adopted the principle of association to communicate two of its major brands Bayer's Tonic and Incidal - to the prescribing physicians. It had chosen clear, powerful concepts for each one of them and more importantly stayed with those for a long time, repeating the main theme with mostly variations in visuals.

For Bayer's Tonic, which had been one of the oldest and traditional brands of the company, had chosen a concept that it is *unique* and *timeless* and *invaluable* and very creatively communicated through a theme that tells it all. The theme was *there are no two of its kind.*

It was supported by pleasing visuals of the *seven wonders of the world* and *other important monuments.* The company presented a series of these visuals to the doctors as collectors' items, giving one at time as a series. The association was unmistakable. The position achieved was enviable. Bayer's Tonic had been enjoying the position of the largest prescribed tonic in the Indian pharmaceutical market.

As regards Incidal, the company had struck on a very powerful, unique concept, that is, the antihistamine that does not cause drowsiness. The company had communicated this unique concept even more dramatically with its - *Alert* theme. Ably supported by superb visualization in the form of photographs of birds and animals depicting *alertness*. The result? Incidal had moved quickly to the number two position and was threatening the brand leader in its heydays (1988).

Case 6.4 Innovative Communication Strategy Pushes a Product into Brand Leadership Position!

One company had found an innovative way to communicate its rather 'me-too' product. The company had fixed a battery-operated electrical display panel board behind the visual-aid, that can light up with the pressing of a button to create a neon-sign effect in the doctor's chamber. Every time the representative announced the brand name, he used to press the button and the brand name was illuminated. The reaction and the response of the doctors to this novel and innovative devise was one of pleasant surprise. It made the brand really memorable. This certainly paved the way for the brand's long march to the leadership position!

Case 6.5 Participation and Involvement Rejuvenate an Old Brand!

A leading pharmaceutical company in India came up with an idea of involving the doctor in detailing. How to make him participate in the detail talk and make it more like an interview? This was necessary because the company was relaunching one of its very old brands. The company finally hit upon an idea of requesting the doctor to give the company's representatives the first prescription for the brand as soon as the detailing was over. The skeptical filed force implemented the strategy rather hesitatingly. But when the first few doctors wrote the brand prescription after the detailing was over without any reservation, the skepticism of the field force was turned into enthusiasm. The *brand name* found its way into the doctor's *pen*. The campaign was an unprecedented success!

Case 6.6 Magic-slate's Magic Formula!

Another company requested the doctor to write the brand name on the magic slate fixed on to the visual-aid, to make the doctor familiar to the writing of the brand name. To the surprise of the company's field force many doctors obliged. The company was successful in getting its new product's brand name on the the pen of the doctor very quickly!

Simple idea well executed, not a magic formula!

Case 6.7 Emotional Appeal Wins the Doctors' Hearts!

Here's a detailing story that had used emotional appeal and won. The detailing story used a case study approach and presented three patient profiles.

Voldys 21 was a progesterone and estrogen combination marketed by Allenbury's division of Glaxo in the 1970s. The product was recommended for treating dysfunctional uterine bleeding. One of the most successful and memorable detailing stories of Voldys 21 was like this:

Doctor, here's a patient with amenorrhea. She needs your reassurance and Voldys 21.

Doctor, here is a patient with a dysmenorrhea. She needs your reassurance and Voldys 21.

Doctor, here is a patient with menorrhagia. She needs your reassurance and Voldys 21.

The story later gave the details of how and why Voldys 21 is superior...etc.

The predominant emotional appeal and concern were very well received by the doctors.

There are numerous success stories about detailing. These five serve only an illustrative purpose of what can be done with detailing stories. Preparing a good detailing story is more hard work than one can imagine. Creativity, of course, is important.

The Times They Are A - Changing!
- Bob Dylan

The times are certainly changing for the healthcare scenario in general and pharmaceutical marketing in particular.

Pharmaceutical marketing media like all other media was unidirectional and relied only on broadcasting its carefully crafted marketing message to its target audience, who were mostly physicians and doctors with good prescribing potential. However, since the mid 1990s the growing popularity of internet offered a huge choice and freedom of access to content dynamically from millions of websites. Content generation during these early years of internet revolution was no doubt huge, but there was not much difference in the type of content. Most of them resembled their traditional websites, which were more like online brochures and e-commerce sites; were merely looking like online versions of their earlier catalogues during this period. This period was later termed as web 1.0.

Later, Web 2.0 or Social Media emerged as a buzz word with the advent of user-generated content such as blogs and wikis. People started participating actively by using the internet discussion boards and started rating the content and posting comments, making it a hub for social communities. What is most interesting about web 2.0 is the fact that some of the most consumed and engaging information was not coming from a small number of media channels but a rather large number of regular internet users. The early social networks started to emerge enabling people to connect with each other more easily. These networks matured and gave rise to services like Twitter and Facebook. Facebook today dominates the social media scene with a whopping two billion users.

Innovative Approaches to Pharmaceutical Detailing

Pharmaceutical industry around the same time was facing challenging times in terms of restricted access to physicians by their sales representatives. Pharmaceutical companies in the US mainly were exploring for ways and means to reach and impact effectively their most important target audience - physicians, with their marketing messages. As many academic medical centers started the partial or complete blockade of sales representatives access to practitioners in their clinics, hospitals, or affiliated professional office settings, the prescribing physicians and healthcare professionals (HCPs) started exploring the emerging new sources of media for medical information on the internet. Pharmaceutical companies too started seeking ways to operate more effectively without losing efficiency in the face of the highly restricted access by medical institutions for their marketing activities. The declining access and the decreasing role of the pharmaceutical sales representatives and the increasing need for physicians to rely on new technology that is within the reach have led to innovative approaches in pharmaceutical detailing. These approaches are eDetailing or remote detailing which gives access to Pharma firms when physical access is restricted. The other is iPad detailing (or tablet detailing), which improves physician engagement significantly during the face-to-face meetings.

Innovations in detailing, however were not enough. When physicians are scanning the ubiquitous internet they are doing it on their terms with respect to time and place that are most convenient to them. They could surf the net whenever they find time to do so on the multiple devices that they have such as a smart phone, laptop, desktop and tablet. Internet too, offers numerous channels to provide the information just about on any subject they want including their therapeutic areas and pharmaceutical products and their clinical trials. When physicians are present on a number of channels, can drug companies lag behind? They have to be present where their key customers are. In addition to doctors, patients too are frequenting internet to look for information about their health, diseases, possible treatment options and physicians to consult.

The technological revolution has in its wake brought a number of technologies such as mobile technologies with smart phone applications, streaming of audio and video capabilities and the omnipresent internet access. Emergence of these highly effective digital technologies and increasing physician acceptance and even reliance on these have prompted the pharmaceutical industry to adopt to these new technologies. And the industry did embrace these and started innovating and implementing a number of new approaches such as digital, multichannel and social media marketing. The drug firms have also created new platforms for delivering their marketing messages from their uni-directional, visual-aid detailing to very engaging conversations about their products and what they can do to benefit the patients across multiple channels in a highly integrated manner. The following paragraphs briefly explain each of these new marketing approaches.

Winning with iPad Detailing

iPad has become the number one digital tool for over eighty percent of pharmaceutical companies in North America and some European countries. But many of them have yet to unleash its real potential to engage the physicians and healthcare professionals. iPad has the potential to be the single device for sales force automation and customer relationship management and closed loop marketing for pharmaceutical sales force.

Closed loop marketing captures information on every interaction with the physicians regardless of the channel being used. It acts on the information gathered in designing subsequent messages thus ensuring target-specific and highly personalized marketing messages.

Tablet detailing can be an excellent tool to start the closed loop marketing experience with additional channels integrated later.

Designing and Delivering Segment-Specific Content

Your iPad can deliver the content that is specific to the segments in each of your physician segments across the *stages of their adoption* of your product. Stages of adoption a is step-wise overview of the possible stages a doctor can be in while considering a brand. Consider the following segments (based on stages in which the physicians currently are) for example:

1. Physicians, who are *unaware* of the treatment or brand or using a different brand
2. Physicians, who have *just started prescribing* and sent their first prescriptions
3. Physicians, who have taken up your brand and *prescribing more or less regularly*
4. Physicians, who are high volume prescribers and *brand advocates* who influence peers proactively to prescribe the brand

Each of these segments require a different marketing message to meet their communication needs. During their calls, the sales representatives will try to find out the stage at which their physicians are. Brand managers accordingly design specific communication messages that are targeted to meet the communication needs of all physicians as per their relative positions on the stages of adoption. The sales representatives can thus access quickly the right information and the required presentation slide-decks or videos on their tablets and deliver an engaging detail. Without the segment-specific content, it would be much harder for the sales force to use their tablets effectively and engagingly.

Improving Tablet Presentation Skills

While iPad is a versatile digital tool for effectively engaging the physicians during a detail, it requires considerable skills and practice. Training to improve the presentation skills in using a tablet is important. Consider training your sales force on these areas:

A. When to use iPad and when not to use

B. How to segment physicians

C. How to use and handle the iPad properly?

D. How to properly use the iPad? A representative for example, should not be looking at his tablet while presenting a detail talk but should be looking at the physician

E. Which message to address first preferably for each segment?

F. How to close the conversation?

G. What to do if no segmentation can be determined?

H. What to do if the physician gives only 30 seconds? What is his elevator speech?

Simple and elementary as they may seem, these basics are important as they make the representatives resourceful in terms of conducting themselves in any situation.

The key question is how are you using your iPad or tablet? The effectiveness of iPad or tablet detailing depends on whether you are trying to unleash its full potential or not. David Ormesher, CEO of Closerlook, one of the leading digital marketing consultancy firms in the US puts it succinctly when he says:

If the tablet is not part of an authentic, closed-loop strategy, it simply replaces a glossy presentation with a shiny one. It is like replacing a traditional hammer with an auto-hammer: it's cool, it's electric, but in the end it still does the same thing.

Closed-Loop Marketing

Multichannel marketing is often tied to closed loop marketing (CLM), because CLM can integrate the use of different digital channels such as website and social media as part of the detailing efforts of a firm.

Pharmaceutical companies identify and refine the marketing promotional materials their physicians find interesting and resonate with. They seek to adapt their promotion efforts and direct it back to the physician - in other words closing the loop. Consider the following steps that a Pharma company may take in implementing the closed loop marketing.

1. A pharmaceutical sales representative (PSR) is provided with an iPad or similar tablet that contains the detailing software. This

software enables the PSR to present an engaging detail talk about his product through a multimedia presentation that may contain PDFs of clinical article reprints, a slide-deck and a video featuring a key opinion leader, or mode of action of the drug or interactive graphs etc. While the physician is engaged in the detail talk and viewing these materials, a record is made of which ones are used and what length of time was spent on each page, slide, graph and video.

2. The recorded information is sent immediately to a central system at the firm's head office via the internet. The feedback data from the tablet is analyzed together with the Customer Relationship Management (CRM) data that the company has (companies that implement CLM strategy will most certainly have CRM in place). The insights derived from this integrated analysis are used in preparing a content that specifically meets that particular physician's needs and communicated to the PSR and brand manager. PSR delivers the message via the preferred channel of the physician and at the time and place the physician wants. This process ensures the delivery of the right message that the physician can resonate with at the right time, on the right channel and at the right place.

3. With these insights, the brand manager may develop branding strategies either nationally or for specific geographical regions based on physician preferences. When you practice closed-loop marketing, you are engaging the physicians optimally because there is a continuity in conversations. Every interaction becomes meaningful as it takes the physicians' needs, concerns and wants into account and addresses them promptly.

Closed loop marketing thus can help the pharmaceutical firms prepare communication strategies that their customers find compelling.

Digital Marketing

Everything these days has become digitized. With the rapid adoption of wearable devices and advances in mobile technology, an increasing number of customers are embracing digital experiences. Digitalization has already disrupted many industries such as media, travel, shopping and finance among others. However, healthcare in general and pharmaceuticals in particular are lagging behind in the rapidly evolving pharmaceuticals in particular are lagging behind in the rapidly evolving digital space. But can pharmaceutical companies continue to be laggards in practicing digital marketing? The question is not whether to digitize or not, but when? Better sooner than later. Why? Consider these reasons for example:

1. As Scott Brinker, blogger and chief marketing technologist says marketing has become a technology powered discipline. Marketing organizations, therefore must infuse technical capabilities with their DNA.

2. Research suggests that vast majority of patients (76 percent) don't just want patient services. They demand them.

3. Patients have become proactive, digitally enabled and continually seek consumer health related services from a variety of channels and sources on internet.

4. Digital's multiple touch points allow us to reach patients and physicians and engage with them on a more personal level across many channels.

5. Digital technology had reached a tipping point in 2014 when 51 percent of healthcare practitioners are digital natives. It is estimated that more than two-thirds of HCPs would be digital natives in a few years. A digital native is a person born or brought up during the age of digital technology and therefore familiar with computers and internet from an early age.

6. Manhattan Research conducted a few years ago suggested that doctors who take part in online patient communities write an average of 24 prescriptions more per week than those with no interest in online communities.

7. Research also suggested that a third of the doctors have changed a patient's treatment as a result of an internet search.

8. An Accenture estimate suggests that effective digitization fuels growth by about 33 percent and profitability by about 40 percent.

Research conducted in North America has found that the average American goes to the doctor three times an year but spends 52 hours in searching for his health related information. Even in the rest of the world too, this should be happening may be to a lesser extent. But, it won't be long before consumers searching for health related information gains speed.

Furthermore, digital's multiple touch points allow us to reach physicians and patients and engage with them on a more personal level by targeting them across the devices and across different channels in an integrated manner. The conversation thus becomes seamless across the devices thanks to the new digital technologies.

The question, therefore, is not whether to digitize or not, but how?

When a company decides to start transforming itself digitally, the best place to start the process is with sales and marketing. There is often a confusion regarding the usage of the terms such as digital marketing, multichannel marketing and more recently omni-channel marketing. Are they same or different? No, they are not the same. Digital is basically a toolset that underpins and supports all marketing efforts. Multichannel marketing is about creating and delivering the right message to the right person at the right place and at the right time. Digital approach and mindset are important because they are effective tools that make your marketing effort cost-effective and highly measurable.

Multichannel Marketing

Multichannel marketing (MCM) as the name indicates is simply the use of multiple channels to reach a target audience. In the case of pharmaceutical marketing the target audience is primarily physicians, followed by healthcare professionals, patients and other stakeholders. The communication channels include both traditional and digital ones. Pharmaceutical marketers, however, have always operated in a multichannel environment that included personal selling, direct mail, journal advertising, meetings and conferences even before the internet era.

Multichannel marketing involves multiple channels - both offline and online. As internet has grown exponentially, the number of channels too increased rather dramatically.

Omni-channel Marketing

The dictionary defines *Omni* as *universal* or *of all things*, whereas *Multi* means *many*. The literal translation of Omni-channel, therefore would mean to communicate across all channels rather than just many channels as in case of Multichannel.

What is the difference between omni channel and multichannel marketing? The difference between omni channel and multichannel really comes down to a company's approach to digital channels. Stacy Schwartz, a digital marketing expert explains the difference between omni channel and multichannel marketing when she says:

Companies that focus on maximizing performance of each channel - physical, phone, web, mobile - have a multichannel strategy. They are likely to structure their organizations in to swim lanes focused on a channel, each with their own reporting structure and revenue goals.

The result is competition that sometimes creates friction between the teams and misalignment. Sometimes it may work for the good. In multichannel marketing, channels are managed and optimized independently. This may result in competition within the marketing department and may lead to a disconnected marketing experience. Whereas an omni channel marketing strategy puts the customer, not the corporate silos at its center. Omni channel is thus more about customer centricity than any thing else. The key differences between multichannel marketing and omni channel marketing are presented in Table 6.3.

Table 6.3 Multichannel Marketing and Omni-channel Marketing: Key Differences

Multichannel Marketing	Omni-channel Marketing
1. Brand is at the center of the strategy. Starts with the brand's view of the world and is then projected on the customer.	1. Customer is at the center of the strategy. Considers how the customer sees the world and then determines internal marketing.
2. Basically a tactical approach. Marketers manage each channel independently and implement tactics that work best for that channel.	2. Internal departments work together and are in-tune with the overall messaging and strategy. The focus is on creating a consistent, cohesive overall strategy.
3. Multichannel marketing is a brand's effort to interact with customers across multiple channels and platforms.	3. Omni channel marketing offers a seamless, integrated customer experience, no matter where or how the individual customer engages with the brand. That's why it is called *Omni-channel*.

Omni channel marketing makes use of data across all touchpoints to build a customer profile to enable the use of contextual marketing. Contextual marketing is an online marketing model in which people are served with targeted advertising based on terms they search for or their recent browsing behavior. In the context of omni channel marketing in pharmaceutical industry this means that if a physician seeks a clarification or some additional evidence in a face-to-face detailing session with a Pharma representative and when he next visits an e-detailing site of that company, he should continue the journey, and not start from the beginning. This translates into seamless customer experience.

It is important to remember that whether it is multichannel or omni channel marketing, you should consider the use of traditional and digital channels in a mutually reinforcing way. Today there are many channels to reach the customer. The multiple channels that have cropped up in the digital era are: website, email, SMS (Short Message Service), Search Engine Marketing, Pay-per-click advertising, eDetailing, online forum, blogs, microblogging, social networks, mobile applications etc.

Website

Website is the foundation of digital marketing. For many companies the website (mobile optimized) is the heart of their digital strategy. It is the hub to which all other marketing activities are directed. According to Inbound Marketing Best Practices, 60 percent of all leads generated should come from inbound traffic and that traffic needs a home. Website is that home.

In the early days of internet, a website was more like a simple online business presentation. However, over the years it has evolved from a oneway promotional channel to an integrated two-way service and educational platform. Today, a website can fulfill many functions in pharmaceutical companies. Consider these for example:

A. *Corporate Websites* give general company information, information for investors and information about employees. It has often limited information for Healthcare Professionals (HCP) and patients. Some pharmaceutical companies have a comprehensive website with multiple sections containing information about their products, research pipeline and other activities.

B. *Product Websites* inform HCP on specific products giving all the relevant product information.

C. *Disease Websites* inform patients about a disease condition, the possible treatment options and the implications of not starting a treatment.

While a detailed discussion on how to optimize your website is beyond the scope of this book, here are a few important points to make your website more effective. Consider these for example:

1. What is the most important page of your website? Every page is equally important. Visitors can enter any page of your website through search engines and social media referrals. Create engaging content on every page.

2. Research suggests that less than 20 percent of visitors ever go to the home page. It is, therefore, important to include a Call to Action (CTA) on every page.

3. Physicians prefer independent websites to those provided by pharmaceutical companies as they perceive them to be more trustworthy. It is therefore, better for pharmaceutical companies to partner with the independent websites to engage with physicians more effectively.

Website is a vital tool for many companies which has many purposes including brand building, fostering customer loyalty and a 360 degree customer engagement.

Email

An email address or Digital ID is the most widely used form of digital verification. It can tell marketers about people who are online, where they have been, what they have done and even what they like. This information enables marketers to improve personalization, deliverability and targeting of their marketing messages to the right customers.

Customers today are more likely to respond to personalized interactions with brands and companies when and where they are most engaged. Technology today made the use of customers' digital ID as the core of who they are, where they have been, what they like and where they might go possible. When you consider the usage of emails today, you would understand how important they are as digital IDs. Research by Radicati Group indicates that there are 3.7 billion email users worldwide, who collectively send 2.69 billion emails every day.

Email has an ability that many other channels do not have. It can create valuable, personal touches at scale. Through email marketing, different types of emails are sent to different target groups to build and maintain customer relationships.

Research indicates that about 57 percent of Pharma marketers consider email marketing as a standard practice in their marketing activity. Best Practices research suggests that Pharma companies would do well with their email strategies if they do three basic things:

1. The subject line of your email determines whether your email will be opened or not. This is because, your recipient's first impression of your email communication is through the subject line. Considering the number of emails we all receive everyday, the subject line has to be really convincing to generate an action.

2. Make it easy to subscribe and make it easy to unsubscribe your emails. When you make it difficult to unsubscribe, people get annoyed and may even mark you as spam, which can be more harmful.

3. In Pharma industry, open rates for representative-directed (sent from sales representatives) emails can be twice as high as those for mass campaigns.

Email is an essential part of every company's communication mix. Investing time, effort, and resources in email marketing is a 'must-do' despite the advent of newer channels of social media sharing.

SMS (Short Messaging Service)

With a whopping 4.77 billion mobile phone users globally, SMS (Short Messaging Service) is a universal communication standard across every mobile phone, smart or not. Research reports that over 90 percent of SMS messages are opened within the first three minutes of delivery. What separates SMS form other communication messages such as email are its easy accessibility. Unlike most other digital channels, it does not require a mobile application or even internet and yet reach a larger segment of audience than many other channels.

With a read rate of 97 percent within fifteen minutes of delivery, SMS (Short Messaging Service) is one of the most immediate channels available for marketers. You can be certain that your time-critical messages will be read almost instantly. When integrated with other marketing channels, SMS can enhance a customer's cross-channel experience.

You need to practice what Seth Godin, the internet marketing guru calls 'Permission Marketing' while sending SMS messages to customers. You need to decide early on how you are going to build a customer database and how you intend to collect mobile numbers for your mobile marketing. It is important that you have the relevant 'opt-ins' and 'opt-outs' covered in the process of collecting them. When you send the SMS to the engaged customers, you need to give a clear opportunity to opt-out for the user in every message.

The standard practice of mobile engagement with SMS is to send information and updates about your company or brand without expecting or requiring any response from the user.

If you want to engage the customers via the SMS, you can direct them to relevant web sources such as a sign-up or landing page. You can use a URL (Unique Resource Locator or simply your web page address) shortener service that supports counting clicks for tracking the user behavior. You can use short codes for simplifying your customers feedback process.

SMS, a great stand alone channel can support and integrate with other channels such as email and social media. It can, for example, serve to remind customers to read an email sent by a brand or company a few hours before. Research shows that a simple follow up SMS asking, 'have you read our email' can help increase email open rates by 20 - 30 percent.

Search Engine Marketing

Google, with 78 percent share in the global search engine market, processes about a whopping 3.5 billion searches on the net everyday. Also, there are over one billion websites on the world wide web today. This milestone was first reached in September 2014. It is quite a challenge to make your website stand out in this huge clutter. How do you make a presence in this heavily crowded cyberspace? Enter Search Engine Marketing (SEM).

Search Engine Marketing (SEM) is a form of internet marketing activity that seeks to promote websites by increasing their visibility in

Search Engine Result Pages (SERP). Search Engine Marketing basically covers two key tactics: Search Engine Optimization (SEO) and Search Engine Advertising (SEA).

Search Engine Optimization (SEO), also known as 'organic results', is mainly achieved by optimizing the content of websites so that they are ranked among the top of the search engine result pages. This is very Important for your website because over 90 percent of all search engine traffic visit or click the links on the first page of search engine results. The second page receives a mere 5 percent of the traffic. What is more, no one types URL (Uniform Resource Locator) or web address any more. While URL remains important to the structure of the web, web users, healthcare professionals and patients alike use search engines virtually. With effective search engine marketing you make sure you are found on the web. If you are not found, you may just as well not exist.

Search Engine Advertising (SEA), also known as 'Sponsored Results' shows specific search related advertisements and works on a Pay-Per-Click (PPC) basis. It is possible for you to get your advertisements placed by a search engine in certain search results. These advertisements, however, do not appear in natural search results. Instead, they usually appear on the right hand side of the results page in response to a corresponding search term. The fee for these advertisements is calculated on the basis of the number of clicks the advertisement attracts. Hence the name pay-per-click ads.

Search engine advertising is particularly useful if a website is not appearing at the top of the search results because it is still new and not yet well known or if there is a lot of competition for the search terms or key words being used.

Online Forum

An online forum is an internet forum or a message board, which is an online discussion site where people can hold conversations in the form of posted messages. Online Forums, since the dawn of the internet have been a very important social outlet that has had a tremendous effect on online society. They have become common place today.

Increasing penetration and use of internet along with changes in the healthcare system have resulted in heavier reliance on the internet for disease and health education. Everyday, millions of users log on to their favorite online health communities, and interact with others to get advice and discuss everything related to their symptoms, disease condition, and treatment options. This trend has increased the expectation for and reliance on peer education and support in many areas, including medical, to precede, supplement, or even replace that of professionals.

Online health forums have become so popular and important that most often, even before they call a doctor, patients go online, when they are facing a health crisis or ongoing illness. More people today than ever before are turning to social media before, during, and after diagnosis. In fact 69 percent of doctors in a survey conducted by Cello Health Insights said that many of their patients look up their conditions online prior to a consultation.

Online health communities, also referred to as treatment or disease state or patient communities represent a tremendous opportunity for pharmaceutical companies to educate patients and to create good will among them.

By creating or partnering with online health communities, Pharma firms have an opportunity to connect with their patients and consumers. They also provide the Pharma brands an avenue to provide the much-needed factual information and patient-centered care and generate good will in the process.

Pharmaceutical companies, through their partnerships with online health communities, can help improve patients' awareness of certain diseases, that take a long time for diagnosis. They can reduce the diagnostic timeline earlier in their disease journey and this early diagnosis would ensure a better quality of life for the patients.

Blogs

Blogging is an opportunity for pharmaceutical companies to share information about their company, their products, and their initiatives to help the patients, physicians and other healthcare stakeholders more often than websites permit. It also allows a highly regulated industry such as Pharma to stay in a regulatory compliance in its informational articles as it is in control of its content. Pharma can create two basic categories of blogs. One is a Branded Blog and the other is an Unbranded Blog.

Branded Blogs are very useful in increasing brand awareness and in increasing the brand's voice in the disease state. They also serve a very useful purpose of educating the patient communities about a specific product or a disease state. The branded blogs also allow influencers to share the content in online forums and communities where the brand might not be able to participate.

Unbranded Blogs can add more value as there are fewer restrictions in content creation. A disease state can be openly discussed in an unbranded blog. Some of the well known unbranded blogs in pharmaceutical industry are:

A. *Discuss Diabetes* by Sanofi Aventis

B. *Your Partner in Epilepsy* by Lundbeck

C. *Between the Lines* by Medtronics

Maintaining a blog gives readers the confidence to trust you, your company and your brand as an expert in your field. It also helps you to build a relationship with readers and encourage them to return for more information. Furthermore, blogging adds new, fresh content consistently to your website that is shareable on social media communities and this generates more inbound links and traffic. Here are four ways to make your blog effective:

1. Create shareable content that strikes an emotional chord with your target audience.

2. Think of infographics when you want to convey complex information in a simple and easy to understand way.

3. Blogs are perfectly linkable with social media platforms like Twitter and Facebook. As communities are built on social networks, alerting followers of your published blog posts on these platforms will drive more traffic to your posts.

4. Add new content and posts on your blog regularly as they are viewed favorably by search engines, which can help your page rankings. In addition, new posts at regular intervals are an effective way to engage your target audience.

Make blogging an important element of your digital marketing mix as it has become an integrated and influential digital marketing tool with endless possibilities.

Microblogs

Microblog is a type of blog that lets users publish micro-posts, which are short text updates. For microblogging, bloggers can use a number of services such as instant messaging, e-mail or Twitter. The messages on Twitter are called *Tweets*. Social networking sites like Facebook also use a microblogging feature called *Status updates* in their profiles.

Twitter is synonymous with microblogging. With the massive rise of Twitter, microblogging has evolved into an effective way for companies to use in a number of ways such as increasing brand awareness and improving customer service. These short, succinct conversational pieces on Twitter and other microblogs allow businesses to talk to the consumer by giving them bitesized pieces of information or updates on their brands and services. What is more, Twitter can be a powerful tool for listening to what your customers are talking about your company, your brands and services. You can even measure the sentiment within the conversation and this analysis will help you to reinforce or improve your act accordingly.

Twitter is the most important microblog you need to be present in. Here are five important points to remember and act on what Virginia Liu suggested for getting the most out of microblogging on Twitter in her Medical Marketing & Media (MM&M) article, *8 ways for Pharma to improve the way it uses Twitter*:

1. Plan your tweets around *Healthcare Events* and *Disease Awareness Days*.

2. Don't sound like a robot when you are tweeting. Make your tweets conversational and sound casual to engage effectively. Create a voice that humanizes your brand. Consider for example how the Novartis brand - *Gilenya* replied to someone in a tweet - *So glad you made it out. Thanks for coming.*

3. Leverage Video, which is the fastest growing creative component being used on Twitter. It is more engaging with sight, sound and movement. Use content based on patient testimonials rather than a television commercial format.

4. Don't ignore tweets, even when they are negative. Being proactive, even when the comments are negative, helps build brand confidence.

5. Include Twitter in the overall marketing strategy.

Social Networks

Social networks are dedicated websites or other applications, which enable users to communicate with each other by posting information, comments, messages, images etc. Originally the social media outlets were designed to attract individuals who use the platform for personal reasons. There seems to be an influx of social networks that cater to specific professions.

For doctors, physicians-only social networks are becoming a valuable resource. These online communities are becoming a valuable resource to turn to for a number of professional purposes. They help physicians to communicate and collaborate with each other in a secure environment. There is more to these physicians-only social networks than sending and receiving messages. They also provide opportunities for receiving CME (Continuing Medical Education) credits and to compete against peers for various rewards. The features differ from site to site. Here are top four social networks for physicians at a glance (Table 6.4).

Table 6.4 Top Four Social Networks for Physicians

Physicians' Social Networks	Important Features
1. Doximity	One of the best physician social networks. Over 50 per cent of U.S. physicians are verified Doximity members. Mobile friendly physician platform giving the ability to instantly connect with their peers in a secure, HIPPA-compliant environment. Offers the opportunity to receive CME credits for reading medical journals provided by the site.
2. Sermo	The most trusted and preferred social network for doctors with over 800,000 doctors in the U.S, and select countries in the West. Exclusively for licensed physicians. High level of anonymity available for physicians who post on the site. Sermo allows the media to conduct polls among its physicians and interview them.

Contd...

Physicians' Social Networks	Important Features
3. Quantia MD	Launched in 2006. One of the best online resources doctors can utilize for collaboration and career development. 1 in 3 physicians visit Quantia MD to keep with new medical information and to learn from their colleagues. Has several features that reward users with CME credits or 'Q' points that can be redeemed for Amazon gift certificates. Another interesting feature is that members can compete against their peers in the monthly general medicine puzzle, the monthly cartoon caption contest and by solving weekly clinical cases and image contests.
4. Docplexus	Largest online community of doctors in India with over 250,000 members. Docplexus aims to provide value to the Indian medical community through innovative, technology-driven offerings. Provides audio-visual coverage for major medical events. Also offers CME courses to fulfill the educational needs of the physician community.

Social networks focused on patients suffering from a specific disease condition have come up over the past few years. They can be vital for people who feel alone in their health struggles. They are particularly helpful to those, who cannot leave home because of their disabilities. These social networks in fact are their social life. At the same time, for all the benefits and support they offer, the patient social networks are not without challenges. Firstly, many physicians are concerned about these networks as most of the medical advice that comes from them is from other users or from unverified articles on the internet. Secondly, many of the patient networks do not generally moderate comments to verify the accuracy. They, however, try to make it clear where the content comes from and whether it is from medical professionals or fellow patients. Table 6.5 presents some of the more influential and important social networks that focus and serve the needs of patients.

Understandably, a business cannot and should not be on every social network. At the same time, you cannot afford to ignore the social networks that are influential. What are the right social networks for your company? To know that, you need to consider what each network is good at doing and how you should meaningfully participate in the conversation. It is important to remember that social media landscape changes very quickly and therefore, keeping abreast of new channels is a part of good long-term social media strategy.

Table 6.5 Some Important Social Networks for Patients

Patient Networks	Their Focus
1. Patients Like Me	Used to be primarily for some neurological conditions, but their fabulous software is available for many conditions now.
2. CureTogether	Has patient communities for a number of conditions
3. Smart Patients.com	An online community where patients and their families learn from each other.
4. Cancer Connect.com	Offers comprehensive cancer information organized by disease and stage. A free social network for patients, survivors, and caregivers.
5. TuDiabetes.org	A space on the web where people with diabetes or their loved ones can find support, help each other and share their experiences and what they do everyday to stay healthy with this condition.

Mobile

Mobile is one of the most recent additions to the digital space today. Literally every digital activity that you can think of such as social sharing, searching the internet, buying things, making payments has gone mobile.

Pharma companies need to have a clear mobile strategy and mindset to survive and grow in the rapidly changing market place. Mobile is a must for Pharma. Consider, for example, the following reasons:

1. There are 4.77 billion mobile users globally.

2. More than one-half of all online searches take place on a mobile. 50 percent of all web activities are mobile.

3. 52 percent of smart phone users gather health-related information on their phones.

4. Even HCPs (Healthcare Professionals) are turning to mobile. About 80 percent of physicians use smart phones and medical apps.

5. It is estimated that by 2017, 50 percent of mobile users would have downloaded mobile health apps.

When your target audience are on mobile more often, you cannot afford to ignore the mobile. Going mobile is the way to engage them when and where they want it. It's no longer an option.

mHealth

mHealth is a term used for the practice of medical and public health, supported by mobile devices. It refers to the usage of mobile communication devices such as mobile phones, Personal Digital Assistants (PDAs) and tablets for health services and information. Mobile devices are changing the way patients and healthcare professionals access internet and find health information.

mHealth is helping track some of the healthcare challenges such as aging population, non-compliance (patients not taking medicines), management of chronic diseases and even helping with strategies for prevention of chronic diseases. Here is a partial list of areas where mobile device applications are used:

1. Reference
2. Decision Support
3. Monitoring
4. Compliance
5. Disease Management
6. Chronic Disease Prevention

Increasingly patients are depending less on HCPs and more on online for healthcare information. It is therefore, important that pharmaceutical companies and other healthcare organizations provide accurate information. Pharmaceutical firms and healthcare marketers can make use of the new technologies such as geo-fence locations, video assets and text messaging to reach their audiences, even while they are in the doctors offices or near a pharmacy.

Furthermore, applications for mobile phones and tablets have provided a new and easy way for patients suffering with chronic diseases to manage their conditions and guide them toward healthier lifestyles.

Social Media Marketing

What is Social Media?

Social media generally refers to Internet-based tools that allow individuals and communities to gather and share information, ideas, personal messages, images, and other content. It also facilitates real time collaboration with other users. Social media is referred to as *Web 2.0* and *Social networking*. Social media includes blogs, social networks, video-and photo-sharing sites, wikis and a number of other media. Here is an example showing some of the media grouped by purpose and functions. The list is only indicative and not exhaustive by any means:

A. Social networking (Facebook, MySpace, Google Plus, Twitter etc.,)

B. Professional Networking (LinkedIn)

C. Physician Social Networks (Sermo, Quantia MD, Doximity, Docplexus)

D. Media sharing (You Tube, Flickr)

E. Content Production (Blogs, Blogger, WordPress, Tumblr, and Microblogs such as Twitter)

F. Knowledge / Information aggregation (Wikipedia)

G. Virtual reality and gaming environments (Second Life)

Social Media Marketing

Social media marketing in pharmaceutical industry combines a wide variety of social media tools and platforms to establish conversations with physicians, patients and other stakeholders. These online conversations help pharmaceutical companies build relationships with customers. Brand messages can be spread through the electronic word-of-mouth.

While traditional marketing media was more of a monologue, social media has created an opportunity for engaging in a dialogue and conversation with consumers. Consumers can express their questions and concerns enabling the brand to build a relationship. Social media users in the process generate a lot of content. In fact they post over 30 billion comments to Facebook and more than two billion tweets on

Twitter every month. What is more, about twenty percent of this huge generated content mentions a specific drug or disease. When one in every five conversation pieces is in the pharmaceutical and healthcare space, can Pharma afford to remain a silent spectator?

Physicians on Social Media

While the exact numbers vary, most studies indicate that about 80 percent of physicians use social media for personal interactions as well as professional communication and research. Physicians' social media usage seems to follow a typical 1-9-90 pattern. Approximately 1 percent of physicians using social media are content producers creating and publishing original content to other healthcare professionals and ePatients. They provide this information on blogs, forums and information-sharing websites. A further 9 percent of physicians engage with others on social media by commenting on posts and participating in online discussions and chats sharing useful information and links to other members online. The remaining 90 percent of physicians consume information. They use the internet and social media to find and read information that is relevant to their patients and practice.

Patients are in Control

Increasingly patients are turning to a number of sites such as *Patients Like Me* and other patient and disease communities online to research their symptoms and arrive at a self-diagnosis before visiting their physicians. The availability of massive healthcare information on the social web is impacting the relationship between patients, physicians and brands. Increasingly, doctors today are facing the self-diagnosing patients who have already researched their symptoms seeking prescriptions for conditions they think they have. The patients may even post reviews of their experiences in case of a pushback by their doctors. Patients today are taking greater responsibility than ever for their health.

Insights From Social Media Conversations

Patients seem to be more forthright and descriptive in their online conversations about their disease conditions and feedback on treatments etc, as they afford greater privacy than in-person consults.

These conversations are very useful for Pharma Marketers as they provide a richer understanding of how patients are perceiving the current product or service offerings and what their unmet needs are. With insights gained from this deep understanding, marketers can develop better, more relevant marketing materials including packaging, educational and promotional tools aimed at physicians and patients.

Challenging Regulatory Environment

Pharmaceutical companies as they are operating in a highly regulated industry, face many challenges such as how to handle incomplete and misinformation about their products both offline and online. According to the US Federal Drug Administration (FDA) Guidance on how Pharma should use social media, the pharmaceutical companies should provide fair and balanced information about their products in their social media posts. They need to include the side effects, adverse reactions, and contraindications in their product information.

Furthermore, FDA clearly stated that it will not be taking a lenient approach towards either tweets or sponsored links. Social media posts even in sites with limited character-spaces such as Twitter need to incorporate full and balanced information about their products. It is not enough to provide links in the post to your webpages for detailed product information. Pharmaceutical companies face serious penalties by the FDA if they do not make the proper disclosure. Drug firms must be careful not to mislead consumers on Twitter. Otherwise they will open themselves for liability. Kim Kardashian's instagram post is a classic example of what happens when you don't follow the regulations governing social media. The following case is classic example of this:

Case 6.8 How Kim Kardashian's Instagram Post Got Drug Firm That Makes 'Diclegis' Gets the Company into Trouble with the FDA.

In July 2015, Kim Kardashian, a leading supermodel with a huge following on social media posted to her 45 million followers on Instagram and 35 million followers on Twitter, about Diclegis, a prescription drug brand of a morning sickness tablet manufactured by Rosemont-based Pharma company, Duchesnay in the US. Here's a transcript of that post:

OMG. Have you heard about this? As you guys know my #morning sickness has been pretty bad...i tried changing things about my lifestyle like my diet, but nothing helped, so I talked to my doctor. He prescribed me #Diclegis, and I felt a lot better and most importantly, it's been studied and there was no increased risk to the baby. I'm so excited and happy with my results that I'm partnering with Duchesnay USA to raise awareness about the morning sickness. If you have morning sickness, be safe and sure to ask your doctor about the pill with the pregnant woman on it and find outmore

www.diclegis.com;www.diclegisImportantSafetyInformation.com

This is not a typical post by an average morning sickness sufferer, who recommends a product online. Kim Kardashian is a celebrity with a massive online following and is paid to endorse the brand. The FDA took objection to this post as it failed to mention important information like the drug's side effects, adverse reactions and contraindications. The social media post is false and misleading in that it presents efficacy claims for 'Diclegis', but fails to communicate any risk information. The FDA demanded that Duchesnay immediately cease its 'misbranding' of the drug and has given time until August 21 2015 to respond to the Agency. The company withdrew the social media posts. Here's what Dean Hopkins, general manager of Duchesnay said in this regard:

In the original post, which we developed with Kim, we provided her with a link to risk information and limitation of use for Diclegis. But the post did not meet the FDA requirements for communicating important product information.

Kim Kardashian had posted a long corrective ad on August 30, 2015.

FDA Guidance on Social Media: Implications for Pharma

What this implies for pharmaceutical companies is that they will not be able to send a series of *tweets* containing the full benefit and risk information of a product, but will instead need to provide the entire information in a single tweet.

How Pharma Can Comply with the FDA Guidance on Social Media?

Pharmaceutical companies need to connect with patients and physicians on social media to offer reliable information about their products and about improving health and wellbeing. But how can they comply with the FDA regulations while providing this information and control the conversations on various social media platforms and ensure delivery of fair and balanced information? Henniger Bullock and Collen Tracy Jones suggest a five-way approach to achieve this in their Law 360 article of April 21, 2017, *5 Social Media Pitfalls in the Pharmaceutical Industry.*

1. *Set A Clear Internal Policy:* Develop a clear policy that includes a centralized social media hub such as a company-sponsored website, twitter handle, facebook page etc. for posting messages on behalf of the company. Create a concrete social media advertising policy and clearly define who may engage on social media on the company's behalf. Ensure that all employees understand their role on social media whether it is in their personal or official capacity and how they need to conduct themselves on social media sites. The content must cleared by the legal department for regulatory compliance.

2. *Create A Controlled Environment:* When its consumers (patients) and customers (HCPs) are frequently on social media, the Pharma cannot afford to shy away. Pharma should embrace social media, but maintain control of it. By creating a company website or a company-initiated chat area, a pharmaceutical company can create a controlled environment and foster relationships with patients and communicate useful, fair and balanced information about its products and services.

3. *Create A Compliance Strategy:* It is not enough if you define the roles of engagement and rules of conduct on social media for your patients in your social media policy. You need to ensure compliance. Put in place a compliance strategy and a monitoring system to ensure total compliance.

4. *Comply With All HIPAA Act Privacy Laws:* Pharmaceutical companies need to do more than comply with the FDA Guidance on social media. They need to comply with HIPAA (Health Insurance Privacy, Portability and Accountability Act). Complying

with patient privacy laws is equally important. Therefore, educate all employees on patient privacy laws and how they are related to business. Remember, even an individual posting of a patient's picture is a privacy violation. Create a social media working group to discuss any concerns and issues.

5. *Keep Future Litigation in Mind:* Ensure that you prepare a carefully coordinated message and have it approved. Ensure compliance with the standards and policies governing social media before embarking on a social media campaign.

Pharma Must Embrace Social Media

Although there are many regulations over how pharmaceutical companies should conduct themselves on social media that are challenging, Pharma must find way to comply with them and participate actively in social media as it offers many opportunities. Pharma must embrace social media. Consider these reasons for example:

A. More and more patients are using social media today as a major source of information and an integral part of their healthcare research journey. Typically, their journey begins when they notice their symptoms. This leads to their searching social channels often before their visit to a physician or simultaneously with their visit to the doctor. The second phase of online search follows the diagnosis to seek more information about their condition from credible sources, and from people like themselves. Patients, who share their stories on social channels become a significant source of information to those actively seeking their perspectives. This information at times could be unbalanced and even irrelevant.

B. The information on the social media may not always be from reputable and accredited sources. It may be marginally accurate at best and significantly harmful at worst.

It is crucial, therefore, for Pharma companies to provide balanced and credible information on social media where their patients are seeking meaningful information and help them in getting balanced and accurate information that is essential for their wellbeing.

6 Ways Pharma May Use Social Media

Dr. Kevin Campbell, an internationally recognized cardiologist suggested six ways in which pharmaceutical companies can use social media in an interview with Joanna Belbey, a columnist with Forbes magazine. He said that social Media is an ideal channel for pharmaceutical and device companies to educate, market, listen to and connect with customers. Pharma firms can do all this while complying with the guidelines of industry regulators. Here's a summary what he suggested:

1. *Education:* Pharmaceutical firms may offer disease-specific, unbiased educational information on broad topics to consumers. The purpose of such educative information is to help patients understand their disease state better so that they can engage with their healthcare professionals better for improved outcomes.

2. *Marketing:* Pharma can use social media as another channel to share press releases on new products, clinical trial results, community service, major contributions to charities and their major commitment to develop new and better treatments etc.

3. *Connecting with Physicians*: Social media is an efficient and effective means of connecting with physician customers. It is also less expensive than the sales force costs. Through social media, Pharma can engage with a large number of physicians at one time with its own best and brightest scientists and researchers. It is also a great opportunity to ask questions and have a dialogue with each other than being 'detailed-to' by a sales representative, which is simply a regurgitation of a memorized script of a new study. The physician would have already read it in all probabilities.

4. *Connecting with Patients*: Pharma can use social media to create patient support groups and communities. These groups allow the patients with common interests and needs to connect with each other and discuss about their conditions, treatments and experiences.

5. *Clinical Trials*: Social media can become a powerful tool to enroll patients in clinical trials. Clinical trial enrollment is one of the biggest barriers to complete a clinical trial.

6. *Listening*: Social media can be a big help for Pharma in gaining insights to the unmet needs of the patients through social listening. These insights can be of immense use in developing its communication strategies to physicians and even in directing the future course of their product development.

Content is King!

The internet is the starting point for most people researching on health information. Digital Pharma reported that over a 12-month period, 72 percent of internet users mentioned in a survey that they looked online for information on health. Pharmaceutical companies can take advantage of this opportunity for creating informative and engaging content on health information related to their therapeutic areas and brands.

Who and what rules the internet? Content, of course! Content is really the king when it comes to marketing online. Content is the fuel that drives your digital marketing activities such as Search Engine Optimization (SEO). Content i2s what gets you noticed in social media. It is content that gives you something of value to offer your customers in emails and paid search advertisements.

Create content that is not promotional in nature, but educates and inspires and gives you visibility. Content that offers valuable and relevant information ensures that your customers stay tuned in. The key to good content, therefore, is that it avoids being overtly promotional and it is useful or valuable to the customer. If the content is not valuable to the consumer, whether it is the patient or HCP, they will go elsewhere. They are looking to understand the condition and the treatment options available to them. Therefore, you need to give the information they need to make a decision in a language they fully understand, through the medium they want and when they want it. Quality of content is crucial to engaging them on their terms. The aim of a good quality content is to create a two-way engagement rather than delivering a one-way sales pitch. Once you generate a good quality content, you need to market it effectively. How do you market your content? Content marketing as defined by the website, Whatistechtarget.com is:

Content marketing is the publication of material designed to promote a brand (or service) usually through a more oblique and subtle approach than that of a traditional push advertising. The essence of good content marketing is that it offers something the viewer wants such as information or entertainment. Content marketing can take a lot of different forms including Youtube videos, blogposts and articles. It shouldn't really seem like marketing - in some cases, in fact, it should only be identifiable as marketing because the advertiser is identified as the content provider.

Pharmaceutical marketers need to provide engaging content that meets the needs, wants, aspirations and goals of all their key stakeholders, namely, patients, HCPs, providers and payers. Meeting the needs and interests of the target audience is crucial for success. Pharma should create different content for each of its customer segment in a way that directly addresses their particular issues. A one-size-fits-all approach is outdated now. The key questions to ask and answer are:

A. Who is your target audience? Are they patients, general practitioners? Specialist physicians etc.?
B. What information do they want?
C. What issues do they have and how can you solve them?

Remember that to be engaging, content should be interactive, interesting, informative and shareable. Your content should not really seem like a marketing strategy or be obviously promotional. Content, however engaging it may be, cannot promote itself, unless at least you share it on social media.

The key to a successful and sustainable content strategy for a pharmaceutical company hinges on developing a trusted relationship using content. And trust is an emotion based on credibility. It can be built only on aligned values. Pharmaceutical marketers need to be very objective in developing their content and focus more on building credibility than on grabbing attention. Of course, you need to grab attention and sustain it, but credibility is more important in building a trusting relationship. In healthcare it is even more important. You can draw attention and build trust only when you have a strong point of view based on facts in your content. Otherwise, it would be a series of mere facts that anyone can find with a google search. In sum, your content must resonate with all your key customers - patients, physicians and payers. All of them should feel that the pharmaceutical company understands their values and beliefs and that it is not just educating them to a prescriptive solution.

Robert Rose, chief strategist at Content Marketing Institute and co-author with Joe Pulizzi of the book, *Managing Content Marketing*, advised that:

Content marketers should start thinking of themselves as media companies - with a distinct point of view. Their goal is to develop an audience for their content. But they have to balance that with how, when and where they will show their distinct and unique point of view.

Gamification

You can find gamification everywhere today - from boardrooms to classrooms and even on social media. Over the last few years, gamification has gained wide acceptance and recognition in a number of areas such as marketing, healthcare, business, politics and technology design. Pharmaceutical industry too, has been embracing this recent trend in healthcare gamification to meet the ever-increasing challenges in creating value and brand building. Initial research and case studies provide evidence that gamification improves both patient compliance and health outcomes.

Five Key Elements

Gamification uses the mechanics of gaming to engage users and solve problems in a non-game context. There are four key elements in a gamification strategy:

1. Reward or recognition for the players' achievements.
2. A goal and a sense of purpose.
3. Rules and a framework for participation that motivate participants to tackle challenges strategically.
4. Continuous challenge. Achieving each next step should be harder but not too hard. The best option is that level one prepares the user for level two. There should be a flow that will keep the users fully engaged.
5. Feedback that tracks the players' status informing them how close they are to reaching the end goal.

How Gamification is Beneficial

1. Gamification can promote therapies. By creating interactive, educational health content, gamification can be utilized to promote new and existing therapies.
2. Gamification can increase engagement between Pharma , HCPs, and patients. HCPs' use of interactive technology to communicate

with their patients is gradually increasing. With gamification, Pharma can provide responsible, educational, health content and improve health awareness among patients. Consider the case of Sanofi-Aventis, which has successfully used gamification as a strategy to improve patient adherence.

3. Gamification allows showing patients first hand how their condition is affected by their daily habits and choices.

4. Gamification helps in creating and regulating virtual patients by inserting actual medical record information.

5. Gamification can facilitate physician education. Physicians are interested in improving health outcomes of their patients in less time. Pharma companies can help achieve this by implementing gamification. Here's how Sanofi, the international drug major used gamification to increase awareness and adherence among patients (case 6.9).

Case 6.9 Sanofi Has Got Game!

1. Sanofi's *GoMeals* mobile app is a good example of gamification in pharmaceutical marketing. *GoMeals* is a set of applications developed for Sanofi-Aventis, U.S. by Intouch Solutions, a specialized digital Pharma marketing agency.

   GoMeals is designed for people living with diabetes to promote Sanofi's diabetes drug Apdria. The app available for the web as well as for smartphones encourages users to make healthy choices in terms of nutrition as the name *GoMeals* suggests. The app comes with features for eating healthy, staying active and tracking blood glucose levels. *GoMeals* allows patients to see how their daily habits in terms of nutrition and exercise impact their diabetes.

   GoMeals uses the game design elements providing users clear reports on calorie-intake from their meals, calories burnt from their exercise and physician activity and glucose readings.

2. Sanofi-Aventis has developed with Vancouver-based Ayogo *Monster Manor*, a game that rewards children with Type 2 diabetes for checking their blood glucose regularly. The app uses short mini games that add up to unlock features and

---

characters. It automatically sends the results to the parents' smartphones. The parents can give kids rewards to the children directly through the app.

3. Sanofi Diabetes, a division of Sanofi-Aventis has launched in the U.K. another mobile game called *Mission T1D* to educate and teach children as well as their parents, caregivers and friends about Type 1 diabetes.

   The game is set in a school. When players complete levels and get points, they unlock short practical messages about living with Type 1 diabetes and longer shareable educational videos. The videos cover important topics such as:
   A. What is Type 1 diabetes?
   B. Everyday life with diabetes
   C. What is hypoglycemia and how to help
   D. What is hyperglycemia and how to help
   E. How to have a healthy diet with or without Type 1 diabetes

   The entire program can run on a P C and a smartphone designed to be used either by individuals or in a class room setting.

   Sanofi has certainly made a pioneering effort in developing these apps for diabetes and in engaging patients as well as HCPs.

   (*Source: Mobile Health News*)

More Apps

Pharmaceutical companies are realizing the importance of gamification as yet another tool to engage their key stakeholders such as patients and HCPs mainly, and have been developing more and more apps for them. Here are some examples of successful apps:

1. *Respimat inhalation demonstrator by Boehringer Ingelheim.* Designed for HCPs, the app provides medical information on the next generation device and facilitates physicians training patients on how to use Respimat. The app enables inhaler interaction, a

key issue, provides hands-on experience with an intuitive interface and is available at no additional cost.

2. *Back-in-Play* by Pfizer. Designed as a game, this app aims to boost knowledge of a little known disease, ankylosing spondylitis. Through this, patients in Europe learned about this condition that causes inflammation in their spine and pelvis joints.

3. Boehringer Ingelheim's *HealthSeeker,* is a game that helps those with diabetes make better lifestyle choices about their condition and overall wellness.

4. Bayer created the diabetes *Didget* game for use with Nintendo's DS handheld game system, to encourage children with diabetes to regularly test their blood glucose levels. Players receive rewards for testing consistently. Bayer's *Didget* blood glucose meter fits in with the Nintendo's handheld game system and allows children with diabetes to play *Knock-'em-down*, the World's Fair Board Game, which inspires pediatric patients to keep up with their testing schedule.

5. *Johnson & Johnson's Care4Today* is designed to improve adherence to treatment regimens through reminders to take medication, refill prescriptions and visit healthcare providers. The mobile adherence program can be used for any kind of prescription or OTC medication or nutritional supplement, including but not limited to Johnson & Johnson group of companies.

6. *Janssen's Sorted App* is designed for patients in the UK with Attention Deficit Hyperactivity disorder (ADHD) in the U.K. The app acts as a daily organizer to help patients create, categorize, and prioritize daily tasks with a point-scoring element to motivate the users. Janssen's key product for ADHD is Concerta XL. Developed with the concurrence of Physicians in U.K. the app is developed to utilize the functionalities of iPhone such as its calendar, reminders, and voice memos. The app is targeted for people above 12 years.

7. Sun Pharma's *RespiTrack* app is a mobile application that connects doctors with their asthma patients. The app's focus is to improve treatment compliance and minimize instances of non-adherence and dropouts in the asthma treatment regime. RespiTrack allows complete monitoring of asthma attacks, symptoms, medications prescribed by the physicians. It enables patients to record time,

place, duration and triggers of attacks along with medication details on the mobile app. The patient can easily send this data to his physician through over-the-air mode on a weekly or monthly basis. A review dashboard in the app provides a snapshot of all parameters to monitor over a period of time. What is more, through *RespiTrack*, a doctor can access his patient's details through a personalized tracker module , which is directly synced with the patients' app. This module allows doctors to access patients' ailment history, attack patterns, symptoms, medication patterns and reports. A doctor can remotely view patient reports and also connect with him through an integrated messaging app.

A research study by Research2Guidance (R2G) observed that between 2008 and 2016 the top Pharma companies had 65 apps in the Apple and Google Play app stores on average compared to 1 or 2 apps from other health app publishers. However, even the Pharma companies with the most downloaded apps have accrued 6.6 million downloads since 2008, had less than a million active users. Why is the rate of adoption slower in case of Pharma as compared to other healthcare and fitness apps?

Slow Rate of Adoption

If gamification offers so many benefits why is it that there are relatively fewer downloads for Pharma apps as compared to other healthcare apps? Here are the possible reasons:

- **A.** Many of the Pharma apps have highly targeted audiences like HCPs.
- **B.** People with specific disease states.
- **C.** Pharma apps tend to target local markets, say in three or fewer countries, which makes them unlikely to compete on download numbers with fitness, health or diet tracking apps that appeal to a larger segment of the market.

Engagification, not Gamification!

While gamification has a positive impact on participant engagement, message recall and patient outcomes, there is one problem. And it is the name itself - gamification. When you say that you are going to gamify the participants' interaction with your content, the term -

gamification lends itself to trivializing the most serious experience related to improving health and wellbeing. Patients, physicians and other stakeholders of pharmaceutical industry still cling to the idea that games should not be part of the conversation in such a serious realm as healthcare. In Pharma marketing, it is crucial to steer the discussion away from the word *Game* - and towards terms like engagement, retention, adherence. Therefore, do not call it a game. Call it an app. Extending the same thought, your strategy is not gamification. It is engagification!

It is estimated that about three billion hours are spent on an average per week playing online games. For Pharma, especially in areas such as medication adherence, and medical education gamification has a huge potential.

Pharma and Social Media: The Indian Presence

Global pharmaceutical industry in general and Indian pharmaceutical industry in particular has been a laggard in its adoption of social media. D Yellow Elephant, a leading digital marketing consultancy firm conducted research among 40 pharmaceutical companies in India across 10 key digital parameters ranging - across websites, social network platforms, and applications and published a study titled, *Indian Pharma Digital Health Report 2015*. The study revealed that only 9 out of 40 - less than 25 percent of the companies managed to score 50 out of 100 on these parameters.

Presence Vs. Engagement

What has emerged out of this study is a pattern of presence vs. engagement by Indian pharmaceutical companies on social media. While Pharma companies in India are present and registered on most social media platforms, only a few of them are active. Here is a brief summary of some key findings:

A. **LinkedIn:** Only 14 companies were present

B. **Google+:** Two companies have a presence while one of the 40 companies was active

C. **Facebook:** 8 out of 40 companies had an India-specific page

D. **Twitter:** 29 percent of the companies have a presence but only 16 percent are active

E. **YouTube:** 24 percent of the companies have a presence

F. **Blog:** 12 companies had a blogger presence

Patients on Social Media

Patients in India have a better adoption rate to social media, than Pharma industry. Consider these facts:

A. 47 percent of people consulted a doctor based on an online search.

B. 60 percent of people discuss the information they found on the web with their doctor.

C. As high as 69 percent of people said that they did not find India-specific information on the web.

These clearly indicate the low engagement of Pharma with patients on social media and amplify the need to improve their presence.

Physicians on Social Media

Physicians too, in India are increasingly taking to online media. Medical professionals are using online media for a number of activities ranging from knowledge updates to peer interactions. Docplexus, India's largest community of doctors conducted a survey recently among12,635 doctors that revealed the following insights towards the online behavior of physicians in India:

A. 83 percent of the doctors surveyed agreed that online learning is beneficial as it overcomes geographic constraints

B. 71 percent found it easy to gain knowledge from online Key Opinion Leaders (KOLs)

C. 78 percent preferred video content (KOL interviews, webinars, surgical videos) as they are easy to grasp

D. 72 percent feel that it is easy to source drug-related information online

E. 26 percent used online media for networking with peers

F. 75 percent of doctors spend a maximum of 5 minutes online and only 10 percent spend 10 minutes or more of their time on online activities. Pharmaceutical marketers, therefore, should create online content that is concise, clear and devoid of complexities

G. Mobiles and laptops are the most preferred devices of doctors. 78 percent of medical professionals accessed online media through mobiles and laptops

H. There seem to be three peak surf times for doctors - at 10 am when they check into their offices; at 2 pm, after the morning rush of patients is over; and from 9 to 10 pm before signing off for the day

Pharmaceutical marketers, with the help of these insights can plan their online strategies more effectively.

Digital Initiatives of MNCs in India

Unlike their counterparts in the domestic sector, some of the more progressive MNC pharmaceutical companies are taking initiatives to exploit the emerging opportunities in the digital era. Here is a partial list of MNCs in India and their digital marketing initiatives:

1. *Abbott Healthcare*: As a consumer healthcare company, Abbott over the past few years has built a digital ecosystem for a doctor and consumer education comprising mobile apps and technologies such as augmented reality and virtual reality over ten therapy areas including heart health, liver health, vertigo management, thyroid, women's health etc. In addition the company has also created one-of-a-kind initiative - *Knowledge Genie* that provides Indian physicians with a single platform access all kinds of medical information. Doctors stay updated with the latest advancements in their specialties to ensure the best clinical outcomes.

2. *GlaxoSmithKline*: GlaxoSmithKline India believes that pharmaceutical companies will have to hone their digital skills because a large portion of their customers will operate in that space in the years to come. As of now, at least 20 to 30 percent of GSK's own customers are already in the digital world, says Annaswamy Vaideesh, managing director of GSK, India. The company is already leveraging a number of digital platforms such as webinars, video chats, information portals etc. It has also equipped its 3000-strong field force with iPads to improve the

quality of interactive presentations to the physicians. Furthermore, GSK has invested about Rs. 10-crore in India for designing its digital platforms. The company has also developed a cloud based application, which enables direct communication between practicing physicians and the company's medical department. The company has also hired about 20 doctors to respond to medical questions from physicians. Furthermore, Glaxo is also test-marketing with a software company in rural setting to improve access to healthcare in remote areas. The company is pulling out all the stops to become and stay digitally savvy.

3. *Pfizer*: Pfizer has pioneered several digital initiatives towards enhancing customer engagement and providing result-driven outcomes. The Rep-Triggered-Email (RTE) campaign is one example. The company has launched a multi-therapy area HCP portal, *Inquimed*, on which 18,000 doctors have already registered. In addition, the company's webcasts, Meet the Expert (MTE) have seen an attendance of approximately 9,000 doctors across different specialties.

4. *Janssen*: Janssen Pharma, although has been active in the digital marketing space with a few initiatives, the company is best known in India for its awareness campaign for increasing migraine awareness, 'Me without Migraine'. It has won many awards for its campaign. Many patients don't realize they have migraine, confuse it with headache and continue taking painkillers. For the first time, Janssen has launched a campaign in migraine space across digital (website, Facebook, Twitter and a launch video) and non-digital channels (in-clinic promotion, PoP activities, and corporate outreach programs). The campaign has achieved within an year 40,000 followers on its Facebook page and almost 22,000 people visiting its website every month.

5. *Sanofi*: Sanofi in India has equipped its sales force with iPads for delivering engaging detail talks to physicians across the country. The company is also toying with the idea of developing a messaging application, which will give flexibility and convenience to seek a meeting with company's medical representatives.

These few examples illustrate that multinational companies understand the advantages of digital marketing better than their counterparts in the domestic pharmaceutical sector. This may be due to their experience in the other markets which are more developed and have become digitally savvy. They also realize that when the Uniform Code of Pharmaceutical Monitoring Practices (UCPMP) is made mandatory, which seems to be round the corner, most of the companies, which are practicing the transactional marketing methods will have to mend their ways and resort to ethical and science-based marketing. Digital marketing can provide the much needed power to engage all stakeholders in an ethical transparent manner.

Social Media and Indian Pharma

Aman Gupta, managing director of D Yellow Elephant, said that in view of this data, Indian Pharma sector - whether Indian companies or global players lag behind their international counterparts by at least 5 - 7 years. Indian drug majors use of social media is considerably low resulting in their negligible presence on social media. Social media presence of the top five Indian drug firms illustrates this (Table 6.6).

Table 6.6 Social Presence of Top Five Indian Pharma Companies in March 2017

Company	Facebook	Twitter	YouTube	LinkedIn
1. Cipla	26,475 Followers	1,681 Followers 1,593 Tweets	402 Subscribers 72 Videos	1,05,802 Followers 253 updates
2. Dr. Reddy's	1,72,558 Followers	3,845 Followers 3,561 Tweets	180 Subscribers 19 Videos	1,31,607 Followers 380 Updates
3. Sun Pharma	15,434 Followers	3,284 Followers 528 Tweets	47 Subscribers 12 Videos	1,12,120 Followers Only 1 Update
4. Lupin	3,762 Followers	2,090 Subscribers 212 Tweets	Absent	21,181 Followers Only 1 Update
5. Aurobindo Pharma	469 Followers	Absent	127 Subscribers 2 Videos	30,387 Followers No Updates

(**Source:** moneycontrol.com The information is as on March 6, 2017)

Table 6.7 Social Media Buttons on Home Page of Top Five Indian
Pharma Companies in 2017

Company	Social Media Buttons
1. Cipla	Facebook Twitter YouTube LinkedIn
2. Dr. Reddy's	Facebook Twitter YouTube LinkedIn
3. Sun Pharma	Twitter LinkedIn
4. Lupin	None
5. Aurobindo Pharma	None

(**Source:** moneycontrol.com The information is as on March 6, 2017)

Less than half of India Pharma giants have a token presence in online media. Most seem to have given up after dabbling with networking platforms for a short while. Cipla had created CiplaMed, an online resource for doctors to keep themselves updated. However the portal is yet to include interactive features such as blogs and discussion forums. Only a few companies such as Biocon have an active blog page named *Bio-conversation*. Some other companies have featured active blog pages on their websites in other countries, but not in India.

All these findings show the reluctance of the pharmaceutical companies in India to engage with their stakeholders on digital platforms. Indian pharmaceutical industry still seems to be sitting on the fence when it comes to social media marketing. This could be due to any one more of the following reasons.

1. Indian pharmaceutical market is predominantly branded generic with 90 percent of products being branded generics or generic-generics. There is very little new scientific information that a branded-generic firm can provide to physicians, which they do not know already.

2. A number of pharmaceutical companies seem to think that transactional approach to marketing is the way to go and take the short cut. They also seem believe in huge price discounts, high value gifts, sponsorships, and even cash payments for

getting prescriptions for their products and invest in those things rather than on technology, innovative marketing, training and development. Customer relationship management (CRM) to them has a totally different meaning.

3. The branded-generic firms in India may not be perceiving a pressing need to engage physicians differently and though online channels, as access to physicians in India, although is decreasing, is not yet a serious issue today. But it could be a very serious issue, when the Department of Pharmaceuticals (DoP), which is determined to make the UCPMP Code mandatory and puts an end to the current transactional marketing model. The industry that is focusing on a promotion mix that largely comprises of freebies, sponsored seminars, foreign junkets, even payments for prescriptions etc, would have to suddenly change its tacks of tactics. Social media marketing, which is ethical, transparent is the only way to build a sustainable way of building enduring relationships with all stakeholders of the industry. But, then that's what vision is about. Seeing the future before it arrives. Companies with foresight are the ones who would take to social media before others do.

Summary

Promotion, which is one of the four classic elements of marketing-the four P's of the marketing mix - is a far more crucial element. Literally speaking, promotion means to move forward. It is common knowledge that aggressive promotion is absolutely essential to move your products and services in the highly competitive market place today than ever before.

Pharmaceutical promotion covers a very large area of operations that include advertising, sales promotion, public relations, and personal selling. Personal selling is a very crucial element of the pharmaceutical promotional activities and we shall discuss this separately in a chapter on personal selling. Public relations, which has been treated as a sub function of promotion all the while seems to be coming of age. Its scope is becoming broader. We shall discuss this separately in a chapter on public relations. We have discussed in pharmaceutical promotion all the aspects related to advertising and sales promotion.

Understanding how communication works is important to formulate effective advertising communication strategies. Only when we know about the communication hierarchy and what advertising appeals are likely to have the desired impact on the physician, can we prepare engaging detailing stories that can generate more prescriptions for our products.

There are simply no rules governing the preparation of an effective detailing story. We can, however, arrive at some useful guidelines based on learning theories, experiential insights from case studies of some companies that carried memorable campaigns and using that important-but-fast-becoming-extinct common sense approach.

If the purpose of promotion is to move the company's goods and services forward in the market place that can only be achieved by a persuasive and convincing detailing that can move the doctors to prescribe your products. The whole focus of pharmaceutical promotion should be directed to raise the standard and improve the quality of detailing effort of your company. Reinforce it. That is the cardinal principle of pharmaceutical promotion.

For a number of years, pharmaceutical marketing media like all other media relied only on broadcasting its carefully crafted message to its main target audience - physicians, with good prescribing potential. Ever increasing restrictions of physician access, dwindling product pipelines, rapid growth of internet and the consequent availability and accessibility of medical and scientific information has forced pharmaceutical industry to explore new approaches of pharmaceutical marketing and their promotion of their products and services.

In North America, Western Europe and select other countries, iPad has become the number one tool for detailing pharmaceutical products almost replacing the long standing visual-aid binder. Pharma companies have also been improving their access and reach to no access physicians through their e-Detailing strategies and delivering their messages where physicians want it, when they want it and how they want it.

Everything these days has become digitized. Digitization has already disrupted many industries such as media, travel, retail, and finance among others. Pharmaceuticals is lagging behind in the rapidly evolving digital space as it is a highly regulated industry. But, it cannot continue to lag behind for long. Consider these reasons:

- Research suggests that a third of doctors have changed a patient's treatment as a result of an online search.
- Accenture research indicates that effective digitization fuels growth by about 33 percent and profitability by about 40 percent.
- Average American spends about 52 hours on the net searching for his health related information and visits doctor three times a year.
- Digital technology has reached a tipping point in 2014, when 51 percent of healthcare practitioners were digitally native.

When a number of patients and physicians are going online increasingly, can Pharma industry afford to lag behind? The question, therefore, is not whether to digitize or not, but how?

Furthermore, digital's multiple touch-points allow pharmaceutical companies to reach physicians and patients and engage with them on a more personal level by targeting them across the devices and across different channels in an integrated manner. The conversation thus becomes seamless across the devices thanks to the new digital technologies.

Enter multichannel marketing and omni-channel marketing. Multichannel marketing as the name suggests is simply the use of multiple channels to reach a target audience. Multichannel marketing involves multiple channels - both offline and online. In multichannel marketing brand is at the center of the strategy. Marketing strategies in other industries continued to evolve from product-centricity to customer-centricity. In customer centricity you have to reach the customer on his terms - where when and how he wants to be reached. Marketers have a found way to meet these new customers' needs and wants in omni-channel strategy.

Omni means universal or of all things according to the dictionary. The literal meaning of omni-channel marketing, therefore, would mean to communicate across channels and devices rather than many channels as in case of multichannel marketing. The difference between omni-channel and multichannel really comes down to a company's approach to digital channels. In multichannel marketing, companies focus on maximizing performance of each channel - physical, phone, web and mobile. In omni-channel marketing companies put the customer in the center and strive to create a seamless customer experience across channels and devices.

The exponential growth of internet has brought a dramatic increase in the number of channels. Customers and stakeholders of Pharma have been willingly embracing these channels. Pharmaceutical companies, therefore have to reach their customers and stakeholders through their marketing effort with meaningful content across these channels such as website, email, SMS, online forums, blogs, microblogs, social media, gamification to provide a seamless customer experience. That is integrated marketing at its best.

For over sixty years, product detailing has been the center of all promotional activities in pharmaceutical industry. Detailing is still important. But not as it has been - as a broadcast of a well crafted message delivered through multiple channels to persuade the physician to prescribe their products. Product messages and medical content today are available from multiple sources as a result of the internet's exponential growth and the consequent social media presence that is almost ubiquitous. Today's internet savvy customers want to be engaged in a dialogue rather than a monologue. The rules of engagement have changed. To effectively promote your products and services, therefore, you need to create a compelling message that is engaging and deliver it to your customers when, where, and how they want it!

Personal Selling

Crucial Determinant Factor

Personal selling is a crucial determinant factor of success in pharmaceutical marketing. Personal selling is an important element of marketing mix in a number of areas like industrial marketing, consumer product marketing and marketing of services such as insurance etc., but nowhere it is as as important and as crucial as a determinant factor of success as in pharmaceutical marketing. The major reason for this is that pharmaceutical marketing is a highly specialized form of direct marketing, which does not lend itself to mass adverting. It markets products and services to intermediary customers like physicians, who advice and recommend the products to the end users (patients) through their prescriptions.

Pharmaceutical products cannot be purchased by patients without the prescriptions of the physicians, excepting OTC formulations such as certain analgesics, cough and cold remedies. The law requires this and the technical nature of the products dictates that. The ever intensifying competition and the unending proliferation of brand space places a premium on personal selling element of pharmaceutical marketing. In a fiercely competitive market that is flooded with 'me-too' products, the competition is no longer between products and strategies. The competition is between the talent of one company and another. It is the quality of your sales force that determines the success of your company in the market place.

An Important Function

Selling is an important function. Selling may be defined as the process of analyzing the potential customers' needs and wants, and assisting them in discovering how such needs and wants can best be satisfied by the purchase of a particular product, service or idea. The focus of selling, thus is on the needs and wants of customers rather than on the features of a product. The emphasis, therefore, should be on the benefits (need-satisfying entities) to the customer. In pharmaceutical selling the sales personnel are popularly known as medical representatives or detail men, since they detail the products to the members of the medical profession.

Personal selling refers to face-to-face attempts to persuade prospective buyers (prescribers) to consider acquiring particular products or services.

Made, Not Born!

Have you ever heard people commenting that *he is a born salesman,* when they refer to a fast-talking, smart-looking, enthusiastic and aggressive person? Are salesmen born? Salesmen are not born. People are born babies, to repeat the old but enduring cliche. Salesmanship is a skill that can be learnt and acquired.

Super Sales-Person

A study conducted among several thousand highly successful sales persons isolated the seven most common drives or motives needed to make it to the top of the sales club in any organization. These are:

1. **Need for Status:** Top sales people are conscious of and enjoy their image and reputation. They seek recognition as proof of their ability and performance.
2. **Need for Respect:** They want to be treated with respect. They want to be perceived as experts capable of advising on what is right and appropriate in their field.
3. **Need for Routine:** Sales people do not shun routine or hate to be disciplined as is popularly believed. Most top performers like routine and hate having it disturbed.
4. **Need for Control:** Top performers in sales enjoy people. They are not unduly concerned whether other people like them.
5. **Need for Achievement:** While money is a prime motivator, top sales performers are keen to accept newer challenges and to break their previous performance records for the sheer excitement of achievement.

6. **Need for Stimulation:** While the top sales people are normally calm and relaxed people, they thrive on challenge. They welcome any stimulation by way of challenges from outside, to satiate their higher-than-average energy levels.

7. **Need for Honesty:** The best sales people have a strong need for honesty, which gives them the moral courage and conviction necessary to excel in their vocation of persuasion. At the same time, they are not rigidly moralistic. They have faith and belief in the products they sell.

What Do Doctors Expect From A Medical Representative?

The best way of identifying and deciding on the attributes required for recruiting medical representatives, is to find out the expectations of doctors from medical representatives. What do doctors look for in a medical representative? What do they expect from a medical representative? Who do they consider as an ideal representative? That would be a good point to start the selection process of medical representatives for your firm, since these are derived from the prospective customers point of view. Medical profession, the world over considers medical representatives as an important source of new product information and as a vital communication link between the pharmaceutical industry and themselves.

Research indicates that doctors look for the following qualities and attributes in medical representatives.

1. Pleasant manners and appearance
2. Confidence
3. Good communication skills and voice
4. Product knowledge
5. Sincerity

Selecting and Recruiting Medical Representatives

Before you actually start the selection and recruitment process you should decide on the number of medical representatives. This depends on a number of factors like:

1. Your product mix
2. The extent of competition in the therapeutic segments in which you are present or you want to enter

3. The degree of market penetration required and your marketing objectives

4. The level of customer coverage in terms of both reach and frequency required to achieve your marketing objectives and

5. Financial capability

A number of companies have been launched during the recent past on a regional basis by having fewer medical representatives and gradually increasing their geographical coverage by increasing the number or representatives to cover the new customers in new markets. Once you decide on the number of medical representatives you would like to recruit, write down the specifications regarding a job profile for medial representatives, field sales managers, divisional managers etc. and determine the criteria for selection. If your company is an ongoing one, it is worth reviewing the job profiles and selection criteria and periodically update them. Updating may be necessary to keep pace with competition. The standards at entry level may have to be upgraded when competition is intensifying. Today, there are far more pharmacy graduates working as medical representatives than in the past. The changing face of competition, the introduction of more complex products and the consequent need for disseminating technical information are raising the standards for recruitment.

What should you look for while selecting a medical representative? What should be the basis for selection? What are the criteria? Here is a checklist (Table 7.1).

Table 7.1 Criteria for Selecting A Medical Representative: A Checklist

---

1. **Age:** What should be the age group? It is advisable to select them young, usually between 21 and 25 years.
2. **Education:** Should be a pharmacy or a science graduate
3. **Experience:** Should he be an experienced or fresh graduate? It is advisable to select a fresh graduate with a good scholastic record and extra-curricular activities. Some companies prefer limited experience of a year or two in similar companies. In the case of an experienced candidate look for his accomplishments, track records etc.
4. **Appearance:** Is he pleasant looking? What about his dress, grooming, bearing and health?
5. **Manners:** Does he look confident, and sound enthusiastic? Is he pleasant mannered?
6. **Voice and Expression:** Does he speak clearly, with proper

---

Contd...

modulation? What about his communication skills? Does he write with proper grammar?

7. **Reactions:** Is he alert? Are his responses quick enough?
8. **Drive:** What is his drive like? Is he enthusiastic?
9. **Intelligence:** How are his comprehension, reasoning and problem solving skills?
10. **Interest:** Does he sound cheerful? Ambitious? Sincere? What are his personal goals? Does he show interest in others?

These are by no means exhaustive, but they are very important attributes to be considered. These are the positive characteristics, which should be considered for selecting a medical representative. Here is a checklist of negative characteristics, which disqualify the applicant for the job of a medical representative. Since it is based on a study of a number of companies, this serves as positive proof of what managers don't look for when they select a medical representative. Here is a checklist of what selectors do not look for while selecting a medical representative.

1. Poor personal appearance

2. Over aggressive, Mr. Know-all syndrome

3. Poor verbal communication skills

4. Lack of enthusiasm

5. Poor scholastic record

6. No specific interest in career

7. Limp handshake

8. Cannot look the interviewer in the eye

9. Gives excuses, evades unfavorable factors in record

10. Over emphasis on money

Orientation and Training

After selecting the medical representatives, almost all companies give an orientation or introductory training. This training program is very important. It can play a vital role in shaping the attitudes of the representatives towards the company, towards the job, and towards themselves. The training program usually covers:

- An introduction about the company, its policies, objectives, and philosophy

- Product information, basic pharmacological, pharmaceutical and medical knowledge required to communicate the product benefits to medical profession persuasively
- Handling objections
- Selling skills
- Interpersonal communication skills
- Monitoring and analyzing competition

What is even more important is to build and inculcate a value based culture, good working habits, sense of achievement and pride in selling as a career. There should also be refresher-training programs to positively reinforce the earlier learning periodically. On-the-job training is far more important in the selling profession. The best person, who can provide continuous on-the-job training is the first-line manager or field manager. It is therefore, essential that field managers should be adequately trained and competent enough to ensure congruence between classroom training and on-the-job training.

A Medical Representative's Role

A medical representative is naturally expected to achieve the product-wise, unit-wise and value-wise sales targets monthly and cumulatively. But then, there is more to a medical representative's job than meeting the target. The means to achieve the end are equally important, if not more. A medical representative, who understands his role clearly and develops a broader perspective about his job would be able to achieve much more than his sales target. There are two important aspects to his role in the organization. A medical representative is a vital communication link between the pharmaceutical company and the medical profession. The medical representative is the source of communication in so far as doctors are concerned. He is also an important source of feedback from the company's point of view. He can provide very important and valuable feedback on what is happening to the company's products in the market place, how they are being perceived, what competition is doing and what are the customers' complaints etc.

Improving the Effectiveness of a Medical Representative

Understanding the role of a medical representative from communication principles point of view will help you evolve strategies to improve the effectiveness of medical representatives. Here are some important ways to improve the effectiveness of your medical representatives. These are based on research findings. Table 7.2 lists some of the more important research findings and their implications.

Table 7.2 Improving the Effectiveness of Medical Representatives

Research Findings and Implications
1. The medical representative's initial impression upon his customer largely determines his future interactions with the doctor and the degree to which the customer will like him.
2. First impressions are the best impressions even in selling. One has to create in the first visit a positive impact and reinforce it subsequently. Pleasant manners, well-groomed appearance, sober, conservative dress-sense, confident approach, will help create a favorable first impression. One should avoid flashy dresses and flamboyant approach.
3. Familiarity helps up to a point. The more familiar a medical representative to his customer the more his doctor will like him. The marketing implication is to decide on the right frequency. Frequent visits will certainly help more than infrequent visits. Experience suggests that two visits a month may be appropriate in a number of cases and a greater frequency may not have any positive advantage. (The latest research findings in 2017 suggest that about 68 percent of doctors said that they would prefer once-a-month visit by medical representatives in India).
4. The more a medical representative rewards his customers (particularly psychological rewards), the more his customers will like him. Frequency of visits in themselves can be considered as psychological rewards to some extent. Samples and giveaways too can also be perceived as psychological rewards as they symbolize attention and importance to customers.
5. The medical representative is more persuasive if his customers perceive him as credible. Source credibility is a very important factor. The level of product knowledge and the confidence with which the representative can communicate often determine the effectiveness of source credibility.

Improving the credibility of your medical representative as source of communication is difficult. Source credibility is a multifaceted concept, which can be established by the perceptions of your customers regarding the source's knowledge, expertise and trustworthiness. Product knowledge therefore, is crucial in enhancing a representative's credibility.

One major hurdle in achieving source credibility is that, when your customers perceive any *manipulative intention* on the part of the source, the credibility is reduced. In the context of pharmaceutical marketing, the customers certainly see that the medical representative as source has a lot to gain (and hence the intention to manipulate). A medical representative therefore, has to fight an uphill battle to establish some degree of credibility in the eyes of his customer. A medical representative, who can detail confidently about his products and demonstrate his product knowledge convincingly enhances his chances of being perceived as a credible source. Sincerity, well modulated delivery of message, pleasant manners, well-groomed appearance, conservative dress sense can enhance the perceptions of the customer regarding the credibility of the source. The organization too can enhance the credibility of its medical representative as a source of communication through its:

- Innovative marketing communication strategies
- Training programs to improve the product knowledge of its field force
- Communicating not only about positive features of the product, but also about its limitations such as side effects and adverse drug reactions, if any transparently
- Creative public relations efforts and publicity campaigns; and by improving the quality of its existing products, developing superior new products etc.

Feedback

So far we have discussed the role of the medical representative as source of communication and the ways in which, his credibility with the customers can be enhanced. The medical representative is also very important source of feedback for the organization. He can provide very valuable feedback, which has important strategic implications. He can provide feedback on:

- Customers' perceptions regarding your products
- Customers' complaints about your products
- Distinctive strengths and weaknesses of competing products and services
- Price and credit policies of competitors
- Competitors's performance in relation to sales volume, reputation, financial health, research activities etc.

The most important means of obtaining qualitative feedback from customers often are overlooked in a discussion on personal selling. It is also ignored in sales training and in practice and that is listening. Listening is the most important skill that can enhance the quality of feedback. Listening can also help a medical representative in overcoming objections and solving problems. It enables him to understand the needs of his customer and to adjust his message to meet those needs. The four basic principles to remember when you want to improve your listening skills are:

1. Stop talking. You cannot listen if you are talking.

2. Be patient. Do not be anxious to put across your point of view. Allow plenty of time. Do not interrupt.

3. Do not make him defensive by arguing or criticizing. Don't argue even if you are right. You may win your argument but lose an opportunity.

4. Show interest. Ask questions. This encourages him and shows you are attentive. It helps the points to develop further. It clarifies.

Four Key Areas

A medical representative has to perform four crucial tasks. Even a slight improvement in the effectiveness of anyone of these will lead to a significant increase in results. If a representative can improve his effectiveness in all these four crucial areas, his performance will truly be outstanding. There are no heights that he cannot reach. These four crucial tasks are:

1. Detailing

2. Monitoring

3. Sampling

4. Retailing (retail booking)

These are no doubt very fundamental and basic tasks. They are very simple to look at. That is why they are often taken for granted. Please do not be carried away by their simplicity and their seemingly obvious nature. These are the very basic functions, tasks and duties and responsibilities of a medical representative. It is common knowledge. There are no representatives who are not aware of these. but, then awareness is not enough. Action is the key!

Detailing

Detailing is singularly the most important task that a representative has to perform. Effective detailing is the only way to increase prescription generation for your products. The basis for this golden rule is one of the most enduring theories regarding the principles of communication. It dates back to the period of the great Greek philosopher, Aristotle. It was Aristotle, who postulated first that there are four indispensable basic elements to communication and these are:

1. Speaker
2. Occasion for speech
3. Speech itself
4. Listener (the receiver)

These basic elements have remained unchanged till date. All these elements of communication have a purpose. A goal. An objective. Communication should lead to action. In our case, prescription is the action and detailing is the process of communication. One of the encouraging features of this communication process is that many of these elements are under the control of the speaker. Careful attention and thorough preparation are what are needed to achieve uncommon success in generating prescriptions. Consider these facts:

Speaker

The medical representative is the *speaker* in the context of detailing to a doctor. To be successful and effective, the speaker has to be confident. He has to have faith in himself, in his abilities to detail effectively. This does not come automatically. Not even with autosuggestion and self-hypnosis. To have faith and belief in his detailing skills he has to have first and foremost faith in his company, his products and his company's communication strategies. He should also have a relaxed mental attitude. This can come only from regular, constant practice. Practice makes perfect has become a cliche that most of us have stopped realizing its real significance and started taking it for granted. There can never be a substitute for practice. Take the case of any professional, who loves his skills. He practices regularly, devotedly and unceasingly. Any medical representative who considers his job as a profession and not merely as a means to earn his livelihood will certainly practice. He is bound to achieve uncommon success. He is sure to achieve a greater credibility with his receivers (doctors). He can get an interview from his doctors instead of a call or visit. He does not simply call on doctors. He does not consider detailing as a chore. He enjoys detailing as a true professional.

Occasion for Speech

Occasion is a significant event. For a medical representative, who considers himself a professional every interview with doctor is an occasion by itself; A special event and not a routine matter. Therefore, he prepares thoroughly for each occasion. He tries to make the most of each interview. Utilization of time is very important for nothing is more precious than time.

Speech

Speech is the detail talk of a representative on his products. Detail talk has to be complete and yet precise. The emphasis here too is on preparation since precision and completeness can be achieved with adequate preparation. It is almost impossible to keep your detail talk concise and complete without preparation. Extempore detailing cannot achieve this. A number of experiments have confirmed this. Consider this case, which describes an experiment, conducted in the U.S. to evaluate extempore and canned sales presentations.

Case 7.1 Extempore Presentation Becomes Canned!

One of the very aggressive salesmen in a Pittsburgh company had protested against the introduction of a canned sales presentation introduced by his company. His argument was that canned presentation took the individual creativity of a salesman away and such a stereotyped presentation was not going to meet the varying needs of the customers. A salesman could tailor his sales talk to suit the individual needs of the customers only through extempore sales presentation.

His sales manager, who was open-minded, agreed to give it a try and told the salesman that they would conduct an experiment on this. The salesman agreed, confident of approaching different prospects with different approaches that were tailor made to their needs.

Arrangements were made with a number of prospects on whom the salesman was to call. The plans included the concealment of an expert stenographer in each office, where every word of the salesman and prospect could be taken down. The prospects selected for the experiment were specially chosen for their differences with the idea of determining whether the salesman did really vary his techniques appreciably.

The results of the experiment were typed and handed over to the salesman to follow his own judgment whether or not he would change his methods in practice to meet the varying needs of his prospects.

The salesman went through the reports carefully and confessed that he had no idea that his presentation to the different prospects was so similar on all occasions and further that it was so poor. He sincerely believed that he was varying his methods and emphasizing on the salient features to meet the different needs of his customers. He was so much chagrined to realize that it was not so. He realized that his presentation would be greatly improved by preparing in advance.

Many companies, subsequently conducted similar experiments using concealed microphones connected to a tape recorder instead of the stenographers, with similar results. The playback was always an eye-opener!

Adapted from *Textbook of Salesmanship by Frederick A. Russel and Frank Herman Beach, McGraw Hill; 3rd Edition 1941*

Listener

All communication objectives are listener-centered. They are aimed at gaining and sustaining the attention of the listener. The marketing implications of this are identifying the right doctor for the right product. In other words this is effective segmentation based on proper prospecting. Secondly, visiting the doctor at his most convenient time and place. This fundamental aspect is often overlooked.

These principles of communication are valid and applicable even in the emerging era of digital marketing. The channels of communication will undergo a dramatic change, not the communication principles.

Visiting the Trade

Retailers and wholesalers are also very important. Visits to the trade too have to be planned in a systematic manner. Visits to the retailers and wholesalers will give vital feedback on:

- What is happening to your products and how they are moving
- Competitors' activities, their product movement, their future plans etc.
- Identification of major prescribers of your products as well as your competitors'
- Basic information leading to effective prospecting

Another neglected area in visits to the trade has been retail order booking. The common argument for the declining emphasis on retail order booking is that there are far more wholesalers today to cater to the retailers than in the past. Retailers, as a result are always stocked with the company's products at the time of the representative's visit. The ever increasing number of wholesalers has made retailers reduce their shelf-stock levels. Such thinking leads to complacency. One should not reduce emphasis on retail booking. Availability and optimum stock pressure at the retail level is essential for your product's success. The visits to the trade are as important as the visits to the doctors. The difference exists only in approach and objective but not in emphasis or importance.

Changing Scenario

The industrial relations scenario concerning medical representatives has been rapidly changing during the past few years. Medical representatives are increasingly getting unionized, consequent to the amendment of the Sales Promotion Employees Act, 1976 in india.

The amendment *per se* has not got anything to do with this increasing tendency towards unionization of medical representatives, for there has not been any significant addition to the protective measures or new benefits in the amendment. The Industrial Disputes Act has been made applicable, and casual leave has been increased. Leave accumulation rules have been made more favorable to employees. But then, responsible employers have always been observing many of these provisions much before this amendment. What is responsible for this phenomenon of increasing unionization? What is the cause for the concern is not so much in the unionization itself, but in the increasing militancy of their unions. What are the reasons for this lack of harmony?

Is it the persuasive power of the unions or their coercive power? Or the inadequate communication of the management teams of the various companies with their respective employees? Is it lack of assertive sales management? Or is it an indifferent attitude of the employers towards the needs, wants and aspirations of medical representatives?

Whatever be the reason, one thing is certain. Improving quality of field force management is the only way to solve the problem. A proper understanding and appreciation of the problems of the representatives is essential to pave the way for better industrial relations. At the same time, management must be assertive in doing what is right. Assertiveness implies the recognition of the legitimate rights of the other party. Performance can be improved by teamwork alone.

The Changing Landscape of Pharmaceutical Selling

What is happening in the pharmaceutical selling arena? What is changing and what remains unchanged? Pharmaceutical sales representatives' access to physicians has been getting increasingly difficult. Representatives have been the main channel for transmitting marketing information through 'detailing' to physicians for over fifty years. The personal selling effort has been accounting for 60 percent of all sales and marketing expenditures in the US. Even in a branded generic market like India, the total cost of personal selling effort accounts for the biggest chunk of total sales and marketing expenditures.

Declining Physician Access

Physicians' access to pharmaceutical representatives has been steadily declining over the past 10 - 12 years now in the research-based Pharma markets like the US. Today almost one-half of the physicians in the US have moderate-to-severe restrictions on representatives' visits. A dramatic increase in the number of representatives over the years, turbulent market conditions with dwindling R&D pipelines, drastic cost-containment methods, increasing generic competition, and a frenzy of M&A (Merger and Acquisition) activities are some of the major reasons for the steadily declining physician access. In fact, it is observed that 19 out of 25 mergers corresponded with additional decreases in Pharma sales representative access with in one year following the merger. What is more, an increasing number of medical schools and university-affiliated health systems (especially top-tier programs) are restricting access to physicians by pharmaceutical companies - a behavior these graduates often take with them when they enter the work force at hospitals or start their practice. With minimal exposure to Pharma representatives during their medical training and fellowship, the new generation of physicians limit in-person visits with pharmaceutical representatives. Another important reason is that today, physicians do not see much value addition in the information provided by pharmaceutical sales representatives as much of the information is already available to them at the click of a button thanks to the internet explosion.

While it is discouraging that doctors may not meet as often as before with pharmaceutical representatives, most physicians still view these representatives as valuable sources of information.

Compared to the physician-access restrictions in the US, the access restrictions in India are not that severe but they are declining albeit gradually. The restrictions are more of quality than quantity. There are a few 'no-see' doctors in India too. The restrictions are more in terms of frequency of visits by a representative and the time allotted to him. The duration of a call is anywhere between 30 seconds to 2 minutes to day as compared to an average of four to five minutes a few years ago. Very few representatives who have thorough product knowledge and good communication skills are able to get more time with doctors.

The main reason for lack of interest and apathy towards personal visits of representatives and their detailing is the significant drop in the quality of information and presentation skills of the sales force. In a study conducted by Mumbai-based brand communications consultancy firm, *Brandcare* a few years ago, over 85 percent of doctors said that the communication skills of medical representatives are very poor and their knowledge about the drugs too is very low. Many doctors felt that majority of the representatives are working like a postman, delivering samples and gifts. A representative with inadequate product knowledge and very poor communication skills cannot get the attention of the physician let alone engage him fruitfully.

Despite all these reasons discussed, majority of the physicians the world over think that pharmaceutical representatives would be an important source of information provided they add value. What is needed is a paradigm shift from the current transactional selling to transformational selling.

Accessing the In-accessible

How do you meet the challenge of this declining access to physicians? How do you gain access to the less accessible and inaccessible physicians who matter? Pharma companies internationally are trying to make up for the reduced access to their representatives through other channels. These include telesales (call center), direct mail, e-mail marketing, e-detailing, speaker programs, self-serve digital content (content that is available on the physicians' professional social media sites, clinical product presentations, Pharma branded sites, e-detailing and other digital channels) mobile alerts etc. An Affinity Monitor Study conducted a few years ago by Z S Associates, a leading consultancy firm specializing in pharmaceutical sales and marketing showed that some Pharma companies had sent nearly 50 percent more digital messages including emails and mobile alerts - than the number of personal face-to-face calls attempted. The physicians' response to this avalanche of digital messages can be understood from this comment of a specialist physician, who said:

More than anything they (the Pharma companies) are taking a big dart board and picking up the darts and just flinging them and hoping one of them will stick.

It's like Pharma companies saying that here's all our ammunition and that's the target - let's throw. Blanketing customers with marketing messages is not likely to yield the desired results because even if some messages hit the target, the customers may not pay attention to them. What is the solution? How do you get the attention of the physicians? Empathy is the solution. Yes, Pharma companies need to apply some empathy and consider the situation from the physician's point of view. There is no single channel that always works today. Therefore, it is important to understand what kind of content doctors want to receive, which channels they prefer, and how frequently they want to be contacted so that they can tailor their marketing communication. That way they can make sure that messages resonate. *Focus on the quality of the customer interaction and not on reach at all costs.*

New Rules of Engagement

It is the steady onslaught of marketing messages that is causing an information overload, which is making the physicians deliberately tune out. Like you label the unwanted and unsolicited information as spam, physicians are labeling most of the marketing messages as spam. To avoid this and to more effectively engage with physicians Pharma companies need to do three things. These new rules of engagement suggested by Pratap Khedkar, Principal at ZS Association are:

1. *Empathize*: Determine the type of content that interests physician and that will engage him. Understand their preferences. Some prefer clinical information communicated by a peer. Others may want patient education material. Some others may want to access the information themselves from a library of self-serve content. Pharma companies should also understand the channels by which physicians prefer to be contacted.

2. *Be Relevant*: Pharma companies that understand the preferences of physicians can design and deliver the most relevant communication to their target doctors through the channels of their interest.

3. *Resonate*: Pharma companies should also understand the impact of frequency. Different channels show different saturation points. It is important to know how often is too often? Research shows that doctors tend to open the first few e-mails for a given brand, but after receiving about ten e-mails they stop. In case of messages through mobile apps the saturation point is lower - doctors stop responding after four or five messages. Direct mail on the other hand, has a higher saturation point, but a lower engagement rate.

Pharma companies can use the alternative channels to access the 'hard-to-see' and 'no-see' doctors and reinforce their access to currently accessible physicians. It may be difficult to determine the preferences of individual physicians, but it is increasingly feasible to systematically track and measure the types of content that the companies put out and the relative response to different types of content. It is also possible to analyze the new highly granular data like representative-doctor interactions on iPad.   In addition, Pharma companies can use analytics to understand how marketing channels reinforce each other. They can, based on this understanding develop the desired set of actions - at the right time, and in the right sequence to support the sales representatives to increase their engagement with individual physicians.

Pharma companies can optimize their engagement with physicians in general and 'hard-to see' and 'no-see' doctors in particular by using the data to understand the affinities of the doctors they are trying to reach and tailoring the content, channel, and frequency of their marketing messages accordingly.

What is needed is a higher engagement rate and a better customer experience than a higher message transmission rate. In marketing, as in medicine - a little empathy goes a long way!

Detailing Today

Detailing remains a core part of any pharmaceutical company's marketing strategy and is a very large part of the promotional spend.

The ubiquitous Visual Aid of Pharma industry certainly has lost its shine and seems to be on the way out. The visual aid even today is the most cost-effective communication tool. A tool that is not sharpened enough by most of the sales reps. When communication is taken away from a 'communication tool' what remains is just a tool. When a medical representative opens his bag and takes out his visual aid, the doctor spontaneously says, "*I know all your products. Just tell me the brand names of your products.*" The reasons for this casual indifference towards the visual aid are that mostly they do not contain any worthwhile information for the doctor. More over, the visual aids of all the companies look the same in terms of size, layout, and even the visuals. What is more, the communication skills of most medical representatives are so poor lacking in enthusiasm, confidence, pronunciation. An average busy doctor on a typical day is exposed to thirty or more such listless visual aid-based presentations.

iPad or Tablet Detailing

Pharma companies have started using laptops for detailing their products to physicians to gain better attention. While the laptop detailing has some advantages over the paper detail-aids or visual aids as they are called in India in terms of audio and video content and some graphics links, it was not very convenient to use. The time taken for the laptop to boot was longer and the navigation too was challenging. Furthermore, the internet speed too was grossly inadequate. The laptops were good for offline presentations of powerpoint slides and videos. The detail-aids as a result were mere electronic versions of paper based detail-aids or visual-aids as they are known in India. Some of the multinational and large Indian Pharma companies used laptops for detailing their new products and major products by their managers in the field.

But the introduction of iPad by Apple in 2010 changed all that. iPad, by virtue of its capabilities has become the most convenient, versatile and effective tool for detailing and the pharmaceutical industry quickly embraced it. Within six years of its introduction, iPad has achieved a phenomenal adoption rate with over 80 percent of Pharma companies using it as their device of choice for detailing their products in North America and some European countries. While iPad has become the numero uno digital tactic for Pharma Industry, some companies have started using other tablets too as detail-aids. The share of other tablets, however is very low.

Why iPad is Pharma's Device of Choice?

Pharma has embraced iPad as their device of choice for detailing by their sales force as it offers a number of advantages. Consider these for example:

A. Great visual quality with large screen for delivering video, graphic and animation content

B. Sleek touch screen and light weight make it easy to carry

C. 3G a 4G wireless connectivity built into the device for speedy internet connection

D. Capability to combine Customer Relationship Management (CRM) system that includes content visualizing, call planning, signature capture, tracking, scheduling, showing videos, presenting detail-aids, GPS, integrated e-mail, and Closed-Loop-Marketing (CLM) system into the device making it an ideal device for sales force automation (we have already discussed about Closed-Loop-Marketing in the chapter on Promotion).

Furthermore, it is also possible to perform on iPad, the sales management side of sales force effectiveness such as territory planning, sales operation, sales forecasting, promotion response planning analysis and some return on investment (ROI) calculations and marketing planning. In addition, Pharma industry will be able to measure which sales campaigns are getting the most response rates or leads with the data input captured through the closed-loop-marketing system on iPad.

3 Ways to Get the Best Out of Your iPad Detailing

Here are three important success factors that can significantly improve your medical representatives' performance of iPad detailing.

1. Use the iPad detail-aid to support the verbal conversations of your sales representatives. spelling out everything leads to an overload of presentation sildes or PDF pages. Experienced pharma sales reps used the printed detail-aids to strengthen their detail talk and never read the text verbatim. Likewise, iPad-aid too should make the conversation impactful and not replace it. A good tablet detail-aid helps strengthen the delivery of the message. A logical structure, example and cases add support to the product story. The representative should always lead the conversation.

2. Engage. Do not broadcast. Invite the physician to interact. Create more engagement. The tablet is an ideal device to capture data on treatment practices and brand perception of physicians. Continuous content refinement will get the attention and more importantly sustain the attention of HCPs (Healthcare Practitioners) and reinforces the motivation of Pharma sales representatives.

3. Maximize the graphical opportunities of the iPad to strengthen the marketing message. iPad and other tablets have huge potential to go beyond text and images. You can, for example,

include treatment class, product's mode of action animations, video statements by Key Opinion Leaders (KOLs) patient cases and much more. You can make the content come alive and make the detail-talk interactive and a lively experience with the help of iPad.

Common Mistakes to Avoid

1. Do not create a digital version of a paper visual-aid. The early adopters of iPad detailing made a mistake of creating exact copies of their visual aids with out utilizing any additional functionalities such as video, animation and data capturing that iPad allows.

2. Do not overload iPad with too much content. It is possible to add almost an infinite stream of content. Therefore, it is tempting to equip the sales force with almost encyclopedic information to handle any objection and any question. That will only make it difficult if not impossible for the sales representatives to search for the relevant content during the detail-call. Furthermore, it is observed that most representatives use only three to five pages or slides of tablet detail-aid to support their conversation. However, when you do want to add more content, make sure that it is not a part of the main navigation stream and add it in a sub-menu. Always ensure that the main detail-talk flows are short and to the point. Let the rest of the content be a part of the sub-menu.

3. Do not over-do it. Never use animation for the sake of animation and video content just because it can be done well on an iPad. Use them only when they are clearly strengthening the key messages.

Implementing iPad Detailing Effectively

Many sales reps feel somewhat uncomfortable about the tablet detailing platform because they can monitor if and how much the detail-aid is being used in the field. You need to explain to them clearly the benefits that it can offer to make their message more effective and their engagement with the physicians much better.

1. Remember to involve your sales representatives right from the very beginning when you are launching a tablet detailing program.

As they have to use the device and the detail-aids every day, they are best positioned to provide valuable input on what is required to make tablet detailing a success.

2. Leverage the call expertise of your sales representatives and show them how iPad detailing can support their conversations with the physicians and take it to the next level. The best way is to demonstrate how it will help them in engaging physicians which is getting increasingly difficult.

3. Train your sales representatives on how and when to use the iPad or any other tablet that you may be using. Use role-play as a part of the training exercise and record the role-play sessions and show it to representatives so that they can know exactly where and what they need to correct. It is observed that a number of representatives today look more at the visual-aids rather than at the physician they are detailing to. Same is the case with the sales representatives who were early adopters of tablet detailing. It is observed that they too were looking more at iPad than at the doctor they are presenting to.

Tablet Detailing: Future Outlook!

The Indian Pharma companies are rather slow to adopt to tablet detailing. Multinationals such as Abbott Healthcare, GlaxoSmithKline, Sanofi and Pfizer and a few others have equipped their sales forces with iPads to help them engage better with their physicians. Majority of Indian companies have yet to adopt to changing technologies such as iPad detailing. The continued heavy reliance on transactional business model and quick success tactics based on heavy rewards - monetary, expensive gifts and huge discounts for purchasing physicians may be one of the key factors. The few companies, which are investing on technology are the ones that are implementing tablet detailing. But, the tablet detailing in India is currently a digital version of the paper based visual-aid with a few bells and whistles. It is not yet exploiting the full capabilities that tablets in general and iPad in particular can offer. It is like a glossy presentation being replaced by a shiny one.

As competition intensifies and when the current race of discount and gratification-based selling begin to recede because they no longer can deliver, Pharma companies that have ignored the telltale signs of the changing landscape of the market place would realize the need to invest in technology, development and the implementation of the best practices. The innovators and early adopters of technology are sure to reap the rich rewards in the changing market place.

Tele-Detailing or e-Detailing

Doctors often rely on pharmaceutical companies for drug information. For the past few years, for various reasons doctors are not able to find time to have face-to-face meetings with Pharma sales representatives. A number of large hospitals and Group Practices have been restricting their access to the pharmaceutical companies. How do you improve access to physicians in times such as these where physician access is increasingly getting restricted? Tele-detailing provides an opportunity for drug companies to provide this interaction remotely on the doctors' terms. Tele-detailing, which is also known as 'e-Detailing, or 'remote detailing' or 'web calls' is engaging remotely with doctors and Healthcare Professionals (HCPs). It is an interactive, online, real-time meeting with a physician. As physician access for Pharma companies is increasingly getting restricted, Tele-detailing or e-detailing helps extend reach and contact frequency to create greater impact.

Two Basic Types

There are two basic types of eDetailing. One is Interactive (Virtual or Remote) detailing. A physician can access the interactive detailing at his convenience. A typical virtual eDetailing call contains multimedia content such as a slide deck, video or an animation lasts between 5 and 15 minutes. It is mainly used by many pharmaceutical companies in North America and some European countries. The virtual detailing offers an advantage to the physician as he can control the time of the detailing and also the contents he would like to access. He can also request for a face-to-face detailing with a sales representative of the company and samples of the products he would like to try at the end of the detailing session.

Live or video detailing, on the contrary is a face-to-face video conference with the physician speaking to a pharmaceutical sales representative on a smartphone, tablet such as iPad, or a computer webcam. Here, the Pharma sales representative directs the detailing and takes him through the presentation containing similar multimedia elements as in virtual or live detailing. This is more or less similar to the traditional detailing except that it is a video and not real.

Three Models

Currently the pharmaceutical industry follows three models for implementing e-Detailing.

1. *The Outsourced Model* where all components and activities of e-Detailing of a company are managed by an external agency. External sales representatives are contracted for making the remote detail calls.

2. *The Dual Model* is one where most activities such as scheduling and arranging for appointments with physicians are conducted by an external agency except the actual call delivery.

3. The *Hybrid Model* is one where the initial setup, training and the platform configuration are done by an external agency and the call scheduling and call delivery are done internally by the company employees.

Implementing e-Detailing

The three basic steps in implementing an e-detailing program are scheduling a meeting, running the meeting (e-Detail) and evaluation of the meeting.

1. Scheduling a meeting involves taking a prior appointment from the physician as to when he would like to log in at the appointed website for participating in the e-Detail of the company.

2. Running a meeting is actually presenting the e-Detail by the Pharma company's representative or MSL (Medical Sales Liaison) if the meeting is about only clinical or medical issues and not about the product. The meeting takes place over Skype, FaceTime or a similar web-based platform or at the designated website for this purpose.

3. Evaluating the e-Detail is the final step in the process. It is for collecting the essential feedback to improve the future e-Details and also to provide the physician with any additional information

such as clinical trial reports, web-links and samples that he or she requires.

Following the e-Detail, physicians would most like to have new product information, educational programs, links to other sources and drug formulary updates (mainly for the reimbursement status of the prescribed products).

e-Detailing Strategies

e-Detailing offers many advantages to a pharmaceutical company. The most common strategies followed by Pharma companies are:

A. *Coverage*, as e-Detailing extends the reach towards customer groups that are currently not seen by the field force.

B. *Frequency*, which is the number of calls a Pharma sales representative can make may be increased as compared to face-to-face calls more cost-effectively. There are no commuting charges and waiting times in web-based, remote calls.

C. *Vacant Territories* can be covered effectively.

D. Companies can offer *Services On Demand* to physicians by addressing their online requests for product or clinical information, samples etc.,

E. e-Detailing makes *Differentiated Messaging* possible. With e-Detailing you can target your message specific to the individual physicians based on the feedback from the previous interactions whether face-to-face or e-Details.

Objectives of e-Detailing

It is important to set clear objectives before implementing an e-detailing program. Consider these objectives for example:

1. To increase the length or duration of an e-Detail. This is possible when the e-detail is more interactive and intuitive, and more interesting with appropriate animation and video built into the communication.

2. To increase the effectiveness of e-Detail by delivering a personalized, target-specific communication that is relevant to each physician.

3. To decrease the cost of sales force without losing effectiveness

Training is Important

Prior training of the Pharma sales representatives, who deliver the e-Detailing is very important as it involves new technology. The training focuses mainly on two broad areas. One is on How to *Present the Content* using the technology and giving the physician access to the meeting and sharing the relevant content in a secure way. The second aspect of training focus is on *Remote Communication.* Pharma representatives will often not be able to see the physician during an e-detail call and still have to ensure that physicians are paying attention to them instead of doing something else during the call.

Three Key Factors for e-Detailing's Success

There are three main factors that influence the success of e-Detailing. One is cost. E-Detailing cost on average per physician is estimated to be between US $ 100 - 150 as compared to the face-to-face detailing cost of US $ 200 - 250 per physician. Secondly, e-Detailing is more effective. The duration of an e-Detail is about 10 minutes on average as compared to 2 minutes of a face-to-face detail. Increasing physician acceptance is the third success factor. A study by quintiles (IQVIA now) observed that a whopping 97 percent of physicians are likely to repeat an e-Detail. Almost three-quarters of them agree that e-Detailing is the future of pharmaceutical contact.

Why Do Physicians Like e-Detailing?

Here are some reasons why physicians like e-detailing.
1. Ease of scheduling.
2. Fits into their schedule better
3. Convenient. Have the option to take the detail at office or home.
4. Saves time.

e-Detailing in the Indian Context

What we have discussed so far is a very brief overview of e-Detailing in research-based Pharma markets such as the US and Europe. e-Detailing as we have discussed here is not yet practiced by the Indian pharmaceutical industry. One major reason could be that e-Detailing is not a one-size-fits-all type of strategy. e-Detailing is more beneficial in the pre-launch and post-launch phases of a product lifecycle. In the pre-launch phase e-Detailing is levenged to create and increase awareness and in the post-launch to accelerate the rate of adoption. During these stages there is a great need for product and clinical information. Perhaps, marketers in branded generic markets do not yet feel a pressing need for e-Detailing. The current transactional model of pharmaceutical selling which is based more on gratification and the consequent complacent attitude by some of the Pharma marketers may be another reason. A few MNC pharmaceutical companies, however seem to be exploring the possibility of using e-Detailing for launching their original patented products.

That said, e-Detailing is certainly important as it offers the same advantages in branded generic markets too as it does in the research based Pharma markets. The new product launches are crucial for companies in branded generic markets too. Physician access is also increasingly getting restricted even in branded generic markets such as India. To reach the 'difficult-to-see' or 'even no-see' physicians e-Detailing offers a cost-effective solution.

Pharma Marketers, who are progressive and forward looking would be better off understanding the best practices of e-Detailing and design strategies to implement would be ahead of the curve and reap the rewards of e-Detailing.

Customer Relationship Management (CRM)

The general perception of customer relationship management in Indian pharmaceutical industry is rather very narrow and transactional in nature as it is based on gratification of customers through high value gifts, foreign junkets, and even cash for prescriptions to physicians. This practice of transactional marketing is not CRM. What is CRM then?

CRM is first and foremost a strategy. CRM is all about identifying, satisfying and maximizing the value of a company's best customers. CRM is about the ways and means that companies interact and engage with customers at all the touch points through out their journey. CRM is also about a set of software tools for customer relationship management. They should be implemented only after a well defined strategy and operational plan with all the monitoring mechanisms are put in place. It has four major components:

1. *Operational CRM:* Stores customers' contact histories with all the relevant details so that sales and marketing people can retrieve it whenever they need it. Operational CRM as the name indicates provides support to the sales and marketing teams (front office). This also provides customer data for managing campaigns and facilitates sales force automation.

2. *Analytical CRM*: Helps in analyzing customer data for designing and executing targeted marketing campaigns that are very useful and even essential in acquiring customers, cross-selling, up-selling, and in making product related decisions such as product augmentation, and pricing etc.

3. *Sales Intelligence CRM*: Provides the much needed insights into customer acquisition and retention strategies in terms of planning, implementing and monitoring customer specific strategies.

4. *Collaborative CRM*: Customer service management is not just the function of marketing department alone. It requires teamwork. A number of people belonging to various other departments come into picture in the process of customer service management. Marketing is the front end of it. Collaborative CRM, as the name suggests covers all aspects of a company's dealings with customers that are handled by various departments within a company and shares it with the respective people as needed.

CRM, thus is a process sponsored from the highest levels of an organization, embedded into the corporate culture and pervades through out the organization.

MSL (Medical Science Liaison)

It was the Upjohn company in the USA that first introduced the concept of Medical Science Liaison in 1967. They created the position of Medical Science Liaison to provide educational awareness and to build rapport with the leading doctors (Key Opinion Leaders or Thought Leaders) for their new drug Tolbutamide (Orinase). Since the Key Opinion Leaders are perceived by their peers as experts in a given therapeutic area, they wield considerable influence among their peers. The key task of Medical Science Liaisons therefore is to influence the influencers!

Medical Science Liaison has grown in importance and size significantly during the last fifteen to twenty years. What are the reasons for this growth? Samuel Dyer, CEO of Medical Science Liaisons says, "*The Key Opinion Leaders are demanding it!*"

The Eureka Moment

The Cutting Edge Information consultancy conducted a benchmark study a few years ago and found that the average time spent by the Pharma sales representative with a doctor was less than two minutes while the MSL spent a little over an hour on average with a doctor. That made companies sit back and realize that doctors valued that exchange.

Growing Importance of MSLs

Today's thought leaders are looking for detailed information as they engage in clinical conversations with Pharma, Biotech and Medical Device companies. Growing scientific sophistication is another reason for this increasing role of medical science liaisons as it requires scientifically trained medical experts.

The traditional sales force is suffering from restricted access to physicians. MSLs despite their non-promotional role, provide a valuable link between doctors and the company.

What is more, a field-based MSL may provide a strong strategic asset for any company. They can collect crucial insights from the field on current and new therapeutic approaches and generate important new data.

What's in a Name?

Although originally called Medical Science Liaison (MSL) by Upjohn, over the years pharmaceutical, biotechnology and medical device companies have used different titles to describe the MSL job. The job titles vary even though they typically have the same role and responsibilities. Some of the more commonly used job titles for the MSL function are:

A. Clinical Liaison

B. Clinical Science Consultant

C. Medical Liaison

D. Medical Manager

E. Medical Science Consultant

F. Medical Science Manager

G. Scientific Affairs Manager

Tasks and Responsibilities of MSLs

Irrespective of the job title the primary responsibility of an MSL remains to establish and maintain peer-to-peer relationship with leading doctors who influence other doctors. Most of the activities of MSLs, therefore revolve around engaging Key Opinion Leaders, building and strengthening relationships with them and educating them about the company's product development and research activities. Here are some of the important activities that the MSLs perform:

A. KOL relationship management

B. Educating KOLs and other leading HCPs

C. Identifying and training speakers

D. Attending medical conferences

E. Coordinating company-sponsored clinical research

F. Delivering scientific presentations

G. Coordinating and participating in Continuing Medical Education (CME) activities

H. Medical publications

I. Gathering competitive intelligence

J. Training or supporting sales force

MSL: Prerequisites and Key Competencies

What qualifications and competences should MSL aspirants need to have to perform such a wide range of scientific and academic activities? They should possess:

A. Advanced degree such as M D, Pharm D, or PhD in life sciences

B. Understanding of Clinical Trial and Drug Development guidelines

C. Demonstrated Scientific Aptitude

D. Strong Communication Skills - both oral and written

E. Strong Interpersonal Skills

F. Ability to Collaborate, Persuade and Motivate

G. Ability to Teach and Learn

H. Working knowledge of internet, computers and technology

I. Strong Scientific and Business Acumen

J. Creativity

Different Role

Sales and Marketing and Medical Science Liaison are field based activities. Both the functions interact with Healthcare Practitioners. Some of the customers may even be common for both the functions. That is where the similarity ends and the difference begins. Table 7.3 presents the key differences between Pharmaceutical Sales Representatives and Medical Sales Liaison Managers at a glance.

It is important that MSLs should be perceived as neutral scientific experts on company's products. They should respond when KOLs and other HCPs have technical questions on a company's products or studies. They should not act as a surrogate sales force.

Table 7.3 Roles of Pharma Sales Representative and MSLs at a Glance

Pharmaceutical Sales Representative	Medical Sales Liaison
1. Part of Sales and Marketing Department	Part of Medical Affairs or Regulatory Department
2. Trained to sell and persuade prescribers to prescribe the company's products	Non-selling function. Establishing and reinforcing relationships with KOLs through a number of scientific activities
3. Prescriber focus	KOL Focus

Contd...

Pharmaceutical Sales Representative	Medical Sales Liaison
4. Works with 'doctors in the trenches' or clinically based physicians	Works primarily with the physicians researching and teaching
5. Redirects unsolicited complex inquiries to Medical Affairs	May respond to unsolicited complex questions from KOLs and HCPs
6. May have technical background	Most often have technical background
7. Sells products based upon integration of key brand messages and appropriate use of product	Works on scientific education and clinical research studies to disseminate product related and non-product related scientific information in therapeutic areas of KOLs' interest
8. Performance and goals are based on sales of a product	Performance and goals are based upon outcomes with academic thought leaders and Continuing Medical Education Objectives as per organizational goals set

What MSLs Don't Do

Since pharmaceutical sales representative and MSL positions are field based and visit some of the same customers it is important to clearly define what sales representatives and MSLs do and don't do. It is even more important to draw a clear boundary in terms of what MSLs don't do. If you remember that 'S' in MSL stands for 'Science and not Sales', what MSLs should not do becomes very clear. Consider these 'Don'ts' for example:

- MSLs do not generate noise or buzz about products prior to approval
- MSLs do not drive sales or otherwise promote products
- MSLs do not proactively discuss off-label information
- MSLs do not make patient-specific therapy or treatment recommendations
- MSLs do not render general practice related medical or business services

It's All About Providing Value

MSLs too are facing physician access issues today. The only key to open the physicians' doors is delivering information that the physician values. MSLs, who consistently create value and differentiate themselves from the rest of the pack get the face-time with thought leaders.

How does an MSL deliver value? Value can be found in a number of things. Consider these for example. Understanding the doctor's needs, targeting the right KOL with the right information can improve credibility and build trust. If MSLs are approaching KOLs with clinical information only, they may be missing the value proposition, which lies in the insights.

As Mr. Paul Meade, President, Thought Leader Select says, *"if doctors are closing to sales representatives at healthcare systems, then closing the door to MSLs is probably not far behind unless they can create value in that conversation. The value is not in the data. It is in the insights the MSL can bring to the discussion. This is a necessary skill for today's MSL."*

MSLs: The Indian Context

The current practices in terms of medical sales liaisons in India differ slightly from those of the first world markets. Their main focus is new product promotion by key opinion leaders, who are the main presenters of the product to the practicing physicians in Pharma company-sponsored product symposia. They also focus on any other relevant topic for a product or therapy area symposium, where the sponsoring company's product is used. Very often the target audience for a KOL is carefully chosen based on the KOL's circle of influence. The sponsoring company usually prepares the speaker notes and even the presentation slide deck, of course in consultation with the KOL. The target audience for these symposia (product or therapy area) are physicians, who normally send referrals to a KOL, who is a super specialist and an expert in that therapeutic area. It is more like a *quid pro quo* arrangement.

Things would certainly change in the years ahead with competition intensifying further, and the market evolving slowly but steadily from a predominantly branded-generic market to an increasing share of the patented, research-based new drug market. The MSL and KOL engagement practices would be more objective, science-based with focus on delivery of value to the patient and improved outcomes.

KOL Management

KOL is an industry term and an acronym. KOL stands for Key Opinion Leader. Key opinion leaders are physicians and members of medical community, whose opinions are highly regarded and who influence other physicians. Managing KOLs effectively is, therefore, essential to pharmaceutical company's future products and market expansion.

Key Opinion Leaders possess by virtue of their knowledge, years of experience, medical affiliations and publications and therefore, enjoy unique credibility among their peers. Physicians in their daily practice strive to choose from a wide range of drug and treatment options for their patients. Very often they turn to fellow physicians who are KOLs for knowledge and advice on specific drugs.

That is why pharmaceutical and life science companies have begun relying heavily on KOLs to help establish the knowledge base about their drugs to influence practicing doctors, regulatory authorities, to create and expand markets.

Why KOLs are Important

Key opinion Leaders are very important in pharmaceutical industry and they are rather indispensable. As the science behind pharmaceutical products grows more complex the importance of KOLs becomes even more crucial. Pharmaceutical companies use KOLs in a number of ways transcending many functional areas within the company. Consider these for example:

A. Clinical research department can seek opinions on trial design, outcome measurements and other needs within the medical community

B. Marketing and Sales departments might seek their advice in lifecycle management of their products

C. Medical Affairs department need KOLs as speakers at their CME programs and their advice on current medical trends

Identifying KOLs

KOL identification is done in a number of ways. One is by the in-house medical affairs department, or by a consultant or through the use of software programs. Here are some of the important criteria used by pharmaceutical companies in identifying a thought leader or a key opinion leader:

A. Faculty position either as full Professor or Associate Professor at a major medical college or an academic and research center

B. Proven expertise in a therapeutic area of the company's interest by either multiple research grants in that area or publications in that area in prestigious, peer-reviewed journals

C. A frequent invitee as a speaker at national and international medical meetings

D. Participant in consensus and guidelines preparation committees

E. Leader in medical associations

F. Leading prescriber in his specialty area

A word of caution here. Prescription data are traditionally not used for identifying for top-tier KOLs, although the prescription leadership makes him the expert in that area in terms of clinical experience. There are two basic reasons for this. First, if the physician is engaged in research, publishing and teaching, he is less likely to have time for treating patients and therefore does not *show up* as a high prescriber. Second, selecting KOLs on the basis of high prescribing of a product could be viewed as a kickback or reward for that prescriber.

Building Relationship with KOLs

It is important to build enduring relationships with key opinion leaders. KOLs can be of great help to a pharmaceutical company in many ways. At the same time it is important to remember that KOL relationships take time to develop. And enduring relationships can be built only on mutual trust and respect for each others' capabilities and competencies. There should be transparency in a relationship for making it sustainable. Here are some of the important areas where KOLs can help a pharmaceutical company:

1. KOLs have influence among their peers during both-pre launch and post-launch phases of a product lifecycle

2. KOLs provide competitive insights throughout the entire lifecycles of products

3. KOLs are effective advocates of your products. High prescribers too, can be effective advocates as they have deep product experience, which makes them so authentic

What KOLs Want

What do KOLs want and expect from pharmaceutical industry? They want and expect what they value most. Consider these for example:

A. KOLs desire contribution and involvement and wish to be on the cutting edge of their fields. They want to be involved in changing science and participate in clinical studies. They would like to be a part of innovative products, be it dissemination of scientific information on the products, and new uses. They would like an active role in engaging their peers and advising them.

B. What appeals to them most? Rewards and benefits such as support to their research activities, sponsorships to medical conferences and events, publishing their work, honoraria and other perks.

C. KOLs also appreciate, expect and respect integrity, ethical behavior, transparency, patient focus and service orientation.

Effective KOL Engagement

Pharma companies must do two things effectively to engage KOLs. The starting point of effective engagement of KOLs is a right list of KOLs. The list must be consistently refined and validated to provide a meaningful value and data to the company.

To engage the Key Opinion Leaders (KOLs) effectively, pharmaceutical companies must make their Medical Sales Liaisons (MSLs) become credible sources of valued information. The MSLs should deliver actionable insights on their products and treatment in their therapy areas to KOLs, not just medical and scientific information.

Ten Rules of KOL Engagement

1. Segment your KOLs

2. Deliver segment-specific communication strategies that resonate

3. Clearly define the engagement goal

4. Develop an engagement plan for each KOL

5. Anchor in consultation, win an engagement

6. Anticipate the KOLs' needs

7. Create opportunities for development

8. Embrace KOL feedback

9. Follow the 80:20 rule in your KOL activities

10. High level scientific content is always the winner.

Key Account Management

The customer landscape has been changing in pharmaceutical industry for quite some time now. It is changing from a '*get-the drug approved and then convince a large number of physicians to prescribe it'* model to a *multi-stakeholder decision making* process.

In the traditional transactional model of selling, the Pharma sales representative used to represent the company to present all the information related to medical, marketing, regulatory and commercial to the physician who was the chief decision maker whether of independent practice or representing a hospital. This *transactional model* is changing rapidly to a consultative model as hospitals and healthcare organizations are evolving into large, complex organizations.

The Transactional Model

In the traditional transactional model of pharmaceutical selling, Pharma sales representative represented all internal departments of the company and attempted to convince the physician, who represented all the stakeholders of the hospital to prescribe and buy his company's products and services. This model is very reliant on the relationships between the Pharma sales representative and the physician. The physician is expected to share all concerns that stakeholders inside the hospital (which is an account) have, which the representative in turn needs to share with the relevant functions inside the Pharma company. Table 7.4 presents major internal (Pharma Company) and external stakeholders (Hospital).

Table 7.4 Major Internal and External Stakeholders

Company	Hospital
Internal Stakeholders	**External Stakeholders**
Medical	Patient
Marketing	Pharmacist
Regulatory	Physician / HCP
Sales Rep	Purchase / Insurance

Changing Marketing Environment

The changing marketing environment is becoming more complex for a number of reasons. Firstly, physicians' access is increasingly getting restricted for Pharma sales representatives. Secondly, the specialty focus of Pharma companies is increasing and they are introducing a number of highly complex products. Thirdly, in many countries, the individual physician is handing over the decision maker role to larger entities (Group Practices, Physicians' Network, etc.). Finally, governments, healthcare institutions in all countries are trying to contain the escalating healthcare costs.

If multiple products are sold in the same hospital it is difficult to coordinate all the activities, which may involve in the engagement of multiple activities with different physicians by multiple representatives. To resolve these challenges, Pharma companies need to share all medical, technical, and commercial information pertaining to their products across the functional areas, plan, liaise and come up with a strategy to present and convince the decision makers of their key accounts.

Key Account Management, A Consultative Selling Strategy

Recognizing the emergence of new influencing groups due to the changing scenario, pharmaceutical companies have come up with a consultative selling strategy called Key Account Management (KAM). With Key account management, pharmaceutical companies can revitalize their sales model and regain their consultative status and influential role in the choice of medicines by physicians and other stakeholders of hospitals and healthcare institutions. Key accounts for a pharmaceutical company can be hospitals, pharmacy chains, or non traditional customers such as payers (insurance companies). Payers are quickly emerging as critical stakeholders in the first world markets such as North America, Europe, Japan etc., Payers might emerge as important stakeholders of healthcare delivery in India and other markets too in future.

In Key Account Management, the focus is on coordination of the activities performed by internal functions at each of the accounts. A key account manager thus becomes the coordinator of multichannel activities (Medical, Marketing,Regulatory, Sales Representative etc.) that are targeted at multiple stakeholders inside complex customer organizations (Hospitals and other Healthcare Organizations).

Three Basic Steps

What is Key Account Management? The Financial Times defines Key Account Management as a customer-oriented coordination unit within a company, in which activities associated with very important customers (Key Customers) are consolidated. The focal point for the coordination of marketing tasks is a small number of customers who are of great significance to the company.

Therefore, it very important for the company to gain a thorough understanding of its key customers. Furthermore, it is important that all the communication is well integrated so that its approach to these customers is uniform even if presented by different employees. Viewed from this angle, Key Account Management is more of a process than a function.

There are three basic steps in the key account management process. Segmenting the accounts according to their importance is the first step. Companies commonly use the potential and performance of the accounts as a criteria for this. In its simplest form, potential for hospitals can be defined as the number of beds as criteria. A more refined and complex measure of potential can be the determination of patient numbers per disease in a therapeutic area, in which the Pharma company offers product solutions. Based on these inputs the company can arrive at the total financial value of the hospital potential.

Once the key accounts are ranked by their potential, the second step is to understand the possible gateways and barriers for entry into these institutions. Based on this understanding, one can formulate a winning strategy.

The third step is to understand and define the functions and roles of stakeholders of key accounts in terms of their nature and scope detailing whether they are gatekeepers, influencers or decision makers. A gatekeeper, for example, might be a nurse or an assistant who manages the agenda of his or her boss. An influencer is someone whom the decision maker will consult before making a decision. A purchaser may be an administration head and may not really have a decision making power in a hospital. Understanding the needs, motivations, and concerns of all these stakeholders will be of immense help not only in selling to the hospitals but also in building sustainable long-term relationships with the key accounts.

A full-fledged key account management system, thus focuses not just on portfolio level discount negotiations. It goes further to achieve synergies that include services, mutual logistic cost savings and all sorts of other win-wins. An illustrative list of a key account manager's responsibilities is provided in Table 7.5.

Table 7.5 Illustrative List of A Key Account Manager's Responsibilities

Role: To oversee, acquire and maintain enduring relationships of the company with its most important customers and clients by their identifying and understanding the needs and requirements.
Responsibilities are:
1. Develop trust and relationships with a portfolio of major clients and customers and ensure that they do not turn to competition.
2. Acquire a thorough understanding of key customer needs and requirements.
3. Expand the relationships with existing customers by continually proposing solutions that meet their objectives.
4. Ensure that correct products and services are delivered to customers in a timely manner.
5. Serve as the link of communication between key customers and internal teams.
6. Resolve any issues and problems faced by customers and deal with complaints to maintain trust.
7. Play an integral part in generating new sales that will turn into long lasting relationships.
8. Prepare regular reports of progress and forecasts to internal and external stakeholders using the key account metrics.

Changing Role of the Pharma Sales Representative

Information today is easily available thanks to the internet revolution. This means that Pharma sales representatives cannot focus on simply informing about products and selling in the traditional sense of persuading physicians to prescribe their products. The Pharma sales representatives in future will be expected to handle a much larger and more diverse customer base such as prescribers, patients, payers (as private health insurance companies continue to grow). They also need to operate across various engagement channels. Here are some of the important changes that are taking place on the healthcare scenario:

1. The focus of pharmaceutical selling is shifting from volume to value. Pharma sales representatives, therefore, need to understand their role in the evolving sales model and learn to maintain the balance between product promotion and product-related services. Their new role involves less of really selling a product and more of showing how their drug benefits patients and payers (Health Insurance Companies) in ways that go beyond clinical efficacy. They need to demonstrate the value of their drug in terms of patient outcomes and cost-effectiveness. They need to communicate more than pharmacological advantages. They need to demonstrate the benefits of their drug pharmacoeconomically.

2. Slowly but surely, the patient is taking his rightful center stage on the healthcare scene. It is important that Pharma companies learn to keep patient in mind at every step. They need to demonstrate how their products benefit the patient.

3. The focus of the future Pharma sales representatives is not just on how they can visit the doctors, but also on providing the full spectrum of sales and marketing information to doctors through their preferred channels. They need to orchestrate all communication channels including digital to reinforce their interactions with doctors.

The new role will be significantly different in the years to come and it is not just a close cousin of the traditional Pharma Representative as we know now. The new role would be a sum of a trusted advisor to key stakeholders in healthcare such as physicians, patients and payers. To be successful in the changing environment Pharma companies need to reimagine their recruitment, selection and training processes.

Widening Gap

There seems to be a gap that is widening between the needs and wants of the physicians and the deliverability of those by medical representatives. Physicians today have a plethora of online resources to learn about new drugs. Fifty-one percent of physicians surveyed in an e-Pharma study stated that they are already aware of the drug information that medical representatives provide. They expect Pharma representatives to provide information beyond the basics and deliver higher value to their practice. They want to be engaged in a more meaningful and useful scientific dialogue rather than the current detailing that mostly reminds them the brand names and revolves around requesting prescriptions and other commercial transactions. Most medical representatives of today are unable and ill-equipped to meet the physicians' needs in this regard. This is a major gap.

Another major reason for this gap is that while medical community has grown comfortable with digital tools, many pharmaceutical companies have not equipped and trained their sales force with these digital tools. The representatives are unable to engage doctors in terms of how they want, where and when they want. Consequently, both these developments have left doctors extremely dissatisfied and the representatives disillusioned. Decreasing product differentiation in a branded generic and generic-generic market, reduced physician access, inability to communicate effectively - all these factors are making the pharmaceutical representatives feel redundant and irrelevant. If the current marketing practices that are on a path of obsolescence continue, it would be very difficult to regain the preeminent position they enjoyed not very long ago.

From Obsolescence to Relevance

What is the way out? How can pharmaceutical companies regain the trust and respect they once enjoyed? They need to change the course from obsolescence to relevance. They need to make their marketing relevant to the current needs and wants of the physicians. Phanish Chandra, CEO of Docplexus suggests an action-plan in his insightful article, Medical Reps 2.0 - *Reinventing Pharma Field Force in India.*

1. A Sermo survey indicates that 87 percent of doctors would like medical representatives to talk about clinical studies and evidence based medicine. Some of them wished for a more educated and

better trained field force. Pharmaceutical companies, therefore, must re-skill and re-tool existing sales force and hire better qualified people with good knowledge, communication skills, analytical ability, problem solving skills and good personality.

2. Transform your sales force from merely pushing and selling your products to achieve a partnership status with the physician community. Train your medical representatives not only on product knowledge but also on overall organizational strategy and vision. Train them on using the digital tools and social media listening. Your representatives should be able to engage physicians on their terms - where they want to be engaged, when they want to be engaged and how they want to be engaged.

3. When medical profession has become highly speciality oriented, can Pharma lag behind? Rather than have the same set of medical representatives deal with doctors, stockists, retailers and institutions, should not pharmaceutical companies think of nurturing specialists for each segment of customers?

4. If Pharma has to position itself as an equal partner in improving healthcare delivery, then it should adopt a patient-centric strategy. For physicians as well as Pharma, Patient health is the top most priority, nay it is the very purpose for which physicians and Pharma exist. To achieve a partnership status, pharmaceutical companies should assist doctors in their patient education and monitoring efforts. Pharmaceutical companies should also train their representatives in delivering patient-focused services like clinical health educators. That is going beyond the pill.

5. With current high attrition rates among sales force, it is not uncommon for doctors to have a medical representative pushing one brand for a month and then returning to promote a rival brand the next month. High attrition rates do not allow a company to build enduring relationships with its customers. Make retention a priority.

6. In today's rapidly changing and hyper competitive market place, a good product and a thrust on generating its prescriptions Is not enough. Today's physicians expect a much more comprehensive and personalized engagement. Follow a strategy of physicians-first. Go beyond prescription generation. Physician-centricity is no longer an option.

7. Smart Pharm consulting suggests a three-way segmentation of physicians - information seekers, service seekers, and emotion

seekers. Such a classification helps medical representatives tailor their messages according to specific needs of doctors. Delivering what physicians want, where they want, when they want and how they want is crucial for developing an enduring relationship with them.

8. To deliver superior customer experience across its broad group of stakeholders, pharmaceutical companies must ensure coordination between sales and non-sales functions. They should adopt technology that facilitates seamless interaction of sales with related functions such as marketing and medical sales liaison.

9. Make digital technology work for you. It is your medical representative's best friend, not foe. Digitization will be of immense help to your medical representatives in taking their relationship with doctors to the next level by equipping them with analytical insights leading to more fulfilling interactions.

10. Develop and deliver meaningful content that is relevant to the needs of physicians. Doctors seem to be dissatisfied with the type of content that pharmaceutical companies are producing in India. They feel that it is too detailed, time consuming and even misleading. Pharma should develop content that is concise, accurate and easily accessible in digital format.

Summary

Personal selling is one of the most crucial elements of pharmaceutical marketing. The nature of the competition and its intensity in the Indian pharmaceutical market have made personal selling the crucial determinant factor for success that it is today. In a market, where both products and strategies are 'me-too' rather 'me-me-too' in nature, the battle is more between the talents of the different selling teams. A well-trained, highly motivated sales force plays a decisive role in winning the marketing wars.

There is more to personal selling than achieving sales targets. A company's medical representatives are its most important source of communication to its prospective customers. They are also the most important source of feedback regarding customers' perceptions of their products and also of the competitors' activities. They are the most vital two-way communication link between the company and customers. Companies, which perceive this important role of their sales force clearly and focus their attention, efforts and programs to improve the effectiveness of their medical representatives as a source of communication and competitive advantage are sure to win.

There seems to be a gap that is widening between the needs and wants of the physicians and the ability to deliver those by medical representatives. Physicians today have a plethora of online resources to learn about new drugs. They expect pharmaceutical representatives to provide information beyond the basics and deliver higher value to their practice. Unfortunately most medical representatives are unable and ill-equipped to meet the physicians' needs in this regard.

Pharma should change its course from obsolescence to relevance to achieve an equal partnership status in the delivery of better healthcare alongside the physicians. It should re-skill and re-tool its existing sales force and recruit better talent. It should train its field force not only on product knowledge but also on the overall corporate strategy and vision. Medical representatives of today should possess sound product knowledge, good communication skills, analytical abilities, problem solving skills, proficiency in using digital tools and social media listening skills. Pharmaceutical companies should train and equip their representatives on all these areas in order to elevate them from their current selling role to that of a partner in delivering better healthcare.

Another important area that requires immediate attention of pharmaceutical companies is reducing the current high attrition rates among its sales force. You cannot build enduring relationships with customers with such high attrition rates.

The nature of sales force management is changing and challenging. The increasing unionization of medical representatives and the militant attitudes and approaches of some of their associations are causing concern to many managers. These are also making the task of sales force management more challenging than ever before.

Management of industrial relations depends entirely on good interpersonal relations that are based on mutual respect for each others competence and view points. It cannot be based on convenience. What is needed is the creation of assertive climate in an organization. Assertiveness by definition recognizes and appreciates the other person's rights. Assertiveness, therefore, implies mutual respect for each others' rights and value systems. Assertive teams can accomplish any task.

To build a team of assertive, responsible medical representatives, the companies should build a strong team of assertive, responsible, committed and competent team of first-line managers. They should be able to improve the effectiveness of their teams of medical representatives.   For medical representatives are not just the important sources of communication. They are the company's source of competitive advantage!

The Prescription

Symbol of Power! Prime Mover!

When you consider that the prescription of approximately over eight-hundred and fifty thousand doctors in various specialties across the country determine the fate and existence of a chemical entity, would not prescription be a symbol of power?

The small piece of paper containing the prescription of a physician literally can shake the slow-moving or non-moving pharmaceutical products out of their deep slumber on a retailer's shelf and wholesaler's warehouse.

Prescription certainly is the prime mover of goods and services in pharmaceutical marketing.

How would you define the pharmaceutical business? What do you say your business really is? Selling pharmaceuticals? Marketing ethical drugs? Generating prescriptions? Prescription generation is the bull's eye! Prescription generation is the name of the game!

Broad Spectrum of Prescription

What is a prescription may be a simple question. But the answer to that is not so simple or obvious. A prescription has many functions, both apparent and latent. Let us first discuss briefly the different definitions of the prescription.

- The art of compounding defines the prescription as an order written by the physician, dentist, veterinarian, or any other licensed practitioner directing the pharmacist to compound and dispense medication for a patient and usually accompanied by directions for its administration or use.

- Prescription can also refer to the finished product (which is dispensed by a retail chemist or a hospital pharmacist on a physician's prescription).
- Prescription, in its verb form may also refer to the act of issuing the order by the licensed practitioner. A physician may prescribe rest, diet and exercise without giving any medicines on certain occasions.
- Dictionary definition of prescription may refer to the directions for administration.

The most familiar functions of a prescription are that it serves as:

- A means of communication between the physician, patient and the pharmacist.
- Legal authorization for dispensing legend drugs.
- Therapeutic record source
- A method of therapy
- A means of clinical trial

Indeed, the prescription serves a broad spectrum of functions!

Symbolic Power

E. D. Peregrino, a George Town Professor and Bio-ethics founder in his paper, Prescribing and Drug Ingestion: Symbols and Substances, eloquently examined the symbolic importance of the prescription. When you consider this, prescription clearly becomes:

- A visible sign of the physician's power to heal
- An indication of the physician's concern
- A symbol of patient's control
- A symbol of the advancement of modern technology in drug discovery
- Evidence that the physician has fulfilled his contract
- A valuable source of information to the pharmaceutical marketer

Thus we can see that prescription is more than an exchange process. For quite sometime prescriptions have been used to study treatment patterns and predict and analyze markets for various therapeutic categories in a number of countries.

In today's highly competitive pharmaceutical marketing arena, discerning marketers are increasingly concentrating on studying the prescription trends and the prescribing behavior of physicians.

Decision Making

When you think of it, the prescription really is a decision of the physician. A decision, simply stated, is choosing between different alternatives. The alternatives or options available to a physician are whether to prescribe or not and if the decision is to prescribe, then what therapy to prescribe, what drug, which brand etc.

Rational or Emotional?

If prescription is a decision, is it a rational decision of the physician or an emotional one? Marketers have been rather obsessed with the classification and study of the decision making process into two broad categories - rational and emotional.

A rational buyer, as the name suggests, makes his purchase theoretically at least, in a logical manner, with clear-cut objectives before him. He evaluates all the alternatives available and matches his needs with the need-satisfying capabilities of the product and makes his decision accordingly. The emotional buyer, on the contrary, may be swayed away by product attributes or advertising appeals, that may not have anything to do with the actual need-satisfying properties of the product.

A word of caution, however. There is a tendency to equate the rational buying with intelligent buying and the emotional buying with irrational or unintelligent buying. It may be noted that more often than not, rational buying and emotional buying may occur together.

Take the case of a physician deciding on prescribing in an acute case of urinary tract infection (UTI). He has decided on giving a course of a newly introduced antibiotic, norfloxacin. He has chosen this new antibiotic not because it is the latest and most expensive, or as a matter of therapeutic fashion. He has weighed all the pros and cons. Firstly, it is a case of acute UTI. He needs a potent, effective antibiotic. Secondly, sensitivity tests indicated that the organism responsible for the infection is resistant to a number of widely used broad-spectrum antibiotics like tearacycline, ampicillin, cephalexin, doxycycline etc. Norfloxacin is a new antibiotic, potent and broad-spectrum, and has a high cure rate in UTI. His choice, therefore, is logical and rational in choosing a therapy i.e., a course of norfloxacin.

But, when it comes to selecting a particular brand of norfloxacin it is quite possible that his decision may be more emotional and less rational. It may depend upon a number of factors like the confident, pleasant mannered, friendly, persuasive medical representative, reputation of a company, easy to remember brand name and many other factors that may not be directly related to the need-satisfying properties of the product. That brings us to the subject of prescriber motivation, which has always been eluding the pharmaceutical marketer.

Prescribing Process

Every decision involves the selection of the best among the alternatives available. Therefore, by definition a decision, in the process, causes some amount of stress, tension or disequilibria for the individual, who has to make a decision. No doubt, this stress is transient and is limited to the point of decision making. Once the decision is made and the goal accomplished the individual is relieved.

Prescription too is a decision, and an important one at that. The physician is very much concerned with the wellbeing of his patient and therefore tries to select the best possible therapy and drug for treatment. Naturally, he has to process all the information he receives from various sources and selects the best suited drug for accomplishing his goal of treating the particular ailment that his patient has been suffering from.

Prescription is a reflection of a physician's ultimate selection of a drug. It is never a simple operation involving only a symptom and treatment, intended to relieve the symptom and cure the ailment. There are a number of components involved in the process. Some of the important variables in the prescribing process are:

A. Clinical manifestations and behavioral characteristics of the patient

B. Needs and expectations of the patient regarding treatment such as expectations and attitudes towards the physician, use of medication etc.

C. The level of knowledge, expertise and training of the treating physician

D. Organizational impact on the doctor-patient relationship. For example, the doctor-patient relationship and the consequent sets of mutual expectations are likely to vary in the organizational context of a government hospital, a large private hospital, a nursing home and a clinic.

Prescriber Motivation

What motivates the physician to prescribe a particular drug? What factors influence the prescribing decision process of the physician?

While the prescriber's drug selection process can be like any consumer's purchasing decision, it is distinctly different on two major counts. One is that there are more number of input variables. The other major aspect to be considered is that a physician's decision to prescribe involves a very high degree of responsibility and concern towards his patients' well being.

There are over a hundred studies done abroad and a handful of studies in India that attempted to find answer to the specific question - what motives physicians to select a specific drug? How does he choose what he chooses?

Here is a brief summary of the observations, propositions, postulations and findings of some of the more important studies:

1. Physicians use and rely more on professional sources like colleagues, while treating difficult conditions, particularly where effects of drug therapy are less clearly defined.

2. Physicians tend to treat wealthier patients with newer and more expensive drugs.

3. Positive attributes that are likely to influence drug adoption by physicians are social reward, consistency of therapeutic response, and relative advantage. Negative factors influencing the prescribing behavior are risk and high continuing cost of therapy.

4. Specialists and well-informed doctors with large practices, who are socially active, use new drugs early in the course of treatment and may be better prescribers (Innovators and early majority).

5. Education appears to influence the quality of prescribing positively.

6. Colleagues do have a positive influence on prescribing, but their influence is secondary to other factors such as education, advertising and promotion by drug companies.

7. Physicians in medical college hospitals sought more drug information than their counterparts in smaller hospitals.

8. Advertising and promotion by pharmaceutical companies is an important source of information on new drugs.

9. Most of the drug choices a physician makes through his prescriptions are habitual.

Scientific or Commercial?

Which sources or information do the physicians in their decision making consider more important? Scientific sources? Or commercial sources? Scientific sources include editorial contents of medical journals, articles published in medical journals, other physicians, clinical pharmacologists and other research publications. Commercial sources include product information monographs, and literature published by pharmaceutical companies, advertisements in medical journals, detail talks by medical representatives, clinical trial reports, seminars and other symposia conducted by the drug companies. Which out of these do physicians perceive as a credible source and as more important?

One study involving about one hundred physicians conducted to determine the roles of various information sources in influencing the prescribing behavior of the physicians revealed that promotional information by pharmaceutical companies (commercial sources) plays a greater role in the decision process of the physicians to prescribe the drugs than even the scientific sources of information. More than two-thirds (68 percent) of the physicians in the study indicated that either representatives, journal advertising or direct mail advertising led to their prescriptions, where as only 32 percent of the physicians mentioned that scientific sources of information were responsible for their prescriptions.

A summary of the findings of the study is presented in Table 8.1.

Table 8.1 Relative Importance of Information Variables

Source of Information	Per cent of Physicians
Medical Representatives	46
Medical Journal Articles	32
Medical Journal Advertising	12
Direct Mail Advertising	10
Other Doctors	8
Staff Meetings	6
National Conventions	5
Other Sources	3

It is apparent from the studies on prescribing behavior that physicians use drug information from various sources. They seem to rely on certain sources more than others at certain stages of the decision making process while selecting a particular drug. The weightage and importance they give to the source of information, therefore, seems different at different stages of the drug selection process. Consider this scenario:

A physician becomes aware of a particular drug through a pharmaceutical company advertisement or journal articles. Interest is aroused when he encounters clinical situations warranting the use of the drug or an increased frequency of the reporting on the drug.

Discussion on the usage of the drug by his peers may also enhance his interest in the drug. Subsequently, at some point, the physician decides to consider the drug for use and starts the evaluation process. It is at the evaluation stage that the physician looks for a third party endorsement and seeks more information necessary for weighing pros and cons and for doing a cost-benefit (or risk-benefit) analysis related to the drug's use.

If all the information received is positive, he may try the drug on a few patients. If the outcomes of these trails are also positive the physician may continue the use of the drug in more patients. Continuous positive reinforcement thus ensures continuous usage of the drug, leading to regular prescribing of the drug by the physician.

Convenience and availability of information sources are two important factors to be considered in influencing the physician's prescribing behavior. Physicians place a high value on convenience and availability of information. Pharmaceutical companies have recognized this fact long ago and orient their advertising and promotional campaigns around the physician's office. They make prescribing information on their products available to the physician within his office. They reach the physician through different media like direct mail, product monographs, clinical research abstracts and full text articles on their products, well-trained medical representatives, samples, attractive give-aways etc. to induce trial and usage. The major advantages of the drug industry's information programs are that they are convenient and free. The only criticism against it is that it may be biased. Pharmaceutical companies can however attempt to overcome this by designing their communication package in a more objective manner.

New Drug Adoption by Physicians:
A Two Step Approach

The study of new drug adoption by physicians, particularly in India involves two steps. This is particularly important for pharmaceutical marketers in India, since the basic research effort is very minimal and consequently 'new-to-the-world' drugs are scarce. The moment a new drug is discovered elsewhere in the world, it is launched by more than one company in India in quick succession. The new drug launch thus is virtually a 'me-too'-new-drug launch. It is this simultaneous introduction of the same new drug (the same new molecule or the generic drug) by various companies that makes pharmaceutical marketing in India a totally different ball game as compared to the highly regulated markets in North America, Western Europe and Japan. This, however is changing gradually after India recognized the product patents in 2005.

The marketing tasks involved here are two-fold. Firstly, the marketer has to facilitate the new drug adoption process by physicians at the molecule level. Secondly, he should ensure adoption of his brand of the newly adopted drug in preference to competing brands within that molecule or generic drug category. The strategy, tactics and the relative emphasis on the promotional elements at each of the different stages would obviously be different for the new drug adoption and new brand adoption.

The pharmaceutical marketer may have to adopt a rational approach - a strong, reason why communication to convince the physician to accomplish the new drug adoption. This is the vital first step. The second logical step is to gain the preference of the physician towards his brand of the newly adopted or accepted drug. The motivating factors behind these steps could be different.

We have already discussed that the basic motivations behind a physician's choice of drug therapy must be considered rational. On the other hand the physician's choice of a brand of the drug (which he has already selected) could be based on certain emotional criteria also and need not necessarily be a rational approach alone.

Communication Hierarchy

The Adoption Process

The communication objectives for the new drug adoption and new brand adoption are different. To get to the root of the difference, a brief discussion on communication hierarchy would be helpful. The widely accepted communication hierarchy in any buying process tells us that the consumer moves from a number of stages - be it an idea or a tangible product. These stages are:

- Unawareness
- Awareness
- Understanding
- Comprehension
- Liking
- Preference
- Conviction
- Action

The consumer passes through these stages every time he makes a purchasing decision. These stages are not isolated. They are on a continuum. All these stages may not be elaborate, apparent, and obvious. It depends on the type of purchasing decision and the extent of stakes involved for the consumer. The marketer through his skillful and creative communication strategy attempts to make the movement of the consumer as swift and as sure as possible. These stages may appear condensed or sandwiched at times. They may not be visible but certainly they are all there in every buying decision we make. The discerning marketer would also realize that these stages include both rational and emotional components. All these elements concerned with knowledge and information can broadly be grouped under rational elements. The emotional elements include all other aspects concerned with liking, preference and action.

Compare this with the physician's new drug adoption process we discussed earlier. Physician's decision process on the selection of a new drug includes the following stages:

- Awareness
- Interest
- Evaluation
- Trial
- Adoption

These stages are similar to those in the communication hierarchy model we discussed earlier. On closer examination, one would observe that the physician's new drug adoption model is a more rational model of decision-making. The marketing implications of these should be clear by now. Since the physician's choice of drug therapy is more rational, the task of marketing communication should be to convince the doctor regarding the new drug, its superiority and advantages over the current line of therapy. The orientation therefore, is relatively more technical and product-oriented. The product claims should be substantiated with the results of clinical trials, success rate etc. to reinforce confidence in the new drug. The importance of this becomes clear when we understand that every time a physician chooses a new drug, he is obviously taking a risk. That is why he should be given all the reassurance and confidence that one can. It is possible only when you have all relevant details backed by evidence. That is the first vital step.

Having gained his acceptance and conviction regarding the choice of the new drug, the second crucial step is to make the physician prefer your brand of the new drug selected and more importantly to get him to act. To prescribe. This step is second only in terms of sequence and not in terms of importance. This step may often be simultaneous. There need not be any time-lag between the first step and second step.

The preference or the new brand adoption have certain emotional components in the decision making process of the physician unlike the new drug adoption process. Favorable predisposition towards the company in general, his experience with the company's earlier products, his response to advertising communications, his opinions and attitudes towards the company's medical representatives and their persuasive power - all those factors are likely to influence his choice of a brand considerably.

There are a number of new drugs like naproxen, piroxicam, cimetidine, ketoprofen, which were very successful abroad, where they were discovered, but failed to take-off in India. It is not that these drugs were not needed in India. In fact, these drugs were substantially advanced alternatives for many of the drugs being used in the respective therapeutic groups at that time. What could be the reasons? Here is a possible explanation or reason.

These new drugs, which were very successful abroad, were discovered abroad and marketed by the companies that discovered them. These companies had gone whole hog with their irrefutable evidence and convinced the physicians in those countries regarding the superiority of these new drugs over the current line of therapy. They had also gained, as a result, acceptance and preference of their brands of the new drugs. The drug choice and brand preferences were almost simultaneous in the western world, where international patent law is recognized. There are very few brands available with the same generic drug. The competition is more at the choice of the generic drug level itself and not so much between different brands of the same new molecule or drug. This is because in the first-world markets, a patented new molecule is marketed as a brand exclusively till the patent expires. The molecule and the brand are one. Only the names differ in the sense the molecule has a chemical name, and a brand name is simpler catchy name. Only on patent expiry do other generics enter the market. Whereas in India, the competition is almost always between different brands of the same drug. Moreover, none of the companies that discovered these drugs were the first to introduce them in India. Some of the companies that discovered these drugs did not introduce them in India at all. As a result, the companies that introduced these drugs earliest in the country may not have had the same degree of commitment, pride, conviction, detailed documentation of research results, as those companies that discovered these drugs would have. That is why and how, the companies that introduced drugs in India have probably not exploited the opportunities completely. Instead they could only tap the peripheral segments of the physician populations, like innovators and early adopters, whose awareness and acceptance of anything new and worthwhile are naturally high. These companies probably have not persisted adequately to gain a firm conviction in the minds of prescribing physicians. Instead, these companies probably have got a tiny, insignificant share of the prescriptions more out of the novelty element than on conviction. That explains why these new drugs never took-off in the Indian market despite a definite need for similar products (those therapeutic groups were rapidly growing) and despite their overwhelming success abroad. The following cases would further amplify this point.

Case 8.1   Fasigyn Gives A Shot-in-the-arm to Tinidazole!

Tinidazole, an anti-amoebic drug, was introduced some years ago by a number of companies in India. Some of the companies that introduced tinidazole in India were considerably large in size and known for their marketing skills. But, tinidazole, after an initial spurt in prescriptions and sales, began to plateau rather prematurely. It could not stand against the mighty metronidazole and its combinations, which accounted for over two-thirds of the anti-amoebic market in the late 1980s. Pfizer, the company that discovered the drug - tinidazole, could not introduce it earlier in India due to certain government regulations applicable to multinationals. Later Pfizer, after diluting its equity to attain non-FERA status under the then Foreign Exchange Regulation Act, introduced tinidazole, its research product in India under the brand name Fasigyn.

The introduction of Fasigyn, if the initial response was any indicator, gave tinidazole a much-needed shot-in-the-arm. The tinidazole market, which was hitherto not progressing, has all of sudden become buoyant.

Pfizer quickly gained the conviction of the prescribing physicians regarding the superiority of tinidazole over other amoebicides in the first place and gained preference to its Fasigyn brand of tinidazole. The two-step approach of new drug adoption and new brand adoption could be seen at work.

Tinidazole had found at long last an ardent spokesman, an advocate in Pfizer, its discoverer, to gain a firm foothold in the physicians' minds. Other companies who had been marketing tinidazole so far, were quick to realize that the drug was gaining conviction among the prescribing doctors and joined the tinidazole bandwagon with renewed promotional effort and communications strategies aimed at gaining brand preference. The result? A resilient tinidazole market with a number of tinidazole brands showing rapid growth apart from Fasigyn, which moved to the brand leadership position within a very short period showing a very progressive trend!

Case 8.2 Pioneer Fails to Take Off!

Cimetidine, the popular anti-ulcer drug is an original research product of Smith Kline Corporation, Philadelphia. The drug was indeed a pioneer among the H2 receptor antagonists. Tagamet, Smith Kline's brand of cimetidine had reached a preeminent position the world's largest selling prescription drug before it was dislodged from that position by another H2 receptor antagonist, ranitidine, a research product of Glaxo, U.K. Zantac was the brand name.

When Cimetidine was introduced in India, the government did not allow brand names for new single-ingredient drug formulations. Eskayef, the subsidiary of Smith Kline Corporation in India (GSK now) could not introduce the drug due to government regulations covering multinationals. A number of Indian drug companies introduced cimetidine under the generic name in India. The doctors, who were aware of cimetidine quickly took up the product. The product was picking up in prescriptions and sales but its progress was no way comparable to the success that it had achieved in the first world markets, where product patents were recognized and brand names were allowed.

Subsequently, due to a stay order of the Supreme Court of India in the mid 1980s, even the new single ingredient formulations were allowed to be marketed with brand names. All companies marketing cimetidine christened their products appropriately.

In the meantime, Zantac brand of ranitidine by Glaxo (GSK now) was remaking history in the anti-ulcer market worldwide. As soon as ranitidine was cleared for marketing in India, a number of companies including Glaxo had introduced their respective brands of the drug. Glaxo had gone all out to make their Zantac brand of ranitidine (Glaxo used a phonetically similar but a different brand name Zinetec in India) the leader in the fast growing anti-ulcer market in India. Ranitidine did not face any competition from its arch-rival cimetidine in India, against, which it had to fight with all its might in the rest of the world.

Instead, the competition in India was centered around different brands of ranitidine. This is because cimetidine did not really gain the conviction of the prescribing physicians. Had Eskayef introduced their Tagamet brand in India before the introduction of ranitidine, probably cimetidine would have found a spokesman and strong advocate for itself. But then, Eskayef had introduced their brand of cimetidine very late and after the introduction of Glaxo's Zantac brand of Ranitidine.

It was rather too late for Tagamet to make any impact! The reason why cimetidine, the pioneer among the H2 receptor antagonists, did not even take off in India was that - even before the drug was adopted by prescribing physicians, its marketers in India shifted the competitive focus to brand preference. The brand preference in the case of cimetidine was literally the company preference, as brand names were not allowed at the time of its introduction. Cimetidine never really gained a firm conviction and a strong foot-hold in the prescribing doctor's mind.

Case 8.3   Zinetec's Cakewalk!

The success of Glaxo's ranitidine brand of Zantac is all too familiar to the pharmaceutical marketers the world over. Zantac quickly marched forward to become the first-ever prescription drug to cross the coveted US $ 1-billion mark in the world.

In India, Glaxo was one of the earliest companies to introduce ranitidine, the world famous anti-ulcer drug. Glaxo had put a never-before-kind of promotional effort towards gaining the conviction of the doctors regarding the superiority of ranitidine over cimetidine and then their preference for Zinetec brand of ranitidine.

The result of this well-orchestrated two-step approach towards gaining the conviction of the prescribing physicians in the new drug adoption and the subsequent preference of the brand Zinetec over others is brand leadership with almost one-quarter of the Indian anti-ulcer market under its belt!

Conquering the Indian anti-ulcer market was a relatively tame affair for Glaxo, for neither cimetidine nor Tagamet were a force to reckon with in India. The real growth of the anti-ulcer market started only with the advent of ranitidine and Zinetec in India. From that point, winning the anti-ulcer market in India had been literally a cakewalk for Zinetec!

Physicians' Brand Choice

What factors do physicians consider as more important while deciding on prescribing a new product? A study involving about one-hundred physicians revealed the following (Table 8.2).

Table 8.2 Factors Influencing Physicians' Choice

Factors Responsible	Per cent
1. Superior Therapeutic Merit	61.0
2. Ease of Administration	11.1
3. General Merit of Product or Ingredient (Generic Drug)	8.3
4. Absence of Side Effects	5.6
5. Price	5.6
6. Confidence in Manufacturer	2.8
7. All Other Motivating Factors	5.6

Accentuate the Positive

Apparently the physician's choice tends to accentuate the positive. Negative characteristics of the product seem to be relegated to secondary importance. The reasons for these are not difficult to understand. There is a very high degree of awareness regarding the safety profile of a product today more than ever before. Furthermore, prescription drugs are prescribed to achieve a predetermined therapeutic end. Whether the drug prescribed by the physician achieves this predetermined therapeutic objective (relief or cure depending on the condition of the patient as well as the drug) or fails to achieve it will determine to some extent the patient's evaluation of the abilities of the physician. For this reason, the performance of the prescribed medication is of paramount importance in the total treatment regimen.

Company Preference

When you consider the fact that every new drug prescribing decision is a threat to both the doctor and the patient, the importance of the company preference as a factor influencing the new drug adoption becomes clearer. The major concern involved in this is the safety margin and the possible incidence of side effects. On the other hand the physician is inclined to treat his patients with the best possible and the most advanced therapy, despite the uncertainty and risks.

The natural tendency of the rational decision making physician is to seek all available information concerning the new drug. The information sources are really wide ranging, and equally wide ranging is the credibility of different sources. The physician, ideally is expected to prefer only the unimpeachable sources to obtain the required information. But in practice the producer of the drug itself provides the major part of the information regarding the new drug to the physician. Therefore, confidence in the manufacturer, both as a producer of the drug and also as a reliable source of information, would be an important factor in influencing the physician's choice of the new drug. Confidence and credibility in the manufacturer would lead to preference of the manufacturer as well.

Studying the Prescribing Behavior

Regular, continuous study of the prescribing behavior of physicians is essential for the pharmaceutical marketer. He can formulate winning strategies only when he understands the prescribing behavior and the prescription habits of physicians. The intense competition in the Indian pharmaceutical industry implies that practicing physicians are exposed constantly to various competing stimuli. The prescribing behavior of doctors too, as a result, undergoes frequent, rapid changes. This makes the continuous study of prescribing behavior of physicians rather mandatory. But how does one go about the study of prescribing behavior? A number of studies conducted in this area revealed that:

- There is a marked relationship between the personal preference for the company and the preference given for a given drug for both mild and severe conditions.
- Preference for a given company may predispose to trying out a new product, but will not necessarily influence use for any prolonged period after the introduction of the drug.
- The preference for a given company will predispose the physician not only towards trying the product, but also towards preferring it.

It is obvious that one should know the prescription habits of doctors and their prescribing behavior, to do anything with the marketing of ethical or prescription drugs. But then, you cannot go to a doctor and ask the doctor about his opinion regarding a particular line of therapy or what he would prescribe to a 50-year old male patient suffering from acute bronchitis. Of course, no one can prevent you from asking such questions. The doctors too, may respond to your questions in a favorable manner and even enthusiastically. Nothing could be more useless than the information obtained in that manner. What you get as responses to such questions are mere intentions and not necessarily the truth or what they (the doctors) would have really done. The medical profession is a knowledge-based science and it presupposes a minimum amount of expertise and knowledge for every practicing doctor. Thus there is certainly a certain amount of homogeneity among doctors as far as knowledge component is concerned. The differences tend to surface in the application area. The gap between intention and practice increases proportionately with the increase in knowledge. The more knowledgeable we are, the more we tend to express our intentions. Therefore, when you ask doctors some hypothetical questions, you get some hypothetical answers based on what they intend to rather than what they actually do. That is why one should actually study the prescribing behavior by observing the actual prescriptions. Not the intended prescriptions. This should not be treated as one-time exercise. Prescriptions should be studied continuously. This is necessary because a doctor's prescribing behavior changes as competing stimuli change. What else can any one except in the dynamic market place other than change? You can expect change, but you cannot predict it. That makes it all the more necessary to study the changing prescribing behavior on a continuous basis. To prepare yourself to face the challenge of change. Remember what the revered military strategist and the famous Chinese general Sun Tzu said? *Forewarned is forearmed*!

Six Honest Serving Men!

In marketing research asking the right questions is more important than obtaining right answers, because there is no such thing as a right or wrong answer. The question, however, should be right in the sense that should elicit a response that could be used as an information input in formulating strategies. By this token, Rudyard Kipling must have been a very good marketing researcher too, apart from being a celebrated author, for once he wrote," *I have six honest serving men. They tell me all I need to know about everything I want to know. Their names are: what, when, where, who, how and why.*"

This six-man army is what every marketing researcher would dream of and die for.

Why do people do what they do is a question that has been plaguing psychoanalysts, psychiatrists and psychologists alike for ages. No one seems to have a found a satisfying answer. There are different schools of thought and the only thing that is common among all of them is that they disagree with each other. Marketing researchers in the pharmaceutical industry are often intrigued to find an answer to this rather enigmatic question. It is futile to ask this question, because even the doctor, who prescribes would not be able to answer the why part of the question. What you get when you attempt it is a rational explanation rather than a real answer. Instead, one can find out the answers for the who, what, when, where, which, whom questions are, and then infer why the doctor has probably prescribed.

That answer would be more dependable than any other, because it is based answers obtained for the other questions through the observation of behavior. And not by asking and knowing the intentions. Intentions cannot be observed. Behavior can be observed. Behavior can be compared. Behavior can be measured. Attitudes and intentions cannot be measured.

Prescription Research: Key Questions

Now that we agree that the only way of studying the physician's prescribing behavior is by observing it in action, let us discuss the key questions and find out how the answers to these questions can be used to formulate winning product strategies.

The small piece of paper called the prescription is virtually a gold mine of information. If you dig carefully enough, long enough (perseverance) and deep enough (probe), you are sure to strike rich rewards.

Here is a checklist of some of the important questions to be answered by the prescription research findings. The answers would serve as very useful inputs for formulating profitable product strategies.

Who Questions
- Who is prescribing my brand?
- General practitioner? Gynecologist?
- Pediatrician? Surgeon? Any other specialist?
- Is he a young doctor? Middle aged or elderly doctor?
- Male doctor or female doctor?

What Questions
- What does the doctor prescribe my brand for?
- What are the indications?
- What is the diagnosis?
- What dosage schedule does the doctor recommend for my brand?
- What type of practice does the doctor have?
- Dispensing? Prescribing?
- What is the frequency of his prescriptions of my brand? Regular? Occasional?

Where Questions
- Where does the doctor prescribe my brand?
- At hospital? At his clinic?
- In the out-patient department? In the ward?

When Questions

- When does the doctor prescribe my brand?
- In acute condition? In chronic condition?
- As a prophylactic? As a first-line therapy? As a second-line of treatment?

Which Questions

- Which other brands does the doctor prescribe when he prescribes my brand?
- Which other products does the doctor prescribe with my brand (co-prescribe)?
- Which competitor is gaining from my brand?
- Which competitor is losing to my brand?

Whom Questions

- To whom does the doctor prescribe my brand?
- To young patients? To middle-aged patients or elderly patients?
- To children? Infants? To male patients? To female patients?

From the answers to these who, what, where, when, which and whom questions, one can find out how the doctor has been prescribing one's product as compared to other competing products. Based on this one can infer why the doctor probably has been prescribing the way he does. This information indeed is an invaluable input for strategic marketing. In fact, it is indispensable. Prescription drug marketing cannot simply do away with it.

Analytical Framework

To convert the mass of prescription data into information and to use it as a strategic input for decision making, here are some simple guidelines. It can also be a frame work for analysis.

All the questions and answers of our prescription research can broadly be grouped into three categories:

A. **People-related:** People-related questions and answers cover all the areas pertaining to prescribers (intermediary customers) and patients (consumers). Based on this information we can sketch the profiles of - prescribers as well as patients for our products, which is a valuable input for deciding on segmentation strategies.

B. **Product-related:** Product-related questions and answers will tell us how the prescribers as compared to our competitors' products are prescribing our product. This feedback is very important as it enables us to find out any perceptual gaps that may exist with respect to our products, so that timely reinforcement or modification can be made.

C. **Performance-related:** Performance in terms of prescription response feedback and the extent of competitive sharpness or lack of it, is crucial to make necessary improvements or modifications in our strategic and tactical plans.

Ambivalent Attitude

The attitude towards prescription research of the pharmaceutical marketing practitioners in India can be described at best as one of ambivalence. There are of course, exceptions to this. You ask the person involved in some manner or other with pharmaceutical marketing to define the pharmaceutical business in one sentence. Almost everyone without exception will either say or agree on a two word answer - prescription generation. They surely hit the bull's eye in so far as answering this question is concerned. But when it comes to practice, they seem to be preoccupied with many other things to generate sales now, somehow, putting off the prescription generation aspect to tomorrow. It is not due to lack of awareness or knowledge that prescription generation is the essence of pharmaceutical marketing. What is it then? Is it lack of conviction? Or excessive, almost myopic preoccupation with sales? Whatever it is, there seems to be a perceptual gap resulting in an ambivalent attitude towards prescription generation. The gap is between words and deeds, conviction and action and between intention and behavior. Marketing folklore abounds in examples of such ambivalence. Consider the folklore and facts.

Prescription Generation: Folklore and Facts

Folklore #1

Prescription generation is of course important. Monitoring the retailers regularly will give me the necessary feedback whether there are adequate prescriptions or not for my products. I can accordingly step up the promotional efforts for my products.

Fact

While retail monitoring is important, that would provide feedback only to the extent of giving a very rough idea of the movement of your products vis-a-vis your competitors' products. This information by itself cannot serve as an input for formulating your strategy. It does not give you a complete picture of your prescriber profile (detailed account of the prescriber of your product), patient profile and also the response profile (how your products are being perceived by the prescriber when he prescribes it). All these are very essential information inputs for formulating profitable product strategies.

Folklore #2

If sales of my products are steadily and continually growing, that clearly indicates that my prescriptions are increasing. Only when my sales are declining I should really be concerned with my prescriptions because that may be a storm signal.

Fact

Increasing sales need not necessarily be indicating increase in prescriptions. On the contrary, it may cause complacency or a false sense of well being. Sales can be increased by a number of ways even when the prescriptions are declining. Such a myopic view would only lead to disaster because by the time one realizes that the prescriptions declining, it may be too late to take any corrective action. On the other hand if prescriptions are increasing, sales should certainly be increasing. If the increase in prescriptions is not reflecting a proportionate increase in sales that is indicative of some untapped or unexploited opportunity and calls for a detailed investigation.

Folklore #3

My product has a very good OTC profile. Therefore, prescription analysis is not very important for this product.

Fact

Nothing could be more shortsighted. As long as one is marketing a prescription drug, prescription research cannot be dispensed with. How did your product gain this OTC profile in the first place? How did it develop such a franchise with the patient population and the consuming public? Chances are that 9.9 times out of ten, your product would have been leading on the prescription front during the years when it was developing an OTC profile. OTC profile has been acquired in product category after category in the Indian pharmaceutical industry by the brands that were largely prescribed. The brands that were leading on the prescription front were the same brands that were leading on the OTC front. Over time, some brands that were having considerable OTC profile, when taken off from active promotion, continued to show increase in sales, but prescription support started declining before long. Subsequently their OTC profile too has become weaker resulting in premature plateau of their sales growth.

When you examine clearly enough, you will observe that prescription support gives the OTC profile of a brand the much-needed back-up power. Call it confidence, reassurance or what you will, prescription power is what reinforces OTC profile both with the trade and the consuming public. Consider the leading brands in the Indian pharmaceutical market like (in the 1980s) Becosules, Benadryl Expectorant, Phensidyl, Avil, Crocin, Betnovate etc. They all had strong prescription base being the leaders in their respective categories and growing above the market growth rate on the prescription front. They all had a very strong OTC profile at the same time.

Summary

That the prescription is the single most important element to be studied in pharmaceutical marketing is universally recognized and accepted. Yet the attitude of many a pharmaceutical marketing practitioner towards the study of prescription research can be described as ambivalent. The purpose of this chapter is to bridge that perceptual gap and turn the ambivalence to active participation.

No Magic Formula!

Apparently there is no magic formula that can enhance or accelerate the rate of prescription generation. But the active ingredients of successful prescription generation are universally acknowledged. They are: precise positioning backed by relevant segmentation strategy and tactics, perceptible product differentiation, creative communication that is target-specific and above all persuasive detailing by the medical representatives. What is probably missing in this success formula is the relative weightage that is to be given to each of these elements or the exact strengths or concentrations in which, each of these ingredients should be mixed.

Prescription research can provide insights into these areas. What is more important than everything else is the firm conviction that increased prescription generation is the only way to successful pharmaceutical marketing. A conviction that is devoid of any preoccupations with shortcuts and short-sighted approaches, or missing-the-forest-for-tree syndromes. That is the secret of success. The real magic formula is not significantly different from the one suggested by the great inventor - Thomas Alva Edison, who gave the recipe for genius long ago. Prescription generation can successfully be enhanced to any level with two percent imagination and 98 percent perspiration!

Policy

Aware—! Alert! Adapt!

The nation's legal and political environments have a profound effect on a firm's marketing decisions. Marketing practitioners should have a thorough understanding of the laws of the land pertaining to their business operations. They should understand public policy in general and industrial policy (related to the industry in which they are competing) in particular. They should be aware of the legislation protecting consumers' rights and interests and observe laws forbidding certain business practices. Marketers must also be alert to anticipate the likely shifts in public policy and respond to consumer complaints. A country's legal environment is one of the strongest forces that marketing decision makers must face. It consists of a number laws and even more interpretations that regulate, control and compel business to operate under competitive conditions and observe consumer rights. Marketers have to adapt themselves in formulating their company policies within the framework of the legal and regulatory environment prevailing. The best policy regarding policy matters is to be Aware, Alert and Adapt!

Taken for Granted?

Policy, probably is one of the most often used and the least-understood words in the English language in the complete sense of the word. If not, it is probably taken for granted. Consider these not-so-unfamiliar situations:

- A front-line manager telling a recalcitrant sales representative, whom he was unable to convince, why one should not take leave immediately after a sales conference, that it is a matter of *company policy.*

- A not-so-confident representative trying to placate an agitated retailer demanding the reason why damaged goods are not being replaced by the company by stating that it is not his *company policy.*
- An accounts assistant with a patronizing look telling the supplier's representative who has been frequenting him rather helplessly to collect payment for the material supplied, that it is not the *company policy* to release payments before time.

Situations like these are many. What do you think is the meaning of policy in situations like these? Buck-passing? A shelter or cover for giving excuses?

Why is that policy is often taken for granted? Why is that even employees refer to policy cynically? Why this indifference to policy?

What is a Policy?

The dictionary defines policy as any overall plan of action adopted by the government, business or a political party designed to influence and determine immediate and long term decisions or actions; a course of action, guiding principle or procedure considered to be expedient, prudent, shrewd or sagacious in practical terms.

The meaning and scope of policy are much broader than is being perceived. This perceptual gap has to be bridged. In practice *policy* is being reduced to a mere *procedure*. A policy manual, if a company has it, degenerates largely into a rule book.

Policy can be a pathway within which, an employee moves towards an objective. Policies are broad guidelines for achieving the organizational goals and they encompass all the functional departments of the organization. Procedures are laid down to ensure that all employees who have to work within the framework of the policy understand the broad guidelines of policy. In other words, to implement the policy, procedures are not and can never be a substitute for a policy.

How can you change, transform, or turn the prevailing indifferent attitude towards policy to one of deference? In other words, what should be your policy on policy?

A thorough understanding and examination of the concept of policy is essential before we proceed further. Policy is considered as a broad guideline within which employees of a particular firm can act towards discharging their tasks according to the western management school of thought. Western mangers consider *policies* more often than not, as short cuts to thinking in the sense that when considering alternatives, an employee can automatically exclude those matters that are outside the designated areas.

In some areas, where a policy is not determined or thought earlier, it is *precedence* that guides the further policy decisions. Therefore, *policy* is considered as some guidelines that are necessary to grease the wheels of organizations without consuming the top management time in the operational problems which are of routine in nature. Compare it with the meaning and implications that the same word has in Japanese management and to Japanese managers. It presents a totally contrasting picture.

Policy in Japanese Management

The term policy is used in Japan to describe long and medium-range management orientations as well as annual goals or targets. Furthermore, policy is used to describe both goals and measures. Policy thus suggests both ends and means.

Goals are established at the corporate level by top management in terms of sales, profits and market share. Measures or the means are the specific action plans and programs to achieve these goals. Goals should be specific, otherwise they become mere slogans. The top management determines both the goals and measures and deploys them down the line, throughout the organization. Top management involves the line management down the line according to their relevance.

Another important aspect to be considered in such *policy deployment* strategy is the recognition, appreciation and involvement of the cross functional departments and their roles. Implementation of corporate policies obviously transcends the boundaries of functional areas in an organization. The goal-setting process by the top management is based on a series of consultations with the mangers down the line. The line managers too are thus involved in working out the details of measurement and formulating the annual goals. Line managers feel that they are the owners of these policy decisions. It is this process of internalization that ensures the highest level of implementation. The basis for setting these goals and criteria for measuring them is of course, past performance.

Once top management determines the goals for the next year and the subsequent five years, they are deployed throughout the lower levels of management. Sub-goals are determined for every business unit and specific action programs for each department are set. However skillful and thoughtful your policy formulation at the top management level may be, unless they are implemented and put to practical use by the managers down the line they are no better than castles in the air.

As the policies are transferred down the line, the broad statements become more specific, actionable programs with precise, measurable objectives. This indicates the top management commitment and determination to internalize the process.

The next most important aspect of management policies in Japanese companies is that they create an atmosphere for promoting a very high degree of teamwork. The policy formulation, statement and programs transcend the functional areas. For example, the product policy aims to improve quality, reduce cost, and ensure timely delivery of new product as well existing products. Thus policy crosses the functional boundaries and is deployed to quality assurance, finance, manufacturing, materials department, engineering department and product management. All these departments set specific, measurable targets leading to the achievement of the overall objectives of product policy decisions.

Deploying and Internalizing the Policy

Policy deployment and involvement of management at all levels in the formulation of policies is necessary to achieve firm commitment of all employees towards its implementation. The whole process has to be internalized. Unless employees of an organization are made to feel that they *own* the policy decisions, they will not show deference to the policies.

Indifferent attitude towards policy clearly indicates lack of conviction. Implementation of the policy without conviction reduces the credibility of the organization among its customers, work force, creditors, debtors etc. To achieve a higher degree of responsibility and commitment towards policy implementation by employees, the organization has to:

- Involve the managers and employees appropriately at different stages of formulating the policies.
- Communicate the policies clearly.
- Make the policy statement concise.
- Translate the policy into specific, measurable, actionable programs rather than making them sound like platitudes.
- Review them periodically and update them to keep up with the changing times.

Conviction increases commitment. Internalization creates a sense of responsibility and a feeling of ownership. Deployment of policies literally spreads the culture of *deference* throughout the organization replacing the earlier indifferent attitudes towards them. In the final analysis, what you achieve is more than mere compliance and adherence to the organizational policy. Now that we have discussed organizational philosophy and policy, let us look at the implications of the study of the policy for marketing practitioners, at a macro level.

Policy implications for the Marketer

Marketers should understand and appreciate the role of government in marketing of goods and services. They should also identify the various public policy instruments in the form of Acts and Statutes that impinge on various marketing decisions. It is not possible for a marketer to know all about the various Acts that affect his decision-making. But, nevertheless, it is essential for him to have a good working knowledge of the major laws protecting competition, consumers and larger interests of society. Such an understanding of public policy would help him examine the legal implications of his own decisions. A marketer should have a clear understanding of the impact of specific policy instruments on all the major *Ps* of marketing.

Some of the important Acts and Statues and the impact on the various of elements of marketing mix are presented in the Table 9.1. While the impact of these instruments of public policy is on the organization as a whole, an attempt is made to show their likely direct impact on important elements of marketing mix in this. Government policies evolve gradually and are greatly influenced by the political parties in office. Marketers must constantly stay alert to subtle shifts in the public and political attitudes towards business in general and their products in particular.

Table 9.1 Public Policy and its Impact on Pharmaceutical Marketing

---

Three Recent New Policy Moves

The GoI (Government of India) has taken three policy initiatives recently:

A. A proposal to make the Universal Code of Pharmaceutical Marketing Practices (UCPMP) Code enforceable by making it into an ACT. This is to curb the unethical marketing practices in Indian pharmaceutical industry by putting an end to the growing Pharma - physician nexus (UCPMP Act), and to make prescription drugs affordable to its 1.2 billion population, majority of which lives under US $ 2 a day. The Indian government is planning to enforce the UCPMP Code, which it introduced in 2015 as a voluntary code to be practiced by the pharmaceutical industry.

B. Got a new NMC (National Medical Council) Bill 2017 approved by the cabinet. The new NMC Bill replaces the existing medical education regulator, MCI (Medical Council of India) to weed out corrupt practices in medical education system and bring transparency to it. IMA (The Indian Medical Association) expressed its deep concern about the proposed NMC Bill and requested the government to change it to make it more meaningful. In its current form, the IMA believes that it will cripple the functioning of the medical profession by making it completely answerable to the bureaucracy and non-medical administrators.

C. In May 2017, India's prime minister Narendra Modi announced a government plan to introduce a law requiring doctors to prescribe only non-branded drugs to their patients. However, the experts are cautioning that the policy, which is designed to make medicines more affordable in a country where majority of the population lives in poverty, could actually do more harm than good.

When you look at closely these three new policy moves you realize that they are a part of the process to correct the total healthcare system and to curb unethical and corrupt practices. The framework of these policies, however shows that not adequate homework was done in terms of analyzing the pros and cons and ways of implementing them effectively. The interrelationships of these three initiatives can be better understood from the following blogpost, *Generics-only policy, Treat the Cause, Not the Symptom* (Table 9.2).

Table 9.2 Generics-Only Policy: Treat the Cause, Not the Symptom

In April 2017, the Prime Minister of India announced that a legislation on *Generics-Only* prescription by physicians is round the corner. While the determination of the Prime Minister to bring down the prices of generic drugs is laudable, the theme is nothing new. The first-ever *generics-only* policy was conceived in 1981. For over three-and-half decades every government has been making resolutions to bring down the prices of drugs and making healthcare more affordable even to the very poor. All attempts and efforts till date towards ensuring generic drug prescriptions in place of branded generics have been in vain.

There are a number of questions that need to be addressed before you insist doctors to prescribe only the generic drugs and not the branded generic drugs. The government has ordered the public sector doctors to prescribe only generic names and not brands. In a country where over 90 percent of the drugs consumed are branded generics, how can the move from branded generics to generic-generics be possible? Not only that, most of country's pharmacies are staffed by unqualified personnel. How will they dispense chemical names and contend with difficulties of this change? Furthermore, more than 50 percent of the drugs currently used are combination drugs. How will the doctors prescribe a combination drug as a generic?

Why did the earlier attempts to make physicians prescribes generic drugs instead of branded generics fail? Will the proposed legislation to make *generics-only* prescriptions mandatory achieve what the earlier efforts did not? Let us briefly consider the factors that affect generic prescribing behavior and reasons for our lack of success so far in this regard. A number of studies conducted elsewhere in the world point out the factors influencing the generics prescribing behavior. Factors that positively affect the generic prescribing behavior are patient's financial status, patient's welfare, compliance, and fear of punishment. Factors that negatively affect the prescribing behavior are quality concerns, lack of regulation by Food and Drug Administration, poor recall of generic names, patient's preference and personal experience.

A physician checks the symptoms, administers a few diagnostic tests to understand the cause of the patient's ailment and then

Contd...

prescribes a drug (brand-name drug or branded-generic or generic-generic) to cure the patient. A physician tries his best to treat the cause and not symptom. Only quacks treat the symptom. Similarly let us try to identify the causes - apparent or hidden, understand the pharmaceutical eco system better to treat the cause of our current healthcare ills. Here are some facts for your consideration:

1. *Too Many Brands, Loan licensing and Pharma-Physician Nexus.* One may wonder. What is the relationship between too many generic brands, loan licensing and Pharma-Physician Nexus. When you examine the current loan licensing scenario in India you would observe there are too many branded generic formulations in the market. There are close to 100,000 branded generic formulations today. The objective of a loan license should be to augment the current manufacturing capacity. It should not be for the purpose of trading with a view to get higher margins. Today it is very easy to start a pharmaceutical company. A pharmaceutical representative, manager or for that matter a physician or a group of physicians with sizable clinical practice can start a company. They can approach a drug manufacturer with a fast moving (largely prescribed molecules or fixed dose combinations) generic formulation and get it manufactured from any of the existing manufacturers under the loan licensing system. They enter into a contractual relationship with some physicians, who can prescribe a pre-determined quantity of prescriptions for select products for a mutually agreeable consideration of cash or kind. Most of these marketers have no intention of manufacturing these or other products anytime in the future. Naturally, transactional marketing arrangements like these are not difficult to copy as one cannot earn customer loyalty and trust through such marketing tactics. There are always competitors, who have deeper pockets and can easily convert these prescribers towards prescribing their products by increasing the transactional sum. This leads to a continuous escalation of marketing costs at the expense of patients.

2. *All Generic Formulations are not low-priced:* That all generic formulations are low-priced is a myth. There are many regional and local drug firms that have less than one percent of a particular product category. These do not come under the Drug Price

Contd...

Control Order (DPCO) scanner and therefore are allowed to price their products without any restriction. Some of these companies price their products at prices that are comparable or even marginally higher than their branded counterparts.

3. ***Regulatory Standards and Monitoring:*** India's current drug regulatory mechanism, like other regulatory systems is known for its inherent inefficiencies and inadequate infrastructure. That brings us to the next question concerning the quality of the generics. In the US and other highly regulated markets, there are very stringent quality control measures to ensure that the generics are effective in treating the patients. Every generic drug should submit a bio-equivalence test comparing it with the innovator drug as they believe that therapeutic equivalence is important and chemical equivalence does not necessarily mean that it is therapeutically equivalent. Moreover, the generic applicant should conduct this test at the US FDA approved laboratory only. All this costs a lot and puts an entry barrier for fly-by-night operators. Contrast this with the current scenario in the Indian drug regulatory environment. The technical infrastructure is grossly in adequate for quality testing and certainly not comparable with the West, with whom we want to align. Almost all of the generic-generic formulations are not tested comparing them with the leader of the branded generic formulation or the brand-name drug for bio-equivalence (unless they are the very first branded-generic formulation to be marketed in the category) and yet they are approved. The government is not yet ready to address and ensure all these quality issues. Many of the reported close-to-ten-thousand drug companies do not have a manufacturing facility that conforms to and approved by WHO GMP (World Health Organization's Good Manufacturing Practices). Under the loan licensing system, literally anyone with less than a million rupees can start a company marketing his own version of generics. As a result, there are companies competing at national level, regional level and local level. How will the Drug Controller General of India (DCGI) ensure that the patients get the same quality of generic-generic that is identical to that of the brand-name drug? A brand-name manufacturer has got his entire reputation at stake. What does a generic-generic manufacturer got to lose?

Contd...

4. *Continuous Escalation of Medical Education Costs*: Pharma - Physician nexus is deepening by the day and along with is the increase in irrational prescribing and prescribing of expensive branded generics. More and more physicians are entering into contractual obligations to prescribe a particular quantum of prescriptions for a negotiated consideration of cash or kind. Even some of the young super specialists, who are starting to set up clinical practice are already entering into negotiations with Pharma firms. The reasons some of them cite are: The escalating costs of medical education with exorbitant capitation fee for post graduate admissions in private medical colleges. A super specialist by the time he sets up his clinical practice would be in his early thirties and would have spent about INR 20 to 30 million in a private medical institution (seats in government medical institutions are very few). His entire focus right from the day he joins the workforce is on how to maximize his return on investment. Neither the government nor the Medical Council of India are able to do anything to curtail the capitation fee system in private medical colleges.

5. *Shortage of Qualified and Trained Pharmacists in Retail Pharmacies:* Let us take a look at our distribution system to ensure availability and dispensing of the generic-generics or plain generics, which carry only the generic name on all their packaging, such as strips and outer cartons, if any and there would not be any brand name. There are over 850,000 retail pharmacies in the country and many of these do not have a full time qualified pharmacist on their premises. Without adequate knowledge of the the drugs they are supposed to dispense these generic-generic drugs. How do you expect majority of chemists to dispense the generic prescriptions correctly? The government is aware of this shortage of qualified pharmacists and even proposed a training program for all the salesmen with an experience of five years or more across the country. However, there is no news of its implementation. Even if such a program is implemented, it is at best a compromise and cannot be a solution. What is more, the curriculum at the graduate level in our pharmacy courses does not include many of the new drugs that are recently developed. Empowering the 'not-so-qualified'

Contd...

pharmacist to dispense generic drugs can do more harm than good to the patients.

6. ***Breaking the Pharma - Physician Nexus to Create a New Pharma - Pharmacist Nexus?***: Think for a moment about the root cause of this problem. When you look at the hierarchy of pharmaceutical products, innovator or brand-name drugs are at the top with the maximum product differentiation, which enables them to command a price premium. Next in the pecking order are value-added generics such as drug delivery products of the same molecule with a perceptible and patentable degree of differentiation, which helps them get some price premium. Branded generics are next in the line with a smaller degree of differentiation in terms of quality perception, availability, customer service, etc. Generic-generics are at the bottom with a commodity status with virtually no differentiation. When there is no product differentiation, gratification rules the strategic roost. That explains, but doesn't justify the unabated corrupt practices of drug manufacturers in wooing the prescribers. A legislation *on generics only* prescription by physicians is unlikely to end the Pharma - Physician Nexus. It may reduce the prescription freedom as the physician can probably insist on the company's name along with the generic prescription. It is a possibility. But the most dangerous outcome of this move will certainly give more power, the power of therapeutic substitution of a prescription to many of the *'not-so-qualified'* retail chemists, who would dispense the drug on which they get the best margin. Pharmaceutical companies may target these chemists and win them over to push their generic drugs over competition in the ways that they know best. It may not stop the Pharma - Physician Nexus totally, but it certainly will facilitate a new Pharma - Pharmacist Nexus!

7. ***Lack of Good Governance***: That there is clearly a lack of good governance is evident from the fact that the government has been unable to ensure compliance from all the stakeholders despite the presence of a well defined legal system governing the manufacturing and selling pharmaceutical products in India such as the Drugs & Cosmetics Act, Voluntary UCPMP (Universal Code of Pharmaceutical Marketing Practices), MCI

Contd...

(Medical Council of India) etc. Another legislation is unlikely to have any greater impact when governance falls short of its objectives and purpose.

The Way Forward: A Prescription

Why do physicians prescribe what they prescribe? They prescribe what they prescribe because of what happens to them when they prescribe what they prescribe. In other words, the consequence. When they prescribe a brand-name drug or a branded-generic drug they are confident of getting what they prescribed. That confidence and trust are the result of a long standing relationship based on empirical evidence of their prescriptions and the delivery of promise - relief, cure and the patients' well being. When they prescribe a generic-generic they are completely at the mercy of the pharmacist who dispenses the generic drug on which he gets the maximum profit margin. The physician does not know anything about the quality standards and and the state of manufacturing of that manufacturer. Here is fixed dose combination of a prescription for your consideration:

1. To change this negative perception of the generic drugs all we have to do is approve every generic formulation based on a bio-equivalence test comparing it with the reference drug (either the brand name drug or leader brand of the branded-generic drug). If this is made mandatory the quality and perception of the generic drugs would improve significantly.

2. Ensure that all the retail pharmacies are manned by a qualified and trained pharmacist, who has adequate knowledge about drugs and diseases, so that they can improve health awareness among the patients whom they serve.

3. Institute recognition and reward systems among physicians who prescribe more generic drugs and make them publicly. This would accelerate the rate of generic drug prescription as positive reinforcement alone can bring a sustainable and lasting change in one's behavior.

4. Strengthen the Drug Administration Department with adequate manpower to ensure compliance and establish GMP (Good Manufacturing Practices) among all manufacturing units.

5. Make it mandatory to loan-licensees marketing generic

Contd...

formulations without any value-addition to start their own manufacturing unit within a prescribed time limit failing which the licenses would be canceled. This will rationalize the number of drug manufacturing units, improve their productivity and the overall quality of generic drugs. It would also help in stopping the Pharma - Physician nexus.

6. Currently, there are an estimated 100,000 pharmaceutical products in India, of which about 50 percent are different versions of branded-generic or generic versions of single ingredient drugs. Do we require 100 versions of Ciprofloxacin and 150 versions of Omeprazole for example? How many generic versions of a drug we need to cater to the patients? Can we think of putting a cap on the number of generic formulations for each single ingredient drug?

This is by no means exhaustive. It is only to start the process of thinking holistically with a singular purpose of treating the causes and not merely the symptoms.

Monitoring the Policy Environment: Key Questions

Changing social attitudes also exert a powerful influence on marketers, particularly in the areas of consumer rights and environmental protection. Special interest groups like Drug Action Forum, patient advocacy groups and other consumer protection societies also exert pressure on business and government, and influence public policy. Marketers should be alert to such changing attitudes and anticipate them.

Understanding leads to awareness. Monitoring the policy trends and governmental attitudes towards business in general and your industry in particular will enable you to anticipate the likely changes or shifts. Anticipation will help you to prepare for and cope with impending changes. Consider for example the drug policy and the new policy movies such as UCPMP Act, 'Generics-only' policy and some their implications.

A. The government's attitude towards improving quality of production and the direction in which it has been moving have been evident for some time through emphasis on GMP, phasing out of loan licensing etc. What changes do you anticipate in these areas during the next few years? How do you plan to prepare yourself to meet those challenges and changes?

B. The introduction of schedule Y has made new product introduction more difficult. Brand proliferation rate is most likely to be changed with this. How is it going to affect your new product plans? How do you plan to meet this challenge?

C. If the 'generics-only' policy becomes a law, how would it affect your business? Your organization? How would it affect your marketing? What would be your promotional strategy? How do you plan to create differentiation in a 'generics-only' market that is commoditized?

D. If the UCPMP Code becomes an Act tomorrow as it is likely to be what are the implications for many of the pharmaceutical companies that are relying heavily on transactional marketing methods on a *quid pro quo* basis? Since many of these current practices would become illegal and the companies practicing them today will have to stop them immediately. How will they market their products? How will they ensure best practices? Should they not start thinking about changing their marketing practices for better today itself as the warning signals are already there for everyone to see?

Marketers, who have been monitoring the trends and are able to anticipate these and other shifts and changes, will have a distinct advantage over the others.

Leading All the Way

If your organization wants to achieve leadership position or has already become a leader in your industry, naturally it has to fulfill certain other responsibilities. Apart from achieving the highest sales and profit levels, it should also set the pace for the industry. It should demonstrate its leadership qualities to the public at large. Apart from fulfilling its obligations and discharging responsibilities towards its customers, shareholders and employees, it has to discharge its share of social responsibility. The public expects this from the business organizations. Their expectations have been increasing over the years. Any organization, which has achieved or wants to achieve the leadership position should not only meet the public expectation but also move one step ahead, by leading the rest of the industry in the area of social responsibility. Only then can it achieve total leadership and sustain it.

Summary

A number of government regulations and legislations influence and intervene in the monitoring of operations of a business organization. The regulations and controls have been steadily increasing over the years. The corporate policy is therefore, governed to a considerable extent by the public policy.

A number of advocacy groups and special interest groups like Drug Action Forum and consumer protection groups are also increasing their pressure and influence on the government and business in formulating their policies.

In April 2017, the prime minister of India announced that a legislation on 'generics-only' policy is round the corner, which mandates all physicians to prescribe drugs to patients with their generic or chemical names only and not the brand names. While the prime minister's determination to bring down the drug prices is laudable, the generics-only policy theme is nothing new. It was first conceived in 1981. For over three-and-half decades, every government has been making resolutions to implement 'generics-only policy' to make the best of healthcare affordable to the very poor. A legislation attempts to treat only the symptom. What is needed is treating the cause. To bring down the healthcare costs and drug prices, you need to treat the cause, not the symptom. Consider these causes for example:

1. Too many brands, loan licensing, and Pharma - Physician nexus
2. All generic-generic formulations are not low priced
3. Regulatory standards and monitoring
4. Continuous escalation of medical education costs
5. Shortage of qualified and trained pharmacists at retail pharmacies
6. Generics-only policy - Breaking the Pharma - Physician Nexus only to create a Pharma - Physician Nexus?
7. Lack of good governance

Many of these policies, regulations in the form of Acts and Statutes by Government legislation, evolve gradually. Seldom, if at all, are they sudden. They are greatly influenced by the political party in power. Therefore, it is possible to anticipate the likely shifts by monitoring the changing trends and social attitudes. Anticipation helps marketers to prepare for impending changes.

An understanding and awareness of public policy is essential for any marketing practitioner. They should have a clear idea of the legal implications of their decisions, for these regulations affect all the elements of the marketing mix.

Achieving leadership in a given industry brings certain responsibilities to be fulfilled by the organization towards the society, that is, the general public. The business leader should be a leader in this area too.

10

Public Relations

Image Makers?

What are public relations? A senior public relations manager once defined public relations as simply a matter of treating public as your relations. There is more to public relations than treating the public as your relations. Public relations present the personality and philosophy of the organization to its various publics. While in other functional departments like marketing, finance, manufacturing, personnel have specific tasks and responsibilities, the task of public relations is much broader. It runs across the organization. While the public relations department may design campaigns and programs to present a favorable image of the company to the public at large, the actual implementation of these programs involves all the employees of the organization. At least that is what it should be. Viewed in this context, the public relations effort is the business equivalent of the *foreign affairs* department of a nation's government.

Contrary to the popular notion, public relations people cannot create an image. An image can be created out of a personality. Public relations efforts aims at presenting a positive image of the personality that an organization has. The personality of the organization is the result of the attitudes of its employees towards their company, their products, services, the management policy, philosophy and other factors. To project a positive image, a company must have a positive personality. The best public relations will not compensate for the weak personality of the organization. On the contrary, an active P R policy will expose rather than hide weakness. Therefore the best policy that can make the public relations effort of an organization effective is basic sincerity itself!

Two-way Communication

Public relations can be defined as the organized two-way communication process between the organization and the audiences critical to its success. An Organization requires understanding and support of various other public groups apart form employees, customers and shareholders for its aims, policies and programs. People develop their perceptions about organizations and their personality and the character of the organization based on their previous experiences.

The character and personality of an organization are often a result of the cumulative effects of the organization's policies, attitudes and actions towards certain key issues like product quality, customer service, social responsibility etc. To really develop a strong character and a positive personality, the organizational attitudes towards these key issues must be consistent. These attitudes are derived from the style of the organization. At the same time, they also help to create that style. Consistency can be achieved only from a planned effort.

Pull Strategy

Philip Kotler in an article entitled, *Mega Marketing* in Harvard Business Review argues that public relations are a pull strategy. Mobilizing public opinion takes a longer time, but when energized, it can help pull the company into the market. Favorable public opinion can help pull customers to a company's products and services and create an enduring franchise, in a highly crowded or relatively undifferentiated segment. Public opinion can also help pull the best talent available in the job market to join the company's work force.

Information, Opinion and Attitudes

Any communication program has an essential element i.e., information, which is used to shape opinions. Information based on facts can help in reinforcing opinions. An attitude, on the other hand, reflects a position or stance adopted by someone. Attitudes may be shaped by the influence of others' opinions or by one's own experiences. Attitudes need not necessarily be shaped or formed by facts. Public opinion shapes the attitudes of the public towards an organization and it need not necessarily be based on facts alone. Very often it is based on what is reported. The implication therefore, is that there should not be any gap between what an organization says and what it does.

A Necessity for the Pharmaceutical Industry

The pharmaceutical industry must take the initiative to talk about the good news, about its accomplishments and the contribution to the world of medicine. The industry should increase consumer awareness of the positive features of the pharmaceutical industry. Dr. Lloyd Millstein, Director of Drug Advertising and Labeling for the USFDA advised the pharmaceutical advertising association that the industry should fight back with the good that the industry has done, at a meeting of the association some time ago. Dr. Millstein reminded the audience of the negative halo effect, where bad press for one company is bad press for all. The public never gets to hear the industry's side. It was only highly publicized actions like Johnson and Johnson's Tylenol case and Pfizer on its Partners in Healthcare series that got noticed by the public.

There is a strong need that public even in India need to be acquainted with the workings of the industry and the development of products. The public perceptions of drug manufacturers even today in India is they are making enormous profits, whereas in reality there are a number of drug companies that are struggling to achieve an acceptable rate of return. Another popular misconception is that it is the brand names that are pushing the drug prices in India and if brand names of drugs are abandoned and only generic drug prescriptions are made mandatory, the prices of drugs would come down. This is a grossly mistaken point of view. Industry should mount a public relations campaign and educate the general public regarding the fallacy of this notion.

Public Relations and Crisis Management

The public relations is to help stabilize the environment by developing messages and public relations strategy, which results in prompt, honest, informative and concerned communications with all important audiences - internal and external, explains Professor Jonathan Bernstein founder of Bernstein communications.

A crisis may be defined as a significant threat to operations or reputations that can have negative consequences on the organization and its stakeholders. Crisis management is about dealing with the threat of potential damages that a crisis can inflict on an organization and its stakeholders and even an industry. A crisis can create a threat three in three areas, namely, public safety, financial loss and loss of reputation.

Crisis management is a process designed to prevent or lessen the damage a crisis can inflict on an organization and its stake holders. It can be divided into three phases:

1. **Pre-crisis**: The pre-crisis phase is connected with prevention and preparation.

2. **Crisis response**: The crisis response phase is when management actually responds to a crisis.

3. **Post-crisis**: The post-crisis phase looks for ways to better prepare for the next crisis and fulfills commitments made during the crisis, including follow-up that is necessary.

13 Golden Rules of Public Relations Crisis Management

Forbes Agency Council members suggested 13 Golden Rules for managing a public relations crisis effectively. Don't take them lightly as they are deceptively simple and self explanatory. Stick to them firmly and you are well-equipped to manage any crisis situation that you may have to face:

1. Take Responsibility.
2. Be proactive. Be transparent. Be accountable.
3. Get ahead of the story. Don't wait till you formulate a complete strategy.
4. Be ready for social media backlash.
5. Remember to be human.
6. First apologize, then take action.
7. Monitor, plan and communicate.
8. Seek first to understand the situation.
9. Listen to your team first.
10. Develop a strong brand culture. Remember, you can develop an organization with strong brand culture only, when you treat your customers and employees (internal customers) with respect.
11. Turn off the fan. When you-know-what hits the fan, the first rule of crisis management is turn off the fan, says Kim Miller of Ink Marketing. Don't fuel the fan. Step back, put yourself in the

shoes of the customer and ask, *If this happened to me how would I feel?* And then decide the course of action. It ensures that we do the right thing.

12. Avoid knee-jerk reaction. Freeze all external communication until you can assess what is going on, suggests Coltrane Curtis of Team Epiphany.

13. Be Prepared.

Tylenol: A Classic Example of Crisis Management

To understand how to manage a crisis, one has to study the classic case of Tylenol. The case is illustrative and instructive at the same time.

Case10.1 Tylenol Scandal and Crisis Management

The Crisis

Tylenol, the leading OTC painkiller drug in the United States faced a tremendous crisis in October 1982. Tylenol was the market leader with a dominant 37 percent of the OTC analgesic market at the time. An unknown suspect(s) tampered Tylenol capsules and put 65 milligrams of deadly cyanide into them. The tampering occurred once the product reached the shelves. They were removed from the shelves, infected with cyanide and returned to the shelves.

The poisoning of the Tylenol capsules resulted in seven deaths in Chicago. The company, Johnson & Johnson immediately after this incident lost major chunk of its market share, which was reduced to 7 percent .

How The Company Responded: McNeil Consumer Products, a subsidiary of Johnson & Johnson, which markets Tylenol responded immediately in the most appropriate and even an exemplary manner.

1. The company following a principle of protecting people first and property second, conducted an immediate product recall from the entire country, which amounted to about 31 million bottles worth more than $ 100 million. Although Johnson & Johnson knew they were not responsible for the tampering of the product, they assumed responsibility for public safety first and recalled entire stock from the market.

2. Stopped all advertisement for the product.

Later, in 1986 when a woman was reported dead from cyanide poisoning in Tylenol capsules, Johnson & Johnson removed all of the capsules from the market. The company had come up with a campaign to re-introduce the product and more importantly restore the confidence of the consumers in the product. Here is how they did it and Tylenol won its leadership back.

A. The company reintroduced Tylenol capsules in a triple-seal tamper resistant packaging and called them caplets and promoted the tamper-proof concept of the packaging that was the first of its kind.

B. They offered a $ 2.50 discount coupon on the purchase of the product to motivate consumers to buy the product. They (the coupons) were available in the newspapers as well as by calling a toll-free-number.

C. In addition, the company made a new pricing program that gave consumers up to 25 percent off on the purchase of Tylenol caplets to recover any stock loss from the crisis.

D. To restore confidence on the product, over 2,250 sales people made presentations to the medical community.

Living up to the Mission Statement

How did Johnson & Johnson do what it did so brilliantly to manage such a huge crisis? By living up to their Credo, written in the mid 1940s by Robert Wood Johnson, who stated that the company's responsibilities were to the consumers and medical professionals using its products, employees, the communities where its people work and live, and its stockholders.

The company's responsibility to its publics first proved to be its most efficient and effective public relations tool. It was the key to brand's survival. Tylenol is a brand to reckon with even today!

(Source: Adapted from Interactive Media Labs, College of Journalism, Crisis Management, University of Florida)

Publicity

Publicity is a public relations function. Although a firm is responsible for the good publicity it receives, it has virtually no control over the bad publicity it receives. Publicity is defined as any form of non-paid, commercially significant, news or editorial comment about ideas, products or institutions. Publicity enjoys a much greater degree of credibility than advertisement because of its news-worthiness and non-manipulative intentions. Another major advantage of publicity is that it can catch customers off-guard and pass through selective filters of their defense mechanism and gain their attention.

What Public Relations Can Do?

A well planned public relations effort can do a lot of things for your company. It can:

1. Project an aura of credibility and professionalism.
2. Project a high profile and improve product awareness.
3. Supplement and support the advertising effort of your company.
4. Attract talent and help in recruiting high caliber employees in all departments.
5. Instill enthusiasm and a sense pride among existing employees.
6. Project the company's image as an ethical and responsible organization.

Public relations effort can be measured. Consider the fact that goodwill is a measurable asset. Goodwill is shown on the balance sheet. Goodwill can only follow from support for the aims of the organization. Support follows understanding, which is a result of the knowledge gained from the communication effort. In addition, the P R effort can be measured in terms of public opinion and their attitude towards the organization, increase in awareness of knowledge about the organization among the defined audience, the level and tone of the news coverage during the period under review and even increase in share prices.

Reputation Management

Once considered as one of the most reputed industries, the reputation of pharmaceutical industry across the world has fallen considerably to a level not much better than financial sector or tobacco industry. What contributed to this fall? And why is reputation important? Let us explore and find out whether and how it can be restored.

Importance of Reputation

A company's reputation is among its most valuable assets. Research confirms this. The percentage of a company's value attributable to tangible assets has dropped from 90 percent to just 25 percent over the past three years according to the research conducted by the New York-based consultancy firm, Ethisphere. Other estimates too confirm this. They suggest that it is intangible assets of a company (including reputation) that currently represent as much as 40 to 60 percent of its market capitalization.

Declining Reputation

A recent patient view survey revealed that there was a 19 percent decline on the reputation of pharmaceutical industry in general and its leading companies in particular from the previous year. Furthermore, the research found that only 34 percent of the patients surveyed believed that multinational drug companies have an excellent or good reputation. What are the reasons for this declining trend in pharmaceutical industry that has greatly contributed towards health and wellbeing of populations across the world over the years? Here are some of the more important reasons:

A. Pharmaceutical companies have become increasingly marketing focused and started highlighting only favorable clinical trial results that drove product sales. They were hiding clinical trial results that were unfavorable and the information, therefore, was misleading the physicians as it was neither complete nor accurate. This has corrupted the scientific literature leading to erosion of trust.

B. In addition, some of the industry's leading pharmaceutical companies have been communicating about the damaging side effects of some their major products in an evasive manner, encouraging the physicians to prescribe their products even in inappropriate clinical conditions.

C. Pharmaceutical companies have been increasing their unethical and illegal marketing practices leading to an increase in their litigations. Some of the more prominent litigations brought by the law firms involved are Pfizer's Rezulin, GlaxoSmithKline's Paxil, Pfizer's Bextra and Merck's Vioxx. As a result of these litigations, lawyers who have targeted asbestos and tobacco manufacturers in the past are increasingly turning their attention to drug companies alleging that they have hidden the harmful side effects of their medicines from consumers.

D. Pharmaceutical companies' corrupt marketing practices such as paying hospital doctors to prescribe, allegations of price-fixing kickbacks, payments to generic companies to delay generic drug access to the public - all these activities are widely publicized in and across various media channels.

All these activities and law suits have resulted in creating a public perception that pharmaceutical industry cares less about their patients than profits. In addition the following missteps of pharmaceutical companies have reinforced that negative perception.

1. Pharmaceutical companies have failed to assist patients in securing medications in a difficult economic environment.

2. Pharmaceutical research for some time now, has been focusing on patentable research and consequently been able to offer drugs with only short term benefits.

3. Pharmaceutical industry is not serving the needs of neglected patient groups.

4. Drug companies have been engaging in inappropriate marketing practices.

5. Pharmaceutical pricing policies clearly lack fairness.

6. Pharmaceutical companies talk about patient-centricity these days, but do not practice what they preach.

7. Lack of integrity is evident from the industry's corrupt practices and the huge fines they pay for illegal marketing activities such as off-label promotion and suppression of facts in terms of adverse effects and unfavorable trial results etc.

One can observe that much of the decline in the reputation of pharmaceutical industry over the years is rather self-inflicted. It is possible to undo what it has done. Research suggests that once a company's reputation declines, it would take about 3.5 years to rebuild it even in the best of circumstances. In case of pharmaceutical industry it could take even longer considering the complexities and the number of stakeholders involved. Moreover, it requires both the industry as a whole and individual drug companies to come together and address the factors that precipitated the decline in the first place.

Mark Kessel suggests the steps that pharmaceutical companies need to take to restore their reputation in his insightful article, *Restoring the pharmaceutical industry's reputation* in Nature (October 2014). Here is the essence of what he has suggested:

1. R*efocus on Patients' Needs:* The pharmaceutical industry seems to have failed mainly on two counts in living up to its earlier reputation. One is its ethical conduct and the other is its customer focus. They need to improve the perception of all the stakeholders that the company cares about patients and is committed to all its customers. The company also needs to demonstrate their ethical conduct through their actions.

2. *Cease DTC Advertising:* Does DTC (Direct-to-consumer) advertising of prescription medicines strengthen the perception of patients that drug companies care more about improving their sales to enhance their earnings than they do about improving patients' health? The pharmaceutical companies should examine and reflect on this and desist from DTC advertising.

3. *Follow a Responsible Pricing Strategy and Justify the Pricing:* The cost of developing a new drug and the time it takes to bring a new drug from concept to the market are very expensive costing over a billion dollars. The pharmaceutical industry should educate all its stakeholders about this. In addition, it should justify the pricing new drug by explaining the benefits the new drug offers

the affected patients and the cost savings that it brings to the healthcare system. Above all, a drug company should consider whether its pricing policy should be tempered to avoid the potential outcry from its stakeholders and the long term impact of its pricing on its reputation.

4. *Restore and Demonstrate an Ethical Culture:* Ethical conduct of a company is at the top of the reputation measurement system. In fact a company's ethical behavior determines its reputation. If companies tolerate unethical behavior of its senior management, it sends a message or a signal within the organization that it is fine to be unethical as along as you get the results and can circumvent potential liability. Despite adverse media publicity of pharmaceutical industry's unethical behavior in terms of billions of dollars of fines it paid for its illegal marketing activities, the public does not believe that senior management was held accountable. To change this perception, the industry needs to restore ethical behavior, put in place better controls and punish misconduct of executives responsible for such misdeeds.

5. *Implement Data Transparency:* There are a number of allegations that pharmaceutical companies publish successful trial data only, and withhold negative data from publication and even rig study designs to foster favorable outcomes. The only way to erase this negative perception in the minds of the industry stakeholders is to implement data transparency by publishing both positive and negative trial results.

6. *Change Industry Messaging:* Send the Right Messages. Although actions speak louder than words, you also need to communicate the right things and accentuate the positive. Pharmaceutical industry did not have an effective and consistent program to inform and educate consumers and other stakeholders on how it has contributed to the health and improved lives by bringing new life saving therapies to the patients. In its heydays, pharmaceutical companies were run by CEOs who had both scientific training and credibility in the market place. They were perceived as individuals concerned about patients health and well being. Today most of the pharmaceutical companies are being run by lawyers or individuals coming from sales and marketing (Novartis is an

exception), who are not likely to command the same level of respect from stakeholders. In addition, the focus on stock market and on the quarterly results lead one to believe that the focus is more on stockholders than patients, who are the most important stakeholders for a pharmaceutical company. The pharmaceutical companies need to change this perception. Pharmaceutical companies would do well to encourage their research and development or medical department heads to interact more frequently with stakeholders and explain how their new drugs benefit and why it is worth the price, its development expenses and company's assistance programs to improve its access to patients.

7. *Counter the Misinformation:* Certain academicians, politicians and others seem to claim that it is academia and the National Institutes of Health in the United States that bring new drugs to the market and not the pharmaceutical industry. The pharmaceutical industry, therefore, needs to counter this misinformation. The industry should consider investing in a communication strategy to inform and educate all stakeholders rather than squandering funds on DTC advertising.

8. *Reduce Government Lobbying:* The pharmaceutical industry in the United States has been spending well over US $ 200-million per year for years now on lobbying activities with the government. The lobbying effort in other countries too seems to be considerable. Despite its high lobbying efforts, the pharmaceutical industry in the US has been criticized by both the Congress and the FDI on several occasions. What is more, this type of lobbying efforts makes the government bodies look at the drug companies with suspicion. Pharmaceutical companies, therefore, need to present the facts with candor and restore confidence in both their testimony and data.

9. *Being Good by Doing Good:* Business history is replete with examples where companies that addressed social issues were the companies that performed well in the market place. For pharmaceutical industry, restoring reputation will mean placing more emphasis on patients and their needs and convincing the

shareholders about the importance of patient focus and how it helps improve their value in the long term.

Pharmaceutical industry can and should start working on restoring its reputation immediately if it has not started already. The industry can draw inspiration from what George W Merck, the legendary CEO of the world's most respected pharmaceutical company, Merck & Co, during his time, said on December 1, 1950 on the occasion of the 50th anniversary of the company at Medical College of Virginia:

We try to remember that medicine is for the patient. We never try to forget that medicine is for the people. It is not for the profits. The profits follow, and if we have remembered that, they have never failed to appear. The better we remembered it, the larger they have been.

Summary

Public relations seem to have come of age. Public relations managers are indeed shedding their con-men image. Indeed the profession as such is growing out of its image makers image. The shift in emphasis is from image to personality. Yesterday's public relations professionals were supposed to have been busy creating a corporate image among the public. Today they are engaged in building a distinct personality for the organization in the minds of the general public and in creating favorable public opinion and attitude towards supporting the aims and actions of the organization. There is more than mere semantics to this shift in emphasis from image to personality.

The pharmaceutical industry should say good-bye to its current low profile. It is time to publicize the good things that the industry has been doing and its contribution to society. The negative halo effect could be dangerous. It must be countered with publicity campaigns and renewed PR efforts.

For restoring the reputation, all the industry needs to do is to remember what George W Merck, the legendary CEO of the world's most respected pharmaceutical company Merck & Co., during his time, said on December 1, 1950 on the occasion of the 50th anniversary of the company at Medical College of Virginia and live up to those words:

We try to remember that medicine is for the patient. We never try to forget that medicine is for the people. It is not for the profits. The profits follow, and if we have remembered that, they have never failed to appear. The better we remembered it, the larger they have been.

Power

Power Begets Power!

Power is not a traditional element of marketing mix. But without power, marketing objectives cannot be achieved. Power is in fact, synonymous with effectiveness. There is something that is self generating about power. Power begets power! Philip Kotler, in a Harvard Business Review article on Mega Marketing suggests that marketers should understand power and build it into their strategies. He also argues the need to go beyond marketing and beyond creating preference for products and services. What we are discussing here is an understanding of power, its types, inter-relationships and its positive reinforcement. Such an understanding will help the marketer to plan more powerful strategies.

The Many Faces of Power

There are many types of power. Proper channeling of power in one area will help generate power in another area. While this may be common knowledge, one should not take it for granted. Consider these various sources of power.

Resource Power

Resources give an organization the necessary power to start something. Proper utilization of these resources, can give the organization its staying power. For proper resource utilization, expertise, skills in the relevant functional areas are needed.

People Power

It is people who really generate power out of a firm's resources and make an organization achieve its goals effectively. That people are our greatest asset is at best cliche in practice. A number of companies, which consider and treat people as their greatest resource, have become the most powerful organizations in their respective industries. Despite this observable evidence, a number of organizations continue to take their people for granted. The consequence? Instead of power generation, a number of power breakdowns occur. The importance of people and the power of their contribution to any organization can never be overemphasized.

Andrew Carnegie, the industrialist, entrepreneur and visionary par excellence, expressed his faith in people and their importance to the organization unequivocally when he said:

Take away our wealth. Take away our factories. Take away our products and money. But give us our organization and people. We shall rebuild every thing again in four years time.

Size Power

The size of an organization gives it considerable power. If it is a large manufacturing organization, it will invariably be able to have the power of economies of scale. A large manufacturer will be able to get better prices, better schedules and better credit facilities from the suppliers of raw materials and packaging materials. The production efficiencies too, will considerably increase because of the experience curve effect. The consequent economic power will give the organization a distinct competitive edge.

Technology Power

Superior technology gives the organization a distinct competitive advantage. A more cost effective production technique or process may enable the firm to achieve cost leadership. That is a significant competitive advantage. It can also be used as an entry barrier and prevent any likely competitors from entering the market. In India, Dr. Reddy's Laboratories have achieved cost leadership in the manufacture of norfloxacin, an Active Pharmaceutical Ingredient (API) for treating a number of infections. Cheminor Drugs (a group company of Dr. Reddy's Laboratories) has achieved cost leadership in the manufacture of ibuprofen, another API, which is an Non-Steroidal Anti-inflammatory Drug (NSAID). Another Indian drug major, Wockhardt has achieved cost-effective manufacturing technology in the manufacture of dextro-propoxyphene and has become the third largest producer of the drug in the world.

Coalition Power

To ward off a competitive threat or to create an entry barrier, some companies from different power blocks may temporarily form a cartel. Cartels use their coalition power to control prices and to prevent the entry of new competition. A classic example of this is the OPEC (Organization of Petroleum Exporting Countries) cartel, which has wielded a tremendous impact on the world economy by its control over oil prices.

To break the competitive threat from the Indian drugs and chemical manufacturers in international market, multinational pharmaceutical and chemical giants including Hoechst, BASF, Monsanto and Rhone-Poulenc had reportedly formed a cartel in the past.

Indian drug manufacturers, too may take a cue and use coalition power to conquer international market for their APIs in certain therapeutic segments.

Franchise Power

The company image has considerable power, which gives a franchise to its products in the market place. This goodwill gives even its new products the much-needed penetrative power during the introductory stage.

Niche Power

Companies, which identify a unique position or slot for themselves and carve out a niche, have a distinct competitive advantage. The niche gives them the power that differentiates them from the rest of the crowd and makes them effective. Consider these companies that effectively carved out a niche for them and entered the fast lane.

- NATCO in its initial years (1990s) carved out a niche for itself as company specializing in time-release technology and marketed a number of formulations using that technology.

- Torrent's niche power has already earned it a reputation as company that is among the first to launch all new drugs in India. Torrent's record in new product introduction is really enviable. It has been moving at such a fast pace that it has reached the 18th position in the Indian pharmaceutical industry (March 1990) virtually out of nowhere in fourteen years.

- American Remedies had carved out a niche for itself as the company with a difference. The company had managed to introduce all its branded generic formulations with a differentiation. The company had been growing at a much faster rate than industry and competition till it was acquired by Dr. Reddy's Laboratories later.

- Dr. Reddy's Laboratories has carved out a superior high-tech niche. It has been living up to its corporate theme of *the national company with an international reach* during its early years. It was force to reckon with in the international bulk drug market in its initial years. The company later refocused itself to become a leading International generic company that it is today.

- Citadel Fine Pharmaceuticals, a medium sized company, entered the market by carving out a niche for itself. It was the first company to make its formulations in the amoxycillin and ampicillin market that was crowded, with a differentiated dispersible formulations for the first time and established its Prescillin and Presmox brands. The company was later acquired by Aurobindo Pharma.

Integration Power

As in the case of nations, an organization's ability to integrate its resources and strengths will give it considerable power. Integration can gain better access to suppliers and to distribution in addition to spreading the overheads and providing economies of scale.

When suppliers decide to take advantage of the higher margins downstream they adopt a forward integration. One major advantage of such a forward integration is that they can rely on a sure source of supply. Marketing is one area where they have to strengthen themselves because marketing downstream products may be a totally different ball game. They have to resist the temptation of using the same marketing techniques and strategies that made them successful as suppliers.

Manufacturers of bulk drugs often enter into manufacturing and marketing of formulations. Few of them realize and appreciate the importance of taking a totally fresh look at the marketing of formulations. The factors responsible for success in the marketing of bulk drugs and formulations can be quite different.

Producers want to enter into competition with suppliers by manufacturing the major items, which they were buying from them, to reduce their costs and to increase profitability. This is called backward integration. Backward integration gives the organization a better control on its operations.

Horizontal integration takes place when new competitors enter your industry from closely related industries. Major pharmaceutical companies have entered the animal health industry, Ayurvedic formulations, and diagnostics during the 1980s. This kind of related diversification or horizontal move may enhance the resources power of an organization by optimizing it. One word of caution, however. Too much of diversification even if it is related to the core may result in reducing the focus of the organization's core strengths. Some of these companies have exited from their animal health, diagnostic and other areas today to sharpen their focus on their pharmaceutical business. A number of pharmaceutical companies have been starting a new division or another trading face to market greater number of branded generic formulations in a focused manner to multiple specialist physician segments.

Innovation Power

The innovative abilities of firm give it the distinct competitive advantage. Innovation sharpens the competitive edge of a firm and enhances its power to cut through the clutter of competition. The innovation could be in any area. It could be in the discovery of a drug due to superior R & D capabilities, or in planning a marketing strategy, or it could be a process innovation, or even a product differentiation strategy.

Prescription Power

In the business of ethical drugs, prescription is the most important factor that determines success in the market place. The firm's ability to generate more prescriptions from physicians for its products than the competition gives it the leading edge and the power to win the race to the top position. All the marketing efforts of the firm are synchronized to achieve just one single objective - to enhance the prescription generating power. It is increased prescriptions that propel the growth of a company's products.

Quality Power

Superior quality of a company's products and services gives the firm greater credibility. Quality stimulates growth by increasing the repeat-usage for a company's products and services. A satisfied customer is a very good asset for a company and spreads the message across by sharing his experiences and recommending the products and services to his friends, relatives and others who seek his opinion. This kind of word-of-mouth communications can over a period of time build a good franchise for the company's products and services by virtue of its ever-increasing number of satisfied customers. Quality, therefore, does not mean the quality of products alone. Without an improvement in the quality of people and their skills in every department of the organization, attitudes and beliefs towards customer service and social responsibilities, quality cannot be accomplished in its complete sense. Quality, when accomplished can give an organization an enormous staying power.

Summary

Power is a multifaceted concept. Power is essential to make an organization effective. In fact, it is the power of an organization that makes it effective. Power gives the organization the much-needed competitive edge to win at the market place. The many sources of power in the context of an organization are its:

A. Resources

B. People

C. Size

D. Technology

E. Coalitions

F. Franchise

G. Niche

H. Integration strategies

I. Innovation

J. Prescription generating ability

K. Quality

What is the outcome when power from all the sources is synchronized and focused to accomplish the corporate objectives? Uncommon success. That is what happened in the case of the Indian pharmaceutical industry. Power by definition generates power. Consider the spectacular successes of companies such as Sun Pharma, Dr. Reddy's Laboratories, Cadila Healthcare, Cipla, Lupin, Mankind, Intas, Torrent, Alkem, Wockhardt and others have achieved during the past few years. And reflect on the reasons behind the enormous staying power demonstrated by companies such as GlaxoSmithKline, Pfizer, Abbott, Sanofi, Alembic and others. On closer examination of the reasons behind their successes, the reinforcing and regenerating nature or property of power becomes obvious.

The message is clear. Accentuate the positive. Build on your strengths. What is true of a nation is also true of an organization. Proper use of power propels the organization to the top. Misuse or abuse of power pushes them down into oblivion.

12

The Patient

Everyone wants it, Not everyone gets it

The most unused person in healthcare is the patient, wrote Professor David Cutler in MIT Technology Review some time ago. We have come a long way since then to when the patient is becoming the focus of healthcare. Enter patient centricity.

Patient centricity seems to be the Holy Grail of modern Pharma, but it will take time for the firms to embrace it as they have to understand it and overcome many cultural barriers to put it into meaningful practice.

What really is patient centricity? Why has patient centricity become essential? How can you build it into your overall strategy? How do you really put it into practice and how do you make sure that your whole organization embraces it?

Before we find answers to these important questions, let us first take a look at how some of the pharmaceutical companies are communicating their patient-centric intent over the past few years. Table 12.1 presents a snap shot of how some of the leading drug firms have been doing it.

For all these companies (Table 12.1), as we can see patient centricity is a stated priority. The concept of patient centricity, therefore, can be defined as offering solutions (products and services) - directly or indirectly - to patients from which, they can benefit in terms of outcomes and/or quality of life. Let's now look at the official definition of patient centricity. Patient centricity is defined as *the process of designing a service or solution around the patient*. The essence of patient centricity concept is best summed up by the NHS (National Health Service) of U.K's visionary thinking - *No decision about me, Without me.*

Table 12.1 Patient Centricity As Some Pharma Companies See it

Company	Patient Centric Approach
AstraZeneca	Our business is focused in making the most meaningful difference to patients' health through great medicines
Janssen	Driven by our commitment to patients, we bring innovative products, services, and solutions to people throughout the world
GlaxoSmith-Kline	We are dedicated to improving the quality of human life by enabling people to do more, feel better and live longer
Leo Pharma	We make products and services with the purpose of making a difference and having an impact in people's everyday lives
Novartis	Our mission is to discover new ways to improve and extend people's lives
UCB	UCB is inspired by patients and driven by science. Patients are at the heart of everything we do
TEVA	Everything we do from producing pharmaceuticals to numerous other relevant services is patient driven

Lode Dewulf, Chief Patient Affairs Officer at UCB describes patient centricity as:

The truth is we are trying to find value points in a process - whether it is writing a protocol, whether it is designing a marketing campaign - where you should really get Patient's insights and connection.

Increasing Patient Power

Every pharmaceutical company seems to be talking about patient focus these days. Why this sudden interest in keeping the patient at the center of their activity? Consider these for example:

A. Patients are becoming more aware and knowledgeable. Medical information is accessible easily on the internet.

B. Their power is increasing with digital technologies, social networks, and the support of patient advocacy groups (PAGs)

C. Patients are becoming more demanding. They want the most effective drugs that are safe and easy to use at affordable prices.

Patient advocacy groups (PAG) are also becoming more influential and exert a growing power that can make them a part of the policy-making process of the payers. Pharmaceutical companies would do well if they partner with PAGs and take their needs, wants and concerns into account while formulating their strategies.

It is important to remember that patient advocacy groups can damage the corporate reputation of companies they do not have good relations with and they do not share the same strategic vision. As the patient voice is gaining power and reach, its impact on corporate reputation and consequent product performance also will increase. Pharmaceutical companies should, therefore, make sure that patients will get the best medical outcomes and quality of life with respect to their diseases and treatments, which have been provided by physicians throughout the patient's journey.

Patient Centricity in Practice

Some of the more progressive companies have been taking strategic initiatives to put patient centricity into practice. These initiatives are different in nature and importance from company to company. Top ten patient centric services offered by pharmaceutical companies are:

1. Disease education
2. Segmentation insights
3. Experience management
4. Medication delivery and support
5. Patients' risk management
6. Wellness and health information
7. Creation and management of Healthcare Professionals' and Patients' Access portals
8. Medication treatment reconciliation
9. Patient outreach and reminders
10. Medication Adherence programs

Offering patient services is a good decision, provided these services are actually used and demonstrate their positive impact with the help of reliable metrics. The objectives of these patient services are:

A. To improve patient outcomes and quality of life

B. To improve HCP relationships

C. To improve patient satisfaction

D. To restore and enhance corporate reputation

E. To reinforce preference of stakeholders

Why is patient centricity is so important? When the differentiation between products is dwindling, service is an important point for differentiating your brand and company for reinforcing their preference among all the stakeholders such as patients, physicians, policy makers and payers. When used effectively, patient services can reinforce your brand and company preference. The more robust the brand (and company) preference is, the more exceptional will be the brand performance. In addition, offering valuable services to patients reinforces the reputation of pharmaceutical companies and preference for their brands.

Broadly speaking there are two types patient services. One is services around the pill and the other is services beyond the pill. An outline of each of these services is presented in Table 12. 2.

Table 12.2 Two Types of Patient Services

Services Around-the-Pill	Services Beyond-the-Pill
1. Around-the-pill services can be adjacent or directly linked to drugs marketed by pharmaceutical companies.	1. A strategy for the long-term. The business model and the metrics to monitor the progress clearly are yet to evolve.
2. The basic objective of these services is to optimize medical outcomes and quality of life of the patients, while strengthening preference of the brands marketed by the company.	2. Can also deliver results in the short-term through better usage of marketed drugs.
3. Services around the pill can be of many types such as: • Training and tools to help physicians choose the right	3. Services to address unmet needs, solutions, devices and tools to measure, monitor the progress along the patients'

Contd...

Services Around-the-Pill	Services Beyond-the-Pill
drug to the right patient for prescribing	journey. The purpose of these beyond-the-pill services too is
• Programs and tools to improve patient adherence • Devices and Apps to monitor the treated patients' conditions.	improve health outcomes and give the company a competitive advantage.

A growing body of empirical evidence suggests that patient-centric initiatives may have a positive impact on pharmaceutical companies' profitability. What is more, patient-centric strategy improves the Pharma companies' overall business outcomes by increasing:

1. HCPs trust
2. Employees' engagement
3. Stakeholders' engagement
4. Stakeholders' trust
5. Patients' outcomes
6. Patients' trust
7. Companies' abilities to attract and retain employees

Patient Centricity or Customer Centricity?

Patient centricity is part of the customer centricity cYoncept, which has become one of the strategic priorities for Pharma companies in the past few years. Customer centricity is about building positive experiences with customers through the quality of interactions and the benefits provided by products or related services offered by the companies. Patients occupy an important position amongst all the customers of a pharmaceutical company in the sense, that they are the end customers of all its other stakeholders. Among the 7 key Pharma stakeholders, the influence of two of them - patients and patient advocacy groups - has recently increased. The 7 Ps (Pharma's key stake holders) are:

1. Physicians
2. Patients
3. Pharmacists
4. Patient Advocacy Groups
5. Payers
6. Policy Makers
7. Pharma's Competitors

Patient centricity has been the rallying cry for some time now at most of the pharmaceutical companies. That patient is at the center of what we do is no doubt true, as the patient is not only the ultimate consumer of pharmaceutical companies' products and services but also the customer for all other stakeholders of Pharma. And yet, patient centricity remains more of a talking point than a standard business practice at many pharmaceutical companies. Here are some probable reasons why this is so:

A. Pharmaceutical companies have little control over ensuring that a patient benefits from a particular medicine. As Pratap Khedkar of Z S Associates says the patient may be at the center, but Pharma is at the periphery.

B. Prescription drugs account for less than a sixth of the total healthcare costs in the U.S. This is more or less the case in number of other countries too. The control of the vast majority of intermediate costs and influence lies with the physicians, the providers and the payers.

C. Until about ten years ago, the physician was the driving influencer for pharmaceutical companies, but today they have to work with multiple stakeholders such as payers and providers and wade through a large organized business entities to provide their products and services to the patients. It is these systems that control the delivery and payment of patient care and pharmaceutical companies are unable to focus their attention on the patient, without the co-operation of the increasingly complex healthcare eco system in the highly regulated markets like the US.

Pharmaceutical companies today need to serve at least four types of customers. They are:

A. Consumers (patients)

B. Physicians (intermediate customers and influencers)

C. Provider organizations

D. Payers

It is not a question of patient centricity or customer centricity in the final analysis. It is how to balance the act. The patient centricity is no doubt very important. In fact it is the reason for the existence of pharmaceutical companies and all its stakeholders. Pratap Khedkar offers a way to this dilemma in his eye for Pharma article, *Patient Centricity is Important, but Customer Centricity is Imperative:*

Yes. Patient centricity is one of the keys to Pharmaceutical industry's success, but it would be worth your while to focus on serving your myriad stakeholders more comprehensively - and in a more customized fashion. It's time to change the conversation from how Pharma can get closer to the patient to how Pharma can be a more influential player throughout the healthcare eco system.

Summary

Patient centricity has been the rallying cry at most of the pharmaceutical companies today. This is because patients are becoming more knowledgeable as medical information is easily accessible on the internet today. Patients are also becoming more demanding as their power is increasing with digital technologies, social networks and the support of PAGs (Patient Advocacy Groups). Patients today are becoming more demanding and they want the most effective drugs that are safe and easy to use at affordable prices.

These changes are driving pharmaceutical companies to explore various avenues to sharpen their focus on patients and implement patient-centric strategies to improve medical outcomes and quality of life. Some of the more important initiatives taken by Pharma companies are in areas such as disease education, patient outreach, medication adherence programs etc.

There is an increasing amount of empirical evidence that suggests patient centric initiatives have positive impact on pharmaceutical companies in terms of improved trust by all their stakeholders - patients, physicians, providers and payers and performance.

When you think of it, patient centricity is part of customer centricity. While patients are very important and central to a pharmaceutical company, it has to satisfy the needs, wants and aspirations of three more broad customer types such as physicians (the intermediary customers and influencers), providers and payers. Patients are the focus of these three customer groups too, as they are also the end consumers of these three groups. Pharmaceutical companies, therefore, need to balance their strategic focus on these three key stakeholders, while sharpening its focus on patients.

As Pratap Khedkar, of Z S Associates aptly observed, *Patient centricity is important, but customer centricity is imperative!*

Managing New Products

Not just Desirable! Rather Mandatory!

Yes. In today's intensely competitive business environment new products are not just desirable. They are rather mandatory. Without innovative, profitable new products companies cannot hope to survive even, let alone grow.

Standing Still Is Going Backwards!

It is said that in today's business world, where competition is at its fiercest, standing still is tantamount to going backward. A company that only wants to defend its existing markets with its existing products and not to venture into new markets or update its product mix with newer and better products, is not really planning for the future. It will certainly cost the company very dearly in the long run. Business history is replete with such examples. There are many reasons for this. One is product obsolescence.

A company must plan for new products even to defend the market share of its existing products in its existing markets. Otherwise it will be caught in the whirlpool of product obsolescence. It must offer replacements for products that are on their way to obsolescence. If not, the products, which once ruled the market may become extinct like dinosaurs.

No corporate function, probably, has a greater impact on successful long-term growth of a company than new product development. As David J Luck in his book *Profitable Product Management* said, *a product mix can remain competitively viable only when it is replenished with timely new products and strengthened with improvements in current products.*

Developing and managing new products of course, is a very expensive and risky business. Expensive because of the huge investments required in R & D for the development of new products. Risky because of the high degree of uncertainty and high rate of failure of new products. The high rate of failure further makes new product development even more expensive. General statistics for over fifty years in the U.S. have shown that four out of five new products fail. While such statistics are not available in India, it is reasonable to presume that the failure rate is even higher, since research and development is still in a stage of infancy in India. All this puts greater premium on planning, developing and managing new products. Whether it is a breakthrough product, an improvement of the existing product, or even a cosmetic change of an old product, it requires innovative thinking and application.

Innovation naturally implies risk. If you are unwilling to experiment and take risks, then you cannot innovate. If you decide not to take risks, you are in fact taking the biggest risk of all - the risk of doing nothing. It is not enough to do what our predecessors did even if what they did was excellent. Managers need to generate new ideas and better ways of doing things for future growth.

Success with new products requires a very disciplined approach. Innovation is neither a mystical nor mysterious process. It is a functional skill that can be taught, learned, assimilated and practiced.

Managing new products effectively and successfully involves a disciplined approach. It involves skillful, creative planning, innovation and plain hard work. Innovation cannot be achieved by mere inspiration. To paraphrase Thomas Alva Edison, the greatest inventor known to mankind, innovation is one percent inspiration and ninety-nine percent perspiration.

Whether you agree with this composition of the formula or not, you will have to agree with this axiom. Companies that pursue success in the ever-changing market place must promote and encourage an innovative culture, and institute a systematic new product planning and development process. Otherwise success will elude them. The writing on the wall is large and clear. Innovate or Perish!

Exorbitant Costs of New Product Development Process

The internationally known management consulting firm, Booz Allen & Hamilton Inc. conducted a study of 51 companies with very good track records in new product development. It found that an average of 58 new product ideas was required to produce *one* successful new product.

Further analysis of their study revealed that out of every fifty-eight ideas, about twelve passed the initial screening test, which showed them to be compatible with company objectives and resources. Only about seven of these twelve remained after a thorough evaluation of their profit potential. Out of these seven too, only about three survived the product development stage, two the test marketing stage and only one was commercially viable. Thus about fifty-eight new ideas must be generated to find a good one that is commercially viable. This one successful idea must be priced at a level profitable enough to cover all the money lost by the company in researching the fifty-seven other ideas that failed.

Types of Risks

The product planners need to judge the degree and likelihood of possible losses that would result from a number of risks that a new product faces. David J Luck categorized them broadly into four types:

1. Technical failure is the risk that no viable product may emerge even after long and expensive development risk.

2. Product failure may be due to the various faults and snags that may develop in a product after it presumably has been perfected and placed in use.

3. Demand failure occurs when the expected demand for a product proves to be non-existent or when the actual demand fades.

4. Competition is an omnipresent product risk unless firmly protected with patents.

The pharmaceutical industry in India has become so fiercely competitive because international patents and intellectual property rights (IPR) were not protected till 2005. That is why some of the large trans-national companies were hesitant and apprehensive to introduce their research products in India. Now that India recognizes the product patents multi-national pharma companies are gradually introducing their major research products in India too.

Why Develop New Products?

If new product development is such a costly process and a risky undertaking why develop new products?

Products need to be resurrected, rejuvenated and replaced. This is vital to ensure a steady flow and growth of profits into company both in the short term and the long term. By studying the life cycle of new products, one can conclude that sooner or later every product is preempted by another, or else it may degenerate into a profitless price war.

When a company does not update or modernize its product-mix, sales growth is not only difficult to achieve, but also becomes an expensive affair. The competition intensifies its attack with new products. The company's selling and distribution costs keep on increasing. The profits stop growing along with sales, reach a plateau, and start declining. This is because the company in order to maintain the sales volume in the face of stiff competition with newer and better products is forced to offer profit-less price cuts, discounts, trade offers etc. Discounts and price cuts can never be a substitute for newer improved products with better profitability. Furthermore, there will be little or no impact of such price cuts on sales after a particular point.

Another important reason is that since business success tends to be governed not only by what you do but also by what others do, you have to stay ahead of competition in your planning and execution of business strategy. You can do this by differentiating your products and introducing new products with better margins. Profits, generally can be sustained in the long run only by a continuing flow of successful new products.

The Impact of New Products on Profits

New products can have a profound impact on the entire firm. They can change the fortunes of the companies. Here are two cases illustrating and amplifying the kind of impact new products can have on a firm, its sales and profit volumes.

Case 13.1 Tagamet Pushes SmithKline into the Forefront!

The SmithKline Corporation is a pharmaceutical company headquartered in Philadelphia, Pennsylvania. In 1976, SmithKline introduced a new product in the United Kingdom followed by its introduction in the U.S. a year later. The new product was Tagamet, an anti-ulcer drug. Tagamet is now sold in over one-hundred countries around the world. It was one the most remarkable successes of the 1970s.

By 1979, SmithKline's revenues reached US $ 1.35 billion, a gain of 125 percent over 1975, the year before Tagamet was introduced. Profits during the same period shot up by a staggering 266 percent . Tagamet accounted for more than a third of the entire company's sales about half of its profits in 1979. By 1980, Tagamet's worldwide sales were over US$ 649 million. This was more than the entire company's total sales before Tagamet.

Tagamet surely pushed SmithKline (GSK now) into the forefront of the international pharmaceutical industry.

Case 13.2 Zantac Wins the Anti-ulcer Race!

Glaxo (GSK now), the British pharmaceutical giant subsequently introduced Zantac, also an anti-ulcer drug in the United Kingdom. Following its success there, Glaxo introduced Zantac in the US and many other countries. Zantac has become the first-ever prescription drug in the world to cross the coveted US$ 1-billion mark, a landmark that eluded its predecessor, Tagamet. Not only that, by 1989, Zantac pushed Glaxo into the prestigious fourth position on the world pharmaceutical league table. Zantac continues to defend its prestigious position as the number one prescribed drug brand in the world with a sales turnover of US$ 1.7 billion. Glaxo"s fortunes have indeed changed with the introduction of Zantac.

Closer home, the success of Burroughs Wellcome's Septran is all too familiar to us. Septran had catapulted Burroughs Wellcome from under twenty-fifth position into the top ten of the pharmaceutical league table in India. Septran continued to be the largest prescribed drug in

India even in 1990. Such is the success that winning new products can bring to a company.

Companies that have been growing faster than their competitors in the Indian pharmaceutical industry are the ones that have pursuing new product development and launch strategies very aggressively. There seems to be no exception to this rule. Another validating factor for this no-exception rule is the fact, that all those companies that have been sliding down in terms of rank and market share in the industry are the ones that have insignificant new product development and planning activity. New product planning and development seems to be the common denominator between winners and the 'also ran'. Consider these cases.

Case 13.3   Cadila's Climb!

Started sixty-seven years ago in 1951 at Ahmedabad, Cadila Laboratories had made very rapid strides and reached the coveted fourth position in the Indian pharmaceutical industry in 1986. Cadila's progress can only be described as spectacular.

Cadila, in 1976 was ranked 37th in the industry with a sales volume of Rs 3.87 crore. Ten years later in 1986, Cadila had catapulted itself into the fourth position. How did Cadila achieve this? By careful, systematic new product planning, market expansion plans and timely execution and implementation of those plans.

Cadila had expanded into newer markets by increasing its market coverage substantially during this period. From around 140 representatives in 1976, Cadila had increased the customer coverage markedly by adding more than two-hundred and fifty medical representatives thus bringing the field force strength close to 400 by 1986.

At the same time, Cadila had pursued a very aggressive new product planning and development strategy. Cadila had diversified into fast growing product groups. In 1976, the size of Cadila's directly competing market was around Rs. 164-crore, a mere 39 percent of the industry's total sales. By 1986, Cadila had improved its therapeutic coverage up to 90 percent of the total pharmaceutical market in India by launching new products in all the key therapeutic segments. As a result, the company had registered a staggering growth of 705 percent in increasing the size its competing market. Cadila's market share too, had grown from a meager 0.9 percent in 1976 to a very respectable 3.1 percent by 1986.

Cadila had introduced as many as 19 new products in the fastest growing therapeutic groups like systemic antibiotics, psychotropic drugs, non-steroidal anti-inflammatory drugs, and anti-peptic ulcer drugs between 1978 and 1986. These 19 new products had contributed to about 60 percent of the increased sales volume of Rs. 42.15-crore.

Not content with the dramatic progress achieved so far, Cadila embarked on a new game plan. It was relatively easy for Cadila to diversify into new product groups and new market all these years because:

A. Earlier (1976) the size of its directly competing market was only 39 percent of the total industry's sales. By 1986 Cadila had expanded its directly competing market to 90 percent of the total industry's sales.

B. The company's base was also very low with 0.9 percent share of the total market in 1976, which had grown to a sizable 3.1 percent by 1986.

Cadila, realizing that it could be very difficult to maintain the same pace of progress from its current position (rank 4, Market share 3.1 percent in 1986), had appropriately changed its game plan to move further up in the Indian pharmaceutical market faster than the competition.

Cadila continued its aggressive stance in introducing new products. To facilitate a stronger and faster new product introduction program, Cadila started a second trading face - Alidac. The dramatic success achieved by Glaxo in managing multiple trading faces effectively to promote a wide range of products, probably had inspired Cadila to start Alidac.

After 1987, Cadila had introduced a number of new products through its two trading faces i.e, Cadila and Alidac. Cadila had introduced a number of new products in the rapidly growing therapeutic segments such as cardiovascular (Envas, Linvas, Diltime) , quinolones (Negafloz, Ciprobid, Ciprodac), anti-pepticulcerants (Famonit, Aciloc), antihistamines (Stemiz, Zoter) and protein supplements (GRD) etc.

All these new products introduced after 1987 by Cadila had accounted for about 50 percent of the company's overall growth between 1987 and 1991.

One can thus conclude that it was the new product planning, development and their effective implementation of the plans were responsible for the phenomenal growth (from a a 37th position to a prestigious 3rd place) that Cadila achieved between 1976 and 1991.

Later in 1995, Cadila had restructured itself into two different companies - Cadila Pharmaceuticals and Cadila Healthcare (later re-christened as Zydus Cadila Healthcare).

Case 13.4   Ranbaxy's Runaway Progress!

Ranbaxy, established in 1961, has been showing a very impressive and enviable growth rate. Ranked only 30th in 1976, Ranbaxy leaped into the big league by reaching the sixth position in the Indian pharmaceutical industry by 1986.

Ranbaxy, during this period of accelerated growth, meticulously followed a three-pronged strategy. Firstly, it expanded into newer markets and increased its customer coverage substantially in the domestic market. Secondly, it diversified into new product groups and launched as many as 23 new products between 1976 and 1986. Thirdly, Ranbaxy went international by setting up joint venture projects in countries like Nigeria, Thailand, Malaysia, and marketing operations in a number of other countries. Ranbaxy increased its group turnover from around Rs. 6-crore in 1976 to Rs. 96-crore by 1986. The pharmaceutical division of Ranbaxy alone increased its turnover from Rs. 4.9-crore to Rs. 38.9-crore during this period.

A closer look at the product-mix of Ranbaxy would reveal that it expanded in the fastest growing therapeutic groups like systemic anti-bacterials (Roscillin, Sporidex, Grmoneg) anti-tubercular (Tibrim, Tibrim-INH), non-narcotic analgesics (Fortwin), tranquilizers (Calmpose) during the first phase of its acceleration. Ranbaxy introduced about 23 new products between 1978 and 1986, which contributed to over 60 percent of the increase in the sales volume of Ranbaxy's pharmaceutical division.

In the five years that followed, Ranbaxy changed its focus from the therapeutic groups like tuberculostatic drugs that were price controlled to rapidly growing decontrolled product groups like anti-pepticulcerants (Histac), quinolones (Norbactin, Cifran), rejuvenators (Revital), antihistamines (Trexyl). It had further consolidated its leadership position in the largest therapeutic segment of the Indian pharmaceutical market, I.e., antibacterials with another new-generation cephalosporin drug (Keflor).

All these winning moves earned the coveted second place for Ranbaxy in the industry. Ranbaxy, in addition started a second marketing division - Stancare in the late 1980s. Stancare, in the late 1980s introduced a number of successful brands like Gramogyl in intestinal anti-infective segment, Zanocin in quinolone segment etc. This further reinforced Ranbaxy's position at the top, bridging the gap between Ranbaxy and Glaxo, the industry leader.

One of the key factors of Ranbaxy's rapid growth from a 30th position in the industry to the top two (group turnover Rs. 333-crore in 1991-92) in just fifteen years, was a systematic approach towards new product planning and implementation while exploiting opportunities all the way!

Case 13.5   Lupin's Leap-frogging!

Started in 1968, Lupin was able to reach only an obscure 98th position in the Indian pharmaceutical industry by 1976, with a mere Rs. 2-million in sales. In the ten years that followed, Lupin chose the rapidly growing anti-tubercular segment as a vehicle for its rapid growth. A number of new anti-TB drugs were introduced between 1976 and 1986. Lupin introduced its brands of all the new molecules that dramatically changed the approach towards anti-tubercular therapy like ehtambutol (Combutal), pyrizinamide (Pyzina), rifampicin (R-cin) and Rifampicin combinations (R-cinex) etc. Lupin also started manufacturing these bulk drugs. Lupin very aggressively promoted all its anti-TB brands with the sole objective of achieving the leadership position in that segment. The company achieved a formidable leadership position with a dominant 35 percent share of the total anti-tubercular market in India by 1986. The anti-tubercular range of Lupin accounted for almost one-half (49 percent) of the company's total sales in 1986-87.

Lupin, thus moved from a token presence (98th rank) in 1976 to a very prominent 20th position in the Indian pharmaceutical league table by 1986-87.

Lupin continued to accelerate its growth with the objective of reaching the top of the league. In five years, i.e., by 1991-92, the company had moved to the coveted ninth position. During this process of acceleration, Lupin further consolidated its already formidable position (1986-87) with 8.4 percent of the total anti-tubercular market to an un-impregnable portion with virtually one-half of the market tucked under its belt (50.5 percent in 1991-92).

Having leapfrogged during the past fifteen years to secure a place among the top ten of the Indian pharmaceutical industry, what is Lupin up to now? Lupin seems to move further up at faster pace. Its objective of crossing Rs. 1,000-crore mark is now common knowledge. Lupin had set up a joint venture at Thailand, stepped up its effort on the export front and integrated backward to manufacture its major product - Rifampicin, right from the basic fermentation stage.

All these plans notwithstanding, Lupin's massive concentration in the anti-tubercular segment is also indicative of its vulnerability. Its anti-TB range accounted for 60 percent of the company's formulation sales in India and these drugs are price controlled. Even during the last five years it is the anti-TB range that has contributed significantly to the overall growth of the company (over 40 percent). Other new products introduced by the company contributed around 20 percent. Having realized this, Lupin had become active in the rapidly growing cephalosporin segment (Ceff, Odxyl, Cezolin) and also planned an ambitious new product development program in the anti-viral segment as well. Lupin, though belatedly made an entry into the fastest growing segment - quinolones with its Ciprova. This move propelled Lupin once again from its 9th position into the top 5 in Indian pharmaceutical industry by 1995.

Case 13.6 Torrent True to its Name!

Torrent Pharma seems to be living up to its name. There had been an abundant stream of new products ever since Torrent Pharma appeared on the Indian pharmaceutical industry in 1959.

In 1976, Torrent did not have national operations and was not listed in the ORG retails store audit's 165 companies. But by 1986, Torrent stormed its way into the top fifty companies in the Indian pharmaceutical industry. It was ranked 50th with a sales volume of Rs. 10.8-crore in 1986.

Torrent seems to be following the *firstest with the mostest* policy in terms of new product planning. Torrent was the first company to introduce new products in a number of therapeutic categories.

Between 1980 and 1986 Torrent chose the psychotropic drugs segment as the major avenue for growth, subsequently achieving and maintaining the leadership position in the segment till 1992.

New products introduced after 1980 accounted for 84 percent of the sales volume of Torrent in 1986. Torrent introduced new products in three of the fastest growing therapeutic segments, namely, pshycotropic, cardiovascular and anti-peptic ulcerants.

Torrent identified the rapidly growing anti-peptic ulcerant and cardiovascular segments to accelerate growth and to consolidate its position in the late 1980s and the early 1990s. True to its tradition of being the first to introduce a new drug in segments of its choice, Torrent introduced the first brands of different molecules like ranitidine (Ranitin), famotidine (Topcid), and omeprazole (Omizac) among anti-peptic ulcerants. This move of entering all conceivable sub-segments secured a third place for Torrent wit a 11.3 percent share in this crowded and fast growing segment that is Rs.80-crore large (1992).

In the cardiovascular segment, Torrent introduced Dilzem, the first brand of diltiazem in India. This placed Torrent firmly in the saddle riding the cardiovascular market that is Rs 137.6-crore large, with an unassailable share of 13 percent in 1992.

Even in the relatively smaller antihistamine segment, Torrent was among the first two companies to introduce two new molecules namely astemizole (Astelong), and terfinadine (Tefril). Torrent's steady stream of new products was responsible for its uncommon success. New products introduced between 1980 and 1986 contributed about 80 percent to the growth of the company during that period.

The secret of Torrent's success can be attributed to its very aggressive new product planning and management. In just about twelve years, the company virtually out of nowhere really galloped into the 13th position in the Indian pharmaceutical industry.

A Program for New Product Evolution

Prior to birth, a new product goes through a gestation or prenatal process that may be short or long depending upon the complexity and the degree of newness, that virtually shapes the nature and survival of a product. These evolutionary phases, originally christened by the well known consultancy firm, Booz Allen and Hamilton have become a standard. These are:

A. **Exploration:** The search for a new product idea to meet the company objectives and goals.

B. **Screening:** A quick analysis essentially to determine which ideas are relevant and practicable, requiring a detailed investigation.

C. **Business Analysis:** The expression of accepted ideas through a detailed analysis into concrete business recommendations including product features, action programs and financial implications.

D. **Development:** Turning the idea-on-paper into a product-in-hand that can be demonstrated.

E. Testing: Designing and conducting commercial experiment to verify the early business judgments.

F. Commercialization: Launching the product in the market.

There are no rigid rules governing this six-stage new product development process. These stages may be called by different names by different practitioners. These stages may either be coupled or sub-divided depending upon the company's needs, goals and policies.

Basic Principles

Admittedly, there is no magic formula for new product success. If you study the success stories and failures of companies with their new products and analyze them carefully, you will find that there is a common thread running through them all. Some basic principles emerge. These basic principles are:

1. You need effective market research to understand and track changing customer needs. Market research helps you in identifying the new product opportunities on which you can capitalize. You minimize the chances of success if you fail to do effective market research. Market research does not necessarily mean all the sophisticated and latest techniques and multivariate analyses. What you need from market research at this stage is to know what new growth opportunities it has uncovered here and now.

2. The second logical step of course involves innovation. How can you innovatively develop a new product to meet the needs of customers that your market research has helped uncover? To be successful, new products must have a clear, significant, perceptible difference - a true reason for being - that is related to a need in the market place. Perceptible differentiation is the name of the game.

3. The formulation and implementation of the most aggressive marketing strategy is the crucial third step, without which, even the most effective market research and product development efforts will be seriously undercut.

4. To execute this effectively, you need the total support and commitment of the top management.

New Product Development Process

While there is no formula for success in developing new products, a systematic approach towards new product planning and execution will certainly help minimize the failure rate. Here is step-by-step approach towards planning and implementing new product development in the Indian pharmaceutical market. The suggested steps are:

1. Develop a new product blue print and strategy.

2. Analyze and rank potentially attractive therapeutic categories.

3. Generate ideas and develop concepts within the selected therapeutic categories.

4. Screen concepts and set priorities.

5. Conduct business analysis of selected concepts.

6. Work with R & D closely and help them develop the product as per the selected concepts and identified market needs.

7. Develop launch plan and commercialize the new product.

8. Prepare a detailed marketing and communication strategy and tactical plans for the launch year.

9. Monitor the performance regularly as per the plan.

1. **Developing a New Product Blueprint:** Your blueprint for new product development should clearly define the direction and role of new products as related to the company's overall objectives of growth and strategy. For example, you should spell out the role that new products have to play in the achievement of growth objectives of the company. Do they have a modest growth role, high growth role or only a survival role? What type of new products should the company develop in the future?

   This, to a large extent depends on the role you envisage for the new products. If you envisage a survival role, you will only be preparing a 'me-too' new product plan. Your approach to new product development is merely reactive. On the other hand, if you assign a high growth role, your posture towards new product development is proactive and an aggressive one at that. You will be directing your energies towards developing truly innovative, even 'new-to-the-world' type of products. In the Indian pharmaceutical industry, it is extremely difficult tho think of the 'new-to-the-world' type of new products, as the development costs are truly prohibitive. You can, however, plan to be the first in introducing a truly new product developed abroad. No matter what roles you assign to the new products and what objectives you set for them, your blueprint for new products should include:

- A description of the role that new products will play in the overall growth plan of the company.
- Budget estimates that indicate all developmental expenditure and capital investment for the new product effort.
- Product-wise sales and profit volume objectives for the five-year period, for all new products.
- Guidelines and benchmarks for successful new product performance.

2. **Analyzing and Ranking Potentially Attractive Categories**: What product categories should you defend (in your existing markets) and what new categories should you enter by introducing new products? The answer to this question depends to some extent on the growth roles you assign to your new products. Your new product blueprint would have prescribed some guidelines. In addition, you have to determine the therapeutic or product categories you want to enter based on their attractiveness in terms of:

A. Size of the potential market

B. Growth rate of the potential market

C. Extent of competition

D. Compatibility with your existing product lines in terms of manufacturing facilities and marketing capabilities like customer coverage, distribution channels etc.

E. Degree of newness

F. Profitability

It is important that you defend your share of your existing markets with existing products as well as update your product mix by preempting competition and planning in advance for product obsolescence that is inevitable in any case. If you want to stay ahead of competition, introduction of new, improved products in your existing markets (therapeutic categories) is a must. The case of Ranbaxy in urological market amplifies this point.

Case 13.7	Ranbaxy Defends its Leadership Position by Updating Its Products In Urological Market

Ranbaxy occupied the No.1 position in the Rs. 6.6-crore urological market in India in 1986 with its Gramoneg brand of nalidixic acid. Gramoneg continued to be the largest selling brand of nalidixic acid in the urological market even after the introduction of norfloxacin, the broad spectrum antibiotic with a high cure rate in urinary tract infections. But norfloxacin as a sub-category has carved out a 51 percent share of the total urological market.

Cipla, another company on the fast track in the Indian pharmaceutical industry, introduced Norflox, which had become the largest selling brand of norfloxacin in the country. Ranbaxy too had introduced Norbactin, their brand of norfloxacin almost simultaneously in 1987, and aggressively promoted it to retain its leadership position in the urological market. Even though, Ranbaxy had to contend with a No. 2 position for their Norbactin in the norfloxacin sub-segment after Cipla (Cipla's Norflox had a market share of 19.4 percent and Ranbaxy's Norbactin had a market share of 16.3 percent), Ranbaxy did defend its leadership position in the urological therapeutic category with a formidable share of 44.2 percent (Gramoneg, Norbactin combined).

The introduction of cirofloxacin, a new quinolone molecule in 1989 changed the complexion of the quinolone market by making it the largest and fastest growing subsegment among anti-bacterials in India.

The ever-alert Ranbaxy grabbed this opportunity and made Cifran, their brand of ciprofloxacin the fifth largest brand in the Indian pharmaceutical industry in less than three years (sales Rs. 18.9-crore in 1991-92). Consequently, Ranbaxy could further consolidate their leadership position in the quinolines sub-segment with a formidable share of about one-fourth of the total market under its belt.

Updating the product mix certainly helped Ranbaxy not only to defend its market share but also to remain far ahead of competition!

For determining the attractiveness of the therapeutic categories identified, and ranking them in order of their importance you can allot certain weights to each of the six attributes discussed earlier and develop evaluative criteria. The values or attributes to use, the scoring system , the weights and other details of this screening process are unique to each company. There are simply no prescribed rules for how to do it and that is how it should be.

There is however, one point to remember. Use items where decision can be made on low-cost, quickly available information. If you try to focus your attention on the details, on the point of precision at this stage, that will only diffuse your resources instead of focusing them on the essentials. Moreover, precision in new product development is more often an illusion.

The purpose of doing a category attractive analysis is to determine the priorities in terms of category selection in an objective manner. In pharmaceutical marketing, defending your market share and leadership position in a given therapeutic category involves some degree of cannibalization. Product obsolescence is a matter of fact and way of life in pharmaceutical market. When a new, more effective and superior therapeutic agent is introduced by some other company, it is bound to affect your product position. It is therefore, better to plan for product obsolescence yourself, at least in therapeutic categories where you enjoy a dominant position. Like Ranbaxy did it in the urological market and indeed even in the antibiotics market as such. That is what the industry leader Glaxo had done in the corticosteroid market even in 1990s. Glaxo introduced the latest topical steroid combinations with an anti-bacterial and anti-fungal under their new Eumosone brand, thus making their position even more formidable in the topical corticosteroid market with over half-of the market under their belt. The moral, therefore, is that if cannibalization despite imaginative positioning is inevitable, it is better if your own new product does it rather than your competitors'.

3. Generate Ideas and Develop Concepts within Categories Selected:

Idea generation is a very important first step. How many ideas should you generate? One way to answer this difficult question is to ask another question. How many new products do you want to market each year? If you want to introduce one major new product each year, then on an average you should plan to generate about 50 to 60 ideas each year. Remember the general statistics indicating the new product success rate in the US show that only one in 58 new product ideas is commercially successful.

What is even more important is that you should track and monitor the changing customer needs in the market place. What new needs are to be fulfilled in the market place? What new sub-therapeutic groups or categories are emerging? What changes are taking place in the line of treatment of certain major ailments? What newer and more potent drugs are currently under development abroad? You should be alert in monitoring these changes pertaining to the therapeutic categories where you are actively involved. Your priority in idea generation too should take this into cognizance.

Concept Development

Once you generate some ideas and initially screen them, the next step is to develop a concept statement for each of the selected ideas. A concept statement is a statement of the problem that the product is supposed to solve, and brief description of the need that you think exists. It also should define briefly the characteristics or attributes of the new product that makes the solution possible.

You must keep the language simple and direct while writing down a product concept. Do not be vague. Don't make statements that are judgmental such as, that it will be better, superior etc. Be precise and clear.

A clear, precise concept statement can ensure the success of your new product. It makes the task of product development and the preparation of communication strategy easier and more meaningful.

4. **Screen Concepts and set Priorities:** Once you define the product concepts, screen them carefully and set the priorities after evaluating them. Here are a few questions you should answer, when you are evaluating new product concepts.

   A. Are they likely to enhance the company's present position in the market place?

   B. Can your sales force handle these new products successfully? Is there a need to train them especially for the new products?

   C. What about distribution? Are the existing channels adequate?

5. **Business Analysis:**The next step is to conduct the business analysis of selected product concepts. The major factors to be considered during a business analysis are:

   A. **Sales Volume Potential:** Before making any estimates of expected sales, it is important to size up the opportunity. What is the size of the total market? What is the extent of competition, both direct and indirect? The indirect competition includes all the products that can be used as substitutes for the same condition or indication. Adding up the sales volumes of all competitive products, you can arrive at the size of the total market. You should also find out the growth trends of the market. What share of the market could your *product-entry* reasonably expect to capture during the first year and second year? Answers to these questions will be helpful in shaping up your product strategy and plans.

   B. **Profit Potential:** The key questions to answer in evaluating or assessing the profit potential of your product are:

      1. What will be the product's gross margins? How are they comparable to your existing products? To competitive products in the same category?

      2. What levels of marketing expenditures are needed to achieve the projected sales volumes in the first year and second year?

      3. What is the breakeven point? By what time are you likely to achieve the breakeven point as per the projected sales volumes?

      4. Are the raw materials and packaging materials freely available and their costs stable? Are there any shortage forecasts for these that might lead to cost escalation?

      5. Do the returns on investment projections for the product under consideration offer the best alternative use of capital?

      6. Considering that the product is priced at par with competition and since the trade margins are virtually the same for all competitors in a given product category (the retail margins are fixed by the DPCO 1987), will the product generate a gross margin equal to or more than for current products?

7. What is the projected pay-back period or breakeven point in capital investment?

8. Introductory marketing investment in terms of months after the product introduction date?

C. **Product Line Compatibility:** If the proposed new products are compatible with the existing product lines of your company, then the risk and expenditure of developing them is minimal. The degree of compatibility can be measured in two broad functional areas, namely marketing and production. The important aspects to be considered from the marketing point of view are:

1. The degree of competitiveness of the proposed new products with the existing products is important as it indicates the likely extent of cannibalization among your products. You can plan to minimize or avoid this if you are aware of it. If cannibalization of your brands is inevitable then you can still decide to introduce the new products, provided your company can achieve a better position in the category than before or balance the likely loss of sales and possible gain from new product sales.

2. Whether your existing distribution channels are adequate for marketing your product profitably? Are additional distribution channels needed? Are they cost-effective?

3. Whether the proposed new products can be handled by your existing sales force effectively? Do they require new skills and knowledge? What are their new product training needs?

4. Whether the target customers for the proposed new products are currently on your company's visiting list? If not, should you include them after proper prospecting? Can they be reached effectively without affecting the coverage of existing customers? Or is there any possibility of rationalizing the existing customer list? For example if you are planning to launch some cardiovascular drugs for the first time and if you company is not covering cardiologists currently, you will have to naturally include them in your visiting list of customers. Whether you can

cover these new doctors effectively with your existing sales force or you have to add more medical representatives to your sales force is what you have to decide.

From the production point of view you have to consider:

A. Whether the proposed new product can be manufactured in your existing manufacturing facilities.

B. If not, what is the level of capital investment needed to create the facilities and to acquire the new equipment required?

C. Competitive strength evaluation.

The extent of competitive intensity in the category or market you are planning to enter with your proposed new products is also a very important factor to be considered. The key questions to be answered while evaluating the competitive strength are:

(a) The intensity of competition in the market, whether it is highly fragmented or dominated by a few competitors.

(b) The production facilities and capabilities of your major competitors.

(c) The marketing strength of the major competitors, their coverage, distribution network, sales force capabilities etc.

(d) The relative strengths and weaknesses of the products of your major competitors.

(e) The levels and expenditure of the promotional efforts of your major competitors.

You can give a rating to the financial evaluation, product line compatibility, competitive intensity, and other aspects of business analysis for the purpose of determining the relative attractiveness on a ten point scale, as you have done earlier to rank the categories in order of their importance.

6. Product Performance, Customer Acceptance and Market Tests: Working closely with R & D and production in translating the selected concept into an usable product and testing its performance in the market place is the next step. Test marketing is not a common practice in the Indian pharmaceutical industry. As regards to product acceptance tests by customers, only the mandatory clinical trials for registering the drug are conducted by the company launching a product for the first time in the country. Some companies as a part of their promotional strategy, organize focal clinical trials with a number of doctors. However, if you have a truly new concept it is worthwhile to conduct multi-center clinical trials as well as the focal clinical trials with all the opinion leaders.

7. **Product Development and Preliminary Marketing Plans:** Now that you have decided that your product idea is viable, it is time to really look into all other aspects of product development and preliminary marketing plans. Here is a checklist:

- Write down the raw material specifications
- Develop the production specifications
- Determine the shipper sizes
- Select the brand name. Since getting the brand name registered takes a minimum of two to three years in India, it is better to have a number of brand names registered before hand in the categories you would like to enter. Whenever you are ready with a new product, you can select a brand name from your already registered list.
- Develop the packaging including specifications of packaging materials. Check whether you labeling is in accordance with the drug laws.
- Decide on the price.
- Fulfill all the licensing and other legal requirements. For example, test license is required for development purpose. Drug license for manufacturing and DGTD registration for commercializing the product are required. Price approval is required before you actually market the product.

8. **Marketing Strategy and Tactics:** Prepare a detailed tactical plan for marketing the new product. The plan should cover all the details for the launch year and be based on the core concept. Broad guidelines for follow-up promotion in the second and third years should also be written. This is necessary to maintain continuity and consistency for building the brand image. Here is a checklist:

- Develop the advertising strategy
- Develop the sales training program
- Develop the sales and promotional material including product monographs, literature, leave-behind leaflets, brochures, visual-aids etc.
- Fix territory-wise the sales targets
- Develop the feedback systems
- Select the key customers depending upon your segmentation strategy
- Anticipate competitive reaction
- Chalk out detailed tactical plan for launching the product

This list is by no means exhaustive. You may add some more details, which you consider appropriate and important. Many of the items on this list are very close to your everyday business activities. Commercializing a product concept means translating the idea into everyday business reality and activity. These items are very important, if not crucial. If they are not given due importance and attention, they can become critical. If you allow them to be critical, you will put your new product project into jeopardy.

Speed by All Means but not Rush

There will be a lot of pressure to get your new products to market as quickly as possible. Top management wants to recover investment as soon as possible. The project team wants to complete the project at least on schedule, if not ahead, because time is really money. Speed, therefore is vital. A new product project should move at a brisk pace. At the same time, one should not rush things. All these pressures should not lead you to introduce a product into the market before it is really ready and not, until is one hundred percent marketable. Do not even be tempted to say or listen to the danger words - *we will take care of that later.*

9. **Monitor Your Performance Regularly:** Elementary and fundamental as it may seem, monitoring performance of new products on a regular basis is an almost forgotten step in many companies. Once the product is commercialized, probably the *novelty* and the consequent or in-built excitement are gone. The common temptation is to revise the forecasts of new products

for six months or even longer instead of analyzing and finding out reasons. Monitoring the performance of new products regularly against the original plan forecasts can provide significant insights and help you leverage the development of successful new products.

Evaluating New Products

What makes some companies more successful in new product planning, development and management than others? What is that quality that separates the men from the boys? Well, the answer is experience. By experience, we mean here the learning experience. The experience of learning from past mistakes and the ability to build upon previous successes. Learning from past performance requires capitalizing on the things that were done right and correcting the things that were done wrong. Tracking, monitoring and evaluating the new product performance of both past and present new products (past new products being the ones that were introduced less than five years ago). If your rate of new product introduction is higher, you can set even a shorter time limit. There are no rigid rules. But it is advisable to determine the phase of the life cycle of the product group before you set any time limit.

A new product diagnostic audit is a very useful tool that can be used to pick up the blueprint to guide the future. Here is what it can do to your new product development program:

1. Quantifies the past new product performance in terms of revenue generated and profit earned.
2. Identifies the reasons and underlying causes for each new product success and failure.
3. Compares actual performance to original product forecasts.
4. Helps identify the company's strengths and weaknesses.
5. Helps in estimating the developmental and launch costs with a reasonable degree of accuracy.
6. Helps in improving the success rate of new products.

There are five major steps in evaluating new product performance. These are:

1. Review the new product performance in terms of sales volumes and profits for preceding five years.
2. Assess the new product performance against the original objective.
3. Check new product survival rate.
4. Identify the causes behind the new product's success or failure.
5. Identify the strengths of top new products' competitors.

1. **New Product Performance Review:** The key questions to ask during a new product performance review are:

   A. How much money was generated by each of your new products during the past five years? List all new products introduced by you year-wise during the past five years and the revenues generated by them each year and cumulatively.

   B. How much profit volume was generated by each of these new products each year and cumulatively?

   C. What were the developmental costs and the marketing expenditure of these new products each year and cumulatively?

   D. What were the net profits (before tax) earned by these new products each year and cumulatively?

   E. What were the payback periods for each of these new products?

2. **New Product Performance Vs. Original Objectives**: Is there a performance gap? The next step of the new product diagnostic audit is to assess the new product performance against the original plan objectives.

3. **What is Your New Product Survival Rate?**: How many new products did you introduce during the past five years? How many of them are moving out of the chemists' shelves today actively? How many of them are gathering dust on the retail counters currently? How many of them are non-existent, whether in the market place or in the doctor's mind? How many of them are actively promoted even today? What is the survival rate of your new products?

4. **Secrets and Reasons**: While the hard data is arranged in the formats suggested for the purpose of conducting the new product diagnostic audit, an in-depth analysis based on these facts is likely to unfold very valuable information. The secrets of your

new product success and the reasons behind the failure of other new products are hidden behind these facts. An open mind, a questioning attitude and analytical ability are what you need to uncover these facts. The many lessons that one can learn from such an analysis will be of immense help in planning and implementing a winning new product program. To identify the reasons behind the successes and failures, you have to examine:

- The assumptions made in the business analysis; how did your information and interpretation differ from your observations in the market?

- Data and analysis behind the original forecasts and the variance between planned objectives and actual performance.

- Whether any external factors influenced your performance - like competitive responses, distribution and consumer-demand shifts etc.

- Whether any internal factors affected your performance - insufficient research, inadequate funds, top management commitment, inadequate facilities and so on.

- The quality of implementation of the launch plans.

5. **Analyze Your Major Competitors**: How are your major competitors faring with their new products? What is their success rate? What is the survival rate of their new products? As a first step to this analysis you have to identify top two or three competitors, for each your new products. You may find that one or two competitors, who pursue a very aggressive and dynamic new product program, turn up more than once as common competitors for several new products. Prepare a list of competitors for each new product launched and the type of new products developed by each competitor during the same period. Collect as much data as you can pertaining to their sales volume, growth rate, market share, advertising to sales ratio, cost of manufacturing etc, from published sources and the feedback reports of your own sales force.

Compare the performance of your major competitors with your own performance in each new product category. Ensure that you evaluate the reasons behind the varying degrees of success. The major advantage of identifying and analyzing a competitor's new products activity is that you are sure to gain insight on how they might respond to new products that are launched in their served markets.

Organizing for Success

The single most important part of a successful new product development strategy is people. There is no doubt about that. All the models, analyses and methods are of no value if the wrong people, or worse by the right people in the wrong organization use them. Assigning the right people and ensuring the right organizational structure for them to function effectively is, therefore crucial for the success of any new product development program. That is the critical responsibility of the top management. What is the right organization structure for new product development? Where should the responsibility lie? Should it be with the R & D department since it is the scientists, technicians and engineers, who finally assess the feasibility and develop the physical product? While this seems and sounds logical there are a few drawbacks.

A majority of new product failures are not technical failures, they are market failures. Since R & D personnel are not likely to be close to the market they may end up a developing a product that has no market. The second drawback is that since R & D people are likely to think far ahead into the distant future, there is a possibility that they will focus on products that are simply far ahead of their time and not on those, which can earn profits immediately.

Is the marketing department a logical choice for shouldering the new product development responsibility? Since marketing personnel are closest to the market, are they the logical and automatic choice? Convincing as it may seem, there are certain drawbacks even with this type of organizational structure.

Experience has shown that new products developed by marketing departments tend to have minor product differentiation of the existing product lines, and that too, very often no more than cosmetic changes. The second major drawback is that since marketing personnel have full-time jobs managing existing products and are rather bogged down with their day to day problems, they are not likely to focus the kind of attention that new product development demands.

That leaves two more options - starting a new product

development department or forming a new product development committee. What should be the composition of these? Ideally they should comprise of talented people from marketing, R & D, and production. Many companies seem to be paying lip service towards the formation of such committees. Instead of seconding the most talented and innovative personnel from their respective departments, they seem to be sending people who can be spared to such committees. Furthermore, in a committee, accountability is not clearly defined.

The new product development department is usually is not given adequate importance in the organizational hierarchy and does not create the much-needed atmosphere of *involvement and commitment* of the other functional departments. They are (the new product people) usually labeled as dreamers.

The key question is how to create a climate that nurtures and develops the spirit of innovation? Some companies seem to have found an answer. Companies that are more aggressive on the new product front have created *venture teams.* The talented personnel from all major functional areas such as marketing, finance, R & D, and production are brought together to form a venture team for a specific new product project. They are empowered to cut through the red tape. They are made accountable for the specific task they are chosen to accomplish. They have a team leader who coordinates the activities of the venture team and provides feedback to the top management. Only the best performers from all the functional areas are chosen for the venture teams. The importance, the recognition and the rewards given to these venture teams are the major motivating factors. These factors also act as optimum pressure points and ensure that the venture teams accomplish the tasks for which they are created. *Product champion* is another concept that is followed in some of the companies that have accomplished an enviable strike-rate with their new products. A *product champion* is an empowered, committed, and die-hard new product development manger. The idea is to promote *entrepreneurship* with in an organization.

Whatever organization structure a company may choose, the most important factor to remember and act upon is that the new product program must have the unqualified support of top management.

Summary

New product development is a very expensive process. It can also be a very risky proposition. But then, it is rewarding as well. Rewarding is probably an understatement. New product development is crucial for the success of any business enterprise. With increasing and intensifying competition, new product development is fast becoming mandatory even for the survival of business.

The new product development process involves six steps that are universally acknowledged. These are - idea generation, screening, business analysis, development, testing and commercialization.

What are new products? Any product that is new to your company is a new product as far as you are concerned. If it (similar product) is already in the market, your new product is a 'me-too' new product. The new products can broadly be classified into products that are:

A. New to the world

B. New to the company

C. Line extensions and

D. Flankers

The risk and cost of developing new products increase with the degree of newness. Developing new products that are new to the world involves a very high degree of risk but then, the rewards of successful 'new-to-the-world' new products are equally high.

Why is it that only a few companies are very successful with new products whereas many others are not? Are there any secrets behind their success? Is there any formula for effective, successful new product development? Of Course, there is no magic formula and there are no secrets of success. If there are secrets, they are open secrets. They can be seen, heard, or felt by the discerning observer. There are many lessons to be learnt from the successes and failures of the new product development programs of various companies. Here is a synthesis of these valuable lessons.

In fact, these are not just lessons. They are more than that. They are the commandments. They are mandatory for successful new product development. The Ten Commandments of successful new product development program are:

1. **Prepare a blueprint for a new product development program:** Define the overall direction of the new product development. Spell out the objectives, goals, resources needed, and their strategic roles clearly.

2. **Plan a new product strategy:** Prepare a well thought out new product strategy. Role clarity and goal clarity for your new products are essential. Identify new product categories and the types of new products you want to launch. Determine the screening criteria. Set performance benchmarks. Anticipate the likely moves of competition.

3. **Consistency in implementation:** Implementing and executing the tactical plan thoroughly right from concept to commercialization is of vital importance.

4. **Homework:** The quality of your strategy and tactical planning depend on the extent and quality of the homework you have done. Meticulous homework is needed to collect and analyze, consumer information from the market on competition, business analysis and category selection etc.

5. **Tracking:** Tracking rather than monitoring the progress of your new product performance against planned objectives and the competitive responses to your strategies is crucial for your new product success. It provides valuable feedback.

6. **Clear Accountability**: The importance of clear accountability can never be over-emphasized. New product development must be a specific responsibility. The persons in charge of this important task must be made accountable and their performance should be evaluated on objective criteria.

7. **Teamwork**: Involvement and commitment are the key words. The new product development team must clearly perceive that their role is really important to the organization and must know what is expected of them. Teamwork can be developed only by mutual respect for each others' competence among all the team members.

8. **Motivation and Rewards**: Rewards and motivation must match the accomplishment of tasks. It is not enough if you say that you are the future of the company. The new product development people are interested in their present as well, even while they are thinking about the future of the company (by developing new products).

9. **People Decisions**: Staffing the new product department is the most important and crucial task of all. Perseverance, optimism, enthusiasm, initiative and creativity are some of the essential attributes that a product champion should have.

10. **Top Management Commitment**: Top management commitment, above all, is what determines the success or failure of a new product program for a company.

Companies that believe in and pay attention to these ten commandments or key success factors are bound to succeed. Companies that pay only lip service to new product development and do not pay heed to these commandments are sure to end up quietly as a whimper. It does not really matter even if they had started once upon a time with a big bang!

Winning Game Plans

Changing Rules!

The rules of the game at the market place are constantly changing. What made one company successful yesterday may not be good enough even for that company, let alone for others to succeed either in the present or future. Changing rules call for changing approaches and changing strategies. Companies should constantly be monitoring the changes in the environment and upgrading themselves to outperform the competition in every department of the game, in order to reach the top, and more importantly to stay there happily ever after.

How Does One Outperform the Competition?

One of the best ways to answer this is to observe, examine, and study how some companies have successfully outperformed their respective competitors. Such a study would provide valuable insights into the principles behind formulating winning strategies.

The following are a few cases highlighting how some companies have successfully fought their way through crowded competition and captured the commanding positions to which they are able to hold on dearly even today. The discerning marketer can certainly learn an invaluable lesson or two and realize the importance of the role of the *grand strategy* or *game plan* in the business of winning at the market place.

These *cases* are not exhaustive studies and they lack a detailed financial performance analysis, in terms of resource allocation and profitability achieved in each therapeutic segment. The financial data pertaining to product-mix allocations, cost data and margins on products is closely guarded and not available for private scrutiny.

These cases are brief enough to sustain the interest of the reader and long enough to cover the salient strategic issues so that marketing scholars and practitioners can draw the necessary inferences.

Case 14.1   The Giant Learns to Dance!

For over thirty-two years in a row (1976 to 2008) Glaxo Laboratories (GSK now) in India has been holding on to its leadership position very firmly. Glaxo's staying power had been truly remarkable. Adversity seems to have brought out the best in Glaxo from the early 1970s, for it was after the promulgation of the DPCO 1970, that Glaxo started its process of consolidation and stayed on top happily ever after. How did the company achieve what it achieved? Here is a brief account of its key strategic actions.

Structuring for Success

Glaxo had been a very large, almost monolithic organization for many years. The take over of British Drug Houses (BDH) in the late 1960s made it even bigger. For an organization that was as big as Glaxo, any change over from the existing scheme of things would naturally be a painfully slow process if not an impossible one. The sheer size makes it difficult to move. The marketing and regulatory environment made it even more difficult.

The 1970 DPCO made optimization a theme song for the pharmaceutical industry. The message was loud and clear. Optimize or perish! Glaxo in the early 1970s restructured its business and implemented a divisionalization program effectively. The purpose was to optimize the resources, ensure enhanced accountability and achieve a greater penetration to gain a bigger share in certain therapeutic segments.

Around the 1980s, it became mandatory for multinational companies operating in India to reduce the foreign equity to less than fifty percent, in order to compete effectively with Indian companies. Indian companies had an advantage over multinationals in terms of new product licenses etc.

Glaxo, despite being the giant that it was, reacted to these rather quickly and persuaded its parent company to bring down the equity so that it could maintain its leadership position in the Indian pharmaceutical industry. Glaxo U.K. bought the idea and diluted the equity and then let its giant Indian subsidiary exploit the marketing opportunities in the sub-continent.

To successfully exploit these dormant opportunities after non-FERA status, Glaxo started a new division, Pulsar, essentially to launch the company's international winner and the world's largest selling prescription drug, Zantac. The company had to rename it as Zinetec in India as regulations in the country did not allow international brand names under the same name (it was supposed to give them an unfair advantage. Now that rule has been changed and international brand names are allowed in India).

Through the creation of Pulsar division, Glaxo India achieved the twin objectives of making Zinetec the unquestioned leader in the rapidly growing anti-peptic ulcerant market and building its corporate image as a trendsetter and opinion leader, among the medical profession. Glaxo till then had an excellent franchise among general practitioners, dermatologists and certain consulting physicians but not among the opinion leaders as it was not focusing on them. Pulsar division bridged the vital gap, which facilitated Zinetec's uncommon success.

In the 1990s the bottom line of Glaxo started eroding due to the escalation of material costs and overheads and a virtual freeze on finished formulation prices. The company once again moved swiftly and restructured its Pharma business as two SBUs (Strategic Business Units) sharing common services like medical distribution, legal and corporate communications. The two SBUs are:

1. Glaxo
2. Glaxo Allenburys

Pulsar had been merged with Glaxo- Allenburys. The basic objective of this reorganization was to achieve greater market penetration, a sharper competitive edge and optimization of resources towards improving the market share and profitability.

Who says that giants cannot move swiftly? Of course, they can! Giants can even dance if they learn to, and if they want to!

Pace Setting

Glaxo India had been an innovative company, particularly in the area of marketing. While Glaxo, the parent company in the United Kingdom was busy inventing new drugs, Glaxo India had been creating continuous innovation in marketing, living up to its leadership status. Glaxo had been playing a pioneer's role till the 1990s in the area of marketing. Consider these facts:

- The use of Visual-aid for medical detailing was a pioneering effort Glaxo in the 1970s. Today, virtually all pharmaceutical companies in India use a Visual-aid for detailing their products as a standard practice.
- Glaxo introduced systematic approach towards product prescription monitoring in the early 1970s, based on the scientific practice of survey based marketing research method.
- Many innovative marketing communication strategies to get nay, to grab the attention of prospective prescribers have been introduced.
- Preparation and distribution of media abstracts on the proceedings of medical conferences was yet another innovative feature in Glaxo's marketing-mix. This was indeed a very creative use of product publicity.
- Glaxo had also launched what was probably the country's first comprehensive patient eduction program for patients with asthma in the 1980s. A pioneering effort indeed.
- Furthermore, Glaxo had also sponsored around the same time the first-ever patient education telephone service - ASMALINC, at St. George Hospital, Bombay. The Asthma and Bronchitis Association of India conceived the project. It is however, discontinued now.

- The twin-brand strategy through its two marketing divisions was another pioneering marketing strategy in India in the late 1970s. Glaxo had introduced similar formulations under two different brand names through its two marketing divisions in a number therapeutic categories like Vitamin B-complex oral solids (Cobadex Forte and Vibelan Forte), Multivitamin Mineral combinations oral solids (Becadexamin and Multivite FM), Cough preparations (Piriton Expectorant and Dilosyn Expectorant) etc. Both the divisions aggressively promoted their respective brands. The company, thanks to its twin-brand strategy has achieved and maintained formidable leadership positions in all these therapeutic categories.
- In 1983, Glaxo was the only company with two separate pharmaceutical divisions to promote formulations in India. Inspired by the success of Glaxo's multi-division and twin-brand strategies, a number of other leading companies such as Cadila , Cipla, Ranbaxy, Alembic, Torrent, Wockhardt had started a second and even a third trading face or division to promote different formulations.

Teamwork

Glaxo's major strength was that it has a well trained and highly motivated sales force. Its restructuring in marketing and the change of guard seem to have further reinforced the 'never-say-die' spirit of the sales force positively. No wonder the entire marketing team was seen humming the catchy tune of their audio-visual's theme song - *nothing's gonna stop us now!*

Restructuring - A Way of Life

Glaxo was on a consolidation mode since 1995. The company had acquired Burroughs Wellcome in 1995 through an international merger. It had later in 1997 acquired an Indian drug company - Biddle Sawyer in India. Subsequently, in 1998 it began a restructuring exercise to achieve sharper marketing focus among major specialty prescriber segments and therapeutic areas. It had created seven SBUs (Strategic Business Units) to achieve this. Hardly a year after the formation of these seven SBUs.

Glaxo had engineered another global merger with SmithKline Beecham to become the world's largest Pharma corporation - GlaxoSmithKline. It was back to the drawing board again for yet another reengineering exercise to further rationalize its product mix and marketing mix and reinforce its specialty focus and customer franchise among the major prescriber segments. Restructuring indeed had become a way of life at GlaxoSmithKline.

Case 14.2   Ranbaxy: No Tail Lights Ahead, No Headlights Behind!

Ranbaxy is the only Indian pharmaceutical company with a truly global outlook. It had many distinctions to its credit. Consider these for example:

Ranbaxy had moved into the top 100 pharmaceutical companies' league in the world. It was the first Asian company to achieve this in the early 1990s. Later it moved up to become one of the top 50 Asian companies that were best prepared to excel in the global market place of the 21st century, according to a survey of 4,500 listed companies from 14 Asian countries by Arthur D. Little and Asia Inc. The survey ranked Ranbaxy in the eleventh place: one of only five Indian companies in the top 50 and the only pharmaceutical company in the top 25. Ranbaxy topped the US $ 1-billion mark in 2002 and became the first Indian drug firm to do so.

Dominant Player

Ranbaxy had achieved a consistently high growth rate since 1988. Its sales had grown from Rs. 17.59-billion in 1999 to over Rs. 55.32-billion in 2004, a compounded annual growth of around 34 percent over a six-year period.

Ranbaxy had also become during this period, India's leading pharmaceutical exporter accounting for about 15 percent of the country's exports of pharmaceutical substances and finished dosage forms. Exports, which accounted for less than 20 percent of company's total sales in 1978-79, accounted for over one-half of the company's total sales in 2004.

The company became a leading player in the domestic market, with an undisputed leadership position in the anti-infective segment, which accounted for almost a quarter of the Indian pharmaceutical market. Ranbaxy had achieved a dominant leadership position in the domestic market with a market share that was nearly twice as much as its nearest Indian rival. Ranbaxy's total sales were around Rs. 55.32-billion, where as Cipla, the second largest Indian player recorded a total sales of only Rs. 23-billion during the same period. Ranbaxy's sales from international operations alone were more than the total sales of other Pharma majors in the Indian sector.

Strategic Vision

How did Ranbaxy achieve all this? The company had a clear vision. It had clearly defined goals, milestones and inflection points in its journey to the top. The company reformulated the goals once it reached the milestones. Consider for example the vision of its chairman Dr. Parvinder Singh, when he reformulated the company's goal to be among the *top three generic drug companies in the world,* almost immediately on making it to the prestigious list of the world's top hundred pharmaceutical companies. He had clearly seen the future before it arrived. On becoming an international generic drug company, he had reset and articulated the mission for his company that it should become a *research-based international pharmaceutical company.* And it did become a research-based international pharmaceutical company with its discovery of a new molecule for the treatment of Benigon Prostatic Hyperplasia (BPH) and its licensing arrangement with an international drug major.

Ranbaxy had realized the importance of achieving cost leadership in order to be globally competitive and had achieved this through a combination of planned technological up-gradation and backward integration. The company's manufacturing plants for bulk actives as well as formulations have approvals of international regulatory authorities like US FDA, UK MCA etc. The company had an enviable portfolio of bulk actives and intermediates, making it a vertically integrated drug firm. This dual strategy had helped the company in achieving a competitive position internationally. The company also achieved world-class quality and predictable control on its costs, quality and timely delivery of inputs. Barring Teva, the rapidly growing international generic drug firm from Israel, there are not many international generic drug firms that were as vertically integrated as Ranbaxy in the 1990s.

The Marketing Mindset

Ranbaxy had been a market-driven company. Three of its brands were among the top ten of the Indian pharmaceutical industry. The company had 12 of its prescription drug brands among the industry's top 250 brands in 1998. In addition to its brand building activity in the domestic market, Ranbaxy had also been investing in a global brand building exercise. It had identified 25 molecules that were going off patent before 2005. The company had planned to channelize its integrative power and manufacturing infrastructure at home and abroad to achieve synergies in building these into 25 global generic brands.

Structure was another area where Ranbaxy was distinctly different from other pharmaceutical companies in India. It was trying to shed the typical headquarters mentality of management and had created four well thought out regional headquarters to manage its far-flung business operations. The four regions are the Americas, with Raleigh as the headquarters, Europe, Common Wealth of Independent States (CIS) and Africa with London as the Headquarters, India and the Middle East with New Delhi as the headquarters and Asia Pacific with Hong Kong as the headquarters.

Harnessing the Alliance Power

The company was very well poised to exploit the big opportunity of the generic markets in the west, particularly in the US. It already had approvals for two products. Ten more Abbreviated New Drug Applications (ANDA)s were awaiting approval. The company was planning to file ten ANDAs every year to build an optimum product portfolio of 35 to 40 generic formulations by

2003. Ranbaxy was confident of generating a sales turnover of US $ 150 million out of these by 2003. To achieve this ambitious objective, the company had already acquired a generic company in the US and formed, in addition strategic alliances with Schein Pharma and HMS to market its generic formulations. Ranbaxy was already preparing to have full fledged marketing team in the US by the 2003.

Important Initiatives

1. Ranbaxy had been building on its core competencies over the years. The company had been investing on both acquisition and nurturing of talent. It had a more competent and better-informed management team in place, compared to most other Indian drug companies.

2. Ranbaxy was the first Indian drug firm to have invested in sophisticated Enterprise Resource Planning (ERP) systems. Ranbaxy was planning to implement five modules of ERP: sales and distribution, materials management, production planning, finance and costing. The company was investing about one percent of its turnover on information technology. The company was planning to digitize its operations across all its markets in the next two to three years by creating an ubiquitous digital network to be competitive externally.

3. Another significant strategic differential that Ranbaxy had chosen was creating value through communication. The company was planning to achieve this through e-mail, intranet and website. It had planned to use intranet extensively. The company was regularly putting up the chairman's messages on the intranet. All employees were able to download corporate presentations made anywhere in the company from the intranet. The company was targeting potential employees using InfoTech.

4. Ranbaxy was implementing this project to bring in a perceptible culture change in its management team. To implement this project called *Project Diamond*, the company had put up a team of 30 young people with diverse backgrounds from within Ranbaxy and from its consultancy firm - Price Waterhouse Coopers. This team, aptly called *Team Diamond* acted as a change agent to usher in an era of digital culture.

5. Ranbaxy was also planning to build, around its website, communities of physicians, medical students, consultants, and final users from different therapeutic segments. The company was also building a database of doctors to create an eclectic club. It had already set up various centers across the country in hospitals and medical colleges that have access to Medline International.

6. Ranbaxy had also planned to use information technology for filing and managing electronic dossiers. The company had more than 900 different dossiers for clearance of different products in different countries with different regulatory regimes. This would facilitate faster clearance and take the products quickly to the market.

7. Further, the company had planned to use Info Tech in combinatorial chemistry and high-throughput screening in the area of new drug discovery research. The companies, which were using information technology in research area, were talking about screening thousand compounds a month as compared to one-hundred a year in the past.

Research and Development

Ranbaxy had set up an independent research center with an investment of Rs. 200-million. The company had spent 6.1 percent of its sales on research in the year 2000 and increased it to about Rs. 4-billion, which was about 10 percent of its sales in 2004. Ranbaxy had already licensed the exclusive development and global marketing rights for an oral once-a-day dosage form of ciprofloxacin to the German drug major, Bayer AG., who discovered ciprofloxacin. It has already received about US $ 15-million in upfront and milestone payments and will further receive payments in excess of US $ 50-million over the next two years depending upon the speed and scope of development and regulatory approvals. Ranbaxy also had five New Chemical Compounds (NCEs) in therapeutic segments like urology, respiratory, anti-fungal and anti-bacterial at different phases of development.

Winning Combination

Ranbaxy had clearly emerged as a winner in Pharma industry not just from the subcontinent but also from the entire Asian continent. Apart from all its winning moves and strategic initiatives, what separated Ranbaxy from others had been its winning combination of strategic vision and execution capabilities. A leading international strategic consultant had observed that he found in Dr. Parvinder Singh, the Chairman and D.S. Brar, the President of Ranbaxy, a world-beating combination. Dr. Singh was a visionary and Brar was impeccable in execution.

Later in 2007, Daichi, the Japanese drug major had acquired Ranbaxy. Sun Pharma more recently in 2014 acquired Ranbaxy from Daichi.

Case 14.3   Dr. Reddy's Labs: It's Time to Dream Again!

Dr. K. Anji Reddy had a dream in the mid-eighties when he founded Dr. Reddy's Laboratories (DRL) - *to put India on the bulk drug map of the world.* He had helped many of his scientists master the reverse engineering of process technology and achieved phenomenal success in developing cost-effective processes for many of the new molecules.

Research Focus

After reaching a critical mass in sales of Rs. 18.35 billion in 2004, and after India had implemented product patents, Dr. Anji Reddy had another dream. This time it was t*o put India on the drug discovery map of the world.* He had already started Dr. Reddy's Research Foundation (DRF), a world class research and development centre in 1994, as soon as India became a signatory to the GATT agreement. He started the drug discovery program and put the country on the drug discovery map of the world with the historical agreement between DRF and the Danish drug major, Novo Nordisk for taking the new insulin sensitizing molecules through further stages of development to commercialization. Later the project was shelved as the molecules were found to be not so promising.

The company raised R & D investments significantly from Rs. 2.26-billion in 2004 to Rs.2.97-billion in 2005. Dr. Reddy's Labs also commenced the first-ever clinical trials project outside India on two NCE assets and completed the phase I trials for DRF 10945 in Canada and RUS 3108 phase I trials in Ireland.

DRL had by 2005 a very impressive portfolio of 65 Drug Master Files (DMFs) and 45 Abbreviated New Drug Applications (ANDAs) with the US FDA. The company stepped up product filings in several international markets. This placed the DRL group in the forefront of the Indian pharmaceutical industry - not because of its present size or performance but based on future potential. The company's performance in the first decade of the new millennium too was nothing short of spectacular, with a growth rate that was three times faster than the average for the domestic industry.

The company had already been granted 19 US patents out of 55 filed by 2005. It had set up a US $ 2-million state-of-the-art laboratory at Atlanta, Georgia in the US to reinforce and accelerate its drug discovery process.

Critical Mass

The company had been on a brand acquisition spree to maintain a high growth rate. The company had acquired two brands Riflux and Clamp from SOL Pharma and Becelac brand from Pfimex in 1996. Later it had acquired five brands - Styptovit, Styptomet, Styptochrome, Doxt, and Trichodol from the Calcutta based Dolphin Laboratories.

These brand acquisitions were aimed at consolidating the company's position in the therapeutic segments of its focus and also in extending the therapeutic coverage. The company had acquired more brands such as Dinoprine Gel, Deviprost and PG Tab from Dai -ichi -Karkaria to strengthen its product portfolio in the woman's healthcare segment.

The company had become even more aggressive in the new millennium and changed the acquisition gears from brands to companies. It acquired the Rs. 92-crore American Remedies Limited to move into the top five position in the Indian pharmaceutical industry.

Marketing Focus

DRL had changed its focus to the value-added formulations business in the late 1990s and pursued a brand building strategy aggressively. This had paid off handsomely. In the process, three of the company's brands had become the brand leaders in their respective categories. In addition four of the company's brands were among the industry's top 250 brands contributing to 54 percent of the total formulations sales.

Technology Focus

Dr. Reddy's Labs had built an impressive manufacturing infrastructure that is comparable to the best in the world. All its plants either conform to international regulatory standards or they had been approved. The company had also developed highly cost-effective alternative processes for a number of bulk drugs, making DRL one of the most integrated among the Indian Pharma companies.

International Operations

Dr. Reddy's Laboratories had been one of the leading exporters of bulk drugs from India. The company had 204 product registrations in various countries by 2004 and added many more in later years. DRL had a strong presence in the CIS markets including a joint venture.

The company has been actively pursuing joint ventures for penetrating important international markets in Latin America and China. It had set up a joint venture company - Aurantis Pharmaceuticals in Brazil with Biochimico to penetrate the Latin American Market. The company also acquired the European generic firm, Betapharm to reinforce its position in the European Union.

The Right Move

The company had merged and integrated Cheminor Drugs Limited, Dr. Reddy's Laboratories and American Remedies in 2000. Cheminor Drugs has world class manufacturing infrastructure and technological capabilities with three US FDA approved facilities for manufacturing pharmaceutical substances and one US FDA approved finished dosage form facility. The merger gave the company access to the rapidly growing generic markets in the first world countries, which are highly regulated. American Remedies merger helped optimize its marketing resources and expand therapeutic coverage and improve market share faster.

Speaking on the occasion of the merger, Dr. Anji Reddy, the indefatigable chairman of the company said: *The merger gives me a feeling of having arrived. We are in the big league now, third only to Ranbaxy and Glaxo. So far, we have enjoyed leadership in basic research. Now we have the size as well. The cultural identities of the three individual constituents - DRL, CDL, and ARL are well matched.* In deed it is the right move!

DR. Reddy's Labs today (2017), has commercial presence in 26 countries with annual sales of Rs. 140.8-billion. The company has 15 state-of-the-art manufacturing facilities and 5 R & D centers in India and in the US.

Case 14.4   Cipla: Capable! Confident! Committed!

If there is one word to describe Cipla's performance over the years that is consistency! With a turnover of Rs. 23.36-billion for the year ending March 2005, Cipla had consolidated its coveted position as the second largest pharmaceutical company in the Indian pharmaceutical industry.

Marketing Focus

The company's product portfolio of bulk drugs as well as formulations has both width and depth. They cover a very wide range of therapeutic segments and disease areas virtually from A to Z - from Asthma to Zollinger-Ellison Syndrome. In each therapeutic segment, the company offers a range of molecules from conventional to the most modern and is better suited to offer almost total solutions for a disease management approach.

The company has an enviable customer franchise in all key prescriber segments. It has one of the most efficient and effective distribution networks with the company's own depots, stockists and retailers. As the company is one of the front-runners in terms of prescription generation in the Indian pharmaceutical market, it enjoys considerable franchise even in the trade.

Cipla has dominant leadership position in the anti-asthmatic market in India, way ahead of even the leading multinational, GSK. It also has sizable presence in the antibacterial and anti-infective segments. The company was among the top seven in the cardiovascular segment in 2005. The company had eleven of its brands among the industry's top 250. All these facts amply demonstrate that Cipla has been carefully nurturing its brands and building brand equity steadily in a strategic manner. The company defends its market share in all its key therapeutic segments with regular promotion and appropriate new product introductions.

Technological Capabilities

Cipla's technological capabilities in process development are exemplary. This explains why the company always has been among the top three companies, which have successfully copied, or reverse engineered a number of new molecules and brought these to the market before the product patent era began in India. The company has also demonstrated its product development capabilities when it introduced the world's first oral drug for treating thalassemia. Its technological capabilities can also be gauged from the fact that in almost all its strategic alliances with overseas partners, Cipla has been the technology provider.

Cipla over the years has built a world class manufacturing infrastructure. Three out of its five plants are approved by international regulatory authorities like US FDA, UK MCA, Australian TGA, and South African Medicine Control Agency (MCC).

Internationalization

The company was rather a late entrant in terms of exploring the foreign shores. The company made rapid progress in internationalizing its business ever since the company had made up its mind. The company had achieved an export turnover of Rs. 10.53-billion by the fiscal 2004. What was the secret of Cipla's rapid progress in such a short time? Cipla had successfully harnessed its win-win strategic alliances in all its overseas forays.

The company had sealed as many as nine alliances within this short time that include marketing arrangements, technical collaborations and even equity-based joint ventures. The structure of these alliances was clearly defined and is aimed at achieving synergies. In all these alliances, Cipla provided the products, technology and the overseas partners provided the marketing, marketing knowledge and the distribution support. As the alliances progress, the joint venture companies could set up a manufacturing base to produce formulations sourcing the bulk actives and intermediates from its Indian partner - Cipla. Later, once the joint venture company reaches a critical mass, it could even start manufacturing the bulk drugs with technical support from Cipla. The company planned to set up one manufacturing base in each of the key regions in the foreseeable future.

Operational Excellence

Cipla has always been strong on systems. Considering the high turnover of employees during the past few years, one tends to think that it is more task oriented rather than people oriented. Even the high turnover of people did not affect the company's performance, which only proves its relentless focus on tasks and objectives. The company's move to de-layer the management structure may have caused some amount of insecurity and reduced motivation levels among its ranks, but it did not reflect in its performance. Overall, the company is well managed. It is systems driven. Swift decision making, empowerment and accountability, well-defined processes and strict budgetary control are the principles on which the company runs effectively.

Drug Discovery

Cipla, the industry's No 2 company (2005) may be a late entrant to the drug discovery program. Considering its process development skills and technological capabilities, one can expect it to be among the front-runners before long. Cipla had identified four new chemical entities in therapeutic areas like asthma, anti-infective, antihistamine and Central Nervous System (CNS). The company filed 55 ANDAs and received approvals for 11 products in FY 2004-05.

Cipla continues its fight against the AIDS pandemic. Its medicines are helping to treat over 200,000 HIV positive patients worldwide. The company is also one of the major suppliers of antimalarial drugs and medicines for neglected diseases like schistosomiasis to international markets.

Achievement - A Way of Life!
- Cipla had achieved a turnover of Rs. 23.36-billion in fiscal 2004. Exports grew to Rs. 10.53 billion during the same period. The company's net profit too had gone up by 38.5 percent to Rs. 4.09-billion.
- Cipla had built up an enviable customer franchise, as a result of which it is among the top 3 companies in all key therapeutic segments. At Cipla, achievement truly has become a way of life.

Cipla today (2017) recorded an annual worldwide sales of US $ 2.2 billion for its APIs and formulations. The company has 43 state-of-the-art manufacturing facilities with certified cGMP practices. Cipla posseses tremendous strength in research and development with over 100 patents.

Case 14.5   The Rising Sun!

From a turnover of less than Rs. 1-million in 1982, Sun Pharma had achieved a sales turnover of Rs. 12.46-billion for the year ending March 2005. A spectacular achievement by any standard!

The Marketing Mindset

Sun Pharma is a master of Niche Craft. The company has chosen the path of least resistance (as Dilip Shanghvi, its ebullient chairman and managing director would like to call it) to enter the Indian pharmaceutical industry in 1982. The road to specialty segments like psychiatry, neurology, cardiology and gastroenterology, which was less travelled in the late 1970s and 1980s, has become most widely traveled by the late 1990s.

Sun Pharma has been a sort of a trial-blazer in structuring its marketing operations around select therapeutic and prescriber segments. The trend that it has started in 1993 has become almost an industry standard today. Many companies are making a beeline to start specialty focused marketing divisions. Sun Pharma is more focused in its specialty orientation than any other Indian drug firm. It had nine Strategic Business Unit (SBU) with a focus on fifteen different specialties by 2002 (Table 13.1).

Table 14.1 Sun Pharma's Marketing Focus in 2002

Strategic Business Unit (SBU)	Therapeutic Areas of Focus
1. Synergy	Psychiatry, Neurology
2. Symbiosis	Psychiatry, Neurology
3. Aztec	Cardiology, Diabetology
4. Arien	Cardiology, Diabetology
5. Sun	Gastroenterology, Orthopedics
6. Spectra	Gynecology, Pediatrics, Dermatology
7. Solares	ENT, Respiratory, Orthopedics
8. Inca	Anesthesia, Oncology, Critical Care
9. Milmet	Ophthalmology, ENT

Sun Pharma, as a result of its very sharp specialty focus, had been able to achieve leadership position in neurology and second place in cardiology by 2002. The company aims to be among the top two companies in its therapeutic areas of focus.

Critical Mass

Sun Pharma had chosen the acquisition route to reach the critical mass faster. The company was ranked 34th in the Indian pharmaceutical industry in 1994. It had moved into the top ten at a breakneck speed since then. It had acquired TDPL (sales Rs. 60-crore) and the entire prescription drug brand portfolio of NATCO (annual sales Rs. 52-crore). The company is currently is an undisputed leader of the Indian pharmaceutical industry.

In 2014, Sum Pharma had acquired Ranbaxy, one of the leading international generic companies for $4 billion and became the fifth largest speciality generic company in the world.

Acquisitions have fueled growth and helped Sun Pharma reach the critical mass even in manufacturing infrastructure, process technology and strategic integration.

Technology Up-gradation

Sun Pharma has created a huge manufacturing infrastructure through green-field ventures and acquisitions and received several regulatory approvals for its facilities across the globe.

Internationalization

To tap the North American generic market, Sun Pharma had acquired a controlling interest in Michigan-based Caraco pharmaceuticals, with an investment of US $7.5 million and a transfer of technology for 20 generic drugs in 1997. By 2010, Caraco became a fully owned company of the Sun Pharma group.

If Sun Pharma can focus on consolidation without being complacent and concentrate on the productivity, it can continue grow further. It does not have to see the sunset. The company acquired a stake in a Hungary-based pharmaceutical company -

ICN company Hungary Limited from Valeant Pharmaceuticals, USA in August 2005.

Building Capacities and Capabilities

Sun Pharma has added new capacities to meet the increased demand from domestic and international markets. Sun Pharma is among the few select companies that have set up manufacturing facilities for the production of peptides, anti-cancer and hormones and steroidal groups in India.

The company stepped up its investment in research and development. It added 250,000 square-feet area for its two high capability sites in Vadodara and Mumbai during the fiscal 2004. This expansion would help the company to take projects in drug discovery, New Drug Delivery Systems (NDDS), Active Pharmaceutical Ingredients (APIs) or bulk drugs, and formulation development for highly regulated markets.

From humble beginnings in 1983, Sun Pharma today (2017) has evolved into a behemoth of an organization as one of the world's leading international specialty Pharma company, which is fully integrated. The company has recorded a whopping Rs. 30,264-crore in world wide sales for FY 2017. Sun Pharma has 40 state-of-the-art manufacturing facilities across the globe, that are approved by virtually all regulatory authorities in the world. Sun Pharma with its 30,000 plus employees, and 2,000 products serves the ailing millions in 150 countries around the world.

Case 14.6   NPIL: Taking over to Overtake!

Ajay Piramal entered the Indian pharmaceutical industry in 1987 rather quietly through the acquisition route. He acquired Nicholas Laboratories of Sarah Lee Corporation for Rs. 16-million. No one would have visualized that this small step would mean a giant leap into the top league of the Indian pharmaceutical industry. But, that is precisely what he did in about ten years time. He steamrolled into the Industry's prestigious top-five by 1998. How did he achieve this? By doing what he knows best, taking over three mover companies and a famous research center between 1993 and 1998. Here are the details (Table 14.2).

With this spate of acquisitions, Nicholas Piramal reached the critical mass of Rs. 5.67-billion in the Fiscal 1997 from a mere Rs. 250-

million in 1988. The company had also by that time reached a critical mass in terms of manufacturing infrastructure for bulk actives as well as formulations and an R&D structure that was among the best in the country.

Table 14.2 Piramal Healthcare's Acquisition Route

Year	Acquisition
1987	Nicholas Laboratories
1993	Roche India
1995	Sumitra Pharmaceuticals and Chemicals
1996	Boerhinger Mannheim India
1998	Glass Division of Gujarat Glass Bulk Drugs Division of Sumatra Pharma Research Center of Hoechst Marion Roussel
2000	Rhone Poulenc (India)
2002	ICI Pharmaceuticals Formed a Joint Venture with Dr. Golwikar Laboratories as NPIL - Dr. Golwikar Laboratories Pvt. Ltd. for Pathlab Business
2003	Global Bulk Drugs and Fine Chemicals

Powered by Alliances

Strategic alliances are another approach Nicholas was banking on. In a short span of three to four years, the company had forged as many as fifteen alliances with leading players around the world. Alliances are the quickest way to gain access to world-class products, technology, know-how and even markets. Most of these alliances, however, are marketing alliances. The company pursued the alliance and licensing route with Multinational Companies (MNCs) for manufacturing and marketing their products in India. The strategy seemed to have worked well for them. Consider these facts:

- First-half results for the Fiscal 1998 indicated that over one-third of its turnover had come from these alliances. The company had planned to achieve 50 percent of its total turnover from alliances within the next two years.
- The company had introduced as many as 12 new products of Roche in India since the acquisition.

- Boots Plc and Reckitt & Coleman, who are competitors internationally, had chosen Nicholas Piramal as their partner in India.

The key differential in Nicholas Piramal's strategy is its alliance-bias. It is based on sound logic. The first premise is that when multinational drug companies are excited about the future prospects of the Indian pharmaceutical market, why can't Indian companies exploit it? In the coming product patent regime, alliances and licensing arrangements are necessary to gain access to new products. The second premise is that even in the post-GATT era, there will be a number of multinationals, who would not like to set up a full-fledged manufacturing and marketing in India. Nicholas Piramal wanted to tap that segment of the market.

The company had clearly understood that to be an attractive suitor for all the alliance partners-to-be, you need to have certain qualities and qualifications. The company had been preparing to:
- Marketing infrastructure comprising one of the India's largest sales forces
- Penetrating the distribution network of C&F agents, stockists, and retailers
- Manufacturing infrastructure for bulk actives and formulations that meet international standards
- World-class R & D facilities
- All the acquisitions had extended the therapeutic coverage of the company to 60 percent

Research & Development

The company had five major discovery projects underway in 2004 and an additional one licensed-in. All these were being developed for domestic and international markets.

Size Does Matter!

Ajay Piramal, the chairman of Piramal Enterprises in his presentation at a seminar on corporate restructuring organized by the Federation of Indian Chamber of Commerce and Industry (FICCI) said: *Size does matter. The organic growth of their*

Pharma group has been at compounded anual growth rate of around 50 percent.

The pharmaceutical group of Primal Enterprises had achieved Rs. 13.41-billion in sales and 1.64-billion in net profit for 2004-05.

Piramal Pharma Group was one of the most integrated pharmaceutical companies in India. It had either already a strong presence or building one in all related areas like pharmaceutical formulations, bulk drugs and intermediaries, OTC formulations, research and development, penetrating international markets and clinical research. It had also been steadily investing in building a strong sales and distribution network. The sales force had increased from 191 in March 1990 to 2000 in March 1999 (including Joint Ventures like Sarabhai Primal, Reckitt & Coleman).

Piramal had grown at a phenomenal rate ever since it entered the Pharma business by acquiring Nicholas Laboratories from Sarah Lee Corporation of the US in 1987.

What was the secret of this success? The Piramal prescription for success is: Build state-of-the-art technology, invest in research and development, boost sales and distribution network, rope in international partners, seek international listing, get access to global funding.

Later in 2010, Abbott, the international drug major acquired the pharmaceutical solutions business of Piramal Healthcare for US $ 3.72-billion (Rs. 17,500-crore)

Case 14.7   Lupin: Leapfrogging into the Top League!

Started with the small change of an investment of five thousand rupees in 1968, Lupin has leapfrogged into the top league of the Indian pharmaceutical industry in the 1990s.

Strategic Vision

Lupin entered the pharmaceutical market with a clear focus on the anti-tubercular segment. The segment was perceived by multinationals and other leading Indian drug companies to be unattractive as its margins were very low. Lupin had found an opportunity in this segment as India accounted for about fifty percent of the total tuberculous patients in the world. The company had rightly chased the volumes, integrated backwards to achieve cost efficiencies and became a leading player in the world anti-tubercular market.

Having tasted the success of a focused strategy, Lupin had once again followed a focused strategy - this time in the high-margin cephalosporin segment. Lupin's expansion strategy literally pivots around cephalosporins. The reasons are not difficult to understand. Consider these for example:

- The world cephalosporin market was around US $ 10 billion.
- A number of major molecules in the sterile cephalosporin segment were going off patent in the next few years.
- There were only three to four integrated players in the world cephalosporin market.

Alliance Power

Lupin had spotted a big opportunity and had become a fully integrated player in this segment. It also used strategic alliances to gain access to the 'difficult-to-penetrate' generic markets for off-patent formulations in the highly regulated western markets. The company had acquired Eli Lilly's cephalosporin plant in Puerto Rico and had entered into a joint venture with the US-based MOVA for marketing these generic formulations. It had also entered into a strategic alliance with Merck Generics, which had a strong generic presence in Europe to market its generic formulations.

Winning Moves

Lupin recorded a turnover of Rs. 11.79-billion for the year ending March 2005. The company was aggressively planning to sharpen its focus. Some of its winning moves were:

- To fuel its growth plans, Lupin had increased its acquisition fund of US $ 10-million to US $ 30-million to acquire companies internationally.

- Lupin increased its R & D investment by 82 percent to Rs. 83-crore in 2004-05.
- The company's focus has always been on regulated markets. Its research activities are accordingly aimed at developing non-infringing processes for APIs and finished dosage forms, NCEs (New Chemical Entities) and NDDS.
- The company had filed 42 patent applications in the fiscal 2004 alone and cumulative filings till the end of 2004 were 152.

Lupin has what it takes to be competitive and more importantly to stay competitive even in the product patent regime.

Lupin today (2017) has achieved the distinction of being the 7th largest international generic drug company in the world with an annual sales of Rs. 171.2-billion, having operations in over 100 countries. The company has 18 state-of-the-art manufacturing facilities and 9 R&D sites.

Case 14.8   Wockhardt: Working Hard!

Wockhardt and hard work may not be synonymous in a semantic sense, but they do have phonetic similarities. The sounds Wockhardt and work hard are pretty close!

The Marketing Mindset

Wockhardt has a diversified portfolio. In the domestic market it concentrated on formulations. Its top five brands accounted for half-of the company's total domestic formulations' sales. Wockhardt had a strong presence in the pain management and wound care segments. The company had restructured its domestic marketing operations to increase thrust on fast growing therapeutic segments such as cardiac, pediatric care and gynecology. The company had plans to increase its presence in oncology and gastroenterology segments as well.

Technology Up-gradation

Wockhardt had invested consistently in upgrading its technology for both bulk drugs and formulations over the years. As a result it had manufacturing facilities for both bulk drugs and formulations approved by US FDA and other international regulatory authorities. The company had also created manufacturing bases overseas through acquisitions in the US and the UK.

In 2004, the company had commissioned its Biotech Park, the largest biopharmaceutical complex in Aurangabad, Maharashtra. It had six dedicated manufacturing plants to US FDA standards. These plants have a capacity to cater to about 15 percent of the global demand for major biopharmaceuticals.

Focused Research

Wockhardt had prioritized biotechnology research and planned to introduce at least eight biotechnology based products in the next three years. These include insulin and erythropoietin (the second recombinant product from the company, the first being the hepatitis- B vaccine). The company also markets erythropoietin, and recombinant human insulin in India and the the emerging markets.

Integration Power

Bulk drugs were mainly for the captive consumption and the balance was exported. It was amongst the world's largest manufacturers of the analgesic - dextropropoxyphene and one of the few global manufacturers of Captopril, which went off-patent in February 1996. Its acquisition of Merind had made Wockhardt one of the major producers of vitamin B12 in the world. Overall, the company had an impressive bulk drug portfolio, paving the way to become one of the vertically integrated manufacturers who are internationally competitive.

Internationalization Strategies

Bulk drugs have been providing the thrust for exports over the years for Wockhardt. The company's manufacturing facilities were approved by international regulatory authorities such as US FDA, UK MCA. Forty seven percent of its bulk drug exports were to highly industrialized markets in the west by 2005. After acquiring C P pharmaceuticals of UK, the company became one of the top 10 generic drug companies in the UK. Wockhardt had spread its global network with subsidiaries in the US, UK and joint ventures in China, Saudi Arabia and Egypt. It was one of the early entrants in the captopril generic market in the US.

Wockhardt had acquired Wallis Laboratories in the UK to gain a foothold in the rapidly growing generic market. It had rechristened the acquired company as Wockhardt UK Limited to create a brand equity for Wockhardt in the UK. The company launched 16 new products in 2001 to achieve a sales of US $ 14-million.

Another feather in the Wockhardt cap is that it could successfully market its generic version of Vasotec, the cardiac blockbuster of Merck in the fiercely competitive US generic drug market immediately after Vasotec's patent expiry. Vasotec's patent expired on August 22, 2000. Wockhardt's generic version of the product was available in the market on August 23, 2000.

Wockhardt! Work Smart!

Wockhardt had recorded a sales turnover of Rs. 14.58-billion in for the year 2005 with a PAT (profit after tax) of Rs. 2.6-billion.

Wockhardt had chalked out a blueprint for succeeding in the post-GATT era. It had made many right moves - it focused on the right therapeutic segments, technology up-gradation, stepping up of export thrust and internationalization of its business.

The company with a view to regain focus on its core business is de-merging its hospitals' business. This de-merging will sharpen its focus on pharmaceuticals and help the company stick to the knitting.

Wockhardt today (2017) has recorded an annual turnover of Rs. 4,015-crore in worldwide sales. The company has 14 manufacturing facilities in India, US, and EU, that are certified by international regulatory authorities such as US FDA, UK MCA among others. The company has also 3 R&D centers with 665 scientists working on various projects on value-added formulations, NDDS, Biosimilars and drug discovery.

Wockhardt is one the few Indian Pharma companies, who have prepared well to meet the challenges in the post-GATT era. Wockhardt's motto - Wockhardt! Work smart!

Case 14.9   Zydus Cadila: The A to Z of Alliance Power!

What was really commendable about the Zydus group (Cadila Healthcare) was that it could return to the top five in the pharmaceutical league table in India (a position held by the un-divided Cadila in 1995) with in just four years!

The first thing that they had done is to give a distinct identity to their group. This was absolutely necessary since both the companies after the division wanted to capitalize on the corporate brand equity of the Cadila name.

Cadila Healthcare group chose the name of the Greco-Roman God - *Zeus* - and spelt it as Zydus due to proprietary reasons. They added a *D* in between signifying *the dawn of a new era in healthcare.* That is how the new identity of Zydus was created by, for and of the Cadila Health group, to paraphrase Abraham Lincoln.

Strategic Vision

Pankaj Patel and his team got their act together immediately after the division and outlined a clear strategy to become competitive in the post-GATT era:

1. Achieve an organic growth of at least 20 percent every year.
2. Acquire businesses and brands to reach the critical mass of Rs. 10-billion by 2002.
3. Harness the power of alliances. Enter into strategic alliances and joint ventures with leading international companies to gain access to new products, technologies and markets.
4. Step up R & D effort and conduct focused research on niche segments.

The Silk Route

What is the silk route to growth and prosperity of pharmaceutical companies in these changing times? Acquisitions and alliances of course! Zydus had chosen this proven path to reach the critical mass faster. In 1996, it took over the loss making Indo Pharma, turned it around and merged it with the group in 1998, catapulting the Zydus group into the top 5-6 companies in the Indian pharmaceutical industry. The company had earmarked Rs. 1.5-billion for acquiring businesses and brands. The company had also acquired Reckon Remedies in the year 2000 to expand its therapeutic coverage and market share. Later, Zydus acquired German Remedies in 2002 to further strengthen its position in the domestic market.

Alliances have been the growth engines for Zydus. The company entered into thirteen strategic alliances of various types, shapes and sizes by 2004. Its alliances covered a wide spectrum of areas including marketing, manufacturing, technology transfer and research in bio-pharmaceuticals, bulk drugs and dosage forms with leading international companies like Mallinckrodt Pharmaceuticals Generics (US), Mayne Pharma (Australia), Zambon Group (Italy) etc.

In addition, the company had set up a 50:50 joint venture with BYK Gulden of Germany to develop, manufacture, distribute and market pharmaceutical products in the area of gastrointestinal disorders.

Marketing Thrust

Zydus has been changing and sharpening its focus on the fast growing therapeutic segments such as cardiovascular, gastrointestinal, bio-pharmaceuticals and antiinfectives. The company had restructured its marketing units into strategic business units (SBUs) to remain focused on different therapeutic groups and manage its diverse product portfolio effectively.

Technology Up-gradation

Zydus had created a world class manufacturing facility with an investment of Rs 1-billion at Moriaya, in Ahmedabad. This probably was one of the largest investments at a single-location in the Indian pharmaceutical industry. The facility conformed and obtained international regulatory approvals and followed cGMP. What is more, the company had also set up a swanky R & D center adjacent to its new plant with an investment of Rs. 30-crore. The mission of this center is to create intellectual property rights for the group in select therapeutic areas. The company had also launched its drug discovery program. Research and development will be a major driving factor in determining the bottomline. Zydus had also planned to spend over 5 percent of its turnover on R&D every year up from the present 2 percent.

The research center of Zydus had over 300 scientists focusing on creating new molecular entities (NMEs) in therapeutic areas such as metabolic disorders including dyslipidemia, hyper cholesteremia, diabetes, obesity, inflammation, pain and bacterial infections. The company filed 24 ANDAs and 28 DMFs by 2004. The company had around this time 100 patents filed in India and another 23 in other countries.

Performing Organization

The Zydus group is determined to build a performing organization. The company has created a the culture of high performance based on the foundation on three solid building blocks - the Es that are - *Enrich, Empower and Excel.* The company had chosen five key result areas where it would like to benchmark the best practices and excel at. These are: market share improvement, exports, technology (up-gradation and transfer), human resources development and cost leadership.

Focus on Performance

Zydus is both clear-headed and level-headed as an organization. Clear about its goals. Level-headed because it knows where it stands, what it needs to do, and what it takes to do so and that it cannot be complacent ever.

From a turnover of Rs. 250-crore in 1995, Zydus Cadila posted revenues of Rs. 9,600-crore today (2017). The company has a strong presence in regulated markets such as the US, EU (Spain and France mainly). The manufacturing infrastructure of Zydus comprises 8 manufacturing facilities that are certified by various international regulatory authorities. The company aims to become a research-based international pharmaceutical company. Zydus understands that success is not only the vision and the strategy to achieve the goal but it also is about, who is in a better position to implement it. At Zydus, the focus is clearly and sharply on performance.

Case 14.10 Aurobindo Pharma Moves into the *A* League!

Started in 1986 by P. V. Ramprasada Reddy and K. Nityananda Reddy for manufacture of semi-synthetic penicillin bulk actives at Pondicherry, Aurobindo Pharma today has grown to be among the top ten leading companies in Indian pharmaceutical Industries.

With sales of Rs. 10.85-billion for the year ending Mach 2005, and 13 manufacturing facilities, and a host of regulatory approvals from the first-world countries, Aurobindo Pharma has truly catapulted itself into the 'A' league of the the Indian drug companies.

Aurobindo Pharma today is a multi-product company with an impressive list of over 120 APIs including both antibiotic and non-antibiotic products. The company had filed over 64 DMFs and 25 ANDAs internationally including regulated markets by fiscal 2004.

The company had also set up a number of joint ventures and 100 percent subsidiaries covering manufacturing and marketing activities internationally (North America, China, and

Europe) to meet the challenges of the future. These strategies had helped the company to make a presence in all its target markets.

Aurobindo Pharma, one of the top-ten pharmaceutical companies in India in terms of consolidated revenues of US $ 2.2-billion in FY 2016, has 22 manufacturing facilities for APIs and formulations. The company exports to 125 countries across the globe and earns over 70 percent of its sales from these markets.

Aurobindo Pharma with all the right moves had truly evolved from an API manufacturer to a fully integrated international generics player of repute!

Case 14.11 Torrent: Torrential Still!

Torrent, one of the front runners in the Indian pharmaceutical industry had recorded Rs. 4.97-billion in sales for the year ending March 2005.

Marketing Focus

Torrent Pharma is focused on formulations with a bias for specialty therapeutic segments such as cardiovascular (23%), CNS (19.5%), gastrointestinal (12.5%), antibiotics (11%). Five of its brands - Dilzem, Alprax, Qunitor, Domstal and Listril were among the industry's top 250 in the year 2005. Torrent had been experimenting its marketing operations for some time and had carved out three strategic business units around 2005.

Focus on Research

Torrent had planned to make its R &D a profitable proposition. It had signed up for research collaboration agreements with international research institutes such as William Harvey Research Institute in the UK. The company's objective was to generate at least a third of its revenues from collaborative research.

The company had set up a state-of-the-art research center with an investment of Rs. 75-crore, with over 100 scientists working on various product development projects including a drug discovery program. The company had a research team of 525 scientists by 2005, who had put in 2,456 scientific man-years in the drug discovery development.

Torrent had invested Rs. 1.72-billion on research between 1994 and 2005. The company had during this time filed for 85 patents in drug discovery and 22 in process development areas.

Strategic Integration

The quest for greater economies of scale has been the driving force at Torrent. Torrent Gujarat Biotech Limited (TGBL), the joint venture company of the group had invested Rs. 75-crore to double the capacity of penicillin-G to an extent where it can be internationally competitive with this capacity expansion. In addition, Torrent had developed an impressive bulk drug portfolio, which reflects its process development capabilities.

International Operations

Torrent has been one of the country's leading exporters of pharmaceutical formulations. Exports accounted for close to 40 percent of the company's total turnover in 2005. Torrent had 668 product registrations in 70 countries by 2005. The company also planned to create manufacturing bases in certain key geographical regions such as Africa, East Asia, Eastern Europe and Latin America either through acquisitions or green-field ventures as a part of its internationalization process.

Torrent Pharma today has posted consolidated revenues of Rs. 4,593-crore for FY 2016. The company has 8 state-of-the-art manufacturing units for APIs and formulations. The company has an advanced research center with over a thousand scientists working on innovation and product development. The company has received 361 patents so far.

Every which way you look at it, Torrent is still Torrential!

Case 14.12 Ipca: Improving Constantly!

Ipca has achieved a dominant and formidable leadership position in the domestic anti-malarial market - both in formulations as well as in bulk drugs. It had a 40 percent share of the chlorine bulk drug market but margins are low due to price controls and the high level of competition.

Expansion Strategy

Ipca has been expanding its product portfolio of formulations as well as bulk drugs from antimalarials to antiemetics, cardiovascular, antibiotics and bronchodilators. Its top four brands contributed to two-thirds of its domestic formulations' sales in the fiscal 2004. It had increased its product portfolio by entering into 'difficult-to-penetrate' cardiovascular market. The company had expanded its field force to 660 medical representatives by 2005, and created a new marketing division to cover about 120,000 medical practitioners in the country.

Manufacturing Infrastructure

Ipca has created an enviable manufacturing infrastructure over the years through a steady stream of investments. Its bulk drug facility at Ratlam in Madhya Pradesh has the approval of US FDA. In addition, UK MCA and Ministry of Health of Germany had approved Ipca's formulation plant at Athal in Gujarat.

Power of Integration

Ipca enjoys considerable scale of economies and is more integrated than many other firms. Interms of volume, Ipca consumes close to 40 percent of its total bulk drugs and intermediates for its own use.

Exports

Exports drive the growth at Ipca. The Company's exports had crossed the Rs. 3.91-billion mark in fiscal 2004. Formulations accounted for almost 45 percent of exports during this period. The product mix for exports is extremely diverse. Ipca manufactures some formulations exclusively for exports to suit the requirements of buyers and agents in 65 countries in addition to its popular domestic brands. Formulation exports of products under patent are mainly to developing countries. Ipca also carried out contract manufacturing for SmithKline Beecham (GSK now). The company stepped up its efforts to increase exports to the US, China, Japan and Australia. It also has been actively pursuing contract manufacturing alliances with other Pharma MNCs.

Research and Development

Ipca had set up three R & D centers at Mumbai, Ratlam and Indore, which are recognized by the Department of Science and Technology. The company had spent Rs. 33.65-crore in fiscal 2004 on research and development.

Moving up the Value Chain

Having established an impressive manufacturing infrastructure, Ipca (sales in 2004-05 Rs. 7.18-billion) had achieved the status of one of the most attractive alliance partners in India for international suitors.

The company started focusing on formulations business to move up the value chain. Ipca has a long way to establish in formulations business, which is a different ball game altogether. If the company can demonstrate the same degree of determination, which it had shown in upgrading technology and manufacturing, Ipca can move up the value chain and stay competitive in the post-GATT Era.

Ipca Laboratories is a fully integrated pharmaceutical company producing branded and generics formulations, APIs and intermediates. The company's consolidated revenues for FY 2016 are Rs. 3,178-crore. Exports contribute to 50 percent of the company's total revenues.

| Case14.13 | Glen On the Mark...In Making its Mark in the World of Pharma! |

Started forty-years ago in 1977, Glenmark seems to be hell bent to make a mark in the world of pharmaceuticals by the time it turned twenty. With a number of right moves and plenty of determination and single-minded focus, Glenmark is making its mark in the world of Pharma. The company with a total sales of mere US $ 31-million in the year 2000, had achieved a consolidated revenue of a US $ 1.4 billion in 2017. Not only that, the company was ranked 75 in the Scrip List of top 100 pharmaceutical and biotechnology firms in the world. The company also has emerged as a top-ten Pharma and Biotech company among the firms based out of emerging markets. A snapshot of Glenmark's progress is presented in table 14.3.

How did Glenmark achieve what it has achieved? What is its secret of success? What is its success formula? The success formula of Glenmark if there is one, is its judicious mix of growth strategies of organic and inorganic growth and one hundred percent determination. Glenmark has a well defined, clear strategy and followed it unflinchingly. To reach the critical mass that is essential to fuel its growth plans, Glenmark like many other pharmaceutical companies before they became what they are today followed the inorganic growth route of acquisitions and alliances. Table 14.4 presents a brief glance at the company's alliances and acquisitions.

Table 14.3 Glenmark: A Snapshot of Progress

Criteria	In The Year 2000	In The Year 2017
1. Total Revenues Generated	US $ 31-Million	US $ 1.4-Billion
2. Manufacturing Facilities	2 Formulation Facilities in India	A. 16 Facilities across Formulations, APIs in Four Continents Across the Globe. 7 Facilities are US FDA Approved. B. GMP-Grade Biologics Plant in Switzerland.

Contd...

Criteria	In The Year 2000	In The Year 2017
3. Revenues from International Operations	8 per cent of Total Turnover	Over 70 per cent of Total Turnover from operations in more than 50 Countries Across the World.
4. Research and Development	NME (New Molecular Entity) Research Initiated	A. 7 Out-licensing Deals Signed with Pharma Majors - Eli Lilly, Merck KGaA, Sanofi-Aventis, Teijin Pharma, and Forest Labs. B. 9 Novel Compounds in Pipeline in Therapeutic Areas - Oncology, Respiratory and Dermatology. C. 120 Scientists based in India Researching on NCEs D. 120 Scientists researching on NBEs (New Biological Entities) based in Switzerland E. A Facility in the US Supporting Clinical Development
5. Employees	About 1,000	About 13,000 from 60 Nationalities.

Table14.4 Glenmark: A Glance at its
Acquisitions and Alliances

The Year	Acquisitions	Alliances
2000	Acquires 3 brands - Alex, Flucort and Sensur from Lyka Labs	
2003		A. Enters into a marketing arrangement with Philadelphia-based Lannett Company in the US to market ANDAs

Contd...

The Year	Acquisitions	Alliances
2003		B. Ties up with Apotex, the Canadian generic drug firm for the supply of a new generation bulk drug in cardiac segment
2004	A. Acquires Laboratories Klinger in Brazil for US $ 5.2-million through its wholly-owned subsidiary in Brazil, Glenmark Pharmaceutica B. Acquires two FDA-approved products (ANDAs) from Clonmel Healthcare Limited	Signs development and marketing agreement with K V Pharmaceutical Company in the US
2005	Acquires an Argentine marketing company, Servycal SA, through its wholly-owned Swiss subsidiary Glenmark Pharmaceuticals SA	A. Forges alliance with two US firms to sell products in the US. B. Signs development and marketing agreement with InvaGen
2006	A. Glenmark USA acquires exclusive marketing rights to 3 additional Generic products B. Acquires the South African Sales and Marketing company, Bouwer Bartlett through its wholly-owned Swiss subsidiary company, Glenmark Holdings SA	A. Signs unique royalty deal for US $ 27-million to build US Generic Dermatology Portfolio B. Signs an agreement with Lehigh Valley Technologies for manufacturing and marketing 7 generic products for the US market C. Enters into a development and licensing arrangement with Celon Labs for generic Seretide Accuhaler
2007	Acquires 90 per cent stake in the Czech pharmaceutical company, Medicamenta through is wholly-owned Swiss subsidiary, Glenmark Holdings SA	Enters in to a US $350-million out-licensing deal for some of its novel compounds in development with Eli Lilly and receives an upfront payment of US $ 45-million
2008	Acquires Cital (Citalopram), Lmotrix (Lamotrigene) and five other brands from Actavis, the generic drug firm from Iceland and Biovena, its Polish affiliate	

Contd...

The Year	Acquisitions	Alliances
2010		Enters into a settlement and license agreement with Separcor Inc to market Eszopiclone tablets in the US
2012		Signs a product development agreement with Forest Laboratories, USA for novel drug candidates to treat chronic inflammatory conditions
2014		Receives US $ 5-million upfront payment from Sanofi for its monoclonal antibody under development
2015		Enters into a strategic development and licensing agreement with Celon, Poland for marketing generic Seritide Accuhaler in Europe

What makes Glenmark stand out from the rest of the international generic companies is its clear strategic vision and sharp focus. Having achieved the critical mass, Glenmark is redefining its strategy. Glen Saldana, the ebullient Chairman and CEO of Glenmark said some time ago while speaking on the company's strategy: *In the short-term, acquisition is not our strategy. Valuations are high and it would be easier to grow organically. Our focus is to introduce new products to the market.*

Glenmark's strategy seems to diversify risks and aims to unlock high growth and profitable revenue generation opportunities across the entire pharmaceutical value chain. Here are some of the strategic snippets from Glenmark's game plan.

A. Glenmark plans to file 20 - 25 ANDAs each year over the next five years and launch about 10-12 new products annually. It has already about 70 ANDAs pending with the US FDA for approval.

B. Generics to fuel the growth for the next three to four years, during which period the company would build a specialty product pipeline.

C. Specialty products would be the company's defense against generic price erosion. The company plans to achieve about 30 percent of its revenues from its specialty products by 2025 and this would pave the way for the specialty innovation products from its research laboratories. The company has already several NCEs (New Chemical Entities) and NBEs (New Biological Entities) under various stages of development and some of them out-licensed to the Big Pharma companies.

Glen Saldana, Glenmark's chairman and managing director knows he is on the mark when he says that, *With this blueprint as our guide, we are prepared to transition from being a generics-driven organization to one that has an optimal mix of generics, specialty and research-driven innovative products.*

With an impeccable track record to its credit, all the stake holders of the company too are confident and agree that Glenmark is indeed making its mark in the world of pharmaceuticals!

Case 14.14 Mankind Pharma: Changing the Rules of the Game!

For a long time, the game of pharmaceutical business has been dictated by a rule book largely filled with unwritten rules. Rules such as:

A. The pyramidical structure of the business comprises factors such as type of therapy, doctor specialization, drug pricing, with leading companies at the top and majority of the firms competing fiercely in the middle.

B. Pareto's principle is at work in pharmaceutical marketing too, with almost all the companies competing for a share of the mind of the top twenty percent of the doctors, who are specialists and are practicing in metros and Tier-one cities.

C. Specialty focus in terms of therapy area as well physician speciality are crucial for success.

D. There is value at the top of the pyramid.

Changing the Rules of the Game!

Pharmaceutical industry in India too has been governed by these rather unwritten rules. At least till Mankind Pharma started its operations. Ramesh Juneja, the founder of Mankind Pharma and his brother Rajeev Juneja, who has been heading the marketing operations since its inception in 1986, changed the rules of the game unknowingly. They knew that to start a pharmaceutical company and compete with established players in metro cities and Tier-1 cities would be next to impossible.

They would not even get a second glance from the specialists and super specialists. They also knew from their experience as medical representatives and first-line sales managers in pharmaceutical industry that the large and mid-size pharmaceutical companies focused their entire attention on top prescribers in metro cities and Tier-1 cities (remember the Pareto principle that says 20 percent of your customers account for 80 percent of your market) and completely neglected general practitioners and doctors in small towns totally.

The Juneja brothers asked a seemingly innocent question. Everyone is thinking that there is value only at the top of the pyramid and focusing there. It is very crowded and it is impossible to compete in that space for a start-up company. What if there is value at the bottom of the pyramid? Can we unlock it? It is eminently possible to compete in this rather *no-competition zone.* They focused their total attention on the so far un-served, and under-served market of general practitioners and all other doctors. The doctors welcomed Mankind Pharma with open arms and rewarded them with their prescriptions making the company a leader in terms of number of prescriptions written in India in 2014 as per IMS Health Report.

Rapid Growth

Coming into existence in 1986, Mankind Pharma became a corporation in 1991. The company has been highly-customer centric since its inception. The company's real growth phase started in 1995. For the next 10 years or more the company has been growing at a break-neck speed of 30 percent per year as compared to the industry's 12 percent. How did Mankind Pharma achieve this uncommon success? What is its secret sauce? Here it is in the words of Rajeev Juneja himself when he spoke to the press on different occasions:

A. *You become creative when there is scarcity. When you have less money, no experience, no name, no background, it makes sense to tap doctors in small towns and villages. The top doctors in the metros would not have given us a second chance.*

B. *The idea is to create a presence in small towns and villages and then work our way up to cities.*

The Company's Secret Sauce!

The essence or the secret sauce of Mankind's strategy has been:

A. To unlock the value at the bottom of the period. The company told its medical representatives to tap as many doctors as possible and generate prescriptions. Mankind has the most extensive physician coverage in the Indian pharmaceutical industry.

B. To market their products at affordable prices. Mankind Pharma priced its products to patients at prices that are lower by 40 - 60 percent as compared to competition.

The company followed the Walmart's business model in marketing its products. Walmart strives to consistently lower purchasing and operating costs and then pass the savings to consumers. Like Walmart, Mankind strives to keep its overheads and all other manufacturing and operating costs low and offers the savings to patients. The company follows a penetrative pricing strategy. Mankind bombarded the Indian pharmaceutical market with low priced drugs - up to 50 percent cheaper than prevailing prices, which made competition sit up and take notice of this new entrant. That is why and how the company is able to deliver quality products at affordable prices.

C. The company has also entered the OTC (Over-the-counter) drugs and invested over Rs. 350-crore on advertising over a period of six years to tap the OTC market and to improve brand recognition. The company today has become well known with successful brands such as Manforce (Condoms), Unwanted 72 (Emergency contraceptives), and Unwanted (Home Pregnancy kits). OTC drugs account for about 8 percent of Mankind's total sales.

The strategy is working. Mankind today has become a behemoth of a company with its revenues of around Rs. 5,000-crore and a total employee strength of about 14,000. What is noteworthy of Mankind's achievement is the fact that its entire growth has been organic except for two acquisitions. The company acquired Magnet Labs in 2007 to enter the areas of CNS (Central Nervous System) disorders and three years later in 2010, acquired Longifene a brand for improving appetitive in children belonging to the Multi National Pharma Company, UCB.

What Next?

The key question is can Mankind continue its growth spurt? Can the company maintain the high growth rate that it has been used to for such a long time? Mankind seems to be determined to grow faster than the fastest competitor and grab market share to reach the top in the coming years. The company is not complacent and does not take itself for granted. The company recognizes and realizes the challenges ahead and crafted a strategy accordingly. What brought Mankind up to here will not take the company where it wants to go. What is needed is a changing of the gears. The game changer needs a new game plan. The growth drivers of Mankind's new game plan are:

1. Increase the company's presence in chronic therapy segment. Chronic therapy segment is growing at a higher rate of 14 percent than acute therapies which are growing at 9.6 percent. Magnet Mankind is already making rapid strides in the segment.

2. Push OTC segment further. It has already started contributing to the profitability of the company.

3. Domestic market alone cannot provide the opportunities to grow at the current rate. Expanding into the international markets and increasing exports is vital to continue the company's frenetic pace that it has been used to. The company plans to enter the international markets in a phased and focused manner. To focus on South East Asia, Africa, CIS and Latin America in the first phase and then graduate to the developed markets. The company plans to sell certain APIs (Active Pharmaceutical Ingredients) in the developed markets such as the US.

4. Even in export markets, Mankind will follow its winning strategy of unlocking the value at the bottom of the pyramid. The company will target smaller towns and and cities in the export markets too and offer differentiated products and not 'me-too' products, since most of these export markets are already crowded with 'me-too' products.

5. Move in to drugs for life threatening diseases such as cancer.

The company is planning to enter the oncology segment with a penetrative pricing strategy. Mankind plans to price its oncology drugs too at 40 - 60 percent cheaper than its competitors. The strategy is to approach oncology segment with Mankind prices.

6. Foray into diagnostic space, which is going rapidly with an investment of Rs. 305-crore over a period of four years. *Pathkind* is the name of the proposed diagnostic arm of the company's business. The aim of Pathkind is to reach out to the masses in tier 2 and tier 3 cities in India to provide easily accessible diagnostic services at affordable prices. The company is planning to open 12 large labs, 20 rapid response labs and 150 collection centers in U P and Uttarakhand states of India in the first year. The company's planning to go pan India with 1300 collection centers and130 labs in the next five years.

In its second phase of rapid growth strategy, Mankind is banking on higher growth from international markets. In fact, that is what has happened to all successful Indian Pharma majors ever since India became a signatory to GATT and a member of WTO. All the leading Indian pharmaceutical companies have started getting a large share of their revenues from international markets, because, India accounts currently for about 5 - 6 percent of the total world Pharma market and there is a limit to what a company can exploit if it chooses to compete only in the domestic market.

Mankind is working on building the required competencies such as international marketing, formulation development and competing in metro cities and tier-one cities. Looking at the company's impeccable track record since its inception, there is every reason to believe that Mankind might as well change the rules of the game for the second time around!

Source: Adapted from: Shabana Hussain, *Mankind Pharma : Formulating strategy to ensure the big league, Forbes.com.*
May 8, 2014.

A Prescription for Success

A detailed analysis of all these successful companies reveals the basic elements of a winning game plan. The strategic approaches of all these companies are similar. The differences exist only in terms of:

A. Relative emphasis on certain strategic elements

B. The stage of evolution at which a company currently is

C. The levels of knowledge, skills and core competencies

D. The point from which they started the business and strategic integration process

E. The capabilities to execute and implement the strategic action plans

What is the prescription for success in the post-GATT era? First things first. It is important to have a clear objective of where the organization wants to be in the foreseeable, and in the distant future. Then draw up a blueprint for reaching where it wants to reach. Here's the prescription for success or the winner's *know-how* and, what other companies are eager to *know how* the successful companies have been doing it!

1. **Reach the Critical Mass:** Do not just sit there on your laurels. Do something to improve your market share, sales and above all profits. Grow organically. Buy businesses. Buy brands. Buy facilities in India and abroad. Do something. Do anything to reach the critical mass.

2. **Make Yourself an Attractive Partner:** To be an attractive alliance partner, one needs to have a strong marketing infrastructure, a strong presence in more than one therapeutic area, world class manufacturing facilities, wide distribution network and good customer franchise. Once you have all these, it is easier to license-in new products and technologies from multinationals currently not having any representation in India. You can keep your product pipelines flowing freely with new products even in post-GATT era. Remember, new products are the life blood of any business. They are not only essential for growth, but are vital even for survival.

3. **Increase Your R & D Effort and Investment:** It is important to enhance the process and product development capabilities of your organization even if you want to retain your current position. To accelerate growth and stay head of competition, the R & D

efforts need to be at a much higher level. Process development capabilities can help the organization to achieve a higher level and degree of strategic integration into bulk drugs and intermediates. This, in turn, will enable the firm to achieve greater control on costs, quality and even strategy. An international generic firm needs to achieve cost leadership in order to be competitive. Product developmental capabilities will help create the much-needed product differentiation, which is crucial for success in the fiercely competitive market place. The organization needs to have a clear strategy for research and graduate into analogue research and its own drug discovery program before the window of opportunity is closed.

4. **Step Up Exports and Draw a Blueprint for Internationalization:** Exports can bring in higher price realizations even in the current era of cost containment strategies practiced by various national governments. It is important to draw up a clear strategy to gradually move up the value chain in exports, from exporting bulk drugs and intermediates, generic and branded generic formulations and to even innovative products over time. Moving up the value chain will also involve a movement from markets with weak or no IPR protection to highly industrialized, hard currency countries with very strong IPR protection and stringent regulatory requirements. Again, all this has to be achieved in compressed time if one is starting now. Buying up a manufacturing facility or an existing generic business overseas is an alternative to the creation of a beachhead through a green filed venture in these 'difficult-to-penetrate' markets.

5. **Use Benchmarking as a Strategy to Excel at Operations:** Successful organizations the world over, no longer set goals. They benchmark against the best practices of firms across the board. One needs to excel in all departments of the game in order to win. Today, the basic knowledge about what strategies should be adopted to succeed in the post-GATT era is widely known. The degree of insight and understanding may differ from firm to firm, but the basic strategy is clear to all. When the strategy is common and broadly understood what is the most crucial success factor? Operational excellence and implementation capabilities. It is the ability of an organization to execute its strategy effectively that determines success or failure. It is the vital difference between winning and running a race.

Post-GATT Scenario: Indian Pharmaceutical Industry - Action Agenda for the Future

1. Indian pharmaceutical industry today probably is in its most challenging phase ever. On the one hand it is poised for a massive growth from the present US 6-billion in 2005 to US $ 55-billion by 2020 as per a McKinsey report on the future of Indian Pharma industry. On the other hand, it had already shed its most protective armor (Indian Patents Act 1970) and amended its patent laws to cover product patent protection and a stronger IPR regime.

2. Change - rapid change can be seen in the Indian Pharma market - be it in industry structure, strategic approaches or tactical moves. In fact change is quite palpable.

3. Yesterday's mighty companies are giving away their hard-earned market share to the once-fledgeling companies with initiative in the emerging specialty segments.

4. A careful look into the high profile initiatives that have been launched by some of the innovative companies reveals a shrewd strategy of organizing their marketing operations around specific therapeutic and specialty prescriber segments.

5. The marketing-mix too has been undergoing rapid changes. Some of the fastest growing companies are those who have revisited their marketing mix through fresh initiatives such as reaching a very large customer base through scientific seminars, symposia, sponsorships of medical conferences, scientific information services and the rapidly emerging digital platforms such as blogs and social media channels that are not product related.

6. Competition in Indian pharmaceutical industry has always been severe. Consider this equation of over 10,000 companies, each fighting for a share in the US $ 29.65-billion market. The going for Indian Pharma can only get tougher in the coming years.

7. While it is difficult to predict at this point of time, the impact of GATT on Indian Pharma precisely, experts based on the experiences of other developed countries, who have accorded the product patent protection over the past two decades opine that:

   • Proliferation of the companies would be checked. The number of companies would dwindle.

- some of the more efficiently run smaller companies would be acquisition targets for newly entering MNCs or large Indian companies on an expansion spree.
- Smaller companies with good manufacturing facilities would become contract manufacturing organizations for the more aggressive, larger marketing companies.
- New product introductions would be reduced and restricted to new products under licensing arrangements.

8. Like Dinosaurs threatened by cataclysmic changes, companies often find it impossible to cope with a radically altered environment. It is only the fittest that survives.

9. Four things are crucial to seize the opportunity in any changing scenario at a broad level:

   (a) An understanding of how competition for the future is different.

   (b) A process for finding and gaining insight into tomorrow's opportunities.

   (c) An ability to energize the company top-to-bottom for what may be a long and arduous journey towards the future.

   (d) The capacity to outrun competitors and get to the future without taking undue risks.

10. Companies, therefore, need to raise their antennae higher to spot, track and monitor the signals of change. Like in war, in business too, *forewarned is forearmed.*

11. The challenges faced by the Indian Pharma industry are at two levels. One is at the functional level of marketing, which essentially revolves around the improvement of operational efficiency and effectiveness. The other is at the organizational level. Marketing here is not viewed in the relatively narrow functional level but in a much broader perspective encompassing the whole organization. Management scholars as well as practitioners have emphasized this holistic view of marketing. Remember what Peter Drucker, the management guru said:

   There is only one valid definition of business purpose: To create and keep a satisfied customer. It is the customer who determines what the business is. Because, it is its purpose to create a customer, any business enterprise has two - and only two- basic functions. Marketing and Innovation. Marketing is the whole business seen from the point of view of its final result, that is, from the customer's point of view.

12. Marketing, therefore it is not a mission for the marketing managers, while the rest of the organization goes about its business as before. It is the responsibility of the whole management of the company, where the goal is to see the business form the customer's view point.

13. The key questions to ask and answer by the senior management towards meeting the future challenges are:

- Is our action agenda mostly offensive or defensive?
- Are we devoting too much energy to preserving the past and not enough to creating the future?
- What percentage of our improvement efforts (quality, customer service, operational efficiency) focuses on merely catching up to our competition?

14. Catching up is necessary, but it is not going to turn an 'also-ran' into a leader. Defending today's leadership position is no substitute for tomorrow's leadership. And market leadership today certainly does not equal market leadership tomorrow. It requires clear, well-defined answers for certain key questions of today as well as for tomorrow (5 to 10 years in the future). Table 14.2 presents these key questions.

Table 14.5 Key Questions for Today and Tomorrow

Questions for Today	Questions for Tomorrow
1. Which customers are you serving today? In which markets?	1. Which customers will you b serving in the future? In which markets?
2. What are your marketing channels for reaching customers today?	2. What are your marketing channels for reaching your customers
3. What are your distinctive competencies today?	3. What distinctive competencies do you need for competing tomorrow?
4. Where do your profit margins come from today?	4. Where will your profit margins come from tomorrow?

(Adapted from *Competing for Future* by C.K. Prahlad and Gary Hammel)

Action Agenda

Some Indian Pharma companies have started asking these questions about the future even before the GATT came into effect. They have been gearing up to meet the challenges of the future. A careful analysis of the high-profile initiatives taken by some of the more aggressive and active Indian drug majors such as Ranbaxy, Lupin, Cipla, Torrent, Sun Pharma, Dr. Reddy's Labs, Zydus Cadila Healthcare, Glenmark, Mankind Pharma among others - a pattern emerges. There is a common thread that runs through their carefully woven strategies. Here is a broad outline of their Action Agenda, for effectively competing in the product patent era.

A. **Reaching a critical mass in terms of size:** It is essential for any company to reach a critical mass in terms of size to effectively generate and leverage resources. In the new economic order, where entry barriers are slowly dissolving, the level and intensity of competition are bound to increase significantly. Unless a company achieves a critical mass in terms of sales and profits, a dominant position in select key markets, it would not be able to compete effectively and make strategic investments required for future growth.

B. **Marketing Focus:** Achieving a dominant position in a therapeutic segment requires a focused marketing strategy like careful selection of product mix in terms of both width and depth, superior customer relationship management, target-specific communication strategies etc, in relevant specialty therapeutic area prescriber segments.

C. **Operating Efficiency and Effectiveness:** In the final analysis, the key determinant of effectiveness or success is a healthy bottomline. This can be achieved only by a systematic approach to all aspects of business and uncompromising adherence to well-defined standards. Generating surplus is essential and only companies with high profitability can invest strategically for future growth.

D. **Export Thrust:** The importance of earning valuable foreign exchange in today's business can never be over-emphasized. Large markets and remunerative prices are the major motivating factors that drive the companies for export performance. Leading Indian drug companies, who have gained a strong foothold in export markets through bulk drugs are gradually shifting their emphasis to more value-added formulation exports. Some companies like Sun Pharma, Ranbaxy (Sun Pharma now), Cadila, Torrent, Lupin and Wockhardt have been registering and promoting their branded generic formulations in South Asia, Africa, CIS countries and even in highly regulated markets such as USA and European Union.

E. Technology Up-gradation: Technology up-gradation is a must not only for growth but vital even for survival in the rapidly changing pharmaceutical business scenario. Up-gradation of manufacturing facilities to international standards and certifications of those facilities by international regulatory authorities such as US FDA, UK MCA, and Canadian HPB are essential prerequisites to export pharmaceutical substances and formulations to those respective countries.

F. R & D effort: Pharma industry is highly research intensive. Process development is an area where Indian companies have excelled over the years and brought the country a net-exporter status in the Pharma industry. The R & D investment had been a meager 1.5 percent of sales on average by Indian companies as compared to 12 to 18 per ent by international drug companies. The introduction of new products is likely to be reduced to a trickle now that product patents are in place. A number of progressive companies that are driven by their ambitious growth plans have been stepping up their investment on research and development nearly to a level of their international counterparts.

While the basic research (considering the cost of developing a new molecule is close to a billion dollars) is unaffordable in India, increased R & D effort is a must, even to assimilate transfer of technology and to pursue applied research. A small number of companies in India, whose cases, we have discussed in this chapter have taken the initiative and stepped up their research effort and even launched their own drug discovery programs.

G. Resource mobilizing capability: Technology up-gradation, R & D efforts are highly investment intensive. They require huge outlays of capital. Export thrust too requires large upfront investments for product registration and marketing activities. A company that is profit making, with an impressive track record, clearly defined and well-crafted strategy and a high degree of transparency in its transactions can attract huge investments from the capital markets. A detailed analysis of the public issues a few years ago would reveal an impressive track record and a well-crafted, powerful communicated corporate strategy and mission. Some of the Indian drug majors such as Dr. Reddy's Labs, Sun Pharma, and Wockhardt have been able to attract even international investors for their New York Stock Exchange (NYSE) listings or Euro issues.

H. **Strategic alliances:** Collaborate to compete seems to be the new stratagem in the international business arena. In a research-intensive industry like Pharma industry more and more strategic alliances are being formed every day. Alliances are important to pool up resources and compete cost-effectively by optimization. They are also powerful sources of synergy. Access to markets, products and technology are some of the important advantages of strategic alliances.

I. **Strategic Integration:** Strategic integration - be it backward integration to manufacture pharmaceutical substances by a manufacturer of formulations or a forward integration to manufacture formulations by a manufacturer of Pharmaceutical raw materials - offers a distinct competitive advantage. Control on input costs, continuous supply, quality and even unique customer perceptions are some of the important advantages that strategic integration offers.

J. **Building core competencies:** Since a core competence is most decidedly a source of competitive advantage, a company must invest considerable amount of time, effort and resources in building a portfolio of core competencies. There are five important steps involved in building core competencies:

1. Identifying existing core competencies
2. Establishing a core competence acquisition agenda
3. Building core competencies
4. Deploying core competencies
5. Protecting and defending core competence leadership

K. **Human resource development:** The competence of the people working in any company gives it the winning edge. People therefore, are not only the greatest asset of a firm but also its source of its distinctive competence. Neither the people nor their competencies can be taken for granted. They must regularly upgrade their skills. Their will must be positively reinforced, rather charged. Upgrade and keep abreast must the watch words and key deeds. Training and retraining, which are a must, therefore, be an integral part of the corporate development program.

All these successful companies have been paying increasingly greater attention to these training and developmental programs. To paraphrase Peter Drucker, any company is only as competent as its least competent employee. Investment in people by an organization is, therefore, not a matter of choice. It is mandatory.

All these companies, which we have discussed here have been continuously improving their capabilities and sharpening their competitive edge to stay ahead of the game. While the game plan in retrospect (since the model is available) is easy to understand and deceptively simple, transforming and translating this into an action plan is very difficult. It takes one-hundred percent commitment, determination and total support of top management to make it happen.

Summary

The nature and intensity of competition in the Indian pharmaceutical industry are in for a big change. As the Indian government has recognized product patents and agreed to protect IPR (Intellectual Property Rights), many companies have realized that the cozy, protective marketing environment that the earlier Indian Patents Act provided would gradually disappear. They realized that they no longer are insulated from international competition. And that they should acquaint and develop the skill and will to match or even outmatch, to out-perform competition in the international arena.

One has to achieve world-class standards to win at the global market place. That requires foresight, lots of hard work, a clearly defined game plan and abundant will to make it happen. Companies which can develop these capabilities are going to be the major players, who will be successful in this new ball game. Companies, which are determined to excel in every department of the game are going to win.

An analysis of the game plans of some of the more progressive Pharma companies in India reveal a carefully crafted strategy. A common thread runs through their action plans of every one of these companies. In fact, the degree of commonality is so high among their strategic approaches as it were, a common action agenda may indeed appear like a a formula for success. Consider these salient features, which are virtually common in all the game plans of these select companies.

A. Reaching a critical mass in terms of size

B. Marketing focus

C. Operating efficiency and effectiveness

D. Export thrust

E. Technology up-gradation

F. R & D effort

G. Resource mobilizing capability

H. Strategic alliances

I. Strategic integration

Towards Excellence in Marketing

Excel or be Extinct!

Excel or be extinct! Well, that may sound a bit harsh. But then, that is the reality of the ruthless market place, where competition is fierce. Excellence, the dictionary defines as t*he state or quality of outdoing, outstripping, outperforming, and doing better...* Implied in this definition is the necessity of competitive edge. If you are not able to outperform and out do your competitor and do better than your competitor, he will outstrip and outperform you. The outcome is the extinction effect.

Excellence and the pursuit of it is no longer a matter of choice or nice to have in a highly competitive industry like Indian pharmaceuticals. It is mandatory. The message the pharmaceutical marketers is clear. Excel or face extinction!

Achieving Excellence - Ten Major Principles

How to excel? How to do better? Better than what we did in the past and better than what we can do. And more importantly, how to do better than the competitor?

There are no magic formulas or right answers to these questions. No easy solutions either. Excellence is a state of mind. It is a constant quest, a burning desire to do better. An organization that can inculcate this at least in the core team of managers is bound to excel.

The spirit of excellence has to be Internalized by all they members who can spread it across the organization.

A detailed analysis and a study of successful organizations reveals that there is a common thread that runs through the firms that achieved excellence and continue to excel. Excellence is not a goal. It is continuous obsession. Here are ten major principles, which can help your organization achieve excellence and more importantly, continue to excel.

1. **Customer Orientation:** All marketing practitioners the world over are only too familiar with these words. The whole business of marketing is concerned with customer orientation. But what do you see in practice? To what extent do you practice customer orientation in your organization? Customer orientation, as normally understood or popularly believed is not restricted to the marketing department of an organization. The whole organization should understand and practice customer orientation. That is what the marketing concept is in reality. A customer comes into contact with your company's telephone operator, security and receptionist first. He is likely form an opinion based on the way he is received and treated by them. If they are courteous, he will think that you are a warm, friendly organization. The importance of customer service and that an organization exists only to satisfy the needs and wants of a customer must be understood not only by the marketing staff, but by all the people working in production, purchase, finance and distribution departments. All the departments should be working as a team to deliver a need-satisfying entity called the product (or service). Every employee of the organization should be made to understand this. In fact, customer orientation should be an important part of the corporate philosophy of every organization. Mahatma Gandhi best expressed the importance of customer orientation. He said:

   A customer is the most important person on our premises. He is not dependent on us.

   We are dependent on him. He is not an interruption on our work. He is the purpose of it.

   We are not doing him a favor. He is doing us a favor by giving us an opportunity to do so.

2. **Quality:** The quality of your products and services must truly be outstanding. The importance of quality is too well known to all marketers and manufacturers to elaborate upon it here. What is needed is an uncompromising attitude to practice it. Quality above everything should be the motto. Quality gives the organization an enormous power to succeed in the market place. Quality wins!

3. **Innovation**: Innovation gives an organization its cutting edge. It keeps the organization ahead. Innovation could virtually be attempted and accomplished in every functional area. Innovation is an essential ingredient of excellence. Innovation is spotting an unmet need and exploiting it with a matching product or service. A number of companies achieved uncommon success by exploiting the latent needs in the market place. Consider how two companies have achieved uncommon success by exploiting the untapped potential in Indian pharmaceutical market:

Case 15.1   Ranbaxy Revitalizes an Opportunity!

Ranbaxy spotted an opportunity hitherto untapped by any other company in the Ginseng containing rejuvenator market and introduced Revital, a combination of ginseng and all other known multivitamins and minerals in a single capsule in 1989. The company put all its might behind it and put up a massive, well synchronized promotional effort. The whole organization right from the chairman of the company to the medical representative in the field was determined to make it a success. The company had gone whole hog with its innovative product strategy and achieved uncommon success. The differentiating feature of the product is that Revital was the only product containing ginseng and vitamins and multivitamins. All other products in the category at that time contained only ginseng.

Revital was one of the biggest product successes in Indian pharmaceutical industry since its launch. Later Revital has changed the tacks and gone over-the-counter route and promoted through mass media. Revital has been unprecedented success. Later the company was acquired by Sun Pharma, which not only continued the OTC promotion but also stepped it up. Revital crossed the Rs. 160-crore mark in sales in India alone in 2012.

Case 15.2 Ajanta Pharma's Thirty-Plus

In the same ginseng and rejuvenators' market in India, a little known company in the domestic market, Ajanata Pharma spotted another opportunity, i.e., the OTC formulation of ginseng. Ajanta Pharma combined ginseng, a herbal product from South Korea with Ashwagandha, a well known Ayurvedic product and marketed it under a catchy brand name, *Thirty Plus*. The company targeted men who are above thirty-years and chose a different route - the OTC, route which was virtually free from any direct competition. The company promoted the brand through the lay press and and television. Thirty Plus, too had become an outstanding success. Ajanta Pharma sold the Thirty Plus brand in 2011 to Dabur Pharma for an undisclosed sum.

---

4. **Perceptible Product Differentiation:** To create perceptible differentiation in your products and marketing strategies, you must stay close to the market at all times, listen to what it says and above all, act on what you hear. That is the only reliable way of spotting the unmet needs and exploiting them. Once you create a product differentiation, reinforce that differentiation by creating a distinctive feature in every element of the marketing mix for that particular product and communicate it with all the force you can muster. Listen to what the market feels and says about it. Once you are convinced that the perceptual response is in the right direction stay with it. That is the way to create winning brands.

5. **Distinctive Competence:** What is your single most important strength that separates you from the competition? The product quality? Productivity? Manufacturing efficiencies? Marketing muscle? Distribution? Technology? R & D? Financial planning? Resources? Size? Economies of scale? Image? Sales force competence? Identify the most distinctive strength and build it into your product and market strategies.

In pharmaceutical marketing in India, sales force competence and commitment are very important determinants of success. In addition to your own distinctive competence (if it is other than the sales force competence) improve your sales force competence and commitment by investing in appropriate training and development activity by instituting proven positive reinforcement programs.

6. **Effective Segmentation:** In a complex marketing situation like pharmaceutical marketing, segmentation assumes even greater importance. Segmentation of the product strategy, at the market level (therapeutic category), customer level (by prescriber specialty and gender) and at the consumer level (patient by age, gender and the stage of disease) has to be synchronized and must achieve a product-market-customer-consumer fit. Once a segmentation strategy is decided upon, you must stick to it with guts, and conviction. Segmentation implies exclusion. For example, when you want to concentrate on gynecologists for your multi-hematinic brand, can you ensure that you promote your brand only to gynecologists and no one else? Or do you yield when your sales force pressurizes you, stating that general practitioners and surgeons also can and do prescribe hematinics? Effective segmentation can be achieved only by concentrated efforts backed by conviction.

7. **Strategy:** In the era of fierce competition, strategy is always the king! What is your corporate strategy? Corporate strategy determines marketing strategy. Innovative corporate strategies have pushed many small and medium sized pharmaceutical companies in India into the big league during the past few years. Some of these companies have aggressively pursued vertical integration strategies and some winning horizontal moves.

8. **Competitive Analysis:** Competitive analysis becomes all the more important in the context of excellence. When you are in the pursuit of of excellence, a systematic approach to competitive analysis is vital. If you want to excel, you should know how your competition is doing. Otherwise how can you outperform them?

9. **New Product Development**: New product development is not only crucial for the growth of the company but also vital even for

its survival. Concentration on building winning brands is necessary to overcome product obsolescence. Over the years, companies that have achieved the most spectacular growth are those, whose new product development and new product strike rate have been very high.

10. **Build a Winning Team:** People in any organization make all the difference. They make the vital difference between excellence and mediocrity, winning and losing and between success and failure.

Build a team of positive-minded, strong-willed, intuitive managers. This is crucial. A winning team of committed managers can help your company achieve uncommon success. Remember your greatest obstacles to competitive success don't lie outside your organization but inside your own management. By demonstration, delegation and decentralization and by empowering, you can build a winning team of managers. A winning team of managers can set the pace for marketing in your industry by excelling and outperforming. Look closely for the key success factors in any organization that achieved excellence. You will find that it is the people who are responsible for excellence. Invest in your people. Make innovation and pace setting a part and parcel of the work of every manager with profit responsibility.

Summary

Excellence implies sharpening of a firm's competitive edge. If you do not develop a distinctive competitive advantage, how can you outdo or outperform your competitor?

In today's fiercely competitive, desire-driven, differentiated, ruthless market place, achieving excellence is no longer a matter of choice for any firm. It is mandatory. When you study the companies that achieved uncommon success, you will find a common thread running through their strategy. The ten essential principles that lie beneath the winning strategy can help you achieve excellence in marketing. These principles are:

1. Customer orientation
2. Quality

3. Innovation

4. Perceptible differentiation

5. Distinctive competence

6. Effective segmentation

7. Strategy

8. Competitive analysis

9. New product development

10. Winning team

To achieve excellence in marketing you should ensure that all elements of the marketing mix are integrated and synchronized to exert the maximum impact. The various elements of the promotional mix should reinforce each other and present a consistent, continuous message to the target audience, which is fulfilled by the product. Only then, it can outperform and outcompete. And outdoing the competition is a must. If you don't outdo you will be outdone. The market place has no mercy. It has only one rule. You excel or be extinct!

16

The Winning Edge

Omnipresent! Pervasive!

Yes, competition is omnipresent. Take any industry, any market - there is competition. Infinite needs, wants and aspirations and finite resources to fulfill, satisfy and realize them further intensify the competition. To be successful in the market place, you have to perform better than the competitor. Outperform your competitor in all major areas of your operations.

Every year, the world over, a number of businesses go bankrupt. A number of products die a premature death on the retailers's shelves, and in distributors' warehouses. Why? There may be many reasons. It may be due to poor management, inept marketing, inefficient manufacturing and so on. When you probe deeper, you would find that all companies that fail in the market place share a single characteristic. They were not able to compete in the market place.

Competition is all pervasive. Not only in the market place but even within the organization. We are not talking about the internal competition., that is, competition between managers of two or more departments to move ahead in the company's hierarchy, when we say that competition is all pervasive. What it really means is that everyone in the company is competing with his counterpart in the rival (competing) organization. In a pharmaceutical company, for example, a medical representative is competing with the rival firm's medical representative for getting prescriptions for his products from the doctor. An R & D scientist of one company is competing with another R &D

scientist of another firm to win the race for new product development. A personnel manager of one company is competing with his counterpart of the rival firm for recruiting the best talent from the job market. Materials managers of two rival firms are directly in competition with each other for getting a better price, timely delivery, and longer attractive credit terms from their suppliers. The list can go on and on.

The implication of this is that competition in the market place is not just between the marketing departments of two different companies competing in the same segment. The competition runs across the entire structure of each of the rival organizations. Companies that are aware of this fact are bound to do well in promoting a competitive spirit among all their members. This is essential to develop a distinct competitive advantage based on a systematic competitive analysis. That is what gives the successful companies their most powerful weapon. Their winning edge.

Three Phases

Business theorists have identified three different phases of management orientation. This first was *product orientation*. The emphasis during this phase was clearly on the product - on what was being sold, production methods and innovation. Orientation during this phase was characterized by Henry Ford's view, who had revolutionized automobile manufacturing with his Model T car. Ford's statement of *my customers can have a car of their choice as long as it was black* was symbolic of the product orientation era. Gradually, many managers changed their thinking. They shifted their emphasis from product orientation to market orientation.

Customer satisfaction became the top priority. Management consultant Peter Drucker declared that the basic objective of all businesses was to create and keep a customer. This *customer - orientation* meant finding better ways to satisfy the customers' needs. The focus was on what customers could use rather than on trying to sell them what was produced. Products were still important. But product development was based on market research to identify unmet needs.

Another change has emerged in the past few years. Competition is intensifying in a number of industries. Managers are finding it increasingly difficult to *ride the market*. Managers, therefore adopted a new approach - *competition-orientation*. This new approach takes a different view of *success* and *failure* in the market place. Improving your market share means winning a battle or two with competitors. And that is not all. You have to win the struggle with your competition in terms of personnel, resources and product development.

Products and customers are of paramount importance even to competition orientation. While quality products targeted at satisfying the customers' needs are crucial to the success of a competition-oriented firm but that is not enough. Quality and efficient service are two elements and sources of competitive advantage. But then, there are many more to be considered. They are process innovation, marketing skills, financial management capabilities, cost control, effective distribution channels. All these are sources for obtaining a competitive advantage over rivals. Winning customers is the ultimate goal of any business. But competition-orientation looks beyond satisfying customer needs and takes into account various other aspects towards developing a distinct competitive advantage. Towards creating the winning edge.

A Zero-Sum Game

When you are competitor-oriented, you are in fact and in effect playing a zero-sum game. In a zero-sum game, what one party wins, another party loses. Competition is fierce and increasing. Here the customers are limited. As a result, what counts in a business game is not how well you do, but how others are doing and what your performance is in relation to your competitors'. The quality of your product, your innovative appeal and your marketing skills - all these have to be evaluated in relation to your competitors' business. You cannot, therefore, stop with the conventional customer-oriented questions like:

- What do they want?
- Which are their currently unmet needs?
- Which customer segments are growing?

You now have to ask questions related to competition:

- How vulnerable are our products and services?
- Which competitors pose a threat to us?
- From which competitors are we currently taking market share?
- How can we defend our market segments?
- What are the areas where our competitors are vulnerable?

Four Major Purposes

Analyzing your competitors' actions becomes a necessity when you are competition-oriented. You have to be competitor-oriented in today's intensely competitive market place. While competitive analysis involves collection of information about the competition, it is much more than a data-gathering exercise. It is a process by which, you can understand your competitors' moves and strategy. This enables you to anticipate their moves. Anticipating your competitors' moves is very important because it lets you plan the strategy for defending your territory and preparing for opportunities resulting from the competitors' weaknesses and mistakes. Otherwise, if you want to react to the competitors' moves after they are made and revealed, you will find yourself falling far behind in the struggle.

Analyzing your competition is essential. A systematic approach to competitive analysis is beneficial. It provides very useful insights regarding your competitors' activities. This information is a prerequisite to anticipating their moves. Here are four major purposes, your competitive analysis can serve:

1. **Defending your market share:** It helps you to defend your market share. It gives you an early warning signal regarding, which competitors are clawing at your door. What strategies are your competitors trying to adopt to lure your customers away. Are they trying to give superior, better quality products? Are they following a product differentiation strategy? Are they reducing their prices? Have they achieved cost leadership? Questions like what Dr. Reddy's Laboratories asked in case of ibuprofen, norfloxacin. Are they extending the image of their products? Are they following new selling strategies? New sales approaches? Your competitive analysis can provide answers to all these questions and more.

2. **Increasing your market share:** One of the major ways of increasing your market share is by luring customers away from your rivals. Unless you analyze your competitors thoroughly, it is not possible to identify their strengths and weaknesses. Where is your competitor vulnerable? How best can you exploit opportunities? How can you develop a competitive advantage to

increase your market share? A systematic competitive analysis should provide the right answers to these questions.

3. **Improving the efficiency of your operations:** A detailed analysis of your competitors' operations gives you a clear idea of their total operations. You can use this information to reinforce your competitive advantages. This may include innovation, new product development, special promotional strategies, process innovation etc. By monitoring his activities closely, you can learn what works for him and what does not. You can learn from his successes and failures. It is less expensive to learn from others' mistakes than your own.

4. **Preparing yourself to be combat-fit:** Competitive analysis can save you from being caught napping and unaware. One can ill-afford such a luxury of unpleasant surprises and shocks. Changes and developments taking place in the market place and the competitors responsible for those should be monitored. Only then can you prepare contingency plans. Only then can you be combat-fit.

A Continuous Program

Competitive analysis is not a one-time exercise. It is a method for monitoring change. Therefore, it must be a continuous program. An ongoing exercise. It must be made a part of your planning process. You must assign the responsibility to a specific manager. You must also inculcate and incorporate competitive thinking into every single employee of your firm. If all your employees are competition conscious, their alertness in monitoring any significant competitor information is certainly going to positively reinforce your competitive analysis. And that will help you counter any bash with your competitor.

A number of companies neglect competitive analysis. Some companies do not give it the necessary importance. The reasons could be many. Complacency is one. Some companies, which are resting on their laurels may suddenly wake up to realize that they are faced with tough competition. The second reason for the inadequate attention paid by companies to competitive analysis is that they take it for granted. The typical response is:

We have the information already. The sales people know their competitors. The purchase people are very competent and they get better terms than our competitors. Our R & D teams are the best in the industry and they track all technological advancement. Why duplicate the effort?

It is not a question of wasting time or duplicating the effort or complicating things. It is a question of getting the whole picture of your major competitors and not getting information in bits and pieces. The parable of the blind men and the elephant amplifies this point.

What you want to see is the whole elephant, and not just different parts of the body. You can see and get useful insight into the activities of your major competitors only when you follow a systematic, organized, and continuous competitive analysis. And above all your competitive analysis should be action-oriented.

Sharpening the Focus: A Three Step Approach

To maintain and improve a competitive position in every facet of your business, you must first evaluate your current position. This involves three steps, namely, defining your business, analyzing your customers and mapping your competitors.

1. **Defining your business:** What business are you in ? This is very simple, in fact a deceptively easy question to ask. But it requires a great deal of clarity of thinking to answer this question. You should begin your competitive analysis with this question, because the answer determines your competitors, and unfolds the key factors required to remain competitive. Consider this case (16.1).

Case 16.1   Redefining Success!

Glaxo, the British pharmaceutical giant in the late 1970s redefined its business as ethical drugs and pharmaceuticals and divested other businesses like health foods, generics, hospital products and animal health products. This redefinition sharpened the focus of the company identified the single most important success factor in ethical drugs as the new product development. Glaxo pursued research and development with renewed vigor. It had put all its might behind new product development. As a result the company unleashed a number of winners such a Zantac, Fortum etc, which pushed Glaxo to the prestigious No 2 portion on the world pharmaceutical league table in 1988. Later in 1990, Glaxo has moved down to the 4th position in world pharmaceutical industry due to two major international mergers - one between SmithKline and Beecham and the other between Bristol Myers and Squibb, both in 1989.

Two years later, in 1992, Glaxo with its sharpened focus not only defended its No 2 position but also narrowed down the gap between Glaxo and Merck, which was No.1 company in the world at that time.

Glaxo in 2000 has become Glaxo SmithKline due to a merger and sharpened its focus further on research based pharmaceutical business.

2. **Analyzing Your Customers**: Knowing your customers closely and analyzing their needs, wants, aspirations hold the key to mapping an effective competitive strategy. In any marketing battle, the customer is the most important prize.

In pharmaceutical marketing, it is an established fact that the doctors are the most important intermediate customers. Doctors make the purchasing (prescribing) decisions for the customers (patients).

A pharmaceutical marketer, therefore, should closely monitor, analyze and anticipate the needs, wants of the intermediate customers (doctors), who are the decision makers and the customers' (patients), whose needs your products are going to satisfy. Such an analysis helps you uncover the key factors, which determine competitiveness in the market. The important questions to ask for in identifying the key factors for determining the competitiveness are:

- Who are my customers?
- What is my product going to do and for whom?
- Which doctors are most likely to use my product and why?
- What do those doctors look for in a product in these conditions

(indications)? Do they look for complete cure, rapid relief, better tolerance, convenience of dosage, ease of administration, patient acceptance or economy?

- How does my product rank along with the competitors' products in terms of satisfying those needs of doctors?
- What is the gap like?
- How else can these needs be met?

Your answers to these questions would reveal the key factors necessary to improve your competitive advantage. While doctors are the decision makers as regards the usage of ethical drugs, the important customers include the pharmacists in hospitals and nursing homes and all the members of the marketing or distribution channels. Wholesalers and retailers are very crucial to your success in the market place. The difference between success and failure may often rest on the availability of the drug. A detailed analysis of your distribution channels vis-a-vis your competitors' is important. Identifying the key factors are necessary for two reasons. One is that substitution can represent one of the most potent form of all competitive threats. Substitution can be at two levels in pharmaceutical marketing. One is in the area of technological advancement, that is, a superior, better or more convenient product replacing an existing one. A new compound, a new dosage form, a new drug delivery system can take a greater share of or even replace the market for existing drugs.

New packaging materials are slowly replacing the existing ones even in pharmaceutical industry. What are the implications for the marketer? Other types of substitution occur in the marketing channels. If a product is not available it can lead to substitution. It is most likely to be substituted with another product having similar, if not the same properties. This type of substitution is not restricted to trade channels alone. Even prescribing doctors advise their patients sometimes when they are not sure of the availability, to take brand B or brand C if brand A is not available. If the product continues to be unavailable, the doctor before long, may drop your product from his prescription. Availability of your products, when they are wanted and where they are needed is most crucial for achieving success. A detailed analysis of all your customers, their needs, expectations and how you are faring with those, as compared to your competitors is a must.

Such an analysis helps you unearth the key factors that determine competitiveness.

Product uniqueness has always been the key factor on which competition in the drug industry has turned. New product development has been the key factor even in Indian pharmaceutical industry. In every industry, the best competitors are those companies that recognize which factors are important and base their competitive strategies on them. Less successful companies often fail to look for the key factors, or concentrate on the wrong ones.

The major issues of a customer analysis therefore, are what the customer is wanting, and what is available to satisfy these needs and desires. An awareness of these things helps you to anticipate changes, especially in the form of new substitute products and services. Such an understanding can help making tomorrow's superstars. By the same token, the lack or absence of an understanding the other ways that customers can be satisfied and the fact and their needs and wants are changing may strip today's complacent superstars of their star status.

3. **Mapping your competitors:** Competitive advantages are sometimes difficult to distinguish. You cannot simply label your competitors as winners or losers based on their sales volume and gross profits alone. The purpose of a competitive analysis is not just to identify which competitor among all the players had more profits. The basic purpose is to find out how he made them in the first place, and where did he make (which segment) them? What are his competitive advantages in those segments? What is winning edge?

How do you start mapping your competitors? You start from the beginning by visualizing a broad functional need, and all the ways of satisfying that need. This presents the big picture - the macro map of the market. Figure 16.1 illustrates an attempt at mapping the Indian health care industry on the lines of the mapping approach provided by the center for information policy at Harvard School. The content-related businesses are grouped on the right side of the map, conduit-related businesses on the left side, and those overlapping, in the middle. The vertical axis is used for product service distinction.

This shows at a glance all the participants in the healthcare industry with inter-relationships and their dimensions. This also indicates the directions of change and the likely shifts that may be taking place. In urban areas the conventional clinical and pathological laboratories are slowly giving away to sophisticated diagnostic centers with all modern equipments and facilities. Electronic medical equipment is making inroads and gradually taking away the share of the conventional ones. Disposable syringes are just rearing their needles. Hospital chains with super specialties like cardiovascular surgery, urology etc. are taking away the share of the private hospitals and nursing homes. Some of the major hospital chains are pursuing aggressive marketing strategies to make their services transcend the barriers of price sensitivity. Health insurance schemes and health cards are on the increase. The increasing literacy levels and the consequent awareness among public, the emergence of super specialties - do they have any significance for pharmaceutical marketing?

Are there any hidden opportunities? The next logical step is turning to competition. Who are the major players in the healthcare business? What are their moves? Where are they active? To chart the competitors' moves you have to focus on more specific areas.

Probing Deeper

As a next step, you select the area or segment where your competitors are fairly entrenched and do an in-depth analysis. Probe deeper. Take for example ethical formulations. That is where the competition is at its fiercest. In ethical formulations you have various therapeutic segments. A detailed analysis of your major competitors in all the segments of your interest and other segments where your major competitors are vulnerable, provides useful inputs for your strategic marketing planning.

Once you gather all the facts and do an in-depth analysis you will be able to spot the opportunities that may be dormant and find out the vulnerable points of your major competitors. This will help you in improving your competitive sharpness and prepare you for an offensive attack. Such an analysis would also enable you to take stock of your vulnerable areas so that you can take the necessary corrective steps and reinforce your position and defend your markets in time.

* Physicians	* Government hospitals	* Diagnostic centre	* Govt.medical colleges
* Surgeons	* Primary health centres	* Chemical laboratores	* Private medical colleges
* Cardiologists	* Private nursing homes		* Medical seminars
* Paediatricians	* Hospital chains		* Medical symposia
* Gynaecologists	* Health insurance		* Clinical trials
* Orthopaedicians	* Health cards		* Medical associations
* Neurologists	* Prosthetic devices		* Medical journals
* Opthalmologists	* Lithotripsy		* Medical representation
* Anaesthetists	* Total body scanner		* Medical exhibitions
* Pathologists	* C.A.T. scanners		* Advertising
* Psychiatrists	* Electronic medical		* Product monographs
* ENT specialists	equipment	* E.E.G. machines	
* Dental surgeons		* E.C.G. machines	
* Radiologists		* X-ray machines	
* Veterinarians		* Erkameters	
* Nursing staff			
* Pharmacists			
* Retailers	* Poultry farms		
* Wholesalers	* Ayurvedic drugs		
	* Homeopathic preparations		* Diagnostic reagents
			* Radiologicalsu
* Bulk drugs			* Surgical equipment
* Pharmaceutical formulations			* I.V. fluids
* Biological products			* Disposable syringes
* Health foods			
* Animal health products			

Figure 16.1 Healthcare Industry

Sources of Competitive Intelligence

Competitive intelligence is not just collecting data periodically and submitting a quarterly or half-yearly report to the chief executive. Competitive intelligence is a way of thinking. It is an ongoing process. The dictionary defines *intelligence* as *the faculty of perceiving and comprehending meaning.* The key word is meaning. Competitive intelligence is an activity of collecting data from all possible sources and processing it into meaningful information that can be used as a strategic input for decision making. It is a means to evaluate your current business strategy and to determine the need for making changes in the light of what competitors are doing, or not doing as the case may be.

Most managers feel that competitive analysis is a very difficult exercise because no competitor will be willing to give realistic information and what you collect from them is more of a misinformation and not really dependable. This is totally a wrong notion. Competitive information is not really available for the asking but there are numerous sources from which you can collect the data and organize it into a meaningful information. If you approach it in a systematic manner, gathering competitive intelligence information is less difficult than you think. All you have to do is design a simple system for facilitating regular, smooth flow of information. You should also provide a periodic feedback to employees regarding how the information has been put to use and how important and significant their contributions have been.

Sources Outside the Organization

Your competitors themselves may be revealing more information in the course of their business, despite the fact that like any other company, they would like to keep their plans and activities secret from rivals. If you are alert, you can gather a lot of competitive intelligence information and make meaning out of it. And then, you have the information from the trade press, government sources, trade shows and exhibitions etc. to supplement it. Consider the sources presented in Table 16.1.

Table 16.1 Important Sources of Competitive Intelligence

1. **Annual Reports:** These give general financial information for the year that ended and the previous financial years on earnings, cash flow, balance sheet etc. if you have been keeping track of these reports over a period of time you can spot trends, and notice any changes in emphasis. The annual reports also give details of the company's business segments, details of their products, their corporate social responsibility initiatives and their future outlook etc.

2. **Speeches:** The speeches of chairmen and managing directors at the annual general meetings will often reveal something about management philosophy and assumptions. If you have been following these over a period of time, you will be able to spot any possible changes in emphasis or reinforcement.

Contd...

3. **Company Publications:** Company publications like employee newsletters, company brochures and any materials published by a company's public relations department may contain useful information. These are often available on request.

4. **Press Releases:** Press releases issued by companies on new products, new projects, joint ventures and any other important events are easy to pick up and often contain important information, which is of interest to direct competitors.

5. **Recruitment:** Recruitment advertisements often carry in them a wealth of information regarding market penetration, diversification plans, remuneration packages at various levels advertised etc.

6. **Trade Press:** Trade publications are one of the most fertile sources of information regarding your industry and you should pay considerable attention to them. Industry-wise newspaper clipping services are very convenient to use.

7. **Trade Shows:** Excellent source of information on competitors' new products.

8. **Promotional Material:** Competitors's promotional material can provide at no cost, very useful information regarding the products they are pushing aggressively, and the advantages they are emphasizing.

9. **Government Sources:** You can get important information relating to the expansion, diversification and export plans and strategies of your competitors from government sources like DGTD, drug controller's office, customs department etc.

10. **Visit to Facilities:** Many companies allow the public to visit their facilities. Sending your key people on a visit to your competitors' facilities will be very beneficial.

11. **Company Websites:** Last, but not least, your competitors' websites are a very rich source of information. They give you all the details about their company like their mission, vision, people, composition of the board, their current performance, activities, future plans, future outlook, details that prospective investors look for such as annual reports, presentations to investors etc.

Putting the Pieces Together

Competitive analysis is a complex task. If you gather too much data from too many sources that will complicate your task further. You should collect the right amount of relevant data. Data and sources therefore, must be evaluated. Evaluate the source in terms of reliability and the date in terms of its relevance.

The data must be first organized to interpret it meaningfully. The interpretation of the information should either add to or alter the perceptions of the situation. In either case, what is the significance? Is it congruent with other known facts? Does it confirm other information or conflict with it? Which is more authentic? What should be used as a strategic input? These are some of the questions that your interpretation of information should answer.

Timely dissemination of information is essential to take any prompt action. The action may be corrective or reinforcing. Dissemination of competitive intelligence information to the respective departments for follow up action, apart from improving your firm's combat fitness, will also increase the competitive consciousness of the company as a whole. This in turn will improve reliability and relevance of the data.

Who Are Your Competitors?

When you are setting up a competitive intelligence system and are determined to monitor and update it, have a broad perspective of who your competitors really are. Who are your competitors may appear to be a naive question. But always consider three classes of competitors.

A. Direct competitors, who are current market participants

B. Potential competitors, who are waiting on the sidelines, ready to join the fray at any time

C. Indirect competitors, who provide substitute products

Focus Your Analysis

To get the best out of your competitive intelligence system, you have to sharpen the focus of your analysis. You may find the two-step approach suggested here useful. Firstly, identify the most important and distinct competitive advantages perceived by all the key players in your industry. These should be the factors determining their success.

This identification of competitive advantages will either improve the position of one company over the other or act as an entry barrier for those companies, who do not possess any of these distinctive competitive advantages.

Secondly, prepare a complete dossier or file on each of your major competitors covering the whole range of their operations, strengths, and weaknesses in each of the functional areas, their distinctive competitive advantages. Constantly update it. Your endeavor should be to know as much as you can, about their activities. This means that you should know about your competition as much as you know about your company especially the past or historical data regarding their performance, perceptions, and also their current progress. Studying their past performance also is important, because it is indeed a good predictor! It helps you to anticipate their likely moves. People are *victims* of their past and their experience. They tend to build on strengths and replicate what made them successful. If delegation was what made them successful in the past, they continue to delegate. If doing things themselves was responsible for what they are today, they continue to do things themselves. Under normal circumstances they normally do not change. They change slightly. This is not to say that people are like robots and cannot adapt themselves. What it really means is that there will be more consistency than inconsistency.

Major Competitive Advantages

1. **Differentiation:** Differentiation is a very important competitive advantage. Differentiation could be real if the product is unique. Or it may be the result of any apparent uniqueness through creative and innovative marketing. The strategic implications of differentiation are that it parallels segmentation. Differentiation of a product makes it more appealing to a particular segment. How do your firm's products compare with your major competitors in their strategies of *differentiation* - apparent or real? What opportunities exist for you in their area of differentiation? What are the possible threats and from whom?

2. **Economy of Scale:** This is clearly a major advantage. Economy of scale comes through manufacturing efficiencies as well as marketing efficiencies. Increase in demand leads to increase in production. A large manufacturer can get more attractive terms

from suppliers. He has also more resources to invest in R & D to further improve product quality and manufacturing efficiency. How do you rate your company in terms of manufacturing efficiencies, productivity in comparison with your major competitors.

3. **Technology:** Technology gives a company very sharp competitive edge. Take the case of bulk drug manufacturing in India. It is technological superiority that gave the winning edge to Cheminor drugs of Dr. Reddy's Laboratories group of companies in the manufacture of ibuprofen, and methyldopa. The company had become the third largest producer of these drugs in the world in a span of few years. It is technological advancement that gave Dr. Reddy's Laboratories the cost leadership in the manufacture of their bulk drug norfloxacin. The company marched on to become the largest manufacturer of that drug in the world. Where does your company stand in the area of technology, along with your major competitors? What is your R & D effort as compared with your major competition?

4. **Marketing Strength:** Marketing is rapidly becoming more than a functional area. Marketing strength is crucial in determining the success of a company. This is particularly true in a highly competitive industry like pharmaceuticals. How strong is your marketing as compared to your major competitors? You should evaluate the relative strengths in all elements of marketing mix such as product-mix, promotional strategies, pricing, distribution, market penetration etc.

5. **Access to Capital:** The ability of a firm to raise the required capital and its access to capital is a very important indicator of its financial strength. Access to capital usually results from good banking relationships, a low debt/equity ratio and conservative liquidity position. Financial strength of a company is an important competitive advantage during a growth situation, or where competition is intense. How is your financial strength as compared to your major competitors?

6. **Management:** The experience, skill, vision, and talent of a company's management is the most crucial factor for achieving success. Take stock of the executive talent in your company and compare it with what your competition has.

7. **Organization Structure:** Organization structure indicates the ability of a company to act fast, how agile it is and how quick its

reflexes are. A highly centralized organizational structure usually indicates a long-drawn process of decision making. A decentralized organization often can move fast. What is needed is a balanced structure based on the organizational priorities and objectives. You can evaluate the organization structure of your firm in this light. Compare it with the competitors'.

These are some of the major competitive advantages from a strategic point of view. These are not exhaustive. These are only indicative. A comparative evaluation of the competitive intelligence information in these areas will sharpen your focus and help in arriving at a useful strategic direction.

Evaluating Competitors' Operations

Take the major players in your industry. Evaluate their operations thoroughly from all angles that is, in all functional areas like manufacturing, marketing, financial management, R & D, etc. Compare their performance in these areas. Such an analysis will highlight the areas where you have to improve and areas where you will have to reinforce to maintain your lead. That is the whole purpose of competitive analysis.

Summary

We have clearly moved into an era of competition-orientation. Today much of your success depends not on what you can do or what you are doing. It rather depends on what the competitor is doing and what the competitors can do. This emphasizes the necessity of analysis. Competitive intelligence is a not necessarily an act of industrial espionage. It is a systematic approach towards gathering, evaluating, processing and interpreting data on competitors' operations and activities from various sources and transferring it into meaningful information input to formulate winning strategies, to march ahead of competition by stealing the thunder from them. Competitive analysis gives the firm, the much-needed competitive advantage to win in the market place. Be it a marketing battle, in one segment, or full-fledged marketing war against the competing corporation, truly competitive analysis gives a firm its winning edge.

17

Corporate Score Board

Keeping the Score to Keep Scoring!

Whether it is in sports or in business knowing how your opponents and competitors are playing and faring is as important as knowing how you are doing. You have to do your best and reach your true potential to achieve excellence. But then, you are not operating in a vacuum or in the sterile atmosphere of a laboratory. You are out there in the market place that is bursting at the seams with ever-increasing competition. Your best may be inadequate to meet the competition in which case you have to reinforce your strengths and minimize your weaknesses. Your best may be way ahead of competition and that may lull you into complacency. And before long, you may find to your utter dismay, that the competition has already overtaken you. Therefore, in business, relative measure is more important than the absolute. Knowing your performance as compared to your competition is more important than knowing your progress alone.

You have to keep the score first, so that you know what you should score for an outright victory in the market place. You have to keep the score to keep scoring!

Ratios Rather than Absolute Figures

Contrary to the popular belief, management information regarding the performance of the organization as compared to competition is more useful, if it is presented in the form of ratios rather than in absolute figures. Consider this for example:

Next time when you are sitting in your car, take a look at the dashboard more closely. No doubt you are familiar with all the instruments, which indicate the speed, oil, pressure , engine temperature, and the rate of charge/discharge of the battery. What you have not probably observed previously is the fact that four out these five instruments give their readiness in ratios and not in absolute figures. They give the ratios like kilometers per hour, revolutions per second, pounds per square inch, amperes per hour. Only the temperature is given in absolute figures. Ratios express interrelationships clearly what the absolute figures cannot. That is why ratios are more useful in giving the necessary information to steer your organization to its objectives purely and swiftly.

Three Main Uses

Ratios are a useful management tool to analyze business situations and monitor the performance of the organization as well that of competing organizations. Ratio analysis has three main uses.

1. To help diagnose a situation
2. To monitor performance
3. To help plan forward

Comparison, Not in Isolation

One important point to remember about ratio analysis is that, just as no figure has meaning in isolation, ratios too have no meaning in isolation. They always should be used for comparing with the firm's internal standards as well as its external standards, that is, other competing firms.

When comparing with the internal standards, the firm's own past serves as a good starting point for analysis, but the disadvantages are:

A. The standards of performance achieved in the past may have been poor and any comparison with it may result it in complacency.
B. The state of economy may have improved considerably and any apparent improvement in the performance of the firm may

be a result of this and not an improvement of the efficiency of its operations.

C. The technological advancements have made the standards of the past unacceptable now.

Therefore, comparison in so far as the internal standards are concerned can be made against the budgets, provided budgets are prepared, taking account changing economic, technological and market considerations.

Comparison with Competitor

Comparison with competitor is preferable because it avoids any subjective elements associated with the budgetary comparison of the firm and also takes into account the changing market conditions and the opportunities resulting out of economic progress and technological advancement. Who are our competitors and with whose performance shall we compare our own are the questions that mangers are often faced with. The firms with which a company should be compared are:

A. Competitors

B. Potential competitors

C. Companies operating in the areas the company might enter

The important task of marketing management of a company is to achieve an optimum balance between:

A. Maximization of profitable sales

B. Minimization of marketing costs

C. Minimization of assets used

But in practice, more often than not, managers are preoccupied with accelerating sales growth in terms of volume and increasing the market share. Market share, sales growth, and sales volumes are considered as the vital statistics of business. While these are very important, the marketer should really be aiming for profitable sales and improving profitability must be his endeavor. Profitability improvement and productivity increases are most vital indicators of a company's efficiency of operations. Unless the productivity is increased in every department, efficiency of operations of a company and its competitive sharpness cannot be improved. One has to keep the score of all important aspects of one's business. To keep the score and to keep scoring, consider this corporate score board.

Corporate Scoreboard: Some Important Criteria for Winning in the Market

1. **Sales Growth:** Sales growth of a company as compared to its major competitors and the industry is an important indicator of its progress.

2. **Market Share:** Market share of a company as a whole and its products as compared to its competitors and the various therapeutic groups in which it is competing reflects the company's ability to compete.

3. **Gross Profits**:

   A. Gross profits earned by a company as compared to its major competitors indicate the competitive edge of a company in terms of its margins.

   B. Gross profits as percent of net sales should be compared.

4. **Net Worth and Growth**: Net worth indicates the financial strength of a company and growth in net worth reflects its performance. Net worth is another phrase to describe stockholders' equity of invested capital - what belongs to the owners of the common stock. This means the loans from banks and others are excluded. Deducing the loans from capital employed arrives at net worth.

5. **Return on Capital**: This indicates the efficiency of a company's operations. It tells the investors whether the return earned is in excess of that, which can be earned elsewhere. The return on capital must at a minimum, exceed the prevailing rates of interest and weighted average cost of borrowings. This ratio is an important comparison to a company's capital.

6. **Inventory Turnover Ratio**: The inventory turnover ratio measures the number of times inventory is turned over in a year or the number of days inventory is held by a company to support sales. This is arrived at by:

Inventory measured in number of days' sales = 365x Average inventory / Cost of Goods Sold

A ratio of 8 times indicates that the company holds enough inventory to support sales for 45 days.

The optimum inventory should be maintained. It should be neither be excess to block the capital nor less to lose the opportunity of sales.

7. **Sales to Average Collection Period**: This ratio represents the length of a period a company takes to actually collect the cash for the sales made. This ratio is calculated by:

Average Receivables x 365 / Sales

This ratio is important in assessing the effectiveness of the credit administration of a company. It also indicates the product movement. If the number of days exceed the targeted period of collection, that may be due to artificial sales. If the number of days is considerably less than the targeted days of collection period, that indicates a positive demand for the company's products in the market.

8. **Quick Ratio**: Quick ratio is a more stringent test of the liquidity position of a company in the sense that it concentrates on those assets, which can quickly be turned into cash, like debtors and marketable securities and cash itself. Stock is excluded. Quick ratio is arrived at:

Quick Ratio = Quick Assets / Current Liabilities

If current liabilities are rising faster than the build-up of current assets, it could indicate that the company is facing financial trouble.

It is important to assess the asset quality while analyzing the company's liquidity ratios. The analyst should look for whether there is any window dressing in the form of fictitious or deferred assets such as deferred advertising expenditure included in current assets. These do not have any en-cashable value.

These ratios are by no means exhaustive. They are the broad indicators of efficiency at the corporate level. The corporate score board at a glance is shown in Table 17.1.

Table 17.1 Corporate Score Board

Corporate scoreboards criteria	Your objective	Your actual performance	Variance (±)	Competitors		
				A	B	C
1. Sales growth						
2. Market share						
3. Gross profit as a percent of sales						
4. Growth in net worth						
5. Return on capital employed						
6. Inventory turnover						
7. Average collection period						
8. Quick ratio						

Summary

Business too, has got its own rules and criteria to determine the winners at the market place. *Ratios* are the means or methods of keeping the score since they express the interrelationships that are necessary to determine the causal effect.

The ratios have to be used in comparison and not in isolation. Firstly, these have to be examined in comparison with the firm's own past performance, performance of current competitors and industry average.

There are eight important ratios, which broadly speaking, indicate the efficiency of an organization's operations. These are sales growth, market share, growth in net worth, return on capital employed, inventory turnover, average collection period and quick ratio. This ratio analysis helps a firm to diagnose a situation, monitor performance and to prepare forward plans based on its strengths.

Keeping the score is essential to keep scoring over competition.

GMP

A Way of Life!

Yes. That is what it should be! GMP should be a way of life! An integral part of the system of a company. What is GMP? GMP is used as an acronym for Good Manufacturing Practices. In pharmaceutical industry, GMP has already become a global standard that is mandatory for your products' acceptance in the market. Without GMP you cannot market a pharmaceutical product.

There is more to GMP than good manufacturing practices when you think of it. GMP means much more to responsive, responsible, progressive organizations that are in pursuit of excellence. GMP could mean to such an organization apart from good manufacturing practices, Good Management Principles and Good Marketing Practices. All these are essential to achieve excellence in performance. Like quality, GMP is not and should not be restricted to manufacturing and the factory floor. Quality and GMP are closely related and they should be practiced and internalized by every single employee of the organization. GMP transcends all the boundaries of the functional areas and that is how it should be.

Good Manufacturing Practices

The significance of consumer protection in the pharmaceutical industry is certainly greater because the consumer (patient) has no way of knowing if the product he has bought and intends to use, will be safe and effective. He has, perforce to be guided by his physician, who prescribes that drug. The physician too, has to rely on the people, who manufacture , distribute, promote and sell the drug in the market. The social responsibility of pharmaceutical manufacturer should certainly be of a very high order. The World Health Organization, recognized this long ago in 1969, at the 22nd World Health Assembly, when it adopted a statement on good practices in the manufacture and quality control of drugs. This statement emphasized the point that:

The manufacturer of a drug must assume responsibilities for the quality of drugs he produces. He alone can avoid mistakes and prevent mishaps by exercising adequate care both in his manufacturing and control procedures.

The purpose of good manufacturing practices is to achieve the production of consistently uniform batches of high quality drugs.

Narrow Perspective

The popular misconception of GMP has been association of good manufacturing practices with high degree of overall cleanliness of manufacturing premises. Cleanliness of manufacturing premises is, of course very important. But then, there is more to GMP than cleanliness. In fact, the 1998 amendment of GMP clarifies and elaborates the various aspects of GMP. The important aspects of GMP include:

A. **Facilities:** Layout and construction of the plant, lighting, ventilation, air filtration, air heating and cooling, plumbing sewage and refuse, sanitation, washing and toilet facilities.

B. **Drug Formulation Development Facilities:** Pre-formulation drug stability evaluation, detailed specifications of various inputs like raw materials and packing materials.

C. **Vendor Selection and Development**

D. **Good Warehouse Management Practices**

E. **Good Production Management Practices:** Selection and validation of equipment, detailed documentation and preparation of standard operating procedures.

F. **Good Maintenance Practices:** Proper lay out of equipment, spares maintenance, equipment maintenance, and preventive maintenance.

G. **Good Control Laboratory Practices:** Analysis and testing procedures, standardization and sampling plans etc.

H. **Good Distribution Practices:** Proper storage conditions and appropriate transportation.

GMP is not the responsibility of manufacturing or production department alone. GMP really is a corporate responsibility and reflects a company's commitment to quality. It, therefore, requires the cooperation and support of almost all the functional departments within the organization. It calls for a high degree of coordination between various departments of the organization.

Good Management Principles

When you are talking of effective management, you are essentially talking of how to make your people more effective on the job. How to make them perform better? How to make them committed and loyal? These are some of the important questions every responsible manager asks himself. You may have the best of technology, the best of equipment, but unless you have a competent, dependable team of people who can man them, you can hardly achieve any thing. Even in a highly automated organization, without people there cannot be any achievement.

All this is too familiar to all of us. It is common knowledge that people are the greatest resource that an organization has. Nobody denies it. But what do you see in practice? Quite the opposite. Personnel polices, that are inconsistent with and contrary to the human resources development philosophy and doctrine. The companies that are truly people oriented are bound to succeed. Organizations that only pay lip service to the human factor will not be able to do well. It is not the these organizations and their managers do not want to motivate their people. They probably do not understand what it is that turns people on.

Human management is what determines the success of an organization. Call it pride, commitment, loyalty, willingness to work, or by other name, it is people who spell success for any organization. What is central to this superior quality of performance is the psychological component - motivation. A highly motivated team of people can achieve just about anything. Nothing is impossible for them.

What is Motivation?

Motivation is a word that is rather overused. But its use as a means to improve productivity is very much below the optimal level. Motivation can be defined as a mental process, function or instinct that produces and sustains incentive or drive in human and animal behavior. John D. Rockefeller said that it was the primary goal of management to show average people how to do the work of superior people. But then, how do you do it? How do you turn people on to something? How do you motivate?

Every manager knows that motivation is critical. Every year a number of programs are conducted throughout the world on themes like improving the productivity, effective people management, and productivity through people. A number of managers both in management schools and in executive development programs discuss, debate and deliberate on the various motivational theories starting from Abraham Maslow's classic hierarchy of needs to Douglas McGregor's Theory X and Theory Y. What is needed is not knowledge about motivation and its importance. How can we translate our understanding of motivation into simple, implementable, down-to-earth, pragmatic programs to improve productivity in our organizations?

Three 'R's

The good management principle revolves around the three 'R's. These are Reward, Recognition, and Responsibility. Sounds simple? Yes. But this basic, simple management tenet is difficult to practice. Not many organizations seem to be practicing it.

Reward

Michael LeBouef, in his best selling book, *How to motivate people* argues that *Reward* is the greatest management principle. According to him, the greatest single obstacle to the success of today's organizations is the giant mismatch between the *behavior we need* and the *behavior we reward.*

It is important to note that people do not change their behavior unless it makes a difference to them to do so. Three basic facts of behavior shaped by behavior are:

A. Good behavior that is reinforced with a reward tends to continue

B. Good, productive behavior that is not reinforced in any way tends to decrease over time

C. Negative reinforcement of bad behavior by way of punishment tends to decrease it

Reward and Managerial Implications

Since what gets rewards is likely to be repeated, a manager first of all should look into what is being rewarded. Then he should decide on what needs to be rewarded.

To build and bring a productive climate and culture into an organization, Michael LeBouf suggests that we should reward:

- Solid solutions rather than quick fixes
- Risk taking instead of risk avoiding
- Applied creativity and not mindless conformity
- Smart work instead of busy work
- Working together instead of working against

Instituting an Objective Reward System that Works

Any reward system that you want to institute should increase productivity. Here are some important guidelines that can make your reward system work for you.

- Set objectives that are specific, simple and easy to understand.
- Ensure that objectives and the performance (which is reflection of behavior) are measurable.
- Set objectives that are realistic and meaningful. If objectives are unrealistic they remain on paper as objectives.
- Involve your team members in the process of setting objectives. When they *own* the objectives, they strive much harder to achieve them.
- Observe the progress that your team members make in achieving objectives. Acknowledge every stage and give them a positive feedback. A feedback demonstrates your interest in them and your concern for their progress.
- It is important to be alert and catch your team members doing something good. Most employees have been traditionally exposed to the fault-finding methods of supervision. You have to change

that perception. Positive reinforcement is far more effective than negative reinforcement.

Recognition

Recognize and acknowledge the progress and contribution of your team members. You can build winning teams of people only through recognition and by acknowledging their progress and contribution.

The late Paul Bryant, one of the finest team builders of the previous century, a professional football coach from the USA said it best about the importance and the magic power of recognition. Here are his words telling us how to lift some men up, how to calm down others until finally the've got one heartbeat together as a team. He said that there are just three things he would ever say:

- If anything goes bad, I did it
- If anything semi-good goes, then we did it
- If anything real good goes, then you did it.

That is an invaluable message for all winning coaches.

Michael LeBouef articulated the most important words to build cooperation, trust and team spirit. They are very few indeed. They are presented in Table 18.1.

Table 18.1 Team-Building Words

The six most important words	I agree I made a mistake
The five most important words	You did a good job
The four most important words	What is your opinion?
The three most important words	Let's work together
The two most important words	Thank you
The single most important word	We

Responsibility

When you reward the right behavior, you are ensuring its continuity. When you recognize good behavior and acknowledge it, you are sowing seeds for building a winning team. You can get commitment and loyalty from people by giving it to them.

When you make people responsible for a specific task or project and make them own it, you are building a much more valuable element - responsibility in to your team members. By building responsibility, you will be able to build *intrapreneurial* culture into your team. An intrapreneur is an entrepreneur within an organization. He is a champion of his product or project and cuts through the red tape and makes things happen. He does not take no for an answer. He is not problem-centered. He is solution-focused. When you make people responsible they will rise to the occasion. Progressive policies like promotions from within and investing in the development of people will further enhance the process of building and nurturing a winning team of responsible mangers and workforce.

Good Marketing Practice

Marketing is the communication link between the organization, its customers and the general public. An organization has to be sensitive to the needs of its customers, employees, shareholders and the expectations of the general public. An organization that wants to achieve leadership in the marketplace must also play the leadership role in fulfilling its obligations and responsibilities to society. It should be one step ahead and anticipate the expectations of the public. It should set the pace for the industry and follow the good marketing practices. The marketing practices recommended by the International Federation of Pharmaceutical Manufacturers' Association (IFPMA) are presented in Table 18.2.

Table 18.2 IFPMA's Code of Marketing Practices

Obligations of the Industry

International Federation of Pharmaceutical Manufacturers' Association (IFPMA) recommends Code of Marketing Practices of its member associations, recognizing the difficulty of setting out simple Code, which will be applicable in all parts of the world. It seems clear that national and regional conditions and legal restrictions will continue to vary to such an extent as to make a simple word code impracticable. Nevertheless, the Federation believes that it has a duty to encourage its member associations to either introduce such Codes or Practices or where such Codes already exist, to continually re-examine and

Contd...

where necessary revise them so that a voluntary system based on such a Code keeps pace with modern medical knowledge and changing health services and conditions.

The obligations of the industry, according to IFPMA, may be identified as follows:

The pharmaceutical industry, conscious of its special position arising from its involvement in public health, and justifiably eager to fulfill its obligation in a free and fully responsible manner undertakes:

A. To ensure that all products it makes available for prescription purposes to the public are backed by the fullest technologic service and have full regard to the needs of public health

B. To produce pharmaceutical products under adequate procedures and strict quality assurance

C. To base the claims for substances and formulations on valid scientific evidence, thus determining the therapeutic indictions and conditions of use

D. To provide scientific information with objectivity and good taste, with scrupulous regard for truth, and with clear statements with respect to indications, contraindications, tolerance and toxicity

E. To use complete candor in dealings with public health officials, healthcare professionals and the public

Suggested Code of Marketing Practices

A. General Principles

1. The term 'Pharmaceutical Product,' in this concept means any pharmaceutical or biological products intended for use in the diagnosis, cure, mitigation, treatment or prevention of disease in humans or to affect the structure of any function of the human body, which is promoted and advertised to the medical profession rather than directly to lay public.

2. Information on pharmaceutical products should be accurate, fair and objective, and presented in such a way as to conform not only to legal requirements, but also to ethical standards and to standards of good taste.

3. Information should be based on an up-to-date evaluation of all the available scientific evidence, and should reflect this evidence clearly.

Contd...

4. No public communication shall be made with the intent of promoting a pharmaceutical product as safe and effective for any use before the required approval of the pharmaceutical product for marketing such use is obtained. However, this provision is not intended to abridge the right of the scientific community and the public to be fully informed concerning scientific and medical progress. It is not intended to restrict a full and proper exchange of scientific information concerning a pharmaceutical product, including appropriate dissemination of investigational findings in scientific or any communications media, nor to restrict public disclosure to stock holders and others concerning any pharmaceutical product as may be required or desirable under a law, rule or regulation.

5. Statements in promotional communications should be based upon substantial scientific evidence or other responsible medical opinion. Claims should not be stronger than such evidence warrants. Every effort should be made to avoid ambiguity.

6. Particular care should be taken that essential information as to pharmaceutical products. Safety, contra-indications, and side effects or toxic hazards is appropriately and consistently communicated subject to the legal, regulatory and medical practices of each nation. The word safe 'must not be used with qualification.'

7. Promotional communications should have medical clearance, or where appropriate, clearance by the responsible pharmacist, before their release.

B. **Medical Representative**: Medical Representatives must be adequately trained to possess sufficient medial and technical knowledge to present information on their companies, products in an accurate and responsible manner.

C. **Symposia, Congresses, and Other Means of Verbal Communication**: Symposia, Congresses and the like are indispensable for the dissemination of knowledge and experience. Scientific objectives should be the principal focus an arranging such meetings, and entertainment and other hospitality shall not be inconsistent with such objectives.

Contd...

D. Printed Promotional Material: Scientific and technical information shall fully disclose the properties of the pharmaceutical product as approved in the country in question based on current scientific knowledge including:

- The active ingredients, using the approved names where such names exist
- At least one approved indiction for the use together with the dosage and methods of use
- A succinct statement of the side-effects, precautions, and contra-indications

Except for pharmaceutical products where use entails specific precautionary measures, reminders need not necessarily contain all the above information providing that a form of words is used which indicates clearly that further information is available on request.

Promotional material such as mailings and medical journal advertisements must not be designed to disguise their real nature and the frequency and volume of such mailing should not be offensive to healthcare professionals.

E. Samples: Samples may be supplied to the medical and allied professions to familiarize them with the products, to enable them to gain experience with the products in their practice upon request.

It is recognized that if any individual member associations of IFPMA have laid down their own Code of Marketing Practices and this recommended code is not intended to replace similar codes or instruments already in force by members of the Federation. The IFPMA Code is a voluntary Code and therefore put forward as a model to its member associations.

Source: IMS News Letter

Guidelines Are Not Enough

Despite such voluntary codes and official guidelines such as IFPMA's Code of Marketing Practices, Universal Code of Pharmaceutical Marketing Practices (UCPMP) Code by Department of Pharmaceuticals in India and specific guidelines to physicians by Medical Council of India, unethical marketing practices and even corrupt marketing practices continue to grow unabated. The trend of these unethical practices seem to happen not just in India but in many countries in the world. The nexus between pharmaceutical industry and physicians seems to continue in a number of markets. In India, however it is much more evident, open and appears commonplace.

Ethics and Pharmaceutical Marketing

Ethics and Pharmaceutical Marketing

The dictionary defines ethics as the basic concepts and fundamental principles of decent human conduct. Ethics is the study of standards, good conduct and moral judgements. Ethics is the practical study of *what ought to be*. Ethics is the branch of knowledge that deals with moral principles.

For over two decades now, pharmaceutical industry's marketing practices have been more often than not are being associated with the word unethical rather than ethical. Pharmaceutical companies in India have been stepping up their incentives and freebies to physicians with high prescription potential. This is despite the code of ethics in Indian Medical Council rules. A 2010 parliamentary committee report pointed that:

There is no let up in this evil practice and the Pharma companies continue to sponsor foreign trips to many doctors and continue to shower high-value gifts like air-conditioners, cars, music systems, gold chains etc. to obliging prescribers, who then prescribe costlier drugs.

Transactional relationships such as these between physicians and pharmaceutical companies influence the clinical decisions of physicians. Consider this example. If there are two drugs, equally efficacious, the doctor is influenced by a particular company may prescribe their drug instead of another, which might be costlier. Furthermore, many critics have observed that doctors after attending sponsored conferences and receiving high-value gifts are likely to write irrational prescriptions.

To curb this ever-growing nexus between pharmaceutical industry and physicians and the corrupt practices that are increasing, the apex body of the medical fraternity, the Medical Council of India (MCI) had come out with guidelines to its members on how they should conduct themselves in their relationships with the Pharma industry in 2002. As it did not result in any improvement of the situation, MCI issued revised guidelines to its members on their ethical conduct in 2009. The revised guidelines too did not make any impact. Finally, the Department of Pharmaceuticals (DoP) came out with a Uniform Code of Pharmaceutical Marketing Practices (UCPMP) in 2015, made it voluntary leaving its implementation to the industry. The industry did not implement it. The corrupt practices continued unabated. Table 18.3 presents the key features of these guidelines by MCI as well as the DoP.

Table 18.3 MCI Guidelines and UCPMP Code

MCI Guidelines To Doctors	UCPMP Code - Key Features
MCI notified all its member-doctors on December 10, 2009 regarding relations between doctors and pharmaceutical companies. Here are some of the important guidelines. This adds a new regulation (Regulation No. 6.8.1) to the pre-existing regulation of 2002 of Indian Medical Council's guidelines on professional conduct, etiquette, and ethics in dealing with pharmaceutical and allied healthcare industries. Medical Practitioners shall follow and adhere to the stipulations given below:	In 2015, Department of Pharmaceuticals (DOP) established a voluntary uniform code of pharmaceutical marketing practices (UCPMP) to promote ethical marketing practices.
1. **Gifts:** A medical practitioner shall not receive any gift from any pharmaceutical or allied healthcare industry and their sales people or representatives.	1. **Gifts:** No gifts/pecuniary advantages/ benefits in kind should be given to drug prescribers or suppliers. No gifts for personal benefit of healthcare professionals and family members (both immediate and extended) should be offered.
2. **Travel Facilities:** A medical practitioner shall not accept any travel facility inside the country or outside, including rail, air, ship, cruise tickets, paid vacations etc. from any pharmaceutical or allied healthcare industry or their representatives	2. **Travel Facilities:** No travel facility inside or outside the country, including rail, air, ship, cruise tickets, paid vacations etc. to doctors and their family members for vacation or for attending conference, seminars, workshops,

Contd...

MCI Guidelines To Doctors	UCPMP Code - Key Features
for self and family members for vacation for attending conferences, seminars, workshops, CME programs etc. as a delegate. The ban on travel facilities for attending conferences, seminars, workshops, CMEs etc. seem to be applicable to delegates and speakers seem to be excluded from this.	CME programs etc. as a delegate should be extended.
3. **Hospitality:** A medical practitioner shall not accept individually any hospitality like hotel accommodation for self and family members under any pretext.	3. **Hospitality:** Any hospitality like hotel accommodation to healthcare practitioners and their family members under any pretext should not be provided.
4. **Cash or Monetary Grants:** A medical practitioner shall not receive any cash or monetary grants from any pharmaceutical or allied healthcare industry for individual purpose in individual capacity under any pretext. Funding for medical research, study etc. can only be received through approved institutions by modalities laid down by law/ rules/guidelines adopted by such approved institutions in a transparent manner. It shall always be fully disclosed.	4. **Cash or Monetary Grants:** Payment of cash or monetary grants to any HCP for individual purpose, in individual capacity, under any pretext may not be made. Funding for medical research, study etc. can only be extended through approved institutions by modalities laid down by law/rules/guidelines adopted by those institutions, in a transparent manner.
5. A consumer can complain to the consumer court that the service provided by a doctor was deficient or negligent because he prescribed a medicine or appliance or test etc. wrongly or unnecessarily in return for favors granted by the pharmaceutical company, even though acceptance of such favors was illegal.	5. Free samples of drugs should be handed to only the person who is qualified to prescribe such product or to a person authorized to receive the samples on his/her behalf.

Even after close two two decades of the announcement of these voluntary guidelines and codes for establishing ethical marketing practices by both the regulatory bodies, the MCI and the DOP, it has been business as usual for pharmaceutical industry and physicians. The nexus between the pharmaceutical industry and physicians has been getting stronger by the day. Clearly, guidelines are not enough.

UCPMP Act

Realizing that most Pharma marketing practices have not been adhering to these voluntary guidelines, the government of India is deciding on taking a stricter approach. What is needed is an enactment to ensure compliance.

The Department of Pharmaceuticals (DoP) announced that it will soon introduce the UCPMP under Essential Commodities Act to make it more deterrent thereby ensuring Pharma industry's compliance with the code that has been optional so far. The DoP started working on a revised draft of UCPMP under the ambit of Essential Commodities (EC) Act. The draft involves CEO penalties and penal provisions as per EC Act. DOP sent the revised draft of UCPMP to the law ministry for vetting it.

The law ministry expressed reservations over certain provisions of the revised draft of UCPMP and suggested modifications to make it compatible with the Act. Sudarshan Pant, joint secretary of DoP said in this context in 2017:

We are working to overcome the hurdles pointed by the law ministry. The revised code, which is in making will be a good deterrent. Our aim is to provide a level playing field for small and large firms. As of now only big firms are complying with UCPMP.

Expressing concern over DoP decision to bring UCPMP under the ambit of Essential Commodities Act, D G Shah, secretary general of Indian Pharmaceutical Alliance (IPA) observed:

The government should bring UCPMP under Drugs and Cosmetics Act instead of E C ACT administered by DoP. Essential Commodities Act is a draconian Act next to Narcotics Act, which hardly offers any hearing opportunity to concerned persons before arrest. There is no provision for condonation in E C Act.

He further suggested that the DoP should focus on creating conducive environment for industry's compliance rather than fear psychosis, which will not work.

When this happens, many pharmaceutical marketers will have to let go of almost all of their habitual marketing practices such as high-value gifts, paying cash for prescriptions, paid holidays etc. on which they have been depending for over two decades. Rather than waiting till then, it would be better if Pharma proactively embraces ethical marketing practices.

Summary

The pharmaceutical industry has an even more specific social responsibility, since it deals with the health and well being of people. The WHO realized and recognized the need for ensuring quality and safety of pharmaceuticals and adopted a statement in July 1969, on Good Manufacturing Practices, which has come to be known as GMP.

But then, the scope of GMP is much broader indeed crossing the functional boundaries of the organization. Social responsibility is really a corporate responsibility and cannot be restricted to production department alone.

GMP, apart from standing for Good Manufacturing Practices, could also mean Good Management Principles and Good Marketing Practices. Good Management Principles are essential to accomplish corporate objectives effectively. Quality control and Good Manufacturing Practices have to be achieved in an organization. An organization that is people-oriented and invests in the development of its people will achieve uncommon success.

Good Marketing Practices too, are important since marketing is the vital link between the organization and, customers and the general public. An organization that is truthful and honest in its communications effort and follows fair trade practices will be able to improve its credibility and image in the society.

GMP should be a way of life, an integral part of the system and a corporate philosophy. And more importantly the organization should live up to it!

Bibliography and Webliography

1. Actando, Social Media - Does It Have a Place in Pharma? May 18, 2017, www.blog.actando.com/social-media-pharma-marketing-mix/
2. Alex Timlin, V P, Client Services, Emarsys, What is Multichannel Marketing? January 16, 2017, www.emarsys.com
3. Alexander Gaffen, FDA Guidance: How Can Pharma and Device Companies Use Twitter? Not Easily, RAPS (Regulatory Affairs Professionals Society), June 17, 2014, www.raps.org/regulatory-focus/news/2014/06/19521/FDA-twitter-social-media-guidance/
4. Allen Frances, M.D., Saving Normal: An Insider's Revolt Against Out-of-control Psychiatric Diagnosis, DSM-5, Big Pharma and The Medicalization of Ordinary Life, William Morrow, A Division of Harper Collins, New York
5. Amber Tiffany, 10 Expectations of Omni-channel Marketing That Will Make You Rethink Your Strategy, Invoca Blog, June 21, 2016, www.blog.invoca.com
6. Amy Kazmin, Indian Drugs: Not What the Doctor Ordered, Financial Times, September 09, 2015
7. Amy McNeil, SMS Programs: Making the Most of Multichannel Marketing, Yes Life Cycle Marketing, www.yeslifecyclemarketing.com/resources/experts/sms-programs-making-most-multichannel-marketing
8. Andrew Mathias, Why Social Listening Has Become Essential to Pharma, PM360, April 2, 2015, www.pm360online.com/why-social-listening-has-become-essential-to-pharma/
9. Anthony Gucciardi, 90% of Big Pharma Spent More on Marketing Than Research in 2013 Alone, Natural Society, February 11, 2015, www.naturalsociety.com

10. Anubhav Pandey, Lawsuits on Patent Infringements in India and Pharma Patents, IPleaders, April 19, 2017, www.blog.ipleaders.in

11. Ash Rishi, How to Develop An Effective Pharma Content Marketing Strategy, Couch, April 20, 2016, www.wearecouch.com

12. Ashley Wazanna, M.D., Physicians and the Pharmaceutical Industry: Is A Gift Just A Gift? JAMA, 2000; 283 (3): 373-380

13. B V Mahalakshmi, Indian Bulk Drug Industry Faces Chinese Threat, Financial Express, July 28, 2015

14. Banana IP Reporter, Posted in Patents, Patents and the Misunderstood Case of Compulsory Licensing in India, BIP Counsels, September 20, 2015, www.bananaip.com

15. Ben Goldcare, Bad Pharma: How Medicine is Broken And How We Can Fix It, Fourth Estate, New York

16. Bobby George, PhD, India's Draft Pharmaceutical Policy - A Game Changer, Guest Column, Biosimilar Development, September 26, 2017, www.biosimilardevelopment.com

17. Brent L Rollins, Matthew Perri, Pharmaceutical Marketing, Jones and Barlett Learning, Burlington, MA

18. Burleigh B Gardner and Sidney J Levy, The Product and the Brand, Harvard Business Review, March - April 1955, (33-39)

19. C. Lee Ventola, Social Media and Healthcare Professionals: Benefits, Risks, and Best Practices, Pharmacy & Therapeutics Journal, July 2014, v. 39 (7)

20. C.A. Westwick, How to Use Management Ratios, Gower Publishing Company, England

21. Caitie Gonzalez, Do You Know What Omni-channel Marketing Really Means, Invoca Blog, January 20, 2016, www.blog.invoca.com

22. Cari Thompson, 3 Reasons Omni-channel and Multichannel Are Not the Same Thing, Invoca Blog, Feb 7, 2017, www.blog.invoca.com

23. Carl R. Rogers and F J Roethlisberger, Barriers and Gateways to Communication, Harvard Business Review, July - August 1952

24. Charlene Li, Josh Bernoff, Groundswell: Winning in A World Transformed by Social Technologies, Forrester Research, Harvard Business Review Press, Boston, Massachusetts

25. Chris Morgan, The Journey to Key Account Management for Pharmaceuticals, Sales & Marketing Insights, Z S Associates, www.zsassociates.com

26. Christina Search, Pharma Companies Spend 19X More on Marketing Than Research And Returns Are Dropping, Natural Society, December 21, 2016, www.naturalsociety.com

27. Christopher Watson, What is Digital Asset Optimization? Mollify, May 20, 2015, www.mollify.biz

28. Colette De Jung, B.A: Adams Dudley, M.D., MBA., Reconsidering Physician - Pharmaceutical Industry Relationships, JAMA, 2017; 317 (17): 1772-1773, May 2, 2017

29. Corstjens & Edouard Demeire, Good Pharma: How Marketing Creates Value in Pharma, Corstjens, 2014.

30. Dale Archer, The Dark Side of Big Pharma, Forbes, December 26, 2013, www.forbes.com/sites/dalearcher/2013/12/26/the-dark-side-of-the-big-pharma

31. Daniel Ghinn, Five Lessons From GSK in Social Media, Pharmaphorum, March 24, 2014, www.pharmaphorum.com/articles/five-lessons-from-gsk-in-social-media/

32. Daniel Ghinn, Pathways for Engagement for Healthcare OrganizationsL Lessons, Strategies and Insights from Pioneers of Healthcare Engagement, Creation Healthcare 2012

33. Daniel Ghinn, Pharma Gets Social: Top 10 Pharma Social Media Firsts in 2013, Pharmaphorum, December 16, 2016, www.pharmaphorum.com/articles/pharma-gets-social-top-10-pharma-social-media-firsts/

34. Danny Sullivan, Does SEM = SEO + CPC Still Add Up? Search Engine Land, March 4, 2010, www.searchengineland.com

35. David Edleman and Brian Salsberg, Beyond Paid Media: Marketing's New Vocabulary, McKinsey Quarterly, November 2010, www.mckinsey.com

36. David Healy, Pharmageddon, University of California Press, Berkeley

37. David J Luck, Product Policy and Strategy (Foundations in Marketing), Prentice Hall, 1972

38. David Ormesher, CEO, Closerlook, Pharma's Digital Transformation Should Start With Marketing, www.closerlook.com

39. Dawn Lacallade, Pharma Must Embrace Its Social Media Role, PharmExec.com, May 12, 2017, www.pharmexec.com/pharma-must-embrace-its-social-media-role

40. Dawn Papandrea, How Cleveland Clinic Became One of the Most Visited Healthcare Destinations, Content Marketing Institute, July 25, 2016, www.contentmarketinginstitute.com

41. Deirdre Coleman, 7 Tips for Successful Pharma Content Marketing, Eye for Pharma, September 19, 2013, www.social.eyeforpharma.com

42. Digital India Health Report 2017, D Yellow Elephant, www.dyellowelephant.com/Registration/india-digital-health-report.pdf

43. Dinesh Chindarkar, Role of Social Media in Pharma Industry, The Financial Express

44. Dipesh Majumder, Need of the Hour: Pharmaceutical Sales Training 2.0, www.medismotech.com/need-for-pharmaceutical-sales-training-2.0/

45. Divya Rajagopal, Compulsory Licensing Hits India's Image: Hetero Pharma, The Economic Times, March 31, 2015, www.economictimes.indiatimes.com/industry/healthcare/biotech/pharmaceuticals/compulsory-licensing-hits-indias-image/hetero-pharma/articles-show/46751947.cms

46. Divya Rajagopal, How Ramesh Juneja's Mankind Pharma Has Changed Pharma Game With Pulp Marketing, The Economic Times, June 13, 2012

47. Divya Rajagopal, Patented Drug Launches Help MNCs Score Over Indian Peers, The Economic Times, September 12, 2017, www.economictimes.indiatimes.com

48. Doris Iarovici, M.D. The Challenge of Doctor - Patient Relations in the Internet Age, March 1, 2018, The New York Times, www.nytimes.com

49. Dr. Andree Bates, iPad and Tablet Use in Detailing: Where Pharma is Going Wrong? July 27, 2016, www.eularis.com

50. Dr. Arun Gadre, Dr. Abhay Shukla, Dissenting Diagnosis: Voices of Conscience From the Medical Profession, Random House, India.

51. Dr. Edmond Differding, The Drug Discovery and Development Industry in India - Two Decades of Proprietary Small Molecule R&D, ChemMedChem, 2017, June 7 12: 12(11): 786-818

52. Dr. Kamal Kumar Mahwar, The Ethical Doctor, Harper Collins Publishers, India

53. Eularis, eDetailing: A strategic analysis of implementation and ROI, www.eularis.com

54. Export-Import Bank of India, Working Paper No. 37, Study on Indian Pharmaceutical Industry, March 2015

55. Gary Hamel, C. K. Prahlad, Competing for Future, Harvard Business Review Press, Boston

56. Geeta Anand, Inside India: India's Fight Against Big Pharma Patents is a Just War, India Realtime - Commentary, The Wall Street Journal, March 19, 2015, www.blogs.wsj.com

57. George Gruenwald, New Product Development, Crain Books, Lincoln woods, Illinois, USA

58. Hally Pinaud, 3 Strategies to Transform Your Organization for the Digital Age, webinar, Marketo, www.marketo.com/webinars/ 3strategies-to-transform-your-organization-for-the-digital-age/

59. Heather Fletcher, Content Marketing in Pharma: Worth Revisiting, Target Marketing, September 13, 2016,

60. Henniger Bullock And Collen Tracy James, Mayer Brown LLP, 5 Social Media Pitfalls in the Pharmaceutical Industry, Law 360, www.law360.com/articles/915911/5-social-media-pitfalls-in-the-pharmaceutical-industry

61. How to make eDetailing relevant, March 16, 2016, http:// worldofdtcmarketing.com/make-edetailing-relevant/marketing-to-healthcare-professionals/

62. Ida Morris, Digital Marketing 101/Pharma, Targeted Media Health, www.targetedmediahealtch.com

63. Jack Trout and Al Ries, The Positioning Era Cometh, The Advertising Age, April 24, 1972

64. Jeff Gaus, Are Digital and Multichannel Marketing Now Are One And the Same? Pharmaphorum, July 15, 2011, www.pharmaphorum.com

65. Jennifer Hague, The Importance of Blogging in Pharma, Pharmaphorum, January 28, 2014, www.pharmaphorum.com

66. Jim Ruiz, Omni Channel: It's Time for Pharma to Get On Board, In Touch Solutions, March 13, 2013, www.intouchsol.com

67. Joana Belbey, 6 Ways Pharma May Use Social Media, March 9, 2016 www.forbes.com

68. Joanna Belbey, Big Pharma and Social Media: How to Avoid Trouble With the FDA, Forbes, May 25, 2017, www.forbes.com/sites/ joannabelbey/2017/05/25/big-pharma-and-social-media-how-to-avoid-trouble-with-the-fda

69. Jodi Harris, Feed Your Hungry Content Channels With A Powerful COPE-ing Strategy, Content Marketing Institute, November 17, 2016, www.contentmarketinginstitute.com

70. Jodi Harris, Pharmaceutical Content Marketing: How to Cure What Ails You, Content Marketing Institute, June 4, 2017, www.contentmarketinginstitute.com

71. John L LaMattina, Devalued and Distrusted: Can the Pharmaceutical Industry Restore Its Broken Image? John Wiley & Sons Inc., New York

72. John LaMattina, India's Solution to Drug Costs: Ignore Patents and Control Prices - Except for Home Grown Drugs, Forbes, April 18, 2013, www.forbes.com

73. John LaMattina, Pharma's Reputation Continues to Suffer - What Can Be Done to Fix It? Pharma and Healthcare, Forbes, January 18, 2013

74. Jonah Berger, Contagious: Why Things Catch On, Simon & Schuster, New York

75. Jonathan Crossfield, When Followers Attack: A Monty Python Guide to Maintaining Social Media Harmony, Chief Content Officer Magazine, Content Marketing Institute, November 15, 2015, www.contentmarketinginstitute.com

76. Jonathan Govette, Referral MD, 30 Amazing Mobile Health Technology Statistics for Today's Physician, www.getreferralmd.com/2015/08/mobile-healthcare-technology-statistics

77. Juan Mendez, 5 Types of Video Content Perfect for Each Stage of Customer Journey, Content Marketing Institute, March 17, 2017, www.contentmarketinginstitute.com

78. Kamal Biswas, Pharma's Prescription: How the Right Technology Can Save the Pharmaceutical Business, Academic Press, Elsevier

79. Katie Thomas, Glaxo Says It Will Stop Paying Doctors to Promote Drugs, The New York Times, December 16, 2013, www.nytimes.com/2013/12/17/business/glaxo-says-it-will-stop-paying-doctors-to-promote-drugs.html?

80. Kaustubh Kulkarni, Ben Hirsche, India Revokes Roche Patent in a New Blow for Big Pharma, Business News: Reuters, November 2, 2012, www.reuters.com

81. Kiran Kabtta Somvanshi, Top Five Indian Pharma Companies Together Spent Over Rs. 8,000 crore on R&D Spend in FY17, The Economic Times, Pharmaceuticals, www.economictimes.indiatimes.com

82. Kiran Patange, Landmark Case of Compulsory Licensing in India, Slide Share, April 02, 2016, www.slideshare.net

83. Kotler, Philip, Marketing Management: Analysis, Planning and Control, Prentice Hall

84. Krishna Kant, How India's Pharma Growth Story Fizzled Out, Rediff Business, July 05, 2017

85. Laxmi Yadav, DoP to Introduce UCPMP Under Essential Commodities Act to Ensure 100% Compliance by Pharma Cos, Pharmabiz - Policy & Regulation, September 7, 2017, www.pharmabiz.com

86. Lea Prevel Katsanis, Global Issues in Pharmaceutical Marketing, Routledge, Taylor & Francis Group, New York

87. Lin Pophal, Multichannel Vs. Omni-channel Marketing: Is there A Difference and What Does It Mean To You? E-Content, March02, 2015, Issue-March 2015, www.econtentmag.com

88. Lisa La Motta, How Pharma is Using Twitter to Connect With Patients, Biopharma Dive, October 26, 2016, www.biopharmadive.com/news/how-pharma-is-using-twitter-to-connect-with-patients/

89. Lisa Manthei, 4 Important Differences Between Multichannel and Omni-channel Marketing, Emarsys, October 3, 2016, www.emarsys.com

90. Make in India: Pharmaceuticals, www.makeinindia.com/sector/pharmaceuticals

91. Marcia Angell, M.D., The Truth About the Drug Companies: How They Deceive Us And What To Do About It, Random House, New York

92. Maria Riefer Johnston, Intelligent Content: What Does 'Reusable Mean?' Content Marketing Institute, May 25,2015, www.contentmarketinginstitute.com/2015/05/intelligent-content-strategy-reuse-definition/

93. Mark Kessel, Restoring Pharmaceutical Industry's Reputation, Nature Biotechnology, Volume 32, Number 10, October 2014

94. Max Flitzer, The Big Pharma Conspiracy: The Drugging of America for Fast Profits, Make Profits Easy LLC.

95. Michael LeBouf, How to Motivate People, Sidgewick & Jackson, London

96. Mickey Smith, Principles of Pharmaceutical Marketing, Lea & Febiger, Philadelphia, USA

97. Nadia Giuffrida and Kym Ellis, Strategic Thinking: How Pharma Can Benefit From A Digital Marketing Strategy, EPM, www.epmmagazine.com

98. National Pharmaceutical Pricing Authority, NPPA Pharma Directory 2007, www.nppaindia.nic.in

99. Neha Bhayana, Doc, Here's A Selfie of my Sore Throat, The Times of India (Pune), July 13, 2014, www.epaperbeta.timesofindia.com

100. Nisha Biswal, Indo - US Trade: Time to Seize the Initiative, The Hindu Business Line, February 23, 2018, www.thehindubusinessline.com

101. Nishith Desai Associates, Uniform Code for Pharmaceutical Marketing Practices (UCPMP) Decoded, November 2017, www.nishithdesai.com/fileadmin/user-uploads/pdfs/Research-papers/uniform-code-for-pharmaceutical-marketing-practices-decoded.pdf

102. Nora Aufritte, Julian Boudet, Vivian Weng, Why Marketers Should Keep Sending You Emails? McKinsey Quarterly, January 2014, www.mckinsey.com

103. OPPI, 51st annual Report 2016-17, www.indiaoppi.com

104. Optimization Glossary, Optimizely, www.optimizely.com/optimization-glossary-landing-page-optimization/

105. P B Jayakumar, Patently Justified, Business Today, March 15, 2015, www.businesstoday.in

106. P. B. Jayakumar, Booster Dose, Business Today, July 19, 2015, www.businesstoday.in

107. P. L. Narayanan, The Indian Pharmaceutical Industry, NCAER, New Delhi

108. Pankaj R Patel, Developing on the Pharma Success Story, The Hindu Business Line, November 30, 2017

109. Peter Vigliarolo, Pharma Needs to Fearlessly Innovate in Social Media, O-Dwyer's, October 20, 2017. www.odyerpr.com/story/public/9599/2017-10-20/pharma-needs-fearlessly-innovate-social-media/

110. Phanish Chandra, 9 Ways Digital Engagement Benefits Pharma, July 5, 2016, www.docplexus-insights.com

111. Phanish Chandra, How Can Pharma Marketers Make the Most of Social Media, March 9 , 2017 www.docplexus-insights.com

112. Phanish Chandra, Medical Reps 2.0 - Reinventing Pharma Field Force in India, Docplexus, www.docplexus.com

113. Phanish Chandra, Securing Doctors' Trust: Has the Pharma Lost Plot, LinkedIn Pulse, April 11, 2017

114. Piyush Gupta, Trends in Pharma Export Industry in India, Pharma Focus Asia, Editorial Section - Strategy, Issue 26, 2017, www.pharmafocusasia.com

115. Priyanka Vora, Big Pharma: Why There is a Problem With Pharma Companies Sponsoring Medical Conferences in India? January 05, 2017, scroll.in

116. Quintiles, Evaluation of Live! Remote e-detailing: Assessing physicians' channel preference - Infographic, www.quintiles.com/services/integrated-channel-management/remote-edetailing

117. Ranjana Smetacek, National Drug Policy - Fair Treatment Needed, Health Files - E T Health World, November 01, 2016, www.health.economictimes.indiatimes.com

118. Rashmi Pant, Indian Pharmaceutical Exports: The Growth Story, Business Standard, January 06, 2017

119. Reuters Staff, India Rejects Patent on Pfizer's Anti-arthritic Drug, September 7, 2015, www.reuters.com

120. Richard Meyer, 'Good Enough' Digital Marketing Not An Option for Pharma, Pharmaphorum, May 11, 2016, www.pharmaphorum.com

121. Richard Meyer, Pharma Websites: A Great Time to Get Closer to Patients, Pharmaphorum, November 6, 2017, www.pharmaphorum.com

122. Robert Rose, New Era of Marketing Requires New Skills, Content Marketing Institute, April 17, 2015, www.contentmarketinginstitute.com

123. Rogerwood, All About P R, McGraw Hill Book Company, London

124. Rudd Kooi, Fonny Schenck, and Beverly Smet, Evidence-based multichannel - Delighting Pharma customers in the omni-channel age: The Missing Manual, Across Health, London, June 2016

125. Rupali Mukherjee, Indian Pharma Cos Get Record 300 US FDA Generic Drug Nods in 2017, ET Health World, January 25, 2018, www.health.theeconomictimes.indiatimes.com

126. Rx India-Pharmacy of the World, Pharmaceutical Industry Analysis: Market Research

127. Sakshi Behl, Digital Marketing in Healthcare Industry: A Complete Guide, August 10, 2016 www.digitalvidya.com

128. Sammy Almashat, M.D. M.P.H, and Sidney Wolfe, M.D. Pharmaceutical Industry Criminal and Civil Penalties: An Update, Public Citizen, September 27, 2012, www.citizen.org

129. Search Engine Advertising, Search Metrics, www.searchmetrics.com/glossary/search-engine-advertising/

130. Seema Singh, Last Man Standing in Indian Pharma, Forbes, September 27, 2011, www.forbes.com

131. Shabana Hussian, Mankind Pharma: Formulating Strategy to enter the big league, Forbes.com, May 8, 2014.

132. Sharon Lurye, How Kim Kardashian's Instagram Post Got A Rosemont Drug Company in Trouble With the FDA, Philly Voice, September 01, 2015, www.phillyvoice.com/kim-kardashians-instagram-post-got-drug-co-trouble-fda/

133. Shilpi Tyagi, D. K. Nauriyal, Profitability Determinants in Indian Drugs and Pharmaceutical Industry: An Analysis of Pre and Post TRIPS Period, Eurasian Journal of Business and Economics, 2016, 9 (17) 1-21

134. Simon Revell, Digital Marketing: Current Opportunities and Challenges in Adopting Digital Marketing in the Pharmaceutical Industry, Slideshare Presentation, www.linkedIn.com/in/simonrevell

135. Simon Wentworth, What Does e-Detailing Entail? How Digital Marketing is Shaping the Pharmaceutical Industry, Base Case, June 18, Base Case, www.basecase.com

136. Social Media & Healthcare by the Numbers, July 12, 2017, www.sma.org/social-media-by-the-numbers/

137. Social Media Trends in the Pharmaceutical Industry, Unmetric, www.unmetric.com/pharma-social-media-trends-report

138. Sophia Bernazzani, The Dark Side of the Pharmaceutical industry, American Journal of Managed Care Markets (AJMC) Network, April 14, 2016, www.ajmc.com/contributor/sophia-bernazzani/2016/04/the-dark-side—big-pharmaceutical-industry

139. Steven Niles, Pharma's Foot Prints Over iPad, MedAdNews, February 2011, Volume 29, Number 10

140. Subba Rao Chaganti, Are We Aligning or Aping? Building Pharma Brands, www.buildingpharmabrands.com

141. Subba Rao Chaganti, Evolution or Devolution, Building Pharma Brands, May 13, 2013, www.buildingpharmabrands.com

142. Subhash Tambe, Kanchan Bhat, Mahesh More, Padmavathy Nair, Perceptions of the Use of Social Media in the Indian Pharmaceutical Industry: A Survey of Marketing, Advertising, and Medical Professionals, SIES Journal of Pharma-Bio Management, Vol 2 (1), 2014, SIES College of Management Studies (SIESCOMS), Nerul, Navi Mumbai

143. Supriti Agrawal, Navjot Kaur, Influence of Social Media Marketing in Indian Pharmaceutical Industry, International Journal of Advance Research and Innovation, Volume 3, Issue 4, 2015

144. Swati Bhaskar, Examining Physician Use of Social Media in 2017, PM 360, May 31, 2017, www.pm360online.com/examining-physician-use-of-social-media-in-2017/

145. Teena Thacker, Code for Pharma Marketing Practices May be Enforced Soon, Live Mint, e-paper, December 25, 2017, www.livemint.com

146. The Dark Side of Big Pharma: How Marketing to Doctors Really Works, Healthcare Global, February 09, 2015, www.healthcareglobal.com/supply-chain/dark-side-big-pharma-how-marketing-doctors-really-works

147. The Editorial Board - Opinion, Editorial - India's Novartis Decision, The New York Times, April 11, 2013, www.nytimes.com

148. Theodore Levitt, The Marketing Imagination, Free Press, New York

149. Tim Smedley, Patent Wars: Has India Taken On Big Pharma and Won, Guardian Sustainable Business, The Guardian, May 14, 2013

150. Tracy Staton, Top Ten Pharma Companies in Social Media, Fierce Pharma - Marketing- Special Report, www.fiercepharma.com/special-report/top-10-pharma-companies-social-media-0

151. Van Eck, Indian Pharma: Analyzing the Tailwinds for Growth, Market Realist Beta, March 21, 2016

152. Virginia Lau, 8 Ways for Pharma to Improve the Way It Uses Twitter, Medical Marketing & Media, July 28, 2016, www.mmm-online.com

153. William Rothschild, How to Gain Competitive Advantage in Business, McGraw Hill Book Company, New York, USA www.targetmarketing.com

154. Zoe Dunn, Is It Finally Time for Pharma to Change the Way It Uses Facebook? Medical Marketing and Media, August 31, 2015, www.mmm-online.com

Index

About the Author

Subba Rao Chaganti, has a masters in business administration and over fifty-two years of experience in pharmaceutical marketing covering the whole gamut and all facets of the industry from selling to sales management, product management to heading the total marketing activity. His experience covers domestic and international marketing, and also Indian and multinational sectors.

He also taught for a few years a course on Advertising and Brand Management at Gitam Institute of Foreign Trade (now part of Gitam University) at Visakhapatnam as an adjunct professor and also taught a course on Marketing at the School of Management, Jawaharlal Nehru Technological University (JNTU), Hyderabad as a visiting faculty.

He lives in Hyderabad and can be reached at subbarao.chaganti@gmail.com

Here is a list of his publications:

1. Pharmaceutical marketing in India: Concepts, Cases, Strategy
2. Game Plans for Post-GATT Era: Action Agenda of Indian Pharmaceutical Industry
3. Compete or Forfeit: Strategies for Sustainable Competitive Advantage in Pharma Product Patents Era

www.ingramcontent.com/pod-product-compliance
Lightning Source LLC
Chambersburg PA
CBHW050658190326
41458CB00008B/2616